THE LITERARY MESSAGE

OF ISAIAH

THE LITERARY MESSAGE
OF ISAIAH

AVRAHAM GILEADI

Hebraeus Press
New York, NY

Dedicated to the great men and women whose marvelous help made it possible to bring forth this work.

First printing September 1994

Library of Congress Cataloging-in-Publication Data

Gileadi, Avraham
    The Literary Message of Isaiah
    Bibliography: pp. 610
    1. Bible. O.T. Isaiah—Criticism, interpretation, etc.
    2. Bible. O.T. Isaiah—Theology
    3. Bible. O.T. Isaiah—Literature
BS1515.2.G55   1994   224.1055   94–76821
ISBN 0-9626643-1-6

CONTENTS

INTRODUCTION

The Hebrew prophet who said, "I foretell the end from the beginning, from ancient times things not yet done,"[1] did just that, and his words are still with us. More than that, his writings resolve many of the anomalies that have vexed Jews and Christians for millennia: Is the New Testament really a continuation of the Old? Is the spiritual Messiah of the Christians the same as the temporal Messiah of the Jews? Was the gospel Jesus taught known before his time? Are the ancient Hebrew prophecies to be fulfilled literally, perhaps in our day? This same prophet, known to us as Isaiah, also said, "The people are taken captive for want of knowledge"[2]—and then spent a lifetime providing us with a means of gaining such knowledge. We have only to plunge into his eloquent predictions to see their relevance to the modern world. We have only to immerse ourselves in his mysterious words to come to a realization of their significance.

Surely, the Book of Isaiah is a handbook for all time, a gift from God, not for us to ignore but to receive with joy. Yet, Isaiah communicated his message in what is called the "manner of the Jews"— a veiled way of speaking to those with "eyes to see" and "ears to hear." This does not mean that the Book of Isaiah is impossible to understand. However, it does mean that reaching such understanding requires exertion, both physical and spiritual, with rewards commensurate with the effort put forth. Fortunately, in this day of much information, aids exist to assist us in the study of this puzzling but highly pertinent ancient book.

---

[1] Isa 46:10.
[2] Isa 5:13.

Applying Interpretive Keys That Help Us Understand Isaiah

The rich Judeo-Christian tradition we have inherited yields not only the Book of Isaiah but several scriptural keys for comprehending the book.[3] These interpretive tools lay the foundation for a unique approach that penetrates to the inner workings of Isaiah and helps uncover the prophetic message within. I call them the keys to a *sealed book*, because without them Isaiah's writings, in effect, remain sealed, almost impossible for anyone to understand. We may sense the significance of Isaiah's words, and even comprehend them in part, but without such keys the prophet's message still escapes us. On the other hand, as we apply these keys and see how they work, we begin to better understand the nature of Hebrew prophecy. We grow not only in our love for the prophet Isaiah, but in our appreciation of his marvelous prophetic message.

There is a second reason I draw an analogy to a sealed book. Sealed books are supposed to reveal the events of the "last days," the time of the end of the world as we know it. When we apply these interpretive keys to Isaiah, just such a vision unfolds. That vision makes Isaiah's writings a guidebook for humanity, a consolation in troubled times for all who understand him. We may even discern parts of a picture that deal with political and spiritual realities existing in our world, that condemn evil practices, even, and perhaps particularly, among the Lord's own people. Yet, we always sense that Isaiah holds out hope for those who repent. In fact, his book serves as a call to such repentance. In language unequaled by any other prophets, Isaiah balances his harsh indictments with the promise of a glorious salvation for those who live on the earth. Perhaps those who comprehend Isaiah will be spared the agony of learning too late the need for us all to repent and to obtain the Spirit of God.

The Spirit of Prophecy

The fact that Isaiah wrote things that are difficult for many people to understand may be explained in part by our being unfamiliar with the manner of prophesying practiced among the Jews. The art

---

[3] See also the Book of Mormon, 2 Ne 25:4–5; 3 Ne 23:1–3.

of prophesying in ancient times, which has only begun to be appreciated in our own time, was developed as much as a defense against those who *should not* understand a prophet's message as it provided a vehicle for those who *should* understand it. The inscrutable nature of Isaiah's prophecies—their complexity and formidableness—thus served a twofold purpose. On the one hand, Isaiah hid the meaning of his words from the wicked, those whom his message would condemn because they were not prepared to receive it. On the other hand, those who diligently sought to know the truth of Isaiah's words would understand his message because they were ready to receive it. The first interpretive key, therefore, has to do with being spiritually qualified or prepared.

The highest spiritual preparedness a person can attain in order to comprehend a prophet's words is surely to be imbued with the same spirit of prophecy that inspired the prophet in the first place. In effect, the *spirit of prophecy*—to a greater or lesser degree—will make Isaiah's words plain to the reader when both prophet and reader are attuned to the same spirit. When the spirit that inspired Isaiah dwells in us, then we are aided in understanding Isaiah's words.

But what is the spirit of prophecy? According to Peter, "Prophecy came not in old time by the will of man; but holy men of God spake as they were moved by the Holy Spirit" (2 Pet 1:21). Paul, too, says that prophecy is a gift of the Holy Spirit (1 Cor 12:4, 10) and notes that "the things of God knoweth no man, but the Spirit of God" (1 Cor 2:11). In other words, we cannot comprehend the revelations God gave through the prophets except by the Spirit of God that gave the prophets utterance. Isaiah tells us that God will imbue with His Spirit those who perform justice and righteousness in the earth (Isa 32:15–17; 42:1–4). These, God will send to minister to others of His people (Isa 48:16; 61:1). Isaiah equates the influence of the Spirit of God upon His people with God's words being "placed in [their] mouth" (Isa 59:21).

Our possessing the spirit of prophecy, or the gift of prophecy, thus depends on our spiritual preparedness or worthiness. This first key hinges on how we relate to God. We qualify for the gift of the Holy Spirit when we show ourselves righteous by His standards, when we truly desire to live His law. There is no getting around this key. Without it we cannot become enlightened, for it guarantees our comprehension or ensures our lack of it, depending on who we are before God.

The Manner of the Jews

A second key for understanding Isaiah concerns the literary aspect of Hebrew prophecy with its many intricate ways of expression. The Jewish method or *manner of the Jews*, as anciently taught in the schools of the prophets (compare 2 Kgs 4:38; 6:1), deals with the mechanics behind a prophet's language—with the literary art of prophesying. Evidently, we cannot obtain this key to Isaiah from any source other than the Jews; it originates within their tradition. Yet, the Jews do not advertise or disseminate among non-Jews their method of interpreting the prophets. The very language, script, and contents of their books are unique to themselves. They hand down their methodology orally in the rabbinic schools, where interpretive devices such as types and foreshadowings, allegorical language, literary patterns, parallelisms, double meanings, key words, code names, interconnections, and other mechanical tools are transmitted individually from teacher to student.

The Jewish approach to scripture is entirely analytical. The Jews even analyze each letter of a word and the significance of that letter within the word. (Every letter of the Hebrew alphabet, for example, possesses a numerical value. Thus, the word "serpent" [*nāḥāš*] equates numerically with the word "messiah" [*māšiaḥ*], the word "serpent" being a symbol for "messiah." We see such symbolism in the brazen serpent Moses lifts up in the wilderness [Num 21:8–9] and perhaps in the Mesoamerican emphasis on the serpent figure.)[4] Such care for the scriptures is reflected in Jesus' statement that "one jot or one tittle (the smallest Hebrew letter—the *yôd* with its serif, which together look like a comma) shall in no wise pass from the law, till all be fulfilled" (Matt 5:18).

In their oversized books, in the center of each page, the Jews place a small square that encloses a single verse or passage being studied. Filling up by far the greater part of the page (in fine print, completely surrounding the small square) appear large columns of the best-known rabbinic commentaries on the verse or passage in the center. I recall spending an entire month of my time in rabbinic

---

[4] See also the use of numerology in the New Testament, for example, in the three sets of fourteen generations from Abraham to Jesus (Matt 1:17)—fourteen being the numerical value of the name "David"—alluding to Jesus' lineage from the loins of King David and in the numerical value of the name of the Beast (666) in the Book of Revelation (Rev 13:18).

school debating just one such verse, exploring it from every angle, studying all its potentialities, its varied ramifications, its several levels of applicability, its definable limitations, and so forth, until we (the group of students around the table, with the rabbi at the head) had wholly assimilated that passage.

For me, such an analytical mind-set constituted a new and fruitful approach. That kind of perseverance, though difficult and at times exacerbating, brought home an important dimension in studying the scriptures: a unique point of view that allows for great flexibility in interpreting a given scripture. Far from a dogmatic, superficial approach that assigns a single interpretation to any verse—thereby denying other intended levels of meaning—the Jewish method recognizes the broad applicability of the word of God. It is the opposite of proof-texting, which first accepts a doctrine and then seeks support for it by drawing on passages of scripture of perhaps entirely different contexts. The Jewish method is essentially open minded. It seeks to elicit meanings from the scripture itself, not to impose or read doctrinal presuppositions into it. It lets the scripture speak.

Analyzing the words of the prophets with such detail requires effort and takes time. Christians, unfortunately, know little of such analysis. In reading the scriptures, they emphasize the spirit of prophecy. Yet, we also know that the Spirit of God tends to increase in proportion to the amount of intelligence we seek and the degree of diligence we apply to the scriptures—studying them out in our minds, making connections with what we have learned, assimilating their message, putting them into practice. Such study generates in us a positive spiritual climate. It paves the way for the influence of the Holy Spirit.

Searching

A third key for understanding Isaiah is *searching*. We cannot comprehend Isaiah without searching his words. In effect, Isaiah is not to be understood simply by reading the words—we must look into them, explore them, analyze what they say. In order to do so, we must approach God's words with a degree of reverence, allowing them to teach us.

Those Jews who, through Paul's preaching, believed in Jesus were considered "more noble" than those who did not believe because they "received the word with all readiness of mind, and searched the scriptures daily, whether those things were so" (Acts 17:11). Immersion in the primary sources of God's word—the scriptures—rather than in human commentary and interpretation, separated the believers from nonbelievers. The spiritual preparedness of Jew and Gentile, today as anciently, is an individual thing characterized by a humble searching for the truth.

Searching is a process: we cannot come to a complete comprehension of Isaiah all at once. We should recognize the implications of this truth and its effect on us. Those who give up before completing the process will fail to understand Isaiah's message when it may be most needed—perhaps to our condemnation and calamity in the day of judgment. On the other hand, those who undertake to search Isaiah diligently will know what to expect, how to obtain God's help and the help of His Spirit. Isaiah represents a deliberate challenge. If we meet this challenge, Isaiah's message will eventually crystallize in our minds, bringing greater recognition of his words. Gaining a mastery of Isaiah's message will prepare us for the events of which he prophesies—we will know clearly what the Lord requires of us.

Of course, the key of searching relates to all other keys. When we search the scriptures, we often experience the Spirit of God, which leads us to further searches and additional knowledge. As stated, the Jewish method requires searching. We cannot analyze Isaiah's words the way the Jews do without searching. To become proficient at the Jewish manner of interpreting the prophets requires practice. In fact, it involves us in an ongoing quest. The Jews themselves, not unusually, may spend fifteen years of their lives studying aspects of the law and the prophets—some, an entire lifetime, supported in their endeavor by their wealthy brethren.

The key of searching, however, goes beyond ferreting out multiple meanings and ancient literary techniques. Searching the words of Isaiah may draw on the manner of the Jews and invite the spirit of prophecy, but it transcends intellectual analysis. Diligent searching leads to a spiritually mature perspective, a deep and abiding commitment to the word of God. To investigate the scriptures is, in and of itself, rewarding where those who have a question, and sincerely seek an answer, may obtain it. For that reason, searching often becomes a spiritual experience. We must all taste such fruits in order to gain our salvation. What we ourselves search out, we assimilate best—it becomes a part of us, our spiritual forage. In short,

6

there is no substitute for searching—others cannot do it for us. Each must undertake it personally; it is a prerequisite for the full flowering of God's word in our lives. It forms a basis for our very spiritual progression.

Types

A fourth key for understanding Isaiah concerns the manner in which Isaiah prophesies—that is, using ancient events as *types* on which to model prophecies of the future. The idea that what happened in Israel's past may happen again reflects a well-known definition of typology. The writer of Ecclesiastes says, "The thing that has been, it is that which shall be; that which has been done, is that which shall be done: there is nothing new under the sun" (Eccl 1:9). In other words, what has occurred once, setting a precedent, will occur again. The Jewish writer continues, "Is there anything of which it may be said, See this is new!—it already has been in ancient times that were before us" (Eccl 1:10). Events repeat themselves; history works in cycles. Isaiah's writings illustrate this concept of typology.

The Jews have long recognized a double fulfillment of Hebrew prophecy. They traditionally interpret the prophets from a typological perspective.[5] First, the Jews apply a prophecy to the time of the prophet himself—to the historical and spiritual crises of his day that caused him to seek answers from God. God gave those answers, which the prophets wrote down as revelations. We thus have prophecies in Isaiah that name the ancient entities of Zion, Babylon, Assyria, Egypt, and so forth—names familiar to us from that period. At the same time, the Jews acknowledge that the word of God transcends time; it has eternal value. In particular, the Jews apply the prophetic word to a parallel context of fulfillment: the last days or latter days. They thus view the ancient entities and events that the prophets mention as types of latter-day entities and events.

Ezek 12:27, for example, shows that the people of Ezekiel's day were all too well aware of this double dimension of prophecy. They exonerated themselves, not wishing to apply Ezekiel's censuring words to themselves. They insisted that Ezekiel must be speaking

---

[5] See Daniel Patte, *Early Jewish Hermeneutic in Palestine* (Missoula, Mont.: Scholars Press, 1975).

of someone other than them. His prophecy, they said, must be intended for "the far-off time"—the latter days. On the other hand, we, who may be living in the latter days, do the reverse. The ancient Hebrew prophecies apply to the time of the prophets themselves, do they not? We, too, exonerate ourselves of hard sayings and unpleasant implications. We keep such at a comfortable distance; human nature has not changed.

Isaiah himself sums up the idea that what has been shall be—that an initial, historical fulfillment of his words prefigures a latter-day fulfillment. In a classic statement, he represents the Lord as saying, "Who predicts what happens as do I, and is the equal of me in appointing a people from of old as types, foretelling things to come?" (Isa 44:7). The ancient Israelites, as God's covenant people, foreshadowed what would befall in the latter days through their history, through the very things they experienced. As Isaiah is quick to point out, only the Lord can predict the future in that way—it is a proof of his divinity (Isa 45:21). That is how, in the Book of Isaiah, the Lord "foretell[s] the end from the beginning, from ancient times things not yet done" (Isa 46:10). It is Isaiah's unusual ability to encapsulate the future in Israel's past, and vice versa, that makes Isaiah's words inimitable and great.

Of course, such a dual fulfillment of prophecy does not mean that history repeats itself in exactly the same sequence. I do not suggest that the same chronology of events that existed anciently applies in the last days or that all things repeat themselves in precisely the same way. Rather, Isaiah often fuses certain ancient events in order to create a picture of something new that will contain elements of the old. He chooses selectively the events in Israel's past that best serve as a type, model, or precedent of what will happen in the future.

This selectivity explains why Isaiah employs no explicit chronology in his writings. Isaiah has scrambled both his chronology and the unfolding of the events themselves. We can unravel them only by diligent searching, linking individual events, domino fashion, to others in the Book of Isaiah to form an implicit sequence. We achieve a complete picture of the last days only when we identify each piece of the puzzle and link it to the other pieces that relate to it. This challenge should not dismay us; it does not lie outside the reach of the reader.

Discovering Isaiah's Message through Literary Analysis

My own serious study of Isaiah began in rabbinic school in Israel, where I was introduced to the Jewish method of analyzing the prophets. Later, academic studies in the United States and Canada introduced me to Hebrew poetic and literary features, which I integrated with my background in Jewish method. Graduate work in the Hebrew Bible, particularly Isaiah, made me realize, however, that something was amiss: neither Jews nor scholars seemed to use a holistic method for studying the scriptures, for analyzing the prophets' words. The result was that neither group obtained a comprehensive prophetic picture. The Jews believed in prophecy and acknowledged multiple meanings, but they lacked literary expertise. Scholars, on the other hand, possessed literary expertise but did not believe in prophecy or acknowledge multiple meanings. I knew that both approaches, of Jews and of scholars, must combine as part of a holistic method for interpreting the scriptures.

Because the prophets were poets as well as inspired men of God, they developed their message by means of every literary device at their disposal. In their minds, the word of God deserved to be written using the highest literary talents and skill. They carefully crafted their prophetic writings so that all their words would have meaning, so that even the way they organized their material would carry a message. Indeed, their literary creations were a reflection of God's creation of the universe; everything counted.

Over the course of years devoted to scripture study, primarily the study of the Hebrew prophets, I discovered many literary features in Isaiah, each of which can communicate a message apart from the literal text. As I would proceed to analyze the scriptures—without preconceived notions of what would develop—I became aware that prophetic dimensions existed that most of us have scarcely begun to explore. When I used both the literary approach and the Jewish method, letting the scriptures simply unfold, many profound messages emerged that I did not realize were there.

I eventually formulated a holistic method of literary analysis that I find extremely effective in studying the scriptures. That method combines the open-ended, multiple-meaning approach of the Jews with the analysis of literary features. It consists primarily of three

9

parts: first, structural analysis, which examines prophetic meanings embedded in the manner of organizing the material; second, rhetorical analysis, which examines the meanings of individual terms and expressions, particularly as they connect different parts of the text; and third, typological analysis, which examines events out of the past that may foreshadow the future.

This threefold method, which lends itself naturally to the study of the scriptures, incorporates the manner of the Jews without limiting itself to it. It analyzes what the scriptures say from what the prophet-writers have built into them. Thus, it helps prevent the reader from distorting the prophetic message, from imposing personal interpretations. This method of literary analysis builds on a foundation of the four interpretive keys for understanding Isaiah. It allows each of us to uncover the whole message of the scriptures, to determine for ourselves what they say, independent of scholars or academic "experts." It accords with the divine injunction that we ourselves search the scriptures.

Determining the Messages Conveyed by Structure

Because of its illuminating effect on all else, structural analysis is a good starting point when considering the literary dimensions of Hebrew prophecy. It involves examining blocks of material, looking for prophetic patterns and themes that grow out of how a prophet-writer arranges his words. Such literary structures may cover individual passages, entire chapters, or even groups of chapters. These structures may function alone or interdependently on several levels, some as broad governing patterns, others as fulfilling a secondary function. Inherent in every structure is a message that serves as a framework for what is being conveyed in the body of the material. Analyzing structures in the scriptures is as important to understanding a prophet's message as is taking into account his individual words; they are two halves of the same equation.

Structural analysis may at first seem a formidable challenge because we are dealing with literary devices that are not always easily apparent. Because we are sometimes on more familiar ground among the trees, we do not readily discern the forest with its contours, expanse, and diversity. But the broader view brings its own rewards. It gives us the overall perspective we need in order to know what is happening at ground level. Don't good authors, before they write a book, determine the story line or organizing principle they will follow that will lead the reader from one connected episode to another? And doesn't satisfaction come to a reader as he or she is able to unravel the pattern? The Book of Isaiah, which is both literature and prophecy, surely ought to be read in that manner.

Governing Structures

We find, when we examine Isaiah, that he employs and adapts the literary patterns of many ancient Near Eastern peoples. For example, long before Isaiah's time, the Egyptians wove narrative stories around a certain literary structure. The story of Sinuhe forms a classic model.[6] The hero of the story, who is of royal origin, finds himself in trouble, political or otherwise, in his homeland. He is exiled from his country—forced to flee for his life. Making his way among a foreign people and culture, he comes to understand himself. At the point where he attains this self-awareness—realizing who he is, what he must do with his life—there arises in him a desire to return to his homeland. Oddly enough, at that point those in authority welcome him back, escort him home with much fanfare, restoring him to a high position.

This, of course, is also the story of Israel, and Isaiah frames his entire book around it as a literary pattern. In the first part of the Book of Isaiah, the Lord's people find themselves in trouble in their homeland (chaps. 1–39). Because of their rebellion and apostasy, the Lord exiles them into the world at large, where they interact with people and events (chaps. 40–54). At a certain point, when the Lord's people repent of their follies and come to themselves—realizing their true identity, renewing their allegiance to the Lord—they return home in a glorious homecoming, a great and marvelous event (chaps. 55–66).

Fittingly, Jacob, father of the nation Israel, typifies this structure: Jacob flees from Esau into the land of Haran. There he interacts with people, marries and has children, and acquires flocks and herds, attaining considerable stature. At that point, the Lord summons him back to the land of Canaan, where he dwells in strength as one

---

[6] See the stories of *Sinuhe*, *The Two Brothers*, *The Enchanted Prince*, and others, in Adolf Erman, *The Ancient Egyptians* (New York: Harper & Row, 1966); Alan H. Gardiner, *Hieratic Papyri*, Third Series (London: British Museum, 1935); John A. Wilson, in J. B. Pritchard, ed., *Ancient Near Eastern Texts* (Princeton: Princeton University, 1969).

of Israel's patriarchs. Going even further back, we note that this pattern reflects the story of man himself. God casts Adam out of paradise—and out of His presence—into a dreary world. There he makes his way, comes to himself, realizes who he is and what his destiny is to be. Then begins his struggle to return home. If he succeeds in returning to his Heavenly Father, he assumes great glory: Adam attains a state far more splendid than he enjoyed formerly. Each one of us resonates with this cycle, or hero journey, as a paradigm of life itself.

Isaiah uses this literary pattern to great effect. It both reveals and conceals his message. Isaiah's structuring of his book according to this pattern, however, has proved a great stumbling block to scholars, most of whom view the different historical settings of the book—Israel before, during, and after the exile—as grounds for dividing the book's authorship. To account for the diverse, sustained historical settings found in the three parts of the book, scholars allege that the book must have had at least three authors. A misunderstanding of a literary structure has caused scholars to pursue a mistaken course, not believing that Isaiah saw the time of exile and beyond. In reality, a broad governing pattern to Israel's history exists. The themes of *trouble at home*, *exile abroad*, and *happy homecoming* reflect a divine plan for the Lord's people and for the world. It foresees "the end from the beginning" (46:10).

An important complementary idea with which Isaiah permeates his book consists of the progression of thought from nationalism to universalism to individualism. A national Israel apostatizes and is exiled. A universal Israel reawakens to her national identity. Individuals who repent are able to return home from their scattered condition to resume this identity. The basic plot of this literary pattern tells us that Israel's history does not end when she goes into exile. It resumes when Israel returns home—all part of a divinely ordained plan. According to this structure, the Lord foreordained Israel's exile: it forms an integral part of his saving plan for the world. When Israel goes into exile, the intermingling of her blood with the nations of the world gives all peoples a claim to Israel's unique heritage.

Isaiah employs other Near Eastern literary patterns. For example, he adapts a fourfold structure we find in the Ugaritic myth of Baal and Anath. Isaiah's structure consists of the four prophetic themes of *apostasy*, *judgment*, *restoration*, and *salvation*, which parallel the themes of *threat, war, victory,* and *feast* in the Baal myth.[7] One cycle of these themes encompasses the entire Book of Isaiah. Its content as a whole thus deals with Israel's *apostasy* (chaps. 1–9), *judgment* (chaps. 10–34), *restoration* (chaps. 35–59), and *salvation* (chaps. 60–66). Forming a second overarching structure, these themes transcend the narrow focus we have when we read the text verse by verse. Such themes lift individual prophecies from a purely historical base, making them part of and subservient to the book's wider message. This broad message is that Israel's literal existence does not cease with her apostasy and judgment, as might at first appear. It continues with Israel's restoration—according to a predetermined plan—until all the earth's righteous are saved and participate with Israel in a glorious new age.

A third such governing structure in the Book of Isaiah consists of the associated ideas of *destruction of the wicked* (chaps. 1–39) and *deliverance of the righteous* (chaps. 40–66) at *the presence of a righteous Davidic king* (chaps. 37–38). Virtually every time the name *Zion* appears in Isaiah, moreover, these three ideas are present in individual passages as well. I call the close association of these three ideas "Zion ideology." It originates in the concept of Zion as a safe place by virtue of the righteousness of her king, a loyal vassal or servant of the Lord. In the days of Isaiah and King Hezekiah, an Assyrian army of 185,000 men surrounded Jerusalem, demanding its surrender. Because of Hezekiah's righteous intercession, and because the people were loyal to Hezekiah, the Lord smote the Assyrian horde with a plague, so that in one night all died (37:33–36; 38:2–6). Thus were the Lord's people spared in Zion in a great deliverance.

That event of Israel's deliverance was unique in ancient history, one that saw the Lord's word fulfilled or actualized when put to the test. It established an important precedent that Isaiah must have deeply felt and pondered. Upon it Isaiah builds a prophecy of the future. In so doing, he not only duplicates it in many localized instances in his writings, as mentioned, but he patterns his entire book after it. In Isaiah's structuring of his book according to the threefold pattern of Zion ideology, that historical deliverance forms the centerpiece.

---

[7] See William R. Millar, *Isaiah 24-27 and the Origin of Apocalyptic* (Missoula, Mont.: Scholars Press, 1976). Millar's study unfortunately flounders amid historical presuppositions and fails to note the incidence of mythical patterns throughout the Book of Isaiah as well as their transformation into Hebrew prophetic forms.

A fourth governing structure divides the Book of Isaiah into two broad categories. These reflect respective curses and blessings pertaining to the Lord's covenant with Israel. As the Lord's covenant people, Israel inevitably experiences either blessings or curses, depending on the people's loyalty to their divine King. Unlike the covenant Moses formulated (the Sinai covenant), in which Moses enumerates first the covenant's blessings and then the curses (Deut 28), Isaiah emphasizes first the curses (*covenantal malediction*; chaps. 1–39) and then the blessings (*covenantal benediction*; chaps. 40–66). He divides his book to reflect these two broad categories: in the first half, curses predominate; but in the second, blessings.

Many localized exceptions of curses and blessings nonetheless appear in both divisions of Isaiah. Blessings appear in the first half of the book, indicating that not all Israel need incur the Lord's wrath. Even in a time of national apostasy and judgment, the Lord makes provision for delivering the righteous. Thus, in a chapter wholly devoted to censuring the Lord's people—spelling out the many curses they are bringing on themselves—Isaiah inserts a single verse: "Tell the righteous it shall be well with them; they shall eat the fruits of their own labors" (3:10)—*covenantal benediction*. Meanwhile, curses appear in the second half of the book, reminding Israel that not all will inherit blessings, only those who remain loyal to the Lord. In a chapter that depicts the blessedness of strangers and aliens who love the Lord, Isaiah inserts a poignant reminder that even spiritual leaders of the Lord's people may transgress, to be devoured by wild beasts (56:3–12)—*covenantal malediction*. By drawing on the two extremes of Israelite society, the highest strata (the prophets) and the lowest (the alien), Isaiah makes his point well: all in between also stand to be blessed or cursed.

The dominant idea of curses first, followed by blessings, reflects the pattern we find in ancient Hittite suzerain–vassal treaties.[8] If a vassal (a lesser king) rebels against the suzerain (the overlord king), he will suffer the curses; but if he exercises loyalty toward the suzerain, he will enjoy the blessings. Since Isaiah commences his book by calling on the heavens and the earth—witnesses of the Sinai covenant (Deut 30:19)—to testify of Israel's apostasy (1:2), the intent

---

[8] See George E. Mendenhall, "Covenant Forms of Israelite Tradition," *BA* 17.3 (1954): 50–76; F. C. Fensham, "Malediction and Benediction in Ancient Near Eastern Vassal Treaties and the Old Testament," *ZAW* 74 (1962): 1–8.

is clearly maledictory. All the Lord's judgments upon Israel thereafter take the form of common ancient Near Eastern covenant curses. At the commencement of the second part of the Book of Isaiah, the Lord declares Israel's crime expiated—her sins are atoned for (40:2). A new, benedictory chapter in Israel's history begins, marked by a wonderful reversal of her curses. Not only does the Lord reverse Israel's curses, but that same reversal transcends and far exceeds Israel's former glory.

Isaiah thus adapts ancient Near Eastern literary patterns for a prophetic purpose. He builds his writings around a diversity of structures, superimposing them one upon another. This layering makes Isaiah's a sophisticated book, replete with meaning. It also implies that the book is heavily encoded. Its multilayered structure explains why the material may read unevenly, often changing context without any warning. In Isaiah's writings, time appears irrelevant as sequences of events criss-cross and overlap. Now he describes one scene, now another, perhaps without any apparent connection between the two. All such scenes are governed by overarching literary criteria. We must learn what these tell us so that we may deal more confidently with Isaiah's writings.

The Bifid Structure

A fifth structure pervading the Book of Isaiah—by far the most complex—is the subject of the literary analysis later in this volume. Called the Bifid Structure, it consists of a division of the Book of Isaiah into two halves of thirty-three chapters each. Each half divides into seven categories of parallel subject matter whose themes are arranged chiastically, as follows:

Ruin and Rebirth (chaps. 1–5 and 34–35)

   Rebellion and Compliance (chaps. 6–8 and 36–40)

      Punishment and Deliverance (chaps. 9–12 and 41–46:13b)

         Humiliation and Exaltation (chaps. 13–23 and 46:13c–47:15)

      Suffering and Salvation (chaps. 24–27 and 48–54)

   Disloyalty and Loyalty (chaps. 28–31 and 55–59)

Disinheritance and Inheritance (chaps. 32–33 and 60–66)

The progression of thought that characterizes this structure possesses no known ancient Near Eastern antecedents; it is most likely original to Isaiah. The chiastic nature of the structure tells us that ultimately Israel's destiny, and humanity's, is to be humiliated or exalted (see the structure's centerpiece). The supporting themes, which express human behavior and its consequences, imply that in order to be exalted, Israel must first pass through a period of humiliation—exaltation has a price. On the other hand, the wicked of Israel, and all other wicked entities, experience precisely the opposite. They exalt themselves now, persecuting the humble, but in the end the Lord humiliates them.

In order to attain exaltation, Israel, and individuals within Israel, must exercise compliance (theme #2) and loyalty (companion theme #6) toward the Lord. As the Lord's people thus prove themselves under duress, the Lord delivers them (theme #3). He saves Israel from temporal and spiritual perils (theme #5) despite her initial punishment and suffering because of sin (themes #3 and #5). After being ruined and disinherited to pay for her crimes (themes #1 and #7), Israel experiences a rebirth (theme #1); she gloriously reinherits the promised land (theme #7). Throughout these phenomena, powerful, often dramatic tests present themselves to try Israel's faithfulness. Exaltation does not come until she passes severe trials. Always there appears the specter of some of Israel being unfaithful to the Lord—playing the traitor while others stand fast amid opposition and oppression.

Throughout this structure, Isaiah identifies the dominant sins of the Lord's people as injustice and idolatry. While he imputes all Israel with guilt on account of these and other sins, the righteous repent when called on to do so. The wicked of Israel and of the world, on the other hand, distinguish themselves in that they do not repent in spite of the Lord's warning. As a consequence, they suffer ruin, punishment, humiliation, and so forth, without recourse, such constituting their final state. This, in briefest form, is the message of the Bifid Structure. How the Lord implements these principles in the last days, the structure sets out in detail.

Like the other structures I have discussed, the Bifid Structure consists of overarching themes that must be recognized if we would grasp any one part of Isaiah's message. It would be bold for us to proceed on the assumption that we could understand Isaiah's words without considering such governing concepts. In fact, the tight structuring of the Book of Isaiah from beginning to end suggests that Isaiah composed much of the book, particularly its disputed latter sections, to accommodate structural criteria.

The correlation of so many governing ideas into a single whole did not materialize spontaneously. It was a life's work, precipitated by an extraordinary spiritual experience. At a certain point in Isaiah's prophetic ministry, after he had proved his loyalty to the Lord by fulfilling his first commission as prophet (chap. 6), Isaiah experienced an apocalyptic vision, a vision of the end from the beginning (chap. 40).[9] From then on, Isaiah's ministry was characterized by his writing the substance of the vision. He also arranged, added to, and structured his former prophecies and revelations to match the broad picture he had now obtained. His writing style itself took on an elevated quality. Isaiah succeeded in integrating many layers of ideas, compacting into one prophecy a tale of the ages.

This transcendent view of Isaiah tells us more about the nature of his prophecies than does the sum of its individual parts. Without it, scholars are left to interpret minute segments of Isaiah's writings, seeking constantly to fit them to some ancient person or event. Rather, Isaiah's message eclipses these historical bounds. His overarching design subordinates the historical origins of his prophecies without taking away from history. Isaiah recasts highlights of Israel's history into a new, more expansive mold, his individual prophecies forming pieces of a large puzzle that reveals, when complete, a panorama of the end from the beginning. Only within this totality do we discover Isaiah's message.

Forms of Speech

In addition to governing structures, Isaiah employs secondary literary patterns. He organizes his sayings so that they will compose minor structures of their own, each conveying a message. They include such forms of prophetic speech as the lawsuit, the messenger speech, the woe oracle, the prophetic lament, the priestly sermon, the parable, and the song of salvation.[10]

---

[9] Compare Sirach 48:22–25 and J. Flemming and H. Duensing, trans., "Ascension of Isaiah," in Edgar Hennecke and Wilhelm Schneemelcher, eds., *New Testament Apocrypha, Vol. 2* (Philadelphia: Westminster, 1965).

[10] See an outline of these forms in Claus Westermann, *Basic Forms of Prophetic Speech*, trans. Hugh C. White (Philadelphia: Westminster, 1967). This list by no means exhausts Isaiah's forms of prophetic speech, which also includes a variety of psalms, prayers, and declarations.

The *lawsuit*, for example, may range over several verses of scripture, forming a single passage. In the lawsuit, the Lord indicts Israel in a court setting (compare 1:10–20). Israel has been rebellious toward the Lord, breaking the covenant. The Lord sits as judge, sentencing Israel for her misdemeanor. Typically, Israel receives a probationary sentence, a brief period in which to repent. But when things come to a head, the Lord metes out judgment and Israel must bear her punishment.

In the *messenger speech*, the prophet assumes the role of the Lord's emissary. He delivers the prophetic message to the people or their king (compare 7:3–9; 30:8–17). Often, the message commences with an account of how the Lord sends the prophet. Following such a preamble, the prophet lists the crimes the people have committed and announces the ensuing punishment. The latter announcement usually commences with the prophetic formula "Thus says the Lord."

The *woe oracle* consists of a series of curses the Lord pronounces upon Israel for breaking the covenant (compare 5:8–24). Since Israel's covenants with the Lord largely parallel the framework of ancient Near Eastern suzerain–vassal treaties, these woes mirror ancient Near Eastern curse patterns. All judgments of God upon Israel in the Book of Isaiah assume a curse form. The prophet pronounces the woes, however, only in specific instances of transgression, thus linking cause and effect.

The *prophetic lament* commences with the word "How?" (compare 1:21), a term that identifies a lament. The lament bewails a calamity or misfortune. It expresses thoughts that might paraphrase "How could this evil have happened before our eyes? How has Jerusalem, this great city, become so wicked?" Or, to draw an analogy from Isaiah to our day, "How could this great country in which we live, an exemplar to all the world, become so wicked and be taken over by enemies?" In the Bible, the Book of Lamentations forms a classic prolonged lament.

In the *priestly sermon*, the prophet assumes the role of a priest or preacher, those who anciently taught the people of Israel by expounding doctrines, urging repentance, and schooling them in the straight way (compare 8:11–17). Isaiah frames several prophecies around this pattern, prophecies that often adopt a personal approach by upholding an example for the people to follow (compare 51:1–8).

A *parable* likens one thing to another allegorically and depicts a sequence of things. For example, Isaiah compares Israel to a vineyard that the Lord carefully cultivates (compare 5:1–7). Though the Lord does everything possible to assure the welfare of his people, they do not bring forth good fruit. Instead, they bring forth *bĕ'ušîm* (5:2), the Hebrew term for fruit that does not mature, that rots before it ripens. Hence the Lord allows aliens to break into the vineyard, trampling it down. Briars and thorns rise up in it, signifying that the wicked overrun it. Enemies lay it waste. After the judgment, the Lord reconstitutes the vineyard. Now, however, the vineyard stands for the world at large (compare 27:2–6), whither the Lord scattered Israel. A repentant Israel again bears fruit when the Lord restores his ancient covenant people.

In the *song of salvation*, Israel or her spokesman sings the Lord's praises. They acknowledge the divine intervention that brought about Israel's deliverance (compare 12:1–6; 26:1–6). When things looked darkest, when the Lord tried the faith of his people past the point of endurance, then he delivered his people from their enemies; then he manifested before the world his glorious power. Such mighty acts of God earn him renown, singling out his people as blessed above all.

The intent of all forms of prophetic speech is to convey a deeper message. The apparent or surface meaning is there when we read the prophecies verbatim. But an additional meaning exists within the structure itself, one that may not readily appear at first glance. Though Isaiah modifies, recasts, or combines such structures, particularly in the latter part of his book, we always discern literary forms. The more of them we can identify, the richer and more meaningful the prophetic message becomes for us.

Parallelism

A literary technique Isaiah commonly uses—determining the smallest structure—is *parallelism*. Most of the Book of Isaiah appears in parallel sentences or statements. They are the basic ingredient of Hebrew and ancient Near Eastern poetry. Isaiah employs several types of parallelisms, all important to know and understand. To pass by them, reading the Book of Isaiah superficially, would be unfortunate, because Isaiah carefully organized the book's entire content, even the structure of individual verses.

As a rule, a parallelism consist of two synonymous statements—a *synonymous parallelism*: what the prophet says in one statement, he more or less repeats in a second. The value of such repetition is that the second statement can modify or qualify the first, and vice versa. The reader can thereby obtain a clearer meaning or definition from each verse:

> What do you mean by oppressing my people,
>> humbling the faces of the poor? says the Lord of Hosts.
>>> (3:15)

From this verse we understand not only that the Lord will indict those who oppress and humble his people (see 3:14), but that his people *are* the poor; Isaiah parallels "my people" with "the poor" synonymously. Another parallelism yields some particulars about a sin the Lord's people are committing:

> Their land is full of silver and gold
>> and there is no end to their wealth;
> their land is full of horses
>> and there is no end to their chariots.
> Their land is full of idols:
>> they adore the works of their hands,
>> things their own fingers have made.
>>> (2:7–8)

The expression "their land is full of" occurs three times, introducing three parallel lines. They speak of (1) silver and gold; (2) horses; and (3) idols. Similarly, the synonymous expression "there is no end to" introduces two parallel lines. They speak of (1) wealth; and (2) chariots. The parallelistic structuring of these verses means they are conceptually synonymous. They imply that the people's silver, gold, wealth, horses, and chariots exemplify their *idols*—the people's possessions have become their gods. On the other hand, a surface reading only identifies as idols the "works of men's hands, things their own fingers have made."

An *antithetical parallelism* contrasts one word or idea with another. Through such a contrast we again obtain a clearer definition or meaning of terms. For example, Isa 45:7 (KJV) reads, "I make peace, and create evil." This parallelism contrasts "peace" with "evil." Both terms come from ancient Near Eastern covenant vocabulary. In covenant language, the word *peace* is synonymous with covenant keeping and covenant blessing; the word *evil* is synonymous with covenant breaking and covenant curse—the two terms are antonyms. The Lord, therefore, does not *create* evil, in the abstract sense of the term. No such definition of evil occurs in the writings of the prophets. But the Lord does cause covenant curses to follow those who commit iniquity. That is the "evil" he creates. By this contrast of peace and evil, we also understand better what *peace* is. Peace must be good—a covenant blessing. By the same token, evil must be the opposite of peace—no peace.

A *chiasm* consists of several parallel statements containing a central idea (see a–b–a):

> a_1—I speak, and my purposes take effect;
>> a_2—I accomplish all my will.
> b—I summon a bird of prey from the east,
>> b—from a distant land the man who performs my counsel.
> a_1—What I have spoken, I bring to pass;
>> a_2—what I have planned, I do.
>> (46:10b–11)

The central idea of this chiastic structure is that the Lord will bring a "man"—one who resembles a "bird of prey"—who will perform the Lord's counsel. The Lord purposed this thing "from of old" (see 46:10a). He will therefore surely do what he has said, in spite of some implied resistance to his plan.

Lastly, a *complementary parallelism* conjoins two interrelated but different ideas:

> My righteousness shall be at hand
> and my salvation proceed;
> my arms shall judge the peoples.
> (51:5)

At a first glance, *righteousness* and *salvation* may appear to be paired in a synonymous parallelism. However, the term *arms* in the next line seems to summarize the two ideas. We are thus left to clarify the meaning of this verse elsewhere. When we search further in

Isaiah, for example, we find two synonymous parallelisms that identify the *arms* of God as *righteousness* and *salvation*:

> His *arm* brought about salvation for him;
>> his *righteousness* rallied to his cause.
>>> (59:16; emphasis added)

> O Lord . . . be our *arm* from morning to morning,
>> our *salvation* in troubled times.
>>> (33:2; emphasis added)

From these two synonymous parallelisms, we understand not only that God has two *arms*—one being *righteousness*, the other *salvation*—but that *righteousness* (the first *arm*) brings about, or is a precondition of, *salvation* (the second *arm*). *Righteousness*, therefore, precedes *salvation*, both literally (as a spiritual condition) and figuratively (when signifying divine intervention).

Uncovering the Underlying Rhetoric of Isaiah

Rhetorical analysis, the second part of my approach to the scriptures, examines the way a prophet-writer uses language (imagery, motifs, code names, definitions, etc.) to convey messages not apparent in a surface reading of the text. It involves more detailed study of individual terms and expressions, noting instances, for example, where one term links to another elsewhere in Isaiah. Such interconnections, whether in consecutive verses or many chapters apart, reveal additional important information. Each scriptural passage that contains rhetorical links to passages elsewhere is like one piece of a puzzle. When joined with other, connected pieces of information, a larger picture begins to form that provides yet another dimension essential to understanding Isaiah.

One of the most helpful ways of searching Isaiah—and all other scriptures—is to take a term or expression within a passage and follow that term or expression throughout the text. (We may do this by using the Concordance in the back of this volume.) How do other passages in Isaiah use that term or expression? What do they say in connection with it that sheds further light on the subject? By gathering such additional information, then applying it to the verse or passage we are studying, we understand more fully what Isaiah is saying. I call such an overview of related information a ''rhetorical exposition'' of a term or expression. We can know what Isaiah means when he uses any term or expression—we can obtain *his* definition of it—by analyzing his other uses of it. Rhetorical analysis thus requires patience and some determination. It helps develop our ability to see more of what Isaiah has embedded in his writings, to catch the many levels on which we may read his words.

Rhetorical Connections

Rhetorical links exist throughout Isaiah. They clarify many concepts and provide details, especially concerning prophecies of the last days. For example, why should Isaiah talk about "nations" or "Gentiles" (Hebrew *gôyîm*) "flowing" (Hebrew *nāhărû*) to Zion in the latter days (2:2)? Why should he not describe them as "coming" or "going"? It is because the verb *flow* purposely links to two other contexts in the Book of Isaiah in which he speaks of nations or Gentiles entering Zion (60:5; 66:12). Those two passages yield further information by depicting the return of Israel's exiles from among the nations. They say nothing, however, about when such a return takes place. While the verse above (2:2) identifies the flowing of nations or Gentiles to Zion as taking place "in the latter days," it says nothing about Israel or about Israel's return home; only nations or Gentiles are described as flowing to Zion.

By means of rhetorical links between these passages—the ideas they have in common—we come to understand that the nations or Gentiles flowing to Zion in Isa 2:2 represent Israel's exiles returning home from among the Gentiles and that this return takes place "in the latter days" (2:2). We see a more complete picture. Other terms and expressions in the same passage, such as the verb "go up" (Hebrew *ʿālâ*; 2:3), which denotes pilgrimage,[11] and the instruction the Lord's people receive in Zion (2:3) support these conclusions.

The Use of Metaphors

An understanding of the function of metaphors is essential to the rhetorical analysis of Isaiah's writings. In the Book of Isaiah, metaphors form key words that help us uncover important underlying

---

[11] See Eugene H. Merrill, "Pilgrimage and Procession: Motifs of Israel's Return," in Avraham Gileadi, ed., *Israel's Apostasy and Restoration* (Grand Rapids, Mich.: Baker Book House, 1988), 261–72.

concepts that are linked throughout the text. The term *mountains*, for example, is used as a metaphor that rhetorically links a number of passages. Isa 13:4 reads:

> Hark! A tumult on the mountains, as of a vast multitude.
> Hark! An uproar among kingdoms, as of nations assembling:
> the Lord of Hosts is marshalling an army for war.

In this verse, *mountains* parallels *kingdoms*, signifying (because their two lines form a synonymous parallelism) that the term *mountains* serves as a metaphor of *kingdoms*. In other words, we may read *mountains* as *kingdoms*. The Hebrew preposition "on" (*bĕ*) also reads "in/at/among."

Mountains likewise appears as a metaphor in chapter 64. There, *mountains* parallels a similar term—*nations*:

1. O that thou wouldst rend the heavens and descend,
   the mountains melting at thy presence—
2. as when fire is lit for boiling water,
   which bubbles over from the heat—
   to make thyself known to thine adversaries,
   the nations trembling at thy presence—
3. as when thou didst perform awesome things,
   unexpected by us; thy descent [of old],
   when the mountains quaked before thee!

This passage forms a chiasm of terms. *Nations* (v 2) appears between two instances of *mountains* (vv 1, 3), forming a chiasm (a–b–a). The expressions "melting at thy presence," "trembling at thy presence," and "quaked before thee" all parallel one another. The terms "at thy presence" and "before thee" appear identical in Hebrew (*mippānêkâ*). The three Hebrew verbs—"melting," "trembling," and "quaked"—are also common synonyms. Here, then, by means of three synonymous lines, Isaiah represents *mountains* as a metaphor of *nations*.

In sum, we may read the term *mountains* in the Book of Isaiah, in a secondary sense, as *kingdoms* or *nations*, to yield a transcendent meaning of the scripture. In fact, we may read every instance of *mountains* metaphorically, both meanings—the literal and the metaphorical—being valid. Once Isaiah establishes an idea in one part of his book, it applies elsewhere as well.

By employing our knowledge of these metaphors, linking their use to passages throughout Isaiah, we make some interesting discoveries. For example, chapter 2 refers to mountains and hills in the day of the world's judgment. A passage begins: "The Lord of Hosts has a day in store for all the proud and arrogant and for all who are exalted, that they may be brought low" (v 12). The key idea of this passage is that a day will come when that which exalts itself will be humbled—Isaiah foresees such a reversal of circumstances. He continues:

13.   [It shall come] against all the lofty cedars of Lebanon
           that lift themselves up high,
      and against all the oaks of Bashan,
14.   against all high mountains and elevated hills,
15.   against every tall tower and reinforced wall.

If we read *nations* or *kingdoms* in place of *mountains* in this passage, we see that a divine judgment comes upon all elite peoples, peoples who are "high" and "lifted up." The intent of that judgment, as a concluding verse summarizes, is to bring human pride low, for "the Lord alone shall be exalted in that day" (v 17).

Isaiah's use of metaphors in this passage, however, extends beyond *mountains* and *hills*. Trees, too, may symbolize people. In the Book of Isaiah, certain *cedars* and *oaks* represent people who are hewn down by an archtyrant, who is represented as the Lord's *axe* and *saw* (see 10:15, 33; 37:24). Only the righteous survive this judgment, those who are called the "*oaks* of righteousness" (61:3). Similarly, the *forests* that the archtyrant levels to the ground (see 10:34) may represent *cities*, as revealed by the parallelism of Isa 32:19: "By a hail shall forests be felled, cities utterly leveled." Mountains, forests, and trees can thus all represent people figuratively in the Book of Isaiah.

By identifying the metaphors in the above passage, therefore, we bring to light another meaning of the prophecy. On the surface, Isa 2:13–16 speaks of a series of geophysical objects that the Lord levels during a day of judgment. Isaiah does not mention peoples. If we read these same verses allegorically, however, we understand that what happens to the *cedars* of Lebanon and *oaks* of Bashan will happen to an exalted people, that the leveling of *mountains* represents the leveling of *nations* or *kingdoms*, and that the laying low of tall towers and reinforced walls will be that of other prideful institutions (compare 30:13).

Reading between the Lines

Rhetorical analysis helps us to discover important doctrines and theological concepts that lie hidden between the lines in every part of Isaiah. A passage in chapter 40, for example, speaks of weariness and nonweariness:

> 28. Is it not known to you; have you not heard?
> The Lord is the God of eternity,
> Creator of the ends of the earth.
> He does not grow faint or weary;
> his intelligence cannot be fathomed.
> 29. He supplies the weary with energy
> and increases in vigor those who lack strength.
> 30. Youths grow faint and weary,
> and young men slump down of exhaustion.
> 31. But they who hope in the Lord
> shall be renewed in strength:
> they shall ascend as on eagles' wings;
> they shall run without wearying,
> they shall walk and not faint.

Verse 28 depicts the Lord as Creator of the ends of the earth. The God of eternity, he does not grow faint or weary. Verses 29–30 contrast those who *do* grow weary—namely, mortal men, even the strongest—the young men on whom Israel depends for physical strength. In effect, even at his best, mortal man grows weary and needs a renewed supply of energy. The Lord provides this. Verse 31 returns to the idea of nonweariness. Those who "hope in" the Lord (Hebrew *qiwê*, also "wait for"), he renews in strength. They "ascend" as on the wings of eagles. They run without wearying and walk without growing faint.

The concept of nonweariness—God's capacity not to become weary—thus contrasts with the weariness of mortals; and then the idea of nonweariness recurs: nonweariness designates those who hope in the Lord, who ascend upward. The word *ascend* in Isaiah (Hebrew *ʿālâ*) implies spiritual progression. In sum, those who ascend become like God in the fact that they become nonwearying. Because the four verses are structured chiastically (a—nonweariness, v 28; b—weariness, v 29; b—weariness, v 30; a—nonweariness, v 31), the nonweariness of those who ascend is alluded to as being of the same character as the nonweariness of God. Isaiah here uses language that comes as close to describing human potential for a glorious immortality as any Hebrew terms.

Looking at Israel's Past as a Type of the Future

The third part of my threefold methodology, typological analysis, regards events and episodes in Israel's ancient history as something that could foreshadow the future. In other words, events that occurred in Israel's past could repeat themselves in modern times, particularly in what the prophets call the last days. Isaiah commences his book, for example, by speaking on the subject of Israel's apostasy: as the people of God alienated themselves from him anciently, so they could or would do again. Similarly, as the people suffered the consequences of their transgressions anciently, so they would again. Those who did not transgress or alienate themselves, however, would be delivered from divine justice, as they were before.

Isaiah consistently uses episodes out of Israel's past as types upon which to frame prophecies of the future. Having seen the end from the beginning in a great cosmic vision, he was able to view both Israel's ancient history (particularly his own day) and also the last days, the time of the end. He thus carefully frames his words in such a way as to capture both time periods in a single prophecy. No other prophet accomplishes this quite so successfully. No other prophet fills out this double picture of events so completely. In this manner Isaiah succeeds in speaking about things past, present, and future that concern the house of Israel.

Historical Precedents for Latter-day Events

Scholars have long recognized the prominence in the Book of Isaiah of a new exodus theme. Just as there occurred an exodus out of Egypt, at which time Israel was born as a nation, so a new nation of the Lord's people—Zion—will be born at the time of a new exodus out of "Babylon," an exodus out of bondage (48:20–21; 52:11–12). This time, however, the return to the promised land will lead through all elements that may stand in the way—fire as well as waters—and will be from the four directions of the earth (43:2, 5–8; cf. Jer 23:7–8). Israel's return exodus is nonetheless but one of many such new events, which include a new passover, a new wandering in the wilderness, a new conquest of the promised land, and many other latter-day versions of events that occurred in Israel's past. Whatever set a precedent in Israel's ancient history qualifies as a type for the future.

In the Book of Isaiah, more than thirty major events that set precedents anciently prefigure a series of latter-day events. These include, but are not limited to, Israel's apostasy (1:2–4; compare Amos 3–9; Hos 1–14)—which takes the form chiefly of injustice (1:21–23; 3:14–15) and idolatry (2:7–8; 8:19); the Jews' captivity in Babylon (47:6; 52:5; compare Jer 20:4–6); the raising of the tower of Babel (2:15; 30:25; compare Gen 11:4–9); the call of Abraham out of Babylonia to the promised land (41:8–9; 51:2; compare Gen 12:1–3); Lot's deliverance from Sodom (33:14–16; 57:1–2; compare Gen 19:15–17); Israel's exodus out of Egypt (43:2, 16–17; 51:9–11; compare Exod 14:21–31); Israel's wandering in the wilderness (40:3–4; 49:9–12; compare Num 14:33); the festal pilgrimage to Zion (30:29; 35:8–10; compare Psa 122:1–4); the Lord's protective cloud in the wilderness (4:5–6; 60:2; compare Exod 14:19–20); the destruction of Sodom and Gomorrah (3:9–11; 13:19; compare Gen 19:24–25); cosmic cataclysm (13:10, 13; 24:19–20; compare Josh 10:11–14); chaos (compare Gen 1:2)—which takes the form of darkness (5:30; 8:22), dust (2:10; 5:24), chaff (17:13; 29:5), refuse/litter (1:31; 5:25), fire (1:7; 9:19), clouds/smoke (9:18; 14:31), ashes (44:20; 61:3), waters (8:7; 17:12–13), mud (10:6; 41:25), clay (41:25; 45:9), fog/mist (5:30; 44:22), and dross (1:22, 25); a worldwide destruction as at the Flood (8:7; 28:2; compare Gen 7:10–24); Assyria's world conquest (10:5–14; 37:11, 18; compare 2 Kgs 19:11, 18); Assyria's invasion of the promised land (5:26–30; 10:28–32; compare 2 Kgs 18:9–10, 13); the Israelites' bondage in Egypt (10:24; 52:4; compare Exod 1:8–14); Assyria's siege of Zion (36:1–2; 37:33–35; compare 2 Kgs 19:32–34); the passover (26:20–21; 31:5; compare Exod 12); the Lord's descent on the mount (30:30; 31:4; compare Exod 19: 10–20); the Lord's consuming fire (10:16–17; 66:15–16; compare Num 11:1; 26:10); Israel's victory over Midian (9:4; 10:26; compare Judg 7–8); Cyrus' universal conquests (41:2, 25; 45:1–2; compare Ezr 1:2); Israel's conquest of the promised land (11:14; 54:2–3; compare Josh 1–12);

the rebuilding of Jerusalem and the temple (44:28; 61:4; compare Hag 1–2); the reign of the judges (1:26; 32:1; compare Judg 2:16–18); the Davidic monarchy (9:6–7; 11:1–5; compare 2 Sam 2:4; 5:3); the Lord's covenant (chap. 54); Zion as the Lord's residence (12:6; 24:23; compare Psa 132:13); the Creation (65:17–18; 66:22; compare Gen 1); and paradise (11:6–9; 51:3; compare Gen 2:8).

Around these ancient events Isaiah builds his prophecies. He includes in this sequence the events of his own day or soon thereafter to serve as types of latter-day events. Isaiah's day represented a crucial period in Israel's history, and it set many historical precedents that have a second, latter-day fulfillment. Isaiah incorporates these events into the broader sequence of Israel's history to compose a full spectrum of biblical types, projecting Israel's history on two levels—one ancient, the other based on the ancient types. What will happen in the last days is thus a composite of all that has happened before. In fact, this recurring of typological events characterizes the last days and would enable us to recognize them as such. When the sequence of events Isaiah predicts typologically is set in motion, we would know that the last days had begun.

We must take the words of Isaiah, therefore, as they stand. Modern scholars, notably in the field of archaeology, make remarkable discoveries that verify the history of the Old Testament, including Isaiah's day. We must nonetheless exercise care in reading such historical data back into the Book of Isaiah. Certainly Isaiah did not intend that we should read his book in that way. Isaiah does not fulfill the role of a historian, though his book contains historical material that modern discoveries corroborate. On the contrary, Isaiah takes pains to be selective in what he says about nations, persons, and events. He mentions only those things that apply on two levels at one time. In his writings, he exemplifies first and foremost the role of prophet.

Isaiah does not speak, for example, of Assyria's exile of the house of Israel, though that represents a major event of his day. But he does mention Assyria's invasion, destruction, and oppression of Israel, because that episode applies on both a historical and an eschatological or latter-day level: there will occur an Assyrian type of invasion of the land, a wholesale destruction of peoples, and a siege of Israel's righteous in the last days (see 10:5–11; 36:1–37:13); and Assyria set a precedent for Israel's takeover by an invading foreign power. But to describe Israel's bondage to a foreign power (Assyria),

Isaiah draws on the ancient type of the Egyptian bondage (10:24). Egypt set the precedent for Israel's latter-day bondage, and it, therefore, is the type Isaiah utilizes.

Further, Isaiah does not describe King Hezekiah in a negative light, though historically some grounds for doing so might have existed. Because all things Isaiah spoke have been and shall be, Hezekiah serves preeminently as a type of a righteous latter-day Davidic king. Isaiah, therefore, preserves only the positive attributes of Hezekiah, which are many. On the other hand, Isaiah does describe King Ahaz disparagingly (7:13). Because Ahaz serves as the type of an apostate Davidic dynasty, Isaiah says only those things about him which fit that mold. The books of Kings and Chronicles give a fuller account of the reign of Ahaz.

Many scholars fail to understand Isaiah because they seek to link his prophecies to their historical base—as if Isaiah were not prophesying, but recording history. Whereas Isaiah says, "Never mind the prophecies of bygone events; do not dwell on things of the past. See, I do a new thing!" (43:18–19). Few seem to recognize that the way Isaiah describes what transpired in his day is deliberately fragmentary. For that reason, the historical view of Isaiah has never made good sense. No one has ever understood Isaiah by means of it, finding, at best, an impaired view of a remote age. Only typologically is Isaiah coherent. His prophecies wax eloquent as he depicts scenes of the last days. His "sum of vision" (29:11)—his apocalyptic vision—unfolds to present a detailed and unified picture.

In short, we must accept entities and events as Isaiah describes them. Reading history back into his writings leads to confusion because Isaiah's message is *a*historical—his book is typologically oriented. Its overarching literary patterns, without negating history, nonetheless subordinate all that is historical. Rather, we should adapt our thinking to the prophetic picture Isaiah presents, laying aside presuppositions until we learn the nature of his transcendent message. To that end, Isaiah's own words serve as our best guide.

Ancient Assyria and Egypt as Types for the Latter Days

Let us look, for example, at how Isaiah characterizes the Assyria of his day: as one of two superpowers in the world, the other being Egypt. Isaiah describes Assyria as coming from the North; oppressive and ruthless; a law unto itself; militaristic and bent on world domination; imposing its yoke of servitude on other nations; encroaching on the world by degrees, swallowing up territories; and setting all the surrounding peoples in fear of it. When the world is ripe in iniquity, Assyria makes peace treaties, catching the earth's inhabitants unawares (33:7–8). Then, suddenly, Assyria bursts forth like a flood. With its alliance of nations, it sweeps over the entire earth, conquering, destroying by fire and by the sword, leaving havoc and disaster in its wake—capturing the whole world. Only Zion/Jerusalem, a safe place for the Lord's righteous, does Assyria not conquer. Assyria invades even Egypt, the other great superpower; it penetrates Egypt and ravages it.

After a few years of war and imposing its heavy yoke, Assyria lays siege to Zion/Jerusalem, where a remnant of the Lord's people takes refuge. Then occurs Assyria's demise. Because of his covenant with Israel, and because his people remain faithful to him through many trials and tribulations, the Lord utterly destroys the Assyrian army. The 185,000 men who perished overnight in the days of King Hezekiah (37:36) serve as the historical type of a latter-day Armageddon. As Isaiah depicts it, that event signals the end of one major Assyrian army (compare 31:8–9). Another is fought to the death by a righteous army of Israel (30:30–32). These two victories effectively end Assyrian hegemony.

The other superpower of Isaiah's time, Egypt, was traditionally a civilized nation. Isaiah characterizes Egypt as industrious, but enduring economic woes; stable, but suffering political decay; religious, but also idolatrous; having fertile, irrigated lands, but experiencing drought (19:1–15). To its vast forces of chariots and horsemen, the smaller nations of the world look for protection against Assyria (30:1–2; 31:1). Egypt represents the only military power sufficiently strong to counter Assyria. Many, therefore, ally themselves with Egypt. Their hopes are dashed, however, when Assyria exposes Egypt's weaknesses in a military confrontation (20:1–6; 30:3–5; 31:1–3).

Isaiah represents Assyria and Egypt as two contrasting political entities and shows how the Lord chastises his people for looking to Egypt for help against Assyria. That sort of trust constitutes relying on the arm of flesh, while the Lord requires Israel to trust in him. In Isaiah, trusting in the Lord when enemies threaten death serves as a test that will repeat itself in the last days. As the writer of Ecclesiastes says, "that which has been shall be" (Eccl 1:9). So too, all things Isaiah describes have been and shall be.

Conclusion: Understanding Isaiah
Is within Our Reach

The method of study I have described, relying on four interpretive keys found in the scriptures, forms a holistic approach for comprehending Isaiah's words. Though at the outset it may seem difficult for nonscholars to apply the interpretive tools outlined here, the smallest start will yield results. As we use these tools, we will begin to recognize how various patterns we discover will repeat themselves throughout the text. What Isaiah says in one context, he usually says, with appropriate variation, in another. The things we discover are seldom unique, appearing once, never to recur. Rather, Isaiah's words build upon each other and corroborate what appears before. Such repetition serves as a point of reference, helping us tie any single prophecy to its overall context. When we observe linked phenomena in that way, Isaiah's message soon grows concrete. We see the consistency of his words; a fabric forms. Only by that means—taking note of interrelationships—can we comprehend Isaiah's sweeping vision, his message of judgment and redemption for Israel and for the world.

This threefold literary method also demonstrates that the more tools we have to work with (the more we familiarize ourselves with the mechanics that lie behind Isaiah's prophecies), the more we can test and verify what is true. Recurring literary phenomena, as they appear throughout the text, help us avoid false interpretations. Isaiah did not compose his book to be immediately intelligible, to be transparent to the casual reader. He devised it to be unraveled with effort by those intent on grasping its message. To that end, literary tools serve as a safeguard as well as a key. They enable us to approach with confidence any given prophecy, to know precisely why we interpret something in a given way or why a particular misinterpretation does not make sense.

Finally, given the scriptural interpretive keys, one cannot fail to learn from Isaiah even by making feeble attempts. This almost inexhaustible book provides a fertile field of study for the beginner and the scholar alike. The motivation to know more that comes with making one's own first discovery will propel the reader forward in this fascinating endeavor. Characteristically, Isaiah opens the mind to new dimensions of comprehending the word of God, helping one to view the world through the eyes of a prophet, and thus, it is hoped, to come closer to seeing it through the eyes of God.

THE LITERARY ANALYSIS OF
THE BIFID STRUCTURE

It was during my translation of Isaiah into modern English that I made my first significant literary discovery in the Book of Isaiah. (That discovery, called the Servant–Tyrant Parallelism, is discussed under sections IV and V of this volume.) I found a series of verses in chapters 52 and 53 that contrast or juxtapose a servant of God with an archtyrant who is described in a similar series of verses in chapter 14. Twenty-one consecutive verses in each location clearly characterize one individual as the opposite or antithesis of the other. Imagine my surprise that two such different parts of Isaiah could be so closely related to one another. It was evident that the author had composed these two bodies of material so that they perfectly correlated, hiding a message at once profound and sublime.

Even more important than their interrelatedness, I realized, is the wealth of information these juxtaposed chapters contain. By such an antithetical depiction of persons, the prophet reveals the nature of the true God (the King of Zion) and the nature of a false god (the king of Babylon). At the same time, he teaches a divine ideology—what makes God God, what exalts him. And he describes a satanic ideology, what damns humans and causes them to forfeit their divine potential.

The discovery of that structure added a dimension to my understanding of Isaiah that changed my whole thinking about this book. How could I have supposed to understand about the suffering figure chapter 53 describes without understanding that chapter's full literary context as contrasted in chapter 14? The prophet was doing much more than telling us about the sufferings of a man of grief or sorrows (Messiah) who bore our burdens. He was also revealing the law of opposites, how one course of action leads to exaltation and another to damnation. He was dealing with personifications of good and evil, two role models from which people could choose to follow. Isaiah was teaching about life, eternal life! The Servant-Tyrant Parallelism in the Book of Isaiah was an exciting and a humbling discovery.

After working on this structure for a time, identifying its components and seeking to determine their significance, I was fortunate to study under Professor R. K. Harrison of Wycliffe College at the Toronto School of Theology. He introduced me to a much larger structure in Isaiah that a colleague of his, William H. Brownlee, had discovered. Harrison thought this structure might refute an idea many scholars had begun to espouse—that two or more authors wrote the Book of Isaiah. Brownlee suggested that Isaiah divides into two parts or books, one comprising chapters 1–33, the other chapters 34–66. He had not analyzed the structure other than to identify seven categories of parallel subject matter that could be found in each half of the book. Harrison challenged me to analyze Brownlee's structure for my doctoral dissertation, which I did, and which became the basis of this book.

Analyzing this structure was for me (as I hope it will be for you) a dynamic initiation into how a Hebrew prophet prophesies. It involved discovering many kinds of literary phenomena present in the Book of Isaiah, structural and otherwise. Using every literary technique at his disposal, Isaiah built into his book a veritable treasure of prophetic knowledge. In fact, it is because of the wealth and diversity of literary devices Isaiah employs that he is able to convey so much information in so few words. By our analyzing such structural or literary patterns, that information comes to light.

Fortunately, one does not have to comprehend all of Isaiah's literary devices at once in order to deepen one's knowledge of the message of this prophet. In my own studies, as I have searched and analyzed one literary pattern at a time, another, typically, would appear to view. Proceeding from one to the other, then reviewing the one in light of the other began to compound my search of Isaiah and ultimately to bear good fruit. As I grew more aware of the complexity and depth of truth embedded in this book, I was constrained to reassess many times the information I had previously obtained. Each new dimension I discovered required a complete reevaluation of the book's message until, after many years, I felt I had reached enough of an understanding that I could present the basic concepts to others.

The Division of Isaiah into Two Parallel Halves

William Brownlee published his suggested two-part division of Isaiah in a larger study on the significance of the Qumran scrolls for the Bible.[1] But Brownlee did not consider the twofold division of Isaiah unique. He contended that such a division also characterizes other biblical books. For example, Josephus writes of Ezekiel that "he left behind him in writing two books."[2] Brownlee considered these "books" to consist of the first twenty-four chapters of Ezekiel—"primarily oracles of doom," and the remaining twenty-four chapters—"primarily prophecies of restoration." He noted that besides this antithetical relationship between the two halves of Ezekiel, several parallel features exist. These include the prophet's call to be a watchman in Ezek 3:16–21 and again in 33:1–9; the temple's destruction in 24:15–27 juxtaposed with the temple's restoration in chapters 40–47; and the Lord's glory, which leaves the temple in the vision of chapters 8–11 and returns to the restored temple in the final vision of 43:1–5.[3] Brownlee also noted the division of the Book of Joshua, which consists of twelve chapters of conquest and twelve of allocation of the land; and of the Book of Daniel, which divides into two sets of six chapters.

In citing evidence for the bisection of biblical texts, Brownlee suggested that the practice of duplicating material—a practice that relates to a bifid division of Isaiah—was an ancient literary device that helps establish the authenticity of a work. He noted the significance that the biblical narrative attaches to the two dreams of Pharaoh in Joseph's day: the dreams are "one . . . fixed by God" (Gen 41:25, 32)—they are a unity. Brownlee pointed out that this idea exists as well in Joseph's two dreams and in the dreams of Pharaoh's two servants. As further evidence of literary duplication, he cited the twofold commission of Moses, first at the burning bush and again in Egypt. He regarded the two separate accounts of the giving of the Ten Commandments in the exodus narratives to reflect a kind of editorial ethic, a stylistic feature that flows from a love of parallelism.[4]

---

[1] William H. Brownlee, *The Meaning of the Qumran Scrolls for the Bible* (New York: Oxford University, 1964), 247–49.

[2] *Antiquities*, 10.5.1, quoted by Brownlee, *Meaning of the Qumran Scrolls*, 250.

[3] Brownlee, *Meaning of the Qumran Scrolls*, 250–51.

[4] Brownlee, *Meaning of the Qumran Scrolls*, 259.

Brownlee thus concluded that the two halves of Isaiah were construed editorially as a single entity. This necessitated that somehow they be expounded together. Brownlee pointed out that the Qumran scroll of Isaiah, 1QIsa[a], divides into two sections of twenty-seven columns each, separated by a seam in the skin of the scroll and a gap of three lines at the bottom of the twenty-seventh column. Earlier, Brownlee had presented evidence that 1QIsa[a] was itself copied from two separate scrolls, each consisting of thirty-three chapters.[5]

An analysis of Brownlee's seven categories of parallel subject matter in each book or "scroll" nonetheless yields mixed results. Although his first few categories show resemblances to one another, others appear dissimilar. Brownlee nonetheless admitted that his outline was not intended as a scientific analysis of the book's literary structure. His work represented but an experiment that sought to see possible parallel relationships between the major sections of each "book," with each category in the first thirty-three chapters corresponding to another in the last thirty-three chapters. Sufficient to establish his thesis, according to Brownlee, was the presence of several blocks of material that clearly relate to one another: biography following introductory material in each half of Isaiah (see figure 1);

Figure 1: William Brownlee's Division of Isaiah

I.	The Ruin and Restoration of Judah (1–5)	Paradise Lost and Regained (34–35)
II.	Biography (6–8)	Biography (36–40)
III.	Agents of Divine Blessing and Judgment (9–12)	Agents of Deliverance and Judgment (41–45)
IV.	Antiforeign Oracles (13–23)	Anti-Babylonian Oracles (46–48)
V.	Universal Judgment and Deliverance of God's People (24–27)	Universal Redemption through God's Servant, also the Glorification of Israel (49–54)
VI.	Ethical Sermons, Indicting Israel and Judah (28–31)	Ethical Sermons, the Ethical Conditions for Israel's Redemption (56–59)
VII.	The Restoration of Judah and the Davidic Kingdom (32–33)	Paradise Regained: The Glories of the New Jersalem and the New Heavens and the New Earth (60–66)

[5] William H. Brownlee, "The Manuscripts of Isaiah from Which DSIa Was Copied," *BASOR* 127 (Oct. 1952): 16–21. Brownlee notes that the midpoint of Isaiah according to the Masoretes occurs at 33:20, only shortly before the end of the chapter (Brownlee, *Meaning of the Qumran Scrolls*, 251–53).

the appearance of a new exodus motif in both units of the third category; and the balancing of antiforeign oracles with anti-Babylonian oracles as a fourth category. In short, Brownlee believed that "the two books were probably developed simultaneously."[6]

Were Brownlee's hypothesis correct, it would be surprising that the diligence applied to paralleling the first few categories of each "book" should wane with respect to the latter categories. If the two halves of Isaiah were developed simultaneously, why should their composition lapse into inconsistency? Since it does not seem likely that the parallel features of a bifid or two-part division should decrease in significance as the work progressed, we would have to either discount Brownlee's theory or assume he could not take the time to explore the full development of ideas.

Closer scrutiny of Brownlee's model, in fact, confirms his theory of a twofold division of Isaiah, but invites a revision of the proposed seven categories as follows:

Figure 2: The Bifid Structure

   I.   Ruin and Rebirth—chapters 1–5; 34–35
   II. Rebellion and Compliance—chapters 6–8; 36–40
   III. Punishment and Deliverance—chapters 9–12; 41:1–46:13b
   IV. Humiliation and Exaltation—chapters 13–23; 46:13c–47:15
   V.   Suffering and Salvation—chapters 24–27; 48–54
   VI. Disloyalty and Loyalty—chapters 28–31; 55–59
   VII. Disinheritance and Inheritance—chapters 32–33; 60–66

My revision of Brownlee's model, which I have called the Bifid Structure, essentially maintains the two-part division of Isaiah (see figure 2). However, the categories I have suggested differ from Brownlee's in several ways. First, Brownlee identified three generic categories, namely biography (II), antiforeign oracles (IV), and ethical sermons (VI), which alternate with other specific categories that he distinguished by prophetic themes, such as ruin (I), judgment (III), deliverance (V), and restoration (VII). At first glance, such alternation of genre and theme might appear to indicate structural inconsistency. Yet, I found that the categories Brownlee classified according to genre also exhibit prophetic themes. In other words, all seven categories display prophetic themes, while only the alternate

---

[6] Brownlee, *Meaning of the Qumran Scrolls*, 249, 253–54. In his chapter division, Brownlee does not account for chapter 55.

categories exhibit both themes and genre. Generic features thus appear to be not a primary but a secondary dimension of the structure, in effect, helping to demarcate the structure's sevenfold division (see figure 3).

Figure 3

I		II		III		IV		V		VI		VII
theme	/	theme	/	theme	/	theme	/	theme	/	theme	/	theme
		/	genre	/			/	genre	/			/	genre	/	

Next, Brownlee's classification of prophetic themes appears partial and inconclusive. While several of the seven categories reflect his suggested themes or ideas, others do not. In particular, Brownlee's historical referents and local motifs are not necessarily fully supported in the text of Isaiah. In contrast, the Bifid Structure of the Book of Isaiah, as determined by seven sets of prophetic themes, suggests a carefully conceived development of ideas, designed to convey an important message to a specific audience. Careful analysis of all seven categories reveals that they form a sequence that develops thematically from beginning to end.

Finally, the revised seven categories of themes that make up the Bifid Structure are more uniform and appear antithetical in nature. As stated in the Introduction (see The Bifid Structure, p. 15), these categories of themes are arranged chiastically. The first pair of themes (Ruin and Rebirth) parallels the seventh pair (Disinheritance and Inheritance); the second pair of themes (Rebellion and Compliance) parallels the sixth pair (Disloyalty and Loyalty); and the third pair of themes (Punishment and Deliverance) parallels the fifth pair (Suffering and Salvation). The fourth pair of themes (Humiliation and Exaltation) represents the centerpiece, and as such establishes a key concept. The peripheral themes of the Bifid Structure, in other words, lead up to and climax in the central themes of humiliation and exaltation.

Humiliation and exaltation are thus represented as two alternative conditions that humanity may attain, the other categories of the Bifid Structure being incidental to or supportive of these two. The antithetical nature of each pair of themes reflects the principle of opposites or of ''the two ways''—a kind of dualism found commonly in apocalyptic literature. These opposite human conditions originate as curses and blessings promised by God in his covenant with his people Israel: the Lord's people may experience either benediction (exaltation, etc.) or malediction (humiliation, etc.), depending on their observance or transgression of the laws of the covenant.

How to Read This Literary Analysis

The analysis on the following pages guides the reader through each of the seven categories or themes that make up the Bifid Structure, exploring the literary features and the apparent message of each category in turn. Throughout this analysis, each category is referred to as a "section." Thus, Ruin and Rebirth constitute section I, Rebellion and Compliance constitute section II, and so forth. Each section consists of two units or blocks of material, one from each half of the Book of Isaiah. The first unit of section I, for example, is the material in chapters 1–5 of Isaiah and it parallels the second unit of section I (chaps. 34–35), both thematically and in content. Similarly, the first unit of section II (chaps. 6–8) parallels the second unit of section II (chaps. 36–40), and so forth. Note that the various sections of the Bifid Structure are not necessarily of equal length, nor does the first unit of a section consist of the same number of chapters or verses as does the second unit, its parallel counterpart. The first unit of section IV (chaps. 13–23), for instance, covers eleven chapters, while the second unit of the same section (chaps. 46:13c–47:15) covers only part of two consecutive chapters. The seven sections and their units are determined by their parallel themes and subject matter, not by an exactly matching amount of material.

The analysis of each section of the Bifid Structure consists of my attempt to determine the literary features that make that section unique. Each section builds upon those that precede it, but it also contains a message of its own, based on its own internal literary phenomena. I identify these literary features in several ways: from a dominant theme or pair of themes, such as suffering and salvation in section V; from parallel or antithetical motifs and ideas, such as a "covenant with Death" and a "covenant of Life" in section VI; from generic features, such as prophetic oracles against reprobate peoples in section IV; from internal structural dimensions, such as alternating patterns of chaos and creation in section III; from rhetorical or word links between two units of material, such as the appearance of the "glory of the Lord" during the "day of the Lord" in section I; and so forth.

Because of the text's highly developed literary integrity, the two units of material that combine to form each section thus possess more than a thematic relationship; they evidence literary interdependence on several levels not just because they share a theme or a pair of themes. In the course of this analysis, all these literary phenomena are explored piecemeal, which, at times, may make the discussion seem somewhat methodical or mechanical. Sometimes a digression may be necessary to explore this or that aspect of the structure. Such secondary discussions are called "Discourses" and these are alphabetized, such as "Discourse J: The Woman Figure" in section VII. To help the reader pull these pieces together, a "Summary" of findings—of each section's literary features, and also their prophetic message—appears at the end of each section of the Bifid Structure's analysis.

The reader should keep in mind that literary features, particularly those that link parallel blocks of material, serve an important purpose. They help establish key theological and prophetic concepts. For that reason, the two units of material that form each section must be analyzed together; they are structurally interdependent. The second unit of each section augments or expands upon what the first unit contains. The next section of the structure, in turn, builds upon the literary evidence of those that precede it, as mentioned. For example, the idea of a reversal of circumstances between Zion and non-Zion, established in section I, is accepted as a starting point for section II. Section II uses a reversal of circumstances between Zion and non-Zion as a basis for identifying what Zion is and what it is not. Section III, in turn, builds upon these concepts by showing how the Lord delivers Zion and damns non-Zion in his day of judgment.

As will appear from the analysis that follows, the composition of the Book of Isaiah according to the bifid model binds inseparably all its parts. The parallel structuring of seven categories of material serves to elucidate the book's message, to develop "line upon line, precept upon precept" (28:10), important prophetic concepts. Within the Bifid Structure, all these concepts cohere and are established cumulatively from beginning to end.

Major Discoveries within the Bifid Structure

Initially, the approach I used to analyze the Bifid Structure was merely to determine whether William Brownlee's suggested model was valid. While his broad outline generally worked, it soon became apparent that there was much more than a mechanical significance to a bifid division of Isaiah. Thus, I went beyond Brownlee's findings into analyzing not only structural components of individual sections but also their deeper, prophetic significance. I discovered a purpose in the mechanical seven-part structure, and that purpose was to convey a profound prophetic message—a message for the latter days. Not only did I find Brownlee's conclusions, in the main, correct, but a mass of new data emerged that linked, theologically, the Old and New Testaments.

It first became clear to me that the Bifid Structure contained an important message as soon as I realized that all its categories, not just the alternating ones Brownlee had identified, possessed prophetic themes. Additional discoveries, such as the Servant-Tyrant Parallelism and structural and rhetorical features within individual sections, constantly required me to reevaluate old data in light of the new. The central themes of humiliation and exaltation in section IV, for example, are immediately encompassed by two high points of the Bifid Structure: (1) section III, which reveals the nature of God's temporal deliverance, and (2) section V, which reveals the nature of God's spiritual salvation. Humiliation and exaltation, as two final human conditions, thus play an integral part not only in spiritual but temporal salvation. Moreover, temporal salvation is structurally placed hand in hand with spiritual salvation.

Several discoveries in Isaiah took me quite by surprise. As I began my analysis, I had few preconceived ideas as to what I might find. Like many other persons, I believed that chapter 53 of Isaiah could describe the atoning mission of Jesus, the Messiah of the New Testament. As a scholar, though, I had been taught that the text describes just one "servant" of God, who fulfills a messianic role. I was surprised to find that the Lord's "servant" mentioned in the latter half of Isaiah appears not to be the same person as the suffering figure described in 53:1–10. Their characterizations in Isaiah, and the way the Bifid Structure deals with each figure, mark them as distinct individuals. For example, one dies by way of an atoning sacrifice for guilt, the other's sacrifice is arrested—he is marred and then healed. One is suzerain or overlord, in the pattern of ancient Near Eastern suzerain–vassal covenants, the other is his vassal: his servant and son. One intervenes in the affairs of God's children to save them spiritually, the other intervenes to deliver them temporally within a specific time frame—the Lord's "day" of universal judgment. The ample literary evidence supporting these conclusions (discussed in detail in the analysis) thus creates a bridge between Jewish and Christian concepts of a Messiah.

Another surprise was how the role of king emerged as a type of the Messiah. I understood that Messiah should be both a King and a son of David, but I did not understand the real significance of either of these attributes. With King David, the Lord made a covenant within which the king or his ruling heir served as a protector or savior of his people in a temporal sense. Depending on whether or not he kept the law of the covenant, the king could obtain or lose the Lord's protection of his people. In other words, if the king remained righteous, he could intercede with God on behalf of his people and serve as a model for them to follow.

Isaiah combines the type of a Davidic king who serves as a proxy for his people with that of another proxy, animal sacrifice. Under the Mosaic covenant, sacrificed animals died in place of persons who had sinned. Isaiah fuses these two Old Testament types to establish the concept of the Messiah's proxy atonement for sin. In Isaiah, the slaughter of ritual animals represents, allegorically, the slaughter of people in the Lord's day of judgment (see Discourse A: Edom as a Type [Synecdoche] of the Nations, in section I). Similarly, the "lamb" slain as an "offering for guilt" (53:7, 10) is a person—Messiah—who fulfills these proxy roles on behalf of his people. The Christian concept of Messiah thus finds an important Jewish basis in the Book of Isaiah. Only within the Bifid Structure do these ideas appear fully developed.

I also did not realize how unified the Book of Isaiah is. Reading other books of scripture with their perhaps looser organization did not prepare me for this highly integrated prophetic text. Though I already believed that parts of Isaiah, even large parts, could have some relevance to the latter days, after analyzing the Bifid Structure I was forced to conclude that all of Isaiah may relate to this time frame, that the book could be read both historically and eschatologically. Its numerous literary interconnections—structural, rhetorical, and typological—yield an apocalyptic message, much of which is presented in this analysis. Within the Bifid Structure, even historical narrative—parts of the book that record certain incidents of Isaiah's day—serve a futuristic function. Structurally, such episodes of history perform a typological purpose, foreshadowing some part or other of a latter-day drama.

The nature of Isaiah's literary structure, I realized (as distinct from the nature of Isaiah's content), is to lift prophetic entities and events out of the realm of history in which they may originally have appeared. The literary structure, in other words, creates a new, independent context for the things that are prophesied. Any governing structure of Isaiah establishes such a transcendent context (see Introduction, pp. 11–17). To grasp that idea, however, requires a considerable leap of comprehension. In my own dealings with literary structures, I had to make a completely new adjustment in my thinking about Isaiah. Of course, I related to the interpretive key that "what has been shall be" (Eccl 1:9). But to observe so many episodes of history repeat themselves, to see events and their participants replayed, as it were, within a latter-day context—to see biblical typology so fulfilled—was indeed astonishing.

One of the key messages of Isaiah, particularly as the Bifid Structure develops it, is that the Lord will physically restore his people Israel in the latter days. He will reconstitute them as a distinct people—made up of the righteous of all nations—at a time otherwise marked by universal calamity. For those who love him, the Lord will set in motion a series of covenant blessings that will end with the establishment of Zion and the ushering in of a millennial reign of peace. The earth's barren or cursed state, together with physical death, will pass away, and the earth will assume a paradisiacal glory. Evil and oppressive powers will be uprooted and removed from the earth as Messiah, the Lord God of Israel and the King of Zion, comes to rule over his people.

Isaiah's is a beautiful message of God's love for humanity, of how the Lord sends temporal saviors to deliver his people, but also of how he has reserved for himself that central and most difficult role of all—redeeming his people from their sins. Those who pass the tests of loyalty the Lord sends his righteous people, who uphold him through all manner of trials and hardships, he will uphold in the day of judgment. They and their posterity will inherit a glorious covenantal heritage on earth that will continue throughout eternity. The literary message of Isaiah, like a voice from the dust of time, speaks in our ears this everlasting truth.

SECTION I
RUIN & REBIRTH
(1–5; 34–35)

Both halves of the Book of Isaiah open with the same theme: the ruin of the Lord's wicked people and the rebirth of the people of Zion. According to chapters 1–5, and the parallel material in chapters 34–35, Israel will suffer ruin as a consequence of breaking her covenants with the Lord. These covenants, made with Israel under the direction of Moses at Sinai (the Sinai covenant) and later with King David and his heirs (the Davidic covenant), enable the Lord's people to obtain divine blessings by keeping the law of the covenants. When Israel breaks the law, however, particular curses come upon her (see Deut 27–30; Psa 89:30–32). Israel's ruin, which follows a period of covenantal blessedness, will therefore consist of a series of covenant curses.

The Lord's people, however, will not suffer these curses alone. Together with Israel, the nations of the Gentiles will suffer ruin for their wickedness and for their enmity toward Israel. Ruin, in other words, does not occur as just a local affair but is worldwide, suggesting that the earth's inhabitants in general have ripened in iniquity. In these chapters, the Lord brings to trial both his covenant people Israel and all nations in a day of universal judgment (3:13–14).

Still, such ruin is not absolute. The theme of rebirth also appears in these chapters, though it possesses a much narrower focus. Rebirth takes the form of a reversal of the covenant curses for Zion; that is, curses resting upon the Lord's people may be reversed and become covenant blessings for those of the Lord's people who repent. Again, Zion's rebirth does not occur as just a local affair but is worldwide (2:1–3). Thus, Isaiah prophesies, in effect, a reversal of circumstances between two categories of people in the Lord's day of judgment, a reversal that results in the ruin of the wicked and in a renascence or rebirth of the righteous.

National and Universal Aspects
of Ruin and Rebirth

Because the two units of material that comprise section I are structurally and thematically interdependent, they are most meaningful, as William Brownlee suggested, when they are expounded together. Virtually the entire section accords with the themes of ruin and rebirth,[1] which events take place on both a national and universal level. In the first unit (chaps. 1–5), an emphasis on national ruin offsets an emphasis on universal rebirth: Israel's land lies ruined, her cities burned with fire (1:7); Lebanon and Bashan, mountains and hills, towers and ships are laid low (2:13–16); Jerusalem and Judea suffer a dearth of food and leadership, causing their collapse (3:1, 8); the land's gateways lie bereaved and forlorn (3:26); like a woman in mourning, the Lord's people sit on the ground destitute (3:26); the Lord's vineyard has become a desolation, overgrown by briars and thorns (5:6); the mountains of Israel quake, and the people's corpses lie like litter about the streets (5:25). In the latter days, however, all nations participate in Zion's rebirth (2:2); the Lord's law and word go forth from Zion and from Jerusalem to many peoples (2:3); the Lord's plant grows resplendent and renowned, and the earth's fruit becomes the pride and glory of Israel's survivors (4:2).

In the second unit (chaps. 34–35), this pattern reverses and an emphasis on universal ruin offsets an emphasis on national rebirth: the earth and the world should take warning (34:1); the Lord's rage is upon all nations, whom he dooms, consigns to the slaughter (34:2); when the heavens roll up as a scroll, its starry hosts cast themselves down (34:4). The Lord's ransomed ones, however, return to Zion crowned with everlasting joy (35:10); wilderness and desert blossom like the crocus (35:1); the thirsty place becomes springs of water (35:7); the Lord's holy ones again traverse highways and roads (35:8).

Both units of section I nonetheless show some exceptions to this thematic pattern. Ruin and rebirth each have national and universal aspects in both units of material. This secondary emphasis, however, occurs much less prominently (see figure 4).

---

[1] See ruin, 1:2–24, 28–31; 2:6–22; 3:1–4:1; 5:1–30; 34:1–17; and rebirth, 1:25–27; 2:2–5; 4:2–6; 35:1–10.

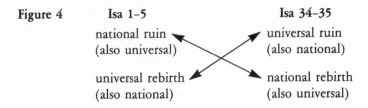

Figure 4   Isa 1–5   Isa 34–35

national ruin   universal ruin
(also universal)   (also national)

universal rebirth   national rebirth
(also national)   (also universal)

Thus, in the first unit, the Lord's judgment of his wicked people occurs synonymously or concurrently with the Lord's judgment of the nations (3:13).[2] The mountains quaking at the Lord's anger, in 5:25 (cf. 2:14), we may read in a metaphorical sense as kingdoms or nations quaking. (The term *mountains*, in Isaiah, appears as a metaphor of *kingdoms* and *nations*, establishing grounds for a secondary, metaphorical meaning of the term. See, for example, the parallelistic synonymity of *mountains* and *kingdoms* or *nations* in 13:4 and 64:1–3.)[3] Yet, Zion will become a city of righteousness (1:26), a place where the Lord's cloud of glory rests (4:5).

In the second unit, the ruin of Edom, a national entity, typifies the ruin of the gentile nations. The people of Edom, the descendants of Esau who sold his birthright for a mess of pottage, here connote structurally all peoples who show enmity toward Israel (see Discourse A: Edom as a Type [Synecdoche] of the Nations). On the other hand, anonymity marks the regenerated wilderness (35:1); its inhabitants, those whom the Lord ransoms and redeems (35:9–10), hail from unnamed origins, presumably universal.

Discourse A: Edom as a Type (Synecdoche) of the Nations

Rhetorical links in the first part of the second unit signify that Edom's destruction represents the destruction of the nations of the Gentiles. In 34:1–8, a series of linking motifs—terms that describe common ideas—tie this material together conceptually, as follows: the Lord sentences both Edom (Idumea) and the nations to

---

[2] An a_1—b—a_2 structure in chapter 3, as follows, establishes a synonymity, parallelistically, between the Lord's people and the nations: "my people," verse 12; "the nations," verse 13; "his people," verse 14. Hebrew *'ammîm* ("nations," 3:13) in MT and 1QIsaᵃ is contradicted by LXX *paon autou* ("his people"). The immediate context of the Lord's indictment of the leaders and elders for causing the ruin of his people (3:12, 14), however, favors the Hebrew reading.

[3] See also this prophetic metaphor in Jer 51:25; Zech 4:7; Dan 2:35.

damnation (*ḥrm*, 34:2, 5), consigns them to the slaughter (*tebaḥ*, 34:2, 6), their blood (*dām*) drenching the soil (34:3, 7) in a day of atmospheric cataclysm (34:4–5). Besides these rhetorical links, an a_1–b_1–c–d–e–d–c–b_2–a_2 structure exists in the same material. That structure, which features the judgment of Edom as a central idea (34:5bc), again places Edom and the nations under a common damnatory umbrella (see figure 5). A pronouncement of the Lord's judgment on the nations and on Edom, respectively (34:1–2, 8), begins and ends the passage.

Figure 5
a_1—nations/peoples (v 1)
b_1—hosts of the nations (v 2)
c—bloodshed (vv 3–4)
d—the Lord's sword (v 5a)
e—Edom's judgment (v 5bc)
d—the Lord's sword (v $6a^a$)
c—bloodshed (v $6a^b c^a$)
b_2—beasts of Edom (v $6c^b$d)
a_2—Bozrah/Edom (v 6ef)

The idea that Edom's slaughter represents the slaughter of the nations appears also in 63:1–6. That passage links rhetorically to the one in chapter 34 by the common motif of the Lord's day of vengeance (*yôm nāqām*, 34:8; 63:4) on behalf of the Lord's redeemed people. The slaughter of the nations, therefore, is not an isolated idea but is directly linked to, and occurs for the purpose of, redeeming Zion from the power of her enemies. In the Book of Obadiah, Edom serves as the type or synecdoche of all nations who, like Edom, did "violence toward your brother Jacob" and whom the Lord slaughters (Obad 9–10, 15–17).

The historical background of the Book of Obadiah throws light on the enmity between Edom and Israel: Edom's treachery toward Judah at the time Babylon destroyed Judah (Obad 11–14; Psa 137:7) perpetuates a tradition of covenant violation (cf. Joel 3:19; Amos 1:11) of which the actions of Esau himself, as father of the nation of Edom, set a precedent (Gen 25:33; 27:40–41). Such treachery appears at the root of identifying the gentile nations with Edom in Hebrew prophecy. The one stands for the other. Like Edom, the nations are reprobate for violating treaties or covenants with

Israel (Amos 1:9; 9:12). Their violation of treaties provides theological grounds, after sufficient warnings by way of oracles against foreign powers, for the nations' destruction.[4]

Chapter 34 thus consists of a series of covenant curses linking Edom and the nations within a common covenantal context. Such curses, which follow upon the breaking of covenants, identify Edom and the nations as reprobate entities. In short, the Lord's oracle against the nations in chapter 34 is grounded in a national type—Edom. Edom epitomizes the nations' treachery toward Israel as the Lord's day of judgment approaches.

Covenant Curses and a Reversal of Curses

Throughout section I, ruin occurs as malediction or "evil" (*rā'âl rā'*, 3:9, 11)—the opposite of "good" (*ṭûb l ṭôb*, 1:19; 3:10)[5]—and rebirth occurs as a reversal of malediction.[6] In biblical and ancient Near Eastern covenant language, good and evil signify the fruits of keeping or breaking covenants. The keeping of a covenant is rewarded with covenant blessings and the breaking of a covenant is followed by covenant curses. These two juxtaposed ideas show that ruin and rebirth in section I are covenantal in nature. They occur precisely because the wicked of the Lord's people and of the nations have broken covenants and because the righteous have fulfilled the terms of the Lord's covenants.

Under ruin in the first unit (chaps. 1–5) appear evils such as the diseased condition of the entire body of Israel (1:5–6), the devastation of the land by fire and by enemies (1:7; 5:5–6, 26–29), the overthrow and desolation of dwelling places (5:9, 17), Israel's destruction almost as Sodom (1:9; 3:9), natural calamities (5:25), the annihilation of those who forsake the Lord (1:28), corpses lying

---

[4] The political and theological background of the nations' covenantal relationship with Israel is also dealt with by G. Ernest Wright, "The Nations in Hebrew Prophecy," *Enc* 26 (1965): 225–37; John Mauchline, "Implicit Signs of a Persistent Belief in the Davidic Empire," *VT* 20 (1970): 287–303; and Gary V. Smith, "Alienation and Restoration: A Jacob–Esau Typology," in Avraham Gileadi, ed., *Israel's Apostasy and Restoration*.

[5] Compare Deut 30:15.

[6] The phenomenon of a reversal of covenantal malediction, as far as is known, possesses no ancient Near Eastern parallel; see F. C. Fensham, "Common Trends in Curses of the Near Eastern Treaties and *Kudurru*-Inscriptions Compared with Maledictions of Amos and Isaiah," *ZAW* 75 (1963): 174. This reversal of malediction therefore represents a prophetic transformation of ancient Near Eastern treaty patterns.

about unburied (5:25), a lack of food and clothing (3:1, 7, 24; 4:1; 5:13), the cutting off of offspring (3:25; 5:24), the abandonment of the land (3:26), the infertility and poor yield of the land (5:2, 4, 10), a lack of moisture and the overgrowing of the land by briars and thorns (5:6), and light turned to darkness—all maledictions or curses attested in ancient Near Eastern texts dealing with treaties or covenants between kings.[7] Whether in biblical covenants or in ancient Near Eastern treaties, such curses were well known and enumerated as following inevitably upon the breaking of covenants. Ruin in the first unit culminates at the Lord's appearance within the context of a "day of the Lord" (*yôm layhwh*, 2:12)—the Lord's day of judgment. Then takes place a final, maledictory abasement of all who exalt themselves against him (2:10–22).[8]

In the first unit, the ransoming of Zion epitomizes her rebirth. A verse identifies Zion by parallelism as those of the Lord's people who "repent" or "return," which verbs are expressed by the same term in Hebrew (*šwb*): "Zion shall be ransomed by justice, those of her [Israel] who repent by righteousness" (1:27). (The same denomination by parallelism occurs in 59:20: "He will come as Redeemer to Zion, to those of Jacob who repent [*šwb*] of transgression.")[9]

Zion's ransoming entails a restoration of political power (1:25–26; cf. 2:4); and in 2:2 we see the mountain of the Lord's house established in the last days as[10] the head of the mountains (*rō'š hehārîm*), implying that when the Lord restores his law and word (2:3) Zion will assume her rightful place as head of the nations.[11] When that event takes place, the nations experience an unprecedented era of peace (2:4). Israel's rebirth as Zion, which

---

[7] Fensham, "Common Trends," 155–75. See also many of these curses in Deut 28:15–68; 29:23.

[8] Fensham, "Common Trends," 173; and F. C. Fensham, "Malediction and Benediction in Ancient Near Eastern Vassal-Treaties and the Old Testament," *ZAW* 74 (1962): 9.

[9] Compare the emphasis on "returning" (*šwb*) in Deut 30:2–3, where Israel's repentance leads directly to her return from exile.

[10] So 1QIsaᵃ; MT has "in" (*bĕ*), which translators accept as *bet-essentiae*; compare RSV, NIV.

[11] See footnote 3. The idea of the Lord's people functioning as the head of the nations first appears as a covenant blessing in Deut 28:1, 13.

consists of a reversal of malediction, culminates with the flowering of a righteous remnant of the Lord's people at the time the Lord regenerates the earth (4:2–3). A cloud of glory forms a protective canopy over the assemblies of Zion during the Lord's day of judgment (4:5–6).[12]

We thus distinguish between those whom the Lord ransoms from ruin—a select group that experiences rebirth (cf. 1:8–9; 3:8–11)—and those whose ruin is identical with the demise of enemies, criminals, and sinners (cf. 1:24, 28), who nonetheless compose the Lord's people. Thus, the Lord says of the reprobate among his people: "Woe to them! I will relieve me of my adversaries, avenge me of my enemies" (1:24); and Isaiah, speaking of the wicked of the Lord's people, prophesies that "criminals and sinners shall be altogether shattered when those who forsake the Lord are annihilated" (1:28). The juxtaposition of these passages with that which describes Zion's ransoming in 1:27 shows that ruin and rebirth occur simultaneously or concurrently, as also the structure of section I establishes.

Typifying ruin in the second unit (chaps. 34–35) are the slaughter of men and nations (34:2, 6–7);[13] cataclysm (34:4); the lying about of unburied corpses (34:3); the infertility of the earth (34:4); the turning of the earth into lava, brimstone, and pitch (34:9–10); a wasteland forever (34:10); a haunt of wild animals and birds of prey (34:11–17)—all variously attested in ancient Near Eastern texts as covenant curses.[14] As in the first unit, ruin takes the form of covenantal malediction within the context of a "day of the Lord" ($y\hat{o}m$ . . . $layhwh$, 34:8). Ruin culminates with the cessation of Edom as a political entity (34:12), implying the political demise of the nations of the Gentiles.

Rebirth in the second unit occurs when the Lord reverses covenantal malediction: the Lord restores his glory to the land (35:2);

---

[12] See the rhetorical use of the term *day* (4:6) throughout Isaiah to denote a time of universal judgment, 2:11–12, 20; 3:7, 18; 5:30; 7:18, 20–21, 23; *passim*.

[13] As in the present instance, the imagery of beasts in Isaianic usage metaphorically denotes persons; compare 5:17; 13:14; 40:11; 51:20; 53:6–7; *passim*. The ritual acceptability of the beasts in 34:6–7, namely lambs, he-goats, rams, bison, bulls, and steers, may allude to the idea that those whom the Lord slaughters have become covenantally alienated. By way of analogy, Gen 15:9–10 implies the slaughter of parties to a covenant, as if of the ritual animals themselves.

[14] See footnote 7.

moisture returns to the wilderness (35:6–7); the wilderness again becomes fertile (35:1–2); the feeble receive strength (35:3); the blind, deaf, dumb, and lame receive healing (35:5–6); beasts of prey depart the land (35:9); and joy and singing occur (35:10).[15] Rebirth culminates at the Lord's appearance, when the Lord delivers and rewards those who hold out faithful to him (35:4). Within this context of rebirth, Zion forms the abode of the Lord's ransomed ones (*pdh*, 35:8–10), those of the Lord's people who repent/return (*šwb*, 35:10).[16] As in the first unit, Zion thus epitomizes Israel's rebirth. In section I of the Bifid Structure, Zion consists of both a people and a place—those of the Lord's people who repent and the place to which they return.

Interpretive Motifs Linking Both Units of Material

Several important rhetorical motifs provide a key to the message in section I about Israel's ruin and rebirth. These motifs include a day of the Lord, the annihilation of enemies, the Lord's appearance, the gain or loss of political power, the ransoming of a remnant that repents/returns (or, alternately, the lack of provision for a surviving remnant), and the glory of the Lord (see figure 6). These motifs are common to both units of material.

Figure 6

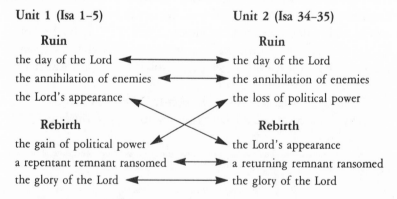

Unit 1 (Isa 1–5)　　　　　　　Unit 2 (Isa 34–35)

Ruin　　　　　　　　　　　　　Ruin

the day of the Lord ⟷ the day of the Lord
the annihilation of enemies ⟷ the annihilation of enemies
the Lord's appearance ↘ the loss of political power

Rebirth　　　　　　　　　　　　Rebirth

the gain of political power ↗ the Lord's appearance
a repentant remnant ransomed ⟷ a returning remnant ransomed
the glory of the Lord ⟷ the glory of the Lord

---

[15] The curses of blindness, maiming, etc., and the stilling of joy and singing—now reversed—also resemble ancient Near Eastern treaty maledictions; Fensham, "Common Trends," 170–72.

[16] Isa 35:10 in part states: "The ransomed of the Lord shall return; they shall come singing to Zion." Compare the similar rhetorical linkage of the verbs *pdh* and *šwb* in the first unit (1:27).

First of all, the parallel incidence of these motifs shows that the themes of ruin and rebirth in both units of material are essentially the same. The literary structure of section I not only juxtaposes ruin and rebirth, it also intersperses these themes with rhetorical motifs that are either identical or antithetical. Such an arrangement clearly ties both units of material together and makes them interdependent from a literary standpoint. Their interdependence is further strengthened by the overlapping national and universal aspects of the themes of ruin and rebirth. This interdependence requires that we view both units as one.

Secondly, by juxtaposing Israel's and the nations' ruin with Zion's rebirth in each unit of material, section I establishes a single stage on which this ruin and rebirth occur. Structurally, there takes place but a single ruin, both national and universal, of those who are covenantally reprobate and there occurs but a single rebirth, both national and universal, of the Lord's people as Zion. The context of these culminating events, in each instance, is the "day of the Lord." The final outcome, also in each instance, is annihilation on the one hand and ransoming on the other.

The literary message of section I, therefore, has to do with a single set of events, not with the separate historical scenarios that appear when the passages are viewed individually. Though Isaiah's prophecies may have originated in these different historical settings and may have dealt with the circumstances of those times, the structure of the material lends it another dimension and lifts the message out of the original time frame—out of history—into another time frame. On a purely structural, and therefore ahistorical, level, a scenario plays itself out that transcends the literal or historical message of the prophecy. On that ahistorical level, the overriding message of the material concerns a reversal of circumstances between Zion and non-Zion and the nature and timing of that reversal. Individual prophecies are therefore relevant within that broader perspective; they are less relevant individually because they are subsumed within this single time frame.

Lastly, the common, pivotal event of the Lord's appearance in both units of section I underscores the oneness of this time frame. The Lord's appearance points to a latter-day context for Isaiah's structural message of a single ruin and rebirth. The time of the Lord's coming is when the great reversal between Zion and non-Zion will take place (see figure 6). Israel's rebirth as Zion is exemplified by

the ransoming of a remnant of the Lord's people that repents/
returns. But within the structure of section I, such ransoming is
represented as taking place concurrently with the ruin of the Lord's
enemies, including those who stem from the Lord's own people—
all who covenantally alienate themselves from him. Both ruin and
rebirth, within this literary context, occur at the Lord's appearance;
the Lord comes simultaneously "to avenge and to reward" (35:4).
His glory rests on nascent Zion to protect his people from harmful
elements[17] and to regenerate them in the blossoming wilderness
(4:6; 35:2). Structurally as well as contextually, therefore, the Lord's
"day of vengeance" on his wicked people and on the nations is
at one and the same time "the year of retribution on behalf of Zion"
(34:8; cf. 1:27–28; 63:4).

Maledictory motifs paralleling the ruin of Israel and the nations
in both units bear out these conclusions. Such linking motifs show
that wicked Israel and the nations share essentially the same judgment. For example, the slaughter of the Lord's people by the sword
(3:25; cf. 1:20) and their corpses lying unburied (5:25) in the first
unit parallel the slaughter of Edom and the nations by a sword
(34:2–7) and the nations' corpses lying unburied (34:3) in the
second. The destruction of the Lord's people almost as Sodom and
Gomorrah and their land's desolation by fire (1:7, 9; 5:5–6) parallel
Edom's cataclysmic destruction and its land's desolation by fire and
brimstone (34:9–10). The desolation of the houses and buildings
of the Lord's people (5:9) and their land's casting of its fruit
(5:2, 4) parallel the desolation of Edom's houses and buildings
(34:13) and its land's casting of fruit (34:4). The cessation of travel
in the Lord's people's land (3:26) and its state of overgrowth by
briars and thorns (5:6) parallel the cessation of travel in Edom's land
(34:10) and its overgrowth by briars and thorns (34:13).

The juxtaposition of Zion's rebirth with the ruin of non-Zion
entities, on the other hand, appears most marked when we consider the Lord's people alone. An antithetical relationship between
the Lord's wicked people and Zion expresses itself from the first
unit to the second. Though the Lord's wicked people experience
malediction—a series of covenant curses—Zion experiences a reversal
of malediction. The deliverance of those in the second unit who

---

[17] See fire and storm imagery (4:6) in Isaianic usage to denote the Lord's retribution on the
wicked in the day of vengeance—while the Lord's righteous people are delivered from these
same elements, 10:16–23; 28:2, 15–19; 30:27–31; 33:12–16; *passim*.

repent/return (35:4, 9–10), for example, counters the annihilation of those in the first who forsake the Lord (1:28). The miraculous healing of those in the second unit who expect the Lord (35:5–6) offsets the general diseased condition of his rebellious people in the first (1:5–6). Similarly, the wilderness that blossoms (35:1–2) supersedes Israel's desolated land (1:7; 5:5–6). The glory of the Lord in the wilderness (35:2) and abundant moisture (35:6–7) contrast the gloom of the land (5:30) and its absence of moisture (5:6). Travel in the regenerated wilderness by the righteous (35:8) replaces the absence of travelers in the land (3:26). In the first unit, the Lord's people perish and go into exile (5:13). In the second, the Lord's ransomed ones return to Zion (35:10). In the first unit, the Lord comes to punish and abase his people (2:10–22). In the second, he comes to avenge, deliver, and reward those who wait for him (35:4).

These structured phenomena confirm that Zion's rebirth directly counters the ruin of non-Zion entities, whether national or universal. Zion's rebirth, in which a representation of all nations and peoples takes part (2:2–5),[18] offsets a concurrent ruin of all nations and peoples (34:1–5; cf. 3:13), including the Lord's wicked people. By paralleling the ruin of the Lord's wicked people with that of the nations while maintaining definitive links between the two entities, section I equates the Lord's wicked people with the nations. For all intents, the one has become as the other.

Such a conceptualization of ideas does not appear apart from the structure of section I. On the basis of content alone, one could contrast the ruin of national entities (Israel, Edom) and universal entities (the nations) with Zion's rebirth, as, for example, in the chronological sense of an *Urzeit* and *Endzeit*—of ancient events that

---

[18] Rhetorical links between 2:2–5 and other passages of Isaiah affirm that this passage depicts the return of Israel's ransomed ones to Zion. The idea of nations (*gôyîm*) streaming (*nhr*) to Zion (2:2) links rhetorically to two other instances of nations (*gôyîm*) streaming (*nhr*) to Zion (60:5; 66:12), both of whose contexts deal with the return of Zion's children from among the nations (cf. 60:3–5; 66:8–11). Neither of these passages, however, gives a time frame for the return of Zion's children, which, rhetorically, is supplied by 2:2—the latter days. The pilgrimage imagery connoted by the verb *ascend* (*'lh*, 2:3; cf. Psa 122:4; Jer 31:6–11), as it depicts the return of Zion's ransomed ones in other Isaianic passages (cf. 30:29; 51:10–11), again suggests a context for this passage of the return of Zion's ransomed ones. The term *judge* (*špṭ*, 2:4) links rhetorically to an ideal Davidic king (cf. *špṭ*, 11:4), whose mission is to gather a remnant of Israel and Judah from among the nations (11:10–12). Lastly, the term *light* (*'ôr*, 2:5) reappears in a passage depicting the return of Zion's children from throughout the earth (60:1–4): the Lord's *light* (*'ôr*, 60:1) attracts nations and rulers to Zion.

evidence Israel's ruin versus latter-day events that deal with Zion's rebirth. But such a contrast does not allow for the structural idea of a single stage of events—the Lord's day of vengeance—in which those who alienate themselves from the Lord suffer destruction and out of which the Lord ransoms those who repent/return. Through Isaiah's literary devices, we learn that these events are not chronological but contemporaneous; they occur at the same time. The idea of repentance and return by some who are then ransomed, for example, implies a general condition of apostasy. It also implies the possibility of not being ransomed, in the day of the Lord's vengeance, on the part of those who do not repent.

Summary

In section I of the Bifid Structure (chaps. 1–5 and 34–35) we find that the juxtaposed themes of ruin and rebirth account for virtually the entire material. The dominance of these themes in parallel units of material helps establish the concept of a political and tangible reversal between Zion and the nations of the Gentiles. Central to this reversal appears, first, the rebirth of Zion, which involves the ransoming of a remnant of the Lord's people—those who repent/return. Second, appears the concurrent ruin of both the Lord's alienated people—those who do not repent/return—and the nations of the Gentiles.

In order to show that the ruin of the Lord's alienated people equates with that of the nations, section I represents their ruin in parallel units of material, at the same time maintaining parallel and also antithetical motifs as common features that bind the two. The theme of Zion's rebirth, also common to both units of material, further suggests a purposeful structural unity in section I. Those nations that are not part of Israel, as represented by Edom in the second unit (chaps. 34–35), suffer a full measure of covenantal malediction, including the loss of political power. Zion, on the other hand, experiences a reversal of malediction, which reversal includes Zion's regaining full political power.

Section I establishes the setting for these events structurally and rhetorically as the Lord's day of vengeance on the wicked and ransoming of the righteous. Within that latter-day time frame, the Lord's appearance forms the pivotal and climactic event. Although this structural message subordinates the material's historical content, that does not imply the structure negates history. Rather, aspects of Israel's history, as selectively represented in this material, repeat themselves in a second, transcendent context. Israel's ancient history thus serves a typological purpose and may be viewed as foreshadowing the future.

Section I of the Bifid Structure is unique in the sense that the concepts it establishes nowhere recur in the form of parallel and antithetical motifs or as the theme of an entire section of material. On the other hand, all concepts the Bifid Structure establishes are cumulative in nature: once they are established, they are maintained throughout the remainder of the book. Thus, succeeding sections continue the juxtaposed themes of ruin and rebirth and the idea of a reversal between Zion and non-Zion, but with less emphasis than in section I.

SECTION II
REBELLION & COMPLIANCE
(6–8; 36–40)

Building on the idea of a reversal of circumstances between Zion and non-Zion established in section I of the Bifid Structure, the ensuing material throws light on the conditions that lead to ruin on the one hand and to rebirth on the other. Section II, in other words, reveals the kind of covenant breaking by the Lord's people that brings upon them such ruin as section I depicts. Conversely, it also reveals the nature of the tests of covenantal loyalty the Lord's people must pass in order to be ransomed from destruction and participate in the rebirth of Zion.

The Contrast between Ahaz and Hezekiah and Their Peoples

Section II of the Bifid Structure (chaps. 6–8 and 36–40) consists of virtually all the biographical material of Isaiah and is thus distinguishable by genre.[1] Structurally, section II contrasts the two

---

[1] See 6:1–11; 7:1–17; 8:1–18; 36:1–22; 37:1–38; 38:1–20; 39:1–8 (see 40:1–8 as a prophetic commission, below). Participants in the historical narratives of chapters 6–8 include the Lord, 6:1, 8–11; seraphs, 6:2–4, 6–7; Isaiah, 6:1, 5–8, 11; 7:3, 13–17; 8:1, 3, 5, 11, 16–18; Ahaz 7:1–4, 10–12; Judah, 7:6; Rezin, 7:1, 8; 8:6; Aram, 7:2, 5; Pekah, 7:1, 5, 9; 8:6; Ephraim, 7:2, 5; Shear-Jashub, 7:3; Uriah the priest, 8:2; Zechariah the son of Jeberechiah, 8:2; and the prophetess, 8:3. The text also mentions "this people," 6:9–10; 8:6, 11–12; the son of Tabeal, 7:6; a young woman with child, 7:14; Immanuel, 7:14; 8:8; Maher-Shalal-Hash-Baz, 8:3; the king of Assyria, 8:7–8; and disciples, 8:16. Participants in the narratives of chapters 36–40 include Sennacherib, king of Assyria, 36:1–2; 37:8–13, 37–38; Rabshakeh, 36:2, 4–10, 12–20; 37:8; Eliakim, 36:3, 11, 21–22; 37:2–5; Shebna, 36:3, 11, 21–22; 37:2–5; Joah, 36:3, 11, 21–22; Hezekiah, 36:22; 37:1, 14–20; 38:1–3, 9–22; 39:2–4, 8; the elders of the priests, 37:2; Isaiah, 37:2–7, 21–35; 38:1, 4–8, 21; 39:3–7; messengers of the king of Assyria, 37:9, 14; the angel of the Lord, 37:36; the Assyrian army, 37:36; Merodach-Baladan king of Babylon, 39:1; God, in the heavenly council, 40:1–2; voices 40:3–9; and a prophet figure, 40:6. The text also mentions the Virgin Daughter of Zion, 37:22; and messengers of good tidings, 40:9. A brief biographical passage that section II does not include (20:1–4) depicts Isaiah in a cumulative role as a paradigm of the demise of Egypt and Cush.

Davidic kings Ahaz (chaps. 7–8) and Hezekiah (chaps. 36–38), and their respective peoples. Together, the two units of material form a chiastic structure that offsets the covenantal rebellion of Ahaz and his people with the covenantal compliance of Hezekiah and his people (see figure 7). The prophetic commissions found in chapters 6 and 40 complement this structural arrangement. Material prefacing chapters 7–38 and 40–54 of the Book of Isaiah also forms a part of the chiastic structure.

Many important concepts emerge out of this structural arrangement. These include covenantal compliance by the king and his people as a formula for obtaining the Lord's protection, the idea of the king as an exemplar of his people, and the idea of the prophet as a paradigm or model of spiritual progression.

Figure 7

a—prophetic commission (6:1–11)

b—historical preface (6:12–13)

c_1—king's rebellion (chap. 7)

d_1—people's rebellion (chap. 8)

d_2—people's compliance (chap. 36)

c_2—king's compliance (chaps. 37–38)

b—historical preface (chap. 39)

a—prophetic commission (chap. 40)

In the first unit (chaps. 6–8), Isaiah confronts Judah's king, Ahaz, at Gihon (7:3), coronation site of heirs to the throne of King David (cf. 1 Kgs 1:38–39). The location of this encounter seems intended to put Ahaz in mind of the Lord's covenant with David and his ruling heirs which promises protection for Israel. Under the terms of that covenant, if the king maintains loyalty to the Lord, the Lord promises to protect the king and his people (see Discourse B: Zion Ideology [1]—the Davidic Covenant). Ahaz, by repudiating the terms of the Davidic covenant, stands to lose the Lord's protection of his people through his unfaithfulness if he does not repent. Ahaz manifests rebellion against the Lord when he rejects the Lord's promise to protect him and his people against a military attack by Aram and Ephraim (7:1–8).

The play on words contained in Isaiah's statement to Ahaz, *ʾim lōʾ taʾămînû kî lōʾ tēʾāmēnû* ("if you do not believe it, [it is] because you are not loyal to him," 7:9), reveals clearly Ahaz' apostasy. As the historical background of that encounter shows, Ahaz rejects the Lord's protection in favor of protection by the king of Assyria. By calling himself the king of Assyria's "servant" and "son" (2 Kgs 16:7), Ahaz repudiates the Lord's suzerainty or lordship and makes the king of Assyria his covenant lord.

Thus, in consequence of Ahaz' disloyalty to the Lord, Isaiah prophesies that Assyria itself will invade the land (7:17–20). The Lord's unconditional guarantee to David of a continuing Davidic dynasty (Psa 132:11), however, will prevent Aram and Ephraim from overthrowing Ahaz (7:4) and forcing Judah to join the alliance against Assyria. The terms *shaken* (7:2) and *intimidated* (7:4) that describe Ahaz betray his distrust of the Lord's protection against the Syro–Ephraimite threat. The contrasting terms *calm* and *unafraid* (7:4), which should reflect Ahaz' attitude if he would trust in the Lord, underscore the Lord's faithfulness to the Davidic covenant and its protection clause. Ahaz caps his rebellion against the Lord by rejecting the sign Isaiah offers that will verify the Lord's faithfulness to the Davidic covenant (7:10–14).

The presence of Isaiah's son Shear-Jashub ("A remnant shall repent/return," 7:3) at the encounter with Ahaz presages the Lord's judgment of his people in the event the king proves unfaithful. At the same time, the son's name denotes that the Lord will cause a remnant of his people to survive—in accordance with the terms of his covenant with Abraham (cf. Gen 22:17). Such a provision agrees with the concept of ruin and rebirth that section I establishes: though evil come, the Lord will deliver a repentant remnant of his people from destruction. Malediction, as represented by a plague of flies and bees (7:18), captivity (7:20), and the overgrowing of the land by briars and thorns (7:23–25), betokens the Lord's imminent judgment.

Ahaz' covenantal rebellion against the Lord coincides with that of Ahaz' people. The people preoccupy themselves with political rather than spiritual realities: they reject the waters of Shiloah, symbol of the Davidic dynasty,[2] endorsing instead the fractious northern coalition against Assyria (8:6; cf. vv 9–10). They live in dread of conspiracy and do not seek refuge in the Lord (8:11–15). They scorn

---

[2] See their source, Gihon, as a coronation site of Davidic monarchs, above. The text contrasts "the waters of Shiloah which flow gently" with the chaotic "great and mighty waters of the River—the king of Assyria in all his glory" (8:6–7) to denote two alternative political dynasts.

the Lord, inquiring instead of mediums and spiritists for doctrine and for a testimony (8:19–20a). As a result of their rebellion against him, the Lord cuts his people off from his presence (8:17), cursing them with military reversals (8:7–10), captivity (8:15), famine, and deprivation (8:21–22).

The northern kingdom of Israel, led by Ephraim, likewise shows rebellion against the Lord by seeking to replace Ahaz with a non-Davidic puppet ruler, the Son of Tabeal (7:5–6; 8:6). That political course, which finds support in Judah, contravenes the Lord's unconditional promise to David of an unbroken dynasty (see Discourse B: Zion Ideology [1]—the Davidic Covenant). The Lord thus esteems the two houses of Israel as one (8:14–15) and sends both, equally, the maledictory portent of Isaiah's other son, Maher-Shalal-Hash-Baz ("Hasten the plunder, hurry the spoil," 8:1–4). Isaiah predicts that the king of Assyria will swarm over the land and strip it bare (7:16–20). In the imagery of Lord Nahar, a mythological power of chaos, the king of Assyria will overflow his banks, sweep into Judea like a flood, and reach the neck (8:7–8).[3]

In the second unit of section II (chaps. 36–40), Assyria's invasion of the promised land and siege of Jerusalem (36:1–20) fulfills Isaiah's prophecy. However, in contrast to Ahaz' rebellion against the Lord, Hezekiah shows compliance: he repudiates the king of Assyria's suzerainty in favor of the Lord's (37:1–5) and relies on the Lord to come to his aid when Assyria invades the land (37:15–20). These acts demonstrate Hezekiah's covenantal loyalty.

Although Judah pays the price of Ahaz' rebellion, Hezekiah's compliance with the terms of the Davidic covenant merits the Lord's renewed protection of his people (37:35). The Lord delivers a remnant of his people by destroying the invading Assyrian army (37:36). Hezekiah caps his covenantal compliance by accepting the Lord's will unreservedly when he falls mortally ill (38:1–3, 9–20). The Lord, in turn, demonstrates his approval by giving Hezekiah a sign vouchsafing that he will recover (38:4–8, 21–22). Hezekiah's fidelity toward the Lord, in both instances, results in the Lord's protection of his people against Assyria (37:1–7, 14–35; 38:2–6); the Lord's testing of the king's loyalty has a direct bearing on the people's welfare.

---

[3] Isaiah's river imagery transforms literary patterns that appear in the Ugaritic myth of Baal and Anat; see *ANET*, 129–31.

Hezekiah's covenantal compliance when Assyria lays siege to Jerusalem coincides with that of Hezekiah's people. The political condition then prevailing in the Near East favored Assyria (cf. 36: 4–10). Not only had Damascus, Samaria, and the greater part of Judea by this time fallen prey to the Assyrian army, so had many nations who composed the ancient world (36:19; 37:11–13). Though the Assyrian general asserts that Hezekiah's loyalty toward the Lord will prove their destruction (36:14–16, 18–20), the people and their representatives stand their ground, following strictly the king's command (36:21).

The people's attitude thus reverses itself from the first unit to the second. Their covenantal loyalty toward the Lord and toward the Davidic dynasty in the second unit counters their repudiation of the Lord and of the Davidic dynasty in the first. The distinction between king and people, moreover, is now not so apparent. Unlike the first unit, in which the rebellion of king and people manifests itself in disparate ways, the second unit links the people's covenantal compliance to Hezekiah's own (36:14–15; 37:22). Their common loyalty suggests that political and spiritual accord now exist between king and people.

Section II's structured contrast of Ahaz and Hezekiah and their respective peoples parallels and builds upon the concepts established in section I. Ahaz' rebellious people and Hezekiah's compliant people share essential features with the antithesis between the Lord's wicked people and Zion. In the first unit of section II (chaps. 6–8), the Lord's rebellious people—the two houses of Israel as a whole (8:14)—suffer the Lord's judgments along with Aram (7:8; 8:4), the nations, and distant lands (8:9). A remnant in Zion survives the time of trouble, as represented by a man who keeps alive a young cow and a pair of sheep (7:21–22), and as expressed individually by the statement, "I will wait for the Lord who hides his face from the house of Jacob, and expect him" (8:17–18). So too, in the second unit (chaps. 36–40), the nations suffer destruction (37:12, 18), along with Samaria and all the fortified cities of Judea (36:1, 19). The text identifies Hezekiah and his people as a "remnant" of the Lord's people (37:4, 31) and as Zion/Jerusalem (37:22).

Thus, section II builds on the idea introduced in section I of a reversal of circumstances between Zion—a ransomed remnant of the Lord's people—and non-Zion. Structurally, those whom the Lord ruins, who ultimately suffer destruction, are those who covenantally alienate themselves from the Lord at a test of their loyalty. Those who experience rebirth, on the other hand, escape destruction when they affirm their covenantal allegiance at a similar test of loyalty.

Though historically the two units of material comprising section II are grounded in different biblical events—events occurring in separate generations of monarchs (Ahaz and Hezekiah)—structurally this material presents a message that again transcends history. That message has to do with the antithesis between two peoples and their rulers and the covenantal choices they make; it has less to do with the historical details of the material, which are subsumed within this literary context. The ruin of Israel and the nations, in effect, follows when many of the Lord's people make improper covenantal choices even as others of the Lord's people make correct covenantal choices. Structurally, these two phenomena are not separated by history but should be seen as occurring concurrently. Though differently nuanced or emphasized, the cumulative concepts of God's judgments upon Israel and the nations and the deliverance of a remnant in Zion in both units of material (see figure 8) confirm the idea of a single time frame for these events.

Figure 8	Unit 1 (Isa 6–8)	Unit 2 (Isa 36–40)
	Covenantal Rebellion	**Covenantal Compliance**
	Universal Judgment	Deliverance in Zion
	(also Deliverance in Zion)	(also Universal Judgment)

The parallelism of the two units of section II, interspersed with such cumulative concepts as just mentioned, thus accomplishes something very similar to the parallelism of the two units of section I. The antithesis of two groups of people in section II answers and builds upon the antithesis of Zion and non-Zion in section I. The covenantal choices of Ahaz and Hezekiah and their peoples have a direct bearing on the reversal of circumstances between the Lord's wicked people and Zion because the ruin of non-Zion and the rebirth of Zion, which themes are continued in section II, are covenantal in nature. Ruin and rebirth, here, as in section I, take the form of curses and blessings pertaining to the Lord's covenants, and such curses and blessings always follow covenant breaking or covenant keeping. The breaking of the Lord's covenants by Ahaz and his people and the keeping of the Lord's covenants by Hezekiah and his people help explain why ruin and rebirth occur in the first place.

Literary considerations, therefore, require that we learn to view Israel's history, as Isaiah here presents it, as being typological in nature or as foreshadowing the future. The idea of concurrent events of ruin and rebirth within the single, latter-day setting suggested by section I makes eminently more sense when we view the contrasting episodes of section II synchronously. In other words, two monarchs of the Lord's people (typified by Ahaz and Hezekiah) will be contemporaries or rivals in a latter-day setting[4] and react disparately to essentially the same political threat—an Assyrian type of takeover. From a structural standpoint, the antithetical relationship between two peoples and their rulers established in section II is ahistorical and typological in nature. It builds upon cumulative concepts established in section I that are also ahistorical and typological and lays a foundation for yet additional such concepts to be developed later.

Discourse B: Zion Ideology (1)—the Davidic Covenant

The idea that Zion is a people with a king who keeps covenant with the Lord is central to Isaiah. Chapters 7–8 and 36–39 within section II reveal an ideology associated with the name *Zion* that demonstrates how keeping the terms of the Davidic covenant leads to Zion's rebirth and deliverance and how such covenantal loyalty forms a basis for Zion's inviolability.

Isaiah uses two rhetorically linked passages, placed in consecutive chapters in the second unit, to underscore the link between the Davidic covenant and Zion:

> 38:6.   I will deliver you and this city
> out of the hand of the king of Assyria;
> I will protect this city.

> 37:35.   I will protect this city and save it,
> for my own sake
> and for the sake of my servant David.

Since these passages appear as one in 2 Kgs 20:6, their division in Isaiah seems intended to link two separate incidents—the threat of Zion/Jerusalem's destruction by Assyria in chapters 36–37 and

---

[4] See Saul and David as a historical type of such rivalry, 1 Sam 16–31.

the threat of Hezekiah's death from a mortal illness in chapter 38—to a common context of Hezekiah's fidelity toward the Lord. In one instance, while praying before the Lord, Hezekiah acknowledges that the Lord alone rules over all kingdoms of the earth; Hezekiah, as king, turns to the Lord, the all-powerful, to save his people in a time of trouble (37:16-20). In the other instance, also while praying before the Lord, Hezekiah asserts that he has been wholly faithful to him; in spite of the threat of death, Hezekiah is a king who has done what is good in the Lord's sight (38:3).

In each passage, Hezekiah—as king and heir to David's throne—considers himself answerable for the terms of the Davidic covenant. Also in each passage, the Lord assures Hezekiah that He will protect the "city"—Zion/Jerusalem (37:32)—called "the remnant [of the Lord's people] that is left" (37:4). Thus, the king's fidelity to the Lord vitally affects the covenantal bond between God and king that results in the people's protection: the Lord's covenant is with David and his ruling heirs (cf. 2 Sam 7:12-16; Psa 89:19-37), and the Lord protects the king's people on account of the king's loyalty to the covenant. When we read the two passages together, therefore, we see the Lord's protection of king and people flowing directly out of the Lord's relationship to David: stated or unstated, divine protection in each instance occurs "for my own sake and for the sake of my servant David" (37:35), as in 2 Kgs 20:6.

It is interesting to note that many Hebrew scholars see in the Lord's covenant with David and his heirs the salient points of Hittite and Neo-Assyrian suzerain–vassal agreements.[5] From such historical parallels we can learn much about the nature of divine covenants in any age, particularly as they relate to the Lord's deliverance of Zion/Jerusalem. A summary of resemblances between the Davidic covenant and suzerain–vassal relationships follows:

1. In the covenant of grant, when a vassal or servant king demonstrates exceeding loyalty toward a suzerain or "great king," the latter may bestow on him the unconditional right of an enduring dynasty to rule over a city-state of the suzerain's

---

[5] See especially Moshe Weinfeld, "The Covenant of Grant in the Old Testament and in the Ancient Near East," *JAOS* 90 (1970): 184-203; Philip J. Calderone, *Dynastic Oracle and Suzerainty Treaty* (Manila: Ateneo University, 1966); F. Charles Fensham, "Clauses of Protection in Hittite Vassal-Treaties and the Old Testament," *VT* 13 (1963): 133-43.

empire.[6] That city-state, in effect, constitutes a promised land granted to a vassal.

2. The establishment of a father–son relationship between the suzerain and the vassal, by a formula declaring the suzerain's adoption of the vassal, creates a legal basis for the suzerain's bestowal of an enduring dynasty on the vassal;[7] in treaty language, the vassal is thus known both as "son" of the suzerain and as his "servant."[8]

3. Bound by the covenant, the suzerain guarantees to protect the vassal or his ruling heir by undertaking to annihilate a common enemy, provided the current ruler remains loyal to the suzerain, does not recognize another as suzerain, and reports any evil word against the suzerain.[9]

4. The suzerain protects the people of the vassal because of the suzerain's agreement with the vassal. On occasion, the suzerain may contract an agreement directly with the people of the vassal. In that case, the separate agreement between the suzerain and the people complements the suzerain's primary agreement with the vassal.[10]

5. In the covenant of grant, formal curses are directed against those who violate the rights of the vassal or his ruling descendants.[11] If a vassal himself proves disloyal, the suzerain disciplines the vassal, often replacing him with an heir of the dynasty loyal to the suzerain.[12]

While scholars have noted that the terms of agreement of secular covenants parallel those of the Davidic covenant, they have nonetheless failed to see the full implication of such parallels, including

---

[6] Weinfeld, "Covenant of Grant," 185, 188, 193, 201; Calderone, *Dynastic Oracle*, 18–19, 34, 52.

[7] Weinfeld, "Covenant of Grant," 190–92, 194; Calderone, *Dynastic Oracle*, 53–55.

[8] Weinfeld, "Covenant of Grant," 185; Calderone, *Dynastic Oracle*, 70–71.

[9] Fensham, "Clauses of Protection," 136–37, 140; Calderone, *Dynastic Oracle*, 19–21, 30–31, 35, 44.

[10] Calderone, *Dynastic Oracle*, 21–25, 49–50.

[11] Weinfeld, "Covenant of Grant," 185; Calderone, *Dynastic Oracle*, 18.

[12] Weinfeld, "Covenant of Grant," 189–90.

the significance of that covenant's protection clause. The key role that the vassal king plays in securing his people's deliverance has a bearing not only on the nature of Zion, but also on important concepts the Bifid Structure develops later, such as proxy salvation from sin. A closer look at the king's role as protector reveals the essence of these concepts.

In the Davidic covenant, the Lord fulfills the role of suzerain, and King David or his ruling heir serves as the Lord's vassal. Thus, in language similar to that of the Neo-Assyrian covenant of grant,[13] when David walks before the Lord in truth and loyalty, and with uprightness of heart, the Lord maintains "loving-kindness" (*ḥesed*) toward him (1 Kgs 3:6). The term *ḥesed* (also "fidelity/charity") is a synonym of *covenant*.[14] To express "loving-kindness" toward someone, therefore, means to keep covenant with that person. On the other hand, when David transgresses against the Lord, as in his peremptorily taking a census of Israel (2 Sam 24:1), the Lord's protection of Israel breaks down (2 Sam 24:13).

In regard to the Lord's agreement with King Solomon, David's heir, if Solomon will walk in the Lord's statutes, perform his laws, and keep all his commandments, the Lord will fulfill his word to David and dwell among the children of Israel and not forsake his people (1 Kgs 6:12–13). But if Solomon will not walk before the Lord as David walked, with integrity of heart and uprightness, and will not keep his commandments and statutes, the Lord will cut off Israel out of the land and Israel will become a proverb and byword among all peoples (1 Kgs 9:4, 6–7). In other words, in Davidic covenant theology, the welfare and protection of the people depend on the king's loyalty toward the Lord.

The movement from inspired war leaders, Israel's judges, to the people's desire for a full-fledged monarch, in fact, occurs in response to a need for national protection (cf. 1 Sam 12:12). Up to that time, the Lord's people were obligated to keep the terms of the Sinai covenant in order to obtain the Lord's protection. The Sinai covenant follows the pattern of a separate and secondary agreement between a suzerain and a people and is a more difficult covenant to keep. The clause of protection in the Sinai covenant operates only if all

---

[13] Weinfeld, "Covenant of Grant," 185–86.

[14] Moshe Weinfeld, "Berîth," in *TDOT*, 2:258–59.

Israel—as the Lord's vassal—maintains loyalty toward him. The Sinai covenant, in other words, demands loyalty toward the Lord by the entire people, rather than by a king on behalf of the people, if the people would obtain divine protection.

Loyalty toward the Lord by the entire people, as under the Sinai covenant, appears briefly when Israel first conquers Canaan. Israel here benefits from the leadership of Moses and Joshua, and Israel consistently gains the victory over her enemies. This generation of Israelites, born during the wilderness wandering, was schooled by Moses in the law of the Sinai covenant. In an instance where one man transgresses by confiscating the spoils of war (Josh 7:21), the Lord nonetheless accuses all Israel of breaking the covenant (Josh 7:11).[15] As a consequence, Israel in general suffers military reverses (Josh 7:4–5, 12–13). Joshua then casts lots, successively, on the tribes, clans, and families of the people to determine who has sinned (Josh 7:14–20). When the people destroy the offender and his house, the Lord again protects Israel (Josh 7:24–8:1).

After the conquest of Canaan, when Israel's loyalty to the Lord lapses, the Lord's protection of his people also lapses, and by the time of Samuel and Saul, the Philistines threaten Israel's very existence. When Israel demands a king, Samuel reminds the people that the Lord is their King—their suzerain (1 Sam 8:4–10; 12:12). If all Israel will keep his commandments—the law of the Sinai covenant—then the Lord is bound to protect them. But the people react to the objections of Samuel with, "We will have a king . . . that our king may . . . go out before us, and fight our battles" (1 Sam 8:19–20). Israel's elders see that the people can no longer maintain loyalty toward the Lord to a man (1 Sam 8:19; 12:12). The Lord therefore answers their demands and gives his people a human king (1 Sam 8:7; 12:13).

The Lord's instituting human kingship in Israel promises a people's protection on the same basis as in ancient Near Eastern treaties. Such protection, however, is put in force, not by virtue of a people's agreement with a suzerain[16]—as in the case of the Sinai covenant—but because a vassal, their king, demonstrates loyalty

---

[15] Later, in the days of Israel's kings, however, when the men of Saul take unlawful spoil, the Lord blames not Israel but Saul (1 Sam 15:1–35).

[16] As in a twin agreement between a suzerain and a people; compare the Hittite treaties with the Mittani and Hayasa peoples; Calderone, *Dynastic Oracle*, 22, 49–50.

toward the suzerain.[17] All that is now required of the people is to exercise loyalty toward their king. A human king, in effect, stands in for the Lord as the people's suzerain, while he himself serves as vassal to the Lord. With the advent of human kingship, the Sinai covenant thus grows less prominent because it follows the pattern of a separate and secondary agreement between a suzerain and a people.

There is nonetheless another dimension to human kingship, that of obtaining a suzerain's, in this case the Lord's, approval. We note, for example, a difference in the actions of Saul, Israel's first king, and those of David, the son of Jesse. When Saul acts presumptuously, and thus fails to keep covenant with the Lord, the Lord replaces him with David (1 Sam 16:1). For a time, however, the two kings exist as contemporaries, and it is evident which king the Lord prospers. Saul's ire at the proverb according to which he kills Philistines by the thousands but David kills them by the tens of thousands (1 Sam 18:8) dramatizes the idea of the king as a divinely sanctioned and divinely prospered warlord. The prophet Samuel's anointing of David results in Saul's losing face with the people even as David gains their favor. Saul's demise takes place soon thereafter.

As in the case of Saul, David's first appointment to kingship occurs largely for the sake of Israel's protection. David becomes the means whereby the Lord will "cut off all [Israel's] enemies out of [her] sight" (2 Sam 7:8–9). Abner's appeal to the northern tribes to accept David as king relies on the premise that "the Lord has spoken of David, saying, By the hand of my servant David I will save my people Israel out of the hand of the Philistines, and out of the hand of all their enemies" (2 Sam 3:18; cf. 5:2). The need for protection leads to the choice of both kings.

Unlike Saul, who loses favor with the Lord for doing contrary to His word (cf. 1 Sam 13:13–14; 15:22–28), David proves loyal when put to the test. He trusts implicitly in the Lord to give him the victory when the Philistines challenge Israel (1 Sam 17:26–47; 23:1–5). He does not so much as speak a word against the Lord's

---

[17] Fensham, "Clauses of Protection," 138–40; Calderone, *Dynastic Oracle*, 24–25., 31, 33. Although the Neo-Assyrian grants, unlike their Hittite models, make no specific mention of a vassal's protection, such protection nonetheless formed an integral part of the agreement, as numerous historical examples show; Calderone, *Dynastic Oracle*, 28–29. Jacques Pirenne, in "La politique d'expansion hittite envisagée à travers les traités de vassalité et de protectorat," *ArOr* 18:1 (1950): 373-82, points to the feudal nature of Hittite covenants.

anointed (Saul), even when Saul seeks his life, and the Lord gives David power over him (1 Sam 24:1–22; 26:1–25). David is a man after the Lord's own heart (1 Sam 13:14).

David's second divine appointment, after the death of Saul, thus confirms the first (as Calderone notes, though he misses its intent).[18] David's second appointment constitutes a suzerain's promise to a faithful and victorious ruler of an enduring dynasty over a people and place—a covenant of grant (cf. 2 Sam 7:10–12; Psa 89:19–29). The idea behind David's second calling, however, which lends permanence to Israel's establishment in the land, is this: thereafter, those who are loyal to the Davidic king obtain the Lord's protection by proxy so long as the king maintains loyalty toward the Lord. The suzerain (the Lord) is bound to protect the people of the vassal (King David) when the vassal fulfills the terms of the covenant.

The conditional aspect of the Davidic covenant—the question of the king's loyalty to the Lord—affects Israel's protection for better or worse. King Hezekiah's loyalty and other kings' disloyalty illustrate that principle. But the covenant's unconditional aspect—that of an enduring dynasty—leaves open the possibility of the Lord's appointing a loyal Davidic monarch should a disloyal monarch default. A suzerain retains the option of replacing a disloyal vassal with another who is loyal. The Lord's protection of his people by virtue of the Davidic covenant can thus be restored at any time.

Although the Lord also guarantees such protection under the Sinai covenant, only in special circumstances can his people merit it. Such a circumstance—loyalty to the Lord by an entire people— would not easily repeat itself. The Davidic covenant, therefore, serves an interim role. That covenant remains in force so long as the Lord's people are unable to fulfill the terms of a higher law, relatively speaking, namely the law of the Sinai covenant. The suzerain–vassal model as a legal framework for both the Sinai covenant and the Davidic covenant nonetheless holds up. It establishes the only basis on which the Lord's people may obtain his protection.

In short, no provision exists for ensuring national protection other than within the framework of a suzerain–vassal type of agreement with the Lord. The Davidic covenant, however, does away with the need for all Israel, to a man, to maintain loyalty toward the Lord

---

[18] Calderone, *Dynastic Oracle*, 46, 59–60.

in order to merit his protection. Davidic kingship thus exemplifies covenantal kingship. As its proxy role shows, one of its primary functions is to secure divine protection for the Lord's people.

As in ancient Near Eastern suzerain–vassal treaties, the Lord establishes a father–son relationship with David and his ruling heirs (2 Sam 7:14–16). The Lord calls David his "servant," "son," and "firstborn" (Psa 2:6–7; 89:3, 20, 27), thus making David Israel's representative. David is the living embodiment of the Lord's covenant people, who are also called the Lord's "servant," "son," and "firstborn" (Exod 4:22; Isa 41:8). To Israel as a nation, and to the Davidic king as an individual, the Lord serves covenantally as "father" (Deut 32:6; Psa 89:26). Concerning Israel's divine protection, the Davidic covenant succeeds the Sinai covenant but only because Israel has regressed in her loyalty toward the Lord (cf. 1 Sam 8:7). The king now stands as an intermediary between the Lord and his people.

An idea flowing out of the Davidic covenant, therefore, is that of Zion/Jerusalem as a safe place (Isa 37:33). Divine protection under the terms of the Davidic covenant is guaranteed for those who are loyal to a righteous king but not for those who are disloyal. That selective element of the Davidic covenant—loyalty by the people—accounts for a "remnant" of Israel surviving a mortal threat such as that posed by Assyria. Where this remnant and its king abide, in other words, constitutes a safe or inviolable place because that is where the Lord intervenes on their behalf.

In short, Zion proves inviolable because Israel's suzerain is bound to come to the aid of his vassal when the vassal keeps the terms of the Davidic covenant. The Lord's dwelling among his people, as the Lord spoke to Solomon, is a sign of the fulfillment of the terms of the Davidic covenant (cf. 1 Kgs 6:12–13; Psa 132:11–14). God's coming to dwell in Zion (Psa 48:1–3) means that all elements of the Davidic covenant, including its protection clause, are operative (cf. Psa 76:2–3). The transition from the Sinai to the Davidic covenant thus coincides with the temple becoming the Lord's fixed abode. Salvation follows for the people when the Lord dwells in their midst (Isa 12:1–6).

Such concepts have a bearing on why the earlier Sinai covenant is linked to the Davidic covenant in 2 Sam 7:23–25: through the unconditional Davidic covenant, the Lord has "confirmed to [himself his] people to be a people unto [him] for ever; and [he has] become their God" (2 Sam 7:24). The covenant formula "your/his people–our/their God" expresses Israel's relationship to the Lord within the Sinai covenant (Lev 26:12; Deut 29:12–13; Isa 51:15–16). In this passage, King David appeals to the Sinai covenant in support of the Davidic covenant. The triad of blessings pertaining to the Sinai covenant—a promised land, an enduring offspring, and divine protection—is now being realized for Israel under the Davidic covenant.

The historical background of the Davidic covenant sheds light on the Lord's promise, "I will protect this city and save it, for my own sake and for the sake of my servant David" (37:35). That promise confirms a suzerain–vassal type of relationship between the Lord and a loyal ruler (Hezekiah), heir of the Davidic dynasty. The city, in this passage, denotes both Jerusalem and Mount Zion (cf. 37:22, 32). The former designates the place that will remain under Davidic jurisdiction (cf. 1 Kgs 11:13); the latter represents the abode of the Lord (cf. Isa 8:18). The expression "for my own sake and for the sake of my servant David" signifies that both parties are meeting the terms of the covenant.

Hezekiah's loyalty toward the Lord is evident from the statement, "I have walked before thee in truth and integrity of heart, in doing what is good ($ṭôb$) in thy sight" (38:3). The Lord acknowledges Hezekiah's loyalty when he heals the king from a mortal illness ($ḥālâ$; 38:1, 21); he prolongs Hezekiah's life by fifteen years (38:5). Both doing good ($ṭôb$) and being ill ($ḥālâ$) express covenantal loyalty in ancient Near Eastern treaty language.[19] Hezekiah's illness and recovery, therefore, themselves imply loyalty toward the Lord. The king's ministering to his people and his suffering on their behalf directly merit their divine protection (38:6).

When Assyria threatens Zion/Jerusalem, Hezekiah summons Isaiah (37:2) to report the king of Assyria's evil word against the Lord (37:4, 17). That act follows the model of the vassal (Hezekiah) reporting to the suzerain (the Lord)—through his prophet or messenger—when the vassal learns of an enemy's plot against the

---

[19] See, respectively, M. Fox, "*Ṭôb* as Covenant Terminology," *BASOR* 209 (1973): 41–42; Weinfeld, "Berîth," 259; and 1 Sam 22:8; Amos 6:6, cited by Weinfeld in "Covenant of Grant," 187. See also the synonymity of good (*ṭôb*) and truth/loyalty (*ʾemet*) in Isa 39:8, and the historical significance afforded a monarch's recovery from grave illness in Isa 39:1.

suzerain. The Lord responds by destroying the common enemy (the Assyrian king and his army), inflicting covenant curses on those who violate the rights of the Lord's vassal (37:36, 38).[20]

These events have an antithesis in the first unit of section II, to demonstrate the opposite phenomenon—a vassal's disloyalty. When the Lord promises Ahaz that Aram and Ephraim's scheme to place a puppet ruler on Ahaz' throne will not succeed (7:6-7), the Lord shows that he intends to stand by the terms of the Davidic covenant, that he will ensure the continuance of Davidic rule.

The name of the proposed puppet ruler, the "Son of Tabeal" (7:6), in treaty language denotes a no-good/noncovenantal vassal. *Tabeal* forms a compound of Hebrew *ṭāb* ("good") and *'al* ("not"). In the light of the Lord's unconditional promise to Ahaz, therefore, the name asserts that the puppet king is not Davidic. Ephraim's demise as a nation, which the Lord decrees in the same passage (7:8), thus represents a covenant curse on those who violate the rights of the Lord's vassal, Ahaz. By sending tribute monies to the king of Assyria, however, and by calling on his aid against Aram and Ephraim (2 Kgs 16:7-8), Ahaz rejects the Lord's suzerainty. By referring to himself as the king of Assyria's "servant" and "son" (2 Kgs 16:7), Ahaz instead identifies the king of Assyria as his suzerain.

As in ancient Near Eastern treaty procedure, the Lord responds by choosing another Davidic son–vassal, Immanuel ("God is with us," 7:14), to replace Ahaz. The Lord also denies his protection to both king and people: the king of Assyria will come "upon you and your people and your father's house" (7:17). Historically, King Hezekiah, Ahaz' son, serves as the prophesied Immanuel. In Hezekiah's day, the king of Assyria invades the land of Immanuel, reaching the very "neck," as Isaiah had predicted (8:5-8; 36:1-2). The neck leaves the head, which is Zion/Jerusalem, where Hezekiah and his people await the Lord's deliverance (37:20).

When Ahaz rejects the sign the Lord offers as an assurance of divine protection (7:10-14), he unwittingly rejects the sign of the Davidic covenant: a sign "in the depths below or in the heights above" (7:10) attests to the Lord's presence and omnipotence. The name *Immanuel* ("God is with us," 7:14) connotes that when the Lord is *with* his people, they enjoy an assurance of divine protection

---

[20] Compare items 3 and 5 of suzerain–vassal relationships, page 67.

(cf. Psa 46:5–7). Where he is not, there exists no such assurance. Hezekiah, as the next reigning king, restores this protective ingredient of the Davidic covenant.

In summing up, the first or conditional aspect of the Davidic covenant—which the words "if his children forsake my law, and walk not in my judgments" (Psa 89:30–31) express—could, as in Ahaz' case, adversely affect the Lord's protection of his people. Nothing, however, could affect the second aspect of the covenant—the continuance of Davidic rule. The Lord had promised that to David unconditionally. Though the Lord may punish his people with the "rod" (*šēbeṭ*) on account of a disloyal vassal, his people's king (cf. 2 Sam 7:14; Psa 89:32), the covenant with David of an enduring dynasty would remain intact.[21]

Ahaz' repudiation of the Lord's suzerainty, therefore, possesses a sequel in the Lord's punishing his people by a "rod" (*šēbeṭ*). In the Book of Isaiah, the term *rod* serves as a metaphorical pseudonym of the king of Assyria (cf. 10:5, 15). The Lord uses the king of Assyria as his instrument for punishing and destroying the wicked of his people. The Lord's promise to Ahaz of a loyal successor, a "son" who would choose the *good* (*ṭôb*, 7:14–15), nonetheless remains unconditional. That promise vouchsafes the Lord's renewed protection of his people and was historically fulfilled in Hezekiah (cf. 38:3, 6).[22]

The King as an Exemplar of the People

As we have seen in section II, severe tests of loyalty evoke either rebellion or compliance toward the Lord by king and people. These attributes surface when the Lord tries Ahaz and Hezekiah and their

---

[21] Compare 2 Sam 7:15–16; 1 Kgs 15:4–5; Psa 89:33–37; Jer 33:17–26. With the advent of Israel's exile the Lord thus transplants Davidic rule among Israelite peoples in other lands (cf. Ezek 17:22–24).

[22] These conclusions may appear to negate the view that John Hayes and others espouse, that the idea of Zion's inviolability can be found in Jebusite mythical traditions concerning Jerusalem; John H. Hayes, "The Tradition of Zion's Inviolability," *JBL* 82 (1963): 419–26. The idea that Zion's inviolability predates Davidic covenant theology appears feasible if the concept of divine protection in pre-Israelite Jerusalem duplicated or preceded Davidic covenant theology. J. J. M. Roberts, in "The Davidic Origin of the Zion Tradition," *JBL* 92 (1973): 329–44, offers plausible arguments for basing the Zion tradition in the Davidic-Solomonic era.

respective peoples under pressure of political expediency. In that regard, the two tests appear similar, though one might argue that Hezekiah and his people undergo the greater trial of faith. A striking feature of section II is that the king's covenantal rebellion coincides with the people's in the first unit—even as the king's covenantal compliance coincides with the people's in the second. Such structuring[23] casts each king in the role of an exemplar of his people: the people's traits, whether of rebellion or compliance, mirror his own.

In the second unit, Hezekiah's role as an exemplar of his people nonetheless appears in part even in the first, in the imagery of eating cream and honey. Both Immanuel—whom scholars identify historically as Hezekiah—and those who survive in the wilderness when the land is desolated eat cream and honey (7:15, 22–25). In connection with that imagery, Isaiah prophesies an Assyrian invasion in the days of Immanuel (7:15–17) that will encompass the land of Immanuel (8:8). The nomadic nature of a diet of cream and honey suggests that, though there occurs no hint of malediction by way of a famine for those who live on this diet, king and people alike will pass through a time of trouble (cf. 7:16–25). (In periods of political upheaval, Israelites at times resorted to the nomadic lifestyle of the patriarchs; cf. 1 Sam 4:10; 2 Kgs 13:5.)

The prophesied time of trouble finds fulfillment in the second unit. That unit depicts Hezekiah and his people as a remnant surviving a protracted period of national distress (cf. 37:30–32). For two years, during Assyria's invasion of the land, both king and people must "eat what grows wild and . . . what springs up of itself; but in the third year sow and harvest, plant vineyards and eat their fruit" (37:30). Hezekiah's mortal illness on that occasion, from which the Lord miraculously delivers him, further reflects Hezekiah's function as an exemplar of his people. Just as Hezekiah survives the threat of death, the Lord's people endure a mortal threat—the Assyrian siege of Jerusalem—from which the Lord miraculously delivers them. Both king and people, respectively, demonstrate compliance toward the Lord sufficient to warrant his intervening on their behalf.

Although no such heroic deeds characterize the first unit, the idea of the king as an exemplar of his people appears in an opposite

---

[23] Were this not a structural device, one might expect any one component of the structure to be absent or show inconsistency (see figure 7).

sense in their common surrender to fear (7:4; 8:12). What typifies Ahaz and his people in the face of the Syro-Ephraimite threat is that "the king's mind and the minds of his people were shaken, as trees in a forest are shaken by a gale" (7:2).

An analogous idea to that of an exemplar—an individual who personifies the Lord's people allegorically—occurs with regard to the Woman figure. While the young woman with child who gives birth to Immanuel (7:14) refers to a real individual (no less than does Isaiah's wife, who, in the same historical context, gives birth to another portending son; 8:3), the Woman figure nonetheless appears throughout Isaiah as a representation of the Lord's people. The second unit depicts her as the Virgin Daughter of Zion, who, in the presence of the loyal Davidic king now in power (Hezekiah), laughs the Assyrian king to scorn (37:22).

A movement from the first unit to the second thus actualizes the idea of the Lord's deliverance of his people implicit in the name *Immanuel*. In the first unit, the young woman names her son Immanuel ("God is with us," 7:14), presumably with the assurance that the Lord will deliver his people. In the second, a remnant of the Lord's people, represented by the Virgin Daughter of Zion, manifestly experiences the Lord's deliverance (37:31). The Lord delivers the Daughter of Zion's children who have reached the point of birth (37:3), together with the king, their covenantal proxy. This reference to the birth or rebirth of the Lord's people carries forward a theme of section I and is one of many cumulative concepts of the Bifid Structure.

From these phenomena we see that the relationship between the two units of section II is not just antithetical, as reflected in the attitudes of Ahaz and Hezekiah and their peoples. It is also developmental. The second unit actualizes and consummates concepts from the first unit that build upon concepts introduced in section I. Such a structured development of ideas receives an even more heightened expression in terms of Zion/Jerusalem's relationship to the prophet.

The Prophet as a Paradigm of the People

Resembling the idea of the king as an exemplar of his people is that of the prophet as a paradigm or model of his people's spiritual progression. The two ideas appear similar and in some ways overlap, though the idea of the prophet as a paradigm possesses dimensions that the king as an exemplar does not.

The first clue to Isaiah's function as a paradigm of his people appears in the account of his prophetic commission. There Isaiah exclaims, "I am a man of unclean lips and I live among a people of unclean lips" (6:5). The way the prophet so overtly identifies with his people represents more than a casual disclosure. On seeing the Lord in the temple, Isaiah is literally dumbstruck (6:5).[24] But a seraph heals him, declaring his sins expiated, so that he can again speak and accept his prophetic call (6:7–8). Isaiah's change of composure in the Lord's presence—from overwhelming dread to renewed self-assurance (6:5, 8)—reflects the healing sequence.

The seraph formalizes Isaiah's expiation of sins by the symbolic act of cleansing the lips with an ember that he takes with tongs from the altar of atonement (6:6–7). That performance resembles the Egyptian rite of the Opening-of-the-Mouth with an adze of meteoric iron, which, in the older Egyptian temple literature, represents an initiatory phase in the king's ritual ascent to deification. The restoring of the eyes to see, the ears to hear, and the legs to walk accompanies the Egyptian rite of the Opening-of-the-Mouth.[25]

Isaiah's identifying himself with his people by means of the imagery of unclean lips takes on another aspect when we consider that this represents a premeditated account. At the Opening-of-the-Mouth rite, Isaiah seems to be expressing a desire to do for his people as has been done for him. Isaiah does not anticipate that his mission will be to bear evil tidings when he so willingly accepts his call (6:8). He learns the magnitude of his people's rebellion against the Lord only when the Lord commissions him as a hardener of the heart: "Go, and say to these people, Go on hearing, but not understanding; go on seeing but not perceiving!" (6:9).

Isaiah's eagerness to undertake the Lord's errand gives way to an uneasy query: "For how long, my Lord?" (6:11). Instead of

---

[24] The meaning "struck dumb/dumbstruck" appears if we read the Hebrew verb as *nādam*. Others accept *dāmâ* ("ruined"). In view of what follows, possibly more than one meaning is valid.

[25] See Eberhard Otto, *Das ägyptische Mundöffnungritual* (Wiesbaden: Harrasowitz, 1960); A. Moret, *Mystères Egyptiens* (Paris: Colin, 1913). Hugh Nibley, in *The Message of the Joseph Smith Papyri* (Salt Lake City: Deseret Book, 1975), 106–13, gives an overview of the Egyptian Opening-of-the-Mouth rite.

bringing healing to his people, Isaiah must "make the heart of these people grow fat, dull their ears and shut their eyes—lest they see with their eyes and hear with their ears, understand in their heart, and repent and be healed!" (6:10). The implicit formula for the people's healing or salvation[26] that this charge contains, particularly its emphasis on seeing and hearing, reflects, paradigmatically, Isaiah's own seeing the Lord, hearing his voice, and healing (6:5, 8). The Opening-of-the-Mouth rite, moreover, typifies the full function of all the human senses.

Isaiah's tacit desire to help his people achieve a healed and sinless state, expressed in chapter 6 of the first unit, finds fulfillment structurally in chapter 40 of the second unit. In the movement from the first unit to the second, the Lord's righteous people as a whole manifest the attributes that characterize Isaiah as an individual. In the first unit, Isaiah's expiation of sins (6:7) repeats itself in the second in the people's expiation of sins: Zion/Jerusalem has fulfilled her term and expiated her guilt (40:2). In the first unit, the healing of Isaiah's senses, which the Opening-of-the-Mouth rite symbolizes (6:7), repeats itself in the second in the healing of the people's senses: the Lord commissions Zion/Jerusalem to raise her voice mightily as the Lord's messenger (40:9); the Lord instructs his people to see (40:26), hear (40:28), and understand (40:21); those who hope in the Lord, he renews in strength, enabling them to run without becoming weary and walk and not faint (40:31). Isaiah's personal anticipation of the Lord in the first unit (8:17), and his willingness to let the Lord direct him (7:3; 8:11–13), has a sequel in the people who anticipate the Lord (40:10, 31) and are willing for the Lord to lead them (40:11). Isaiah's personal vision of the Lord (6:1, 5) has a sequel in his people's vision of the Lord: "Behold your God!" (40:9).

Isaiah's name, "The Lord will save," encapsulates the development from the first unit to the second: the Lord commissions Zion/Jerusalem as a messenger of good tidings (40:9); she is to declare that "the Lord comes in power . . . his reward with him" (40:10). Such a commission represents a paradigmatic fulfillment, in that Zion/Jerusalem, like Isaiah, now serves as the Lord's messenger. But it also reflects the antithetical relationship between the first unit and the second: Zion/Jerusalem, whom the Lord

---

[26] See, in Isaiah, the synonymity of healing and salvation, 19:20–22; 57:17–19.

commissions as a messenger of good tidings, contrasts Isaiah, who initially serves as a messenger of evil tidings.

Zion's emulation of Isaiah, however, does not mean that Isaiah himself does not emulate someone higher. A prophet's own spiritual progression does not stop with the assumption of prophetic traits. Just as Zion, in the second unit, assumes prophetic traits, emulating Isaiah in the first, so Isaiah, in the second unit, assumes a higher office, emulating the seraph or seraphs in the first. (The parallel structure of section II presupposes that the prophet figure of chapter 40 is Isaiah.) As the seraphs stand in the Lord's council (6:2), so does Isaiah (40:1-6). The seraph's role in declaring the expiation of sins (6:7) is now Isaiah's: the prophet is to announce that Zion/Jerusalem has expiated her guilt (40:2, 6). As the seraph speaks kindly to Isaiah (6:7), so Isaiah speaks kindly to the Lord's people (40:1-2). The seraph's role in healing Isaiah (6:7) is now undertaken by the prophet himself when he heals Hezekiah (38:21).

As the seraphs testify of the Lord's glory (6:3), so testifies Isaiah. Much of the nonbiographical material of chapter 40 is an expansion on the cosmic hymn of the seraphs in chapter 6: "Most holy is the Lord of Hosts; the consummation of all the earth is his glory" (*qādôš qādôš qādôš yhwh ṣĕbā'ôt mĕlō' kol hā'āreṣ kĕbôdô*, v 3). Structurally, chapter 40's cosmology—unparalleled in biblical literature—is part of the revelatory event with which the chapter commences. Yet, like its biographical and paradigmatic content, chapter 40's cosmology further develops in the second unit what appears initially in the first. Rhetorical links between the cosmic hymn of 6:3 and chapter 40 demonstrate this development. The idea of the Lord's "holiness" (*qādôš*, 6:3) reappears in his inimitable title and attribute of "Holy One" (*qādôš*, 40:25). The name "the Lord of Hosts" (*yhwh ṣĕbā'ôt*, 6:3) is eloquently amplified in 40:26, where the "hosts" of the Lord are called forth:

Lift your eyes heavenward and see:
    Who formed these?
He who brings forth their hosts [*ṣĕbā'ām*] by number,
    calling each one by name.
Because he is almighty and all powerful,
    not one is unaccounted for.

The idea of a "consummation" or "fulfillment" (*mĕlō'*, 6:3) reappears in Zion/Jerusalem's consummation or fulfillment of her term (*māl'â ṣĕbā'âh*, 40:2). The idea of a consummation of "all the earth" (*kol hā'āreṣ*, 6:3) reappears in the Lord's creation, sequentially, of the earth and its mountains (40:12), of nations and isles (40:15–17), of Jacob/Israel (40:27–28), and of those who "ascend" (40:31). Lastly, the idea of the Lord's "glory" (*kĕbôdô*, 6:3) characterizes chapter 40 as a whole. It also appears demonstratively in the verse "The glory of the Lord [*kĕbôd yhwh*] shall be revealed and all flesh see it at once" (40:5).

The emphasis on the prophet seeing heavenly beings in the first unit (6:1–3) and hearing heavenly beings in the second (40:1–6) expresses a parallelistic relationship between the two prophetic commissions. It is doubtful, however, that chapter 40 recounts merely an auditory experience, just as chapter 6 does not recount merely a visionary one. There exists no biblical precedent for a prophet hearing more than one voice (40:1, 3, 6) without an accompanying vision.[27] The scope of the chapter's cosmology suggests that the prophet may have had an apocalyptic vision, a vision of the "end from the beginning" (46:10), rather than a typical revelatory experience. The several layers of revelatory phenomena that this account represents preclude it from being a simple vision or audition.

The throne motif illustrates this point. In the first unit, the Lord sits on a throne within the confines of the temple (6:1), commonplace of the Mosaic rite. In the second, he sits enthroned above the earth's sphere, the heavens suspended like a canopy, stretched out like a cosmic tent (40:22). Things are no longer being described from below but from above (40:12, 15, 22, 31). The vision has broadened to the cosmic view that the seraphs enjoy (see 6:3). In effect, the revelation at the foot of the mount, which the Mosaic rite epitomizes (chap. 6), has given way to the revelation on top of the mount, which the cosmos epitomizes (chap. 40). Thus, even a prophet, when he faithfully fulfills his first commission, can attain to a higher office and achieve a higher state of blessedness.[28]

The hierarchy of individuals who appear in chapter 40 reflects a paradigmatic progression in which the prophet himself takes part.

---

[27] Compare Isa 6:1–11; Ezek 1:1–28; 10:1–22; Dan 8:16; 10:1–21.

[28] Compare Enoch, Gen 5:22–24; Elijah, 2 Kgs 2:9–11.

The chapter mentions, in turn, Israel's God (40:1), voices of heavenly beings (40:3, 6), the prophet (40:6), Zion/Jerusalem (40:9), and Jacob/Israel (40:27). The idea of a paradigmatic hierarchy—a hierarchy of entities or individuals who serve as paradigms or models for one another to follow—explains why two prophetic commissions appear in chapter 40. The first commission is of the prophet (40:1–8), who emulates the seraph or seraphs of chapter 6. The second is of Zion/Jerusalem (40:9), who emulates Isaiah. The idea of a paradigmatic hierarchy, and the corollary idea of ascent or progression to a higher functional state, may account for the prophet's anonymity in chapter 40: the prophet figure here is no longer the Isaiah of chapter 6 but one whom the Lord commissions to an angelic mission.

We see another kind of paradigmatic development in the second unit, one that reflects the names of the three portending children who appear in the first. Isaiah asserts, "as for me and the children the Lord has given me, we shall be types [$'ōtôt$] and paradigms [$môptîm$][29] in Israel from the Lord of Hosts who dwells in Mount Zion" (8:18). The actualizing in the second unit of a concept introduced in the first does not limit itself to chapter 40. We have already seen how the son Immanuel ("God is with us," 7:14) in the first unit, though not Isaiah's own, serves as a paradigm: Hezekiah, as the historical Immanuel, typifies those in the second unit designated Zion/Jerusalem, whom the Lord delivers in a time of crisis (37:35; 38:6). The Lord proves to be *with* Hezekiah's people against Assyria when the Assyrians surround the city (37:36).

In addition, Isaiah's son Maher-Shalal-Hash-Baz ("Hasten the plunder, hurry the spoil," 8:1, 3), who is mentioned in the first unit, typifies those of the Lord's people in the second whom the Lord destroys in his day of judgment. The wicked of the Lord's people, together with the nations, fall prey to Assyria's barbarity (36:18–20, 37:12–13, 18; cf. 8:4) when the Lord commissions Assyria "to pillage for plunder, to spoliate for spoil" (cf. 10:5–6). The text represents all those destroyed as idolaters who revere the works of men's hands (36:18–20; 37:18–19). Their ruin, in section II, expresses, cumulatively, a concept that section I establishes.

---

[29] Compare $'ōt$ and $môpēt$, 20:3. Sheldon Blank, in an unrelated study on Jeremiah, accepts the term $mopet$ ("sign/portent") as *paradigm*; Sheldon H. Blank, "The Prophet as Paradigm," in James L. Crenshaw and John T. Willis, eds., *Essays on Old Testament Ethics* (New York: Ktav, 1974), 124.

Lastly, Isaiah's son Shear-Jashub ("A remnant shall repent/ return," 7:3) in the first unit typifies an intermediate, tentative category of the Lord's people in the second. This category of people has yet to repent/return in order to become identified with ransomed Zion (cf. 40:6–8).[30] Included in that category are Jacob/Israel (40:27) and certain cities of Judea, those to whom the Lord sends Zion/ Jerusalem as a messenger (40:9). Zion's mission is to bid the Lord's people to see, hear, and understand (40:21, 26–28). The birth or rebirth of the Lord's people as Zion, a cumulative concept (cf. 37:3), occurs when they assume prophetic traits. They assume prophetic traits upon passing a severe test of covenantal loyalty (40:31).

Thus, several categories of the Lord's people are alluded to in the first unit of section II—the compliant, the rebellious, and those who must yet make covenantal choices. These three categories reemerge in the second unit within a paradigmatic hierarchy. This hierarchy of entities ties together all parts of the second unit (chaps. 36–40). Chapter 40, whose historical setting may be exilic (because it describes conditions during Judah's exile in Babylon), is as much a part of this material as are chapters 36–39. (The latter chapters' historical setting is preexilic because they describe conditions before the kingdom of Judah came to an end.) Though historically chapter 40 may be separated from others in the second unit by Judah's exile,[31] all chapters of this unit consistently portray the paradigmatic categories we have identified.

Isaiah himself represents a superlative category of the Lord's salvation. His celestial accession models itself on the seraphs, who serve less as the Lord's messengers than they exemplify a sanctified state (cf. 40:26).[32] Hezekiah's place within the hierarchy, on the other hand, despite his role as an exemplar of his people, identifies structurally with Zion/Jerusalem. Zion/Jerusalem's forgiveness of sins and healing (40:1–2) mirrors Hezekiah's forgiveness of sins and

---

[30] Compare, in section I, those of the Lord's people who "go up/ascend" (*ʿlh*) from among the nations to Zion/Jerusalem, there to observe the law and word of the Lord (2:3, 5).

[31] Chapter 40 itself, however, exhibits both preexilic and exilic element, as in a reference to the cities of Judea (40:9) and in imagery descriptive of Babylonian idolatry (40:19–20). Such duality is not true of chapter 41 and beyond, whose historical setting is clearly exilic.

[32] See the term *seraph* (*śārāp*, 6:2, 6) as describing the brazen serpent made by Moses in the wilderness (Num 21:8), to which the Lord's people look for healing (Num 21:9). Compare the term's metaphorical use to depict an ideal Davidic king in Isa 14:29.

healing in the same unit (38:16–17, 21), and both follow Isaiah's forgiveness and healing paradigmatically (6:7). The Lord's deliverance of Zion/Jerusalem, following a test of her covenantal loyalty (37:32), qualifies her for a prophetic mission to those of the Lord's people who have yet to pass such a test (40:9).

Forming a lower rung on the paradigmatic ladder, Jacob/Israel ultimately divides into those who grow faint and weary in their allegiance toward the Lord, who lack understanding (40:27–28), and those whom the Lord renews in strength, who "ascend" upward (*'lh*, 40:31). In their healed condition,[33] the latter typify Zion/Jerusalem. We observe their common identity in the motif of waiting for the Lord: those who ascend or progress upward are those who wait for the Lord to intervene (40:31)—evidently at the same test of loyalty that causes others of the Lord's people to faint (40:30)—even as Hezekiah and Zion/Jerusalem wait for the Lord to deliver them from the Assyrian threat (37:20; cf. 40:10). At the same time, both categories of waiters emulate Isaiah's waiting for the Lord in the first unit at another test of loyalty (8:17).

From these descriptions we assume that in order to ascend the paradigmatic ladder, all must pass a test of covenantal compliance. Failure to pass the test forfeits the Lord's saving intervention and eliminates those who manifest rebellion against him.

Such a message can also be gleaned from the two historical prefaces. The historical preface of 6:12–13, for example, delineates essentially the same categories of the Lord's people that the three sons portend. A division of Israel into subgroups, following a test of covenantal loyalty (cf. 6:10), consists of those burned (6:13)—corresponding to Maher-Shalal-Hash-Baz ("Hasten the plunder, hurry the spoil," 8:3); those driven away (6:12)—corresponding to Shear-Jashub ("A remnant shall repent/return," 7:3); and those who, like the stump (*maṣṣebet*) of a tree that is felled, are left standing (*maṣṣabtâh*) after the Lord's judgment (6:13)—corresponding to Immanuel ("God is with us," 7:14). The latter category appears identical with Zion/Jerusalem in the second unit, those who again "take root below and bear fruit above" (37:31).

---

[33] An a_1–b–b–a_2 structure in chapter 40 likens the nonweariness of those whom the Lord renews in strength to the Lord's own, as follows: the Lord's nonweariness, verse 28; the weariness of mortals, verses 29–30; and the nonweariness of those whom the Lord renews in strength, verse 31.

The historical preface of chapter 39, on the other hand, predicts that at some point the Lord will exile Hezekiah's descendants (and, by analogy, the descendants of his people) to Babylon (39:7). Historically speaking, that event, as well as others before or after it, could constitute a test of covenantal loyalty for Jacob/Israel. But about the future exile, Hezekiah is not so concerned. Nor does Isaiah predict it directly as a national event. Hezekiah's response implies that he and his people have passed the test, and others must answer for themselves: "The Lord's word you have spoken is good [*ṭôb*], for he thought, Then there shall be peace and loyalty during my reign" (39:8).

Summary

A chiastic structure of section II (chaps. 6–8; 36–40) divides the material into two tests of loyalty of king and people (chaps. 7–8; 36–38), two prophetic commissions (6:1–11; chap. 40), and two historical prefaces (6:12–13; chap. 39). The structure juxtaposes the covenantal rebellion in the first unit of Ahaz and his people with the covenantal compliance in the second of Hezekiah and his people. Ahaz and his people's failure to pass a test of loyalty toward the Lord causes them to lose the Lord's protection against Assyria. The Lord nonetheless protects Hezekiah and his people against Assyria in the face of a similar threat. The coincidence of rebellion and compliance by king and people in respective units of material establishes, structurally, the idea of the king as an exemplar of his people: what he does, they do. The material supports that idea rhetorically and typologically, as reflected in the people's loyalty or disloyalty toward their king and in their passing through similar experiences.

The correlation between divine protection and covenantal compliance by king and people forms a basis for Isaiah's Zion ideology. Zion ideology, founded on the protection clause of the Davidic covenant, defines the king's role as a proxy for his people in order to merit the Lord's protection on their behalf. Zion/Jerusalem forms a safe or inviolable place when a king exercises loyalty toward the Lord and the people exercise loyalty toward the king.

A development from the first unit to the second establishes a paradigmatic relationship between the prophet and the people. Zion/Jerusalem, in the second unit, assumes functions attributed to Isaiah in the first. The prophet, in the second unit, in turn assumes the role of the seraphs in the first. These phenomena establish the idea of a paradigmatic hierarchy, in which those on a lower spiritual plane emulate and become like those on a higher spiritual plane. Such a hierarchy cements all parts of section II. The imperative to repent/return, pending a test of covenantal loyalty, characterizes a third, lesser category of the Lord's people, Jacob/Israel. On the one hand, Jacob/Israel's covenantal rebellion leads to destruction in the Lord's day of judgment. On the other, covenantal compliance leads to forgiveness of sins and healing, an identity with Zion/Jerusalem, and a prophetic commission.

These delineations accord with concepts established in section I, which defines Zion as those of the Lord's people who, because they repent/ return, are ransomed in the Lord's day of judgment. The themes of ruin and rebirth that characterize section I appear cumulatively in section II: Assyria's destruction of the Lord's wicked people and of the nations, which both units of section II portray, reflects ruin. Zion's rebirth, which appears implicitly in the first unit, flowers in the second. Typifying the themes of ruin and rebirth are the Lord's day of judgment in the first unit (7:17–23) and the Lord's appearance in the second (40:10).

Lastly, the structural message of section II, though based in history, is ahistorical and projects a transcendent fulfillment of the prophecy. Like section I, upon which it builds, section II deals with structured and therefore contemporaneous phenomena that are typological in nature, such as a reversal between Zion and non-Zion in the Lord's day of judgment. The themes of ruin and rebirth developed in section I, in effect, are enhanced when we view section I against the backdrop of section II: covenantal rebellion on the part of the Lord's wicked people results in their ruin; concurrently, covenantal compliance by Zion/Jerusalem results in her birth or rebirth. A single test of loyalty— in a day when the Lord's judgment and appearance are nigh—evokes two opposite responses from the Lord's people and their rulers.

Because section I singles out no individuals, the idea of the king as an exemplar or of the prophet as a paradigm does not appear there. The apposition of Ahaz and Hezekiah and their respective peoples, and other concepts section II establishes structurally, is facilitated by the fact that this section contains virtually all the biographical material in Isaiah, making it unique. As with section I, however, such new concepts are cumulative. Ruin and rebirth, based on covenantal rebellion or compliance, and all associated ideas section II develops, build a foundation for succeeding sections of the Bifid Structure.

Section III
Punishment & Deliverance
(9–12; 41:1–46:13b)

Sections I and II of the Bifid Structure demonstrate that the wicked (those who break covenantal law) will experience ruin while the righteous (those who comply with the terms of the Lord's covenants) will experience rebirth. Section III introduces the concept that both ruin and rebirth, following upon covenantal rebellion and compliance, occur through divine intervention. Such intervention takes the form of agents or chosen individuals who carry out the Lord's punishment or deliverance.

Through parallel descriptions of persons who serve as types, section III creates a picture of an ideal agent or agents whom the Lord employs as instruments of divine punishment and deliverance. The structure of the material, and its use of biblical types, again transcends history, suggesting that these agents of punishment and deliverance are real individuals who will fulfill their roles in a latter-day setting. The ruin of non-Zion and rebirth of Zion, in other words, occur when the Lord sends agents to intervene in the affairs of his people as they make divergent covenantal choices in that day.

Typological Motifs in Common

The first unit of section III (chaps. 9–12) centers on the role of a future Davidic king—one who embodies the righteous functions and attributes of past Davidic kings, such as David, Solomon, and Hezekiah, as well as those of other Israelite heroes, such as Abraham, Moses, and Joshua. In the second unit of section III (chaps. 41:1–46:13b) the roles of three other figures emerge: a Righteous Warrior, a ruler named Cyrus, and a Servant of the Lord. Based on their functions and attributes, these three figures also have antecedents in biblical heroes, including Abraham, Moses, King David, and Cyrus.

All these figures, in both units of material, serve as the Lord's agents for punishing the wicked or delivering the righteous. Sometimes these figures are overtly identified by name; at other times they are covertly identified by metaphorical pseudonyms. In addition, each figure possesses royal attributes, viz., "a son" on the throne of David (9:6-7); a "bird of prey" from the east (46:11);[1] "his anointed one" (45:1); and "my servant whom I uphold" (42:1).[2] The appearance of these figures in parallel units of material helps determine their relationship to one another, each figure serving as the Lord's agent of punishment or deliverance within some context of Israel's redemption.

It could be assumed that the relationship between these figures is complementary, as between two or more individuals who perform separate but related redemptive tasks. It appears, however, that the structure of section III is instead meant to establish the idea of a single prophesied deliverer who possesses the important attributes of each of these figures. Thus, the exilic context of the second unit (Israel's time of captivity), which appears to clash with the preexilic context of so much of the first unit, merely allows this agent of the Lord's redemption to embody the functions and attributes of all Israel's heroes regardless of when they lived. By drawing on diverse historical types, in both exilic and preexilic settings, section III develops the idea of one great archetypal leader or deliverer who will exist in the latter days. On that ahistorical level, the Lord's redemption applies simultaneously to the Lord's people who are to be restored to their land as well as to those requiring deliverance within their land.

The first unit of section III, moreover, juxtaposes the Davidic king in chapters 9 and 11 with a threatening king of Assyria in chapter 10, whereas the three figures in the second unit are not so threatened. Could this structuring of the material mean that the king of Assyria's role in serving as the Lord's agent of punishment will interfere with a similar role by the Davidic king? Or will this Davidic king (presuming a latter-day context of the structure) ultimately triumph over the king of Assyria? Furthermore, what do the roles of the three figures in the second unit have in common with such roles by the Davidic king?

---

[1] The term ʿayiṭ ("bird of prey"), as in the case of an eagle or falcon, serves as a royal symbol in Egypt and Mesopotamia; see *ANEP*, 298, 377, 564, 617. Compare Ezek 17:3, 7.

[2] The title of "King," however, applies to the Lord himself (cf. 41:21; 43:15; 44:6).

Fortunately, the motif of a new exodus, which William Brownlee sees in both units of section III, provides a key to answering these questions. In fact, this new exodus motif is one of a number of typological motifs common to both units. Other motifs include release from bondage, return to the promised land, a new wandering in the wilderness, and a new conquest of the land, all of which events appear in conjunction with the new exodus. These key events establish a common redemptive context, in both units of material, for a single ideal agent of the Lord's punishment and deliverance. Stated another way, that ideal figure, who is described in terms of types, redeems the Lord's people—in both units of material—by releasing them from bondage, initiating their exodus and return, and leading them in a new wandering in the wilderness to the promised land.

Despite the preexilic context of much of the material, the role of the Davidic king in these redemptive events, as described in the first unit, parallels in every essential the exilic roles of the Righteous Warrior, Cyrus, and Servant figures described in the second unit. Such parallels indicate that section III of the Bifid Structure, rather than listing a number of figures involved in identical redemptive events, establishes structurally the concept of a single agent of the Lord's punishment and deliverance based on a number of biblical types.

The Future Davidic King as a Composite Figure

The key motifs of release from bondage, a new exodus, a new wandering in the wilderness, Israel's return to the promised land, and a new conquest first appear in Isaiah in the first unit of section III (chaps. 9–12). A passage in chapter 11 contains three of the motifs:

> 10. In that day the sprig of Jesse,
>   who stands for an ensign to the peoples,
> shall be sought by the nations,
>   and his rest shall be glorious.
> 11. In that day my Lord will again raise[3] his hand
>   to reclaim the remnant of his people—
> those who shall be left out of Assyria,
>   Egypt, Pathros, Cush, Elam, Shinar, Hamath
>   and the isles of the sea.

---

[3] Hebrew *šēnît* ("a second time") has been emended to *šĕ'ēt*; see R. B. Y. Scott, *IB*, 5:251.

12. He will raise the ensign to the nations
     and assemble the exiled of Israel;
   he will gather the scattered of Judah
     from the four directions of the earth.
13. Ephraim's jealousy shall pass away
     and the hostile ones of Judah be cut off;
   Ephraim will not envy Judah,
     nor Judah resent Ephraim.
14. But they will swoop on the Philistine flank
     toward the west,
   and together plunder those on the east;
     [they will take] Edom and Moab
   at the sending forth of their hand,
     and the Ammonites will obey them.
15. The Lord will dry up the tongue
     of the Egyptian Sea by his mighty wind;[4]
   he will extend his hand over the River
     and smite it into seven streams
   to provide a way on foot.
16. And there shall be a pathway out of Assyria
     for the remnant of his people who shall be left,
   as there was for Israel
     when it came up from the land of Egypt.

In this passage, the metaphor of the Lord's *hand* (*yād*, vv 11, 14–15) links, rhetorically, three future events: Israel's return to Zion or the Lord's "rest" (vv 10–12),[5] a new conquest of the promised land (v 14), and a new exodus out of exile (vv 15–16). The raising or sending forth of the hand is an exodus and conquest motif and was literally the means Moses and Joshua used to obtain victories for Israel (cf. Exod 14:21–27; 17:11; Josh 8:18–19). When Moses stretched out his hand over the Red Sea, the waters parted to let the Israelites pass over on dry land, while the same waters overwhelmed the Egyptians (Exod 14:21–27). Likewise, so long as Moses or Joshua stretched out his hand, the Israelites prevailed over their enemies in battle (Exod 17:11; Josh 8:18–19); but when Moses let down his hand, the Israelites did not prevail (Exod 17:12). At both the exodus out of Egypt and the conquest of Canaan, Moses and

---

[4] The phrase "by his mighty wind" has been transposed; in MT, it follows "and smite it."

[5] Compare Deut 12:9–11; Psa 132:13–14; Isa 66:1.

Joshua nonetheless acknowledged the Lord's hand as giving them the victory (Exod 15:6; Josh 4:22–24).

In the preceding passage, the Lord's extending his *hand* brings about a new exodus (v 15); this parallels the Lord's raising his *hand* to bring about Israel's return (v 11). In each instance, the intervention of the Lord's hand causes a ''remnant'' (*šeʾār*) of the Lord's people to be delivered from their scattered condition among the nations (see vv 11, 16). The preceding passage, though it falls within a broader historical context that is preexilic, presupposes Israel's exile.

Further, the Lord's raising his *hand* in verse 11 parallels, synonymously, the Lord's raising an *ensign* (*nēs*) in verse 12. Like the raising of the hand, the raising of the ensign causes the Lord's people to return from exile: they return from many countries (v 11); they gather from the four directions of the earth (v 12). The synonymous parallelism of the Lord's raising his *hand* (*yād*) and raising an *ensign* (*nēs*) in order to effect Israel's return is not limited to this passage but appears cumulatively elsewhere. See, for example, the parallelistic raising of the Lord's *hand* (*yād*) and *ensign* (*nēs*) to the nations that brings about Israel's return in 49:22.

The preceding passage, however, further identifies the term *ensign* as a metaphor describing a future Davidic king—''the sprig of Jesse, who stands for an *ensign* to the peoples'' (v 10; cf. v 1). Like King David himself (see 1 Chr 12:18), his ruling descendants were sometimes known simply as ''the son of Jesse,'' Jesse being David's father (see 1 Kgs 12:16). By identifying the term *ensign* as a metaphor describing a future Davidic king, a ''sprig of Jesse'' (v 10), the preceding passage also establishes an identity for the term *hand* (v 11). Because *ensign* and *hand* synonymously parallel each other in verses 11–12 and elsewhere (cf. 5:25–26; 49:22), and because the *ensign* is clearly identified as a ruler from David's line, the term *hand* must also serve as a metaphor describing the future Davidic king. The synonymous use of the two terms suggests that both identify the same individual.

In a metaphorical sense, therefore, the preceding passage depicts a future Davidic king or vassal of the Lord under the pseudonyms of the Lord's *ensign* and *hand*[6] who, first, rallies a remnant of the

---

[6] The concept of the Lord's ''hand'' in the Jebusite-influenced royal theology of Jerusalem, corresponds to the Babylonian personification of *kittu*—''justice/righteousness'' (Hebrew *ṣedeq*)—the beneficent emanation of the sungod Shamash, called the ''minister of his right hand.'' In Israelite royal ideology this attribute was transferred to the king, the ''man of thy right hand'' (cf. Psa 80:17; 110:1); Roy A. Rosenberg, ''The God Sedeq,'' *HUCA* 36 (1965): 161–78.

Lord's people from exile (v 11)[7] and, second, brings about their return exodus (v 15). In that respect, the metaphors *hand* and *ensign* resemble the metaphor *branch* (*nēṣer*, 11:1), which also describes the future Davidic king (cf. *ṣemaḥ* as a "branch/plant" of David in a similar context of a new exodus and return from exile in Jer 23:3–8). The term *branch* (*nēṣer*) seems to express a full-blown or "fruitful" phase, of which the term *sprig* (*šōreš*, v 10) represents an early or grafting phase.

A third function of the Lord's *hand* is to initiate a new conquest of the promised land: at the stretching forth of the *hand*, Ephraim and Judah unitedly plunder and subdue the surrounding peoples of Philistia, Edom, Moab, and Ammon (v 14), as they did under King David (see David's victory over Philistia, Edom, Moab, and Ammon in 2 Sam 5, 8, 10). All three contexts in which the *hand* motif appears (vv 11, 14, 15) thus describe redemptive events for Israel.

Assuming that the metaphors of the Lord's *ensign* and *hand* hold true, and that the events of Israel's return, new exodus, and new conquest are neither unrelated nor take place in a leaderless fashion, a future Davidic figure thus serves as the Lord's agent for punishing foreign powers and delivering the Lord's people in the typological tradition of Moses, Joshua, and David. As at the exodus under Moses, a Song of Salvation in the first person immediately follows the new exodus to conclude the first unit of section III (12:1–6; cf. Exod 15:1–21). The Lord's "salvation" (*yěšû'â*, 12:2–3), which sums up his universally renowned deeds (12:4–5), is nonetheless celebrated by the inhabitants of Zion (12:6). The reference to Zion signifies that not only the new exodus but the return and new conquest are now accomplished facts.

The name *Zion* in this passage pulls together some important cumulative concepts from sections I and II: those redeemed *in* Zion are those of Jacob/Israel who repent/return (cf. Isa 10:20–27); to qualify for the Lord's redemption, the latter are required to pass an important test of loyalty in a time of trouble (cf. Isa 12:1–3). Historically, the king who serves as a type of deliverer in Zion is

---

[7] An a–b–a structure in chapter 11 identifies the nations whom the *ensign* rallies as the Lord's people as follows: "the nations," verse 10; "his people," verse 11; "the nations," verse 12. Compare a similar structure in section I, footnote 2. The remnant of the Lord's people thus also represents a remnant of the nations.

Hezekiah. Zion's birth or rebirth occurs when the Lord delivers his people from the Assyrian power on account of a righteous Davidic king, the Lord's vassal (see section I and II). The biblical type of Hezekiah as a Davidic king appears cumulatively in chapter 9.

Chapter 9, which opens the first unit, alludes to Israel's return from exile when it describes the Lord's making glorious, at the last, the Sea Route to the territory of the nations (*gôyîm*, 9:1).[8] A psalm of royal accession or coronation of a Davidic king[9] follows the allusion to Israel's return (9:1) and contains several related typological motifs:

> 2. The people walking in darkness
>   have seen a bright light;
>   on the inhabitants of the land
>   of the shadow of death has the light dawned.
> 3. Thou hast enlarged the nation
>   and increased its joy;
>   they rejoice at thy presence
>   as men rejoice at harvest time,
>   or as men are joyous when they divide spoil.
> 4. For thou has smashed the yoke
>   that burdened them,
>   the staff of submission,
>   the rod of those who subjected them,
>   as in the day of Midian.
> 5. And all boots used in battle
>   and tunics rolled in blood
>   have become fuel for bonfires.
> 6. For to us a child is born, a son appointed,
>   who will shoulder the burden
>   of the government.
>   He will be called
>   Wonderful Counselor, one Mighty in Valor,
>   a Father for Ever, a Prince of Peace,

---

[8] From that description it can be inferred that the highway mentioned was made inglorious at Israel's trek into exile through "the land of Zebulon and Naphtali" (9:1; cf. 2 Kgs 15:29).

[9] See Margaret B. Cook, "A Suggested Occasion for Isaiah 9:2–7 and 11:1–9," *JBL* 68 (1949): 213–14; Gerald Cooke, "The Israelite King as Son of God," *ZAW* 73 (1961): 202–25.

7.   that sovereignty may be extended
and peace have no end;
that, on the throne of David
and over his kingdom,
[his rule] may be established and upheld
by justice and righteousness
from this time forth and forever.
The zeal of the Lord of Hosts will accomplish it.

Rhetorical links tie this psalm of royal accession to Judah's victory over Assyria in the days of Hezekiah (cf. vv 2–4).[10] Thus, besides looking forward to the righteous rule of a newly installed king, the psalm may reflect a suzerain's unconditional promise to a faithful and victorious ruler of an enduring dynasty over a people and place—a covenant of grant (see Discourse B: Zion Ideology [1]—the Davidic Covenant). Of all historical Davidic kings, Hezekiah qualifies as a candidate for a suzerain's second appointment of a son or vassal; for such a thing, David, the Lord's "son," set a precedent (Psa 2:6–7). The Davidic king's birth or rebirth, on that occasion (v 6), parallels the rebirth of the Lord's people as Zion of which this king serves, cumulatively, as a paradigm.

The preceding psalm commences with a people wandering in darkness, inhabiting a shadowy land (v 2), representing a new wandering in the wilderness (cf. Psa 23:4). The king, who is depicted as a bright *light* (*'ôr*, v 2), lights up their darkness as the sun. That idea accords with the historical type of King David, whom the biblical narrative describes as a "light" (*'ôr*) and as the sun rising upon his people (2 Sam 23:4). An ancient Near Eastern parallel exists in the Egyptian royal accession ritual, timed for sunrise, which names the king as successor to the sungod Re. His accession to the throne heralds a creative reordering of the cosmos and a regeneration of life; hieroglyphs depict these events as the sun rising over the Primeval Hill.[11]

---

[10] See, for example, the "son" Immanuel (7:14; cf. v 6); the removal of the people's "yoke" as in the day of Midian (10:26–27; cf. v 4); the idea of "harvest" (37:30; cf. v 3) and "spoil" (33:23; cf. v 3); the expression "The zeal of the Lord of Hosts will accomplish it" (37:32; cf. v 7); and David's "throne" established in righteousness after tyrants and oppressors are destroyed from the earth (16:4–5; cf. v 7).

[11] Henri Frankfort, *Kingship and the Gods* (Chicago: University of Chicago, 1948), 148–51.

In Egypt, as in Babylon, sunrise represents victory over the powers of darkness or chaos as well as a restoration of justice and righteousness.[12] The king, a righteous judge in the image of Re or Shamash, personifies these creative attributes.[13] The Jebusites of Jerusalem regard the sungod, as manifested in his personified attribute *ṣedeq* ("righteousness"), to be the judge of all lands who brings hidden crimes to light and rights the wrongs done to the innocent.[14]

The context of the present passage, however, links the Davidic king's royal accession—and thus aspects of its ancient Near Eastern parallels—to the events of Israel's return from exile (v 1), new wandering in the wilderness (v 2), new conquest (v 3), and release from bondage (v 4). The psalm represents the conquest of the forces of chaos as the smashing of the enemy's yoke (*'ōl*), staff (*maṭṭēh*), and rod (*šēbeṭ*, v 4) in a great victory as of light over darkness (v 2). The terms "burdened," "submission," and "subjected" (v 4) all reflect bondage—from which the king releases his people. The reestablishment of justice and righteousness (v 7) portends a new creation of cosmic order.[15]

Chapter 11 conveys the idea of a creative reordering of the cosmos and a regeneration of life more fully: universal harmony ensues among men and beasts (11:6-9) when a righteous Davidic "judge" arbitrates for the lowly in the land (11:3-5); he smites the earth, slaying the wicked (11:4); and the knowledge of the Lord fills the earth (11:9). Such descriptions of cosmic order suggest that chapter 11 is the thematic complement of the coronation psalm of chapter 9. The interrelated events of Israel's release from bondage, return, new exodus, new wandering in the wilderness, and new conquest in the first unit of section III (cf. 9:1-4; 11:10-16), in effect, create a single, redemptive context for the two Davidic passages.

The intervening Assyrian material (chap. 10), on the other hand, structurally offsets both. Rhetorical links in the form of metaphorical pseudonyms tie the two Davidic passages to the Assyrian material.

---

[12] Frankfort, *Kingship*, 157.

[13] See the king as "sun of his peoples," W. G. Lambert, *Babylonian Wisdom Literature* (Oxford: Clarendon Press, 1960), 30.

[14] Rosenberg, "The God Sedeq," 164.

[15] For the imagery of victory over chaos in Israelite royal ideology, see Walter Brueggemann, "Kingship and Chaos," *CBQ* 33 (1971): 317-32.

The terms *staff* (*maṭṭēh*) and *rod* (*šēbeṭ*) in the coronation psalm (9:4), for example, reappear in chapter 10 as metaphorical pseudonyms of the king of Assyria and his oppressive rule: "Hail the Assyrian, the rod of my anger! He is a staff—my wrath in their hand" (10:5); "As though the rod wielded him who lifts it up! As though the staff held up the one who is not made of wood!" (10:15). Because these terms establish a metaphorical identity for the king of Assyria as the Lord's punitive *staff* and *rod*, they imply that the Davidic king's victory over the forces of chaos in the coronation psalm constitutes, in essence, a victory over Assyria. The smashing of the *yoke*, *staff*, and *rod* as in the day of Midian's defeat (9:4) expresses, allegorically, the Davidic king's triumph over the current ruling power—Assyria.

The new exodus of the Lord's people out of Assyria in 11:16 similarly implies such a victory. As at the exodus out of Egypt, the new exodus entails more than release from bondage. Pharaoh's armies of chariots and horses were drowned in the depths of the sea; the new exodus thus involves a decisive victory over the enslaving power itself. In the historical context of chapters 9–12, no power other than Assyria threatens the Lord's people with such bondage. As Israel never achieved a universal victory over Assyria, however, these events relate not to the plane of history but to the pale of eschatology. In that context, Assyria serves as the historical model of an archetypal power of chaos that will emerge in the latter days.[16] The use of metaphorical pseudonyms, moreover, facilitates the description of such redemptive events without infringing on history at the literal level.

The metaphors *yoke*, *staff*, and *rod* represent Assyrian rule in a further passage of chapter 10:

24. Therefore, thus says my lord, the Lord of hosts:
    O my people who inhabit Zion,
    be not afraid of the Assyrians,
        though they strike you with the rod
    or raise their staff over you,
        as did the Egyptians.
25. For my anger will very soon come to an end;
    my wrath will become their undoing.

---

[16] Brevard Childs, in "The Enemy from the North and the Chaos Tradition," *JBL* 78 (1959): 187–98, shows how the prophetic literature mythologizes the historical tradition of Assyria/ Babylon, thus facilitating the transformation of these entities into eschatological archetypes.

26. The Lord of Hosts will raise the whip against them,
    as when he struck the Midianites
    at the rock of Oreb.
    His staff is over the Sea,
    and he will lift it over them,
    as he did to the Egyptians.
27. In that day their burdens shall be lifted
    from your shoulders,
    their yoke [removed] from your neck.

The text here likens the Assyrian oppression of *rod*, *staff*, and *yoke* to Israel's Egyptian bondage (vv 24, 27). Assyria's overthrow by the Lord's counter-*staff* (*maṭṭēh*) and *whip* (*šôṭ*) is compared to the Lord's victory over the Egyptians and the Midianites (v 26). The mention of Midian's defeat in both the coronation psalm (9:4) and the present passage again identifies the Davidic king's victory over *rod*, *staff*, and *yoke* in the coronation psalm as a victory over Assyria.

Chapter 10, accordingly, depicts the king of Assyria as a power of chaos: "I will commission him against the people of my wrath, to pillage for plunder and spoliate for spoil, to tread underfoot like mud in the streets" (10:6). "Mud," a chaos motif, signifies that the Assyrian king reduces the Lord's wicked people to a powerless state. The terms *axe* (*garzen*) and *saw* (*ma'ṣṣôr*) additionally identify the king of Assyria as a power of chaos: "Shall an ax exalt itself above the one who hews with it, or a saw vaunt itself over him who handles it?" (10:15). As the Lord's instrument of punishment, the king of Assyria smites the Lord's wicked people together with all nations (10:9–14). By the same token, such metaphorical terms add to the list of pseudonyms that describe the king of Assyria.

The Lord's lifting of his counter-*staff* over the Sea, in the preceding passage (v 26), again recalls the role of Moses at the Exodus (cf. Exod 14:16). The Lord's *whip* subduing the Assyrians as the Midianites (v 26) recalls Gideon's role in overthrowing the Midianite host (cf. Judg 7:17–8:13); the biblical narrative depicts Gideon's flagellation of his enemies with briars and thorns (Judg 8:7, 16). In chapter 11, however, we saw the Lord's *hand* (*yād*) winning the victory over *Sea* (*yām*) and *River* (*nāhār*, 11:15), and prior material uses the terms *Sea* and *River* to describe the king of Assyria as a power of chaos (5:30; 7:20; 8:7).[17] Such rhetorical links reaffirm that the Lord's *staff* and *whip* subduing Assyria in the present passage (v 26) represent a future Davidic king's victory over a latter-day Assyria. A war to the death with Assyria at the stretching out of a *staff* appears cumulatively in 30:32.

The first unit's juxtaposition of the Davidic king and the king of Assyria thus extends to the use of metaphorical pseudonyms these figures share as well as to divergent metaphors. Terms that describe both figures include the Lord's *hand* (*yād*), *staff* (*maṭṭēh*), and *ensign* (*nēs*); each figure appears under these pseudonyms and does so throughout Isaiah. The shared use of metaphorical pseudonyms, depicting either the Davidic king or the Assyrian tyrant king, suggests an arch-rivalry between the two.[18] Divergent metaphors describing the two figures include the Lord's *anger* (*'ap*), *wrath* (*'ebrâ*), and *indignation* (*za'am*) on the one hand, and the Lord's *light* (*'ôr*) on the other. We recognize the metaphorical function of these terms by the same means noted previously—by the text attributing such a function to them directly or by their synonymous parallelism with other metaphors (cf. 5:25–26; 9:2; 10:5, 24–27; *passim*). Divergent metaphors also identify the king of Assyria as a power of chaos and the Davidic king as a power of creation (see Discourse C: Chaos and Creation [1]).

In sum, the first unit's juxtaposition of the Davidic king and the king of Assyria, supported rhetorically by metaphorical pseudonyms, serves to reveal the Davidic king's victory over the forces of chaos when he fulfills the typological roles of Moses, Joshua, David, Gideon, and Hezekiah. The Davidic king fulfills these roles by releasing the Lord's people from bondage, leading them in a new exodus and new conquest of the promised land, and ending their new wandering in the wilderness with "harvest time" and "spoil" (9:3; 11:14). These redemptive events pave the way for the Lord's establishing a millennial reign of peace (9:7; 11:6–9; 12:4–6).

---

[17] See Yamm ("Sea") and Nahar ("River") as powers of chaos in the Ugaritic myth, *ANET*, 129–31; Herbert G. May, "Some Cosmic Connotations of *Mayîm Rabbîm*, 'Many Waters,'" *JBL* 74 (1955): 9–21.

[18] See the ancient Near Eastern background to such arch-rivalry in the contests between Horus and Seth, Frankfort, *Kingship and the Gods*, 21–22; 25–26; and between Baal and Yamm, *ANET*, 120–22.

As stated earlier, the various roles the Davidic king performs draw on a multiplicity of types to establish an eschatological or latter-day ideal. Even as the text represents events contemporary to Isaiah in terms of ancient types, so it projects events yet future in terms of both contemporary and ancient types. It accomplishes this transformation by using structural and rhetorical devices to build a prophecy within a prophecy. Roles based on the type of King David, such as the reuniting of Judah and Ephraim (11:13–14; cf. 2 Sam 5:1–3), and roles based on the type of King Solomon, such as a divine endowment of wisdom (11:2–4; cf. 1 Kgs 3:12) and the expansion of Davidic dominion (9:7, cf. 1 Kgs 4:21), also appear in the text and augment this unit's portrait of a latter-day Davidic king.

The fusion of typological roles in the person of the Davidic king possesses parallels in Pharaoh. As Horus incarnate, the Egyptian king is a "son" not only of Osiris and Re, but of Atum, Amun, Ptah, and the larger pantheon of gods. Egyptian literature stresses the king's affinity to his divine forbears particularly on the occasion of his winning a great military victory.[19] Pharaoh's ideal rule, in effect, reflects the attributes of all the gods, notably that of Maat, "truth/justice/righteousness."[20]

The list of epithets comprising the Davidic king's titulary in the coronation psalm—"Wonderful Counselor, one Mighty in Valor, a Father for Ever, a Prince of Peace" (9:6)—too, has a counterpart in Pharaoh.[21] These four couplets, however, with the possible exception of the third,[22] do not appear to originate in Egypt. They reflect four phases in the life of yet another biblical type—Abraham. As a biblical figure, Abraham epitomizes human perfection.[23] In successive narratives in the Genesis account, Abraham exemplifies the attributes of counsel—in the dispute with Lot (Gen 13); valor—in the war against the coalition of northern kings (Gen 14); covenantal fatherhood—after two tentative heirs (Gen 15–16), Isaac (Gen 17); and peacemaker/savior (Gen 18). The crowning title, "Prince of Peace" (*'sar šālôm*),

---

[19] Frankfort, *Kingship and the Gods*, 42.

[20] Benjamin F. Lowe, Jr., "The King as Mediator of the Cosmic Order" (diss., Emory University, 1967), 26–63.

[21] Otto Kaiser, *Isaiah 1–12* (Philadelphia: Westminster, 1972), 129, n. *a*.

[22] See the Egyptian king as "father" of the people, Henri Frankfort, *Ancient Egyptian Religion* (New York: Columbia University, 1948), 43.

[23] See the Lord's command to Abraham: "Be thou perfect!" (Gen 17:1).

connotes an agent of the Lord's salvation.[24] Abraham assumes that role when he mediates with the Lord on behalf of the righteous in Sodom (Gen 18:23-25).[25]

In the future Davidic ruler thus merge the typological functions and attributes of many heroes of the biblical narrative. The text creates this prophetic figure in part by transforming Egyptian myth.

Discourse C: Chaos and Creation (1)

A structure consisting of alternating motifs of a return to chaos and a new creation underscores the Davidic king's victory over Assyria. That structure, which spans all of chapters 1-12 but culminates in the first unit of section III (chaps. 9-12), links prophetic material of diverse historical origins. An initial example of the chaos/creation pattern appears in chapter 1:

> 25. I will restore my hand over you
>   and smelt away your dross as in a crucible,[26]
>   and remove all your alloy.
> 26. I will restore your judges as at the first,
>   and your counselors as in the beginning.
>   After this you shall be called
>   the City of Righteousness, a faithful city.

Chaos motifs are "dross" and "alloy" (v 25), creation motifs "as at the first" and "as in the beginning" (v 26). The parallel events of the Lord's "restoring" (*'āšîbâ*) his *hand* over his people (v 25) and "restoring" (*'āšîbâ*) his people's judges (v 26) follow Israel's political demise when the Lord punishes her (1:23-24). The text identifies the people's present rulers/princes (*'śārayik*) contextually as "dross" (1:22-23; cf. v 10); the Lord deals with them as with enemies and adversaries (1:24) and makes an end of them (cf. v 28). The Lord's new order thus consists of creation out of chaos, as the imagery of refining precious metals also signifies (1:25). The "city" motif expresses the idea of a renewal of political institutions: the righteous city that

---

[24] See the synonymity of peace and salvation, 52:7.

[25] Compare Gen 19:29: "And God remembered Abraham and sent Lot out of the midst of the overthrow."

[26] Hebrew *kabbōr* ("as with potash/lye") has been emended to *kakōr*; compare 48:10.

became a harlot (1:21) will be succeeded by another righteous city when the Lord restores his people's leadership (1:26). The city appears elsewhere cumulatively as a new creation (cf. 52:1–3; 65:18).

The parallel restorative events in this passage denote a reinstitution of both monarchy and judges, an idea that occurs cumulatively elsewhere as well (cf. 32:1). The expediency of predicting a new monarchy by way of metaphor seems self-evident because such a reinstitution implies the supplanting of the current, alienated monarchy. In proposing a dual restoration of monarchy and judges, however, the text associates the future Davidic king—the Lord's *hand* (*yād*, 1:25)—with the type of government Moses and the seventy elders conducted (cf. Num 11:16–17; Deut 1:16–17).[27] The biblical narrative relates how the Lord's Spirit rested upon these, as on Israel's judges after Moses, in order that they might judge the Lord's people righteously (Num 11:24–25; Judg 3:10).

Because the judges (*šōptayik*) whom the Lord restores (1:26) possess no typological antecedents that we can support rhetorically other than these ancient judges, we assume that the Lord's ideal government combines the positive features of both monarchy and judges: the king exercises his executive role by purifying the establishment (1:25),[28] and the people's judges maintain pristine judicial functions—"as at the first" and "as in the beginning" (1:26). This synthesis of biblical types in order to create an ideal accords with Isaianic practice we have already observed.

The Lord's *hand* of restoration in 1:25 contrasts with another *hand* of the Lord, that of destruction in chapter 5:

> 25. Therefore the Lord's anger is kindled
> against his people:
> he draws back his hand against them
> and strikes them;
> the mountains quake, and their corpses
> lie like litter about the streets.
> Yet for all this his anger is not abated;
> his hand is upraised still.
> 26. He raises an ensign to distant nations
> and summons them from beyond the horizon.
> Forthwith they come,
> swiftly and speedily.

[27] As a rhetorical contrast, compare Moses as "king" (*melek*), Deut 33:5, and the future Davidic king as "judge" (*šōpēt*), Isa 11:4; 16:5.

[28] Compare the historical parallels of Hezekiah and Josiah, 2 Kgs 18:4; 22:4–24.

In this passage, the Lord's (left) *hand*, which appears twice in parallel with the Lord's *anger* (*'ap*, v 25), causes "litter/refuse" (*sûḥâ*), representing chaos. The text links the Lord's upraised *hand* contextually to the Lord's raising an *ensign* (*nēs*, v 26), again suggesting a synonymity of these two terms. The *ensign* rallies hostile nations from afar, from beyond the horizon, in the classic Enemy-from-the-North tradition (v 26).[29]

That enemy, and the chaos motif associated with it, reappear in the concluding verse of the passage:

> 30. He shall be stirred up against them in that day,
>   even as the Sea is stirred up.
>   And should one look to the land,
>   there [too] shall be a distressing gloom,
>   for the daylight shall be darkened
>   by an overhanging mist.

This verse depicts the king of Assyria as a mythological power of chaos—the *Sea* (*yām*)—which is stirred up against the Lord's wicked people. The text couples that idea with the chaos motifs of "gloom," "darkness," and "mist" to end chapter 5.

Chapter 6 commences with the Lord's sitting on a throne (6:1), while seraphs proclaim the consummation of his creation (6:3). The theophany on the throne in the temple, and the cosmic hymn that the seraphs sing, are classic representations denoting world dominion following a divine victory over the forces of chaos.[30] The patterned motifs of a return to chaos (5:25–30) and a new creation (6:1–3) thus connote the Lord's victory over Assyria, a world power. Assyria's reduction of the Lord's wicked people to chaos prepares the way for the consummation of the Lord's creation when Assyria itself is put down (cf. 10:5–11:9). The chaos/creation pattern, then, links structurally chapters 5 and 6 as well as consecutive sections of the Bifid Structure (chaps. 1–5; 6–8).

Additional chaos/creation cycles occur in the intervening material of chapters 1–5. A return to chaos ends chapter 1: the mighty and their works are but "refuse" burnt up in the fire (1:31). A new creation begins chapter 2: the Lord establishes the "mountain" or

---

[29] See Childs, "The Enemy from the North and the Chaos Tradition," 187–98.

[30] Compare Baal's ascent on the throne upon his victory over Yamm and Mot, *ANET*, 134–35, 141.

nation of his house in the top of, or as the head of, the mountains or nations (2:2); and the Lord's creative "word" goes forth (2:3) like a *light* (2:5). The land's desolation, which expresses a variant chaos motif, ends chapter 3: the land lies forsaken and destitute (3:26) and its inhabitants fall by the sword (3:25). The regeneration of the land commences chapter 4: the Lord's *plant* (*ṣemaḥ*)—a metaphor describing a future Davidic king[31]—and the earth's "fruit" (*pĕrî*) grow illustrious among the survivors of Israel (4:2). Lastly, the Lord cleanses his people of their "excrement" and "bloodshed" (4:4) and "creates" (*br'*) a cloud of glory over them as a protective canopy (4:5).

In chapters 6–8, the motifs of desolation and regeneration of the land repeat the variant pattern: the Lord permits the land and its cities to be ravaged and burned (6:11–13); yet, the live stump of a tree—Israel's holy offspring—survives (6:13d), denoting renewal. Importantly, the text now identifies directly both the future Davidic king—in the person of Immanuel (7:14)—and "the great[32] and mighty waters of the River, the king of Assyria in all his glory" (8:7; cf. 7:20). The transition from pseudonymity for these figures in chapters 1–5 to open identification in chapters 6–8 accords with the progression from ruin and rebirth in section I of the Bifid Structure to rebellion and compliance in section II. Section I features the Lord's people as its subject, while section II features both king and people.

The text's now overt identification of the Davidic king and the Assyrian tyrant king serves to heighten climactically the two figures' contest for supremacy. Chapter 8 depicts the Assyrian king as having the upper hand over the land and people of Immanuel: the chaotic Assyrian "flood" (*šāṭap*) displaces the gentle waters of Shiloah that signify Davidic succession (8:6–7); the king of Assyria overflows his banks, sweeps into the land of Immanuel, and reaches the neck (8:7–8). Chaos imagery prevails through the remainder of the chapter, ending with "gloom" and "darkness" pervading the land (8:22).

Chapters 6–8, like chapters 1–5, thus end with a return to chaos. Chapters 9–12, like chapters 6–8, begin with a new creation: the dawning of a bright *light* dispels the darkness (9:2). The chaos/creation pattern here again links diverse prophetic material as well

---

[31] Compare Jer 23:5; 33:15; Zech 6:12.

[32] Hebrew *rabbîm*, also "many"; compare May, "Some Cosmic Connotations of *Mayim Rabbîm*, 'Many Waters.'"

as successive units of the Bifid Structure. The motifs of chaos and creation repeat themselves with the turning of war accoutrements into "fuel for bonfires" (9:4–5) when the Davidic king accedes to the throne (9:7).

We observe, then, that most instances of the chaos/creation pattern associate the motif of creation with the Davidic king, the Lord's vassal. At this point in the text, however, a transition from an indirect association occurs—by way of metaphor—to a direct association: the metaphorical pseudonyms *hand* (1:25), *light* (2:5; 9:2), and *plant* (4:2) give way to a "son . . . on the throne of David" (9:6–7). Conversely, the text associates a majority of chaos motifs with the king of Assyria: burned refuse (1:31), the darkened or desolated land (3:26; 5:30; 6:11; 8:22), littered corpses (5:25), the *Sea* in commotion (5:30), the *River* in flood (8:8)—all attest to Assyria's handiwork. Two exceptions to this identification of the Davidic king with the motif of creation are the Lord's theophany on the throne (6:1) and the Lord's forming a cloud of glory in Zion (4:5). The latter two examples feature only the Lord, the suzerain or great king. On the other hand, a single creation motif features both the Lord and the Davidic king: when the Lord's house is established in the latter days (2:2), the Lord's word goes forth like a *light* (2:3, 5; cf. 51:4).

The common linkage of the Lord and the Davidic king to a new creation—in contrast to the king of Assyria's sole association with chaos—shows that the Lord and the Davidic king (the suzerain and his vassal) act in concert as powers of creation. The climactic structuring of chaos/creation motifs leading up to the first unit of section III, particularly as it moves from pseudonymity on the part of the Davidic king and the king of Assyria to their direct association with creation and chaos, identifies the Davidic king as the one who now has the upper hand over the king of Assyria. We observe that idea also in the Davidic king's victory over the *staff* and *rod* of the oppressors "as in the day of Midian" (9:4); that event denotes, rhetorically, the Davidic king's victory over Assyria (10:24–26).

We further observe Davidic ascendancy in the way the text identifies the Davidic king with the variant motif of the regenerating land: "A shoot will spring up from the stock of Jesse, and a branch from its graft bear fruit" (11:1). That verse immediately follows the king of Assyria's desolation of the land: the dense forests are battered down with the force of iron and Lebanon falls spectacularly

(10:34).[33] Lastly, we observe the Davidic king's victory when a remnant of the Lord's people exits Assyria (11:16); at that time, the Lord's *hand* subdues *Sea* and *River* (11:15). With the Lord's *anger* (*'ap*) being turned away (12:1) and peaceful waters again flowing (12:3), a Song of Salvation in Zion proclaims the Lord's worldwide victory (12:1–6).

A pattern of alternating chaos and creation motifs in Isa 1–12 thus supports the first unit of section III's structured rivalry between the Davidic king and the king of Assyria. The Davidic power, which the Lord raises up, succeeds the Assyrian power of chaos even as the Lord newly creates his people in Zion. That this chaos/creation pattern transcends historical origins and chapter divisions implies that its message relates not to history but to eschatology. The ideal this structure achieves finds fullest expression in a futuristic or latter-day redemption of Israel.

The Righteous Warrior Figure

In the second unit of section III (chaps. 41:1–46:13b), the metaphors *hand*, *righteousness*, and *light* again identify an ideal latter-day figure. That figure serves as the Lord's agent of punishing the wicked and delivering the righteous within a context of Israel's release from bondage, new exodus, new wandering in the wilderness, return, and new conquest. One manifestation of this ideal agent of the Lord's redemption is the Righteous Warrior figure. Chapter 41 depicts a person called *Righteousness* (*ṣedeq*), who hails from the east, as the Lord's agent of punishing idolatrous nations who are condemned in a lawsuit:

1.   Be silent before me, O isles;
     become still, you peoples!
     Let them come forward and state their case;
     let us stand trial together.

---

[33] The name *Lebanon* represents, figuratively, the Lord's people and their land; see 2:13; 14:8; 33:9; *passim*. Compare Deut 3:25; Judg 9:15; 2 Kgs 14:9; Psa 104:16. See also the king of Assyria as hewer of the cedars of Lebanon, 10:15; 37:24, and the mythological implications of that motif, *ANET*, 79.

> 2. Who has raised up Righteousness from the east,
>   calling him to his foot?[34]
>   Who has delivered nations to him,
>   toppled their rulers,
>   rendering them as dust to his sword,
>   as driven stubble to his bow?
> 3. He puts them to flight, passing on unhindered
>   by paths his feet have never trod.

The motif of a new conquest here takes the form of rendering nations and rulers into dust and stubble (v 2). That imagery signifies the nations' powerlessness or extinction as political entities. If the text intends Cyrus the Persian as the victor (so concur Westermann, McKenzie, *et al.*)—as it does elsewhere (cf. 44:28; 45:1)—it does not make a direct connection to that effect. The events surrounding Cyrus' rise to power may nonetheless constitute a valid premise for the passage, and we may therefore associate these descriptions at least typologically with Cyrus.

The figure *righteousness*, however, possesses a further aspect. That figure relates both contextually and typologically to "Abraham my beloved [friend]" (41:8), progenitor and exemplar of the Lord's corporate servant, Jacob/Israel (41:8). The Genesis narrative depicts Abraham as a righteous one par excellence (cf. Gen 15:6),[35] he too being raised up from the east and called to the Lord's foot (Gen 12:1).[36] Like Abraham, or that aspect of the figure *righteousness* that resembles Abraham, Jacob/Israel is now taken from the ends of the earth, called from its farthest limit (41:9). Such imagery

---

[34] No rhetorical definition of the term *ṣedeq* ("righteousness") justifies the rendering of this verse by Westermann, *et al.*, "Who stirred [him] up from the east whom victory meets at every step"; Claus Westermann, *Isaiah 40-66* (Philadelphia: Westminster, 1969), 62, 64. Rather, the rhetorical use of the terms *ṣedeq*, *ṣĕdāqâ*, and *ṣaddîq* in Isaiah suggests a meaning that carries the traditional connotation of "justice/righteousness/vindication," an attribute of the Lord, which, like *yĕšû*ʿâ ("salvation"), appears in a personified form (cf. 53:11; 62:11). Further, the expression *mimmizrāḥ* ("from the east") is the parallelistic complement of *lĕraglô* ("to his foot")—as the verb *hēʿîr* ("raised up") is of *yiqrāʾēhû* ("called him," v 2). Because the object of the second verb is "him," that of the first must be "Righteousness" (*ṣedeq*) or a breakdown of parallelism results. The precedence of parallelism over a strict conformity of meter does not apply uniquely to this verse.

[35] Gen 15:6 in full states: "He believed in the Lord and he [the Lord] counted it unto him for righteousness."

[36] Compare Zion as the place of the Lord's foot, Isa 60:13.

describes Israel's return. Like the figure *righteousness*, moreover, Jacob/Israel threshes mountains or nations into dust and chaff (41:15), representing a new conquest.[37]

The figure *righteousness*, including its Abraham aspect, can thus be identified in an exemplary sense with the Lord's people through the motifs of Israel's return and new conquest. Within the context of these redemptive events, the figure *righteousness* serves as an exemplar or paradigm of Jacob/Israel, consistent with concepts established in section II. The Lord's assurance, in 41:10, that *righteousness*, his *right hand*,[38] will strengthen, succor, and uphold Jacob/Israel against hostile elements nonetheless implies more than an exemplary relationship: the Lord's intervention directly facilitates Jacob/Israel's return from the ends of the earth (41:9). That intervention suggests a leading function by the figure *righteousness* in serving as the Lord's agent of delivering the Lord's people.

In a second example, in 41:13–15, when the Lord's *right hand* holds and helps Jacob/Israel, the Lord's people are transformed from a worm into a threshing sledge. The Lord's intervention enables Jacob/Israel to render mountains or nations into dust and chaff (41:15). Such a transformation suggests a leading and empowering function by this prophetic figure as the Lord's agent of punishment. Accordingly, the context of this passage asserts that Jacob/Israel's "adversaries" will come to nought and be reduced to nothing (41:11–12).

When we read *righteousness* and *right hand* as allegorically describing a prophetic figure who serves as the Lord's agent of punishment and deliverance, then an exemplary and collaborative relationship appears between that figure and Jacob/Israel.[39] The

---

[37] See section I, footnote 3. Compare Mic 4:13: "Arise and thresh, O daughter of Zion, for I will give you horns of iron; I will give you hooves of brass, and you will break in pieces many nations." John Hamlin, using an entirely different approach, also sees Jacob/Israel's rendering of mountains into dust as a new conquest motif; E. John Hamlin, "The Meaning of 'Mountains and Hills' in Isa. 41:14–16," *JNES* 13 (1954): 189.

[38] Hebrew *yĕmîn ṣidqî* ("my righteous right hand," or, "righteousness, my right hand," 41:10) forms a construct of two nouns with a possessive article, which, like similar constructs (e.g., *har qodšî*), semantically associates the possessive article with the first of its components.

[39] Compare a similar relationship in Mic 2:13: "One who breaks open the way will go up before them; they will break through the gate and go out. Their king will pass through before them, the Lord at their head." An analogous idea, that of the one and the many, has long been recognized as essential to understanding the servant passages of Isaiah; see Herbert G. May, "The Righteous Servant in Second Isaiah's Songs," *ZAW* 66 (1954): 237.

respective contexts of Israel's return and new conquest, within which this relationship manifests itself, implies that the figure *righteousness* of 41:2 fulfills the typological roles of Cyrus and Abraham in serving as an agent of the Lord's intervention. Because this figure's actions reflect neither those of Abraham nor Cyrus alone, and because they express primarily an exemplary and collaborative relationship toward Jacob/Israel, the text uses a pseudonym—*righteousness (ṣedeq)*—to identify him.

A Righteous Warrior figure approaching from the east reappears in the same chapter:

> 25. I have raised up one from the north
> who calls on my name,
> who shall come from the direction of sunrise.
> He shall come upon dignitaries as on mud,
> tread them as clay like a potter.

This figure again identifies typologically with Abraham and Cyrus.[40] On arriving in the land of Canaan from Haran, Abram called on the name of the Lord (Gen 12:8). Likewise, Cyrus' almost effortless taking of Babylonia qualifies him as the kind of conqueror this verse describes. Both biblical figures hail from the east. As with 41:2, however, we cannot relate 41:25 to either Abraham or Cyrus alone.[41] Each of these verses contains elements exclusive to both figures. While, admittedly, Abraham, like Cyrus, overpowered peoples and rulers (cf. Gen 14:13–15), he did not do so in the present context—while approaching from the east. This second passage, therefore, closely matches 41:2; it expresses functions that are exemplary for Jacob/Israel within the context of a new conquest and return.

We conclude, then, that these passages exhibit composites of types in order to project a series of transcendent redemptive events. Though they draw on biblical history, these passages subordinate history in order to create an ideal agent of the Lord's redemption. This material, therefore, is not purely historical but is instead of an eschatological nature. We again see this latter-day intent in the

---

[40] G. H. Jones also points out this identification in "Abraham and Cyrus: Type and Antitype?" *VT* 22 (1972): 311–16. Jones's thesis of Abraham as type and Cyrus as antitype, however, is untenable in view of the evidence here being presented.

[41] So also concludes Jones, "Abraham and Cyrus," 314.

motif of the regenerating wilderness. That motif directly follows Jacob/Israel's new conquest in the same chapter:

17. When the poor and needy require water,
    and there is none,
    and their tongue becomes parched with thirst,
    I, the Lord, will answer their want;
    I, the God of Israel, will not forsake them.
18. I will open up streams in barren hill country,
    springs in the midst of the plains;
    I will turn the desert into lakes,
    parched lands into fountains of water.
19. I will bring cedars and acacias,
    myrtles and oleasters in the wilderness;
    I will place cypresses,
    elms and box trees in the steppes—
20. that all may see it and know,
    consider it and perceive
    that the Lord's hand did this,
    that the Holy One of Israel created it.

Within the structured context of this chapter, the wilderness regenerates (41:18–19) immediately following Jacob/Israel's threshing of mountains into dust (41:15–16)—when Jacob/Israel is strengthened by the Lord's *right hand* (41:10–14). These two land-based events thus complement one another; they conform with chaos/creation patterns, in which chaos precedes creation. The concluding verse of the passage confirms their interrelatedness: the Lord's *hand* and the Holy One of Israel, respectively, are acknowledged as doing (*'sh*) and creating (*br'*) what has been described (41:20). In other words, the rendering of hostile elements into chaos (41:15–16) and the regeneration of the wilderness (41:17–19) form a concerted division of labors between *hand* and Holy One. Within the broader context of this chapter, moreover, such structuring ties together the redemptive events of Israel's return (41:8–9), new conquest (41:10–16), and, in this instance, a new wandering in the wilderness (41:17–19).

In summary, the passages cited speak, with varying emphases, of the same eschatological sequence that links them: a prophetic figure *righteousness* (41:2, 10), alias the Lord's *hand* or *right hand* (41:10, 13, 20), who heralds from the east (41:2, 25), serves as a paradigm and helper of the Lord's corporate servant Jacob/Israel (41:8–10, 13) in heralding from afar (41:9, 17) and making chaos of idolatrous nations (41:1, 5–7, 21–29) while on a march of conquest (41:2, 15–16, 25). For Jacob/Israel, the return march leads through a regenerating wilderness (41:17–19), a new creation succeeding chaos (41:20).

The motif of one coming from the east reappears in chapter 46:

> 9. Review the former things, those from of old!
> I am God, there is no other.
> I am divine; nothing resembles me.
> 10. I foretell the end from the beginning,
> from ancient times things not yet done.
> I speak, and my counsel takes effect;
> I accomplish all my will.
> 11. I summon a bird of prey from the east,
> from a land far off, the man of my counsel.
> What I have spoken I bring to pass;
> what I have planned, I do.
> 12. Hear me, you stubborn-hearted,
> who are far from righteousness:
> 13. I have brought near my righteousness;
> it is not now far off—
> my salvation shall no longer be delayed.

Parallel lines identify the "bird of prey" who heralds from the east as the "man of [the Lord's] counsel" who hails from a land far off (v 11). As does chapter 41, this passage also identifies the figure from the east as the Lord's *righteousness* (*ṣĕdāqâ*).[42] The passage does this by using a chain of linking words: "from of old/from ancient times" (vv 9–10); "my counsel/man of my counsel" (vv 10–11); "from . . . far off/far from" (vv 11–12); and "righteousness/righteousness" (vv 12–13). This linking device expresses the key ideas of the passage, revealing the future figure's exemplary function toward Jacob/Israel. The key ideas consist of ancient origins, fulfillment of the Lord's counsel, arrival from afar, and righteousness. The concluding verse of the passage reveals that the intent of the Lord's intervention is to bring about Israel's salvation/deliverance (*tĕšû'â*, v 13).

---

[42] Rhetorically, in Isaiah, the terms *ṣedeq*, *ṣĕdāqâ*, and *ṣaddîq* are metaphorical variants that describe a single ideal figure.

The chain of linking words thus identifies the bird of prey whom the Lord summons from the east (v 11) with the Lord's *righteousness* who is brought near (v 13). This doubling of directional terms—of one who hails "from the east" and is "brought near"—parallels the raising up of *righteousness* "from the east" whom the Lord summons "to his foot" in 41:2. In addition, a common rhetoric identifies the figure from the east as the Lord's *righteousness*: when the man of the Lord's counsel arrives from a land "far off" (46:11), the Lord's *righteousness* is no longer "far off" but brought near (46:13). By means of such rhetorical devices, the text determines the common identity of the bird of prey and the figure *righteousness*. At the same time, it correlates attributes the future figure possesses that serve an exemplary function for Jacob/Israel. Prominent among these attributes is righteousness, which forms a prerequisite of the Lord's salvation (46:13).

As in chapter 41, both Abraham and Cyrus qualify as types of the future figure. Cyrus resembles a bird of prey (*'ayiṭ*) because of the swiftness of his conquests.[43] Abraham exemplifies a man of the Lord's counsel (cf. Gen 18:17: "Shall I hide from Abraham what I do?"). The Hebrew prophets use the term *'ayiṭ* ("bird of prey") within the context of the overthrow of kingdoms as a covenant curse (cf. Isa 18:6; Jer 12:9; Ezek 39:4).[44] The imagery of a bird of prey and man of the Lord's counsel, then, suggests a function for the future figure as the Lord's instrument of retribution within a covenantal framework. Such a function parallels the role of the figure *righteousness* in 41:1-6. The background of idolatry that comprises the remainder of chapter 46 (vv 1-8; cf. 41:5-6, 21-24) depicts the idolaters' defenselessness against trouble (*ṣārâ*, 46:7), which we may take to mean covenant curses inflicted by the Lord's agent of punishment.

The Lord's appeal to a remnant of Jacob/Israel (46:3) to come to their senses and dissociate themselves from idolatry (46:8) lends a rationale to the Righteous Warrior figure's fulfillment of an exemplary function. At present, the Lord's people are stubborn-hearted and "far from righteousness" (46:12). The Lord brings near his *righteousness* to pave the way for his people's salvation (46:13). The Righteous Warrior figure thus serves as a paradigm of the Lord's people as well as the Lord's agent for delivering them.

---

[43] So also concludes James Muilenburg, *IB*, 5:542.

[44] See also Weinfeld, "Covenant of Grant," 198, n. 132. Compare Gen 15:11, and a similar figure in Hos 8:1.

We understand the eschatological or latter-day intent of the passage from its purporting to foretell "the end from the beginning, from ancient times things not yet done" (46:10). Within that context, the end or last thing (*'aḥărît*, 46:10) is foreshadowed by several former things (*ri'šōnôt*, 46:9). As we have already observed, what constitutes a type in Isaiah is a biblical phenomenon that serves as a precedent as much as it serves as a model. By the text's own criteria, therefore, both Abraham and Cyrus—and the biblical events they exemplify— qualify as former things: their typological synthesis creates an eschatological ideal, or latter thing. Stated another way, the future figure's role in relation to the Lord's people is to embody attributes that Abraham and Cyrus typify. He embodies their attributes and fulfills their roles by acting as the Lord's latter-day agent of punishment and deliverance. The passage thus foretells the end from the beginning (46:10)—thereby proving the Lord's divinity (46:9)—by means of biblical types (46:9). As the text frequently asserts, the capacity to do that belongs exclusively to the Lord (cf. 43:9–10; 44:7–8).

The Cyrus Figure

Against a similar background of idolatry, chapter 44 introduces the figure of Cyrus.[45] The mention of Cyrus' name has been a source of dispute among scholars, many of whom contend that the eighth-century B.C. prophet Isaiah could not have known of this sixth-century B.C. Persian conquerer.[46]

> 26.   . . . who fulfills the word of his servant,
>   accomplishes the aims of his messengers,
> who says of Jerusalem, It shall be reinhabited,
>   and of the cities of Judah, They shall be rebuilt,
>   their ruins I will restore,
> 27.   who says to the deep, Become dry!
>   I am drying up your currents,
> 28.   who says of Cyrus, He is my shepherd;
>   he will fulfill all my will.
> He will say of Jerusalem that it must be rebuilt,
>   its temple foundations relaid.

---

[45] Verses 9–20 of chapter 44 comprise the longest passage on idolatry in Isaiah; verses 21–22 first implicate, then absolve Jacob/Israel—on condition Jacob/Israel repents/returns; and verses 23–28 declare Jacob/Israel's redemption and introduce Cyrus.

[46] That question is resolved in the course of this literary analysis as we discover that Isaiah not only saw the time of Cyrus, he saw the end of time.

The representation of Cyrus as the Lord's shepherd (v 28), within a context of the deep becoming dry (v 27), identifies the figure of Cyrus typologically with Moses.[47] Although the term *shepherd* is a common descriptive title of ancient Near Eastern kings (which connotation here undoubtedly applies to Cyrus the Persian), the Lord's personalizing it to "my shepherd" (*rōʿî*, 44:28), as well as the text's rhetorical use of the term, takes precedence, interpretively speaking, over non-Isaianic parallels.

The term *shepherd* and the exodus motif associated with it coincide elsewhere in Isaiah only with reference to Moses in chapter 63:

> 11. Then his people recalled the days
> of Moses of old:
> Where is he who brought them up out of the Sea
> with the shepherd of his flock?
> Where is he who put into him
> his holy Spirit,
> 12. who made his glorious arm proceed
> at the right hand of Moses,
> who divided the waters before them,
> making an everlasting name for himself
> 13. when he led them through the deep?

Chapter 44 thus combines an ahistorical or transposed element—a Moses typology (vv 27–28)—with another that we recognize as historical or original to Cyrus, namely the word to restore Jerusalem (vv 26, 28). Cyrus' association with the figure of Moses, and with Abraham in chapters 41 and 46, shows why the text now mentions Cyrus by name. As chapter 41 names Abraham because he serves as a precedent of one whom the Lord calls from the ends of the earth (41:8–9; cf. vv 2, 25), and as chapter 63 names Moses because he serves as a precedent of the Lord's shepherd leading his people out of bondage (63:11–14), so chapter 44 names Cyrus because he sets a precedent for restoring Jerusalem. As a biblical type, Cyrus eminently qualifies for that event. Like other biblical

---

[47] Graham Ogden also notes that Cyrus identifies typologically with Moses and shows evidence that "Cyrus can be viewed as having a relationship to the Return analogous to that of Moses to the Exodus"; Graham S. Ogden, "Moses and Cyrus," *VT* 28 (1978): 201. Ogden concludes, "There are some important questions which flow from the demonstrated purpose of this prophet in his locating Cyrus within Israel's deepest soteriological traditions," 203.

figures and the events they typify, Cyrus' name thus receives mention in connection with it.

Yet, none of the figures appearing in the second unit describes Cyrus alone. Abraham, Moses, and other biblical figures, through the well-known traditions associated with them, help form a composite of types that makes up the ideal. The description of the Cyrus figure as the Lord's "servant"—the Lord's vassal—whose word the Lord establishes (44:26),[48] and who, as the Lord's shepherd, "fulfills all my will" (44:28), further idealizes a non-Israelite sovereign beyond what would conceivably conform with historical reality. The text's subordination and synthesis of history—in order to create an eschatological ideal—does not negate history but emphasizes those historical elements that heighten the ideal. As the Lord's ideal agent both of punishment and of deliverance, the Cyrus figure performs functions typified in the lives of select biblical heroes.

That process of selectivity repeats itself in chapter 45, where Cyrus' name receives mention a second time:

1. Thus says the Lord to his anointed,
       to Cyrus, whom I grasp by the right hand,
    to subdue nations before him,
       to ungird the loins of rulers,
    opening doors ahead of him,
       letting no gates remain shut:
2. I will go before you
       and level all obstacles;
    I will break in pieces brazen doors
       and cut through iron bars.
3. I will give you hidden treasures
       and secret hoards of wealth—
    that you may know that it is I, the Lord,
       the God of Israel, who calls you by name.
4. For the sake of my servant Jacob,
       and Israel my chosen,
    I call you by name—
       I named you when yet you knew me not—
5. I am the Lord, there is no other;
       apart from me there is no God.
    I girded you up when yet you knew me not.

---

[48] Within the parallelistic structure of 44:26, the servant's word concerns the restoration of Jerusalem—just as that is the word of Cyrus in 44:28 (cf. 45:13). Compare Nebuchadnezzar as the Lord's "servant," Jer 27:6; 43:10.

A second event for which Cyrus sets a historical precedent—
and therefore his name appears in connection with it—is his conquest
of nations and rulers (v 1) for the sake of Jacob/Israel (v 4). Although
other world conquerors preceded Cyrus, notably the Assyrian and
Babylonian kings, that particular event vouchsafed Jacob/Israel's
release from exile or bondage. The text thus sums up Cyrus' twofold
mission: "He will rebuild my city and set free my exiles for no price
or bribe, says the Lord of Hosts" (45:13).

An ahistorical element nonetheless attaches itself to Cyrus (and
thus to the motifs of a universal conquest and release from bondage
associated with Cyrus), namely the title "his anointed" (*měšîḥô*, v 1).
That title represents a David typology (cf. *měšîḥô*, 2 Sam 22:51;
Psa 2:2) as the Lord's anointing of a king or vassal originates within
Israel's own royal tradition. Further, the Cyrus Cylinder, a record
dating to the time of Cyrus the Persian, attests the rite of grasping
by the hand (v 1) and giving a name (vv 3–4);[49] however, it is the
god Marduk who does so, not the Lord God of Israel. Isaiah's Cyrus
passage, therefore, transforms a Mesopotamian rite of royal accession
by lending it a Hebrew prophetic connotation. It is this transformation, not the possible historical origins of the passage, that
primarily deserves our attention. Although the ancient Near Eastern
parallels are significant[50]—forming a Mesopotamian counterpart in
the second unit to the Egyptian-influenced royal accession in the
first unit—the Isaianic and biblical parallels supersede them, since
it is within the Hebrew tradition that the passage appears.

To carry this point one step further, not only does the Lord hold
the Cyrus figure by the right hand (45:1) but also Jacob/Israel (41:10,
13) and the Servant figure (42:6). According to Mesopotamian patterns of royal accession, the commission of a new king to perform
a particular task follows immediately the gods calling him through
the act of grasping his hand and naming him.[51] The Lord's grasping others by the hand thus implies that they will perform functions
similar to those of Cyrus. Jacob/Israel's task, when held by the Lord's
hand, for example, is to render enemies into dust and chaff

---

[49] *ANET*, 315.

[50] With regard to Cyrus and the Isaianic servant, see the Summerian, Hittite, Assyrian, and
Babylonian parallels Shalom M. Paul notes in "Deutero-Isaiah and Cuneiform Royal
Inscriptions," *JAOS* 88 (1968): 180–86. Compare Weinfeld, "Covenant of Grant," 190–92.

[51] Paul, "Royal Inscriptions," 182.

(41:11–16; cf. Cyrus, 45:1–2), representing a new conquest. The Servant figure's task, when held by the Lord's hand, is to release the Lord's captives from bondage (42:6–7; cf. Cyrus, 45:2, 13), leading to a new wandering in the wilderness as they return from exile (42:16).

Functions attributed to Cyrus, therefore, such as the conquest of nations and the release of captives, do not apply uniquely to Cyrus the Persian. Despite the historical precedents Cyrus set, the Isaianic Cyrus figure fulfills roles that resemble those of the Servant figure and also serve an exemplary function toward Jacob/Israel. By the same token, all these roles fall within the same series of redemptive events of Israel's release from bondage, new exodus, new wandering in the wilderness, return, and new conquest.

Moreover, not only does the Lord call the Cyrus figure by name (45:3–4), but also Jacob/Israel (43:1) and the Servant figure (49:1, 3). Jacob/Israel's endowment of a name, as with the naming of the Cyrus figure, provides immunity when passing through restraining elements upon their return to the promised land: "When you cross the waters, I will be with you; [when you traverse] the rivers, you shall not be overwhelmed. Though you walk through the fire, you shall not be burned; its flame shall not consume you" (43:2; cf. Cyrus, 45:2). Such immunity is essential at the time Jacob/Israel returns from exile from the four directions of the earth (43:3–8).

Beyond section III, the Lord's naming the Servant figure before the womb (49:1), which likewise parallels Mesopotamian prescriptions for royal accession,[52] destines him to become the Lord's secret weapon (49:2). In that respect, the Servant figure serves as a paradigm of Jacob/Israel's election before the womb (44:2, 24) and of Jacob/Israel's function as the Lord's weapon of conquest (41:15–16). On the other hand, the Lord's naming the Servant figure at his royal accession (49:3), as with the Lord's naming the Cyrus figure (45:3–4),[53] endows him with strength to restore the tribes (49:4–6) and bring about Jacob/Israel's return (49:7–25; cf. Cyrus, 45:13). The incidence of such parallels beyond section III reflects the cumulative nature of concepts this and all other sections establish. Once an idea is substantiated through literary devices, it remains valid and receives corroboration through the remainder of the material.

---

[52] Paul, "Royal Inscriptions," 184–85.

[53] The Cyrus figure's naming (45:4) parallels the Lord's girding him (45:5), which girding, in turn, contrasts his enemies' ungirding (45:1).

The pattern that emerges from the parallels just cited is that the Cyrus figure assumes typologies originating with Abraham, Moses, and David, while typologies that originate with the historical Cyrus are assumed by the Righteous Warrior and Servant figures. Cyrus, in effect, nowhere appears in Isaiah as a purely historical figure but more accurately represents a biblical type. That type, together with those of Abraham, Moses, and David, is shared by all three figures who appear from the second unit on, namely the Righteous Warrior figure, the Cyrus figure, and the Servant figure. Even Jacob/Israel assumes typological functions originating with Cyrus where such functions are exemplary for Jacob/Israel. When led by the Lord's ideal agent of punishment and deliverance, Jacob/Israel follows.

Examples of typologies transferred *from* Cyrus to others, besides those already mentioned, include the restoration of Jerusalem and of the land's ruins. The restoration of ruins, for which Cyrus sets a precedent (cf. 44:26, 28), is also undertaken by those whom *righteousness* leads in a new exodus in 58:8, 12. The restoration of ruins is further undertaken by an "anointed" one and certain mourners in Zion in 61:1–4. The Lord's elevation of the Cyrus figure to royal office "in righteousness" (*bĕṣedeq*, 45:13)—a Mesopotamian legitimation formula[54]—similarly applies to the Servant figure (42:6) and, in a variant form, to Jacob/Israel (41:9–10). The term *righteousness*, as it appears in the second unit and elsewhere, thus expresses that aspect of royalty which meets divine approval, the ideal king being justified (*ṣdq*), or a legitimate vassal.

Examples of typologies transferred *to* the Cyrus figure, besides those already mentioned, include being "loved" by the Lord. That term (*'hb*) denotes a covenant relationship between the Lord and the one loved.[55] In the second unit, use of that term identifies Abraham as a biblical precedent: "Abraham, my beloved" (*'ōhăbî*, 41:8). The term also appears with reference to Jacob/Israel,

---

[54] The god's raising up, naming, and choosing of the king "in righteousness" (*bĕṣedeq*), the Hebrew equivalent of Akkadian *kenu/kenis*, all constitute Mesopotamian royal legitimation formulae; Paul, "Royal Inscriptions," 181–82.

[55] W. L. Moran notes biblical examples of covenant love in "The Ancient Near Eastern Background of the Love of God in Deuteronomy," *CBQ* 25 (1963): 77–87. See also D. J. McCarthy, "Notes on the Love of God in Deuteronomy and the Father–Son Relationship between Yahweh and Israel," *CBQ* 27 (1965): 144–47. Although ancient Near Eastern parallels of the love of the god for the king exist, a rhetorical definition of *love* in Isaiah, as in the example of Abraham, carries the connotation of covenantal love (cf. 56:6; 63:7–9).

whom the Lord loves and redeems (43:4). It applies to the Cyrus figure beyond section III, where the latter is described as one whom the Lord loves (*yhwh ʾăhēbô*, 48:14).[56]

The Cyrus figure's status in the second unit as the Lord's anointed (45:1), too, possesses parallels elsewhere, as in the anointed status of the composite figure in 61:1. Among the many rhetorical links between the various Isaianic figures, this motif of anointing illustrates the close typological relationship between two of them in particular, namely the Cyrus and Servant figures. In the Hebrew tradition, the anointing of a king or vassal and his endowment with the Lord's Spirit occur as two complementary phenomena (cf. 1 Sam 10:1, 6–11; 16:13).[57] In the second unit, however, what the Lord confers upon one figure manifests itself in the other: the Cyrus figure features as the Lord's anointed (45:1), but the Servant figure exhibits an endowment of the Lord's Spirit (42:1). Both ideas come together in the figure in 61:1 as a cumulative concept: "The Spirit of my lord the Lord is upon me, for the Lord has anointed me . . . ''

The Servant Figure

The Servant figure appears in a single passage in the second unit, in chapter 42. While the modern scholarly concensus limits what is called the "first Servant Song" to 42:1–4, a closer look reveals a parallelistic structure (a–b_1–c–c–b_2–a) in 42:1–6. Within that structure, verses 1 and 6 depict the election, accession, and mission of the Lord's "servant"—the Lord's vassal; verses 2 and 5 describe the respective attributes of the Servant figure and of the Lord who commissions him; and verses 3 and 4, which the motifs of a bruised reed and dim wick link rhetorically,[58] emphasize the establishment of universal justice as a chief task of the Servant figure. Verse 7

---

[56] That motif represents an ahistorical element—covenantal love—that is attached to the historical event of Cyrus' conquest of Babylonia.

[57] See also Z. Weizman, "Anointing as a Motif in the Making of the Charismatic King," *Bib* 57 (1976): 378–98.

[58] The metaphors of a bruised reed and a dim wick express the universal nature of the Servant figure's mission. The bruised reed (*qāneh rāṣûṣ*) signifies, rhetorically, Egypt and her pharaoh (cf. 36:6) and a dim wick (*pištâ kēhâ*) the Babylonians (cf. 43:17).

of chapter 42, an appendage to this parallelistic structure, expands on the Servant figure's mission as described in 42:6. The passage in full states:

1. My servant whom I sustain,
   my chosen one in whom I delight,
   him I have endowed with my Spirit;
   he will dispense justice to the nations.

2. He will not shout or raise his voice
   to make himself heard in public.

3. Even a bruised reed he will not break;
   a dim wick he will not snuff out.
   He will perform the work of justice
   in the cause of truth.

4. Neither shall he himself grow dim or be bruised
   till he has brought about justice in the earth.
   The isles await his law.

5. Thus says the Lord, God,
   who frames and suspends the heavens,
   who gives form to the earth and its creatures,
   the breath of life to the people upon it,
   spirit to those who walk on it:

6. I, the Lord, call you in righteousness
   and grasp you by the hand;
   I create you and appoint you
   to be a covenant of the people,
   a light to the nations,

7. to open eyes that are blind,
   to free captives from confinement
   and from prison those who sit in darkness.

The parallelistic patterning of this passage implies that the Servant figure of verse 1 is also addressed in verse 6. That conclusion contradicts the theory of Westermann, Muilenburg, and other scholars, who claim that verse 6 makes a sudden shift to corporate Israel as its subject.[59] The same passage nonetheless intends corporate Israel

---

[59] Westermann, *Isaiah 40–66*, 99–100; Muilenburg, *IB*, 5:468–69. Westermann proposes a similar transition of subjects in the so-called Servant Song of 49:1–6. But in that passage, too, an a–b–c–d–d–c–b–a structure suggests that 49:1–8 forms a unit (with a similar expansion on the Servant figure's mission in 49:9) and that the Servant figure, who there appears cumulatively, is its subject throughout.

when it refers to the blind captives to whom the Lord sends the Servant figure (v 7).[60] The Servant figure's mission, in other words, seeks the release and return of the Lord's people who are in bondage among the nations (cf. 42:16, 22–25; 43:1–8, 14–21; *passim*).

Verses 1 and 6 of this passage contain both Mesopotamian and Israelite royal accession motifs. These include, in verse 1, the declaration "I sustain" (*'etmāh*), a Mesopotamian accession motif;[61] the expression "my chosen" (*běhîrî*), a David typology (cf. 2 Sam 6:21; Psa 89:3);[62] the endowment of the Lord's Spirit, an Israelite accession motif (cf. 1 Sam 10:1, 6–11; 16:13) and a Moses typology (cf. Isa 63:11); and the king's task of dispensing justice to the nations, claimed by Mesopotamian monarchs.[63] In verse 6, the Lord's calling the Servant figure "in righteousness" (*běṣedeq*), grasping his hand, and "creating" him (*yṣr*) all resemble Mesopotamian royal accession.[64]

The Servant figure's rendering "justice to the nations" (*mišpaṭ laggôyîm*) in verse 1 parallels, chiastically, his mission as a "light to the nations" (*lě'ôr gôyîm*) in verse 6. The idea of justice as a light for the people appears both in the Code of Hammurabi[65] and in Isaiah. Isa 51:4 calls the Lord's justice (*mišpāṭî*), founded on his law (*tôrâ*), a "light to the nations" (*lě'ôr 'ammîm*).[66] Rhetorically, in Isaiah, only the Servant figure and the Davidic king humanly personify *light* (*'ôr*, 42:6; 9:2; 49:6). In each instance, the *light* dissipates the darkness in which the Lord's people find themselves (9:2; 42:7), exemplifying the ideal vassal's role as the Lord's agent of deliverance.[67]

---

[60] Compare 43:8: "Let go the people who are blind" and the text's rhetorical use of blindness as an attribute that describes the Lord's people in general, 29:18; 35:5; 42:16–19; *passim*.

[61] Paul, "Royal Inscriptions," 182, n. 19. Compare Psa 63:8.

[62] See its Mesopotamian equivalent, Paul, "Royal Inscriptions," 181.

[63] Hammurabi, in Mesopotamia, exemplifies a new king's role of lawgiver (cf. 42:4) in restoring justice to the people (cf. v 1), *ANET*, 164–65, 177–78, 269; compare Lipit-Ishtar, *ANET*, 159. Cyrus universalizes this role; see the Cyrus Cylinder, *ANET*, 315–16.

[64] Paul, "Royal Inscriptions," 183, 185–86. Compare Weinfeld, "Covenant of Grant," 191–92.

[65] *ANET*, 164, 178.

[66] See also G. Vermes, "The Torah as a Light," *VT* 8 (1958): 436–38.

[67] See darkness (*hošek*), rhetorically, as apostasy, 5:20; 29:15, 18; 50:10; *passim*.

A second metaphor describing the Servant figure in this passage is the term *covenant*. That term synonymously parallels the term *light* in verse 6. The Servant figure's personification of the Lord's *covenant* possesses no known parallels outside Isaiah. A rhetorical definition of the term shows it to be an endowment of the Lord's Spirit: "This is my covenant with them, says the Lord: my Spirit which is upon you, and my words which I have placed in your mouth . . . " (59:21). Such a definition appears in the Servant passage itself in the chiastic parallelism of 42:6 and 42:1: "I appoint (*ntn*) you to be a covenant of the people, a light to the nations" (42:6); "him I have endowed (*ntn*) with my Spirit; he will dispense justice to the nations" (42:1). This pairing and paralleling of ideas— of *covenant* with the Lord's Spirit and of *light* with the Lord's justice—suggests that the Servant figure's mission, like that of Moses (cf. Num 11:25), is to mediate the Lord's Spirit/covenant (cf. Num 11:29). The Lord's endowment of the Servant figure with his Spirit thus serves an exemplary function for Jacob/Israel (see Jacob/ Israel's endowment by the Lord's Spirit, 44:3; 59:21).

A second definition of the term *covenant*, one linked to the verb *appoint* (*ntn*), as in 42:6, combines both David and Moses typologies. The two terms coincide elsewhere only in the passage "I will make with you an everlasting covenant: [my] loving fidelity toward David. See, I appoint him as a witness to the nations, a prince and lawgiver to the peoples" (55:3c–4). The term *witness* (*'ēd*), which describes the figure whom the Lord appoints, is itself a biblical synonym of *covenant* (cf. Gen 31:44; Josh 24:25–27).[68] The related titles of *prince* (*nāgîd*) and *lawgiver* (*mĕṣawwēh*) express respective Davidic and Mosaic functions (cf. *nāgîd*, 1 Sam 10:1; 13:14; *tôrâ ṣiwwâ lānû*, Deut 33:4).

The verb *appoint* (*ntn*, 55:4), too, expresses a David typology, as we see in the first unit, in which the Lord "appoints" (*ntn*) a son or vassal to the throne of David who establishes justice and righteousness (9:6–7). Two other such personalized uses of the verb *appoint* occur in Isaiah. The first appears in the context that introduces the Servant figure himself: "To Jerusalem I appoint one who heralds good tidings" (41:27). The second appears cumulatively, also with

---

[68] See Weinfeld, "Berîth," 264, and the term's more expansive connotation of teacher of law, testifier of deity, and sign of the divine presence in John H. Eaton, "The King as God's Witness," *ASTI* 7 (1968/69): 25–40.

reference to the Servant figure: "I appoint you a light to the nations" (49:6); "I appoint you a covenant of the people" (49:8).

Although such rhetorical connections do not, by themselves, establish an identity for the Servant figure, they do support the conclusions we drew based on typological evidence: the Servant figure, like the Cyrus and Righteous Warrior figures, represents a composite of types. Other Isaianic figures share these types, but their particular combination lends each figure a certain emphasis. Chapter 42 describes the Servant figure's mission in terms of "new things" (*ḥădāšôt*), things paralleled, by way of contrast, with "former things" (*ri'šōnôt*, 42:9). The Servant figure's role of lawgiver, for example, possesses both Mesopotamian and Mosaic prototypes. The phrase "The isles await his law" (*tôrātô*, 42:4) expresses a royal role in Mesopotamian tradition; while the Servant figure's depiction as a lawgiver who does not grow dim or bruised (42:4) is a Mosaic feature.[69] The Servant figure's task of releasing the Lord's people from bondage similarly represents a Moses typology but is here aimed at spiritually blind exiles (42:7; cf. vv 16, 18–19).

Mesopotamian typologies inherent in Cyrus that are transposed to the Servant figure—such as the establishment of justice to the nations[70]—and biblical typologies transposed to the Cyrus figure but developed in the Servant figure, such as the former's anointed status and the latter's endowment of the Lord's Spirit, show that these two figures complement one another typologically. The Servant figure, in effect, performs functions that are implicit in the Cyrus figure but that in the Cyrus figure are left undeveloped. Such a division of functions makes these two figures interpretively interdependent. Neither serves as the Lord's agent of Israel's redemption in any ultimate sense. Unlike the roles of punishment and deliverance ascribed to the Cyrus figure, the Servant figure's function as an agent of the Lord's redemption is limited to deliverance, and in that context to nonviolence. In short, the text is typologically selective in how it describes each figure.

We can conclude, therefore, that the Servant and Cyrus figures individually fall short of fulfilling an ideal role as the Lord's latter-day agent of redemption. The question remains as to why their various functions and attributes are divided between them, and

---

[69] Compare Moses: "His eye was not dim, nor his natural force abated," Deut 34:7.

[70] See *ANET*, 315–16; compare the decree of Cyrus as it relates to Judah, Ezr 1:1–4.

beyond that, between them and the Righteous Warrior figure. We now address that question.

Variations of the Ideal

The foregoing evidence shows that the Servant and Cyrus figures typologically complement one another, each forming a composite of essentially the same biblical figures—Moses, David, and Cyrus—which together create the idea of an ideal vassal, an archetypal leader of the latter days. That ideal figure manifests himself as an agent of the Lord's punishment and deliverance within a context of Israel's release from bondage, new exodus, new wandering in the wilderness, return, and new conquest.[71] Because the individual roles of the Servant and Cyrus figures fulfill this redemptive purpose only partially or selectively, neither figure achieves the ideal alone.

When we compare the Servant and Cyrus figures, we find that their roles express respective spiritual and temporal aspects of the ideal. The Moses typologies evident in both figures illustrate this. The Servant figure, the Lord's Spirit-endowed lawgiver (42:1, 4), delivers the Lord's people from *spiritual* bondage: he opens eyes that are blind and delivers captives from darkness (42:7). His mission results in a new wandering in the wilderness for the Lord's people (42:15–16). The Cyrus figure, the Lord's shepherd (44:28), delivers the Lord's people from *physical* bondage: he subdues nations and ungirds rulers, opens doors and levels obstacles—in order to set the Lord's exiles free (45:1–2, 13). A new exodus serves as the context of his mission (44:27). The biblical roles of Moses—of physically delivering Israel at the exodus and of offering spiritual tutelage during Israel's wandering in the wilderness—are thus divided between the two.

It is a fact that no biblical person that this material uses as a type served as an agent of the Lord's punishment or deliverance solely in a temporal or solely in a spiritual sense. We should therefore view this division of roles in Isaiah as something ahistorical and as rendering the Servant and the Cyrus figures incomplete as an ideal. Historically, Cyrus' activity is not limited to physical retribution against nations and rulers, as depicted in 45:1–2, nor to physical

---

[71] See, in the second unit, the motifs of release from exile or bondage, 42:7; 45:13; a new exodus, 43:2, 16–17; 44:27; a new wandering in the wilderness, 42:15–16; 43:20; return, 43:5–8; and new conquest, 42:13; 43:14; 45:1.

restoration of ruins, as depicted in 44:26, 28. Additional roles that could be attributed to Cyrus the Persian, such as restoring justice to the nations, together with typologies of royal accession, are nevertheless transposed to the Servant figure. The Servant figure combines these typologies with that of lawgiver, and with others that are spiritual, to create a spiritual ideal. Yet, only when we combine both spiritual and temporal dimensions do we have a credible agent of the Lord's redemption, whether a figure is modeled after Moses, David, Cyrus, or all three. Isaiah's latter-day ideal, in effect, is not to be found in either the Servant or the Cyrus figure alone.

The need to look beyond just one figure for an ideal agent of the Lord's redemption becomes apparent in the Righteous Warrior figure, who combines both spiritual and temporal functions. The metaphor *righteousness*, which describes him (41:2), expresses a spiritual concept. Its combination with "one who calls on my name" (41:25) establishes an Abraham typology, also spiritual. In conjunction with this, a Cyrus typology—that of making chaos of nations and rulers while marching from the east (41:2, 25)—represents a temporal aspect of the ideal. Additionally, the metaphor *righteousness*, which describes the Warrior figure a second time (46:12–13), combines with the description "man of my counsel" (46:11). That combination, too, is an Abraham typology and is spiritual in nature. In conjunction with it, the metaphor *bird of prey* (46:11)—a Cyrus typology—and the idea of salvation or deliverance for the Lord's people (46:13), express temporal aspects of the ideal. The Righteous Warrior figure, unlike the Servant and Cyrus figures, thus fulfills both spiritual and temporal functions in serving as an agent of the Lord's redemption (see figure 9).

Figure 9: Redemptive Functions of the Lord's Ideal Agent of Punishment and Deliverance

Davidic King	Righteous Warrior Figure	Servant Figure	Cyrus Figure
(spiritual/ temporal)	(spiritual/ temporal)	(spiritual)	(temporal)

Divided spiritual and temporal functions in the Davidic king first appear in the first unit of section III (chaps. 9–12), where the structure of the material separates these twin aspects of the ideal. Chapter 9 depicts the future Davidic king as vanquishing his people's enemies and releasing the Lord's people from physical bondage (9:4). Chapter 11 depicts the Lord's endowment of the Davidic king with his Spirit (9:2) in order that he may establish justice in the earth (9:3–9). Exceptions to this division of temporal and spiritual roles occur by way of metaphor: a *light* lights up the people's darkness (9:2) and a *rod* smites the earth (11:4). Fittingly, the execution of retribution and the universal establishment of the Lord's law, as twin roles of a king, have a prototype in King David himself (cf. Psa 2:8–11).

The combination of spiritual and temporal functions in the future Davidic king and in the Righteous Warrior figure shows that, optimally, an ideal agent of the Lord's punishment and deliverance assumes both these functions. The structured division of these functions in the Davidic king in chapters 9 and 11 is duplicated in the divided functions of the Servant and Cyrus figures, but not in the case of the Righteous Warrior figure. In many respects, however, the Righteous Warrior figure himself imperfectly expresses the ideal. Whereas the Servant and Cyrus figures form composites of Moses, David, and Cyrus, and the Davidic king forms a composite of Abraham, Moses, Joshua, Gideon, David, Solomon, and Hezekiah, the Righteous Warrior figure forms a composite of only Abraham and Cyrus (see figure 10). Moreover, the Abraham and Cyrus typologies that make up the Righteous Warrior figure serve primarily an exemplary function for Jacob/Israel. Abraham serves as a model for Jacob/Israel's righteousness (41:2, 25; 46:12–13) and in returning from the ends of the earth (41:2, 8–9, 25), and Cyrus typifies Jacob/Israel's new conquest (41:2, 15, 25).

Figure 10: Typologies of the Lord's Ideal Agent of Punishment and Deliverance

Davidic King	Righteous Warrior Figure	Servant Figure	Cyrus Figure
(Abraham, Moses, Joshua, Gideon, David, Solomon, Hezekiah)	(Abraham, Cyrus)	(Moses, David, Cyrus)	(Moses, David, Cyrus)

In contrast to the Righteous Warrior figure's exemplary function toward Jacob/Israel, the Moses, David, and Cyrus typologies that make up the Servant and Cyrus figures serve primarily a redemptive function toward Jacob/Israel. Their roles as paradigms for the most part find fulfillment beyond section III, where we would expect all such concepts to appear cumulatively. In the second unit of section III, the typologies of Moses, David, and Cyrus characterize largely the Cyrus and Servant figures: Moses serves as a type of releaser from bondage (42:7; 45:13), of the Lord's shepherd (44:28), and of the Lord's lawgiver (42:4); David serves as a type of the Lord's chosen one (42:1), the Lord's anointed (45:1), and the Lord's Spirit-endowed servant or vassal (42:1); and Cyrus serves as a type of universal conqueror (45:1), establisher of justice among the nations (42:1, 4, 6), and restorer of ruins, principally the temple (44:26, 28).

Meanwhile, the redemptive idea of releasing the Lord's people from exile or bondage that characterizes the Servant and Cyrus figures (cf. 42:7; 45:13), is expressly lacking in the Righteous Warrior figure. The text does not represent the subjugation of nations and rulers performed by the Righteous Warrior figure (41:2, 25) as bringing about Jacob/Israel's release from exile. In the Righteous Warrior figure, the event of Jacob/Israel's release from exile has been separated out. Though it is a Cyrus typology (45:1)—and the historical Cyrus was not an Israelite—the conquest of nations is here an event in which Jacob/Israel participates (41:15): when empowered by the Lord's *hand* or *right hand*, Jacob/Israel threshes mountains (nations) into dust and chaff (41:10–16). In rendering nations to dust and stubble, the Righteous Warrior figure serves as a paradigm of the Lord's people, and thus, by implication, as their leader. His personifying *righteousness* (41:2) and calling on the Lord's name (41:25) additionally express paradigmatic or exemplary functions for Jacob/Israel.[72]

A tension thus exists between the historical origin of an event—in this instance, Cyrus' conquests—and its structural transformation. The text resolves this tension by resorting to metaphor—*righteousness*, *right hand*, *mountains*, *threshing*, etc. This use of metaphor enables one to read the text both to some extent literally—on a historical level; and typologically—on an eschatological or latter-day level. What it depicts historically, though representing only select episodes, the text nonetheless reflects accurately. What it projects eschatologically, though representing a much fuller picture, does

---

[72] See righteousness and calling on the Lord as two attributes in which Jacob/Israel is lacking at the time the ideal figure fulfills his mission, 43:22; 46:12, but which attributes some of the Lord's people acquire as a result of that mission, 51:1, 7; 58:8–9.

not contradict history at the literal level. The text accommodates both prophetic strata.

Cyrus' name does not appear in the Righteous Warrior passage because the new conquest is not represented there as releasing Jacob/Israel from exile. The new conquest, therefore, is no longer a true type of Cyrus; it is no longer something for which Cyrus set a precedent. Although the Righteous Warrior figure's conquests model themselves on Cyrus' victories, they contain the added feature of Jacob/Israel's participation. In establishing an ideal agent of the Lord's punishment and deliverance, the text thus of necessity breaks up the ideal into parts or figures. No one figure meets all the criteria of an ideal agent of the Lord's redemption, first, because historically no such person existed and, second, because historically no such redemption occurred.

Similar considerations apply to the Servant figure. No name appears in connection with the Servant figure because his mission models itself on no singular precedent of biblical history and also because historically no such person existed, only a number of possible "servants" who qualify as partial models of this and other Isaianic figures. Breaking up the ideal into parts in this manner allows all criteria for an eschatological agent of the Lord's redemption to be represented. Yet, each individual part of the ideal is nuanced to portray its incompleteness. At the same time, each part of the latter-day ideal selectively reflects historical phenomena, allowing us to read the text, at least in some measure, historically.

The Davidic king, the Lord's vassal, for example, possesses a model and type in King David. David's second divine appointment set a historical precedent, and David's name therefore appears in connection with it (9:7).[73] To the Davidic type, however, are added Abraham, Moses, and others, suggesting that the future Davidic king or vassal in the first unit complements, typologically, the three Isaianic figures in the second unit, who are also modeled after Abraham, Moses, and others.

The structured parallelism of the two units of section III, moreover, lends a Davidic flavor to the Lord's ideal agent of redemption in the second unit. His Davidic vassalship finds support in the

---

[73] On the other hand, David's name is expressly lacking in the second Davidic passage in the first unit (chap. 11) because the roles the Davidic king performs there do not originate with David. The passage nonetheless establishes a Davidic identity for the future king by characterizing him as a descendant "of Jesse" (11:1, 10).

David typologies used there. As stated earlier, a Davidic redemptive role in an exilic context appears in the first unit itself (11:10–16; cf. 9:1) alongside a preexilic context. In addition, the Davidic king's ideal roles and attributes described there—such as his endowment of the Lord's Spirit (11:1), his function as a *light* lighting up people's darkness (9:2) and as the Lord's *hand* delivering them (11:11, 14–15), his release of the Lord's people from physical bondage (9:4), and his establishment of universal justice (9:7; 11:4–9)—parallel the ideal roles and attributes of the three Isaianic figures in the second unit.

The common redemptive purpose all these figures serve demonstrates their typological interdependence. Within that redemptive framework, the Isaianic figures' functions complement one another. Together, not separately, the events of Jacob/Israel's release from bondage, new exodus, new wandering in the wilderness, return, and new conquest, realize the Lord's redemption. That redemption includes the deliverance of the Lord's people from spiritual bondage and the physical punishment of their oppressors. To achieve that goal, the Lord sends his people an ideal agent of redemption, a kind of archetypal leader or deliverer.

The imagery of the blind and deaf illustrates the common redemptive purpose behind this Isaianic figure's mission. A passage in chapter 42 informs us that blindness and captivity on the part of Jacob/Israel result from disobedience to covenantal law:

19. Who is blind but my own servant,
    or so deaf as the messenger I have sent?
    Who is blind like those I have commissioned,
    as uncomprehending as the Lord's servant—
20. seeing much but not giving heed,
    with open ears hearing nothing?
21. It is the Lord's will that, because of his righteousness,
    he[74] magnify the law and become illustrious.
22. Instead, they are a people plundered and sacked,
    all of them trapped in holes, hidden away in dungeons.
    They have become a prey, yet no one rescues them,
    a spoil, yet none demands restitution.

---

[74] Viz., Jacob/Israel—the Lord's corporate servant (42:19–20, 24)—not the Lord, as in Westermann, *Isaiah 40–66*, 108, 111; John C. McKenzie, *Second Isaiah* (New York:Doubleday, 1967), 45–47. Because of a confusion of subjects, both these authors' translations of this verse are grammatically at variance with the text.

24. Who is it that hands Jacob over to plunder
      and Israel to despoilers, if not the Lord,
      against whom we have sinned?
      For they have no desire to walk in his ways
      or obey his law.
25. So in the heat of his anger
      he pours out on them the violence of war,
      till it envelops them in flames—
      yet they remain unaware;
      till it sets them on fire—
      yet they take it not to heart.

This passage tells us that so long as the Lord's people despise his law, they will remain blind and captive. The idolatry that forms the context of the passage (cf. 42:17–18)—and of the second unit in general[75]—highlights Jacob/Israel's blindness. The Lord now appoints a *light* (42:6; cf. 9:2), alias his *righteousness* (42:21; cf. 41:2), and restores his law (42:4, 21)—that his people might free themselves from spiritual blindness and from physical captivity (42:7, 22–25; cf. 9:2–4; 11:1–5, 10–16; 45:13).

In effect, just as the Lord's people spiritually apostatize before they are physically taken captive, so they must convert to the Lord spiritually before he physically delivers them. These concepts, as we have seen, are established in sections I and II of the Bifid Structure and they here appear cumulatively. Section III describes the setting in which this scenario is acted out. The blind and the deaf in section III are the equivalent of those in sections I and II who have need to repent/return: the Lord's people, to whom the Lord sends Isaiah, do not see and hear as does Isaiah (cf. 6:10). If they now repent, the Lord redeems them; if they do not, he destroys them together with the idolaters (cf. 10:5–11; 20–23).

In section III, in other words, the Lord's ideal agent of punishment initiates the covenant curse reversals for the Lord's people who repent/return described in section I, as well as many of the covenant curses that come upon the wicked. Other covenant curses upon the wicked come through the instrumentality of the king of Assyria, the Lord's agent of punishment. In the first

---

[75] See idolatry, 41:7, 22–24; 43:9–12; 44:9–20, 25; 45:16, 20; 46:1–8; compare idolatry in the first unit, 8:19–22; 10:10–11.

unit of section III, the king of Assyria appears both overtly, identified by name, and covertly under the several metaphorical pseudonyms that describe him. In the second unit, the king of Assyria appears cumulatively, but only covertly, under such metaphorical pseudonyms as the Lord's *anger/wrath* (42:25; 48:9) and *Sea/River* (42:15; 43:2, 16) and as identified through rhetorical links such as those who make "war" upon the Lord's people (41:12; 42:25; cf. 3:25; 36:5), who "plunder" and "spoil" Jacob/Israel (42:22, 24; cf. 8:4; 10:6).

Discourse D: Chaos and Creation (2)

In the second unit of section III, a structure of alternating motifs of a return to chaos and a new creation (chaps. 41:1–46:13b) supports the idea of a single ideal agent of the Lord's punishment and deliverance. That future figure—a kind of archetypal leader or deliverer—manifests himself in the Righteous Warrior, Cyrus, and Servant figures and identifies with the motif of a new creation. The new creation, which comprehends a series of redemptive events, exemplifies Jacob/Israel's salvation. Just as a structure of chaos/creation motifs in the first unit of section III commences earlier than the unit itself but within that unit comes to a climax, so the present structure commences in chapter 40 and ends in chapter 46. The present structure, however, evidences a greater complexity and parallelism of ideas. Such complexity suggests that Isa 40–46 represents a more deliberated literary composition.

Incipient instances of a return to chaos and a new creation appear in chapter 40 at the conclusion of a passage that depicts the infirmity of humanity:

> 6. A voice said, Announce it!
>   And I asked, How shall I announce it?
>   All flesh is grass,
>   and at its best like a blossom of the field.[76]
> 7. Though the Lord's Spirit breathe within it,
>   the people themselves are but herbage—
> 8. grass that withers, flowers that fade.
>   But the word of our God endures forever!

---

[76] MT adds "grass that withers, flowers that fade" (so 40:8), a probable duplication; compare 1QIsa^a; LXX.

"Withering grass" and "fading flowers" are chaos motifs, the Lord's Spirit (*rûaḥ*) and his creative word (*dābār*), creation motifs.[77]

This pattern repeats itself in a passage that attests to the pre-existence of matter:[78]

> 12. Who measured out the waters with the hollow of his hand
>   and gauged the heavens by the span of his fingers?
>   Who compiled the earth's dust by measure,
>   weighing mountains in scales, hills in a balance?
> 13. Who has comprehended the Spirit of the Lord
>   that a man should let him know his plan?

"Waters" and "dust" represent chaos. The heavens and the earth, mountains and hills, the Lord's Spirit (*rûaḥ*) and creative plan (*'ăṣātô*) represent creation.

The chaos/creation pattern moves climactically from subjects of a general nature to more definitive ones. A return to chaos depicts the nations as but drops from a bucket and mere "dust" and "chaos" (*tōhû*, 40:15–17). The idols people arduously fashion for themselves are subject to "decay" and "deterioration" (40:20). Following this, the motifs of creation, chaos, and creation recur in quick succession, their subjects ever narrowing:

> 21. Are you so unaware, that you have not heard?
>   Have you not been told before,
>   that you do not understand
>   [by whom] the earth was founded?
> 22. By him who sits enthroned above the earth's sphere,
>   to whom its inhabitants are as grasshoppers,
>   who suspends the heavens like a canopy,
>   stretching them out as a tent to dwell in.
> 23. By him who brings potentates to nought
>   and makes chaos of the authorities of the world:

---

[77] Compare Gen 1:2–3: "The Spirit of God brooded over the face of the waters; and God said . . ."

[78] Preexistent matter is something to which the pattern of alternating chaos and creation motifs itself testifies. Isaianic theology thus concurs with the Book of Genesis. The Genesis account of creation through God's word similarly presupposes the existence of matter, viz., "chaos" (*tōhû wābōhû*), "darkness" (*ḥōšek*), and cosmic "waters" (*mayim*), Gen 1:2–3.

24. when scarcely they are planted,
    or scarcely they are sown,
    when hardly their stalk has taken root in the earth,
    he puffs at them and they wither,
    and a storm sweeps them off as chaff.
25. To whom then will you liken me,
    to whom can I be compared? says the Holy One.
26. Lift your eyes heavenward and see:
    Who formed these?
    He who brings forth their hosts by number,
    calling each one by name.
    Because he is almighty and all powerful,
    not one is unaccounted for.

The subject of the Lord's creation here narrows from the organization of raw materials (40:12)—by the Lord's Spirit and creative word (40:7-8), according to the Lord's plan (40:13)—to the foundation (*môsdôt*) of the earth as a place of habitation and to the Lord's enthronement in the heavens (40:21-22).[79] A return to chaos involves the great ones of the earth, whom the Lord renders into ''chaos'' (*tōhû*) and ''chaff'' (40:23-24). Then follows the royal accession of the great ones of heaven, whom the Lord calls forth one by one and names (40:26)[80]—a new creation.

Within this creative context, the text introduces Jacob/Israel. But the Lord's people complain that ''our path has become obscured from the Lord; our cause is overlooked by our God'' (40:27). That verse represents a variant form of the chaos motif (weariness), and its imagery implies exile.[81] A creation motif follows: the Lord creates the ends of the earth (*br'*, 40:28), from which Jacob/Israel will soon return (cf. 41:9). As the God of eternity, the Lord is nonwearying (40:28). He supplies the weary—Jacob/Israel—with energy (40:29). The motifs of weariness and nonweariness repeat themselves to end chapter 40: youths and young men (those on whom Israel

---

[79] Norman Habel sees the establishment of a cosmic tent in 40:22 as an act of divine enthronement preparatory to the Lord's coming to earth in theophany. A *Chaoskampf* follows it in 40:23; Norman C. Habel, ''He who stretches out the heavens,'' *CBQ* 34 (1972): 417-30.

[80] See parallel Egyptian concepts that R. O. Faulkner discusses, in ''The King and the Star Religion in the Pyramid Texts,'' *JNES* 25 (1966): 153-61.

[81] See Walter Brueggemann, ''Weariness, Exile and Chaos,'' *CBQ* 34 (1972): 19-39.

depends for exertion and warfare) grow faint and weary and slump down exhausted (40:30). Yet, those who hope in, or wait for, the Lord (*qwh*) renew their strength and ascend upward (*'lh*, 40:31). They run without wearying; they walk and do not faint (40:31).

The subject of the Lord's creation thus narrows further from Jacob/Israel (40:27) to those who hope in, or wait for, the Lord (40:31). The context of celestial accession (40:26) that introduces Jacob/Israel colors this narrowing of subjects. Jacob/Israel's path (*derek*), in effect, is not obscured (40:27): it remains for the Lord's people but to ascend like eagles (40:31), a royal and mythic symbol. Similarly, Jacob/Israel's cause (*mišpāṭ*), the Lord does not overlook (40:27): his people may attain to the Lord's own nonweariness by waiting for or hoping in him (40:31).[82] Jacob/Israel's maledictory condition, in other words, provides the very setting in which a reversal of circumstances may occur, which reversal is here described in terms of creation out of chaos.

At this point of the text's narrowing of the concept—as if presenting a model or paradigm of the Lord's creation—chapter 41 introduces the figure *righteousness* (41:2). The latter serves as the Lord's agent for rendering idolatrous nations into "dust" and "stubble" (41:2), denoting a return to chaos.[83] The motif of chaos repeats itself when Jacob/Israel renders mountains and hills into "dust" and "chaff" (41:15). That event occurs when the Lord's righteous *right hand* strengthens and helps Jacob/Israel (41:10). The concerted function of the figure *righteousness* and Jacob/Israel in making chaos of mountains or nations underscores the paradigmatic relationship that exists between them. The dual incidence of chaos before a new creation reflects the common goal of the Righteous Warrior figure and Jacob/Israel of bringing about the Lord's redemption.

The new creation, which immediately follows, takes the variant form of a regenerating wilderness: streams open up in barren places to provide drink for the Lord's poor (41:17), and the Lord adorns

---

[82] See section II, footnote 33. Brueggemann notes the implication of royal accession associated with nonweariness, "Weariness, Exile and Chaos," 27.

[83] Brueggemann sees being reduced to dust as both royal and covenantal, signifying a deprivation of royal powers upon breaking a covenant relationship. Creation out of dust, on the other hand, denotes royal accession within a covenantal framework; Walter Brueggemann, "From Dust to Kingship," *ZAW* 84 (1972): 1–18.

the desert with trees and lakes (41:18–19). This reordering of elements is something Israel's Holy One "creates" (*br'*, 41:20). Within the latter chaos/creation pattern, both a literal and metaphorical use of the terms *mountains* and *hills* is thus meaningful. The former describes the earth as being desolated before it regenerates; the latter signifies a new conquest of nations by Jacob/Israel and the figure *righteousness*.

A passage on false diviners ends the chapter (41:21–29), a return to chaos forming its centerpiece: the Righteous Warrior figure comes upon dignitaries as on "mud," treads them as "clay" like a potter (41:25). The association of false diviners with "wind" (*rûaḥ*) and "chaos" (*tōhû*) at the conclusion of the passage (41:29) suggests that they are identical with those whom the Righteous Warrior figure reduces to chaos; both instances of chaos precede a new creation. The new creation is the Servant figure of chapter 42, who, by implication, divines truly.[84] The Creator of heaven and earth "creates" him (*yṣr*, 42:5–6) and endows him with his Spirit (*rûaḥ*, 42:1); the Lord appoints him to be a *light* (*'ôr*) to the nations (42:6) and makes him the subject of nonweariness (42:4)—all instances of creation. This prolonged theme of creation reinforces the structural unity of 42:1–6 and its singular subject, the Servant figure.

A return to chaos occurs when the Lord comes forth like a warrior, lays waste mountains and hills, and dries up waters and vegetation (42:13–15). The Lord, as a righteous Warrior, thus serves as a paradigm to the figure *righteousness* from the east (cf. 41:2, 25), even as the figure *righteousness* serves as a paradigm of a righteous warrior to Jacob/Israel (cf. 41:15–16). The Lord's victory over the elements, too, has an allegorical connotation: the Lord's desolation of the elements epitomizes his victory over "enemies" (42:13). The cataclysmic destruction that the Lord causes makes possible a new exodus and a return wandering in the wilderness for the Lord's blind servant Jacob/Israel (42:16). Two creation motifs—a *light* (*'ôr*) lighting up the darkness of the Lord's people as they return and rugged terrain made into a plain (*mîšôr*, 42:16)—distinguish these redemptive events. The verse following contrasts the orderly exodus and its participants with the idolaters' retreat in utter confusion (42:17)—signifying chaos.

---

[84] See also 41:26: "Who announced this beforehand, so we would know; ahead of time, that we might say, *ṣaddîq*?"

A new creation occurs when the people of the Lord, "because of his *righteousness*, magnify the law and become illustrious" (42:21). That imagery narrows yet further the concept of creation. It also expresses the paradigmatic or exemplary relationship that exists between the latter-day figure—the Lord's lawgiver—and Jacob/Israel. The creative activity of those who magnify the Lord's law contrasts with that of others who display no desire to walk in his ways or obey his law (42:24). These reprobates are subject to chaos: they are enveloped in flames and set on fire (42:25). Such divergent fates express, cumulatively, concepts sections I and II establish, namely that Jacob/Israel, as a category of the Lord's people, divides into those whom the Lord delivers, because they repent, and those whom he destroys as idolaters. The new creation, which immediately follows in chapter 43, consists of the Lord's "forming" (*br'*), "creating" (*yṣr*), and "redeeming" (*g'l*) Jacob/Israel and calling his people by name (43:1), signifying royal accession. That sequence again shows—by narrowing the subject of creation—that royal accession in a redemptive context constitutes the ultimate goal of the Lord's creation.

The pattern of chaos/creation motifs in the second unit possesses a midpoint about the middle of chapter 43. From there it spans out into a chiasm, with Babylon appearing at the core of chaos and Jacob/Israel at the center of creation (see figure 11). The Lord brings down Babylon's citizens as fugitives (43:14), representing chaos. As Israel's Holy One and King, on the other hand, the Lord "creates" Israel (*br'*, 43:15). In conjunction with this new creation, at the structure's center, occurs the motif of a new exodus. The new exodus is represented as a conquest of chaos: the Lord provides "a way (*derek*) in the Sea, a path through the mighty waters" (43:16). Babylon then reappears as the subject of chaos: the Lord dispatches Babylon's chariots and horses, her armies of men in full strength. They lie down as one, to rise no more; they flicker and die, snuffed out like a wick (43:17). Following his victory over Babylon, the Lord regenerates the wilderness (43:19–20) and "creates" Jacob/Israel (*yṣr*, 43:21)—a new creation.

Jacob/Israel's "weariness" in serving the Lord (43:22, 24), and his people's "sinfulness" and "transgression" (43:24–27), brings upon them the Lord's punishment (43:28). Jacob/Israel's execration in 43:28 forms the object of an a–a–ab–b–b structure in 43:22–27. That structure establishes a synonymous or derivative relationship

Figure 11

a_1—The Lord raises up *righteousness* from the east (41:2).

b_1—Idolatrous nations and rulers turn into dust and stubble (41:2–7);
mountains and hills become dust and chaff (41:15).

c_1—Jacob/Israel is not forsaken (41:17); Israel's Holy One
regenerates and creates the wilderness (41:17–20).

d_1—Idolaters are an abomination, worth nothing (41:21–24).

e_1—The Lord raises up (*ha'îrôtî*) the Warrior figure from the sunrise (41:25ab).

f_1—Dignitaries are trodden down as mud and clay (41:25cd);
false diviners are but wind and chaos (41:29).

g_1—The Creator of heaven and earth creates the Servant figure, endows him with
his Spirit, appoints him as a *light*—the subject of nonweariness (42:1–6).

h_1—The Lord desolates the earth and its vegetation, dries up lakes
and rivers—the Lord's victory over his enemies (42:13–15).

i_1—The Lord guides the blind by his *light*, levels the uneven ground (42:16).

j_1—Idolaters retreat in confusion (42:17).

k_1—Jacob/Israel magnifies the law and becomes illustrious,
because of the Lord's *righteousness* (42:21).

l_1—Jacob/Israel is a prey, consumed by fire for
transgressing the Lord's law (42:22–25).

m_1—The Lord creates Jacob/Israel (43:1); the Lord's people are
immune to the elements as they return from exile (43:2–7).

n_1—Babylon's citizens come down as fugitives (43:14).

o_1—The Lord, Israel's Holy One and King, creates Israel (43:15).

o_2—The Lord provides a way through the Sea,
through the mighty waters (43:16).

n_2—Babylon's armies of men, chariots,
and horses are snuffed out (43:17).

m_2—The Lord regenerates the wilderness through which his people
travel (43:19–20); the Lord creates Jacob/Israel (43:21).

l_2—Jacob/Israel's weariness and sins bring execration (43:22–28).

k_2—The Lord creates and succors Jacob/Israel (44:1–2); the Lord
pours out his Spirit, regenerates the wilderness (44:3–4);
Jacob/Israel are the Lord's witnesses (44:5–8).

j_2—Idolaters and their works are but chaos and ashes (44:9, 20).

i_2—The Lord creates Jacob/Israel, removes his people's
sins like a cloud of mist (44:21–24).

h_2—The Lord dries up the deep and its rivers (44:27).

g_2—The Creator of *light* and peace names and girds the Cyrus
figure (45:4–7); the Lord creates *righteousness*—
by implication, the Cyrus figure (45:8).

f_2—Those who dispute what the Lord makes and
begets are but shards and clay (45:9–11).

e_2—The Lord, Creator of heaven and earth, raises up
(*ha'îrōtihû*) the Cyrus figure (45:12–13).

d_2—Idolaters retire in shame and disgrace (45:16).

c_2—The Creator of heaven and earth saves Jacob/Israel (45:17–18).

b_2—Idolatrous nations live in darkness and chaos (45:19–20);
their idolatry causes weariness and exile (46:1–4).

a_2—The Lord brings *righteousness* from the east, fulfilling his word (46:10–13b).

between weariness and sin.[85] Immediately following these chaos motifs, in chapter 44, the Lord "creates" (*yṣr*) and chooses Jacob/Israel (44:1–2). A polarity of fates thus again appears for the Lord's people: some become an execration, while others experience redemption. A regenerating wilderness and outpouring of the Lord's Spirit (*rûaḥ*) augment the Lord's creation (44:3–4). Variant creation motifs, such as the regenerating wilderness, an outpouring of the Lord's Spirit, a new exodus, and nonweariness, express ever-widening dimensions of the Lord's creation. These coincide with an ever-narrowing and definitive idea of the Lord's people, the chief subject of the Lord's creation.

A long passage on idolatry (44:9–20) sums up the idolaters and their works as "chaos" (*tōhû*, 44:9) and mere "ashes" (44:20). The Lord nonetheless "creates" (*yṣr*) Jacob/Israel to be his servant (44:21). The motif of creation continues with the Lord's suspension of the heavens and formation of the earth (44:24). In conjunction with that imagery occurs the Lord's "creation" (*yṣr*) and "redemption" (*g'l*) of Jacob/Israel at the removal of his people's sins (44:22–24). This affinity between Israel's creation and the creation of the cosmos reflects the Lord's purpose as the chaos/creation pattern reveals it:[86] the Lord's creation consummates with, and has as its goal, the creation—ultimately in the most definitive sense—of a righteous covenant people. The Lord's redemption of Jacob/Israel— by the removal of his people's sins and by their new exodus, royal accession, endowment of the Lord's Spirit, and attainment to nonweariness—yields a superlative definition of the Lord's creation.

A return to chaos occurs when the Lord dries up the deep and its streams (44:27). A new creation follows, in chapter 45, when the Lord grasps the Cyrus figure by the hand, calls him by name, and girds him (45:1–7). Appearing in a continuum with this new creation is the Lord's "formation" (*yṣr*) of *light* and "creation" (*br'*) of *righteousness* (*ṣedeq/ṣĕdāqâ*)—in order that the Lord's salvation may blossom on the earth (45:7–8). These conjoined instances of creation establish a common identity for the Lord's *light*, the Lord's *righteousness*, and the Cyrus figure. Even as the Servant

---

[85] See weariness, 43:22–24ab; and sin, 43:24cd–27. Jacob/Israel's punishment ensues in 43:28.

[86] On the subject of this affinity, see also the work of Carrol Stuhlmueller, "The Theology of Creation in Second Isaiah," *CBQ* 21 (1959): 429–67; Carrol Stuhlmueller, *Creative Redemption in Deutero-Isaiah* (Rome: Pontifical Biblical Institute, 1970).

figure, the Lord's lawgiver, identifies with the Lord's *light* (42:6) and *righteousness* (cf. *ṣedeq*, 42:21), so does the Cyrus figure. In addition, the chiastic pattern of chaos/creation motifs itself parallels the Cyrus and Servant figures (see g_1, g_2, figure 11). Such parallelism reflects the complementary nature of these two figures. Within the chaos/creation pattern, the Cyrus and Servant figures represent variant manifestations of a single ideal vassal.

Chaos reappears in the form of "shards" and "clay" (45:9). That imagery describes those who disclaim what the Lord makes and begets, that is, Jacob/Israel and the Cyrus figure (45:10-13). The Lord—who "begets" children (*yld*, 45:10-11) as his divine offspring,[87] who "makes" (*'sh*) the earth and "creates" (*br'*) humanity upon it, who suspends the heavens and appoints their host (45:12)—also raises up the Cyrus figure (45:13), a new creation. The Lord's raising up (*ha'îrōtihû*) of the Cyrus figure parallels chiastically his raising up (*ha'îrōtî*) of the Righteous Warrior figure (see e_1, e_2, figure 11). Such parallelism supports the idea that these figures represent a single ideal agent of the Lord's redemption.

A return to chaos occurs when the makers of idols retire in disgrace, utterly dismayed and embarrassed (45:16). He who "creates" the heavens and the earth (*br'*/*yṣr*) nonetheless saves Jacob/Israel everlastingly (45:17-18). Following that, "darkness" and "chaos" (*tōhû*, 45:19) characterize idolatrous nations (45:20-21). Continuous with this chaos appear weariness and exile, in chapter 46. The latter manifestations of chaos, therefore, appear linked to idolatry (46:1-4): idolatry, which is a form of covenant breaking, leads to the covenant curses of weariness, exile, a state of darkness, and chaos. The pattern of chaos to end a chapter, and of creation to begin the next,[88] thus has an exception between chapters 45 and 46. That exception may indicate an irregularity in the chapter divisions at this point.

The Lord causes Israel's deliverance/salvation (46:13b) by means of his creative word: "I speak, and my purposes take effect; I accomplish all my will" (46:10); "What I have spoken, I bring to pass, what I have planned, I do" (46:11). The figure *righteousness*,

---

[87] An a–b–a structure in chapter 45 establishes the Lord as "Father" of his children, as follows: the Lord as Maker, verses 9, 11; and the Lord as Father, verse 10. The Lord's begetting of "children," in verse 10, is confirmed in verse 11.

[88] So chapters 41/42; 42/43; 43/44; 44/45.

whom the Lord brings from the east, serves as the Lord's agent for delivering Jacob/Israel (46:11–13a). An a–b–a structure in 46:10c–11 presents the figure from the east as the object of the Lord's creative word: verse 10cd features the Lord's creative word; verse 11ab depicts the figure from the east, whom the Lord summons; and verse 11cd again features the Lord's creative word.[89] As in the chaos/creation pattern of Isa 1–12, Israel's deliverance/salvation (*těšûʿâ*) sums up the message of the structure (46:13b; cf. *yěšûʿâ*, 12:2–3).

The chiastic structure of chaos/creation motifs in chapters 41–46 and the atypical ending of chapter 40's chaos/creation pattern with a creation motif (40:31) illustrate the integrity of the second unit as a distinct literary entity. Underlying literary criteria evidently determine much of the composition and message of this material. That message includes the Lord's raising up an ideal vassal in the latter days who serves as the Lord's agent for redeeming Jacob/Israel. The new exodus, which forms the pivotal event of Jacob/Israel's redemption (see o_1, o_2, figure 11), separates those whom the Lord creates anew from those who return to chaos.[90]

Lastly, a pattern in the second unit links the mission of the Lord's agent of redemption to the Lord's own role as creator of the cosmos: the Lord God of Israel, who creates the heavens and the earth, now raises up or creates his ideal vassal.[91] This pairing of ideas implies two important things: first, the Lord's ideal vassal possesses divine authority, being sent or appointed by the Lord; and second, he epitomizes the Lord's creation. Of that creation—which, as we have seen, includes royal accession, an endowment of the Lord's Spirit, and a state of nonweariness—the Lord's ideal vassal serves as a paradigm. Just as the Lord has "created" him (expressing the ideal vassal's birth or rebirth), so the Lord will "create" his people who emulate *righteousness*. Such an event, moreover—of creation out of chaos—typifies the Lord's salvation.

Summary

The structural, typological, and rhetorical evidence section III furnishes, determines that the several agents of the Lord's punishment

---

[89] Compare the ability of the Lord's ideal vassal to predict the future, 41:26–27; 44:26–28; 48:14–16.

[90] See also the new exodus as the redemptive event that climaxes the first unit, 11:15–12:6.

[91] See this pattern in 40:28–41:4; 42:5–7; 44:24–45:8; 45:12–13; 45:18–19.

and deliverance who appear in this material represent a single, composite figure—an ideal vassal of the Lord. That figure plays a key role in releasing the Lord's people from bondage, in bringing about their return from throughout the earth, and in facilitating the related typological events of a new exodus, new wandering in the wilderness, and new conquest. These events provide a common eschatological or latter-day context for both units of material.

The first unit (chaps. 9–12) vests a redemptive role in a future Davidic king, who serves as the Lord's agent of punishing the wicked and delivering the righteous. That Davidic king forms a composite of the biblical types of kings David, Solomon, and Hezekiah and of the biblical heroes Abraham, Moses, Joshua, and Gideon. The second unit (chaps. 41:1–46:13b), in building its ideal agent of the Lord's redemption, essentially maintains this composite of types, with the exception that the universal warrior type, Cyrus, replaces the Israelite warriors Joshua and Gideon. Cyrus adds the rebuilding of Jerusalem and the temple to Jacob/Israel's release from bondage, new exodus, new wandering in the wilderness, return, and new conquest as events through which the Lord's redemption manifests itself. Another event for which Cyrus sets a precedent—the treading down of nations for Jacob/Israel's sake—the second unit subsumes under that of a new conquest.

The first unit juxtaposes, structurally, the latter-day Davidic king with a kind of archtyrant, of whom an anonymous and mythologized king of Assyria serves as a type. As an agent of the Lord's punishment, the king of Assyria prevails over the Lord's wicked people. Metaphorical links, however, show that in the end the Davidic king overpowers him. A pattern of alternating chaos and creation motifs in Isa 1–12 confirms the Davidic king's victory over the king of Assyria: within the chaos/creation pattern, the king of Assyria identifies with the powers of chaos and the Davidic king with the powers of creation—creation succeeding chaos.

The second unit divides the Lord's ideal vassal of the latter days—the Lord's agent of punishment and deliverance—into three separate composites of types. Of these, the Righteous Warrior figure serves primarily an exemplary function in bringing about Jacob/Israel's redemption. The Servant and Cyrus figures, on the other hand, fulfill respective spiritual and temporal roles in redeeming Jacob/Israel. No one figure fulfills all criteria of an ideal agent of the Lord's punishment and deliverance but each complements the others. Together, these three figures realize the ideal of the Lord's redemption, while separately they represent fragments of the ideal as reflected in various historical phenomena. The three figures' parallelism in the second unit with the Davidic king in the first unit heightens the Davidic vassalship of this latter-day prophetic figure, which succeeding sections of the Bifid Structure maintain (cf. 55:3–4).

A chiastic pattern of alternating chaos and creation motifs in Isa 40–46 confirms that the three Isaianic figures in the second unit variously manifest a single ideal vassal. Within that chaos/creation pattern, the three figures identify with one another parallelistically as powers of creation. Both of the chaos/creation patterns—in Isa 1–12 and 40–46—define the Lord's new creation in terms of Israel's redemption. The new creation proceeds upon the Lord's intervention: the Lord raises up an ideal agent of punishment and deliverance in order to render Israel's enemies extinct or ineffectual.

The metaphorical terms *hand*, *light*, and *righteousness*, which appear in both units, express attributes the Lord's ideal vassal exemplifies. The rhetorical use of these and other such terms shows that they serve as pseudonyms of this prophetic figure. Metaphorical pseudonyms that the king of Assyria and the Davidic king share in common, such as the Lord's *hand*, *staff*, and *ensign*, may denote an arch rivalry between the two. Metaphorical pseudonyms they do not share, such as the Lord's *anger*, *wrath*, and *indignation*, on the one hand, and the Lord's *light* on the other, identify the king of Assyria as a power of chaos and the Davidic king as a power of creation. In addition, the metaphor *righteousness* (*ṣedeq*/*ṣĕdāqâ*/*ṣaddîq*), an attribute the latter-day figure personifies, expresses an exemplary function toward Jacob/Israel in the second unit.

The ideal vassal's role in the second unit differs essentially from that in the first only in that his acts, physical or spiritual, appear exemplary for the Lord's people and in that this figure and Jacob/Israel act together in order to realize the Lord's redemption. The text characterizes the Lord's redemption as the demise of the wicked and the deliverance of the righteous. These things show that concepts established in sections I and II appear cumulatively in section III and that the Lord's ideal vassal initiates the reversal of circumstances developed in section I. A movement from an Egyptian-influenced ''son'' of the Lord in the first unit (9:6) to a Mesopotamian-influenced ''servant'' of the Lord in the second

(42:1; 44:26),[92] moreover, develops an idea that appears incipiently in section II (cf. "son," 7:14; and "servant," 37:35).

Section III's synthesis of biblical types to form a latter-day prophetic figure, and that figure's role in serving as the Lord's agent of punishing the wicked and delivering the righteous—within a context of Jacob/Israel's release from bondage, new exodus, new wandering in the wilderness, return, new conquest, and rebuilding of Jerusalem and the temple—possesses no parallel in prior sections of the Bifid Structure. Although subsequent sections presuppose this composite of types, it does not recur within so tightly a structured context as this. Section III's juxtaposition of the Lord's ideal vassal with the Lord's enemies, political or spiritual, within patterns of alternating chaos and creation motifs, similarly does not appear elsewhere.

---

[92] On the Isaianic use of the term *servant*, see also J. W. Behr, *The Writings of Isaiah and the Neo-Babylonian Royal Inscriptions* (Pretoria, So. Africa: Rubenstein & Co., 1937), 25–26.

SECTION IV
HUMILIATION & EXALTATION
(13–23; 46:13c–47:15)

As explained in the Introduction (p. 15), the themes of the various sections of the Bifid Structure form a chiastic pattern (see figure 12). Within this chiastic arrangement, the first three pairs of themes resemble or parallel the last three pairs. Section IV thus forms a centerpiece within the Bifid Structure, suggesting that its themes of humiliation and exaltation, which stand alone, express a key concept. Like other sections of the Bifid Structure, section IV builds upon the concepts introduced in prior material. These concepts include a reversal of circumstances between Zion and non-Zion (section I), the coexistence of two peoples contrasting in their commitment to the Lord (section II), and the portrayal of a single, composite entity made up of a number of historical types (section III).

Figure 12

> Ruin and Rebirth (chaps. 1–5 and 34–35)
>> Rebellion and Compliance (chaps. 6–8 and 36–40)
>>> Punishment and Deliverance (chaps. 9–12 and 41:1–46:13b)
>>>> Humiliation and Exaltation (chaps. 13–23 and 46:13c–47:15)
>>> Suffering and Salvation (chaps. 24–27 and 48–54)
>> Disloyalty and Loyalty (chaps. 28–31 and 55–59)
> Disinheritance and Inheritance (chaps. 32–33 and 60–66)

Section IV lends a name to all entities that do not identify with Zion by juxtaposing Zion (those whom the Lord ransoms and delivers in the day of judgment) with an antithetical or opposing category called "Babylon." Babylon epitomizes those whom the Lord punishes and destroys in the day of judgment, who include the Lord's wicked people and all idolatrous nations. Additionally, section IV colors the reversal of circumstances between Zion and Babylon with the idea of glory and ignominy: just as the Lord's righteous people, by ascending the paradigmatic ladder, attain an exalted state, so those who oppose the Lord incur a state of humiliation. Exaltation and humiliation thus express two ultimate human conditions. These conditions modify or redefine the idea of ruin and rebirth and of punishment and deliverance that previous sections of the Bifid Structure describe.

Babylon as a Composite Entity

Section IV consists almost entirely of oracles against foreign nations and is thus distinguishable, from a literary standpoint, by genre. A disproportionately large number of chapters comprising the first unit (chaps. 13–23) parallels a single chapter and part of one verse (chap. 46:13c–47:15) in the second. This unbalanced parallelism of material serves as a structural device that identifies the foreign nations in the first unit with Babylon in the second. Just as section III establishes the idea of a single person—the Lord's ideal vassal—who is composed of a number of historical types, so section IV expands the idea of a composite entity to include nations, in this instance non-Zion or reprobate nations. Section IV, in other words, establishes the concept of a corporate or arch entity—a kind of Babylon the Great (cf. Rev 17:5, 15, 18)—that consists of all entities other than Zion. Babylon, the sole subject of an oracle in the second unit (47:1–15), typifies structurally all foreign entities in the first. By paralleling one with the other, the structure equates one with the other.

The first unit itself, however, commences with "an oracle concerning Babylon, which Isaiah the son of Amoz saw in vision" (13:1). This focus on Babylon continues intermittently through the first unit, emphasizing, as in the second unit (46:13c–47:15), Babylon's fall: Babylon will be thrown down as God overthrew Sodom and Gomorrah (13:19); Babylon will not be reinhabited through all generations (13:20); wild animals will infest Babylon and jackals cry out from her palaces (13:21–22); the Lord will sweep Babylon with the broom of destruction, cutting off her name and remnant (14:22–23); Babylon's king will be hewn down and cast away unburied (14:12, 19); Babylon's idols will be razed to the ground when she falls (21:9); the Lord will lay waste and destroy Tyre (23:1, 11), which the Babylonians founded for shipping (23:13);[1] Babylon will descend into the dust as catastrophe overtakes her suddenly (47:1, 11); fire will consume Babylon's prognosticators, burn them up like stubble (47:14).

The fact that Babylon heads the oracles against foreign nations in the first unit, combined with this unit's parallelism of Babylon in the second, puts all remaining nations and entities in the first unit under a structural umbrella of *Babylon*. The origin of such an idea may stem from that of empire, perhaps harking back to the old Babylonian empire or to the empire of David and Solomon. Both empires established precedents of a cultural–theological arch entity, one allied with the Lord, the other alien to the Lord. In Hebrew prophetic thought, the failure of the Davidic empire leads ultimately to a rebirth of the Babylonian empire. Conversely, in Isaiah, a rebirth of the Davidic empire follows on the failure of the Babylonian empire. The common doom shared by Babylon and the nations (13:1–23:14), the depiction of Babylon as Mistress of Kingdoms (47:5), the mother of "children" (47:8), and the king of Babylon as one who commands the nations (14:12), his sons rising up and taking possession of the world (14:21)—such descriptions support the structurally connoted merger of the nations with Babylon.

A short passage at the end of chapter 46 forms an exception to the parallelism of Babylon and the nations and to the doom that characterizes both. Two lines speak of the Lord's granting "deliverance [*těšû'â*] in Zion, and to Israel my glory [*tip'artî*]" (46:13cd). This passage, though it does not affect the parallelism of Babylon and the nations,[2] expresses the key idea that Babylon's ignominy—a chief feature of section IV—occurs simultaneously with, and in contrast to, the Lord's glorification of his righteous people (cf. 47:3–4). The motif of *glory* shows up an antithetical relationship between Israel or Zion and Babylon: the Lord endows Israel with

---

[1] Hebrew *yěsādâh lěsîyîm* does not justify the RSV rendering, "destined for wild beasts"; the verb *ysd* does not possess a connotation of destiny. Rather, a rhetorical definition of that term yields the familiar meaning of "founded/established"; compare 14:32; 28:16. See also *sî* as "ships," 33:21; Num 24:24; Ezek 30:9.

[2] A transitional fragment to chapter 47, the two lines appear *after* the chiastic structure of alternating chaos and creation motifs that begins and ends the second unit of section III. These lines repeat the idea of deliverance/salvation (*těšû'â*, 46:13b) that concludes both a Righteous Warrior passage and the chaos/creation pattern.

his glory and delivers his people in Zion (46:13cd); but disaster overtakes Babylon when the Lord dethrones her and she dwells, humiliated, in the dust (47:1, 11). The Lord's exaltation of Israel/Zion and his humiliation of Babylon commences a seven-part pattern of alternating motifs of glory and ignominy that continues through the end of chapter 47.[3] This closely knit pattern of linked motifs reflects the structural integrity of the second unit of section IV, including its opening lines.

An antithetical relationship between Israel/Zion and Babylon similarly characterizes the first unit: the Lord establishes Zion as a place of refuge for his long-suffering people (14:32) and Israel rules over her captors (14:1); a nation dreaded far and wide is made to bring tribute to Zion (18:7). But Babylon's glory (*tip'eret*) is thrown down like Sodom and Gomorrah (13:19); her king's glory (*gĕ'ôn*), the Lord casts into Sheol (14:11); the nations' glory, and the glory of the Lord's wicked people, the Lord turns into ignominy (cf. Moab, 16:6–14; Aram, 17:1–3; Egypt and Cush, 20:4; Kedar, 21:16; Tyre, 23:9; and the Lord's wicked people, 17:4; 22:1–5). The idea of a reversal of circumstances between the Lord's righteous people and the nations, which appears cumulatively from section I, here receives the added dimension of glory and ignominy: the Lord exalts and humiliates, respectively, his redeemed people and their oppressors.

This antithesis of two corporate groups or entities—one identified with Zion, whom the Lord delivers, the other identified with the wicked whom the Lord destroys—builds on concepts established in section II. The creation of a greater or arch Babylon, however, lends a corporate dimension to concepts established in section III. In order to create this archetypal Babylon, section IV subordinates history by means of structural and rhetorical devices, transforming peoples identified with ancient Babylon into types of a latter-day Babylon. This latter-day Babylon functions as the counterpart and antithesis of Zion, which itself is a latter-day and transformed entity. Just as a typological precedent exists for any prophecy that the text builds structurally, so section IV builds on the type or precedent of an actual historical Babylon as an arch entity. However, the question remains as to which Babylon forms the basis of the prophecy: the old Babylonian empire (2500–689 B.C.), Neo-Babylon (608–539 B.C.), or both?

---

[3] See glory, 46:13cd; 47:1c; 47:5c; 47:7a; 47:8; 47:9c–10; 47:12; and ignominy, 47:1ab; 47:2–5b; 47:6; 47:7bc; 47:9ab; 47:11; 47:13–15.

Some scholars assume that chapters 13–14 and 21 depict the fall of the Neo-Babylonian empire at the hands of the "Medes" or Persians (cf. 13:17; 21:2).[4] They consider that the Babylonian material in these chapters, therefore, should be dated much later than Isaiah.[5] Seth Erlandsson, in his scholarly work, *The Burden of Babylon*, protests that such a view is unhistorical. Erlandsson illustrates the literary and political integrity of chapters 13–23 on the grounds that from the end of the eighth century B.C. to the Assyrian destruction of Babylon in 689 B.C., all political entities appearing in the series of ten "burdens" or "oracles" *(massâ')* that comprise the first unit of section IV (chaps. 13–23)[6] involve themselves with attempts to overthrow an oppressive Assyrian hegemony. In these attempts Babylon plays a key role.[7] On this political stage, Isaiah's words refute the possibility that the nations will achieve their goal. According to Isaiah, the Assyrian yoke cannot be broken by forming pacts with Egypt nor by the nations collaborating with Babylon, but by the Lord's intervening "in my own land" (14:25).[8] Historically, Erlandsson shows, the dirge against the king of Babylon (14:4–21) actually addresses an Assyrian conqueror of Babylon. Assyrian kings assumed the epithet "king of Babylon" (14:4) as a theological title from 729 B.C.[9]

Erlandsson's arguments for the nations' political affiliation with Babylon find support in the structural device of a Babylon composite or arch Babylon. The content of the first unit reflects both a universal and multinational consciousness, with the theme of a common catastrophe upon all nations pervading the bulk of the oracles against foreign powers.[10] Chapter 13, which is addressed to

---

[4] Otto Kaiser gives detailed but inconclusive arguments for the postexilic period as the setting of these chapters in *Isaiah 13–39* (Philadelphia: Westminster, 1974), 8–13, 29–31, 121–24.

[5] See O. Eissfeldt, *The Old Testament* (New York: Harper and Row, 1965), 312, 319–20; Georg Fohrer, *Introduction to the Old Testament* (Nashville: Abingdon, 1968), 368.

[6] The term "burden/oracle" *(massâ')* occurs eleven times in Isaiah, in 13:1; 14:28; 15:1; 17:1; 19:1; 21:1, 11, 13; 22:1; 23:1; 30:6.

[7] Seth Erlandsson, *The Burden of Babylon* (Lund, Sweden: Gleerup, 1970), 64–65, 102–5, 164–66.

[8] Erlandsson, *Burden of Babylon*, 102–5, 160–66.

[9] Erlandsson, *Burden of Babylon*, 122, 163–64.

[10] See catastrophe, 13:2, 4–22; 14:4–6, 9–31; 15:1–9; 16:1–4, 6–14; 17:1–14; 18:1–6; 19:1–17; 20:1–6; 21:1–17; 22:1–19, 25; 23:1–14.

"Babylon" (v 1), for example, introduces material that appears to condemn only Babylon the nation, but in reality condemns "the earth," "sinners" (v 9), "the world," and "the wicked" (v 11):

> 9. The day of the Lord shall come
>   as a cruel outburst of anger and wrath
>   to make **the earth** a desolation,
>   that **sinners** may be annihilated from it.

> 11. I have decreed calamity for **the world**,
>   punishment for **the wicked**;
>   I will put an end to the arrogance of insolent men
>   and humble the pride of tyrants.

The setting of this oracle as the "day of the Lord" (13:6, 9, 13)—a day that sees destruction throughout the earth (13:5), the earth jolting out of place (13:13), the hearts of all men melting with fear (13:7), everyone fleeing to his own land (13:14), etc.—further universalizes the idea of Babylon. Two concluding references to Babylon affirm, contextually, that "Babylon" is the subject of the worldwide catastrophe (13:19, 22).

Chapter 14, in like vein, depicts the dead kings of the nations— vassals of the king of Babylon—receiving him with wonder in Sheol (14:9–10). He who subdued the nations and made kingdoms quake (14:6, 16), whose vassals filled the face of the earth with cities (14:21), is himself subdued. The whole earth rejoices at his departure and rests from his tyranny (14:7–8). A verse concluding the chapter's Babylon/Assyria content affirms this material's universal perspective: "These are things determined upon the whole earth; this is the *hand* upraised over all nations" (14:26; cf. the Lord's upraised *hand* as the king of Assyria, 5:25; 10:4).

That perspective continues through the remainder of the first unit. A passage that anticipates the universal reign of a righteous Davidic king (16:5) interjects an oracle that depicts the ruin of Moab (15:1–16:14): the Davidic king will accede to the throne "when oppressors are no more and violence has ceased and tyrants are destroyed from the earth" (16:4cd). A passage describing the overnight annihilation of "many peoples in an uproar, who rage like the raging of the seas, tumultuous nations, in commotion like the turbulence of mighty waters" (17:12), concludes a chapter that addresses Aram as well as the Lord's idolatrous people. A verse alluding to the universal nature of the mission of the Lord's ideal vassal appears in an oracle concerning a dreaded nation (Assyria?) that encroaches upon others (18:2, 7): "All you who live in the world, you inhabitants of the earth, look to the *ensign* when it is lifted up in the *mountains*; heed the trumpet when it is sounded!" (18:3).[11]

A universal perspective further appears in the motif of a highway that reaches from Assyria to Egypt (19:23) and in the blessed state of the world that ensues after the catastrophe. In that blessedness, Assyria, Egypt, and Israel share alike (19:25). Babylon's fall (cf. 21:9) affects the uttermost reaches of civilization (cf. 21:11–12), calamity overtaking even wandering nomads (21:13–17). The revelers among the Lord's people perish at the hands of the same army that destroys Babylon (22:1–14; cf. 21:2). An oracle against Tyre that ends the first unit depicts the Lord's stretching out his *hand* over the seas and distressing kingdoms (23:11). Tyre appears as the "merchant of nations" (23:3), an imperial city whose traders (*sōḥărehâ*) were princes, whose merchants were the world's celebrities (23:8). As the mercantile arm of Babylon (23:13), Tyre concludes the first unit.

A common harlot imagery identifies Tyre in the first unit with Babylon in the second: Tyre hires herself out to all kingdoms of the world on the face of the earth (23:17); Babylon, mistress of kingdoms, has exerted herself from her youth for her procurers or merchants (*sōḥărayîk*, 47:5, 15). Tyre, who reared young men and virgins, is rendered barren, bereft of children (23:4); bereavement of children and widowhood overtake Babylon, both in one day (47:9, 13). This rhetorical affinity between Tyre and Babylon adds to the idea of Babylon as a composite entity made up of many nations and peoples.

Babylon's destruction, moreover, resembles that of Edom in section I: Babylon's destruction as Sodom and Gomorrah (13:19) in a "day of the Lord" (13:6, 9, 13) is contextually synonymous with the desolation of the earth and the world (13:9, 11) and structurally with that of the nations; Edom's Sodom and Gomorrah type of destruction (34:9–10) in a "day of the Lord" (34:8) serves as the type of a desolation of the earth and the world and of all nations and peoples (34:1–2). The common evils that befall Babylon and

---

[11] See also the blowing of the trumpet (*šôpār*) as a royal accession motif, 1 Kgs 1:34, 39, and, rhetorically, as signalling the return of the Lord's people from exile among the nations, Isa 27:13.

Edom—including cosmic cataclysm (13:10, 13; 34:4–5); lands infested by wild beasts and birds of prey (13:21–22; 14:23; 34:11–15), never to be resettled (13:20; 34:10); and the cutting off both name and remnant (14:20–22; 34:12)—represent covenantal malediction (cf. section I).

Babylon's idolatry and anti-Lord posture, however, distinguish her from Edom. Affirmations such as "I, the Eternal Mistress, exist forever!" (47:7) and "I exist, and there is none besides me!" (47:8, 10) characterize Babylon as the Lord's rival[12] and heighten the idea of wickedness. Babylon's anti-Lord stance eclipses the covenantal estrangement we find in the identification of the nations (and the Lord's errant people) with Edom. Whereas Edom typifies all nations who covenantally alienate themselves from the Lord or his people, Babylon typifies the nations in a way that goes beyond breaking covenant—that directly opposes the Lord or his people. Babylon thus adds to or augments the idea of Edom as a type or synecdoche of reprobate peoples described in section I. Babylon's self-exaltation, moreover, directly precedes her fall.

Self-exaltation, an ultimate type of wickedness, is the basis on which the Lord humiliates Babylon and all who exalt themselves with her. Babylon's humiliation in section IV subsumes the idea of the nations who suffer ruin in section I. Zion's exaltation, on the other hand, subsumes the idea of Zion's rebirth. While the themes of ruin and rebirth occur cumulatively in section IV, this new material modifies or redefines such concepts to show that ultimately ruin involves humiliation and rebirth involves exaltation. It also typifies non-Zion, which is ruined, as Babylon—all entities who stand in opposition to the Lord. In the anti-Lord climate that Babylon exemplifies, the Lord's people suffer ignominy in the interim before the Lord redeems them.[13] As the motif of glory implies (46:13cd), the humiliation of Babylon heralds the exaltation of Zion, and vice versa (cf. 47:1–3).

---

[12] See Hebrew *ʾehyeh* ("I am/exist," 47:7) as it applies to the Lord in Exod 3:14, and the expression *ʾănî wĕ*ʾapsî *ʿôd* ("I exist, and there is none/nothing besides me," 47:8, 10) as it describes the Lord in Isa 45:6; 46:9.

[13] See Isa 47:6: "I was provoked by my people, so I let my inheritance be defiled; I gave them into your hand, and you showed them no mercy; even the aged you weighed down heavily with your yoke." Compare 14:3.

To sum up, section IV appears to create the idea of a greater or arch Babylon (including that entity's antithesis of Zion)[14] that emerges from several cumulative concepts of the Bifid Structure. These include a reversal of circumstances between Zion and non-Zion first presented in section I, the coexistence of two antithetical peoples or entities found in section II, and the formation of a single, composite entity consisting of a number of historical types first seen in section III. This greater or arch Babylon, as an ahistorical entity that is the contemporary of Zion, has its being, and ultimately perishes, in the latter days—in the "day of the Lord" (cf. 13:6, 9; 47:9). Babylon's humiliation, at that time, leads to Zion's exaltation.

The peculiar structuring of section IV that establishes Babylon as an arch entity finds support in the common catastrophic content of each unit of material, in strategic and intermittent references to Babylon throughout the first unit, and in the historical, cultural, and political ties that existed between the nations and the Babylon of Isaiah's time that provide the basis for a pluralistic entity. Section IV goes beyond the cumulative concepts we have noted thus far by pluralizing the idea of a composite entity and by developing a heightened concept of wickedness. It does this by depicting structurally a multinational Babylon that exalts itself above, and thus diametrically opposes, the Lord and his righteous people.

A summary of reprobate entities within the structure of section IV—which thus make up arch Babylon—includes Babylon itself (13:1, 19; 14:22–23; 21:2–9; 47:1–15), the earth and the world (13:5, 9, 11, 13; 14:7, 16–17, 21, 26; 16:1, 4; 18:3; 23:17), hosts of heaven (13:10), nations and alliances of nations (13:14; 14:2, 12, 26, 31; 15:1–9; 16:2–4, 6–14; 17:1–3, 12–14; 19:1–25; 20:3–6; 21:16–17; 23:1–18; 47:5), aggressive world powers (18:2, 7), Assyria (14:25), the tyrants and oppressors of the earth (13:11; 14:2, 4; 16:4), rulers and men of power (14:9; 23:8), enemies and adversaries (14:8; 17:14; 47:6), the sea and rivers (16:8; 18:2–7; 19:6; 23:4, 11), and the Lord's wicked people (17:3–11; 20:6; 22:1–14).

Discourse E: Zion Ideology (2)— Deliverance and Destruction

A literary pattern involving the name *Zion* supports the idea of a multinational Babylon that is the antithesis and arch rival of

---

[14] See also that antithesis in apocalyptic literature, 2 Bar 11:1–2; 13:3–10; 4 Ezr 3:2.

the Lord's people. This pattern consists of three motifs that appear together cyclically throughout Isaiah. These motifs are (a) the Lord's overthrow of the forces of chaos or evil; (b) the Lord's establishment of the place Zion or his deliverance of the people called Zion; and (c) the presence or accession to the throne of the Lord's ideal Davidic vassal and/or of the Lord himself. Essentially, these three conjoined motifs repeat the pattern of Zion ideology established in section II (see Discourse B: Zion Ideology [1]—the Davidic Covenant), where the Lord delivers his compliant people in Zion/Jerusalem—b—by destroying the Assyrian army that threatens them—a—upon the intercession of an ideal Davidic vassal, Hezekiah—c—(see 37:32-36). The three motifs in this pattern recur in proximity to one another in all parts of the text, though not necessarily in any particular order (see examples of a, b, and c, below).

The first unit of section IV contains three instances of this pattern of Zion ideology, two of which highlight Zion's exaltation. A passage in chapter 14 states:

28. In the year King Ahaz died, came this oracle:
29. Rejoice not, all you Philistines,
     now that the rod which struck you is broken.
     From among the descendants of that snake
     shall spring up a viper,
     and his offspring shall be a fiery flying serpent.
30. The elect poor shall have pasture,
     and the needy recline in safety.
     But your descendants I will kill with famine,
     and your survivors shall be slain.
31. Wail at the gates; howl in the cities!
     Utterly melt away, you Philistines!
     From the North shall come [pillars of] smoke,
     and no place he has designated shall be left out.[15]
32. What shall then be told the envoys of the nation?
     The Lord has founded Zion;
     let his long suffering people find refuge there.

---

[15] Hebrew *ʾēn bôdēd běmôʿādāw* does not accord with the common translation, "no straggler in his ranks"; neither *bôdēd* nor *môʿādāw* possesses a military connotation. Rather, rhetorical definitions of these terms yield the familiar meanings of "left/abandoned" (cf. 27:10), "apart/separate" (cf. Lev 13:46), or "solitary" (cf. Hos 8:9; Mic 7:14); and "appointed time" (cf. Isa 1:14; Hos 2:11) or "designated place" (cf. Isa 14:13; 33:20), respectively. The immediate context of the expression, moreover, features no subject in third person singular other than the Lord (14:32).

Though scholars dispute the traditional interpretation of the "fiery flying serpent" (*śārāp mĕ'ôpēp*, v 29) as Davidic,[16] the context of safety for the Lord's poor (vv 30, 32), and of the Lord's founding Zion (v 32)—b—suggests that the rise of the *fiery flying serpent* alludes to the accession to the throne of a Davidic king—c—who vouchsafes the Lord's renewed protection and who, like Isaiah, functions on the level of a seraph (*śārāp*, v 29). The destruction of the Philistines (v 30cd)—a—completes the trio of literary motifs. The recurrence of this pattern throughout Isaiah suggests not only that this passage is Davidic but that the king in question is the Lord's ideal vassal.

The pattern repeats itself when a righteous Davidic king accedes to the throne (16:5)—c—within a context of the Daughter of Zion ruling in the earth (16:1)—b.[17] That event occurs when the Lord destroys the tyrants from the earth and violence ceases (16:4)—a. Next, the raising of the Lord's *ensign* to all the world (18:3)—c—appears within a context of the Lord's subjugation of a hostile world power—a—that brings tribute to Zion (18:7)—b. The text depicts Zion as the "place of the name of the Lord of hosts" (18:7), alluding to the Lord's theophany or manifestation of his presence in Zion—c. In this instance of the pattern of Zion ideology, the Davidic king—the Lord's *ensign*—and the Lord appear side by side.

These three expressions of Zion ideology in the first unit account for what might otherwise seem implausible references to the accession to the throne of a Davidic descendant in the oracles against foreign nations. As part of the cyclical pattern, however, the motif of Davidic accession appears consistently throughout the text. It underscores a preeminent involvement by a future Davidic king—the Lord's ideal vassal—in the redemption of Zion and in the overthrow of the forces of evil. As in the first unit, this cyclical pattern occurs at virtually every mention of the name *Zion* in the Book of Isaiah. The representation of the Davidic vassal under metaphorical pseudonyms, such as *ensign*, *hand*, *righteousness*, etc., accords with section III's establishment of an ideal latter-day agent of the Lord's punishment and deliverance. That figure, throughout, is Davidic, and it is he who overthrows the forces who oppose the Lord.

---

[16] See O. Kaiser, *Isaiah 13-39*, 50-55; R. B. Y. Scott, *IB*, 5:266. Compare, however, the similar three-part allegory of Isa 11:1.

[17] See the directional parallelism of *'el har bat ṣiyyôn* ("to the mountain of the Daughter of Zion") and *môšēl 'ereṣ* ("ruling in the earth"), 16:1.

Thus, the ransoming of Zion—b—by *righteousness* (1:27), when the Lord restores his *hand* (1:25)—c—occurs when the Lord takes vengeance on adversaries (1:24), when he annihilates those who forsake him (1:28)—a. The reign of a righteous "judge" of the nations (2:4)—c—commences when Zion becomes the head of the mountains or nations (2:2-3)—b—and chaotic entities burn up (1:31)—a. The Lord destroys the wicked of his people (3:25-26; 4:4)—a— but he protects Zion (4:3, 5-6)—b—when the Lord's *plant* blossoms (4:2)—c.[18] As godless nations are routed (8:9-10)—a—the king Immanuel (8:8, 10)—c—ensures the safety of the Lord's people in the Lord's sanctuary (*miqdāš*, 8:14)[19] on Mount Zion (8:18)—b.

Although the Lord carries out the utter destruction he has decreed upon the whole earth (10:23)—a—he spares a remnant of his people in Zion (10:21, 24)—b—because of his *righteousness* (10:22)—c. The Lord overthrows Assyria—a—by his *whip/staff* (10:26)—c—and delivers his righteous people (10:27)—b—when the king of Assyria advances against Zion (10:32). The Davidic king—c—slays the wicked—a—establishing peace among men and beasts in the Lord's "holy mountain" (11:1-9)—b. Zion's inhabitants sing a song of salvation (12:1-6) as the Lord's *hand*—c—subdues *Sea* and *River* (11:15)—a—and facilitates a new exodus (11:16)—b.

Beyond the oracles against foreign powers we find the Lord's manifesting his glory in the presence of his elders—c—as the Lord institutes his reign on Mount Zion (24:23)—b; that event follows the Lord's punishment of the wicked of heaven and earth (24:21)—a. In this instance of Zion ideology, theophany replaces Davidic accession, expressing a variant form of the pattern. Next, the Lord destroys proud Moab (25:10-12)—a—and saves his people (25:9)— b—when the Lord's *hand* alights in "this mountain" (25:10a)—c. The Lord grants salvation in "our city" (26:1)—b—as the nation of *righteousness* (*ṣaddîq*)—c—takes refuge in the Lord (26:2-4)—b; but the elite inhabitants of an exalted earthly city the Lord casts in the dust (26:5)—a. *Righteousness*—c—serves as a sure foundation

---

[18] See "plant/branch" (*ṣemaḥ*) as a metaphor describing a future Davidic king, Jer 23:5; 33:15.

[19] Some commentators do not accept the term *miqdāš* (8:14), which does not appear in the Targum; see Scott, *IB*, 5:227. The term nonetheless forms part of a chain of linking words that includes "this people"/"this people," 8:11-12; "fear" and "awe"/"fear" and "awe," 8:12-13; "sanctify" (*taqdîšû*)/"sanctuary" (*miqdāš*), 8:13-14; and "a snare"/"ensnared," 8:14-15. Compare LXX *hagiasma*; and *miqdāš* as "refuge," Ezek 11:16.

in Zion for those who believe in it (28:16–17)—b—an antidote to the doom that envelopes the wicked (28:17–18)—a. The Lord destroys the nations who war against Ariel/Mount Zion (29:5–8)—a—the city where David lodged (29:1)—c—while Zion revives from the dust (29:4)—b.

Zion's inhabitants survive—b—like an *ensign* on a hill—c—when others perish (30:16–19)—a; they behold the divine Teacher at his coming (30:18–20)—c. In this instance of the pattern, the Davidic king and a theophany again feature side by side. Those who make a pilgrimage to the Lord's "mountain" survive amid rejoicing (30:29)—b—when the Lord's *wrath* consumes the nations (30:27–28)—a; on that occasion, the Lord's *voice/arm/staff*—c—overthrows Assyria (30:30–32)—a. The Lord's new descent on Mount Zion (31:4)—c—is the setting for a new passover of his people (31:5)—b; but the Egyptians and their allies fall beneath Assyria's *hand* (31:3)—a. The Assyrians shrink in terror from the *ensign* in Zion (31:9)—c—as the Lord's fire and sword devour them (31:8–9)—a; at that time, an ideal king rules—c—and men dwell safely (32:1–2)—b.

At the Lord's uprising (*rommĕmūt*), the nations scatter (33:3)—a; but Zion, filled with justice and *righteousness* (33:5)—c—the Lord spares (33:6)—b. The righteous in Zion (33:15–16) live through the fire (33:14)—b—that sets nations ablaze (33:12)—a—and behold the divine King in his glory (33:17)—c. Those whom the divine Judge and King saves (33:22)—c—dwell safely in Zion (33:20–21)—b; but the nations, he condemns to the slaughter (34:1–2)—a. At the Lord's vengeance upon Edom (34:5–15)—a—on behalf of Zion (34:8)—b—the Lord's *hand*—c—apportions each his inheritance (34:17)—b. The Lord protects a remnant of his people in Zion—b—for the sake of his servant David (37:32–35)—c; but the besieging Assyrian horde, the Lord slays (37:36)—a.

This pattern of Zion ideology continues essentially unchanged in the exilic and postexilic settings of Isaiah. Men may perish like withering grass, like fading flowers (40:8)—a—but the Lord's word from Zion nurtures his people (40:9)—b; the Lord's *arm*—c—gathers them like a flock—b—as the Lord's coming to the earth draws nigh (40:9–11)—c. A "righteous one" (*ṣaddîq*)—c—treads down dignitaries as mud (41:25–26)—a; to Zion, however, he heralds good tidings (41:27), delivering the Lord's people from blindness (42:1–7)—b. The Lord grants deliverance in Zion—b—as his *righteousness* comes near (46:13)—c—but Babylon he reduces to dust (47:1)—a. Zion's children return safely (49:14-23)—b—and the Lord slays their oppressors (49:24-26)—a—when the Lord's *hand/ensign* beckons the nations (49:22)—c.

The Lord regenerates Zion (51:3)—b—as his *righteousness* and *salvation* appear—c;[20] these two alone provide surety for the Lord's people—b—while the world perishes (51:5-8)—a. A variant pattern of Zion ideology models itself on the new exodus: those whom the Lord ransoms, return to Zion (51:11)—b—when the Lord's *arm*—c—slays the *dragon* and dries up the *Sea* (51:9-10)—a. Zion takes shelter—b—in the shadow of the Lord's *hand* (51:16)—c—while the Lord's (left) *hand/wrath* desolates his wicked people (51:17-20)—a. At the Lord's coming (52:6-8)—c—Zion rises from the dust (52:1-2)—b—and the Lord turns the tables on her tormentors (51:21-23)—a. The Lord's *arm* of *righteousness* (59:16)—c—gains the victory over enemies (59:16-18)—a—when the Lord comes to redeem Zion (59:19-20)—b, c.

Righteousness rules in place of oppressors (60:17)—c—as the Lord comforts Zion—b—humbling his people's tormentors (60:14)—a. The Lord's anointed one—c—anoints those who mourn in Zion (61:3)—b—as the Lord's day of vengeance draws nigh (61:2)—a. The nations behold Zion's vindication (62:2)—a, b—while her *righteousness* and *salvation* shine brightly (62:1)—c. The Lord's *ensign* to the nations (62:10)—c—heralds the Lord's coming as *salvation* to Zion (62:11-12)—b, c; but the Lord's *anger/wrath* tramples Edom and the nations (63:1-6)—a. Zion delivers a son—c—and a nation of sons (66:7-8)—b—when the Lord's *voice*—c—pays his enemies their due (66:6)—a.

This cyclical pattern demonstrates the integrity of Isaianic Zion ideology as a literary phenomenon. The pattern's threefold structure and supporting metaphors appear consistently throughout the text. Though this pattern transcends historical bounds and chapter divisions, it remains true to cumulative, structurally established concepts. The threefold pattern, for example, supports section II's ahistorical view of the Lord's deliverance of Zion from the besieging Assyrians at the intercession of King Hezekiah. That historical act of divine deliverance, as a focal point of Zion ideology, exemplifies the cyclical pattern. Within the Bifid Structure, and

---

[20] See *salvation* (*yeša'/yĕšû'â*) as a metaphor describing the Lord himself, 12:2; 17:10; 33:2; *passim*.

within the threefold pattern we have just observed, that historical event serves a typological purpose—it prefigures a future deliverance of Zion and destruction of Zion's enemies at the intercession of a Davidic king, the Lord's ideal vassal and agent of punishment and deliverance.

It is thus in the so-called rhetoric of Isaiah, which writers like R. P. Carroll dismiss as superfluous,[21] that we find literary interconnections that support an ahistorical, and specifically latter-day, view of the prophecy. The pattern of Zion ideology, moreover, clearly reveals what Zion is: Zion consists of a people and a place with a righteous Davidic king that survive when the Lord destroys chaotic entities. The few instances of the term *Zion* that do not fall within this pattern still accord with that definition (cf. 1:8; 10:12; 35:10).

Isaianic Zion ideology, in effect, juxtaposes Zion with all other entities. When we take account of those who oppose Zion and thus perish—based on the cyclical pattern we have just observed—we find that these non-Zion entities include Babylon itself (14:22–23; 47:1, 11), the earth and the world (34:1–2; 51:6), hosts of heaven (24:21; 51:6), nations and alliances of nations (8:9; 14:30c–31; 29:7–8; 30:27–28; 31:3; 33:3, 12; 34:1–7; 62:2; 63:1–6), aggressive world powers (18:2, 7), Assyria (10:26; 30:30–32; 31:8–9; 37:36), the tyrants and oppressors of the earth (16:4; 49:24–26; 51:23; 60:14), rulers and men of power (1:31; 24:21), enemies and adversaries (1:24; 59:18; 66:60), *Sea* and *River* (10:26; 11:15; 51:9–10), and the Lord's wicked people (1:24, 28; 3:25; 28:17–19; 30:16–17; 31:3; 33:14; 51:19–21; 66:6). These categories coincide with those defined structurally as arch Babylon (see p. 151), supporting the idea of Babylon as a composite entity and its antithesis of and opposition to Zion.

A Babylon Ideology

The definition of Zion that emerges from the preceding cyclical pattern not only develops a Zion ideology, it also clarifies the nature of Babylon. Just as a Zion ideology functions redemptively, so a Babylon "ideology" functions damnatorily. In light of section IV, all entities that are not Zion, in effect, are Babylon and are seen as reprobate. The definition of Zion as both a people and a place

---

[21] R. P. Carroll, "Second Isaiah and the Failure of Prophecy," *ST* 32 (1978): 119–31.

(those of the Lord's people who repent and the place to which they return, where the Lord delivers them) is the antithesis of Babylon as a people and a place (the sinners, the wicked, the earth, and the world [13:9, 11]—all that the Lord destroys in his day of judgment). Thus, the text defines Zion within a narrow compass but Babylon within a broad compass.

The contrast between these entities is heightened as we compare arch Babylon's characteristics in section IV with those of Zion throughout Isaiah: the Lord forgives Zion's inhabitants their iniquity (33:24), but he does not forgive arch Babylon's inhabitants till they die (22:14). The Lord lays a sure foundation in Zion (28:16), but he removes arch Babylon's foundation (13:13). The Lord protects Zion in his day of judgment (4:5-6; 37:32-35; 51:16), but he will not protect arch Babylon in that day (13:6-19; 14:21-22; 15:4, 9; *passim*). Zion enjoys peace and an absence of fear (33:18-20; 54:14), but fear and terror overtake arch Babylon (13:8; 19:16-17; 21:3-4). The Lord delivers Zion (25:9; 33:15-16; 46:13), but he destroys arch Babylon (13:19-22; 14:23; 15:1; *passim*).

The Lord redeems Zion (1:27; 35:9c-10; 62:12), but he punishes arch Babylon (13:9, 11; 22:5, 14; 47:3). The Lord comforts Zion (51:3), but he discomfits arch Babylon (15:5; 16:2; 23:10-12). Zion's children gather home safely (30:29; 49:7-23; 51:11), but arch Babylon's children scatter and die (13:14-18; 21:14-15; 47:15). Zion's land gloriously regenerates (51:3; 60:13), but arch Babylon's land decays and dries up (14:23; 15:6; 19:5-7). Zion sings with joy (12:6; 51:3, 11), but arch Babylon weeps and laments (14:31; 15:2-5; 23:1, 6). Zion rules in the earth (2:2-4; 16:1; 18:7), but arch Babylon's rule in the earth ends (14:5-6, 21; 17:3; 47:1, 5). The Lord exalts Zion (52:1; 60:12-22; 62:2-3), but he humiliates arch Babylon (20:4; 23:9; 47:1-3; *passim*).

We observe this polarity between Zion and arch Babylon particularly when we compare Babylon in chapter 47—a key component of section IV—with Zion throughout Isaiah: Zion rises from the dust (29:4; 52:2), but Babylon descends into the dust (47:1; cf. 21:9). The Lord clothes Zion in robes of glory (49:18; 52:1; 61:3), but he strips Babylon naked (47:2-3). Zion, jubilant, spreads abroad and inherits nations (54:1-3), but Babylon, speechless, ceases to rule kingdoms (47:5, 8). Zion gathers up the Lord's people who were outcasts (56:7-8), but Babylon shows them no mercy, yokes down young and old (47:6). Zion, forsaken and cast off, the Lord espouses anew (54:4–8), but Babylon, espoused and secure, he widows and bereaves (47:7–10). The Lord empowers Zion (52:11), but he renders Babylon powerless (47:13). The Lord ransoms Zion from catastrophe (51:11–16; 54:15–17; 59:20), but Babylon, unable to ransom herself, he visits with disaster (47:11–13). Zion lives through the devouring fire (33:14–16; 43:2; 66:14–16), but Babylon burns up (47:14–15).

The contrast between Zion and arch Babylon thus obtained may be summed up as redemption on the one hand and damnation on the other—the Lord's exaltation of the righteous and humiliation of the wicked in an ultimate sense. The structuring of this material in order to establish an arch Babylon turns the focus of section IV on arch Babylon. It therefore deals primarily with arch Babylon's humiliation. Indeed, the idea of humiliation, and of a prior self-exaltation, permeates the entire material.

Arch Babylon's humiliation—following its self-exaltation—is evident throughout section IV: the Lord puts an end to the arrogance of insolent men and humbles the pride of tyrants (13:11); Babylon, the most exalted of kingdoms, the glory and pride of Chaldeans, the Lord throws down as Sodom and Gomorrah (13:19); Moab's pride and boasting (16:6), the Lord turns into ignominy and dejection (16:7, 14); Aram's and Jacob's glory wanes as their fatness of body wastes away (17:3–4); an aggressive nation, dreaded far and wide, is made to bring tribute to Mount Zion (18:7); Pharaoh's counselors, who think themselves the equals of Egypt's first rulers (19:11), make Egypt stagger like a drunkard into his vomit (19:14); Egypt, looked up to for help against Assyria (20:6), the Lord exiles naked and barefoot with buttocks uncovered (20:4); Babylon, who indulges herself in feasting and drinking (21:5), the Lord razes to the ground (21:9); the city of revelry, resounding with loud cheers (22:2), shamefully flees in disarray (22:1–5); Shebna the steward, who vaingloriously exalts himself (22:16), the Lord thrusts out of office, a disgrace to his master's house (22:18–19); Tyre, the festive city, whose traders were princes, whose merchants were the world's celebrities (23:8), the Lord lays low—"to make all glorying in excellence a profanity, and the world's celebrities an utter execration" (23:9); Babylon, securely enthroned as mistress of kingdoms, the Lord banishes into obscurity (47:5); Babylon, a pampered lady, delicate and refined (47:1, 8), the Lord reduces to a slave girl (47:2); Babylon, exalting herself as the Eternal Mistress (47:7), the Lord turns into stubble (47:14).

That section IV emphasizes arch Babylon's humiliation, of necessity giving only small space to Zion's exaltation, does not mean that this latter, twin aspect of the structure possesses less significance. Though the reversal of circumstances between Zion and non-Zion appears cumulatively from section I, Zion's exaltation, established in section IV, comes vividly to the fore in section V. Even as section IV establishes a theological basis (an anti-Lord posture) for arch Babylon's damnation, so section V establishes a theological basis for Zion's redemption. Clearly, arch Babylon's damnation represents but one side of the coin. Arch Babylon, which exalts itself, falls into the dust (13:19; 21:9; 47:1); but Zion, humiliated and oppressed under arch Babylon's regime, rises to exaltation from the dust (52:1-2).

Two individuals in the first unit—Shebna, a reprobate steward (22:15), and Eliakim, a righteous Davidic "servant" (22:20)—epitomize this reversal of circumstances between Zion and arch Babylon: the *nail* fastened in a sure place (Shebna), along with the burden hanging on it, the Lord dislodges, and it falls (22:25), even as the new *nail* in a sure place (the Lord's servant) succeeds it (22:23-24). That reversal affirms the somber prospect that the Lord includes entities native to his people among those whom he damns. It also affirms a leading role, whether for good or for evil, by those who have stewardship over the Lord's people.

D. E. Hollenberg, in a scholarly article, gives plausible reasons why in a certain sense the term *nations* in Isaiah refers to Israel among the nations. He explains that as a result of the Servant's mission, some Israelite exiles repent and return. Others, forsaking covenantal obligations, merge and become identified with "the nations."[22] The structure of section IV nuances that idea somewhat: for those who choose not to repent/return to the Lord, *Babylon*, the place to which the Lord exiles his people, typifies such a merger among the nations.

A Babylon ideology thus assumes that some who alienate themselves covenantally (viz., Edom) reject the Lord's redemption and assimilate among non-Zion entities. The pattern of Zion ideology reiterates further that a righteous Davidic king, the Lord's ideal vassal, acts as the Lord's agent of redemption. That idea is consistent with concepts sections II and III establish. Those who make

---

22 D. E. Hollenberg, "Nationalism and 'The Nations' in Isaiah XL–LV," *VT* 19 (1969): 23–36.

up arch Babylon, in other words, reject the Lord's Servant and instead follow a hedonistic, egocentric course, which, after it serves the Lord's purpose of trying his righteous people, dooms the wicked to a humiliating end. In essence, an imposed humiliation turns into exaltation for those whom the Lord redeems; but self-exaltation turns into humiliation for those whom he damns.

A passage in chapter 19, however, asserts that an assimilatory, and thus damnatory, course is not irreversible. The opposite of a merger with the nations—and of being covenantally alienated—holds true for certain Egyptians in the oracles against foreign powers. As do the other entities who make up arch Babylon, Egypt incurs malediction and humiliation (19:4–17; 20:4; cf. 30:3–5). Yet, in a time of adversity (19:4, 16–17), when certain "Egyptians" swear loyalty to the Lord and worship him (19:18–19), the Lord sends them a savior who delivers them (19:20). One city in Egypt of those who worship the Lord is known as the city of *righteousness* (19:18).[23] The Lord answers the loyalty of these Egyptians with an epiphany (19:21).[24] In the time of calamity, when the Egyptians repent, the Lord heals them (*rp'*, 19:22).[25] Thereafter, the Lord recognizes Egypt covenantally as "my people" (19:25; cf. 52:4–6; *passim*).

This example of Zion ideology in the land of Egypt demonstrates not only the inherent idea that Israelites may assimilate into the nations, but that such Israelites may reverse their assimilation: those who merge and identify with the nations may repent/return and resume their covenantal status as the Lord's people. In localized instances, a Babylon ideology may thus be renounced in favor of a Zion ideology: the Lord may save some, even as he destroys others, at the presence of a savior figure and/or the Lord's theophany. The pattern of Zion ideology, moreover, limits the options to two. In Isaiah, deliverance and destruction occur simultaneously within an eschatological or latter-day time frame; that is, both deliverance and destruction take place during the Lord's day of judgment when the Lord comes to redeem Zion.

---

[23] LXX *polis 'asedec* transliterates into Hebrew *'îr hassedeq* ("city of righteousness"). Neither MT "city of destruction" nor 1QIsa[a] "city of the sun" is compatible with the context of the passage as a whole.

[24] Compare the Egyptians "knowing" the Lord (*yd'*) in 19:21 with the Lord's people "knowing" the Lord's name (*yd'*) in 52:6.

[25] Compare the Lord's healing of his people (*rp'*), 30:26; 53:5.

In conclusion, several historical models provide the basis on which section IV builds structurally. First, the old Babylonian empire constitutes a precedent for the kind of cultural and religious arch entity projected. Second, the political collusion of the nations with Babylon in the eighth and seventh centuries B.C. sets the stage for Assyria's catastrophic destruction of Babylon and the other nations. Third, Neo-Babylon's captivity of Judah represents a final and essential component of a Babylon composite and of a Babylon ideology. This greater or arch Babylon allows for Israelites to assimilate into a pluralistic society but also to emerge as Zion when the Lord redeems his people.

Although Neo-Babylon overlaps typologically with earlier phases of Babylon's existence, section IV preserves particularly those characteristics that set a historical precedent. Babylon's self-exaltation in chapter 47 crowns a number of Babylonish (wicked) characteristics that precipitate the Lord's judgment; others include idolatry, self-indulgence, and oppression. The transcendence of historical periods—preexilic (old Babylon) and exilic (Neo-Babylon)—in order to create a latter-day ideal represents a cumulative concept. In this instance, however, the structure creates an anti-ideal, an archetype that epitomizes the evils of an anti-Lord ideology.

The King of Babylon

Babylon's king figure in chapter 14[26] epitomizes a Babylon ideology pursued, consummately, to its ignominious end. That archtyrant's sudden passing from a state of self-exaltation to one of utter damnation receives dramatic expression. When the king of Babylon ascends, godlike, in the heavens, to the utmost heights of Zaphon (14:13–14), the Lord thrusts him down to Sheol, to the utmost depths of the Pit (14:15). After he rises majestically as the morning star, he falls, calamitously, from the heavens (14:12). After

---

[26] Although scholars identify two separate poems or laments in chapter 14, one of the king of Babylon (vv 4b–11) and one of Helal ben Shahar (vv 12–20), an a–b–c–d–e–f–g–h–g–f–e–d–c–b–a structure supports the thematic unity of this material and the common identity of the two figures, as follows: verses 4–5 and 20c lament tyranny; verses 6–8 and 20ab testify of the tyrant's destruction of peoples and lands; verses 9a and 19 identify the tyrant's fate as Sheol or the Pit; verses 9bc and 18 describe the dead rulers of nations; verses 10–11 and 16–17 dramatize the dead tyrant's ignominy; verses 12 and 15 portray the tyrant's fall and demise; verses 13ab and 14 depict the tyrant's ascent in the heavens as a demigod; and verse 13cd depicts the tyrant's self-investiture on Mount Zaphon.

he commands the nations, the Lord hews him down to earth (14:12), his corpse lying unburied in a bed of maggots (14:11, 19–20). After he makes the earth shake and kingdoms quake, dead men mock and revile him (14:10, 16). The king of Babylon, hewer of the cedars of Lebanon, the Lord lays low (14:8).

A historical premise for this king figure rests on several possible types, including the Assyrian kings Sargon II, Sennacherib, and Ashurbanipal, and the Neo-Babylonian king Nebuchadnezzar. Erlandsson's arguments for an Assyrian identity of the king of Babylon, mentioned above,[27] find support in the idea of an archtyrant established in section III (cf. 14:25; 20:4, 6). It also finds support in two almost identical characterizations of the kings of Assyria and Babylon. Both kings come from the north (10:28–32; 14:13, 31), hew down the cedars of Lebanon (10:15, 33–34; 14:8; 37:24), conquer the whole earth (10:12–14; 14:5–7, 21), and, as the Lord's rivals (14:13, 24; 37:10–12, 23–29), impose their yoke of servitude on the Lord's people (10:24, 27; 14:3–5, 25). Both figures also appear under identical metaphorical pseudonyms. These include the Lord's punitive *staff* (*maṭṭeh*) and *rod* (*šēbeṭ*, 10:5, 15; 14:3–5). Finally, both figures meet an inglorious fate (10:16; 14:11–12; 37:29).

Such role-casting and rhetorical usage cast figures that technically appear under two different names into a single archetype. While the Neo-Babylonian king Nebuchadnezzar could fit this archetype as well as any Assyrian monarch, Assyrian kings set the historical precedent for militaristic world conquerors from the north. Accordingly, the first lament (14:4–11) parodies unrestrained military ambition. The Babylonian identity, however, adds to the Assyrian type the archtyrant's blatant anti-Lord posture: he seeks to rise in the heavens, to set his throne above the stars of God, to become as the Most High God—as El Elyon (14:12–14). Here, the second lament draws on ancient Near Eastern mythology. Such mythic imagery, by parodying the archtyrant's aspirations to divinity, expresses the very ideology that the title "king of Babylon" encapsulates.[28] This archtyrant's

---

[27] Erlandsson shows that the dirge against the king of Babylon (14:4–21) addresses an Assyrian conqueror of Babylon, Assyrian kings assuming the epithet "king of Babylon" (14:4) as a theological title from 729 B.C. See footnote 9.

[28] See the work on the possible ancient Near Eastern mythic origin of this passage, and on an Assyrian identity for the king of Babylon, by Alfred E. Krause, "Historical Selectivity: Prophetic Prerogative or Typological Imperative?" in *Israel's Apostasy and Restoration*, 175–212.

self-aggrandizement, in effect, serves as a paradigm of Babylon's anti-Lord ideology—of Babylon's wickedness. In that wicked ideological context, the archtyrant's assumption of a religious title is appropos.

The archtyrant as a composite figure—possessing types in the kings of Assyria and Babylon—builds on the concept of a composite figure developed in section III. Section IV's wicked composite figure, however, juxtaposes the righteous composite figure—the Lord's ideal vassal—developed in section III. As an ideal agent of the Lord's punishment and deliverance, the Davidic king is also made up of ahistorical or transformed elements. He, too, serves as a paradigm, not of an evil but of a divine ideology—of Zion's righteousness.

Additionally, in section IV, the composite entities of Zion and arch Babylon, including their two kings, modify or redefine the coexistence of two antithetical peoples and their monarchs developed in section II. Arch Babylon, however, does not consist only of the rebellious or reprobate of the Lord's people, as those of section II, but of all wicked entities worldwide. That is another reason why the archtyrant is called the "king of Babylon." Within the structural unit of which chapter 14 is a part (chaps. 13–23), the title "king of Assyria" would appear meaningless; an arch ruler whom the Lord damns along with Babylon and the reprobate nations should identify with the arch entity itself—with Babylon. Thus, metaphorical and other descriptions of the king of Assyria/Babylon help us distinguish a composite figure, a single latter-day archtyrant.

A tension, complex in nature, thus exists between a historical or mythical interpretation of chapter 14 and that chapter's function structurally. Babylon's king figure exemplifies section IV's transformation and subordination of biblical history and ancient Near Eastern mythology in order to create an archetype. That archetype is the antithesis of, and thus opposes, the Lord and his righteous rule. Chapter 14's transformation of myth, as it describes the king of Babylon, thus builds on the same typological principle and achieves the same purpose as does the Bifid Structure's transformation of history. In that sense, the king of Babylon, as a latter-day archtyrant, is not just an ahistorical figure; he is an amythical figure as well.

Discourse F: The Servant–Tyrant Parallelism (1)—the Structure

A structure that contrasts Babylon with Zion and the king of Babylon with the king of Zion augments chapter 14's transformation of history and myth and sets in striking relief the opposite activities of the Lord and the archtyrant. That structure consists of an extended parallelism of antithetical verses drawn from chapters 14 and 47, which appear in section IV of the Bifid Structure, and from chapters 52 and 53, which appear in section V. I have named this configuration of antithetical verses the Servant–Tyrant Parallelism (see figure 13). Two short passages (47:1-4; 52:1-3) form a kind of prologue to the main structure (14:1-23; 52:4-53:12). The main structure contains a total of twenty-one antithetical verses; in addition, the structure's third and seventh parallels (marked by asterisks) contain key complementary ideas.[29] The fact that the Servant–Tyrant Parallelism spans sections IV and V of the Bifid Structure demonstrates the thematic interdependence of these two blocks of material, particularly as it concerns Zion's exaltation.

Figure 13

	Isa 47		Isa 52
1-4.	Babylon is dethroned, disrobed, goes into the dust—Israel's Redeemer takes vengeance.	1-3.	Zion rises from the dust, is enthroned, robed in power—the Lord redeems his people.

Isa 14

1.	Jacob/Israel is resettled in the land—strangers cleave to them.	4.	The Lord's people are in exile—foreigners oppress them.
2.	The nations bring back Israel—she rules over her captors.	5.	The Lord's people are taken over without price—rulers subject them.
*3.	The Lord gives rest from sorrow and bondage in that day.	*6.	The Lord manifests his presence in that day.
4.	Bad tidings for Babylon—her king's reign of tyranny ends.	7.	Good tidings for Zion—her God's reign of peace begins.
5.	Babylon's wicked king is deposed.	8.	The Lord returns as King to Zion.

[29] Compare Nah 1:3, 7 for a similar choice of third and seventh elements containing a key message.

6.	The Tyrant strikes the nations.	10.	The nations see the Lord's saving *arm*.[30]
*7.	Jubilation—the whole earth is at rest and peace.	*9.	Jubilation—the Lord's people are comforted, redeemed.
8.	The hewers of cedars depart Lebanon.[31]	11.	Those who bear the Lord's vessels depart Babylon.[32]
9.	The Tyrant is exiled to Sheol, in the company of the dead.	12.	The Lord's people return from exile in the company of their God.
10.	The Tyrant is humiliated, subjected to reproach.	13.	The Servant is exalted and acquires eminence.
11.	The ignominious Tyrant formerly enjoyed eminence.	14.	The eminent Servant formerly endured ignomiy.
12.	He who subjugates the nations is lamented in awe.	15.	He who purges the nations is esteemed in awe.

Isa 53

13.	The Tyrant ascends (*'lh*) the heavens.	1–2.	The Servant[33] grows up (*'lh*) out of the earth.
14.	The Tyrant aspires to be like the Most High.	3.	The Servant submits to being the lowliest of men.
15.	The Tyrant's ignomiy is irrevocable.	4–5b.	The Servant's ignomiy is redemptive.

---

[30] A reversal, in MT, of verses 9 and 10 of chapter 52 appears from the complementary nature of verse 9 to 14:7, the seventh component of the parallelism, viz., *pashû rinnâ*, 14:7; *pishû rannĕnû*, 52:9. An a_1–b_1–b_2–a_2 structure in verses 8–10 of chapter 52 supports the relocation of verses 9 and 10 that the parallelism suggests, as follows: the Lord's watchmen cry out with joy, verse 8; the Lord reveals his *arm* universally, verse 10ab; men see the Lord's *salvation* universally, verse 10cd; the Lord's people break out in song, verse 9.

[31] See Lebanon as a biblical metaphor of the land and people of Israel, section III, footnote 33. See also the metaphor of trees as representing people, Introduction, page 25.

[32] See a rhetorical identity of "vessels" to denote, here, Israel's descendants, 22:24 (cf. 66:20).

[33] Use of the term *Servant* in 53:1–10 of the Servant–Tyrant Parallelism is justified only by analogy with that term as it appears in 52:13; 53:11. Elsewhere I refer to the subject of 53:1–10 as the suffering figure.

16–17b.	The Tyrant causes havoc and destruction.	5cd.	The Servant causes peace and healing.
17c.	The Tyrant keeps men in bondage.	6.	The Servant atones for men's sins.[34]
18.	The kings of the nations are honorable in death.	7.	The Servant goes like a lamb to the slaughter.
19.	The Tyrant is slain for his own crimes.	8.	The Servant is slain for the crimes of his people.
20ab.	The Tyrant is unburied because he did violence.	9.	The Servant is buried because he did no violence.[35]
20c–21.	The Tyrant's offspring are wiped out.	10.	The Servant's offspring continue.
22.	All in Babylon are condemned.	11.	The Servant vindicates many.
23.	Babylon is an inheritance for noxious birds.	12.	The Lord's great ones inherit with the Servant.

Like the Bifid Structure, the Servant–Tyrant Parallelism uses a structural device—an extended parallelism—to establish literary and theological concepts that transcend history. Analogical relationships that function within the structure, such as those suggested by its complementary and antithetical parallels, yield data that we can interpret only eschatologically or in a latter-day context. A polarity, not merely between blocks of diverse material but between two archetypal opposites—the Tyrant and the Servant and the respective chaotic and creative forces each represents—lifts entities within the structure from a historical or mythical plane to the realm of apocalyptic. Babylon and its king here function, on a primary level,

---

[34] See the effects of sin as bondage, 42:24; 43:24c–28; 44:20–22.

[35] The antithetical relationship of 52:9ab to 14:20ab suggests that a reversal of indirect objects—"his burial" (*qibrô*) and "in his death" (*bĕmōtâw*)—exists in MT. Isa 14:20ab represents the Tyrant as unburied because of his wickedness—a covenant curse. Isa 52:9ab, however, represents the Servant as buried, implying his innocence of wickedness; the statement, "he had done no violence," confirms this. Further, 52:9ab, as it stands, contains an anomaly: biblical tradition generally associates violence (*ḥāmās*) with wickedness (cf. Gen 6:11–13) and deceit (*mirmâ*) with wealth (cf. Psa 52:2–7), not vice versa. Isa 52:9ab should thus read, "He was appointed among the wicked in death; among the rich was his burial."

as futuristic types rather than historical realities. Babylon represents an arch entity that stands in opposition to Zion, and the king of Babylon to the king of Zion. Their contrasting ideologies could not receive more eloquent expression.

A thematic division of verses in the Servant–Tyrant Parallelism that is virtually identical to the sevenfold division of the Bifid Structure helps us to evaluate both structures. Whereas antithetical themes in the Bifid Structure show up in both units of each section, in the Servant–Tyrant Parallelism such themes appear simply juxtaposed (see figure 14). The third and seventh parallel verses of the Servant–Tyrant Parallelism (marked by asterisks), which lie outside this thematic arrangement, express the idea of redemption that both structures develop.

Figure 14   **Isa 47**   **Isa 52**

Prol. 1–3.	Babylon is dethroned —*Humiliation*.	1–3.	Zion is enthroned —*Exaltation*.

Isa 14

I. 1–2.	Jacob/Israel is restored —*Rebirth*.	4–5.	The Lord's people are taken captive —*Ruin*.
*3.	The Lord grants rest in that day.	*6.	The Lord manifests himself in that day.
II. 4–6.	The Tyrant is unrelenting —*Rebellion*.	7–8,10.	The Lord fulfills expectations —*Compliance*.
*7.	Jubilation: the whole earth is at rest.	*9.	Jubilation: the Lord redeems his people.
III. 8–9.	The Tyrant enters Sheol —*Punishment*.	11–12.	The Lord's people exit Babylon —*Deliverance*.
IV. 10–12.	The Tyrant is demeaned —*Humiliation*.	13–15.	The Servant becomes eminent —*Exaltation*.

Isa 53

IV. 13–14.	The Tyrant becomes a demigod —*Exaltation*.	1–3.	The Servant is despised —*Humiliation*.

V. 15-17.	The Tyrant causes havoc —*Suffering*.	4-6.	The Servant causes peace —*Salvation*.
VI. 18-20b.	The Tyrant becomes infamous —*Disloyalty*.	7-9.	The Servant is submissive —*Loyalty*.
VII. 20c-23.	Offspring/land are destroyed —*Disinheritance*.	10-12.	Offspring/portion are redeemed —*Inheritance*.

The Servant–Tyrant Parallelism's repetition and reversal of the themes of humiliation and exaltation at the center of the structure, as well as the appearance of these themes in the prologue, suggest that they form a central message of the structure. This message is that humiliation and exaltation constitute two superlative human conditions. Humanity universally, as a result of actual choice, separates into those who incur humiliation and those who inherit exaltation. The pivoting of these themes at the center of the Parallelism divides the structure into two thematic halves: the first four pairs of antithetical themes mirror the last four to form an a_1–b_1–c_1–d–d–c_2–b_2–a_2 structure. In addition, the first three pairs of themes and the last three pairs of themes each form a loose chiastic arrangement of themselves (a_1–b–a_2).[36] Such a configuration of themes, by highlighting key ideas, suggests that the determining principle leading to exaltation and humiliation is compliance or loyalty on the one hand and rebellion or disloyalty on the other. The remaining categories of themes express conditions incidental to exaltation and humiliation.

The Servant–Tyrant Parallelism's reflection of the same progression of themes that governs the Bifid Structure heightens our perception of the Bifid Structure. The archtyrant's exemplifying rebelliousness and disloyalty in the Servant–Tyrant Parallelism, for example, and the Lord's or the Servant's exemplifying compliance and loyalty suggest that these two entities epitomize such traits. All who rebel against the Lord and are disloyal toward him model themselves upon—and thus ally themselves with—the archtyrant.

---

[36] Viz., Ruin and Rebirth—a_1; Rebellion and Compliance—b; Punishment and Deliverance—a_2; and Suffering and Salvation—a_1; Disloyalty and Loyalty—b; Disinheritance and Inheritance—a_2.

All who comply with the Lord and are loyal toward him, on the other hand, model themselves upon—and ally themselves with— the Lord and his Servant. Moreover, each of these archetypal figures functions as a paradigm of both humiliation and exaltation: the Tyrant shows how self-exaltation leads to humiliation, and the Servant shows how an imposed humiliation may lead to exaltation. These concepts appear also in the Bifid Structure. The Lord's servant or ideal vassal, as an exemplar and paradigm of the Lord's people, himself emulates the Lord within a paradigmatic hierarchy. The Servant–Tyrant Parallelism, as a microcosm of the Bifid Structure, thus epitomizes that structure's eschatological message—its latter-day intent. The chief actors in the Lord's redemption of his people and his damnation of the wicked, who feature prominently in both structures, include the Lord himself, his ideal vassal, his people Zion, arch Babylon, and the tyrant king of Assyria/Babylon. The Servant–Tyrant Parallelism, however, heightens the message of the Bifid Structure by directly juxtaposing Zion and Babylon and their ideologies and by personalizing them in their respective king figures. Isaianic concepts and themes that are developed progressively and meticulously in the Bifid Structure are summed up in the Servant–Tyrant Parallelism in a matter of a few verses.

Summary

Section IV parallels a large number of oracles against foreign powers (chaps. 13–23) with a single oracle against Babylon and a part of one verse that emphasizes Zion's deliverance (46:13c–47:15). Such a one-sided structuring (paralleling the first unit with the second) helps establish the idea of an arch Babylon that consists of a composite of non-Zion entities. Key references to Babylon in the first unit of section IV, a common catastrophic context for Babylon and the nations, and literary and historical ties that mark Babylon as an arch entity support the structurally connoted merger of the nations and of the Lord's wicked people with Babylon. This Babylon composite is the antithesis of and stands in opposition to Zion. The Lord's exaltation of Zion and humiliation of Babylon color a reversal of circumstances between these two arch entities.

Section IV's establishment of an arch Babylon draws upon several cumulative concepts, including a reversal of circumstances developed in section I between Israel and the nations, the coexistence in

170

section II of two contrasting peoples and their kings, and the idea of a single, composite entity made up of a number of historical types described in section III. By corporatizing the idea of a composite entity found in section III, and by juxtaposing that entity with Zion as in section II, section IV, in effect, modifies or redefines the reversal of circumstances established in section I between Israel and the nations.

A cyclical pattern present throughout the text, based on Isaianic Zion ideology, confirms that arch Babylon's makeup as a composite entity flows out of its antithesis of and opposition to Zion. Zion ideology thus assists in defining a Babylon ideology in which Babylon and her king typify arch rivalry of the Lord and of Zion. The king of Babylon, a typologically composite figure, serves as a paradigm of Babylon's anti-Lord and anti-Zion ideology, consistent with similar concepts established in sections II and III.

Two alternative destinies for humanity—humiliation and exaltation—emerge from the ideological polarity between the two arch entities and their rulers: a chaotic Babylon and her king, exalting themselves above all, suffer ignominy and extirpation in the Lord's day of vengeance; a nascent Zion, humbled by Babylon's oppression, obtains deliverance and an exalted status in that day. The Servant–Tyrant Parallelism, a structure that juxtaposes Babylon and Zion and the king of Babylon and the king of Zion, exemplifies section IV's transformation of historical and other material to establish two opposing ideologies. The Servant–Tyrant Parallelism also affirms that arch Babylon's humiliation, which follows her self-exaltation, forms a twin aspect of Zion's exaltation, which, in turn, follows Zion's imposed humiliation. The Servant–Tyrant Parallelism's chiastic structure, which parallels the Bifid Structure's own chiastic arrangement, highlights the themes of humiliation and exaltation as two ultimate human conditions and as the central theme of both structures.

Passages from sections IV and V of the Bifid Structure that make up the Servant–Tyrant Parallelism evidence the thematic interdependence of these two bodies of material. Such interdependence extends not only to a contrast between Zion and arch Babylon but to the exaltation of Zion in section V that section IV cannot fully develop. Lastly, section IV's almost entire makeup of oracles against foreign powers makes it unique and facilitates the establishment of the concept of Babylon as a composite entity. Once established, the idea of such an ahistorical or latter-day arch entity is maintained in succeeding sections of the Bifid Structure.

SECTION V
SUFFERING & SALVATION
(24–27; 48–54)

Section V of the Bifid Structure ties a great confluence of concepts from previous sections into the central idea of the Lord's redemption of Zion. Through historical types and other literary devices, these cumulative concepts are modified or redefined in terms of suffering and salvation and a necessary interplay between the two. Section V, in fact, reveals the nature of suffering and salvation: some suffering takes the form of punishment or covenantal malediction, while some is redemptive and leads to the salvation of the Lord's people. Such suffering grows particularly intense just prior to the Lord's coming when he manifests his salvation in Zion.

Because suffering may actually fulfill a redemptive role, agents of divine redemption are seen to suffer. One historical type for such suffering, found in section III, is King Hezekiah, who endures a mortal illness while fulfilling the role of proxy for his people's deliverance (see Discourse B: Zion Ideology [1]—the Davidic Covenant). In section V, such agents of divine redemption consist of a latter-day Davidic king—the Lord's ideal vassal (who appears primarily under his spiritual, ministering aspect of the Servant figure)—and the Lord himself. The Servant figure's role is to implement the temporal salvation of the Lord's people, which he does principally by serving as their righteous proxy and exemplar, thus facilitating a new exodus out of Babylon. The Lord's role, on the other hand, is to personally effect the entire scope of his people's redemption, including such spiritual aspects of salvation as the remission of sins, the reversal of malediction, and the abolition of death.

While the first unit of section V deals with the salvation of the Lord's people within a context of Zion ideology, the second unit establishes a theological basis for Zion's salvation. A nuanced version of Zion's exaltation as presented in section IV, such salvation shows the interdependence of sections IV and V of the Bifid Structure. That interdependence appears most dramatically in the previously discussed Servant–Tyrant Parallelism, which draws on passages from both sections of material.

Cumulative Concepts

Section V of the Bifid Structure includes, as its first unit, the so-called Isaiah Apocalypse of chapters 24–27. This material poses problems for most scholars,[1] who consider it to be the work of an author later than Isaiah and who therefore question its position so early in the book. However, many questions scholars raise can be resolved by viewing chapters 24–27 from a literary standpoint as an integral part of the Bifid Structure. Viewed structurally, much of the first unit forms an aggregate of concepts established in previous sections. These concepts include a reversal of circumstances between Israel and the nations (section I); the coexistence of two antithetical peoples and their kings (section II); an ideal agent of the Lord's redemption made up of a composite of biblical types, who serves as a paradigm of the Lord's righteous people (section III); and an arch entity made up of a composite of historical types that is the rival of Zion (section IV).

These concepts can be summed up in two main ideas: (1) a reversal of circumstances between the Lord's righteous people Zion and a rival arch entity; and (2) an ideal agent of the Lord's redemption who serves as a paradigm of the Lord's righteous people. Underlying concepts consist of the ruin, punishment, and humiliation of a rebellious arch entity on the one hand and of the rebirth, deliverance, and exaltation of a covenantally compliant people of the Lord on the other. All such phenomena occur within an eschatological or latter-day time frame. Apart from section V's own conceptual development, which we will explore after the following summary, the first unit (chaps. 24–27) conforms fully with this aggregate of cumulative concepts.

Taken individually, the cumulative themes of ruin, punishment, and humiliation in the first unit, for example, characterize an arch

---

[1] See Helmer Ringgren, "Some Observations on Style and Structure in the Isaiah Apocalypse," *ASTI* 9 (1973): 107–15; Richard J. Coggins, "The Problem of Isaiah 24–27," *Exp Tim* 90 (1978–79): 328–33.

entity that comprehends all wicked entities worldwide.[2] We observe universal ruin in the Lord's cataclysmic destruction of the earth and the world, entities that form the main subject of the first unit:[3] the earth shakes to its foundation, gets crushed and rent, breaks up and caves in, convulses and lurches, reels to and fro like a drunkard (24:18–20); the Lord lays the earth to waste and empties it, disfigures its surface and scatters its inhabitants (24:1); when the earth is sacked, it is utterly ravaged (24:3).[4] Universal punishment occurs when the Lord's retribution falls upon humanity and upon the earth's/the world's inhabitants, entities that form the second main subject of this material:[5] on account of men's guilt and transgressions, the population of the earth diminishes and little of humanity remains (24:5–6); the Lord comes out of his dwelling place to punish the inhabitants of the earth for their iniquities (26:21); the Lord punishes Leviathan with his sword, slaying the dragons of the *Sea* (27:1).[6] Universal humiliation appears in the consignment of the high ones of heaven and earth to a low estate: the Lord renders wretched the elite inhabitants of the earth (24:4); he herds the hosts on high and rulers on earth together like prisoners to a dungeon (24:21–22); when the Lord manifests his glory on Mount Zion, the moon blushes and the sun is put to shame (24:23).[7]

The Lord singles out for ruin, punishment, and humiliation an anonymous "city"—a city of chaos (*tōhû*, 24:10), high and exalted (*ni'sgābâ*, 26:5),[8] entrenched (*běṣûrâ*, 25:2; 27:10), but cast down (*hešaḥ*), laid low (*yašpîlennâ*), to the ground (*'ad 'ereṣ yaggî-'ennâ*), even with the dust (*'ad 'āpār*, 26:5). Rhetorically synonymous with the city appears proud Moab, whose place of habitation, like the city, is high and exalted (*ni'sgab*), entrenched

---

[2] Compare arch Babylon in section IV as composed of Babylon, the earth and the world, the hosts of heaven, nations and alliances of nations, aggressive world powers, Assyria, the tyrants and oppressors of the earth, rulers and men of power, enemies and adversaries, *Sea* and *River*, and the Lord's wicked people.

[3] See the earth and the world, 24:1, 3–6, 11, 13, 16–21; 25:8; 26:9, 18–19, 21; 27:2, 6.

[4] See also universal ruin in 24:4, 7–12; 25:2, 10–12; 26:5–6, 14; 27:7–10.

[5] See humanity and the earth's/the world's inhabitants, 24:1, 5–6, 17; 26:9, 18, 21.

[6] See also universal punishment in 24:17–18, 20–22; 25:5; 26:11, 14, 16, 20–21; 27:4, 7–8, 12.

[7] See also universal humiliation in 25:2–3, 5, 10–12; 26:5–6, 11, 13–14; 27:8.

[8] Elsewhere, the term *ni'sgab* describes the Lord (cf. 2:11, 17; 12:4; 33:5), signifying, rhetorically, an anti-Lord ideology in 26:5.

(*mibṣar*), but cast down (*hešaḥ*), laid low (*hišpîl*), to the ground (*higgîaʿ lāʾāreṣ*), even with the dust (*ʿad ʿāpār*, 25:12).

Two instances of the pattern of Zion ideology bracket the destruction of Moab and the anonymous city: when the Lord's *hand* rests in "this mountain" (25:10), the Lord saves his people (25:9); but proud Moab goes into the dust (25:11–12). When the nation of *righteousness* (*ṣaddîq*) enters to take refuge in the Lord (26:2–4), the Lord grants salvation in "our city" (26:1); but the elite inhabitants of the exalted city go into the dust (26:5). Rhetorically and typologically, therefore, Moab and the exalted city represent synonymous entities.

The exalted city, however, shares a common identity with other entities in the first unit, not just with Moab. We observe that identity in the city's mutual suffering with them of covenantal malediction. Within that maledictory context, the city identifies with a progressively narrowing series of corporate entities, beginning with the earth and its inhabitants: a curse that overtakes the earth and its inhabitants (24:6), in the form of the silencing of joyful sounds and a lack of wine (24:8–9),[9] repeats itself upon the city and its silence of joy and lack of wine (24:11). The curse passage itself commences with curses upon the earth and its inhabitants, in the form of destruction by fire and withering vegetation (24:6–7), continues with the previously named curses in common, and concludes with curses upon the city in the form of destruction of gates and dwelling places (24:10, 12). Two references in this passage to "the city" (*qiryāʾ ʿîr*, 24:10, 12) are interjected by a reference to "the earth" (*ʾāreṣ*, 24:11).[10] This a₁–b–a₂ structure again connotes an identity of the city with the earth and its inhabitants.

A second passage defines the city as "heathen mansions" or "a citadel of aliens" (*ʾarmôn zārîm*, 25:2) as well as a "city [or community] of tyrannous nations" (*qiryat gôyîm ʿārîṣîm*, 25:3). The rendering of the city into ruins (*mappēlâ*) and a heap (*gāl*), the citadel of aliens never to be rebuilt (25:2), forms a single covenant curse that equates the city with the heathen. A third reference to the city identifies it rhetorically and typologically with Moab, as

---

[9] See these and the following curses in Fensham, "Common Trends."

[10] See also the parallel terms *ʿîr* and *qiryâ* in 25:2 and their separate recurrence in 26:5 and 27:10. The term *earth* (*ʾāreṣ*), which appears sixteen times in chapter 24, does so evenly before and after the city passage.

we have seen. Moab's pride and aggression (25:11) manifest enmity toward Israel by a kindred people. The common fate that Moab and the city suffer—the overthrowing of dwelling places (25:12; 26:5) and trampling underfoot (25:10; 26:6)—again denotes covenantal malediction.

A final reference to the city narrows down its identity to Jacob (27:9). The text cites Jacob's apostasy, which takes the form of idolatry (27:9),[11] as a cause of curses upon the city. These curses include the habitation of the city's ruins by animals (27:10) and the withering of vegetation (27:11). The text sums up Jacob and the city as an undiscerning people, to whom their Maker shows no mercy (*lō> yĕraḥamennû*), whom their Creator does not favor (*lō> yĕḥunnennû*, 27:11). Both expressions denote a broken covenant relationship.[12]

The anonymous *city* in the first unit thus identifies with a wide spectrum of typological entities, including the earth and its inhabitants, alien nations, proud kindred peoples, and the wicked of the Lord's people. These entities represent essentially the same ones that form arch Babylon in section IV (see footnote 2). The theme of covenantal malediction that identifies the *city* with other reprobate entities shows that the *city* metaphor in the first unit of section V modifies a historically based arch Babylon in section IV. The *city*, in effect, redefines the idea of a rebellious (anti-Lord) arch entity whom the Lord ruins, punishes, and humiliates.

Also consistent with cumulative concepts, the first unit of section V juxtaposes the Lord's righteous people with the entities that comprise the anonymous *city*. We see that juxtaposition in a reversal of covenantal malediction for the Lord's people. As with the ruin, punishment, and humiliation of the rebellious *city*, moreover, so the counter phenomenon of the rebirth, deliverance, and exaltation of the Lord's compliant people assumes worldwide proportions. We observe the universality of that reversal in the grape vines of the earth languishing (24:6–7), while the Lord's fruitful vineyard, hitherto a fruitless national locale (cf. 5:1–7), extends to the

---

[11] The Canaanite nature of that idolatry, as well as references to Moab (25:10), Egypt (27:12), and Assyria (27:13), suggests a preexilic, Judaic origin for this material; 27:12–13, on the other hand, reflects an exilic context so far as the Northern Kingdom is concerned.

[12] See Weinfeld, "Berîth," 258. Compare *ḥannûn* ("gracious") and *raḥûm* ("merciful") as covenantal attributes of the Lord, Exod 34:6; Psa 86:15; Joel 2:13.

world (27:2–6). The Lord's punitive vintage and threshing of the nations (24:13; 27:12) is survived by an Israel whom the Lord gleans from the torrent of the River (Assyria) to the streams of Egypt (24:13–15; 27:12–13). The enemies of his people, the Lord utterly banishes (27:7–8); but his lost and outcast people, the Lord restores from exile (27:13). The elite and proud of the earth, the Lord lays low in the dust (25:10–12; 26:5); but his lowly ones, the Lord revives and raises from the dust (25:8–9; 26:19).

The Lord punishes those who misrule in the earth (24:21–22; 27:7), but he delivers his poor and needy (25:4, 9; 26:3, 6). Terrors, pitfalls, and traps overtake the inhabitants of the earth (24:17–18), but to his people the Lord is a refuge in the day of calamity (25:4; 27:2–5). The dead lords of the nations do not rise and live again (26:14), but the Lord's dead rise and live when the earth casts up its dead (26:19).[13] The Lord deposes the earth's rulers in disgrace (24:21–22; 26:13–14), but he exalts his righteous ones in the earth (24:16; 26:15). The Lord counters a universal lack of wine (24:9, 11) by a sumptuous feast of cakes and wine for the righteous of all peoples (25:6). A universal cessation of joy (24:7–9, 11) sees an exception in the renewed joy and singing of the Lord's people throughout the earth (24:14–16; 25:9; 26:19; 27:2).[14] The Lord destroys the wicked city (24:10, 12; 25:2; 26:5; 27:10), but he saves the righteous city (26:1–4).

We thus observe that the first unit of section V forms an integral part of concepts the Bifid Structure has developed. These concepts include, first of all, a reversal of circumstances between the Lord's righteous people and a rival arch entity. That reversal manifests itself in the ruin, punishment, and humiliation of a rebellious arch entity and in the rebirth, deliverance, and exaltation of the Lord's compliant people. Cumulative concepts include, by way of metaphor, an ideal latter-day agent of the Lord's redemption who serves as

---

[13] The above two passages, 26:14 and 26:19, use the identical verbs *ḥyh* and *qwm*. J. Wyngaards notes the covenantal aspects of death and resurrection in "Death and Resurrection in Covenantal Context," *VT* 17 (1967): 226–39. That covenantal aspect agrees with the present context of a reversal of malediction for the Lord's people. See also the prophetic literalness of resurrection that Joseph E. Coleson documents in "Israel's Life Cycle from Birth to Resurrection," *Israel's Apostasy and Restoration*, 237–50.

[14] The motif of joy links all passages in chapters 24–27 in which the Lord's people are the subject.

a paradigm of the Lord's righteous people,[15] and also an archtyrant, this Davidic figure's rival.[16]

Discourse G: The Composite City

Rhetorical analysis of the terms *'îr* and *qiryâ* throughout Isaiah,[17] both of which translate "city," reveals a climactic development of the *city* motif. That development supports the idea that the *city* may represent a wicked arch entity that is juxtaposed with Zion. Chapter 1 introduces the reprobate city in a lament:

> 21. How the faithful city has become a harlot!
>   She was filled with justice;
>   righteousness made its abode in her,
>   but now murderers.

The Lord deals with the city, first, by avenging his "enemies" (1:24). The text depicts that act allegorically as the Lord's smelting away of dross and alloy (1:25). Second, the Lord restores a righteous political government (1:26) in place of the corrupt one (1:23). The Lord initiates this cleansing of his people by restoring his *hand* over them (1:25). The passage continues:

> 26c. After this you shall be called the City of Righteousness,
>   a faithful city.
> 27. For Zion shall be ransomed by justice,
>   those of her who repent by righteousness.
> 28. But criminals and sinners shall be altogether shattered
>   when those who forsake the Lord are annihilated.

Within this context of Zion ideology, the Lord ransoms the city of *righteousness*—Zion, or those who repent/return—while he destroys murderers, enemies, sinners, and criminals. The same thing applies to the city of Zion in 1:8: when Zion comes "under siege" (*nĕṣûrâ*),

---

[15] See the metaphorical pseudonyms, respectively, of the Lord's [right] *hand* (25:10) and *righteousness* (24:16; 26:2, 7, 9–10).

[16] See the metaphorical pseudonyms of the Lord's [left] *hand* (26:11) and *wrath* (26:20), as well as *Sea* (27:1) and *River* (27:12).

[17] The terms *'îr* and *qiryâ* appear interchangeably throughout Isaiah, though the former predominates.

the Lord "preserves" her (*něṣûrâ*), her survivors becoming as those who escape the destruction of Sodom and Gomorrah (1:9). Chapter 1's dichotomy of the Lord's dealings with his people—the Lord's destroying the wicked elements of the city and his passing through the fire and ransoming those who repent/return—eventually gives way to two distinct cities in Isaiah, one wicked and one righteous.

A passage in chapter 22 makes the transition toward this division. It depicts a city of revelry (*qiryâ ʿallîzâ*), a tumultuous city (*ʿîr hômîyâ*, 22:2), which forms a part of arch Babylon developed in section IV. Although rhetorically the city is still the "city of David" (22:9), within its context the city appears anonymously (22:2), as if to denote an alien entity. Enemies batter down the city's walls; they trample its inhabitants underfoot (22:5). For some people, however, a Davidic "servant"—Eliakim—provides surety (22:22-24). The Davidic connection answers, rhetorically, the idea of an inviolable city of David.

Next, we have the anonymous "city of chaos" (*qiryat tōhû*, 24:10). That expression, and the city's description as exalted (26:5), entrenched (25:2; 27:10), a citadel of aliens (25:2), and so forth, portrays an entity that can no longer be reclaimed by appealing to repentance. We observe this foreboding also in the way the text juxtaposes the doomed exalted city (26:5) with "our city" (26:1)—the habitation of the righteous whom the Lord preserves (26:2-4). Those who keep faith with the Lord experience *salvation* in the city and enjoy a perfect peace (26:1, 3). They live to tread the dust of the chaotic city underfoot (26:6) as the Lord makes it a desolation (24:12), a forsaken habitation (27:10), a ruin, a heap, and "no city" (25:2).

Chapter 29 depicts Ariel, the city of David, as an "altar hearth" (*ʾărîêl*) during a siege (29:2-3). A dichotomy of thought surrounding the city prevails through the remainder of the city passage. On the one hand, the Lord lays the city low in the dust (29:4). Its crowds of evildoers (*hămôn zēdāyîk*),[18] its violent mobs (*hămôn ʿārîsîm*), become dust and flying chaff in a fiery conflagration (29:5-6). Zion,[19] on the other hand, remains inviolable

---

[18] So 1QIsaᵃ; LXX. MT reads *zārāyîk* ("aliens").

[19] An a₁–b₁–b₂–a₂ structure in chapter 29 shows the city in this passage to be Mount Zion, as follows: the nations fight against Ariel, verse 7; a hungry man dreams he eats, verse 8a; a thirsty man dreams he drinks, verse 8b; the nations fight against Mount Zion, verse 8c.

against all nations who amass against her; these nations vanish overnight, as if they were a dream (29:7-8). The chapter then restates the above dichotomy:

> 19. The lowly shall obtain an increase of joy in the Lord,
> and the poorest of men rejoice
> in the Holy One of Israel.
> 20. But tyrants shall come to nought and scorners cease;
> all who persist in wickedness shall be cut off.

A final reference to a wicked city combines the motifs of a city of revelry (*qiryâ ʿallîzâ*, 32:13), a citadel (*ʾarmôn*), and a tumultuous city (*hămôn ʿîr*, 32:14). That imagery denotes, contextually, a habitation of the godless, rogues, and carefree ones among the Lord's people (32:5-12). The Lord levels the city by flattening or abasement (*baššiplâ tišpal hāʿîr*, 32:19), and it becomes a place forsaken, the habitation of wild animals (32:14). The same passage, however, juxtaposes the wicked city with the Lord's righteous people. It depicts the latter as dwelling in an abode of peace (*něwēh šālôm*), a peaceable habitation (*měnûḥôt šaʾănannôt*, 32:18). Using this same imagery, the following chapter identifies the righteous city rhetorically as Zion/Jerusalem—a city of solemn assemblies (*qiryat môʿădēnû*), an abode of peace (*nāweh šaʾănān*, 33:20). This juxtaposition of two cities, both of which originate with the Lord's people, thus appears cumulatively, though briefly, beyond chapters 24-27. That the motif of a wicked city now ends, however, signifies that ultimately the righteous city prevails over its chaotic counterpart.

The motif of a threatened city reappears in 36:15, though the city (Zion/Jerusalem) proves inviolable for David's sake (37:33-35; cf. 38:6). Next, the Lord personalizes the city the Cyrus figure builds as "my city" (*ʿîrî*, 45:13; cf. 44:28). The "holy city" (*ʿîr haqqōdeš*, 52:1) continues a series of narrowing definitions of the motif. The city (Zion/Jerusalem) puts on garments of glory and rises from the dust and from captivity (52:1-2). Zion further appears as the "city of the Lord" (*ʿîr yhwh*), the site of his sanctuary and place of his feet (60:13-14). Finally, Zion represents the holy people, those whom the Lord redeems, a city sought for and not forsaken (62:12).

The *city* of chapters 24-27 thus forms a constituent part of a motif whose development commences prior to this unit and culminates beyond it. The wicked city, moreover, which goes into the dust, is the antithesis of a righteous city that rises from the dust and prevails—Zion.[20] These identities suggest that throughout Isaiah the term *city* subsumes, metaphorically, the archetypes Zion and Babylon. That idea finds support even where the city represents the Lord's wicked people, and in that the city becomes two cities from chapters 24–27.

Universal Distress and Universal Salvation

Apart from cumulative themes, the idea of suffering, distress, and agony pervades the first unit.[21] We observe this suffering in the harsh terms used to describe conditions on the earth, viz., batter, blast, crush, raze, ravage, rent, sack, convulse, disfigure, waste away; ruthless, severe, bitter; tears, reproach, gloom, havoc; etc. The distress that the text depicts so graphically occurs worldwide and encompasses both Israel and non-Israel: the earth pines away and the world miserably perishes (24:4); the elite of the earth become wretched (24:4); the inhabitants of the earth who flee at the sound of terror, fall into a pit, and those who get up out of the pit are caught in a trap (24:18); the Lord's people remember the Lord in their distress, pouring out silent prayers when his chastisements come upon them (26:16); like a woman giving birth, who cries out from her pangs, so do the Lord's people at the time the Lord comes (26:17).

The text points to the cause of distress as people's wickedness and rebelliousness: the curse devours the earth because its inhabitants transgress the Lord's law (24:5–6); though the Lord shows favor to the wicked, they do not learn righteousness—in a land of uprightness they remain perverse (26:10); the Lord lifts up his *hand*, but people do not perceive it; too late, they perceive the Lord's zeal for his people when the fire prepared for the Lord's enemies consumes them (26:11).[22]

Although the Lord's people, too, endure distress, a remnant finds hope in the Lord. The latter's preservation contrasts sharply with the rest of humanity: those whose minds are steadfast through

---

[20] See a similar antithesis between Babylon and Zion in the prologue of the Servant–Tyrant Parallelism, section IV, figure 13.

[21] See suffering, 24:1–12, 16–22; 25:2–5, 7–8, 10–12; 26:11, 14, 16–18, 20–21; 27:1, 4, 7–8, 12.

[22] See also wickedness in 24:16de, 20; 25:4c–5; 26:18, 20–21; 27:4, 9–11.

trials, the Lord preserves in perfect peace (26:3); but the oppressors of his people, the Lord appoints to destruction, wiping out all recollection of them (26:13–14). The Lord does not smite his people as he does their smiters, nor slay them as he does their slayers (27:7); the Lord flings his people's enemies far away by his fierce and burning blasts (27:8).[23]

A righteous remnant of the Lord's people ultimately boasts of salvation. Five Songs of Salvation (24:14–15; 25:1–5, 9; 26:1–6; 27:2–6) follow, respectively, passages that depict (1) calamity upon the inhabitants of the earth (24:1–12), (2) cataclysm upon the earth and in the heavens (24:19–23), (3) the abolition of death (25:7–8),[24] (4) the destruction of Moab (25:10–12), and (5) punishment of the earth's inhabitants and Leviathan (26:21–27:1).[25] The songs' contexts suggest that salvation for the Lord's people, like the distress that precedes it, occurs universally. The saved remnant hails from across the sea, from the regions of sunrise, from the isles of the sea (24:14–15), from among all nations, and from throughout the earth (25:6–9; 27:6, 12–13).

The contradistinction between those who suffer distress without hope and those whom the Lord saves out of distress is analogous to the covenantal malediction that overtakes a composite *city* and the reversal of malediction that the Lord's righteous people experience. The criteria for salvation, on one hand, and for a hopeless distress ending in destruction, on the other, are thus covenantal righteousness and unrighteousness. Those who experience salvation are righteous because they keep faith with the Lord through a period of trial (26:1–4). The inhabitants of the earth nonetheless incur malediction when they transgress the Lord's law, change his ordinances, and set at nought his ancient covenant (24:5–6).

The first unit's emphasis on the covenantal nature of calamities befalling the earth and its inhabitants is significant. The Lord's

---

[23] See also hope for the Lord's people in 24:13–16, 23; 25:1, 4–9; 26:1–4, 6–12, 15–16, 19–20; 27:2–9, 12–13; and no hope for the rest of humanity in 24:1–12, 17–22; 25:2–3, 10–12; 26:5–6, 10–11, 21; 27:1, 4, 7–8, 10–11.

[24] See victory over the forces of chaos that 25:7–8 signifies, in William R. Millar, *Isaiah 24–27 and the Origin of Apocalyptic* (Missoula, Mont.: Scholars Press, 1976), 87.

[25] See the idea of chaos or evil that the name *Leviathan* connotes, in Cyrus H. Gordon, "Leviathan: Symbol of Evil," in A. Altmann, ed., *Biblical Motifs* (Cambridge: Harvard University, 1966), 1–9.

wicked people, by assimilating into a universal, composite *city*, in effect, become a direct cause for the inhabitants of the earth suffering covenantal malediction. The Lord's punishment of the inhabitants of the earth for transgressing Israel's law, changing its ordinances, and nullifying the Lord's covenant presupposes that the earth's inhabitants, or at least many of them, are part of Israel and thus possess an obligation toward the Lord's covenant.[26]

Several passages support these conceptualizations. First, we have the premise that salvation, as experienced universally, comes by virtue of covenantal righteousness. Yet, the Lord's people admit that they have not wrought salvation in the earth in order that its inhabitants might not "fall away" or "abort" (*yiplû*, 26:18). Such a confession implies that the Lord has invested Israel with a spiritual mission toward the inhabitants of the earth. That mission, though largely ineffectual, nonetheless aims to bring about humanity's salvation (cf. 42:18–19; 43:10–13).

Second, two components of a parallel structure state: "In the passage of thy rites/precepts (*mišpāṭekâ*) we anticipate thee, O Lord . . . for when thy rites/precepts (*mišpāṭekâ*) are on the earth, the inhabitants of the world learn righteousness" (26:8a, 9c).[27] These statements affirm that the inhabitants of the earth are being taught righteousness based on performances pertaining to the Lord's covenant with Israel. Allegorically, on the other hand, these statements imply that the Lord's ideal vassal, who personifies *righteousness* (26:9c), funtions universally as the Lord's lawgiver and forerunner[28] as well as a paradigm of righteousness.

The larger context of this passage contains a unique example of Zion ideology: among common elements, the text cites covenantal

---

[26] Rhetorical definitions of the terms *law* and *covenant* in Isaiah suggest that it is the Lord's law and covenant with Israel that are spoken of in 24:5; see 2:3; 8:16; 42:21; 56:4, 6; 61:8; *passim*. Since the Lord's ideal vassal also personifies the Lord's *covenant* to the nations (42:6; 49:8), their setting at nought the *covenant* further implies their rejection of the Lord's latter-day agent of redemption.

[27] An a–b–b–a structure in chapter 26 parallels the two lines just quoted, as follows: the Lord's rites/precepts, verse 8a; the soul's desire for the Lord, verses 8b and 9ab; and the Lord's rites/precepts, verse 9c. The Lord's rites or precepts, as in rites of passage, thus lead directly to the Lord himself.

[28] See also the pairing of the person of the Davidic king—the Lord's ideal vassal—with the Lord's theophany in the threefold pattern of Zion ideology (Discourse E: Zion Ideology [2]—Deliverance and Destruction). Such pairing suggests that the Lord's vassal is instrumental in facilitating the Lord's manifestation of his presence.

righteousness and unrighteousness, respectively, as criteria for salvation or destruction. The three common elements of Zion ideology are, first, the presence of *righteousness* (26:9–10), alias the Lord's *hand* (26:11), in a "land of uprightness" or "proving-ground" (*'ereṣ nĕkōḥôt*), where the Lord's glory dwells (26:10);[29] second, the Lord's salvation of his people (26:12, 15); and third, the destruction of enemies (26:11, 14). Those whom the Lord saves are righteous because they follow the straight "path" or "passage" (*'ōraḥ*) of his ordinances (26:7–8); they seek the Lord day and night (26:8–9). Their salvation enlarges or adds to (*ysp*) the nation of the Lord's people and transcends worldly boundaries (26:15). Those whom the Lord destroys are described as wicked and "dead" (26:10, 14); these do not learn righteousness but remain perverse, even when an exemplar of righteousness dwells among them (26:10–11).

Another passage describes those whom the Lord gleans from among the nations as "they" (*hēmmâ*) who shout for joy and give glory to the Lord, the God of Israel, at the time his "vintage" (judgment) of the earth ends (24:13–15). Within that context appears the statement "from a sector of the earth we hear singing: Glory to the righteous/righteous one!" (*ṣĕbî laṣṣaddîq*, 24:16ab). The juxtaposition of the pronouns *we* and *they*, as well as the mention of Israel's God in connection with the latter (24:15), implies that some who are abroad in the earth convert to the Lord.[30]

The remainder of the passage bears out this conclusion, as those in the category of *we* express surprise at the salvation of others: "Whereas I thought, I am wasting away; I am weakening: woe is me; the traitors have been treacherous, the turncoats have deceitfully betrayed!" (24:16cd). Those whom the text identifies as *we* (24:16a)—a local entity of the Lord's people—anticipate nothing but treachery from the nations of the earth, from among whom *they*—a universal entity of the Lord's people—are gleaned (cf. 27:12–13). The term *righteous* or *righteous one* (*ṣaddîq*) in this passage (24:16) denotes, rhetorically, both the ideal latter-day vassal (cf. 41:26; 53:11)—who serves as an exemplar and paradigm of the Lord's

---

[29] See, rhetorically, the place where the Lord manifests his glory or presence as Zion/Jerusalem, 24:23; 46:13; 60:1–2; *passim*.

[30] The idea of Israel's returnees from exile bowing down to the Lord in 27:13 further suggests conversion. Hollenberg, who argues for such conversion in chapters 40–55, sees this as the mission of the Servant, Hollenberg, "Nationalism and 'The Nations.'"

righteous remnant—and the Lord's remnant itself (cf. 3:10; 60:21), the antithesis of the traitors who betray the Lord's people (24:16). A final passage describes a nation of the righteous or righteous one (*gôy ṣaddîq*, 26:2). These keep faith and trust in the Lord through a period of trial (26:2–4). They enter the gates that those already in the Lord's city open for them (26:1–2). This further example of those at home and those abroad who experience the Lord's salvation is part of yet another instance of the pattern of Zion ideology in which the term *ṣaddîq* represents the Lord's ideal latter-day vassal. As in similar instances of Zion ideology in the first unit, salvation thus occurs not only because the Lord's people or the inhabitants of the earth practice righteousness but because the Lord's ideal vassal, who serves as a righteous proxy for his people, personally occasions the Lord's salvation. This latter dimension of salvation— the role that the Lord's vassal fulfills—gains significance in the second unit.

Suffering and Redemption

The second unit of section V (chaps. 48–54) similarly consists of an aggregate of cumulative concepts besides those peculiar to itself. This material, however, counters the first unit's emphasis on universal ruin, rebellion, punishment, humiliation, and suffering by stressing Zion's rebirth, compliance, deliverance, exaltation, and salvation.

Both sets of themes nonetheless appear in each unit. In the second unit, for example, we find the heavens clothed with the blackness of mourning (50:3) and vanishing from view through smoke (51:6); the earth wearing away like a garment, its inhabitants perishing like vermin (51:6); mountains and hills collapsing and moving out of place (54:10); people turned into grass (51:12); the sea and rivers drying up (50:2; 51:10), their fish perishing of thirst (50:2); Babylon suffering defeat (48:14); rulers and tyrants being humbled (49:7, 25); oppressors eating and drinking their own flesh and blood (49:26; 51:21–23); mockers and disputers incurring plagues (50:9; 51:8); mobs being slain (54:15); the sinners of the Lord's people selling themselves (50:1); the reprobate of Israel being cut off (48:19); desolation, ruin, famine, the sword, and captivity coming as a curse upon the Lord's wicked people (51:19–20); and the pseudo-righteous of the Lord's people agonizing at the Lord's judgments (50:11).

Calamity thus overtakes essentially the same universal entities that make up arch Babylon and the wicked *city* in prior material. Whereas the wicked city does not appear in the second unit because of a climactic development of the city motif in the Book of Isaiah as a whole, Babylon appears cumulatively as an arch entity from which the Lord delivers his people.

Those who comply with the Lord's admonition to flee Babylon (48:20) and come out of her (52:11) participate in a new exodus (48:21; 52:12). The exodus determines whom the Lord saves when Babylon falls. The new exodus involves Jacob/Israel's exiting Babylon when the announcement goes forth to the end of the earth that the Lord has redeemed his servant Jacob (48:20; cf. 52:9–11). The expression "end of the earth" (*qĕṣēh hā'āreṣ*, 48:20) denotes the universal nature of this call[31] and thus the universality of both Babylon and the exodus (cf. 49:12, 22). The Lord's salvation, in other words, extends to the end of the earth (*qĕṣēh hā'āreṣ*), and no one is excluded who responds to the Lord's call (49:6).

As in the first unit, cumulative redemptive themes appear upon the Lord's reversing malediction universally for his people. We observe such a reversal of malediction when the Lord restores his law and word to the nations (51:4),[32] refines the house of Jacob for his name's sake (48:10–11), calls his people from afar, like Abraham (51:2; cf. 41:8–9), releases his people from captivity and from bands (49:9, 24–25; 51:14; 52:2), restores his exiles to Zion (49:5–6, 12, 18, 22; 51:11; 52:11–12), sustains the exiles on their return (49:9–10), rebuilds and resettles Zion's ruins (49:8, 19; 51:3; 52:9; 54:3), causes Zion's ravagers and devourers to depart (49:17, 19), ends fear for his righteous people (54:4, 14), restores peace to Zion (52:7; 54:13), restores compassion and comforts to his people (49:13; 51:3; 52:9; 54:7–8, 10), renews joy and rejoicing among his people (49:13; 51:3, 11; 52:9; 54:1), expands Zion's dwelling places (49:20; 54:2–3), regenerates Zion's land (51:3), protects Zion (51:16, 22;

---

[31] See the expression *qĕṣēh hā'āreṣ* (in the singular) to denote, rhetorically, the isles, 42:10; the four directions, 43:5–6; the nations, 49:6; and Zion in exile among the nations, 62:10–11. Compare the declarations "Turn to me and be saved, all you ends of the earth!" (*'apsê 'āreṣ*), 45:22, and "the Lord has bared his holy *arm* in the eyes of all nations, that all ends of the earth (*kol 'apsê 'āreṣ*) may see our God's *salvation*," 52:10.

[32] See also the going forth of the Lord's law and word elsewhere in the second unit, 48:16–18; 50:4; 51:4, 7, 16; 54:13.

187

54:14–17), delivers Zion's children (49:17–22; 51:2; 54:1, 13), returns to rule over Zion (52:6–8, 12), chooses Zion as his bride (49:18; 54:5), causes all flesh to behold Zion's redemption (49:26; 52:10), empowers, enthrones, and exalts Zion (52:1–2), causes Zion's offspring to dispossess the nations (54:3), and beautifies Zion's land with precious stones (54:11–12).[33]

The growing prominence of Zion in this material occurs in direct proportion to the Lord's implementing the redemption of his people. Zion, the Lord's righteous people, epitomizes rebirth, compliance, deliverance, exaltation, and salvation—even as arch Babylon does the contrary.

As in the first unit, both the righteous and the wicked suffer. Now, however, suffering turns from the righteous to the wicked— those who contend with, oppress, and revile Zion. The Servant figure, moreover, who features prominently throughout the second unit, also suffers. The Servant figure represents that cumulative aspect of the Lord's ideal vassal—the Lord's agent of redemption— that originally fulfills a spiritual, ministering function toward Jacob/ Israel (see section III). In exercising that role, he, like his people, endures suffering. His role of physically subduing enemies is kept in abeyance until the Lord endows him with power (cf. 48:14–15; 49:5–8; 51:9). The nature of the Servant figure's suffering nonetheless differs from the suffering that Zion and non-Zion endure. Because the second unit stresses the relationship between the Servant figure's suffering and the Lord's redemption of Zion, the suffering of non-Zion entities, who include the wicked of the Lord's people, receives less emphasis.

As in the first unit, the suffering that the Lord's righteous people endure is infused with hope. We note this in the verse, "I am refining you, though not as silver; I am testing[34] you in the crucible of affliction" (48:10). Although the Lord cuts off (*krt*) from his people many who do not participate in the new exodus (48:19), he does not cut off (*krt*) those whom he refines through affliction (48:9). The latter live to participate in the exodus out of arch Babylon (48:20). For them, a reversal of

---

[33] Compare the opposites of these covenant blessings—the covenant curses—in Deut 28:25, 32–33, 41, 48, 51, 64–67; Fensham, "Common Trends," 158–59, 164–72.

[34] So 1QIsaᵃ; MT reads "choosing."

malediction commences, substantially, at the new exodus (48:21).[35] Nonparticipants in the new exodus—the wicked—on the other hand, inherit a state of no peace (48:22). The idea of "no peace" (ʾēn šālôm), or no salvation,[36] sums up the hopeless suffering non-Zion endures. The same passage contrasts the condition of no peace the wicked suffer with the implied condition of the Lord's righteous: their peace compares to a river, their righteousness to the waves of the sea (48:18; cf. 66:12).[37]

Because the reversal of circumstances between Zion and non-Zion commences at the new exodus, the suffering of the Lord's righteous people occurs most prominently during conditions that prevail before the exodus. The text describes this situation as those in authority taking the Lord's people over (52:5), selling them for no price, before the Lord redeems them (52:3, 9); Zion/Jerusalem's drinking from the Lord's *hand* the cup of his *wrath* (51:17-21), before the Lord gives it into the *hand* of his people's tormentors (51:22-23); Zion, wretched, without consolation (51:19, 21), lying prostrate on the ground, her oppressors riding roughshod over her (51:23), before these same chastisements turn on Zion/Jerusalem's oppressors (51:22-23).

Further such examples of suffering before salvation include those who know *righteousness*, in whose heart abides the Lord's law, enduring reproach and ridicule, before the Lord destroys their revilers (51:7-8); Zion, afflicted, claiming to be forsaken and forgotten (49:13-14) and Zion bereaved, barren, exiled, and banished (49:21), before her children return to her from among the nations (49:17-22), before rulers adore her (49:22-23) and the Lord comforts her (49:13); the followers of *righteousness*, who seek the Lord, living solitary like Abraham, suffering barrenness like Sarah (51:1-2), before the Lord

---

[35] See curse reversals in Isaiah—within the context of a new exodus and a new wandering in the wilderness—as darkness turned to light (42:16), victory over enemies (43:14-17; 51:9-10), return from exile (49:10-12; 51:11; 52:11-12), flowing waters in the desert (43:19-20; 49:9-11), the restoration of ruins (44:26-28), and joy (49:11-13; 51:10-11; 52:8-12).

[36] See the parallelistic synonymity of peace and salvation in the rhetorical chain, "peace . . . salvation," 52:7; "salvation . . . light," 49:6; "light . . . covenant," 42:6; "covenant of peace," 54:10; *passim*.

[37] Because the terms *Sea* and *River* also serve as pseudomyms of the king of Assyria (cf. 5:30; 8:7), their present usage suggests that the king of Assyria, a power of chaos, is in the end subdued.

regenerates their wilderness and multiplies their posterity (51:2–3; cf. 54:1–3); Zion, fearful, reproached, and ashamed (54:4), being forsaken, rejected, and forlorn (54:6), before the Lord receives her back and espouses her anew (54:5); Zion, experiencing the Lord's displeasure (54:8), before she enjoys his loving compassion by an immutable covenant (54:7–10); Zion, living as a wretch, tempest-tossed and disconsolate (54:11), before the Lord blesses her with an endowed posterity (54:13), a bejewelled place of abode (54:11–12), and his divine protection (54:14–17).

In sum, Zion's suffering is not just infused with hope, but it portends an imminent reversal of covenant curses leading to her salvation and exaltation. The very context of covenantal malediction upon the wicked through which the Lord's people suffer turns—for Zion—into covenantal benediction when she endures her trials as a refiner's fire. Zion's suffering provides the setting in which the Lord redeems her, while non-Zion's suffering proves irreversible so long as those who comprise non-Zion do not repent/return.

Agents of Redemption

Although other sections of the Bifid Structure discuss the Lord's redemption of his people, section V differs from others in that it establishes a theological basis for the Lord's redemption in the second unit. The prominence this material gives to an agent or agents of redemption coincides with the idea of suffering, distress, and agony turning from the Lord's righteous people—Zion—to wicked entities, or non-Zion. Such a coincidence of ideas implies that divine intervention forms a necessary ingredient in the Lord's redemption of Zion. We observe this also in the nature of redemption itself—how the text defines it.

Rhetorical analysis of the term *redeem* ($g^{\jmath}l$) and its synonym *ransom* (*pdh*) in Isaiah[38] reveals that the Lord's redemption occurs gratis (52:3) when those who err in spirit convert to the Lord (29:22–24; 44:6–8). Redemption entails the Lord's removal of his people's sins (44:22) and happens when they repent/return and obey his commandments (1:27; 48:17–18; 59:20). The Lord's redemption of his people leads to arch Babylon's demise (47:4) and includes

---

[38] See the parallelistic synonymity of the terms *redeem* ($g^{\jmath}l$) and *ransom* (*pdh*), 35:9–10; 51:10–11.

being released from captivity (49:24–26), participating in a new exodus (43:14–17; 48:20–21; 50:2; 51:10–11; 52:9–12; 63:9–14), being immune to the elements (43:1–4), accepting a new covenant (54:5–10; 59:20–21), acceding to royal status (43:1; 44:21–22; 49:7–8; 52:1–3), obtaining power over enemies (41:14–16; 43:14–17; 47:1–4; 49:24–26), restoring ruins (44:24–28; 52:9), having offspring (48:17–19; 59:20–21), and enjoying plenitude (60:16).

The Lord's role as Redeemer of his people features prominently in Isaiah, starting from the second unit of section III. Such prominence means that deliverance, an idea that pervades section III, forms an integral part of the Lord's redemption. Those passages that identify the Lord as Redeemer, moreover, articulate his divine nature and attributes: "your Redeemer, the Holy One of Israel" (41:14; 43:14; 48:17); "the Lord, the King of Israel, the Lord of Hosts, their Redeemer" (44:6); "our Redeemer, the Holy One of Israel, whose name is the Lord of Hosts" (47:4); "your Redeemer, the Valiant One of Jacob" (49:26; 60:16); "your Redeemer, the Holy One of Israel, who is called the God of all the earth" (54:5); "the Lord, our Father, whose name is Our Redeemer from Eternity" (63:16). The divine nature of Israel's Redeemer, and therefore of redemption itself, impacts our entire understanding of the subject.

Most passages that discuss redemption use the verb *g'l*. Those that use the verb *pdh*, on the other hand, deal primarily with the deliverance aspect of the Lord's redemption (cf. 29:22; 51:10–11). By attributing the "ransoming" of the Lord's people to the Lord's *hand* (50:2) and *righteousness* (1:27), the text associates the deliverance aspect of redemption with the Lord's ideal latter-day vassal.

As in section III, where the Holy One of Israel performs curse reversals and the Lord's *hand* makes chaos of hostile powers (41:20), there appears a division of redemptive roles between the Lord and his vassal. Some aspects of redemption, such as the removal of sins, the reversal of malediction, the conferral of royal status, and an endowment of power, reflect a divine function, one that the Lord himself performs. Others, such as the release of the Lord's people from captivity and their new exodus (cf. 49:9; 51:9–11; 52:10–12), pertain to the Lord's ideal vassal and agent of deliverance, who appears cumulatively as the Servant figure.[39]

---

[39] The cumulative nature of the redemptive roles the Servant figure fulfills is evident in that the release of the Lord's people from captivity and their new exodus (in the second unit of section V) are functions attributed to the Cyrus figure in section III (cf. 44:27–28; 45:1–2, 13).

The Lord nonetheless redeems the Servant figure himself. The Lord names him "my servant, Israel, in whom I will be glorified" (49:1, 3). That description, because it also characterizes the Lord's corporate servant, Jacob/Israel, shows that the Lord's ideal vassal, in effect, personifies the Lord's people (cf. the Lord's calling both King David and his people Israel his "servant," "son," and "firstborn," Discourse B: Zion Ideology [1]—the Davidic Covenant). The Lord's naming his vassal "Israel," a royal accession motif, has a type and precedent in Jacob, whom the Lord named "Israel" (Gen 32:28; 35:10). Such a name accords with the vassal's cumulative role of exemplar and paradigm of the Lord's people and with his cumulative function as a proxy in obtaining their deliverance.[40] The Lord's naming his vassal, as we saw in section III, empowers him to perform a redemptive role: the Lord, the Redeemer of Israel, now delivers the Servant figure from adversaries (49:4, 7–8) and commissions him to deliver his people (49:5–6, 8–9).[41] In Isaiah, the title "Redeemer of Israel" (*gōʾēl yiʾsrāʾēl*, 49:7) is unique to this passage.

Rhetorical analysis of the term *save* (*yšʿ*) and its synonym *deliver* (*nṣl*)[42] also reveals a division of redemptive roles between the Lord and his ideal vassal. These generic terms show that salvation follows upon righteousness (64:5), occurs universally (45:22; 49:6), and is everlasting (45:17; 51:6). Salvation includes being released from captivity (19:20; 42:22; 43:13; 44:20; 49:25), obtaining an endowment of strength (33:6), gaining power over enemies (5:29; 20:6; 30:15; 36:14–20; 37:11–12), receiving divine protection (26:1; 31:5; 37:35; 38:6), and being delivered out of trouble (25:9; 36:14–20; 44:17; 46:7; 47:13–15; 57:13). Salvation occurs

---

[40] These cumulative roles by the Lord's vassal—of serving as a paradigm of the people, and as their righteous proxy—are attributed to the Righteous Warrior figure and to the Davidic king, respectively, in section III.

[41] An a–b–c–d–d–c–b–a structure attests to the integrity of 49:1–8 as a passage dealing with a single individual. Within this chiasm, verses 1 and 8 depict the Servant figure's royal accession; verses 2 and 7 emphasize his chosenness; verses 3 and 6 designate him as the Lord's "servant" and note his exalted status; and verses 4–5 describe the circumstances of his endowment of divine power.

[42] See the parallel use of the terms *save* (*yšʿ*) and *deliver* (*nṣl*)—which express concepts akin to *redeem* and *ransom*—in the rhetorical chain, "save . . . redeem" (*yšʿ/gʾl*), 63:9; "redeem . . . ransom" (*gʾl/pdh*), 51:10–11; "ransom . . . deliver" (*pdh/nṣl*), 50:2; "deliver . . . save" (*nṣl/yšʿ*), 19:20; *passim*.

when the Lord executes justice and vengeance upon the earth (35:4; 51:5; 59:11, 16) and is expressed in terms of the Lord's favor (49:8), glory (46:13), light (49:6; 62:1), and peace (52:7).

He who saves ($y\check{s}^{(}/n\underline{s}l$) is the Lord himself (25:9; 26:1–4; 33:22; 43:12; 45:17; 49:25; 50:2), though the role of saving applies secondarily to the Lord's *hand* (43:13; 59:1) and to the angel or messenger of the Lord's presence (*mal'ak pānâw*, 63:9).[43] Similarly, the title of "savior" (*môšîa'*) describes primarily "the Lord, your Savior, your Redeemer" (49:26; 60:16; 63:8–9); "the Lord, your God, your Savior, the Holy One of Israel" (43:3); the "Savior God of Israel" (45:15); and the "God of righteousness, a Savior" (45:21). The term applies secondarily to a deliverer of a "City of Righteousness" in the land of Egypt (19:18–20). Lastly, the Lord himself personifies *salvation* (*yěšû'â*, 12:2; 17:10; 33:2; *passim*), particularly upon his return to Zion (62:11).

The Lord's personification of salvation expresses something similar to the personification of righteousness by the Lord's ideal latter-day vassal.[44] In the literal sense of these terms, righteousness precedes or is a precondition of salvation: when the Lord's people evidence righteousness, then they experience salvation as a covenant blessing (56:1; cf. 45:8; 64:5). The personified or metaphorical use of these terms, however, suggests that the Lord's ideal vassal serves as a forerunner of the Lord's coming. Thus, both the Lord and the Servant figure fulfill redemptive roles toward the Lord's people, one being the corollary of the other: the Lord brings near his *righteousness* in order that *salvation* may come (46:13; cf. 51:5); *righteousness* leads the exodus of the Lord's people (58:8) and *salvation* characterizes and succeeds the exodus (11:15–12:3); *righteousness* firmly establishes the Lord's people (54:14; cf. 61:3) but *salvation* protects them (26:1; cf. 60:18). In the Lord's day of judgment, *righteousness* and *salvation*—literally and allegorically— alone serve as a surety against calamity (51:6, 8).

---

[43] See the parallelistic synonymity of the Lord's "servant" (*'ebed*) and "messenger/angel" (*mal'āk*) in 42:19; 44:26 to denote here, rhetorically, the Lord's ideal vassal.

[44] See the pairing of *righteousness* and *salvation* in the complementary parallelisms of 46:13; 51:5–8; 59:17; 62:1, though the dissimilar rhetorical use of these terms precludes our viewing them as synonyms. John Chamberlain notes that the Qumran community in part understood the messianic nature of these metaphors; see John V. Chamberlain, "The Functions of God as Messianic Titles in the Complete Isaiah Scroll," *VT* 5 (1955): 366–72.

The concerted, yet distinct, roles of the Lord and his vassal show up again in the Isaianic term *arm*. That term appears as a synonym of both *salvation* (33:2) and *righteousness*[45]—the Lord and his ideal vassal. The term *arm*, in fact, identifies two agents or vehicles of God's intervention. First, the Lord bares his *arm*—his ideal vassal—in the eyes of all nations, in order that all ends of the earth may witness God's *salvation* (52:10); the Lord calls, brings near, and prospers his *arm* to perform his will in Babylon (48:14–15); the Lord endows his *arm* with power to lead the new exodus of his ransomed ones (51:9–11). Secondly, to those who wait for the Lord, the Lord is an *arm* of *salvation* (33:2).

The following verse illustrates the operation of both *arms*: "my *righteousness* shall be at hand and my *salvation* proceed; my *arms* shall judge the peoples—the isles anticipate me, awaiting my *arm*" (51:5). This verse reiterates the twin functions of *righteousness* and *salvation*, the former preceding the latter. It further identifies *righteousness* and *salvation* parallelistically as two *arms*, signifying a twofold intervention universally in order to bring about the Lord's redemption. The verse then restates, chiastically, the concerted function of "me" and "my *arm*." The term *judge* (*špṭ*), which occurs in conjunction with the above metaphors (51:5), supports their meaning rhetorically. In its authoritative sense, the term *judge* (*špṭ*) occurs only with reference to the Lord himself and to the Davidic king (cf. 2:4; 11:3–4; 16:5; 33:22). The mission of the Lord's *arm* to the "isles" (51:5) finds rhetorical support in a mission to the "isles" by the Lord's ideal vassal (41:1–5; 42:1–4; 49:1–6); the Lord ultimately comes to those who return or have returned from the "isles" (cf. 59:18–20; 60:1–9; 66:18–20).

To sum up, the idea of redemption transcends that of salvation in that redemption actualizes the exaltation of Zion to which section IV attests but which it cannot develop. The Lord's people are unable to achieve such an exalted status of themselves. Two vehicles of divine redemption, the Lord's ideal vassal and the Lord himself, intervene to lift the Lord's people from their fallen or maledictory state. In his role of serving as an exemplar and paradigm of the Lord's people, the Lord's latter-day vassal elevates a remnant of the Lord's

---

[45] In connection with the latter term, see a rhetorical chain of metaphors paralleling the Lord's *righteousness* and *right hand*, 41:10; the Lord's *right hand* and mighty *arm*, 62:8; the Lord's *arm* and *righteousness*, 59:16.

people to a state of righteousness that serves covenantally as a precondition of salvation. The vassal's role of lawgiver, his personification of *righteousness*, and his manifestation of other spiritual attributes, qualify him as the Lord's agent of redemption and as the Lord's forerunner. Finally, the ideal vassal's role of serving as a proxy of his people in obtaining their deliverance—deliverance from the full measure of malediction that overwhelms the wicked—forms a vital but preliminary part of the Lord's redemption. The fundamental and transcendent work of that redemption, culminating in Zion's salvation and exaltation, the Lord performs himself.

Discourse H: The Servant-Tyrant Parallelism (2)—the Message

As section IV of the Bifid Structure deals with the demise of arch Babylon and the king of arch Babylon, so section V deals with the victory of Zion and the king of Zion. We observe this structural apposition particularly in the Servant-Tyrant Parallelism. That structure parallels, antithetically, 47:1–4 and 14:1–23 in section IV with 52:1–53:12 in section V (see section IV, figure 13). Within this material falls the so-called fourth Servant Song of 52:13–53:12, which scholars generally regard as a unified passage with a so-called Suffering Servant as its subject. Rhetorically, however, the text identifies more than one subject. Neglect of that point has created many of the difficulties scholars have with this passage:

52:13. My servant, being astute, shall be highly exalted;
      he shall become exceedingly eminent:
14. just as he[46] appalled many—
      his appearance was marred beyond human likeness,
      his semblance unlike that of men—
15. so shall he yet astound[47] many nations,
      rulers shutting their mouths at him—
      what was not told them, they shall see;
      what they had not heard, they shall consider.

53:1. Who has believed our revelation?
      On whose account has the arm
      of the Lord been revealed?

---

[46] Hebrew, *you*.

[47] Or, *startle*; also *purge, sprinkle*.

2. Like a sapling he grew up in his presence,
   a stalk out of arid ground.
   He had no distinguished appearance,
   that we should notice him;
   he had no [pleasing] aspect,
   that we should find him attractive.

3. He was despised and disdained by men,
   a man of grief, accustomed to suffering.
   As one from whom men hide their faces
   he was shunned, deemed by us of no merit.

4. Yet he bore our sufferings, endured our griefs,
   though we thought him stricken,
   smitten of God, and humbled.

5. But he was pierced for our transgressions,
   crushed because of our iniquities;
   the price of our peace he incurred,
   and with his wounds we are healed.

6. We all like sheep had gone astray,
   each of us headed his own way;
   the Lord brought together upon him the iniquity of us all.

7. He was harassed, yet submissive,
   and opened not his mouth—
   like a lamb led to slaughter,
   like a sheep, dumb before its shearers,
   he opened not his mouth.

8. By arrest and trial he was taken away.
   Who can apprise his generation
   that he was cut off from the land of the living
   for the crime of my people to whom the blow was due?

9. He was appointed among the wicked in death,[48]
   among the rich was his burial;[48]
   yet he had done no violence,
   and deceit was not in his mouth.

10. But the Lord willed to crush him,
    causing him suffering,
    that, if he[49] made his life an offering for guilt,
    he might see his offspring and prolong his days,
    and that the purposes of the Lord
    might prosper in his hand.

---

[48] Terms transposed; in text appear reversed. See section IV, footnote 35.

[49] Hebrew, *you.*

11. He shall see the toil of his soul and be satisfied;
  because of his knowledge, and by bearing their iniquities,
  shall my servant, the righteous one, vindicate many.
12. I will assign him an inheritance among the great,
  and he shall divide the spoil with the mighty,
  because he poured out his soul unto death,
  and was numbered with criminals—
he bore the sins of many,
  and made intercession for the transgressors.

Those verses in which the Lord speaks, namely 52:13–15 and 53:11–12, identify their subject as "my servant" (52:13) or "my servant *ṣaddîq*" (53:11). The latter's mission extends to many nations and their rulers (52:15). These descriptions (cf. 42:1; 49:7), and this figure's serving as a proxy and paradigm of the Lord's people—by vindicating many or making many righteous (*yaṣdîq . . . lārabbîm*, 53:11)—mark him, cumulatively, as the Lord's ideal latter-day vassal, who is here represented by the Servant figure. Two parallel lines affirm that this figure "bears the iniquities" of his people "because of his knowledge" (53:11).[50] The text thus implies that he considers himself answerable, as a vassal to the suzerain, for the terms of the Davidic covenant and its protection clause. In the event his people are disloyal to the suzerain, he—the vassal—bears their iniquities.

The part of chapter 53 that "we/us" narrates, on the other hand (53:2–6), or that a representative of "we/us" narrates (53:7–11a), does not identify its subject except by way of descriptive imagery. Such descriptive imagery possesses few literary connections in Isaiah that would enable us to identify the subject of 53:1–10. Depictions such as "sapling," "stalk" (53:2), "man of grief" (*ʾîš makʾōbôt*, 53:3), "lamb," and "sheep" (53:7) lack identifying characteristics that allow us to link them to other material. Rhetorical use of the pronouns *we* and *us* associates them with both the Lord's people and the nations (cf. 1:9; 2:3; 5:19; 7:6; *passim*). We confirm that association by means of the additional identifying marks of "my people" (*ʿammî*, 53:8)—an expression Isaiah uses elsewhere to

---

[50] See "knowledge" (*daʿat*) as expressing a covenant relationship, Hos 6:6–7; and H. B. Huffmon, "The Treaty Background of Hebrew *yādaʿ*," *BASOR* 181 (1966): 31–37; H. B. Huffmon and S. B. Parker, "A Further Note on the Treaty Background of Hebrew *yādaʿ*," *BASOR* 184 (1966): 36–38.

describe his own people (22:4)—and "sheep/flock" ($s'\bar{o}n$, 53:6), which elsewhere describes the peoples of the earth (13:14). These identities suggest that the subject of 53:1–10 provokes universal interest.

The location of 53:1–10 within the Servant–Tyrant parallelism, however, leads us to conclude that it is not the Lord's vassal who is its subject, but the Lord himself. The Servant–Tyrant Parallelism structurally juxtaposes the king of Babylon—an archtyrant (14:4–20)—with the Lord (52:7–12), with the Lord's Servant (52:13–15), and with a suffering figure (53:1–10). A few additional verses, which do not describe the king of Babylon, complete the structure (see section IV, figure 13). The analogical relationships of these figures within the Servant–Tyrant Parallelism serves as a structural device that reveals their identity. First, the structure juxtaposes Babylon and Zion in the prologue of the Parallelism (47:1–4; 52:1–3). Second, it depicts the Lord as coming to assume his role as King of Zion (52:7). Third, it depicts the Lord (52:7–12), the Lord's Servant (52:13–15), and the suffering figure (53:1–10) as the antithesis of the king of Babylon (14:4–21). These analogical relationships thus determine, structurally, that the Lord, the Lord's Servant, and the suffering figure represent a king or kings of Zion.

While that identity as a king of Zion appears directly in the Lord's case, it does so only indirectly in the case of the Lord's Servant. As we observe in Isaianic Zion ideology, both the Lord and his ideal vassal (the latter-day Davidic king) identify with Zion, whether singly or paired. As the Lord's Servant or vassal, moreover, the Lord's ideal agent of deliverance serves as suzerain to the nations (cf. 41:2; 42:1; 45:1; 49:7; 55:4). So do David, Solomon, and Cyrus, his types; and so does the king of Babylon, his arch rival. The attributes of both suzerainty and vassalship qualify the Lord's Servant as a king of Zion. In that role, the Servant–Tyrant Parallelism, as an analogical device, thus briefly features him. Material that depicts the king of Babylon as a deity or demigod (14:13–14), on the other hand, is juxtaposed structurally with the suffering figure (53:1–3). That juxtaposition, together with the Lord's identity as a deity—the King of Zion (52:7)[51]—connotes

---

[51] Isa 52:7, in part, states: "saying to Zion, Your God reigns!"

the suffering figure himself to be a deity, namely the Lord, the King of Zion.[52]

We confirm that conclusion rhetorically by the motif of *peace*, a term that possesses literary connections throughout Isaiah. The suffering figure pays "the price/penalty of our peace" (*mûsar šĕlômēnû*, 53:5), which peace the structure defines elsewhere as the Lord's salvation (52:7).[53] Rhetorical analysis of the term *peace* (*šālôm*) shows it to be the reverse of malediction (33:7–9; 45:7), the effect of justice or righteousness (32:17; 39:8; 48:18; 60:17), a righteous sovereignty (9:7), an enduring calm (*šqṭ*, 32:17), mercy or compassion (*rḥm*, 54:10), healing (*rpʾ*, 57:19), rest (*nwḥ*, 57:2), bounty (66:12), joy (55:12), reconciliation to the Lord (27:5), wrought by the Lord (26:12), obtained at the price of suffering (38:17), established by an immutable covenant (54:10), and denied the wicked (48:22; 57:21; 59:8).

These definitions confirm that the suffering figure's role of serving as a proxy for the peace or salvation of his people is a function of the Lord himself. These definitions also express, quintessentially, the Lord's redemption as the Servant–Tyrant Parallelism reveals it. That redemption includes, but is not limited to, a reversal of malediction (14:1–2; 52:1–3), the effect of a righteous proxy or proxies (53:6, 10–11), the Lord's sovereignty (52:7), an enduring calm (*šqṭ*, 14:7), mercy or compassion (*rḥm*, 14:1), healing (*rpʾ*, 53:5), rest (*nwḥ*, 14:3, 7), bounty (53:12), joy (14:7; 52:8–9), reconciliation to the Lord (53:11–12), wrought by the suffering figure (53:5), obtained at the price of suffering (53:4–5, 10–11), epitomized by good (*ṭôb*, 52:7), and denied the wicked (14:22). Since these contextual descriptions of the Lord's redemption coincide with rhetorical definitions of the term *peace* in Isaiah, they link the Lord's redemption indissolubly to the mission of the suffering figure.

How the Lord's redemption is wrought thus forms a key message of the Servant–Tyrant Parallelism. This transcendent structure throws into perspective all aspects of the Lord's redemption. Its configuration reveals the interrelatedness of such diverse ideas as the effects

---

[52] The idea of divinity applies analogically but less forcefully also to the Lord's ideal vassal. Though the Bifid Structure deals with that idea only indirectly—by means of a paradigmatic hierarchy—other prophetic texts discuss Davidic divinity directly; compare Psa 45:6; Zech 12:8.

[53] See the Lord's messenger announcing peace, heralding salvation, 52:7.

of unfaithfulness to the Lord's covenant, universal tyranny as epitomized by an archtyrant, the Lord's answer to Babylon's oppressive ideology, the self-exaltation and ensuing overthrow of the forces of chaos, the price of suffering paid for the Lord's redemption, the role of the Lord as suffering figure and as King of Zion, the Lord's ideal vassal as a proxy and paradigm of the Lord's people (to a degree emulating the Lord himself), the Lord's reversal of malediction and his exaltation of Zion, the synonymity of Zion's redemption and the world's salvation, and so forth. The Servant–Tyrant Parallelism, by spelling out the nature of the Lord's redemption, in effect presents a brief or synopsis of the message of the Bifid Structure. The substance of the one is also that of the other.

Typological patterns additionally attest to the divinity of the suffering figure in that there exists no biblical type or precedent of one man's death atoning for the sins of others. In Isaianic Zion ideology, the Lord delivers his people by virtue of the righteousness of his ideal vassal, an idea that flows out of the Davidic covenant and its protection clause. Such deliverance nonetheless represents but a limited part of the Lord's redemption, and the king, though he suffers, does not die. Passages in Isaiah declare that the Lord makes deliverance possible because he himself has wrought redemption. The pivotal event of the exodus out of arch Babylon, for example, follows the declaration that the Lord has redeemed his people (48:20; 52:9–12). Jacob/Israel's return from exile follows a similar declaration (43:1–2, 5–6).

The text shows that the deliverance aspect of the Lord's redemption is subordinate to the divine when it represents the mission of the Lord's vassal as deriving from that of the suffering figure, who is the Lord. An a–b–c–d–e–f–g–h–g–f–e–d–c–b–a structure in 52:13–53:12, for example, highlights the governing concepts that appear in this material, as follows: the Lord's exaltation of the Servant figure (52:13; 53:12), the effects of the Servant figure's suffering (52:14–15; 53:11), the role of the Lord's *arm/hand* (53:1, 10d), the ill-fated life of the suffering figure (53:2, 10ac), the suffering figure's execration (53:3, 9), the suffering figure's smiting or death (53:4, 8), the suffering figure's self-sacrifice (53:5, 7), and the suffering figure's function as an atoning proxy for "we/us" (53:6). Within this structure, two parallel statements show (1) that the Lord reveals his *arm* for the sake of those who believe his people's account of the suffering figure (53:1), and (2) that the suffering figure makes his life an offering for guilt in order that the Lord's purposes might prosper in his *hand* (53:10). The ideal vassal's role thus flows out of and is subservient to that of the suffering figure.

As we have seen, moreover, no exception exists in Isaiah to utilizing a biblical type or precedent to portray an ideal eschatological role. The text builds prophecies on such types whether a particular type originates in a person or in allegorical imagery. The book's chief human characters, the Lord's ideal vassal and the archtyrant, possess as types the respective heroes and villains of biblical tradition together with the royal and mythical imagery that tradition associates with them. Even the Servant figure, an ahistorical entity, is a composite of Moses, David, and Cyrus in section III. The Lord's raising his *staff* over the *Sea* (10:26) and *hand* over the *River* (11:15), in the same section, likewise projects an ahistorical Davidic ascendency over Assyria. All such figures rely on types imbedded in the tradition out of which they arise. Since an atoning death by one man for the sins of others (cf. 53:7–10) possesses no human type in this tradition, such an act, typologically speaking, lies outside the sphere of purely human activity.

The language of 53:1–10 itself reflects the uniqueness of such proxy atonement. Though it contains a few distinguishing features, such as the motif of peace (53:5) and the chiastically parallel idea of a sacrificial lamb (*'seh*, 53:7; cf. 66:3), this passage of Isaiah is rhetorically and typologically unique. It stands alone in the entire text, and in all biblical literature, for the kind of phenomenon it describes. Unlike the Lord's ideal vassal, whom we recognize cumulatively in the second unit by the familiar roles ascribed to him—releasing the Lord's captives (49:9), leading a new exodus (51:9–11), executing the Lord's retribution upon the nations (48:14; 52:15)—or by the roles that depict him metaphorically as the Lord's *light* (49:6; 51:4), *hand* (50:2; 53:10), and *righteousness* (51:1, 7; 53:11), the suffering figure lacks identifying characteristics other than those few that mark his role as the Lord's own. Such uniqueness is atypical of the text as a whole, which, as we have seen, abounds with rhetorical and typological interconnections.

Nine biblical types, for example, characterize the Lord's vassal in the adjacent material of 52:13–15 and 53:11–12: Solomon typifies one astute or prudent (*ya'skil*) who grows eminent among the nations, before whom rulers shut their mouths—for "what was not told them they shall see, and what they had not heard they shall

201

consider" (52:13, 15; cf. 1 Kgs 5:29–34; 10:4–7); Uzziah (Azariah) typifies one whose appearance is marred beyond human likeness (52:14)—when the Lord smites him with leprosy (cf. 2 Kgs 15:5; 2 Chr 26:20); Hezekiah typifies one who serves as a righteous proxy and exemplar of his people, vindicating many (53:11)—when the Assyrian army surrounds Jerusalem (cf. 37:14–35); Caleb typifies one whom the Lord assigns an inheritance among the great (53:12)—when Israel conquers Canaan (cf. Num 14:24; Josh 14: 6–15; 15:13–17); David typifies one who divides the spoil with the mighty (53:12)—when he gains the victory over the Amalekites (cf. 1 Sam 30:16–31); Hezekiah typifies one who pours out his soul unto death (53:12)—during his illness, when the Lord promises to deliver his people from the Assyrians (cf. 38:1–20); David typifies one numbered with criminals (53:12)—when Saul outlaws him (cf. 1 Sam 22:1–2); Job typifies one who bears the sins of many (53:12)—upon the feasting and extravagant lifestyle of his children (cf. Job 1:5); and Moses typifies one who makes intercession for transgressors (53:12)—when Israel turns to idolatry in the wilderness (cf. Exod 32:11–13; Deut 9:16–29). These typologies express, cumulatively, the concept of an ideal agent of the Lord's punishment and deliverance who forms a composite of types.

Although 53:1–10 does not lend itself to such visible parallels,[54] analogical relationships within the Servant–Tyrant Parallelism suggest that attributes characterizing one entity may characterize another on the same side of the structure. That both the Lord and his vassal represent kings of Zion, for example, appears virtually without the principle of analogy. A Zion identity links all entities that juxtapose Babylon and the king of Babylon; and royalty, whether enfranchised or disfranchised, characterizes all entities in the Parallelism.

Conformably, the structure's juxtaposition of the Lord's royal accession (52:7) with the king of Babylon's deposition (14:4) by analogy implies royal accession for the Lord's vassal also. The latter's royal accession, which section III establishes, occurs cumulatively in section V: the Lord calls his ideal vassal from before his mother's womb (49:1); the Lord names him (49:1), designates him his

---

[54] Some possible biblical types for the suffering figure include David, who at sundry times was "disdained by men" (53:3), and Job, whom his friends thought "smitten of God" (53:4). These, however, constitute types of suffering rather than role models. Although valid as types, therefore, they fail to identify positively an ideal Isaianic figure.

"servant" (49:3, 5, 6), "creates" him (yṣr, 49:5, 8), "appoints" him (ntn, 49:6, 8), and "helps" him ($'zr$, 49:8; 50:7, 9). The Servant–Tyrant Parallelism, moreover, juxtaposes the vassal's rise to prominence with the king of Babylon's fall (cf. 14:10–12; 52:13–15). An implicit royal accession for the Lord's vassal in the Servant–Tyrant Parallelism would thus coincide with a reversal of circumstances in which a condition of ignominy turns into one of exaltation (52:13–15; cf. 49:1–8). Zion's royal accession from the dust in the prologue of the Parallelism (52:1–2) provides an analogy of such an idea. A paradigmatic hierarchy, therefore, functions consistently as well as cumulatively in the Servant–Tyrant Parallelism: all three entities—the Lord as suffering figure, his ideal vassal, and the Lord's people—rise from a condition of ignominy to one of exaltation on whatever level of the paradigmatic ladder each one appears.

By the same principle of analogy, the ideal vassal's designation as the Lord's "servant" (52:13; 53:11), which term denotes his vassal status, and the Lord's people's concurrent vassal status (14:1; cf. 52:4–7), suggests that the suffering figure assumes a condition of servanthood or vassalship while paying the price of his people's salvation. We confirm that idea by the nature of his suffering: the suffering figure undergoes the trial and punishment of a rebellious vassal (53:8–9) and appears to experience the curses of one who covenantally transgresses (53:4). Two exceptions to his suffering malediction—an honorable burial and offspring (53:9–10)—both covenant blessings, nonetheless signify that the suffering figure is innocent of the crime for which he is put to death (cf. 53:9). (In the juxtaposed verses of the Parallelism, the king of Babylon receives no burial and his offspring are slaughtered [14:20–21], signifying covenantal malediction.)

Lastly, what applies to a figure on one side of the Parallelism may, because of the antithetical nature of the structure, apply to a figure on the opposite side. The king of Babylon's aspiration to attain to an exalted divine status—"like El Elyon" (14:13–14)—for example, may describe, inferentially, the final state of the suffering figure whom the structure contrasts with him (53:1–3). That accords with the Lord's royal accession as Zion's God within the same structure (52:7). The idea of an abhorred "man" ($'$îš, 53:3) who attains to celestial exaltation is thus no less Isaianic than that of a "man" ($'$îš, 14:16) who gains celestial exaltation only to be made an abhorrence. By the same token, the king of Babylon's parody of celestial accession is just as literally intended as the parody of justice inflicted on the suffering figure. In the paradigmatic hierarchy of Isaiah, celestial accession forms an implicit idea. But the king of Babylon's tenure as a demigod represents a counterfeit of such accession because he deviates from the divine paradigm. It is in the very process of establishing that paradigm that the suffering figure suffers death.

The ignominy that the Lord's vassal and the suffering figure endure (52:14; 53:3) may additionally describe the final state of the king of Babylon whom the structure contrasts with them (14:11, 14). That idea, too, finds support in the text: the king of Babylon suffers utter execration (14:16–21) and descends to the depths of Sheol (14:15).[55] The force of such secondary, inferential analogies corroborates the (primary) evidence for concepts the text develops structurally, typologically, and rhetorically.

Redemptive Suffering

The burden of suffering that precedes or lays the groundwork for the Lord's redemption of his people, though common to all, differs from one suffering entity to the next. In the redemptive context of the second unit, the wicked—all non-Zion entities—suffer a full measure of covenantal malediction for their crimes of injustice and idolatry. Secondly, the righteous—those who repent/return and emulate the righteousness of the Lord's ideal vassal—suffer oppression and ignominy in the interim before the Lord redeems them. Their suffering, however, serves as a purifying influence, vouchsafing their repentance rather than itself generating redemption.

---

[55] The Servant–Tyrant Parallelism, as an Isaianic structure, explains an otherwise enigmatic statement that the *Ascension of Isaiah* attributes to Isaiah, namely, that the "Beloved" (i.e., the Lord; cf. Isa 5:1) would descend into Sheol. The *Ascension* apparently derives that idea by linking the passage commencing with Isa 52:13 to chapters 13–14. It states: "The remainder of the words of the vision is recorded in the vision concerning Babylon [Isa 13–14]. And the rest of the vision of the Lord, behold, it is recorded in parables in my words which are written in the book which I openly proclaimed. Moreover, the descent of the Beloved into the realm of the dead is recorded in the section where the Lord says 'Behold my servant is prudent' [Isa 52:13]" (Asc Isa 4:19–21). In Isa 14:15–16, the king of Babylon descends into Sheol, the realm of the dead. Because of the parallelistic (and thus analogical) relationship that the Servant–Tyrant Parallelism establishes between the tyrant and suffering figures, such a descent may, inferentially, apply to both figures. The idea of a god who descends to the nether world occurs commonly in ancient Near Eastern mythology.

Thirdly, the Lord's ideal vassal suffers ignominy and marring while fulfilling his mission as a proxy and paradigm of the Lord's people. As the Lord's vassal, he answers to the Lord for crimes his people may have committed against their divine suzerain. The ideal vassal's suffering for their sake lends substance to his mediatory role on their behalf. His suffering merits or justifies the Lord's deliverance of a remnant of His people from a mortal threat. The Bifid Structure identifies that threat as universal destruction wrought by the king of Assyria in the Lord's day of judgment (see sections I–IV). Lastly, the suffering figure—by his suffering (53:4–8)—brings about the entire scope of the Lord's redemption: the removal of sins, the reversal of malediction, and the deliverance and exaltation of a remnant of the Lord's people—Zion.

From this last category of redemptive suffering thus flows the ideal vassal's own redemption. His reversal of circumstances—from a marred condition, one that appalls many (52:14), to one of healing and universal eminence (52:13, 15; cf. 57:18–19)—derives from the same redemption that the Lord ordains universally. By experiencing this reversal of his condition, the ideal vassal serves as a paradigm of the Lord's righteous people whom the Lord similarly heals and exalts.

That kind of reversal, however, does not apply to the suffering figure of 53:1–10. Although he too suffers, he does not experience curse reversals in his lifetime. Besides being despised, disdained, harassed, pierced, and crushed, he is also led like a "lamb" ('seh) to the slaughter (53:3–7). He is taken (lqh),[56] cut off from the land of the living, and buried (53:7–9). God wills to crush him, causing him "suffering" or "sickness" (ḥlh, 53:10). His very life is an "offering for guilt" ('āšām, 53:10). He is "pierced for our transgressions"; he pays "the price of our peace" (53:5). The use of sacrificial imagery, such as the "guilt offering" of a "lamb," to depict the suffering figure's offering of his life means that the typological antecedent of animal sacrifice most nearly represents what happens to the suffering figure. The price of suffering he pays for his people's peace and healing (53:5), in effect, constitutes an atoning sacrifice for transgression. In the absence of a human precedent for such atonement, the suffering figure's suffering is described in terms of a sacrificial proxy.

---

[56] See the sacrificial and covenantal nature of the verb *take* (lqh), Gen 15:9–10.

The Lord's vassal, on the other hand, does not undergo a sacrificial death. Although he pours out his soul unto death, he receives an inheritance among the "many" or "great" (*rabbîm*) whom he vindicates and with whom he divides the spoils of war (53:11–12; cf. 9:3)—evidence that he survives his ordeal. His reversed condition resembles the ancient Near Eastern pattern of the arrested sacrifice of the king[57] and possesses a type in King Hezekiah. We nonetheless find a reversed condition for the suffering figure in the Servant–Tyrant Parallelism, in the Lord's accession as King of Zion (52:7). That reversal of circumstances possesses ancient Near Eastern parallels in the god who dies, then revives and assumes the throne of a senior deity.[58] The Servant–Tyrant Parallelism contains that idea analogically in the king of Babylon's aspiration to assume the throne of El Elyon—the Most High God (14:13–14).

Other passages in the second unit, such as 49:1–8, depict the Lord's "servant"—the Lord's ideal vassal—as suffering but surviving to attain an exalted state. After supposing his labor to be futile, his strength spent in vain (49:4), he accedes to royal status. When his people despise and abhor him (49:7), the Lord comes to his aid and "creates" him (*yṣr*, 49:8). The Lord appoints him as a *covenant* of the people, causing rulers of nations to see (*r'h*) and prostrate themselves before him (49:7–8).[59] Thereupon, the vassal releases the Lord's captives and leads a return wandering in the wilderness to Zion (49:9–12). The text restates this scenario allegorically by the Lord's raising his *hand/ensign* in order to return his people from exile (49:22). As a *light* to the nations, the Lord's vassal heralds the Lord's salvation to the end of the earth (49:6).

---

[57] See Frankfort, *Kingship and the Gods*, 319–20; Ivan Engnell, *Divine Kingship in the Ancient Near East* (Oxford: Basil Blackwell, 1967), 35, 66–67; Theodore H. Gaster, *Thespis: Ritual, Myth, and Drama in the Ancient Near East* (New York: Schuman, 1950), 36.

[58] See Alexandre Moret, *Kings and Gods of Egypt* (New York: Putnam's Sons, 1912), 69–108, esp. 90; Frankfort, *Kingship and the Gods*, 281–94, 313–33; Gaster, *Thespis*, 34–43; C. J. Bleeker, "Isis as Saviour Goddess," in S. G. F. Brandon, ed., *The Saviour God* (New York: Barnes & Noble, 1963), 1–16; S. G. F. Brandon, "The Ritual Technique of Salvation in the Ancient Near East," in *The Saviour God*, 17–36; Engnell, *Divine Kingship*, 119–23; Thorkild Jacobsen, *Toward the Image of Tammuz* (Cambridge, Mass.: Harvard, 1970), 73–103; James G. Frazer, *Adonis, Attis, Osiris* (New York: University Books, 1961); Thorkild Jacobsen, *The Treasures of Darkness* (New Haven, Conn.: Yale University Press, 1976), 25–73.

[59] Compare rulers who see (*r'h*) and consider the Lord's vassal in 52:15.

A passage in chapter 50 depicts the Lord's "servant" (50:10)—the Lord's vassal—as one whom the Lord endows with a learned tongue in order to preach to the weary a word to wake them up (50:4). In the course of fulfilling his mission, the ideal vassal suffers smiting, plucking of the beard, insult, and spitting (50:6). When his enemies incriminate him, the Lord "helps" him (*'zr*, 50:7–9), signifying royal accession. Those who reject the Lord's *light*, in preference to mere sparks, incur distress (50:10–11); those who reject the Lord's *hand* of deliverance (50:2) suffer the Lord's *hand* of punishment (50:11).[60]

These passages thus build on the cumulative concept of an ideal latter-day vassal who serves as the Lord's agent of punishment and deliverance. In the second unit's context of redemption, however, they emphasize the vassal's suffering in the course of fulfilling his mission; he suffers while performing a spiritual role. His reversal of circumstances—from ignominy to royal accession—enables him to perform a temporal role as well, that of physically delivering his people.

The suffering that the vassal and the suffering figure endure lies beyond that of suffering for one's own transgressions. Their suffering mediates and atones for those who find themselves in a maledictory state—to whom such suffering, in reality, is due.[61] While the ideal vassal's mediatory function limits itself to making intercession (*pg'*) for transgressors (53:12),[62] the role that the suffering figure fulfills greatly exceeds this. In the course of redeeming his people, he takes upon himself "the iniquity of us all" (53:6). He pays the price of his people's peace or salvation by dying like a lamb (53:5, 7).

Yet, in one important respect, the suffering figure's function draws on the biblical type of the Davidic king in that he serves as

---

[60] An a–b–c–d–c–b–a structure in chapter 50 evidences the literary unity of the servant passage, as follows: verses 2 and 11 feature the motif of the Lord's *hand*; verses 3–6 and 10 contrast the people's darkness and apostasy with the Servant's mission to preach; verses 7 and 9 depict the Lord's help toward his Servant as he faces adversity; and verse 8 tells of the Lord's vindication of his Servant when enemies confront him.

[61] Compare 53:11bc: "Because of his knowledge, and by bearing their iniquities, shall my servant, the righteous one, vindicate many"; and 53:8: "He was cut off from the land of the living for the crime of my people to whom the blow was due."

[62] Compare, rhetorically, the Lord's *arm* of *righteousness* intervening/interceding (*pg'*) on behalf of the Lord's people, 59:16.

a proxy for the deliverance of his people. Only in the Davidic king do we find the precedent of a human proxy for the salvation of the Lord's people. Isa 53:1–10 combines the idea of a human proxy with that of an expiating sacrifice to arrive at human atonement for sin. The suffering figure forms a composite of two proxy roles in accordance with cumulative concepts. Such an atonement by "a man" (53:3), however, must additionally be divine: it possesses no prehistory in biblical tradition, nor, indeed, any veracity unless the one making the atonement be himself vindicated by having his maledictory condition reversed. Zion/Jerusalem's royal accession from the dust in the Servant–Tyrant Parallelism (52:1–2) supplies the analogical pattern for such a reversal. The first unit of section V, moreover, affirms the Lord's victory over death (25:7–8) that makes this reversal possible (cf. 26:19).

All three entities—Zion/Jerusalem, the Lord's ideal vassal, and the suffering figure—thus experience a reversal of circumstances from a condition of humiliation to one of exaltation, from malediction to benediction. The pattern such a reversal of circumstances establishes is that lower entities progress up the paradigmatic ladder by emulating one above. In responding to the ideal vassal's mission, Jacob/Israel becomes Zion/Jerusalem, whom the Lord redeems from a maledictory state. Zion/Jerusalem's burden of suffering forms an integral part of the Lord's redemption: the Lord turns ignominy into royal accession for those who follow righteousness, whom *righteousness* ransoms and vindicates (see figure 15).

Figure 15

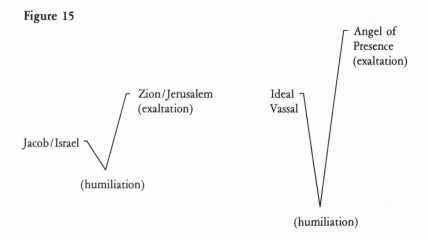

208

In the process of vindicating the Lord's repentant people, the ideal vassal suffers nigh unto death but does not die. Thereupon, the Lord empowers him to redeem his people temporally. The vassal's suffering exceeds that of Zion/Jerusalem to the degree that his mission exceeds Zion/Jerusalem's. From one whose "appearance was marred beyond human likeness," at whom men were appalled, he becomes one "highly exalted" and "exceedingly eminent," before whom rulers shut their mouths (52:13–15). His exaltation is surpassed only by that of the Lord himself, who, as King of Zion, rules as God (52:7).[63] Of the vassal's exaltation, the prophet Isaiah serves as a type when he assumes the function of a seraph (see section II).

By the same token, the ideal vassal's suffering and humiliation is surpassed only by that of the suffering figure, who is the Lord himself. According to the pattern of a reversal from humiliation to exaltation, the suffering figure's suffering is commensurate with the Lord's glorious accession as King of Zion. In short, the greater the glory an entity assumes, the greater the burden of suffering that precedes it—granted that such suffering is redemptive not punitive.

What, then, makes the suffering figure's suffering redemptive? We have seen that Zion/Jerusalem's suffering underscores the repentance process through which the Lord's people must pass in order to experience the Lord's redemption. The ideal vassal's suffering, on the other hand, is inherent in a Davidic king's role of proxy in obtaining his people's deliverance from a mortal threat. But why should the suffering figure suffer? Or rather, what is the Lord's role as suzerain toward his ideal vassal and toward Jacob/Israel, his corporate vassal, that he should suffer at all? Should the Lord, the Holy One of Israel, suffer in the likeness of a sacrificial proxy? Is that conceivable?

The answer to these questions is that the ultimate mortal enemy of the Lord's people is not the king of Assyria/Babylon and the universal destruction that he causes; it is death itself and the potential of an irrevocable damnation associated with death. If the curse of death is not at some point reversed, then divine protection must, in the end, have failed. The Lord's punitive *staff/rod* of *anger/wrath* may indeed serve as the means of destroying the wicked in the Lord's day of judgment; and from that instrument of death, the Lord may

---

[63] Compare the Lord, who, as a paradigm of his ideal vassal, is highly exalted (6:1) and exceedingly eminent (33:10).

save his righteous people. But apart from that, the Lord's people live and die like mortals, even those whom the Lord delivers from a temporary mortal threat. Inevitably, all humanity is subject to death.

Yet, the Lord's covenants with his people and with King David require that the Lord—their suzerain—deliver them from *any* mortal threat when they—his vassal/s—keep the terms of his covenants. As their divine suzerain, the Lord must come to the aid of his people when an enemy threatens, even if that enemy is death: "Bound by the covenant, the suzerain guarantees to protect the vassal . . . by undertaking to annihilate a common enemy . . ."[64] The common enemy, ultimately, is death, Sheol, or the Pit, the realm of the departed (cf. 14:9–10, 15; 38:18). From that "enemy" there is no escape except through a reversal of the curse of death for those who die (26:19). A key question, therefore, is: How can death be conquered or annihilated? Can any mortal abolish death? The first unit assserts that the Lord himself will abolish death for "all peoples" and for "all nations" (25:7–8).

If death threatens the Lord's vassal/s with extinction, therefore, then the Lord—his people's suzerain—must at some point conquer death. In order to conquer death, however, must he not himself undergo death? Can anyone conquer death without experiencing death? We might assume, because the Lord is God, that such would be impossible. But how does one conquer an enemy whom he does not confront? Can one overcome death without first being dead? Moreover, as his people's proxy, the Lord also serves as their paradigm: as he suffers and dies a maledictory death, so do they; as he rises from the grave to exaltation, so do they (cf. 26:19; 52:1–3). These things constitute the message of the Servant–Tyrant Parallelism, which synopsizes the message of the Bifid Structure.

But more than that, in order to abolish death completely, the Lord must also remove the cause of death: he must first account for and remove his people's transgressions of the terms of the covenant, which are the cause of death. As in Mosaic or covenantal law, the man who transgresses—or rather, the animal, his sacrificial proxy—dies (Lev 4–7). Under that dispensation, however, repeated sacrifices are required so long as transgressions are repeated. Animal sacrifice, moreover, cannot itself abolish death but only forestall such malediction for a time.

---

[64] See item 3 of suzerain–vassal relationships, page 67.

Since the Lord is a just God who punishes his people's transgressions, how, then, can he take their transgressions away? How can he, as a just God, both remove the sins of his people and deliver them from a mortal or maledictory state to one of immortality and exaltation? The answer is the same: through the Lord's covenanting with his people and delivering them when they or their king—the Lord's vassal/s—keep the terms of the covenant. Within the Bifid Structure, the conditions for divine deliverance are actually met by the Lord's ideal vassal and by Zion/Jerusalem, those who emulate the vassal's righteousness. The vassal's personification of righteousness (41:2) connotes his perfect keeping of the terms of the Lord's covenant. Those who "follow *righteousness*" (51:1), who "know *righteousness*" (51:7), in the second unit of section V, likewise qualify for deliverance from death. Their righteousness is the precursor of salvation—of the Lord's coming to deliver his people, not only from the king of Assyria/Babylon, but from death itself (51:13–14).[65]

The suffering that the suffering figure endures as an atoning proxy for sin, therefore, allows for the law of a just God to be fulfilled within the terms of his covenants for those who repent/return. In the act of "bearing our sufferings" and "enduring our griefs" (53:4), in the course of being pierced and wounded while answering for "the iniquity of us all" (53:5–6)—in taking his people's malediction on himself—the Lord alone is able to reverse malediction. The implementation of that reversal occurs in the Lord's day of judgment (26:19–21), at the time of his coming (52:7–12), consistent with cumulative concepts.

In section V, therefore, we encounter a high point of the Bifid Structure. Whereas the first unit establishes the idea of a reversal from malediction that includes the abolition of death, the second unit establishes the premise for such a reversal. The Lord himself ordains the removal of sins and the reversal of his people's maledictory state. The Lord himself, as his people's suzerain, delivers them from their ultimate enemy—death—when they keep the terms of his covenants. In addition, by taking upon himself the role of a

---

[65] Compare Zion/Jerusalem's parallel "awakening" and "arising" both from the oppression of the Lord's *hand* of *wrath* (51:17) and from the dust (52:1–3). Such awakening and arising follow the paradigm of the *arm* of the Lord "awakening" and "arising" in order to deliver his people by means of a new exodus (51:9–11).

vassal—a vassal who answers to his suzerain for his people's loyalties—he atones for his people's sins, thereby effecting the entire scope of redemption. As a superlative paradigm of salvation and exaltation, the suffering figure—the Lord God of Israel—paradoxically suffers humiliation and death, thereby bringing hope to all of humanity who show covenantal loyalty toward him.

Summary

Section V of the Bifid Structure emphasizes the themes of suffering and salvation and reveals the interrelationship between these two ideas. The first unit (chaps. 24–27) depicts an inexorable distress overtaking a composite *city* that is analogous to arch Babylon in prior material. The earth and its inhabitants, alien nations, tyrannical entities, proud kindred peoples, and the Lord's reprobate people suffer a full measure of covenantal malediction. At the same time, the Lord saves a remnant of his people out of distress within a context of Isaianic Zion ideology. A reversal of malediction, including the abolition of death, accompanies the Lord's salvation. Besides emphasizing universal suffering, the first unit also fully maintains cumulative concepts of the Bifid Structure.

The second unit (chaps. 48–54) presents universal suffering as turning from the Lord's righteous people—Zion—to the wicked, Zion's enemies. Salvation takes the form of Zion's redemption and consists of the removal of sins, deliverance from distress and destruction, a reversal of malediction that includes victory over death, and royal accession. Two agents of redemption, the suffering figure and the Lord's ideal vassal, intervene in the affairs of the Lord's people in order to bring about their redemption. The suffering these figures endure in the course of fulfilling their respective roles attests to suffering forming an implicit but essential ingredient of the Lord's salvation. A theology of redemptive suffering functions both within a context of Isaianic Zion ideology and within the fuller, transcendent context of the Lord's redemption. These two contexts correspond to the temporal and spiritual salvation of the Lord's people.

The Servant–Tyrant Parallelism identifies the suffering figure of chapter 53, who serves as the principal agent of the Lord's redemption, as Zion's divine King, the Lord. That structure further links Zion's redemption to the overthrow of Babylon and the king of Babylon and the supplanting of these entities with the Lord's righteous rule. The latter idea modifies or redefines a Davidic ascendancy over the Assyrian tyrant king that section III establishes. The Lord's role as divine suzerain of his people, however, requires that he deliver them not only from the king of Assyria/Babylon but from death itself and from the cause of death. In the course of fulfilling his role as Redeemer of his people, thus reversing the curse of death, the Lord assumes the additional function of a proxy of his people in the likeness of both a righteous Davidic king and an expiating sacrifice for sin.

The ideal vassal's function as a paradigm of *righteousness* paves the way for the Lord's people to repent/return and for the Lord to come as *salvation*. Zion's faithful endurance of oppression—in the interim before the Lord comes—serves as the occasion for the Lord's redemption of Zion. That redemption manifests itself in Zion's attaining a state of immortality and exaltation as the Lord's reversal of malediction takes effect. Section V is unique in delineating a theology of redemption based on suffering, more particularly the suffering two agents of redemption experience in the course of fulfilling their proxy roles. The second unit's delineation of a paradigmatic relationship between the Lord, his ideal vassal, and Zion/Jerusalem within a context of redemptive suffering is similarly unique. The confluence of redemptive ideas in this material marks section V as *the* high point of the Bifid Structure. By subsuming and combining with section IV's central themes of humiliation and exaltation, section V sets forth the glorious promise the Lord holds out for his people.

SECTION VI
DISLOYALTY & LOYALTY
(28-31; 55-59)

Section VI of the Bifid Structure consists of homiletic or moralistic material and is thus distinguishable as a literary genre. A reproving and exhortative tone in this material, centering around the Lord's word and covenant, attempts to elicit a loyal response to the Lord's covenant from those flagrantly disloyal. At the same time, the Lord confirms the covenant with those who exercise loyalty toward him. Righteousness and wickedness, reflecting loyalty and disloyalty, thus assume a formal, covenantal aspect: righteousness crystallizes in a covenant of life, and wickedness in a covenant with death. As the Lord's day of judgment approaches, the righteous are sealed up, covenantally, to salvation and the wicked to calamity and destruction.

A Covenant with Death

We note the homiletic or didactic nature of the first unit (chaps. 28-31) in language such as law, word, precepts (29:13-14; 30:9, 12), way (30:21), counsel, inspiration (28:29), instruction, revelation (28:9, 26; 29:24), homage, piety (29:13), devotion, reverence (29:23), justice, righteousness (28:6, 17; 30:18), knowledge, intelligence, understanding (29:14-16), tablets, book, testimony (30:8), words, sayings (29:4, 18), and learning (29:11-12). Loyal responses to the Lord include seeing and hearing (28:14, 23; 29:18; 30:20-21), giving heed and being attentive (28:23), believing (28:16), repenting (31:6), renouncing idols (30:22; 31:7), understanding (29:24), inquiring of the Lord (30:2; 31:1), crying to the Lord (30:19), and waiting for the Lord (30:18). Disloyal responses include going astray (31:6), breaking faith with the Lord (30:9), disobeying the Lord's law (30:9), sinning and causing iniquity (30:1, 13; 31:7), rebelling against the Lord (30:1, 9), becoming drunk (28:1, 7; 29:9), scoffing and scorning (28:14, 22; 29:20), rejecting the Lord's word (30:12), becoming idolatrous (31:7), growing blind and deaf (29:18), perpetrating injustice (29:21), trusting in manipulation and double dealing (30:12), and practicing wickedness and tyranny (29:20).

All four chapters of the first unit commence with a "woe" (*hôy*), the pronouncement of a covenant curse. This material thus focuses on the reprobate of the Lord's people. The Lord singles out for woe or malediction those who seek to implement their own "schemes" or "counsel" (*ʿēṣâ*, 29:15; 30:1) in preference to the Lord's "counsel" (*ʿēṣâ*, 28:29).[1] These go down or regress (*yrd*) in their loyalty toward the Lord (30:2; 31:1). They rely instead on corrupt allies to protect them (29:15; 30:1–3; 31:1). Pharaoh's vast forces of chariots and horsemen cannot save the Lord's people (30:5–7). Depending on an arm of flesh is self-destructive (31:3). The Lord's *wrath/indignation* is kindled against his people (30:27). He will stretch out his punitive *hand* against them (31:3). In a day of great slaughter when the towers fall (30:25)—a day of flight and sudden peril (30:13–17)—a fiery and flooding torrent (*ʾēš ʾōkelet/naḥal šôṭēp*, 30:27–28) will overrun the wicked.

To the righteous, on the other hand, the Lord will show favor and mercy (30:18–19). When enemy shepherds come in full force against them, the Lord will protect them in a new passover (31:4–5). A righteous remnant will survive destruction like a *flagstaff* on a mountaintop, an *ensign* on a hill (30:17), signifying the presence of the Lord's ideal vassal, a latter-day Davidic king who serves as the Lord's agent of deliverance. Those saved will participate in a joyful pilgrimage to Zion (30:29).

A "covenant with death" (*bĕrît ʾet māwet*) epitomizes the reliance of the Lord's wicked people on human counsel (28:15, 18).[2] Parties to that covenant include political and spiritual leaders of the Lord's people (28:14). These scoff at the Lord's living oracle (28:14, 22). For that cause, a "flooding scourge" (*šôṭ šôṭēp*) will overrun them (28:17–19), for the Lord is bringing utter destruction upon the whole earth (28:22).

---

[1] Compare the Lord's ideal vassal as the man of the Lord's "counsel" (*ʿēṣâ*), 46:11.

[2] See also "counsel" (*ʿēṣâ*) as a biblical synonym of "covenant" (*bĕrît*), Weinfeld, "Berîth," 257; and "death" (*môt/māwet*) as an ancient Near Eastern power of chaos, *ANET*, 138–41.

Rhetorically, the imagery of a "flood" (*šôṭēp*) identifies with the Assyrian "flood of mighty waters" (*mayîm kabbîrîm šōṭpîm*) that sweeps the earth in the Lord's day of judgment (28:2; cf. 8:7–8; 17:13). In that metaphorical context, the *scourge* (*šôṭ*, 28:15, 18) the Lord uses against his wicked people describes the king of Assyria, the Lord's instrument of punishment. The king of Assyria functions as the chaotic counterpart of the ideal vassal, the Lord's *whip* (*šôṭ*, 10:26), which the Lord uses against Assyria. The linked motifs of a "flood of mighty waters" and the Lord's *hand* (28:2) support the Assyrian identity.

After serving as the Lord's instrument of universal retribution, Assyria itself suffers destruction: the Lord wages war against all nations who lay siege to Zion (29:6–8; 31:4); the Lord's *arm/voice/staff/ensign* subdues Assyria in warfare (30:30–32; 31:9); and a righteous remnant of Ephraim, whom the Lord empowers, repulses Assyria's attack at the gates (28:5–6). In the end, those who perish include Assyria (30:32; 31:8), Egyptians and their allies (31:3), the nations (29:8), tyrants, scorners (29:20), and the wicked of the Lord's people (28:2–3, 18–22; 29:5, 21; 30:14–17; 31:3)—all non-Zion entities.

The text narrows down those who perish among the Lord's people as those who reject the Lord's counsel and living oracle in favor of a false shelter (28:15, 17). The Lord's counsel excels, his inspiration surpasses men's understanding (28:29; 29:14); he himself guides and instructs common men (28:26; 29:24; 30:21); his living oracle conveys the Lord's words to his people and their leaders (28:14, 22; 30:2, 10–12). But by relying on mortal means of protection, the Lord's people deceive themselves (28:15). By thinking no one discerns their schemes, they mock God, their Maker (29:15–16). As they take refuge in human institutions, these institutions unexpectedly collapse about them, leaving them destitute and disgraced (30:1–5, 12–14).

Those who erred in spirit who accept the Lord's instruction (29:24), on the other hand, the Lord redeems like Abraham (29:22). Those who endure the Lord's sifting of the nations in a sieve of falsehood, who survive his testing of men's loyalties with a bridle of error on their jaws (30:28), sing, rejoicing, as they participate in a pilgrimage to the Lord's holy mountain (30:29).

The first unit's emphasis on divine guidance versus human counsel reflects a heightened spiritual response the Lord expects of his people. The Lord's divine instruction and revelation surpass the schoolmaster principle of "precept upon precept" and "line upon line" (*ṣaw lāṣāw ṣaw lāṣāw qaw lāqāw qaw lāqāw*, 28:9–10). Repetition and assonance parody the rote method the Lord's wicked people use for learning the Lord's word.[3] That approach yields but "a trifle here and a trifle there" (*zĕʿîr šām zĕʿîr šām*, 28:10–13). As priests and prophets fail in their function as seers (28:7), such a knowledge of the Lord's word proves fatefully insufficient to save the Lord's people from calamity (28:13).

As the Lord shuts the eyes of the prophets (29:10), all-encompassing or "apocalyptic vision" (*ḥāzût hakkôl*) becomes a sealed book to the learned and unlearned alike (29:11–12; cf. 48:6). The unsealing of the book, which contains a testimony for the last day (30:8), causes the Lord's blind and deaf remnant to see and hear his words (29:18). Despite that positive result, the lip service and rote commandments the wicked offer as homage (29:13) cause the Lord to overturn their human learning (29:14). At such a time of apostasy, the Lord proceeds wondrously to perform things unexpected (29:14).

A Covenant of Life

The second unit (chaps. 55–59) focuses on a positive response to the Lord's word and is replete with exhortations to righteousness: "Let the wicked forsake their ways and sinful men their thoughts; let them return to the Lord, and he will have mercy on them, to our God, who graciously pardons" (55:7); "Observe justice and perform righteousness, for soon my salvation will come and my righteousness be revealed" (56:1); "They who walk uprightly shall attain peace and rest in their beds" (57:2); "They who seek refuge in me shall possess the earth and receive an inheritance in my holy mountain" (57:13cd).

This material condemns the wicked and expresses approbation of the righteous, as before. The second unit goes beyond the first, however, in describing how the Lord's people respond to the Lord's word. The wicked exemplify straying hearts (57:17), crooked paths (59:8), wantonness (57:12), covetousness (57:17), dishonesty (59:4, 13),

---

[3] The expression "this/these people" (*hāʿām hazzeh*) that describes the Lord's people in this context (28:11, 14; 29:13–14) repudiates the covenant relationship implicit in the expression "my people" (*ʿammî*); compare 6:9–10; 8:11; *passim*.

injustice (59:4, 11), guile, duplicity (59:3), deceit, wrongdoing (59:4, 6), injurious dealings (59:6–7), extortion, manipulation (59:6, 13), strife, contention (58:4), wilful denial of the Lord (59:13), darkness (59:9–10), alienation (57:11), idolatry (57:6–7), blindness (56:10–11; 59:10), sin, iniquity (57:4; 58:1; 59:2–3, 7, 12), lust (57:5), adultery (57:3, 8–10), persecution of the righteous (57:4; 58:9), and murder (57:5; 59:3, 7).

The righteous, on the other hand, are truthful, just, and upright (56:1; 57:1–2; 58:8; 59:14). They have a humble spirit (57:15) and do no evil (56:2; 59:15). They repent of transgression (55:7; 59:20); pray to the Lord (56:7); come to the Lord (55:3; 58:2); call upon the Lord (55:6; 58:9); inquire of the Lord (55:6; 58:2); hear the Lord (55:3); receive the Lord's direction (58:11; 59:21); learn the Lord's ways (58:2); choose what the Lord wills (56:4); adhere to the Lord (56:3, 6); abide by the Lord's precepts and ordinances (58:2); serve the Lord and love his name (56:6); hold fast to the Lord's covenant (56:4, 6); seek refuge in the Lord (57:13cd); keep the sabbath day holy (56:2, 4, 6; 58:13); make sacrifices and offerings (56:7); demonstrate integrity and perfection (59:8, 15); release others from bondage (58:6, 9); and share shelter, food, and clothing with the needy (58:7, 10).

Such characterizations of the righteous and the wicked reflect two definitive responses to the Lord's law and word. How the Lord conveys his law and word, together with how his people respond, forms the substance of this material. The Lord exhorts his people to seek his living oracle (55:6). By definition, the Lord's word constitutes food for the eater (55:2, 10–11). It begets covenantal benediction and peace for those who receive it (55:11–12). Those inherit peace who "partake⁴ of the fruit of the lips" (57:19), while the wicked, who rely on empty words (59:4), know no peace (57:21; 59:8).

A universal appeal to hear the Lord's word, in chapter 55, centers on the Lord's covenant:

1. Attention, all who thirst; come for water!
   You who have no money, come and buy food,
   that you may eat.
   Come, buy wine and milk
   with no money and at no cost.

---

⁴ Hebrew *bôrē)* ("create") has been emended to *bôrê*.

219

2. Why do you spend money on what is not bread,
    your labor on what does not satisfy?
    Hear me well: Eat what is good,
    and your souls shall enjoy abundance.
3. Give ear and come unto me;
    pay heed, that your souls may live!
    And I will make with you an everlasting covenant:
    [my] loving fidelity toward David.[5]
4. See, I have appointed him as a witness to the nations,
    a prince and lawgiver of the peoples.
5. You will summon a nation whom you did not know;
    and a people who did not know you
    will hasten to you—
    because of the Lord your God,
    the Holy One of Israel, who gloriously endows you.

An a–b–c–b–a structure in this passage highlights the Lord's invitation to come unto the Lord's covenant, as follows: verses 1–2b and 5 deal with the summons of the Lord's people, who sometime evidenced alienation; verses 2c–3b and 4 deal with the Lord's living oracle as personified by the Lord's ideal vassal, who here appears cumulatively under his Davidic aspect; and verse 3cd presents the Lord's covenant as vested in the ideal vassal, the Lord's agent of deliverance.

The Lord offers gratis a "covenant" (*běrît*) of survival or sustenance—"that your souls may live" (*těḥî napšěkem*, v 3). An abundance of food and drink symbolizes both the Lord's word as nourishment and the covenantal benediction that accompanies a positive response to the Lord's word. By exhorting all to "eat what is good!" (v 2), the Lord calls them to covenantal loyalty.[6] The appeal to "hear well!" (*šim'û šāmôa'*, v 2), which the passage repeats (v 3), calls attention to the Lord's covenant of life. That appeal points to the Lord's word as the antidote to noncovenantal hunger and thirst (v 1) and to the implicit alternative of death.[7]

---

[5] Compare *ḥasdê dāwid hanne'ĕmānîm* as objective genetive in H. G. M. Williamson, "The Sure Mercies of David," *JSS* 23 (1978): 330–49.

[6] See good (*ṭôb*, 55:2) as a synonym of covenant in Fox, "*Ṭôb* as Covenant Terminology"; and good (*ṭôb*) as yielding fruit for the righteous when the Lord judges the wicked, 3:10–11.

[7] See this expression (*šim'û šāmôa'*) as it applies rhetorically elsewhere to an unresponsive people who are cut off from covenantal blessedness, 6:9.

The Lord's covenant subsists in the ideal latter-day vassal (v 3), who serves as the Lord's spokesman to the nations (v 4).[8] That idea accords with the vassal's personifying the Lord's *covenant* and his serving as the Lord's lawgiver and *light* to the nations (cf. 42:1, 4, 6; 49:6). The second unit modifies or redefines these cumulative concepts by depicting the ideal vassal as the Lord's living oracle. Because the Lord's covenant embodies the Lord's law and word, this vassal's role as the Lord's living oracle flows naturally out of his personification of the Lord's *covenant*. The Lord's appointing him as a witness (*'ēd*), prince (*nāgîd*), and lawgiver (*mĕṣawwēh*) to the nations (v 4) expresses the ideal vassal's redemptive role as the Lord's representative.[9]

Besides a chiastic pattern, a series of word pairs marks this passage as a tightly knit unit. These word pairs underline the renewed covenantal allegiance of a nation of the Lord's people that gathers from among the nations because of the Lord's word.[10] This chain of word pairs, a literary device, links the first and last ideas to appear in the passage, which are the hungry and thirsty hearkening to the Lord's word (v 1) at the time the Lord gloriously endows his vassal (v 5). The words that are repeated highlight the invitation to covenantal allegiance. The renewed allegiance of the Lord's people leads directly to a return wandering in the wilderness—according to the Lord's word (55:11-13).[11]

The Lord's fulfillment of the "word that issues from his mouth" (55:11), in effect, is contingent on the ideal vassal's function as the

---

[8] There is no literary evidence for the idea Otto Eissfeldt and others espouse, that the covenant subsists in the Lord's people and that these corporately represent the Lord's lawgiver to the nations; Otto Eissfeldt, "The Promises of Grace to David in Isaiah 55:1-5," in B. W. Anderson and Walter Harrelson, eds., *Israel's Prophetic Heritage* (New York: Harper and Row, 1962), 196-207. At this point in the text, the Lord's ideal vassal still serves, cumulatively, as a paradigm of the Lord's people, whom he summons from exile through allegiance toward the Lord (55:4-7).

[9] See the less obvious of these terms—"prince" (*nāgîd*)—as "speaker/spokesman," Job 31:37 (cf. Prov 8:6), which meaning relates to the present passage. See also the connotation of *nāgîd* as proxy representative, 2 Kgs 20:5-6.

[10] See, in 55:1-5, the word-chain, "come/come," verse 1; "no money/no money," verse 1; "buy/buy," verse 1; "eat/eat," verses 1-2; "hear/hear," verses 2-3; "souls/souls," verses 2-3; "nations/nations" (*lĕ'ûmîm*, also "peoples"), verse 4; "a nation/a nation" (*gôy*), verse 5; "did not know/did not know," verse 5.

[11] See 49:5-12, where a similar divine endowment of the Lord's ideal vassal leads to a return wandering in the wilderness from throughout the nations (cf. also 52:11-13).

Lord's living oracle, as his *mouth*. Such a function modifies or redefines the cumulative concepts of the ideal vassal as the Lord's prophet (41:26; 48:16) and as a preacher of the Lord's word (50:4, 10). In the first unit of section VI, those who rely on their own counsel do not inquire at the Lord's *mouth* (30:2). Those who respond positively to the Lord's word, on the other hand, hear his *voice* (28:23).[12] In the second unit, the Lord's *voice* declares his people's transgression (58:1) and the Lord's *mouth* schools them in righteousness (58:13-14). The verse "inquire of the Lord while he is present; call upon him while he is near!" (55:6), which follows the Davidic passage, suggests that the Lord grants a brief interval of time (the duration of the vassal's prophetic mission) in which the nations may repent and receive his word (55:7; cf. 56:1).

The remainder of the second unit yields a dichotomy of responses to the Lord's appeal to covenantal loyalty. "Aliens" and "eunuchs," the lowest rung of Israelite society, are included among the Lord's covenant people (56:3-4) when they respond favorably to the Lord's *righteousness* (56:1). These merit royal accession (56:5) and constitute "additional" people whom the Lord gathers, along with Israel's exiles, to become his people (56:7-8). Wild beasts, on the other hand, devour the Lord's blind "watchmen" and insensible "shepherds" (56:9-11)—the highest rung of society. These suffer a full measure of malediction when a drunken preoccupation with personal advantage makes them but dumb watchdogs as the Lord's day of judgment draws nigh (56:10-57:1). Harlot imagery (57:7-13) depicts those who ignore the Lord and alienate themselves from him (57:3-6, 11). The Lord reduces such to vapor and wind—to chaos— in the time of calamity (57:13). Yet, the Lord feeds those who repent of false religious practices with the heritage of Jacob their father (58:1, 14). Their *righteousness* qualifies them for participating in a new exodus and they experience a reversal of malediction (58:8-12).

Such disparate fates follow a universal response to the Lord's ideal vassal. The declaration "according to what they deserve, he will repay them" (59:18) addresses those to whom the Lord extends his *arm* of *righteousness* when he intervenes forcibly to restore justice among his people (59:15-17). The Lord's enemies, worldwide, will

---

[12] See the parallelistic synonymity of the Lord's *mouth* (*peh*) and *hand* (*yād*), 49:2; 51:16; the Lord's *voice* (*qôl*) and *ensign* (*nēs*), 13:2; the Lord's *voice* (*qôl*) and *hand* (*yād*), 13:2; and the Lord's *voice* (*qôl*) and *arm* (*zĕrôaʿ*), 30:30.

suffer his *rage* (*ḥēmâ*, 59:18–19)—the king of Assyria/Babylon. But Zion—those of Jacob who repent of transgression—will receive the Lord as Redeemer (59:19). In that redemptive context, the Lord places his Spirit and words in his people's *mouth* and in the *mouth* of their offspring by an everlasting covenant (59:21).

The Lord's manifesting his covenant through his living word in this manner modifies or redefines the role of the Lord's vassal as an exemplar and paradigm of the Lord's people. Those who receive the Lord's word, as it issues from the Lord's *mouth*, themselves become the recipients of the Lord's Spirit and words. The parallelism, in 59:21—of the Lord's bestowing his Spirit, placing his words in the mouth—further alludes to the ideal vassal's function as the Lord's living oracle or *mouth*: the Lord's endowment of his vassal with his Spirit enables him to convey the Lord's words to his people.[13] Of those twin roles King David is a type (cf. 2 Sam 23:2: "The Spirit of the Lord spoke by me, and his word was on my tongue").

At the Lord's coming to Zion (59:20), all who attain a righteousness that compares with that of the ideal vassal are endowed even as he is endowed by the Lord (59:21). The conferral of the Lord's Spirit and word, together with the blessings of offspring (59:21), a land of inheritance (57:13; 58:14), and divine protection (59:17–20), forms the essence of Isaianic covenant theology. The Lord fully implements his redemption, in other words, as his people renew their allegiance toward him.

Discourse I: The New Covenant

The covenant theme in Isaiah draws on a full spectrum of covenant ideas. Though these come to light sporadically throughout the text, many such covenant ideas appear linked to one another. By piecing them together, domino fashion, we obtain a clearer understanding of the nature of the Isaianic covenant. We learn that this material projects a new covenant the Lord makes with his people in the latter days that is a composite of all former covenants of the Lord.

The main elements of four biblical covenants, for example, appear in variously linked combinations through Isaiah. First is the Lord's promise to Abraham of a numerous posterity and an

---

[13] Compare the Lord's endowment of the ideal vassal with the Lord's Spirit in 11:2; 42:1; 48:16, its purpose being to declare good tidings, 61:1.

inheritance of land (51:2–3; 61:7–9; cf. Gen 17:1–8): the Lord blesses the followers of *righteousness* (51:1)—those who repent/return (51:11)—as he blesses Abraham, their type (51:2–3; 60:21–22). Second, the Lord addresses Zion by the covenant formula, "You are my people" (51:16). That corporate dimension pertains to the Sinai covenant, the Lord's covenant with his people as a nation (cf. Lev 26:9, 12). Third, the Lord endows the righteous and their offspring with his Spirit (32:15; 44:3); the Lord places his words in their mouth (51:16; 59:21). The latter reflects a feature of the Levitical covenant, the Lord's Spirit empowering the Lord's priests to teach his law (cf. Mal 2:4–7). Fourth, the Lord protects Zion in the shadow of his *hand* (51:16; cf. 41:8–13), exemplifying the Davidic covenant and its protection clause (see Discourse B: Zion Ideology [1]—the Davidic Covenant).

Beyond representing these basic covenant concepts, the text transforms the covenant theme to include additional covenantal features. For example, the idea of a land of inheritance (an ingredient of the Abrahamic covenant) is transformed into the Lord's people inheriting a wilderness regenerated to a paradisiacal state—"like Eden" (51:3; cf. 35:1–2; 55:13)—denoting covenant curse reversal. Further, the Lord ordains his righteous people and their posterity as his priests (61:6–10; 66:21), expressing features of both the Abrahamic and Levitical covenants. Additionally, the Lord makes his new covenant "everlasting" or "unconditional" (*běrît ʿôlām*, 55:3; 59:21; 61:8). Such an unconditional aspect characterizes the Lord's covenants with Noah, Abraham, Pinehas the priest, and King David after each proves himself loyal to the Lord.[14] The expression "[my] loving fidelity toward David" (*ḥasdê dāwid hanneʾĕmānîm*, 55:3) typifies that unconditional aspect of the covenant.[15]

Many elements of the Lord's new covenant come together in chapter 54, which is part of the second unit of section V. Offspring and land (vv 1–3), the basic features of the Abrahamic covenant, are transformed into offspring that the Lord himself teaches (v 13)

---

[14] See the Lord's unconditional covenants with Noah, Abraham, Pinehas, and David as *běrît ʿôlām*, Gen 9:16; 17:7; Num 25:13; 2 Sam 23:5, respectively; and the new covenant elsewhere as *běrît ʿôlām*, Jer 32:40; Ezek 37:26.

[15] See the term *ḥesed* as a synonym of the ancient Near Eastern Covenant of Grant, Weinfeld, "Berîth," 270–72.

and a land that the Lord protects (vv 14–17). The Lord makes the new covenant with those who survive a cataclysm of the magnitude of the Flood in the days of Noah (vv 9–10). That idea signifies both a time frame—that the Lord makes the covenant *after* a universal cataclysm—and that those with whom the Lord covenants resemble Noah in righteousness (v 9; cf. Gen 6:9). By calling it a "covenant of peace" (*bĕrît šālôm*, v 10), the text identifies it with the Levitical covenant.[16]

In its context, however, the Lord's covenant of peace in chapter 54 (cf. "peace," *šālôm*, v 13) expresses quintessentially the Lord's redemption of his people as section V develops it: the Lord's people are redeemed and remarried to the Lord everlastingly (vv 5–8). In section V, the suffering figure pays the "price of our peace" or salvation (53:5), which, as we saw, lays the foundation for the Lord's redemption of his people. Lastly, the new covenant's description as the Lord's "everlasting charity" (*ḥesed ʿôlām*, 54:8, 10) reiterates the covenant's unconditional aspect[15]—the new covenant is made with a people (not just with individuals) who have proven themselves exceedingly loyal to the Lord.

The covenant to which the Lord's ideal vassal summons the Lord's people from among the nations (55:1–5), then, combines the exemplary features of the Lord's former covenants, particularly covenants the Lord made with individuals. The structured context of that covenant in the second unit of section VI, and the rhetorical linking of covenantal elements throughout Isaiah, attests to a single ideal covenant that transcends former covenants. Of that new covenant, former covenants serve as a type. This means that those with whom the Lord makes the new covenant evidence covenantal loyalty toward the Lord comparable to that of the ancients. The Lord makes no unconditional covenant except with those who exemplify covenantal allegiance by passing severe tests of loyalty toward him. The Lord's ideal latter-day vassal, who combines the outstanding attributes of many biblical heroes, thus qualifies as the exemplar of those with whom the Lord covenants.

In sum, the Isaianic covenant represents a composite of all former covenants the Lord made with his people and with individuals consistent with the cumulative principle of composite phenomena

---

[16] See the "covenant of peace" (*bĕrît šālôm*) the Lord makes with Pinehas, Num 25:12; compare the Levitical covenant of life (*ḥayyîm*) and peace (*šālôm*), Mal 2:5.

found throughout the Bifid Structure. These former covenants include the Noachian, Abrahamic, Sinaitic, Levitical, and Davidic covenants. The Lord's new covenant embodies in one a promise of offspring whom the Lord endows with the priesthood and with his Spirit and of a land that the Lord regenerates and protects, which covenant the Lord makes unconditionally, after a cataclysm of the magnitude of the Flood, with the righteous who return from among the nations.

The ideal vassal's personification of the Lord's *covenant*—which term serves as a metaphorical pseudonym of the Lord's vassal (42:6; 49:8; see section III)—implies that the latter-day vassal mediates the new covenant. This mediatory role differs from that of Moses to Israel, first, in that the ideal vassal mediates the covenant with a people whom he releases from bondage among the nations rather than from a single nation, Egypt (42:7; 49:5–12; 55:4–5); and, second, that he does so as a monarch, the Lord's vassal, not only as a prophet.[17] Because all elements of the new covenant form an integral part of the Lord's redemption of his people, the term *covenant*, as it applies to the Lord's vassal, also identifies him allegorically as an agent of that redemption.

A Decisive Covenantal Allegiance

Just as in the first unit a covenant with death epitomizes adherence to human counsel and schemes (*'ēṣâ*), so, in the second, a covenant of life epitomizes acceptance of the Lord's living word. These juxtaposed covenantal ideas subsume the various cumulative concepts of the Bifid Structure. On the one hand, covenantal loyalty and compliance lead to the rebirth, deliverance, exaltation, and salvation of Zion as represented by a covenant of life. On the other, covenantal disloyalty and rebellion lead to the ruin, punishment, humiliation, and suffering of non-Zion, as represented by a covenant with death. Such contrasting covenantal fortunes include the abolition of death for the Lord's righteous people (developed in section V), which section VI restates in terms of a covenant of life. Whereas the Lord's righteous people are delivered from death because they reject human counsel in favor of the Lord's living word, the wicked suffer death because they do the contrary.

---

[17] See King Josiah as a type of Davidic mediator of the Lord's covenant, 2 Kgs 23:3.

Isaiah nonetheless juxtaposes adherence to human counsel with acceptance of the Lord's living word within the first unit of section VI, even as he juxtaposes acceptance of the Lord's living word with human dissoluteness within the second unit. The Lord's new covenant manifests itself in a redemptive "peace" for those who are far off and those who are near who receive the Lord's word (57:19). That redemption accords with the ideal vassal's serving a mission to those at home and those abroad, as we noted in section V. Adherence to human counsel, on the other hand, results in the wicked's being utterly destroyed (28:22). Such incur covenantal calamity or cursing (*rā'â*) in the Lord's day of judgment (57:1).

Section VI's structuring of these ideas suggests that the Lord's redemption—or, alternatively, the Lord's vengeance—follows a time when the inhabitants of the earth ally themselves with one or another covenantal entity. At a certain point (in the latter days, when the Lord's coming draws nigh), all persons turn either pro- or anti-Lord. During the period in which the Lord's words issue from his *mouth*, all middle ground vanishes. As the Lord's day of judgment approaches, the Lord reduces the choices to two, life or death. The exhortative tone of the material reflects the exigency of people's allying themselves with the Lord. The juxtaposition of two covenants—one of life, the other with death—underscores an emerging polarization of people. Both groups formally bind themselves to a course of action and thus choose the consequences that follow.

The Lord's witness, spokesman, and lawgiver—the Lord's agent for mediating his words—thus acts as the catalyst of a great division or separation that takes place between the righteous and the wicked. Those who receive the Lord's words are redeemed as Zion; but those who reject the Lord's words are punished as non-Zion. The polarization of peoples that results in Zion's redemption and non-Zion's demise flows out of a definitive response to the Lord's living oracle, the ideal latter-day vassal. Since the Lord personally guides and directs individuals loyal to himself (28:9, 26), these recognize the Lord's vassal as his *voice* and *mouth* and thus respond to his summons (55:5). Those who alienate themselves from the Lord's law and word, on the other hand, emerge as a spurious people of the Lord (30:8–11; 58:1). The latter's repudiation of the Lord's vassal—of his mediating the Lord's word and his exemplifying covenantal righteousness (30:12; 59:9, 14)—in effect precipitates the Lord's judgment of the wicked (28:22; 59:17-19).

Section VI rounds out these concepts in many instances. The first unit, for example, depicts a reversal of malediction for the Lord's repentant people: the deaf hear the words of the book and the eyes of the blind see out of gross darkness (29:18; cf. vv 22-24);[18] but those who mock and persist in wickedness, the Lord cuts off (29:20). That reversal takes place "in a very little while" from the time the Lord speaks to his people (29:17).[19] For those who believe, the Lord lays in Zion a *stone* (*'eben*) as a sure foundation (28:16);[20] but those who reject the Lord's word, he visits with sudden and unexpected calamity (30:12-14). The Lord's righteous remnant benefits from the judgment of a just judge (28:5-6); but the wicked reject the *righteous one* (*ṣaddîq*) for chaos (*tōhû*, 29:21).

The second unit, too, speaks of imminent salvation for those of "humanity" (*'ĕnôs*) who hold fast to the Lord's *righteousness* and *covenant* (56:1-2, 4);[21] impending disaster, on the other hand, awaits the children of the harlot (57:1, 3)—the Lord's alienated people (57:11). To those who accept the Lord's instruction, the Lord's *light* dawns and they participate in a new exodus led by *righteousness* (58:8); but those who make crooked their paths, *righteousness* cannot reach and they have no *light* (59:9). The Lord revives and regenerates those whose stumbling blocks are removed (57:14-15; 58:11); but those who back away from following the Lord become as dead men (59:10, 13). Such portrayals of the righteous and the wicked suggest that these two groups coexist as covenantal entities in the interim before the Lord redeems Zion and damns non-Zion.

---

[18] Compare the ideal vassal's mission to open the eyes of the blind and to release those who dwell in darkness, 42:7.

[19] Compare the prophet Isaiah's three-year mission as a "sign and portent" of Assyria's capture of Egypt, which nation is part of arch Babylon, 20:1-6. Since the message of the Bifid Structure teaches of a destruction of arch Babylon by a latter-day Assyria, Isaiah's mission warning against Assyria's conquest serves as a type of the ideal vassal's latter-day mission. Compare also arch Babylon's three-year "lease" of time before its destruction, 16:14.

[20] Compare, in Gen 49:24, "a shepherd, the *stone* (*'eben*) of Israel."

[21] See the synonymity of *righteousness* and *covenant* that the verb *hold fast* (*ḥzq*) establishes rhetorically, 56:2, 4.

Summary

The homiletic and exhortative content of section VI (chaps. 28–31; 55–59) lends itself to the emergence of two juxtaposed ideas, a covenant of life and a covenant of death. An intrinsic covenant relationship of people or peoples with the Lord thus divides in two: one reflects loyalty toward the Lord, the other springs of disloyalty; one accounts for the Lord's redeemed people, the other marks apostates. Because the Lord's redemption and vengeance occur universally and concurrently, all peoples, Israelite or non-Israelite, fall into one or the other covenantal category. In the first unit, the Lord cuts off those who covenant with death, who rely on human counsel; yet he delivers those of his people who receive his living word. In the second unit, the Lord grants a covenant of life and peace to those from among the nations who heed the ideal vassal's summons. Those who reject the Lord's *righteousness*, on the other hand, incur a state of no peace.

The Lord's redemption of the righteous and his vengeance on the wicked follow their response to the Lord's living oracle. The ideal vassal's personification of the Lord's *covenant* entails his mediating the Lord's law and word and serving as the Lord's *mouth*. Those who receive the Lord's word and repent/return will experience the Lord's redemption. Those who reject the Lord's word harden into an alien entity, sealing themselves up, covenantally, for destruction. The Lord's agent of that destruction—of death—is the king of Assyria.

Section VI thus modifies or redefines cumulative concepts of a nascent Zion whom the Lord redeems and an arch Babylon that represents non-Zion, transforming them into two polarized covenantal entities. In the end, covenantal allegiance distinguishes the righteous from the wicked worldwide. In its emphasis on covenantal allegiance, and in the homiletic context for that emphasis, section VI of the Bifid Structure is unique.

SECTION VII
DISINHERITANCE & INHERITANCE
(32–33; 60–66)

Section VII of the Bifid Structure builds on all prior concepts established structurally and completes their development with its own literary message. By alternately characterizing those who serve God and those who alienate themselves from him, this material contrasts two coexisting covenantal entities, then portrays their inevitable separation. The righteous receive a glorious covenantal heritage; the wicked become an eternal execration. The language rings with finality, its descriptive terms possessing a pointedness that prior material lacks. All prophetic themes that the Bifid Structure develops appear cumulatively and climactically in this section.

One noteworthy phenomenon that characterizes section VII is the idea of spiritual progression. In this final section of the Bifid Structure—as if here, indeed, the goal is realized—we observe spiritual ascent on several levels: according to the cumulative concept of a paradigmatic hierarchy, individual "sons" of Zion ascend and become the Lord's "servants," even as the Lord's ideal latter-day vassal ascends and becomes as the angel of the Lord. The ideal vassal's spiritual ascent, a cumulative concept from section V, parallels the prophet Isaiah's ascent in section II. The spiritual progression of the Lord's "servants" and "sons," on the other hand, follows the paradigm of the Lord's ideal vassal.

A Contradistinction between the Wicked and the Righteous

The first unit of section VII (chaps. 32–33) characterizes both the wicked and the righteous. It speaks of the blasphemy, impiety, and hypocrisy of the godless (32:5–7), who nevertheless pass for the noble among the people (32:5). These include political opportunists who resort to malevolent means and insidious devices in their dealings with others (32:6–7), and teachers of religion who preach perverse things concerning the Lord (32:6). They leave the hungry soul empty and deprive the thirsty soul of drink (32:6). They cause the ruin and social demise of the poor (32:7). Included among the reprobates are complacent and carefree women who suffer the failure of the harvest they so smugly depend on (32:9–13). The text sums up this evil category of people as sinners in Zion and wicked nations,[1] both of whom are ripe for burning (33:11–14).

The righteous, on the other hand, stand up for what is virtuous (32:8). These wait for the Lord amid troubled times (33:2). They prove faithful and wise under duress and at all times exercise a scrupulous integrity (33:6, 15). Such survive the holocaust that consumes the godless (33:14–15). They live to behold the King in his glory (33:17). They obtain healing, forgiveness of their sins, and an abundance of spoil (33:23–24). The cumulative themes of ruin and rebirth, rebellion and compliance, punishment and deliverance, humiliation and exaltation, suffering and salvation, loyalty and disloyalty are all present and interwoven in this material.

Two disparate fates—dispossession and inheritance—complete the contrast between the wicked and the righteous. An enemy lays waste the land of the Lord's people (33:1, 9), and briars and thorns overgrow it (32:13). A hail fells the forests and levels the city of revelry (32:19), which becomes the haunt of wild animals (32:13–14, 19). Though the land is identified as that of the Lord's people (32:13), its desolation attests to the false peace people (*'ĕnôs*) seek in human treaties or covenants (*bĕrît*, 33:7–9). The righteous, on the other hand, dwell safely in cliff fortresses in the day of burning (33:16). They inherit Zion, the abode of peace, an immovable tent never to be uprooted (33:20–21, 24). As the Lord's covenant people, they possess the land in peace and safety (32:16–19). Their crops are well watered and their domestic animals graze unmolested (32:20).

The desert typifies the reversal of circumstances between the wicked and the righteous: the productive lands of the wicked become wilderness and forests (32:12–15), but the Lord turns the desert into

---

[1] An a_1–b_1–c_1–c_2–b_2–a_2 structure in chapter 33 identifies those who are far off as the nations and those who are near as the Lord's people in Zion, as follows: verses 11 and 14cd describe a curse of burning; verses 12 and 14ab identify the nations and the sinners in Zion, respectively; and verse 13 speaks of those who are far off and those who are near.

productive lands for the righteous (32:15-20). Mourning among the wicked (32:12-13) and an outpouring of the Lord's Spirit among the righteous (32:15) accompany this reversal of circumstances. These representations combine the cumulative concepts mentioned above with section VII's own emphasis on dispossession and inheritance.

The characterization of two contrasting covenantal entities assumes a personified form in the first unit's chapter headings. The two headings juxtapose the treachery of an arch "traitor" (*bôgēd*, 33:1) with the righteous rule of an ideal "king" and other "rulers/princes" (*śārîm*, 32:1). As one who violates the covenant or treaties (*hēpēr bĕrît*, 33:8), the former betrays and devastates others but then others betray and devastate him (33:1). The imagery of an archtyrant, one who burns and terrorizes the Lord's people and the nations (33:3, 11-14, 18-19), identifies him, cumulatively, as the king of Assyria/Babylon (cf. 9:18-19; 13:8-9; *passim*).

The ideal king, on the other hand, serves as a shelter from the storm (*zerem*),[2] as shade and water in the desert (32:2). Such proxy protection, within a threefold pattern of Isaianic Zion ideology (see Discourse B: Zion Ideology [1]—the Davidic Covenant),[3] identifies the righteous king as the Lord's ideal vassal. As becomes clear in the second unit, the vassal rules together with certain other "sons/servants"—vassals—of the Lord. The latter emulate the ideal vassal in fulfilling proxy roles on behalf of the Lord's people and in acceding to royal status. Rhetorically, however, the idea of a "king" ruling "in/with/by (*bĕ*) righteousness" (32:1) identifies the Lord himself as the king,[4] and *righteousness* as his ideal vassal. Depending on which level we read this passage, either the Lord or his ideal vassal may thus be intended.[5] Such duality is consistent with the threefold pattern of Zion ideology, in which the Lord and/or his ideal vassal are always represented.

---

[2] See storm, flood, and tempest imagery in Isaiah as denoting judgment, 4:6; 25:4; 28:2; *passim*.

[3] See the destruction of the wicked, 31:8-9; and the deliverance of the righteous, 32:2; at the presence of the Lord and/or his ideal vassal, 32:1.

[4] See, rhetorically, the Lord as "King," 33:22; 52:7.

[5] See a similar interpretive dichotomy in 11:4 (*passim*): "He will judge the poor with [*bĕ*] righteousness." Contextually, the Lord's ideal vassal—the *branch* (11:1) is the subject of this verse (see section III). Rhetorically, however, the Lord is "Judge" (see 33:22) and *righteousness* is his ideal vassal.

A Decisive Covenantal Separation

The second unit of section VII (chaps. 60–66) devotes part of the material to contrasting the fortunes of the wicked and the righteous, as before, and part to lavishly portraying the blessedness of the righteous. Just as the first unit alternately characterizes the wicked and the righteous—suggesting that two covenantal categories exist side by side—so the second unit adds the idea of two fates realized concurrently. One reward for the wicked and another for the righteous occur simultaneously within a common context. The second unit is especially vivid in its portrayal of these contrasts, weaving into its message all cumulative themes of the Bifid Structure—ruin and rebirth, rebellion and compliance, punishment and deliverance, humiliation and exaltation, suffering and salvation, disloyalty and loyalty, disinheritance and inheritance.

For example, the motif of a *light* dawning on the Lord's people in chapter 60, which opens the second unit, contrasts with that of darkness enveloping others, expressing a reversal of circumstances or a concurrent ruin and rebirth:

1. Arise, shine, your light has dawned;
    the glory of the Lord has risen upon you!
2. Although darkness covers the earth,
    and a thick mist the peoples,
  upon you the Lord will shine,
    over you his glory shall be visible.

In a like vein, those who reviled and tormented the Lord's people now bow and prostrate themselves before them (60:14). That scene features the simultaneous humiliation of the wicked and exaltation of the righteous. To punish the nations, moreover, the Lord treads their glory underfoot by his *anger/wrath* (63:3–6); but the Lord's redeemed praise him for his favor (*ḥesed*), goodness (*ṭûb*), and mercy (*raḥămâw*) when the Lord's *arm* intervenes to deliver them (63:5, 7). To some of his people, the Lord serves as a Savior, redeeming them in his love and compassion from their afflictions (63:8–9); but

234

to those of his people who rebel and grieve his Spirit, the Lord turns enemy and he fights against them (63:10).[6]

Those who recall the Lord's former wonders, who cry to the Lord in their distress, participate in a new exodus led by his *arm* (63:11–16). Those who harden their hearts toward the Lord, on the other hand, who stray from his ways and no longer fear him, the Lord dispossesses of their lands (63:17–18); they become as though the Lord had never ruled them, as though they had never been known by his name (63:19). Those who faithfully wait for the Lord, who perform righteousness and walk in his ways, the Lord saves from enemies as he descends in power (64:1–5c). Those who sin against the Lord and defile themselves, on the other hand, who do not call upon him or take hold of him, cause the Lord to hide his face and remain silent at their suffering (64:6, 10–11); a wind sweeps them away, and their inheritance turns to wilderness (64:5d–7, 12).

Those to whom the Lord holds out his *hands* all the day,[7] who manifest rebellion against the Lord, walking in ways that are "not good" (*lōʾ ṭôb*), following their own imagination, who do not seek the Lord, nor inquire of him, who provoke the Lord to his face by sacrificing in parks, making smoke upon bricks, who consume polluted foods and beverages, yet consider themselves "holier than thou"—such receive the maledictory payment that has accrued when the Lord destroys them (65:1–8). But the people of the Lord, those who loyally seek him, he takes out of destruction; they inherit the Lord's mountains, where they dwell in pastoral serenity (65:8–10). Those who forsake the Lord and forget his holy mountain, who spread tables for Luck and pour mixed wines for Fortune, who do not respond when the Lord calls, nor give heed when he speaks, who do "evil" (*raʿ*) in his eyes and choose to do what is not his will—such, the Lord destines to the sword and to the slaughter (65:11–12).

---

[6] The apposite conditions described in adjacent passages of chapters 63–64, though they appear circumstantially, form an integral part of the material's contrast of the wicked and the righteous. In that manner, the second unit illustrates by way of context the idea of the Lord's "day of vengeance" being at one and the same time the "year of [his] redeemed" (63:4; cf. 61:2).

[7] The term *hands*, in the context of a *day* (65:2)—the day of the Lord—suggests the imminence of both redemption and judgment through the agency of the Lord's ideal vassal (the Lord's right *hand*) and the archtyrant (the Lord's left *hand*).

A passage in chapter 65 depicts the separation of the wicked and the righteous that characterizes the second unit; covenantal benediction and malediction manifest themselves concurrently and in full:

13. My servants shall eat indeed,
    while you shall hunger;
    my servants shall drink indeed,
    while you shall thirst;
    my servants shall rejoice indeed,
    while you shall be dismayed.
14. My servants shall shout indeed,
    for gladness of heart,
    while you shall cry out with heartbreak,
    howling from brokenness of spirit.
15. Your name shall be left
    to serve my chosen ones for a curse
    when my lord the Lord slays you.
    But his servants he will call by a different name.

The idea of a curse associated with a name (v 15), like the name *Sodom* (see 1:9–10), implies that a sentence of damnation has been passed upon the wicked. The parallel idea of a new name (v 15), like the name *Israel* (see 49:1, 3), implies the assumption of a higher spiritual function for the Lord's righteous people. These things suggest that an irrevocable separation of the wicked and the righteous occurs—of utter execration on the one hand, and of royal accession and a new covenantal status on the other. The title of "servants" (*ăbādîm*) that describes the righteous and the anonymous "you" (*ʾattem*) that distinguishes the wicked reflect respective pro- and anti-Lord loyalties. The term "servants" denotes individual vassalship by some toward the Lord, in emulation of the ideal latter-day vassal, the Lord's "servant." Rhetorically, we learn that the Lord's servants consist of the "tribes" of the Lord's inheritance (*šibṭê nahălātekâ*, 63:17) as well as "foreigners/aliens" (*běnê hannēkār*, 56:6). The latter experience royal accession (a handclasp and a new name) when they hold fast to the Lord's *covenant* (56:3–6).

The term "you," on the other hand, addresses particularly those who *were* the Lord's people but who alienated themselves from him (65:11–12). Their alienation from the Lord—by their not responding when he calls, nor giving heed when he speaks, but of doing "evil" (*ra'*) in his eyes, of choosing to do what is not his will (65:12)—parallels the alienation of the Lord's wicked people in the following chapter: those who go their own ways, whose souls delight in abominations, who do not respond when the Lord calls, nor give heed when he speaks, who do "evil" (*ra'*) in his eyes and choose to do what is not his will—upon them the Lord brings intrigues, the very things they dread, all that is due them (66:3–4, 6). With those of a humble and contrite spirit, who are vigilant for the Lord's word, on the other hand, the Lord dwells as in his house (66:1–2; cf. 57:15). Such persons the Lord protects (66:5–6).[8]

The text here narrows down the identity of the wicked to "brethren." These brethren hate and exclude the righteous who take upon themselves the Lord's name, but in the end it is they who will suffer shame (66:5). The rhetorical synonymity of 66:4 to 65:12—that describes the alienation of the wicked in identical terms—assists in identifying the wicked as idolatrous brethren of the Lord's servants. The contexts of both passages depict the wicked as indulging in idolatry (65:11; 66:3), whereas those whom they oppress are the Lord's "servants," their righteous counterparts (65:13; 66:5).

The false brethren, moreover, are described contextually as the Lord's "enemies" (66:6). Such generic descriptions—of "servants" on the one hand and "enemies" on the other—reflect the universality of the righteous and of the wicked who oppress them. They also modify or redefine the concept of two contrasting covenantal groups: first, included among non-Zion entities are apostates who are evidently in a position of authority over the Lord's people; second, among the righteous who are persecuted there occurs progression to a new vassal status. A spiritual paradox thus manifests itself.

The idea of two opposite fates realized simultaneously comes clearly into focus when the Lord's *hand* is known among his servants and his *rage* is known among his enemies (66:14). The term *know* (*yd'*), which expresses a covenant relationship,[9] implies that pro- and anti-Lord entities, respectively, affiliate covenantally with the Lord's ideal vassal and with the archtyrant. That affiliation and

---

[8] See the rhetorical identity of those whom the Lord protects as those of a humble and contrite spirit, through the linking phrase "vigilant for my/his word" (66:2, 5).

[9] See section V, footnote 50.

its aftermath, too, represent cumulative concepts. (In sections V and VI, we saw that the Lord and his ideal vassal serve as paradigms of the righteous and the king of Assyria/Babylon as a paradigm of the wicked and that all entities affiliate covenantally either with the Lord and his ideal vassal—in a covenant of life—or with the king of Assyria/Babylon, in a covenant with death.)

The Lord's servants, who feature prominently in the second unit, owe covenantal allegiance directly toward the Lord. As the Lord's vassals, they resemble the Lord's ideal latter-day vassal; like him, they serve as proxies: the Lord delivers some of his people from destruction "for the sake of his servants" (65:8–9; cf. 63:17). Like him, they have ascended the paradigmatic ladder to become the Lord's "chosen" or "elect" (*běḥîray*, 65:9; cf. the ideal vassal, 42:1; 49:7). The enemies of the Lord's servants, therefore, are the Lord's enemies (66:5–6). Moreover, as the ideal vassal suffers affronts by the wicked, so do the Lord's servants (61:7; 66:5; cf. the ideal vassal, 49:7; 50:6–8). As the Lord puts down his ideal vassal's enemies, so he puts down his servants' enemies (54:15–17; 66:5–6; cf. the ideal vassal, 49:7; 50:7–9). The elevation of the Lord's servants and the abasement of the Lord's enemies occur simultaneously (65:13–15; 66:12–16).

The Lord's enemies, who make up non-Zion, include "cultists" (*mitqadšîm*) among the Lord's people and among "all flesh" (66:14–17). These suffer slaughter and burning at the Lord's coming (66:15–16). The Lord's servants, on the other hand, experience peace, comforts, rejuvenation, and rejoicing (66:12–14). Such blessings compare with those the woman Zion and her sons enjoy (66:10–12). Undergoing a nascent birth, Zion is a nation of the Lord's people born in a *day*—the Lord's day of judgment—made up of those who mourn for her (66:7–11). The woman imagery, which expresses the Lord's relationship with his people allegorically, illustrates how the wicked and the righteous, forming two covenantal entities, in the end irrevocably separate (see Discourse J: The Woman Figure).

Lastly, the Lord's re-creating the heavens and the earth (65:17), coupled with the Lord's re-creating his people (65:18), sums up the Lord's redemption. The linking of these ideas shows that the purpose of the Lord's cosmic creation *is* the creation of a redeemed people of the Lord. That creation is here in process of being realized. But the Lord's new creation involving the righteous also contrasts his everlasting damnation of the wicked: as the new heavens and new earth will endure before the Lord, so his righteous people's name and offspring will endure; but the bodies of the people who transgressed against the Lord will return to chaos amid unquenchable fire (66:22–24).

Discourse J: The Woman Figure

Just as a single covenant in Isaiah gives way to two covenants, and a single city to two cities, so a single Woman figure develops into two Woman figures: one affiliates with the Lord, the other disaffiliates from the Lord. The separation of two contrasting covenantal entities that the Bifid Structure develops parallels the destinies of the two Woman figures. In the opening chapter of Isaiah, the Lord adjudges a once faithful city a "harlot" (1:21). The harlot imagery describes the Lord's people anonymously: the text never identifies the harlot directly as the Lord's people, though contextually we understand that they represent the wicked among them (cf. 1:20–24). Such anonymity thus reflects the covenantal alienation of the wicked, those whom the Lord separates from among the righteous.[10] The righteous are those whom the Lord redeems (cf. 1:26–27), whom he espouses anew.

A consequence of the Woman's unfaithfulness toward the Lord is that she loses the Lord's protection. When enemies attack, they ruin her (22:4), leaving her sitting on the ground, mourning and destitute (3:26). Among the children she bore, none remains to guide her (51:18). Calamity overtakes both her and her children in the form of the sword, famine, ruin, and desolation (51:19–20). Neither she nor her children possess recourse to the Lord's protection because "by sinning you sold yourselves, on account of your crimes was your mother an outcast" (50:1). The idea of being sold (*nimkartem*) suggests that the Lord's alienated people become the possession of another lord. Section IV of the Bifid Structure thus develops the idea of an arch Babylon (non-Zion) that incorporates the Lord's people who choose wickedness.

The text depicts Babylon too as a Woman. Her lord, the tyrannical Babylonian god-king (cf. 14:13–14), suffers the same fate as the harlot Babylon (14:4). Protection for the Woman Babylon breaks

---

[10] A parallel example of anonymity signifying alienation appears in the expression "this/these people" (*hā'ām hazzeh*, 6:9; *passim*), in contrast to the covenant formula "my people" (*'ammî*, 51:16; *passim*).

down because of the tyranny of her lord (14:20–23) and on account of her adultery (47:3). The Lord exposes Babylon's nakedness and uncovers her shame (47:3). She who was mistress of kingdoms (47:5), who exerted herself from her youth for her procurers (47:12, 15), sits in the dust, dethroned and disgraced (47:1). Of her consorts, none saves her but each deviates his own way (47:15). They themselves cannot escape the *hand* of the flame (47:14). When her time draws near (13:22), sudden "calamity" or "evil" (*rā'â*) overtakes Babylon (47:11). The Lord razes all her idols to the ground (21:9). None of her children remain (14:22; 47:9).

Forming part of a non-Zion composite, the anonymous harlot and sorceress described in chapter 57 again represents the Lord's apostate people. The text details her adultery:

7. On a lofty mountain
   you have made prominent your bed,
   and there you ascend to offer sacrifices.
8. Behind doors and facades
   you have put up your emblems,
   and have exposed yourself to [others] than I:
   mounting your bed, you have laid it wide open.
   And you bargain with those with whom you love to lie,
   your hand on their nakedness.[11]
9. You bathe[12] with oil for the king
   and increase your perfumes;
   you send your solicitors far abroad
   and debase yourself to Sheol.
10. Though wearied by your excessive ways,
   you have not admitted despair;
   you have found livelihood,
   and therefore have not slackened.

The harlot's use of "oil" in connection with a king other than the Lord, and her debasing herself "to Sheol" (57:9), suggest that she maintains allegiance to another lord, pursuing a chaotic and irrevocable course.

At this point in her career she simply pretends the Lord does not exist, expressing utter fearlessness toward him (57:11). The

---

[11] Lit., "foreparts."

[12] From the verb *śrḥ*.

adulteress meets her doom when the Lord exposes her fornication and wanton exploits (57:12). In her distress, none saves her among those who flock to her (57:13). A wind carries all away (57:13). The same "calamity" or "evil" (*rāʿâ*) from which the Lord's righteous people are delivered overtakes her children (57:1–3).

Those of the Lord's people who repent of unfaithfulness, on the other hand, become a city of *righteousness* (1:26–27). These represent Zion or the Daughter of Zion (1:8, 27). When the archtyrant attacks her (10:32), laying siege to her (*nĕṣûrâ*, 1:8), she shakes her head and laughs him to scorn (37:22). She trusts in the Lord to protect her (37:35). As protection, the Lord extends his nuptial "canopy" (*ḥuppâ*) over her (4:5–6) and preserves her (*nĕṣûrâ*, 1:8). The text depicts the time of her distress as travail with children (37:3). The Lord overthrows her enemies when the Woman gives birth to a deliverer son (7:14; 9:1–6; 66:6–9).

The Woman, having served her term and expiated her sins (40:2), remarries the Lord everlastingly (54:5–8; 62:5). She forgets the shame of her youth and reproach of her widowhood (54:4). Rising from the dust, she sits enthroned, clothed with power (52:1–2). She binds to her the children who return to her as a bride adorns herself with jewels (49:18). She who was banished, exiled, bereaved, and barren (49:21) now sings with joy at her numerous offspring (54:1). Her children who mourned for her now nurse, comforted, at her consoling breasts (66:10–13). As her children increase, she expands the site of her tent (54:2). She becomes firmly established through *righteousness* (54:14) and ultimately encompasses the earth (66:8).

In sections IV and V, we reviewed the structural antithesis that depicts Zion as the Lord's redeemed people and arch Babylon as non-Zion. Yet, here we find a typological antithesis that depicts Zion as the Lord's newly espoused bride and the Lord's alienated people as a harlot. In both cases, Zion appears juxtaposed with a non-Zion composite that includes the wicked or alienated of the Lord's people. One concludes, therefore, that the Lord's wicked or alienated people and the harlot Babylon represent synonymous entities. These things again affirm that ultimately but two covenantal groups exist. The Woman imagery nuances the idea of Zion and non-Zion as parties opposite to one another in nature and destiny.

A Glorious Covenantal Heritage

Besides contrasting the wicked and the righteous, the second unit (chaps. 60–66) elaborates on the covenantal blessedness of the Lord's righteous people. Under the blessing of offspring, it describes Zion's sons and daughters gathering to Zion from afar (60:4, 9). Their gathering appears contextually as nations and rulers coming to the Lord's *light* (60:3–11). The Lord makes his priests those who return (61:6; 66:21). They and their offspring become renowned among the nations (61:9; 62:2) and enjoy the nations' wealth (60:16; 61:6). The Lord establishes the economic stability of his people by his *right hand*, his mighty *arm* (62:8–9), and the Lord prospers their labors (65:21–23). The Lord hears the righteous when they call upon him (65:24) and blesses them and their offspring (61:9; 65:23). They feel joy in place of shame (61:7; 65:14). They live an exceedingly long life (65:20, 22) and become fathers of nations (60:22).

The Lord blesses the righteous with a twofold inheritance in their land (60:21; 61:7)—a land newly restored (60:10; 61:4), a land the Lord regenerates and beautifies (60:13, 17), where the Lord himself dwells (60:1–2, 9, 13–14; 61:9), an everlasting pride, the joy of generation upon generation (60:15), a land where *righteousness* rules (60:17), a land *salvation* protects (60:18), a land the Lord's presence lights up (60:19–20), a land the Lord espouses (62:4), where peace reigns (60:17) and all creatures live in harmony (65:25). The Lord grants the blessings of offspring and land unconditionally—by an everlasting covenant (*bĕrît 'ôlām*, 61:8).[13]

The Lord's righteous people are thus the beneficiaries of a covenant of grant that incorporates the blessings and privileges of all former covenants of the Lord with his people or with individuals. Such a covenant implies that the Lord's people, corporately, have ascended to a higher spiritual status that compares with the spiritual status of Abraham, Isaac, Jacob, David, and others with whom the Lord made covenants of grant. Mediating the Lord's covenant and its blessings is the Lord's ideal latter-day vassal. A passage in

---

[13] The covenant forms the centerpiece of an a_1–b_1–c_1–d–c_2–b_2–a_2 structure in chapter 61, as follows: verses 4–5 describe the land's restoration and verse 11 the land's regeneration; verse 6 depicts an abundant sustenance for the Lord's priests and verse 10 their elegant attire; verse 7 emphasizes a twofold inheritance in the land and verse 9 a blessed posterity; and verse 8 presents the Lord's covenant as a sure reward for the righteous.

chapter 61 depicts the role of the ideal vassal, who serves as an agent of the Lord's redemption:

1. The Spirit of my lord the Lord is upon me,
    for the Lord has anointed me
    to announce good tidings to the lowly;
       he has sent me to bind up the brokenhearted,
    to proclaim liberty to the captives
       and the opening of the eyes to the bound,
2. to herald the year of the Lord's favor
       and the day of vengeance of our God,
    to comfort all who mourn:
3. to endow those who mourn in Zion,
       bestowing upon them a priestly headpiece
    in place of ashes,
    the festal anointing in place of mourning,
       a resplendent robe in place of a downcast spirit.
    They shall be called the oaks of righteousness,
       planted by the Lord for his glory.

The ideal vassal's "anointed" status, his endowment by the Lord's Spirit, his mission as a herald of good tidings, and his liberation of the Lord's blind captives—within a context of the *day* of the Lord (vv 1–2)—express cumulative concepts.[14] The purpose of the Lord's empowerment of the ideal vassal is thus the empowerment of his righteous people when these qualify for redemption. They qualify for the Lord's redemption by enduring faithfully a test or tests of their loyalty toward the Lord. As the Lord's agent of redemption, the ideal vassal fulfills a priestly role toward them (v 3). Drawing on a Moses typology, the ideal vassal anoints the mourners in Zion with oil and clothes them in priestly attire (v 3). Such an act follows the pattern of Moses' anointing and clothing of Aaron and his sons within a covenantal context (cf. Lev 8:12–13).

The anointing of the mourners in Zion again illustrates the concept of a paradigmatic hierarchy: those on a lower rung of the ladder may ascend and become as one who ministers to them. Some among the Lord's people, in other words, now too are anointed and serve

---

[14] See elsewhere the ideal vassal's "anointed" status, 45:1; his endowment by the Lord's Spirit, 11:2; 42:1; his mission as a herald of good tidings, 41:27; 52:7; and his liberation of the Lord's blind captives, 42:7; 49:9. See also, rhetorically, the *day* of the Lord as the context in which the ideal vassal fulfills his mission, 11:10; 49:8; 52:6; *passim*.

as the Lord's priests (61:3, 6). Descriptions of those whom the ideal vassal anoints as oaks of *righteousness* (61:3), and of their priestly adornment in a robe of *righteousness* and garments of *salvation*— "like a bridegroom dressed in priestly attire, or a bride adorned with her jewels" (61:10)—modify or redefine the ideal vassal's role as an exemplar and paradigm of the Lord's people and his mediation of the Lord's covenant. Not only does the ideal vassal fulfill all these functions, but such functions include his empowerment or endowment of the righteous. The ideal vassal, in effect, is directly instrumental in his people's spiritual ascent. He performs for them something akin to what the seraph performs for Isaiah when he empowers him within the ritualistic setting of the temple.[15]

Righteousness and praise springing up before all nations (61:11) express the universal redemptive mission of the Lord's ideal vassal. With the help of additional "servants" of the Lord, that redemptive mission now intensifies.[16] The parallelism of the "year of the Lord's favor" and "day of [his] vengeance" in the previous passage (61:2) locates the priestly endowment of the mourners in Zion within the second unit's contrast of the righteous and the wicked. This context means that the empowerment of the righteous proceeds even as the Lord's judgments are coming upon the wicked.

The metaphorical pseudonyms *righteousness* and *salvation* connected with the priestly endowment of the righteous (61:10) establish a rhetorical link to chapter 62. In that chapter, nations and rulers (who are Zion's sons and daughters, cf. 60:3-4) behold Zion's *righteousness* and glory when the Lord's *mouth* calls his people by a new name (62:2). Zion's *righteousness* serves as a *light*, her *salvation* as a flaming torch (*lappîd yib'ār*),[17] shining brightly to the nations (62:1-2). The Lord's long-awaited coming to Zion

---

[15] See a common imagery of temple ritual and its purpose that runs like a thread through Isaiah, viz., initiation, 6:6-7; 61:1; royal accession, 45:1, 4-5; 56:4-7; investiture, 22:20-24; 61:3, 10; theophany, 6:1, 5; 64:1-4; *passim*. See also the temple as a motif prominent in the second unit of section VII, 60:7, 13; 62:9; 63:18; 64:11; 65:11; 66:1, 6, 20.

[16] Compare *righteousness* as engendering "servants" of the Lord, 54:14a, 17cd; 56:1-6; and 144,000 such servants empowered before the Lord's day of judgment by the "angel" from the east, Rev 7:2-4.

[17] Compare the Lord as a flaming torch (*lappîd 'ēš*) in a covenant ceremony, Gen 15:17; and the Lord's presence in a pillar of fire (*'ammûd 'ēš*), Exod 13:21; Num 14:14. Parallelisms in 62:1-2 establish the synonymity of *salvation* (*yĕšû'â*) and *glory* (*kābôd*) as metaphorical pseudonyms of the Lord; cf. 60:2.

culminates his people's redemption (62:11-12; cf. 63:1, 4). Chapter 62 sums up, allegorically, the ideal vassal's mission as the Lord's forerunner. The raising of the Lord's *ensign* to the nations heralds the Lord's coming as *Salvation*:

> 10. Pass on, go through the gates;
>   prepare the way for the people!
>   Excavate, pave a highway cleared of stones;
>   raise the ensign to the nations!
> 11. · The Lord has made proclamation to the end of the earth:
>   Tell the Daughter of Zion,
>   See, your Salvation comes,
>   his reward with him, his work preceding him.

In conclusion, the new name that the Lord's people receive, which name the Lord's *mouth* gives them, is an integral part of the blessed inheritance of the righteous. Royal accession thus accompanies priestly endowment, being part of the empowerment of the Lord's righteous people. Bride and bridegroom imagery in both benedictory passages—in 61:10 and 62:5—links royal accession to priestly endowment as a twin feature of the Lord's covenant. Such imagery suggests that ascent to a higher spiritual state, in which the Lord's people minister in a priestly role, involves the ordinance of marriage within a covenantal context. As a paradigm of that ordinance, the Lord himself marries the woman Zion: "as the bridegroom rejoices over the bride, so shall your God rejoice over you" (62:5; cf. 54:5). The new name the Lord confers on his people— "her in whom I delight" (*ḥepṣîbâh*, 62:4)—again suggests marriage and links Zion's royal accession to her espousal as the Lord's bride. The idea of covenant and the mediation of the covenant thus governs those passages that elaborate on the blessedness of the righteous.

The second unit's innovative use of the term *servants* (*'ăbādîm*) to describe some among the Lord's people (63:17; 65:8-9, 13-15; 66:14)—which term implies individual royal accession (65:4-6)— reflects a climactic development of the Bifid Structure. Because of individual righteousness, in other words, the Lord's people are helped corporately to become a crown of glory in the Lord's *hand*, a royal diadem in the palm of Zion's God (62:3). Because their shame was double for giving heed to the Lord's word (61:7; 66:5), the Lord doubly endows his servants—with the priesthood and with royal accession (61:6–7; 62:2). In short, through the ideal vassal's mediation of the Lord's covenant, many of the Lord's people—at the time of the Lord's coming—ascend the paradigmatic ladder to become as the ideal vassal himself.

In that light, the woman Zion and her offspring realize ascent within a paradigmatic hierarchy. The text states that before Zion suffers the ordeal of labor—that is, before the Lord's day of judgment[18]—Zion delivers a son (66:7; cf. 7:14). As we have seen, that son is the Lord's ideal latter-day vassal, whose mission commences prior to the Lord's day of judgment. The Lord's vassal, in turn, serves as an exemplar and paradigm as well as mediator of the Lord's covenant to Zion's other "sons" (*bānehâ*, 66:8). According to the text, Zion gives birth to these sons as soon as she goes into labor (66:8), that is, when the Lord's judgments commence. The Lord himself, moreover, begets Zion's sons (66:9; cf. 45:10–11) and endows them with a new name (65:15), signifying royal accession.

Zion's sons thus become the Lord's "servants"—the Lord's vassals—and they, in turn, wed Zion (62:5). Their marrying Zion suggests that they become Zion's ministers and consorts: a common bridegroom imagery identifies those who wed Zion as those whom the ideal vassal anoints as priests (61:10; 62:5). Such sons of Zion are not identical with those still suckling at Zion's breasts (66:11), as the text reflects several degrees of ascent within a paradigmatic hierarchy.[19] Because espousal and redemption are synonymous ideas in Isaiah (54:5; cf. Mic 4:10), Zion's sons' marrying her denotes their serving as the Lord's agents of redemption.[20]

Lastly, as the Lord's ideal vassal fulfills his redemptive mission, he ascends the paradigmatic ladder to become as "the angel/ messenger of [the Lord's] presence" (*mal'ak pānâw*, 63:9; cf. the seraph/s, 6:2, 6).[21] Although the vassal's divine empowerment represents a cumulative concept from section V, the vassal's

---

[18] See the Lord's day of judgment as a time when all peoples, including the Lord's people, are "in labor," 13:8; 26:16–18; 37:3; compare Rev 12:1–6.

[19] See the life cycle of Zion's children, viz., birth, 66:8–10; lactation, 66:11; infancy, 66:12; childhood, 66:13; youth, 66:14ab; and manhood, as "servants" of the Lord, 66:14c.

[20] Compare Boaz' redemption of Ruth and her former husband's inheritance, Ruth 4:1–10.

[21] See the parallelistic synonymity of "angel/messenger" (*mal'āk*, 63:9) and "servant" (*'ebed*) in 42:19; 44:26, to denote here, rhetorically, the Lord's ideal latter-day vassal. Compare the "messenger of the covenant" (*mal'ak habběrît*), Mal 3:1.

description in such supernal language as "the angel of His presence" reflects the spiritual ascent that occurs when one fulfills a divine commission. The ideal vassal's "saving/delivering" (yš') the Lord's people follows the paradigm of the Lord's "saving/delivering" (yš') his people (63:8). Such deliverance by the Lord's vassal represents a cumulative concept (cf. 19:20): upon being empowered by the Lord, the ideal vassal releases the Lord's people from bondage and leads them in a new exodus and new wandering in the wilderness to Zion (see sections III, V).

Summary

The concept of a reversal of circumstances between Zion and non-Zion developed in section I of the Bifid Structure concludes climactically in section VII (chaps. 32–33; 60–66). The Lord separates out and irrevocably ruins, punishes, humiliates, causes to suffer, and disinherits non-Zion at his coming to redeem Zion. The inclusion among non-Zion entities of "sinners in Zion" (33:14) and "brethren" who exclude and persecute the righteous (66:5) suggests that this reversal of circumstances occurs when rebellion and disloyalty among the Lord's wicked people take on an anti-Lord stance. The endurance of such oppression by the righteous among the Lord's people, on the other hand, attests to their compliance and loyalty toward the Lord and qualifies them for a higher state of blessedness. Thus, some are reborn as the Lord's "sons/servants"—the Lord's vassals—and are delivered from enemies. In short, they are exalted as kings and priests and are saved with an everlasting salvation, inheriting all the blessings of the covenant. When the Lord comes to avenge and to reward, those who have served him at all costs merit an endowment of glory.

All cumulative themes of the Bifid Structure are thus present in section VII. The reversal of circumstances between the wicked and the righteous—between non-Zion and Zion—underscores all such themes, including the central expression of that reversal, developed in section IV, of non-Zion's humiliation and Zion's exaltation. Further cumulative concepts color this reversal between non-Zion and Zion, such as the Lord's *day* of judgment (which immediately precedes the Lord's coming to Zion) as the occasion for these events; the covenantal nature of two coexisting arch entities, each with its ideology and human exemplar; a covenant of death juxtaposed with a covenant of life, each of which is administered by a mediator of that covenant; an instrument of the Lord's punishment, on the one hand—the king of Assyria/Babylon—and an agent or agents of the Lord's redemption, on the other; the threefold pattern of the destruction of the wicked and the deliverance of the righteous at the presence of the Lord and/or his ideal vassal; calamities coming upon the wicked at the same time as the righteous experience a series of redemptive events; covenantal malediction overtaking the wicked even as covenantal benediction overtakes the righteous; the reduction of wicked entities to chaos and a concurrent creation or re-creation of the righteous; everlasting damnation upon the wicked, but everlasting salvation, both temporal and spiritual, for the righteous; descent of the wicked *down* the paradigmatic ladder—as these follow a paradigm of wickedness—and ascent of the righteous up the paradigmatic ladder, when the latter follow the Lord's paradigm of *righteousness*.

Contrasting characterizations and fates, depicted within a common eschatological context, distinguish section VII from others. Such contrasts outline a glorious inheritance for the righteous, while the wicked suffer an eternal execration. The second unit goes beyond the first in dramatizing the respective fates of the wicked and the righteous. In more celebrated terms than other material, this unit elaborates on the covenantal blessedness of the righteous. Their priestly endowment and royal accession, which form an integral part of that blessedness, modify or redefine the ideal vassal's role toward them in mediating the Lord's covenant. Metaphorical imagery, such as *righteousness* on the one hand and *anger/wrath* on the other, rounds out this culmination of all concepts that the Bifid Structure establishes.

CONCLUSION: THE LITERARY
MESSAGE OF ISAIAH

William Brownlee's original hypothesis—that the Book of Isaiah divides into two halves, each made up of seven parts of parallel subject matter—holds up when we view Isaiah from a literary standpoint. By looking deeper, however, and applying methods of literary analysis unfamiliar to Brownlee, we bring to light the real significance of Brownlee's discovery: the apocalyptic message of Isaiah, a message that relates to what is called the "last days."

One important discovery resulting from this analysis, therefore, is that within a literary context the events described in the Book of Isaiah appear almost exclusively future. Structurally, typologically, and rhetorically, we are dealing with apocalyptic prophecy—a vision of the end from the beginning—that draws on what transpired anciently, but also transcends it. Israel's ancient history, selectively represented by one who saw all time, is recast into a new latter-day context in which history repeats itself following ancient patterns of events. Thus, the scholarly debate on whether there were one, two, or three Isaiahs (one before, one during, and one after Israel's exile) becomes moot, as does the question of whether events in Isaiah relate partly to the prophet's own time and partly to the future.

In addition, numerous profound theological truths present themselves in the course of a literary analysis of Isaiah. To my knowledge, no other biblical text even comes close to Isaiah's in teaching so completely a gospel of salvation, both temporal and spiritual, for all humanity. We might say that this book, more than any other, bridges the gap between the Old and New Testaments. Yet, nothing of the old or the new is sacrificed; rather, both are seen as pertinent to our time.

Without analyzing the Book of Isaiah holistically—without coming to terms with the mechanics of its composition—neither its apocalyptic message nor its theological truths can be fully brought to light. The Bifid Structure with its many internal literary phenomena both conceals and reveals a treasurehouse so vast as to require a complete rethinking of the Book of Isaiah. Lest the detailed analysis of Isaiah in this volume has caused us to lose sight of some parts of the apparent message, let us summarize the information we have gleaned.

The World Divides into Two Opposite Entities

Two major entities—spiritual and political opposites—appear as the main subject of Isaiah within the Bifid Structure. These two entities can best be described as two kinds or classes of people, one righteous, the other wicked. Although people throughout the earth's history have always chosen one path or the other, in the last days all peoples, Israelite and non-Israelite, will divide into these two categories. As simplistic as it seems that at one critical moment the whole world will polarize, according to Isaiah such is what will actually happen. We learn from Isaiah that the cause of this division is how people respond to their Maker, the Lord God of Israel, at a time when he intervenes in the affairs of his people. Thus, in the end, a separation occurs so that the righteous may be delivered when the wicked are destroyed.

The righteous in the earth are identified with Zion, which is a distinct category of the people of God. Zion is righteous and is delivered from her enemies because her people repent and pass tests of loyalty to their covenants with the Lord. The wicked of the world, on the other hand, are identified with Babylon or rather arch Babylon, which constitutes an alien composite entity. Arch Babylon is wicked and is destroyed because her people do not repent and because they fail the same or similar tests of covenantal loyalty. These two entities, Zion and arch Babylon, coexist in the last days until the Lord irrevocably separates them.

Isaiah likens these opposite entities to two women. One is the faithful "spouse" of the Lord, expressing the covenantal bond between the Lord and his people. The other is a "harlot," expressing people's alienation from their Maker. Isaiah also likens these entities to two cities. One is the city of the Lord, a city of joy and peace where the righteous dwell together. The other is a city of chaos, full of oppression and excesses, of want and misery. Those who make up Zion consist of the Lord's compliant people; they hold fast to the Lord, trusting in him through all the challenges of life. Those who make up arch Babylon rebel against the Lord; they trust in the arm of flesh, relying on human counsel and malevolent schemes. Thus, in the last days, all peoples turn either pro- or anti-God.

The Lord Tests His People's Loyalty to His Covenant

A sure test of whether the Lord's people love him is whether they keep his law—the law of the covenant—and obey his word at all costs. According to Isaiah, the Lord's restoration of his law and word in the last days will mark the beginning of a reversal of circumstances for his people—of deliverance from their fallen or maledictory state. Even amid this divine restoration, however, falsehood and error will temporarily prevail so that people's loyalties to the Lord might be tested.

Out of that paradoxical situation arise the two opposite classes of people. Those who accept the law and word of the Lord will renew their covenantal allegiance toward him. Such covenantal allegiance distinguishes the righteous from the wicked throughout the earth. To the repentant, the Lord's word is food for the hungry; it begets an everlasting peace and salvation. Salvation, both temporal and spiritual, results from covenantal righteousness—keeping the law of the covenant and obeying the word of God. Righteousness precedes or is the precursor of salvation and the righteous are sealed up—by covenant—for salvation. Those who reject the law and word of the Lord, on the other hand, are counted among his enemies and adversaries and are destroyed.

A sifting of the peoples of the earth in response to the restoration of the Lord's law and word thus forms a prelude to a day of judgment during which Zion is redeemed and arch Babylon is damned. All the earth's inhabitants will ally themselves with one or the other party. Acceptance of the Lord's law and word crystallizes in a covenant of Life—an appointment with the God of life when destruction is all around. Rejection of the Lord's law and word turns into a covenant with Death—an appointment with the instruments of death and destruction. The Lord's day of judgment will see all peoples everywhere become subject to the path they have chosen.

In the last days, therefore, the choices for humanity are two: life or death. At a time when the word of the Lord issues from his *mouth*, all middle ground vanishes. Both groups of people, the repentant and nonrepentant, in that day bind themselves to a course of action and to its consequences. While the repentant, at that time, qualify for deliverance, the nonrepentant seal themselves up, covenantally, for destruction. In fact, it is covenantal rebellion among the people of God, in the last days as anciently, that is *the* catalyst in Isaiah of a divine and universal judgment.

The Wicked Align Themselves with Arch Babylon and Choose Death

Within the Bifid Structure, Babylon or arch Babylon forms a composite entity made up of the world in general, certain hosts of heaven, nations and alliances of nations, aggressive world powers, the tyrants and oppressors of the earth, rulers and men of power, enemies and adversaries, seas and rivers (that is, of people, metaphorically speaking), proud kindred peoples, and, notably, the wicked of the Lord's people. Arch Babylon, as both a people and a place, in effect, consists of the world and its wicked inhabitants. As such, arch Babylon is idolatrous, self-indulgent, and oppressive. Ultimately, her people—the godless, revelers, and tyrants of humanity—cannot be reclaimed by an appeal to repentance. Instead of exalting God, arch Babylon exalts herself; she rules, firmly entrenched, as Mistress of Kingdoms. Isaiah's arch Babylon thus consists of all reprobate peoples. In that respect, she resembles Babylon the Great in the Book of Revelation.

Of special focus in Isaiah are those of the Lord's own people who form a part of arch Babylon. These include sinners in Zion, cultists, and false brethren. They merge with or assimilate into arch Babylon upon failing to repent when put to the test. The latter in particular contend with, persecute, and revile the people of Zion above all others. They make themselves the enemies of God because they are enemies to his people, and vice versa. These idolatrous and wicked brethren, who include political and religious leaders, hate and exclude the righteous. They scoff at the Lord's living oracle and instead counsel among themselves for what course they will follow. In so doing, they break their covenant with the Lord and choose to be destroyed with the wicked of all nations. A broken covenant relationship with the Lord thus marks the time prior to his judgment of the world.

The wicked of the Lord's people resemble a harlot because they deliberately disaffiliate themselves from the Lord. They reject the Lord's counsel in favor of a false shelter. Together with other wicked peoples, they seek a deceptive peace in human treaties or covenants. They thus descend down the spiritual ladder to become as the heathen, peoples with whom the Lord has no covenant relationship. Wickedness, particularly among the people of the Lord, may be summed up as disloyalty toward the Lord, which leads to death in the Lord's day of judgment.

Thus do the wicked and idolaters among the Lord's people receive a reward of their wickedness—they are condemned to suffer calamity with all apostate peoples. By rejecting the Lord's living oracle in a day when the Lord's coming to the earth draws nigh, they actually precipitate the divine judgment. They and their disloyal leader or leaders, following the pattern of Ahaz and his people, lose the Lord's protection in the face of invading enemies. Their loss of power and authority and their utter humiliation shows that their ideology—the ideology of Babylon—in the end serves to condemn them. Their self-exaltation and anti-Lord attitude mark them as ripe for an everlasting burning.

The destruction of the wicked and deliverance of the righteous occur concurrently because without the wicked perishing there would be no real deliverance for the righteous—oppression would persist. When arch Babylon exalts herself to high heaven, the Lord humiliates her to the dust. At the same time, Zion, which has suffered humiliation at the hands of arch Babylon, rises from the dust to sit enthroned. Humiliation and exaltation, as two final conditions, are thus realized in the last days and continue forever.

For the nonrepentant among the Lord's people there is no hope of deliverance in the Lord's day of judgment. Together with all the wicked, they suffer a full measure of covenantal malediction because they disqualify themselves for divine help. They incur ruin and disinheritance, being cut off from among the people of God. They become as dross and refuse upon the face of the earth in the day the Lord destroys them. Their idolatry and injustice brings upon them sudden and unexpected calamity from which they cannot escape.

When the Lord rises up in judgment against the wicked, all alike will be reduced to chaos. With fire and with the sword, he will destroy evildoers from the earth. Arch Babylon will be thrown down as God overthrew Sodom and Gomorrah. A worldwide catastrophe will overtake arch Babylon as her elite peoples are cast down. The Lord will wage war and overthrow all who fight against Zion. The enemies of the Lord's people will miserably perish and their lands become desolate. Gloom and darkness will envelop the earth as its inhabitants are burned. The wicked will become an eternal execration and their productive lands turn into wilderness and forests.

The King of Assyria/Babylon Ravages the Earth and Is Destroyed

In this day of judgment, the Lord will use a world ruler, like the ancient king of Assyria/Babylon, as a chief instrument for destroying the wicked. That archtyrant, with his alliance of nations from the north, will serve as a power of chaos in reducing the wicked to dust and ashes. The Lord will empower him against the transgressors of His own people and against all reprobate nations. In the process of serving as an agent of death, the archtyrant will plunder and despoil the whole world. He appears in Isaiah as the Lord's *rod* and *staff*, His *axe* and *saw*, with which the Lord punishes and hews down the wicked. The king of Assyria/Babylon thus personifies the Lord's *anger* and *wrath*, his *fury* and *indignation*. As a personification of *Sea* and *River*—ancient Near Eastern powers of chaos—he typifies the wicked themselves.

The wicked are like the king of Assyria/Babylon in that they follow his pattern of treachery and tyranny. As a model of rebelliousness and disloyalty, he inspires people to do evil rather than good. His self-aggrandizement serves as a model of arch Babylon's self-aggrandizement. Ultimately, the wicked affiliate with the archtyrant because they follow his anti-Lord ideology. Having rejected the Lord, her husband, the harlot (the Lord's nonrepentant people) cleaves to another lord—the king of Assyria/Babylon.

This evil king, however, does not protect his own but rather, like the archtyrant of the Book of Daniel, desolates and destroys as it suits him. After making peace treaties, so that he may catch people unawares, he launches a worldwide flood of conquest. Like the *Sea* in commotion or a *River* in flood, he transgresses his bounds. As a new *Flood*—as destructive of life as the Flood was anciently—the king of Assyria/Babylon overruns the entire earth. As the *scourge*

254

of the wicked, the archtyrant ravages and conquers the world. With fire and with the sword the king of Assyria/Babylon desolates the earth and imposes his yoke of servitude on surviving humanity.

After serving the Lord's purpose of destroying the wicked, however, this wicked king is himself destroyed. After betraying humanity, ruthlessly tyrannizing them, he himself is betrayed. Because he ruled the world as a demigod, rivaling even the Lord, the archtyrant will suffer utter humiliation. Though he rose high in the heavens and set his throne among the stars, his soul will be banished to the utmost depths of hell. His mighty armies will be routed and defeated, as at the battle of Midian and at the ancient Assyrian siege of Jerusalem. When the archtyrant seeks absolute world rule, even over the people of God, he will be put down for ever. He and his kind will be made an execration, never again to rise up and take possession of the world.

Arch Babylon and its king will be supplanted in the earth by the Lord's righteous rule in Zion. Just as arch Babylon contrasts with Zion in Isaiah, so the king of Assyria/Babylon contrasts with the King of Zion—the Lord. Each king serves as the model or exemplar of those who affiliate with him. A reversal of circumstances between Zion and arch Babylon, which commences, substantially, at the Lord's day of judgment, ends with Zion's complete redemption and the overthrow of arch Babylon and its king. Even as the archtyrant's rule ends, the Lord's rule commences, ushering in a millennial era of peace.

Thus, the worldwide chaos caused by the king of Assyria/Babylon will be succeeded by a new creation, the creation of a peaceful world. Zion's redemption, which heralds this world peace, nonetheless begins with the Lord's judgments coming upon the wicked, in large part through the agency of the archtyrant. Zion's exaltation, which is an integral part of Zion's redemption, features simultaneously with arch Babylon's humiliation. The Lord's redemption of his people and his vengeance upon the wicked occur universally and concurrently. All the earth's inhabitants will at that time fall into one or the other category—those redeemed or those damned.

Those Who Repent Become Zion and Are Delivered from Affliction

As we have seen, a reversal of circumstances between the righteous and the wicked takes place in the last days when the wicked fight against God. Even the people of the Lord, those who at one time or another evidenced allegiance toward him, go one of two ways. Some, who serve the Lord at all costs, become his covenant people—Zion or Jerusalem. Others, who turn upon their brethren and persecute them, become the Lord's enemies and are banished.

Yet, such persecution of the righteous by the wicked forms a necessary prelude to Zion's redemption. Though the Lord's people are humbled by arch Babylon's oppression (in the interim before arch Babylon is judged), this very humiliation and oppression leads to deliverance, as suffering, which was the lot of the righteous, suddenly becomes the fate of the wicked. Arch Babylon's oppressive ideology is an integral part of Zion's redemption because divine deliverance implies being delivered *from* something, and divine empowerment involves being empowered *over* something. Deliverance and empowerment by the Lord, in effect, cannot happen until the need arises and the conditions are met. Thus, the righteous will appeal to the Lord for help and be delivered in a new Passover from the very calamities that come upon the wicked. In short, the Lord's day of vengeance upon arch Babylon provides the setting in which Zion is redeemed. The elevation of the Lord's servants and the abasement of their enemies occur together.

In a word, Isaiah juxtaposes Zion with all other entities, including those of the Lord's people who are cut off. He characterizes Zion as a people and a place, with a righteous Davidic king, who survive when the Lord destroys the wicked. He likens Zion's people to the stump of a tree that was cut off but regenerates and grows into a new fruit-bearing tree. The wicked, on the other hand, also appear as trees in Isaiah: they are hewn down by the archtyrant—the Lord's *axe* and *saw*—to rise no more.

The desolation of the earth and its wicked inhabitants thus proceeds concurrently with the regeneration of Zion. Arch Babylon's ruin heralds Zion's rebirth as curses or plagues come upon the one and curse reversals or blessings upon the other. Such a reversal of malediction for Zion includes the transformation of the earth to a paradisiacal state, a new Garden of Eden. It includes also—for the earth's righteous survivors—the abolition of death itself. Royal accession from the dust—the resurrection of the righteous to an everlasting exaltation—epitomizes all such curse reversals. Curse reversals form an integral part of Zion's redemption, becoming prominent in Isaiah at the Lord's day of judgment when the Lord's coming to the earth is nigh.

Zion's suffering, which grows intense just prior to the Lord's coming, is thus infused with hope, while the suffering of arch Babylon is hopeless, yielding no deliverance. Suffering forms an implicit but essential ingredient of salvation in Isaiah because it purifies the Lord's people of their iniquities and attests to their repentance, their willingness to remain loyal in the face of all hazards. Affronts by the wicked, and all forms of oppression and treachery, whether by political authorities or by false brethren, are a sign of the imminent deliverance the Lord has promised.

Divine intervention occurs for the Lord's people worldwide, who, when challenged, repent of iniquities and come to the Lord with all their hearts. Repentance, in effect, reverses the process of assimilation into the nations that characterizes the inhabitants of arch Babylon. The fruits of repentance are forgiveness of sins, healing, and spiritual ascent to the level of Zion. Such Zion status, marked by repentance, qualifies one for being ransomed from destruction in the Lord's day of judgment. As with the woman Zion in the Book of Revelation, provision is made for her divine protection.

The name *Zion*, in Isaiah, becomes conspicuous when speaking of redemption because it is Zion that is redeemed, not Israel or some other entity. If the Lord's people Israel would be redeemed in the day of judgment they must assume an identity with Zion by passing tests of loyalty toward the Lord. Then they may be delivered from the state of spiritual and literal weariness, bondage, and chaos that characterizes arch Babylon. In that day, if one is not a part of Zion, one must be a part of arch Babylon and thus subject to the power of the archtyrant.

Zion Is Redeemed in Fulfillment of the Sinai and Davidic Covenants

According to Isaiah, divine deliverance in the face of a mortal threat occurs in two ways, each of which depends on the Lord's people and their leaders keeping the law of the covenant. The first is based on the protection promised the Lord's people when they covenanted with him at Sinai under the direction of Moses (see Exod 19:3–8; Lev 26:1–9; Deut 29:1–15). According to the Sinai covenant, each individual in Israel must keep the law and word of the Lord in order for the people as a whole to qualify for his protection. As difficult as such complete loyalty to the Lord may be, Isaiah depicts one group that will succeed in keeping this strict covenant. He shows a righteous remnant of Ephraim vanquishing an invading Assyrian army that seeks to conquer, or has succeeded in conquering, much of the promised land. Although Assyria, in the course of overrunning the world, destroys the promised land, the Lord preserves a remnant of his people by empowering them against Assyria.

The second means of divine protection is based on the covenant the Lord made with King David and his ruling heirs (see 2 Sam 7:8-17; Psa 89:3, 19-37; 132:11-18). Under the terms of the Davidic covenant, those of the Lord's people who do not as yet fully keep the law and word of the Lord may obtain his protection by proxy. In their case, a righteous king to whom they give their allegiance may act as their surrogate in keeping the whole law of the covenant. The king may thus merit the Lord's protection or deliverance on their behalf, alleviating the necessity that all the Lord's people, to a man, keep the law of the covenant. That situation presents itself in Isaiah in a repeat of Assyria's siege of Jerusalem in the days of King Hezekiah. A latter-day "Assyrian" army, following the pattern of its ancient counterpart, will perish when it attempts to deal the death blow to the Lord's covenant people.

Those who obtain divine protection under the terms of the Davidic covenant thus keep a lesser law; they are not able to obtain protection under the law of the Sinai covenant. Such protection, however, serves the purpose of saving those newly converted to the Lord—those just renewing their allegiance toward the Lord—at a time when the judgments of God are coming upon the wicked. In the divine economy of deliverance in the last days, the Lord thus makes provision for all who repent and disaffiliate themselves from arch Babylon.

Zion has a counterpart of arch Babylon's human king (the archtyrant) in a righteous Davidic king whom the Lord raises up before the day of judgment. Isaiah portrays the oppression and persecution the righteous suffer before that day as Zion's travail with children. As this oppression intensifies, Zion delivers a son—the Davidic king, the Lord's servant—and, following that, she delivers a nation of children. These righteous whom the Lord delivers from destruction constitute the nation of the Lord's people Zion who are "born in a day"—the Lord's day of judgment.

Divine deliverance under the terms of both the Sinai covenant and the Davidic covenant resembles temporal deliverance of a vassal by his overlord in ancient Near Eastern suzerain–vassal treaties. Such deliverance is based on the protection clause of the treaty, and a similar means of securing protection forms a central message of the Book of Isaiah. The Lord fulfills the role of suzerain or overlord in delivering his people from a mortal threat (the king of Assyria/Babylon) when they or their king, His vassals, fulfill the terms of the covenant. Ancient Assyria's invasion of the promised land and siege of Jerusalem serve as types in Isaiah of a latter-day invasion at which the loyalties of the Lord's people will be tested in full.

Zion Participates in a New Exodus out of Arch Babylon

The idea of a righteous Davidic king is important in another respect in Isaiah. This latter-day figure sets in motion a series of redemptive events for the Lord's people Zion that consists of the release of the Lord's people from bondage and exile; their exodus out of arch Babylon when protected by the Lord; their return wandering in the wilderness to the promised land; their conquest of the promised land from the hands of the wicked; their inheritance of the promised land and rebuilding of its ruins; and their building the temple of the Lord. Just as ancient Assyria's invasion and siege repeat themselves in the Lord's day of judgment, so this cycle of events will repeat itself.

The preceding series of events, in fact, typifies the latter-day redemption of Zion and is again central to Isaiah's message. The great reversal of circumstances between Zion and arch Babylon—in which captivity turns to freedom, sorrow to joy, and so forth—begins, tangibly, at the new exodus out of Babylon. That exodus forms the pivotal event of Zion's redemption, separating those whom the Lord creates anew—his people Zion—from those who return to chaos at the time of judgment. It occurs when the affliction of the Lord's people, evidenced by their bondage under a Babylonian regime, grows intense and unbearable.

The spiritual conversion of the Lord's people in the last days is crucial to their deliverance because the Lord can deliver them only if they keep the terms of his covenants. Just as anciently Israel's spiritual apostasy preceded Israel's physical captivity and exile, so in the last days the spiritual conversion of the Lord's people precedes their physical return. Isaiah thus defines Zion as a people of God, who, when they repent of iniquity, return to the place Zion, where the Lord protects them. The Lord's cloud of glory, as anciently, shields his people from the power of their enemies and signifies the Lord's presence with them.

Those who repent and return include many nations and rulers in the earth. These come from afar, from the four directions of the earth, to the promised land. Isaiah depicts their return gathering as a pilgrimage to the Lord's holy mountain, similar to Israel's ancient pilgrimage to Zion. Those who return are the elect of God, and they journey through the wilderness, over mountain ranges, in the midst of great waters, and through fire. The Lord's empowerment of his people at their return enables them not only to travel unimpeded through the elements, but to render enemies to dust and stubble—to chaos—while on the march.

Zion's rising from the dust—from the chaos of arch Babylon—to sit enthroned, clothed with power, epitomizes this series of redemptive events. Beginning with her release from bondage and exile, Zion's redemption ends with her becoming a new creation. The Lord's people Zion in that day experience a reversal of covenant curses that entails, first, the removal of sins upon repentance. The series of redemptive events just mentioned, which includes the exodus out of arch Babylon, literally manifests this reversal of malediction. An endowment of the Lord's Spirit, royal investiture, and a physical state of nonweariness also form a part of this reversal.

In other words, every blessing had anciently among the people of God, or any divine benediction that ever was manifested among them or their prophets, will now be enjoyed by the Lord's people Zion. Enemies will be put down, elements subdued, wilderness and arid lands will regenerate to a paradisiacal glory, and so forth. The Lord's righteous people will become a nation of kings and priests and fulfill sacred missions as the Lord's emissaries and ministers. That is why Zion's redemption is synonymous in Isaiah with the salvation of the world. The Lord's coming to redeem Zion as a personification of *salvation* will usher in a worldwide peace and rest.

Zion Ascends the Spiritual Ladder
by Passing Tests of Loyalty

What actually occasions the Lord's coming to the earth is the loyalty and compliance of the Lord's people Zion. In effect, the Lord—*salvation*—cannot come to his people until righteousness is established among them. They must ascend to a higher spiritual plane in order for the Lord to manifest himself among them. In the Sinai wilderness, various levels existed on which the Lord manifested himself, and these will also exist in the last days: first, the level of Moses, who talked with God face to face; second, that of the elders on the mount who ate bread in His presence; third, that of the congregation of Israel who received the word of God given through Moses; and fourth, that of the wicked people of Israel and the nations, who perished at the Lord's presence.

The spiritual ascent of the Lord's people through increasing levels of righteousness, as if climbing a spiritual ladder, marks the time just prior to and during the Lord's day of judgment. In all instances, the Lord's people ascend to new levels by passing tests of covenantal loyalty. In fact, such tests present themselves and opposition continues so that the Lord's people can spiritually progress. Overcoming the temptation to worship idols, the works of men's hands; exercising an uncompromising integrity in business dealings; faithfully enduring persecution and betrayal, particularly by false brethren; practicing love and kindness, especially toward the needy; repudiating the king of Assyria/Babylon and his emissaries, even in the face of death; waiting for the Lord to deliver his people in their utmost extremity—passing these and other tests of loyalty qualify the Lord's people to become Zion.

The Lord's people, upon facing tests of loyalty, go one of two ways: either they ascend to the level of Zion, or they descend to join with the wicked, idolatrous peoples of the world—with arch Babylon. Three symbolic names, in Isaiah, represent these three categories of people: (1) Immanuel ("God is with us"), which corresponds to Zion or Jerusalem, those who will receive a prophetic commission; (2) Shear-Jashub ("A remnant shall repent/return"), which corresponds to Jacob/Israel, those who must yet pass tests of loyalty in order to become identified with Zion; and (3) Maher Shalal Hash Baz ("Hasten the plunder, hurry the spoil"), which corresponds to the wicked of Israel and the nations, those who will be spoiled and destroyed.

Above the level of Zion are the seraphs who stand about the Lord and minister in his presence; and above them is the Lord himself. I call this ladder of spiritual levels in Isaiah a "paradigmatic hierarchy" because it is a hierarchy based upon emulating one who stands above. In other words, those on beginning levels of righteousness may progress or ascend upward by following the paradigm or model of one higher. By so doing, they become like the one whom they emulate, leading to more advanced spiritual functions.

Those above serve or minister to those below but are themselves ministered to by one above them. For example, Zion/Jerusalem (those on that rung of the spiritual ladder) ministers to Jacob/Israel but is itself ministered to by the Lord's servant, the Davidic king, and other servants who assist him. The latter, on the other hand, in functioning as seraphs, are ministered to by the Lord himself.

Zion's New Covenant Is a Composite of Former Covenants

All divine blessings these servants inherit, together with blessings inherited by Zion/Jerusalem, are sealed by an eternal covenant upon those who receive them. That new covenant is a composite of all former covenants the Lord made with his people, or with individuals within his people, embodying in one covenant the positive features of the former. The new covenant in Isaiah follows the pattern of a covenant of grant—an unconditional covenant— found in ancient Near Eastern suzerain–vassal treaties: upon a vassal king proving himself exceedingly loyal to the suzerain, the suzerain or overlord king may bestow on him the unconditional promise of a city–state (a promised land) over which the vassal and his descendants may rule forever. The suzerain promises to protect the vassal and his people, provided they keep the terms of the covenant by remaining loyal to the suzerain.

Isaiah transforms the treaty model by adding features to the new covenant that are drawn from the various covenants the Lord made anciently. These include the Lord's covenants with Noah, Abraham, Israel, Pinehas the priest, and King David. The new covenant—a composite covenant—thus consists of the promise of a land regenerated to a paradisiacal glory and protected by the presence of the

Lord, a posterity endowed with the Spirit of the Lord to minister in the priesthood, which promise or covenant the Lord makes unconditionally with a new nation of the Lord's people—Zion—after a cataclysmic destruction of the magnitude of the Flood.

The glorious covenantal heritage the Lord's people receive in the last days, therefore, encapsulates all former covenant blessings. This implies that the tests of loyalty the Lord's people must pass will be equal to the tests passed by those who merited the former covenants and their blessings. The severity of these tests, such as Noah's exceeding righteousness in the face of exceeding wickedness, Abraham's faith and obedience as evidenced by his willingness to give up his only son Isaac, and Pinehas' and David's zeal in turning the tide against wickedness and adversity, may resemble the kind of loyalty the Lord will require of his people.

The royal investiture and priestly endowment of the people of Zion—their exaltation as kings and priests, as vassals or servants to the Lord God—thus come to them as covenant blessings and draw on all former covenants the Lord made with his people. Isaiah depicts the Lord's making the new covenant as Zion's—His bride's—espousal to the Lord, which is another way of expressing Zion's redemption.

Those who espouse the Lord, however, are those who expiate their sins, waiting for the Lord to deliver them through their many trials and afflictions. Isaiah likens their spiritual rebirth, their deliverance from mortal threats, their inheritance of salvation, and their glorious birthright on the earth, to the exaltation of the earth's holy ones. Like the Lord's servant, the Davidic king, such "firstfruits" of the earth attain celestial accession by following the paradigm of the Lord himself. Their divine empowerment includes a state of nonweariness; their ability to ascend as on the wings of eagles expresses their transcendent or seraphic state.

Indeed, in Isaiah, the purpose of the Lord's creation is to exalt the offspring of God. Even cosmic creation has as its goal a redeemed and exalted people of Zion. The creation of new heavens and a new earth concludes an entire series of new events associated with Zion's redemption. That new creation commences in the Lord's day of judgment even as wicked entities revert to chaos. Zion's expansion during an era of unprecedented terrestrial peace ultimately encompasses the earth, thus consummating the Lord's new creation.

The Lord's people Zion, however, do not attain so exalted a state in a leaderless fashion. No people of God ever achieved a condition of righteousness without the leadership of a prophet like Moses or other holy men appointed by the Lord. Paradoxically, the time of greatest righteousness among the people of God will also be a time of exceeding wickedness, as it was in the days of Moses and other ancient prophets. The Lord's day of judgment in Isaiah is thus characterized by the destruction of the wicked—the destruction of arch Babylon—and the deliverance of Zion at the presence or mediation of a righteous Davidic king.

The Lord's Servant Fulfills a Mission to the Nations

In Isaiah, a Davidic king, who is the Lord's servant, arises at a time when the world is ripening in iniquity. The Davidic king and those who assist him ultimately replace a rebellious Davidic king or kings after the pattern of the apostate King Ahaz. They also succeed false religious leaders after the pattern of Israel's drunken prophets. The Lord's reestablishment of both monarchy and judges in that day is thus intended to substitute a righteous government of the people for a wicked and oppressive one.

The Lord sends his servant, the Davidic king, to his people after they have strayed far from righteousness. He is sent to Israel's blind and deaf exiles as a light to dispel their darkness. The servant's mission acts as a brief interval of time in which the Lord's people may repent, a point in the earth's history when failure to repent will mean certain destruction. His mission provides the catalyst for a great division of people into two opposite categories, a division that takes place at the Lord's day of judgment. Those who repent will be redeemed as Zion, while those who reject the servant's appeal to repent will perish.

The Lord's servant, when divinely empowered, fulfills both spiritual and temporal functions. His mission—in heralding deliverance or destruction—follows the pattern of Isaiah's three-year mission in heralding the Lord's day of judgment anciently when the Lord sent Isaiah to his people Israel and appointed him as a sign to the nations of the world. Because the Lord's people in the last days are scattered among all nations, the servant's mission encompasses the earth. The Lord appoints him as a prince, a witness, and a lawgiver to the nations. As the Lord's living oracle, he summons the repentant people of the earth to renew their covenantal allegiance to the Lord. The blind and deaf of the Lord's people respond to the law and word of the Lord as they receive it through his servant. These see and hear in that day and affiliate with the Lord through the mediation of his servant. As the Lord's spokesman or messenger, the servant leads them to the Lord himself.

The servant is able to help the Lord's people ascend the spiritual ladder in part because of his own experience in doing so. At first, he endures humiliation and persecution, even to the point of being unrecognizably marred. Thereupon, the Lord heals him and gloriously empowers him to perform his redemptive mission. His reversal of circumstances is a paradigm of Zion's imminent reversal from affliction to divine empowerment. As the Lord strengthens him, the poor and needy, the blind and deaf, the hungry and thirsty respond to the servant's mission of releasing them from bondage.

The Lord's empowerment of his servant over political and spiritual enemies brings him worldwide recognition and renown. He attains the seraph level of the spiritual ladder and becomes an agent of life (as the king of Assyria/Babylon is an agent of death). He fulfills that role initially as a temporal savior who delivers his people from destruction. Because he functions as a seraph or angel of the Lord's presence, his vision and comprehension of the Lord's plan of salvation are equal to his divine commission. The Lord thus acts in concert with his servant in implementing Zion's full redemption.

As one anointed by the Lord and endowed by his Spirit, this latter-day deliverer fulfills a plurality of roles performed anciently by others, including Abraham, Moses, David, and Cyrus. Isaiah draws on these figures and their functions as types of the mission of the Lord's servant. The servant, therefore, appears in Isaiah as a composite of these ancient types. Isaiah includes in his depiction of the Lord's servant both Egyptian and Mesopotamian symbols of divine investiture, reflecting the universality of the servant's mission to the nations.

The Lord's Servant Acts as a Model of Righteousness

A chief role of the servant of the Lord is to provide a paradigm of righteousness for His people. The Lord sends his servant, the

Davidic king, as an exemplar to His people after the pattern of the righteous King Hezekiah. Additionally, the servant acts as an example of spiritual progression after the pattern of the prophet Isaiah. The servant's personification of *righteousness* in the text illustrates his ability to exemplify righteousness—in the covenantal sense of loyalty toward the Lord—amid the peculiar challenges people face in the last days.

As the Lord's people respond to the servant's mission of establishing righteousness among them, the Lord does for his people as he does for their king. As the Lord heals and exalts his servant, so he heals and exalts his people Zion. As the Lord empowers his servant, so he empowers his people Zion. Like him, they may become kings and priests and assume a prophetic office toward the nations of the earth. When righteous individuals among the Lord's people emulate the righteousness of the servant, they ascend the spiritual ladder and become like him.

Certain "servants" and "sons" of Zion thus become as seraphs together with the Davidic king. Like him, they fulfill a proxy role as temporal saviors toward the Lord's people, their royal investiture and priestly endowment empowering them to deliver others from bondage. As with the 144,000 servants of the Lord in the Book of Revelation, Isaiah identifies these individuals with the tribes of Israel to whom they minister.

Like the Davidic king, these servants suffer while serving others, thus themselves passing severe tests of loyalty. Rising from the dust to sit enthroned, these kings and priests of the Lord's people are reborn as the Lord's servants—his vassals—following intense humiliation and shame. Isaiah depicts their priestly endowment as a reversal of circumstances for those who mourn in Zion just prior to the Lord's day of judgment. As the Lord delivers them from their afflictions, these leaders and rulers of the Lord's people, in turn, deliver others. Their combined latter-day mission, when led by the Lord's servant, brings about the redemption of Zion.

As an agent of the Lord's redemption, the servant (the Davidic king) punishes the wicked and delivers the righteous. He delivers the Lord's people by releasing them from bondage and exile and leading them in an exodus out of arch Babylon to Zion. When led by the servant, the Lord's people conquer the nations who oppressed them and reinherit the promised land. The Lord's righteous people assist the servant in restoring the land's ruins and in building the temple of the Lord. The servant reconstitutes the tribes of Israel, unites Judah and Ephraim, and appoints the Lord's people lands of inheritance.

The servant's conquest of the forces of chaos—his subduing the wicked nations of the earth—includes his overthrowing the Assyrian power. As David slew Goliath anciently, so the Lord's servant, the Davidic king, slays the latter-day archtyrant. Following the pattern of Cyrus the Persian, he reconquers the earth from the king of Assyria/Babylon, delivering all peoples from tyranny. As the Assyrian power is put down, the glorious reign of the Lord and his vassals commences throughout the earth.

Metaphorical pseudonyms of the Lord's servant in Isaiah help identify his redemptive mission. As already noted, a condition of *righteousness*, which the servant personifies, must precede Zion's *salvation*, which latter term identifies the Lord. The servant, therefore, comes as a forerunner or precursor of the coming of the Lord. As a *light* to the nations, the servant acts as a power of creation—of the rebirth or re-creation of the Lord's people Zion. Leading them out of darkness or spiritual bondage, he brings them into the presence of the greater *Light*—the Lord. He serves as the Lord's living oracle, his *mouth* and *voice*, declaring the word of God at a time of change and transformation.

The terms *hand* and *right hand* identify the servant when empowered by the Lord to deliver and empower his people. The terms *rod* and *staff* signify his royal attributes and his power over the nations of the earth. The term *ensign* signifies his function as a rallying point for the Lord's righteous people in the last days. The latter gather to Zion as the Lord raises his *ensign* to all nations. As a personification of the Lord's *covenant*, the servant mediates the new covenant to his people and exemplifies all its blessings. These and other metaphorical pseudonyms, which appear throughout Isaiah, fill out our understanding of the mission and attributes of the servant of the Lord in the last days.

Part of the servant's spiritual mission is to act as a surety for his people's divine protection, as required by the terms of the Davidic covenant. In the course of fulfilling that role, he suffers grievously after the pattern of King Hezekiah, thereby paying the price of his people's deliverance. By answering to the Lord for their acts of disloyalty, the servant is able to mediate on their behalf. In such mediation, he follows the pattern of Abraham, who mediated with the Lord on behalf of the righteous in Sodom. Lot's deliverance from Sodom on the eve of its destruction provides a type in Isaiah for the deliverance of those who repent in arch Babylon on the eve of her fiery destruction.

The servant, like Abraham, thus serves as a prince of peace or salvation, as a shelter from the storm and as shade from the heat in the Lord's day of judgment. In these and other roles, the Lord's servant and son is a type of the Lord himself; however, Isaiah makes clear that the servant's mission derives from and is subservient to the mission of the Lord. The servant depends on the Lord's redemptive suffering for *his* deliverance, he being ministered to directly by the Lord.

The Lord, the King of Zion, Fulfills the Central Redemptive Mission

Isaiah waits until section V of the Bifid Structure—after developing most of the concepts above—to introduce us to the mission of the Lord God of Israel. Though, prior to that, Isaiah describes the Lord as Redeemer of his people, his forgiveness of their sins, and curse reversals, only at this climactic point of the structure does Isaiah establish a theological premise for the Lord's redemption. Only at this juncture in the development of concepts is his audience able to see how the Lord's own mission becomes central to God's plan.

Paradoxically, Isaiah depicts the Lord's redemptive mission on behalf of his people in terms of a suffering figure. The Servant–Tyrant Parallelism, an important complementary structure in Isaiah, helps identify that suffering figure as the Lord himself. Chapter 53, which describes his mission in the most singular terms, forms a part of that structural configuration. Important rhetorical links confirm the suffering figure's identity as the Lord.

This figure's suffering is redemptive in that it leads to salvation that is spiritual in nature and of much broader scope than temporal salvation. Through his suffering, the suffering figure—the Lord—pays the price of the peace or salvation of all humanity. He does that by establishing the basis for a reversal of malediction that includes forgiveness of sins and the abolition of death.

A theology of redemptive suffering in Isaiah thus applies to spiritual as well as temporal salvation. The Lord's servant, the Davidic king, pays the price of his people's temporal salvation; but the suffering figure—the Lord—pays the price of all peoples' spiritual salvation. Though the Lord's people also suffer, they suffer as a consequence of their sins; their suffering serves both to purify and sanctify them. The suffering of the Lord, and also his vassal's, lies beyond that of suffering for one's own sins. Though the Lord's servant, the Davidic king, suffers nigh unto death after the pattern of King Hezekiah, he does not die. The Lord delivers him. However, Isaiah's suffering figure—the Lord—suffers unto death, even though he is innocent of the crimes for which he is slain.

But why does the Lord, the creator of heaven and earth, suffer and die in the likeness of a man? The answer has to do with the Lord's role as suzerain or Redeemer of his people. That role requires not only that he deliver them from the king of Assyria/Babylon, who threatens them, but from death itself. When they and their king, the Lord's servant, fulfill the terms of his covenant, the Lord is under obligation to deliver them from *any* mortal threat. To do that, he must ultimately conquer death, for death itself would continue to threaten them even after the archtyrant's threat had passed. But death, which is a maledictory condition, cannot be done away unless sin and transgression—the cause of death—are also done away. It is in the course of removing his people's sins, taking them upon himself, and conquering death, that the suffering figure suffers and dies.

The suffering figure—the Lord—thus assumes three roles in order to redeem his people. First, he fulfills the role of suzerain in delivering his people from a mortal threat, in this case death itself. Second, he fulfills the role of a Davidic king: he takes upon himself the form of a servant, assuming the proxy role of a vassal in answering to his suzerain for his people's loyalties. And third, he follows the ancient type of animal sacrifice, in which an unblemished animal died in place of a person who had sinned. These latter two types of proxy suffering thus fuse in Isaiah to establish the concept of atonement for sin. As a vassal answering to his suzerain for his people's sins, as an expiating sacrifice for sin, and as his people's divine suzerain, delivering them from death, the suffering figure in Isaiah combines in himself all the roles necessary to redeem his people.

In suzerain–vassal covenants, those who give a vassal king their allegiance are delivered together with him, their righteous proxy. Thus, the reversal of the suffering figure's maledictory condition— from death to life—ensures the reversal of the maledictory condition of his people. That reversal, as with Zion's rising from the dust, establishes a type and precedent for the resurrection of all who, sooner or later, bend the knee in allegiance to him. The Lord's role, therefore, is not only to effect the remission of sins for those who, as an expression of their allegiance, repent of their disloyalties; it is also to reverse their maledictory or fallen state, which includes his removal of death.

His suffering while fulfilling these redemptive functions is commensurate with the magnitude of his mission—he suffers beyond all. Because innocent suffering and ignominy in Isaiah always precede salvation and exaltation, the greater the glory a person assumes, the greater the burden of suffering he endures on behalf of others. The Lord's glorious investiture as King of Zion is thus commensurate with his prior suffering on Zion's behalf.

In fact, the Lord, his servant or servants, and his people Zion— all rise from a condition of ignominy to exaltation, but on different levels. Within that spiritual hierarchy, the Lord serves as the highest or noblest exemplar of his people. He is their supreme model of covenantal loyalty and compliance. All who affiliate covenantally with the Lord inevitably emulate him and follow his example.

The Lord's coming to deliver his people from death is the crowning event of the day of judgment. The Lord's appearance in Zion climaxes the entire series of events dealing with Zion's redemption. It underscores the fact that the Lord alone is Redeemer and that all rests upon his atonement for sin. Like other servants who have ministered to the Lord's people in times past, two *arms* of God— the Lord and his servant—intervene in the affairs of the Lord's people to deliver them from perils both temporal and spiritual. Such deliverance, however, is ultimately divine. Power to put down the enemies of his people—even the enemy death—comes from God alone when the conditions for his intervention are met.

Such is at least part of the literary message Isaiah has embedded in his book. Because this message far surpasses what we learn from a surface reading of the text, the literary features of Isaiah are indeed important to comprehend. In effect, the structure, rhetoric, and typology of Isaiah form an integral part of the book's content; what the one conveys cannot fully be comprehended without the other. It is hoped that this study will bring a broader awareness of the pertinence of the message of Isaiah for our time as well as a deeper understanding of the eternal truths he declared.

THE BOOK OF ISAIAH

A NEW TRANSLATION

HOW TO USE THE NEW TRANSLATION

Passages of Isaiah translated from Hebrew prose extend from margin to margin. Passages translated from Hebrew poetic or verse form are indented from the margins.

Words inserted in the text in order to clarify incomplete or difficult phrasing appear in *italics*.

Metaphorical key words that serve as pseudonyms of the Lord, of the Davidic servant, and of the king of Assyria/Babylon appear in **bold**.

Words or phrases transposed from other parts of the text are set off by brackets [ ].

Passages in Isaiah cross-referenced in the margins may throw light on the adjoining verses. Cross-referenced passages marked by an asterisk* appear out of order in the text.

An italicized letter after a problematic word or phrase in the text,*a* or two identical italicized letters, *b*one before and one after,*b* indicate a footnote.

Footnotes are numbered alphabetically within a chapter and identify a verse by its number.

Abbreviations in the footnotes include—
MT—The Hebrew Masoretic Text from which the New Translation of Isaiah is made.
1QIsaª—The complete Hebrew Dead Sea Scroll of Isaiah.
LXX—The Greek Septuagint Version of the Old Testament.

The Comprehensive Concordance that follows the Translation of Isaiah assists in locating and identifying rhetorically related passages.

THE BOOK OF ISAIAH

1 The vision of Isaiah the son of Amoz which he beheld concerning Judea and Jerusalem during the reigns of Uzziah, Jotham, Ahaz, and Hezekiah, kings of Judah:

² Hear, O heavens! Give heed, O earth!
  The Lord*ᵃ* has spoken:

63:8–10 I have reared sons, brought them up,
    but they have revolted against me.
³ The ox knows its owner,
    the ass its master's stall,
45:6 but Israel does not know;
    my people are insensible.
⁴ Alas, a nation astray,
3:9   a people weighed down by sin,
    the offspring of wrongdoers,
      perverse children:
    they have forsaken the Lord,
30:9–11   they have spurned the Holy One of Israel,
    they have lapsed into apostasy.

⁵ Why be smitten further
    by adding to your waywardness?
9:15 The whole head is sick,
    the whole heart diseased.
⁶ From the soles of the feet even to the head
    there is nothing sound,
    only wounds and bruises and festering sores;
17:11   they have not been pressed out or bound up,
    nor soothed with ointment.

---

*ᵃ*2   Hebrew *YHWH* throughout.

7 Your land is ruined,

5:5–6   your cities burned with **fire**;
your native soil is devoured by aliens in your presence,
laid waste at its takeover by foreigners.

4:5–6   8 The Daughter of Zion is left
like a shelter in a vineyard,
a hut in a melon field,

36:1–2   a city under siege.
9 Had not the Lord of Hosts left us a few survivors,
we should have been as Sodom,
or become like Gomorrah.

28:14   10 Hear the word of the Lord,
O leaders of Sodom;
give heed to the law of our God,
you people of Gomorrah!
11 For what purpose are your abundant
sacrifices to me? says the Lord.

43:23–24   I have had my fill of offerings of rams
and fat of fatted beasts;
the blood of bulls and sheep and he-goats
I do not want.

38:11   12 When you come to see me,
who requires you to trample my courts so?

13 Bring no more worthless offerings;
they are as a loathsome incense to me.

58:13–14   As for convening meetings at the New Month
and on the Sabbath,
wickedness with the solemn gathering
I cannot approve.
14 Your monthly and regular meetings
my soul detests.

46:3   They have become a burden on me;
I am weary of putting up with them.
15 When you spread forth your hands,
I will conceal my eyes from you;

59:2–3   though you pray at length, I will not hear—
your hands are filled with blood.

16 Wash yourselves clean:
55:7   remove your wicked deeds
from before my eyes;
cease to do evil.
17 Learn to do good: demand justice,
58:6   stand up for the oppressed;
plead the cause of the fatherless,
appeal on behalf of the widow.

18 Come now, let us put it to the test,
says the Lord:
though your sins are as scarlet,
43:25   they can be made white as snow;
though they have reddened as crimson,
they may become *white* as wool.
3:10   19 If you are willing and obey,
you shall eat the good of the land.
20 But if you are unwilling and disobey,
3:25   you shall be eaten by the **sword**.
By his **mouth** the Lord has spoken it.

21 How the faithful city
57:7–8   has become a harlot!
She was filled with justice;
righteousness made its abode in her,
but now murderers.
22 Your silver has become dross,
your wine diluted with water.
5:23   23 Your rulers are renegades,
accomplices of robbers:
with one accord they love bribes
and run after rewards;
10:2   they do not dispense justice to the fatherless,
nor does the widow's case come before them.

24 Therefore the Lord, the Lord of Hosts,
the Valiant One of Israel, declares,
59:18   Woe to them! I will relieve me
of my adversaries,
avenge me of my enemies.

²⁵ I will restore my **hand** over you

48:10   and smelt away your dross as in a crucible,*ᵇ*

and remove all your alloy.

²⁶ I will restore your judges as at the first,

and your counsellors as in the beginning.

After this you shall be called

19:18   the City of **Righteousness**, a faithful city.

²⁷ For Zion shall be ransomed by justice,

32:17   those of her who repent by **righteousness**.

²⁸ But criminals and sinners

shall be altogether shattered

13:9   when those who forsake the Lord are annihilated.

²⁹ And you*ᶜ* will be ashamed of the oaks you cherished

65:3   and blush for the parks you were fond of;

³⁰ you shall become like an oak whose leaves wither,

and as a garden that has no water.

³¹ The mighty shall be as refuse,

37:18–19   their works a spark;

both shall burn up alike,

and there shall be none to extinguish.

2 A prophecy concerning Judea and Jerusalem which Isaiah the son of Amoz saw in vision:

² In the latter days

16:1   the mountain of the Lord's house

shall become established

as*ᵈ* the head of the mountains;

it shall be preeminent among the hills,

66:12   and all nations will flow to it.

³ Many peoples shall go, saying,

Come, let us go up

56:6–8   to the mountain of the Lord,

to the house of the God of Jacob,

---

*ᵇ*25   Hebrew *kabbōr, as with potash/lye,* emended to *kakūr;* compare 48:10.

*ᶜ*29   Hebrew *they.*

*ᵈ*2   So 1QIsaª; MT has *bet essentiae: in/as.*

that he may instruct us in his ways,
that we may follow in his paths.
51:4   For out of Zion shall go forth the law,
and from Jerusalem the word of the Lord.

11:4   ⁴ He will judge between the nations
and arbitrate for many peoples.
They will beat their swords into plowshares,
their spears into pruning hooks:
54:16–17   nation will not lift the **sword** against nation,
nor will they learn warfare any more.

⁵ O house of Jacob, come,
60:1–4   let us follow the **light** of the Lord.

⁶ For thou, O *Lord*, hast forsaken thy people,
the house of Jacob, because,
like the Philistines,
they provide themselves with*ᵇ*
mystics from the East
and are content with the infantile heathen.
31:7   ⁷ Their land is full of silver and gold
and there is no end to their wealth;
their land is full of horses
and there is no end to their chariots.
17:7–8   ⁸ Their land is full of idols:
they adore the works of their hands,
things their own fingers have made.

5:15   ⁹ Mankind is brought low
when men thus debase themselves.
Forbear them not!

¹⁰ Go into the rocks; hide in the dust
from the awesome presence of the Lord
40:5   and from the brightness of his glory.
¹¹ The haughty eyes of men shall be lowered
and man's pride abased;
5:16   the Lord alone shall be exalted in that day.

---

*ᵇ*6   Hebrew conjunctive *wĕ* emended to preposition *bĕ*.

¹² The Lord of Hosts has a day in store

13:6, 9, 11   for all the proud and arrogant
and for all who are exalted,
that they may be brought low.

10:33-34 ¹³ *It shall come* against all the lofty
cedars of Lebanon that lift themselves up high,
and against all the oaks of Bashan,

37:24   ¹⁴ against all high mountains and elevated hills,
¹⁵ against every tall tower and reinforced wall,
¹⁶ against [all vessels at sea,]ᶜ

23:1   both merchant shipsᵈ and pleasure craft.
¹⁷ The haughtiness of men shall be abased,
and man's pride brought low;
the Lord alone shall be exalted in that day.

43:11-13 ¹⁸ He will utterly supplant the false gods.

¹⁹ Men will go into caves in the rocks
and holes in the ground,

30:27   from the awesome presence of the Lord
and from the brightness of his glory,
when he arises and strikes terror on earth.
²⁰ In that day men will throw away
to the moles and to the bats

30:22   their idols of silver and gods of gold
which they have made for themselves
to adore.

²¹ Men will go into crevices in the rocks
and fissures in the cliffs,

64:1-3   from the awesome presence of the Lord
and from the brightness of his glory,
when he arises and strikes terror on earth.

²² Desist from *the things of* man,

40:6-8   in whose nostrils is but breath!
For of what consideration is he?

ᶜ16 So LXX; not in MT.
ᵈ16 Hebrew *ships of Tarshish*.

3   Even now, the Lord, the Lord of Hosts,
         deprives Judea and Jerusalem
     of both staff and crutch—

9:20   all food supply and water supply,
     ² the valiant man and soldier,
         the magistrate and prophet, the augur and elder,
     ³ the officer and dignitary,
         advisers, skilled craftsmen, and orators.

1:23   ⁴ I, *the Lord*, will make adolescents their rulers;
         delinquents will lord it over them.
     ⁵ People will oppress one another,
         every man his neighbor.

9:17   The young will be insolent to the elderly,
         the vile to the honorable.

     ⁶ Then will a man apprehend a kinsman
         of his father's house, *and say*,

24:2-4   You have a tunic: be our leader
         and take charge of this ruination!
     ⁷ But he will raise *his hand* in that day
         and swear, I am no physician.

59:4-6   There is neither food nor clothing in my house;
         you cannot make me a leader of the people.

     ⁸ Jerusalem will falter and Judea fall

57:4-5   because their **tongue** and their actions
         are contrary to the Lord,
         an affront to his glory before his very eyes.
     ⁹ The look on their faces betrays them:

1:10   they flaunt their sin like Sodom;
         they cannot hide it.
     Woe to their souls;
         they have brought disaster upon themselves!

62:8-9   ¹⁰ Tell the righteous it shall be well with them;
         they shall eat the fruits of their own labors.
     ¹¹ But woe to the wicked

13:11   when calamity *overtakes them*:
         they shall be paid back
         for the deeds they have done!

¹² As for my people, babes subject them;
women wield authority over them.
9:16 O my people, your leaders mislead you,
abolishing your traditional ways.
¹³ The Lord will take a stand and contend *with them*;
41:1 he has arisen to judge the nations.
¹⁴ He will bring to trial the elders of his people
and their rulers, *and say to them*,
5:7 It is you who have devoured the vineyard;
you fill your houses by depriving the needy.
¹⁵ What do you mean by oppressing my people,
humbling the faces of the poor?
10:1–2 says the Lord of Hosts.

¹⁶ The Lord says, moreover,
Because the women of Zion are haughty
and put on airs, painting their eyes,
ever flirting when they walk
and clacking with their feet,
57:12 ¹⁷ the Lord will afflict the scalps
of the women of Zion with baldness;
the Lord will expose their private parts.

¹⁸ In that day the Lord will strip away their finery—the anklets, head
ornaments and crescents, ¹⁹ the pendants, chains and scarves, ²⁰ tiaras,
bracelets and ribbons, zodiac signs and charm amulets, ²¹ rings for
the fingers and for the ears, ²² the elegant dress, the shawl, the
kerchief and the purse, ²³ hosiery, sheer linen, millinery, and cloaks.

²⁴ And instead of perfume there shall be a stench,
instead of the girdle, a piece of twine,
instead of the coiffure, baldness,
32:11 instead of the festive dress, a loincloth of burlap;
for in place of beauty
there shall be ignominy.^{*a*}
²⁵ Your men shall be felled by the **sword**,
your might *overthrown* in war.
51:19 ²⁶ Her gateways shall lie bereaved and forlorn;
she shall sit on the ground destitute.

---

*a*24   So 1QIsa^a; term not in MT.

4 Seven women will take hold of one man
    in that day, and say,
We will eat our own food,
    wear our own clothes,
32:2   only let us be called by your name—
    take away our reproach!

² In that day the **plant** of the Lord shall be beautiful and glorious, and the earth's fruit the pride and glory of the survivors of Israel. ³ Then shall they who are left in Zion and they who remain in Jerusalem be called holy—all who were inscribed to be among the living at Jerusalem. ⁴ *This shall be* when my Lord has washed away the excrement of the women of Zion and cleansed Jerusalem of its bloodshed, in the spirit of justice, by a burning wind. ⁵ Over the whole site of Mount Zion, and over its solemn assembly, the Lord will form a cloud by day and a mist glowing with fire by night: above all that is glorious shall be a canopy. ⁶ It shall be a shelter and shade from the heat of the day, a secret refuge from the downpour and from rain.

5 Let me sing for my beloved
    a love song about his vineyard:
My beloved had a vineyard
    on the fertile brow of a hill.
27:2–3   ² He cultivated it, clearing it of stones,
    and planted it with choice vines.
He built a watchtower in its midst
    and hewed for it a winepress as well.
Then he expected it to yield grapes,
3:14–15   but it produced wild grapes.

³ Now, O inhabitants of Jerusalem and you men of Judea,
    please judge between me and my vineyard!
⁴ What more could have been done
    for my vineyard than I have done for it?
When I expected it to yield grapes,
64:6   why did it produce wild grapes?
⁵ Let me now inform you
    what I will do to my vineyard:
5:24   I will have its hedge removed
    and let it be burned;

281

I will have its wall broken through
1:7-8   and let it be trampled.
        6 I will make it a desolation:
            it shall neither be pruned nor hoed,
7:23-25   but briars and thorns shall overgrow it.
        Moreover, I will forbid the rainclouds to rain on it.

        7 The vineyard of the Lord of Hosts is the house of Israel
            and the people of Judah his cherished grove.
        He expected justice,
            but there was injustice;
        he expected righteousness,
59:3-4   but there was an outcry.

        8 Woe to those who join house to house
            and link field to field till no place is left,
        and you are restricted to dwell
32:19*   in the centers of the land!
        9 The Lord of Hosts *spoke this* in my hearing:
            Surely many buildings shall lie desolate,
6:11-12   large and fine *houses* unoccupied.
        10 A ten-acre*ᵃ* vineyard shall yield but one bath,*ᵇ*
            a homer*ᶜ* of seed but an ephah.*ᵈ*

        11 Woe to those who go after liquor
            as soon as they arise in the morning,
        who linger at night parties, inflamed by wine!
22:12-13 12 There are harps and lyres,
            drums, flutes, and wine at their banquets,
        but they regard not what the Lord does,
26:11   nor perceive his **hands** at work.

        13 Therefore my people are taken captive
            for want of knowledge;
24:6   their best men die of famine,
            their masses perish with thirst.

---

*ᵃ*10   Hebrew *ten-yoke,* viz., the land plowed by ten yoke of oxen in one day.
*ᵇ*10   About 6 gallons, or 22 liters.
*ᶜ*10   About 6 bushels, or 220 liters.
*ᵈ*10   A tenth of a homer.

¹⁴ Sheol becomes ravenous,
    opening her **mouth** insatiably;

14:11 into it descend their elite with the masses,
    their boisterous ones and revelers.

¹⁵ Mankind is brought low
    when men debase themselves,
    causing the eyes of the high-minded to be downcast.

2:17 ¹⁶ But the Lord of Hosts will be exalted
    by a just judgment,
    the holy God show himself holy
    by *his* **righteousness**.

14:1 ¹⁷ Then shall *his* sheep feed in their pasture,
    and proselytes eat in the ruins of the affluent.

¹⁸ Woe to those drawn to sin by vain attachments,
    hitched to transgression like a trailer,

40:10 ¹⁹ who think, Let him quickly speed up his work
    so we may see it!
    Let the plan of the Holy One of Israel
    soon come to pass, and we will know!

65:2 ²⁰ Woe to those who suppose what is evil to be good
    and what is good, evil!
    They put **darkness** for **light**
    and **light** for **darkness**;
    they make bitterness sweet and the sweet bitter.

29:14 ²¹ Woe to those who are wise in their own eyes
    and clever in their own view!

²² Woe to those who are valiant at drinking wine
    and champions at mixing liquor!

1:23 ²³ *Woe to those* who acquit the guilty for a bribe,
    but deny justice to the innocent!

²⁴ As a blazing **fire** consumes stubble,

37:26–27   and as dry weeds wane before the **flame**,
    so shall their roots decay away
    and their blossoms fly up like dust.

1:10   For they have despised the law of the Lord of Hosts
    and reviled the words of the Holy One of Israel.

10:5   **25** Therefore the **anger** of the Lord is kindled
       against his people:
       he draws back his **hand** against them
       and strikes them;
14:16   the mountains quake, and their corpses
       lie like litter about the streets.

       Yet for all this his **anger** is not abated;
       his **hand** is upraised still.

13:2, 5   **26** He raises an **ensign** to distant nations
       and summons them from beyond the horizon.
       Forthwith they come, swiftly and speedily.
       27 Not one of them grows weary,
         nor does any stumble;
29:10   they do not drowse or fall asleep.
       Their waist-belts come not loose
       nor their sandal thongs undone.
       28 Their arrows are sharp;
13:18   all their bows are strung.
       The tread of their warhorses resembles flint;
       their chariot wheels revolve like a whirlwind.
       29 They have the roar of a lion;
       they are aroused like young lions:
42:22   growling, they seize the prey, and escape,
       and none comes to the rescue.

       30 He shall be stirred up against them in that day,
17:12   even as the **Sea** is stirred up.
       And should one look to the land,
       there *too* shall be a distressing gloom,
8:22   for the daylight shall be darkened
       by an overhanging mist.

6 In the year of King Uzziah's death, I saw my Lord seated on a throne, highly exalted, the skirt of his robe filling the sanctuary. **2** Seraphs stood by him overhead, each having six wings—with two they could veil their presence, with two conceal their location, and with two fly about. **3** They called out to one another, and said,

5:16   Most holy is the Lord of Hosts;
   the consummation of all the earth is his glory!

⁴ The threshold shook to its foundation at the sound of those who called and a mist filled the temple.

⁵ Then I thought, Woe is me: I have been struck dumb, for I am a man of unclean speech, and I live among a people of unclean speech: I have seen the King, the Lord of Hosts, with my own eyes!

⁶ Then one of the seraphs flew to me carrying an ember which he had taken with tongs from the altar. ⁷ Touching it to my mouth, he said, See, this has touched your lips: your sins are taken away, your transgressions atoned for.

⁸ Then I heard the voice of my Lord saying, Whom shall I send? Who will go for us? And I replied, Here am I; send me!

⁹ And he said, Go, and say to these people,

   Go on hearing, but not understanding;
42:18–20 Go on seeing, but not perceiving.
  ¹⁰ Make the heart of these people grow fat;
   dull their ears and shut their eyes,
   lest they see with their eyes
   and hear with their ears,
29:13 understand in their heart,
   and repent, and be healed.

¹¹ And I replied, For how long, my Lord? And he said,

   Until the cities lie desolate
17:9 and without inhabitant,
   the houses without a man,
   and the land ravaged to ruin.

  ¹² For the Lord will drive men away,
   and great shall be the exodus
5:8 from the centers of the land.
  ¹³ And while yet a tenth of *the people*
   remain in it, or return,
1:7 they shall be burned.
   But like the terebinth or the oak
   when it is felled, whose stump remains alive,
4:3 so shall the holy offspring be what is left standing.

285

7 When Ahaz son of Jotham, the son of Uzziah, was king of Judah, Rezin king of Aram and Pekah son of Remaliah king of Israel came up to Jerusalem to wage war against it, but could not overpower it.

² And when the house of David was informed that Aram was leading Ephraim on, the king's mind and the minds of his people were shaken, as trees in a forest are shaken by a gale.

³ Then the Lord said to Isaiah, Go out and meet Ahaz, you and your son Shear-Jashub,ᵃ at the end of the aqueduct of the Upper Reservoir, on the road to the Laundry Plaza. ⁴ Say to him, See to it that you remain calm and unafraid. Be not intimidated by these two smoking tail ends of kindling, by the burning anger of Rezin and Aram and the son of Remaliah, ⁵ even though Aram has conceived an evil plot against you, as has Ephraim and the son of Remaliah, who say, ⁶ Let us invade Judea and stir up trouble there. We will take it for ourselves by force and set a ruler over it—the son of Tabeal.

> ⁷ Thus says my Lord the Lord:
> It shall not occur or transpire.
> ⁸ For as surely as Damascus is the capital of Aram
> and Rezin the head of Damascus,

17:1–3
> within sixty-fiveᵇ years shall Ephraim
> be shattered as a nation.
> ⁹ But as surely as Samaria is the capital of Ephraim
> and the son of Remaliah the head of Samaria,

43:10
> you will not believe it,
> because you are not loyal.

¹⁰ Again the Lord addressed Ahaz, and said, ¹¹ Ask a sign for yourself from the Lord your God, whether in the depths below or in the heights above. ¹² But Ahaz said, I will not. I will not put the Lord to the test.

¹³ Then *Isaiah* said, Take heed, O house of David! Is it not enough for you to try the patience of men? Must you also try the patience of my God?

ᵃ3 That is, *A remnant will return.*
ᵇ8 Many commentators: *six or five.*

¹⁴ Therefore will my Lord of himself give you a sign: the young woman with child shall give birth to a son and name him Immanuel.ᶜ ¹⁵ Cream and honey will he eat by the time he has learned to reject what is evil and choose what is good. ¹⁶ But before the child learns to reject the evil and choose the good, the land whose two rulers you loathe shall lie forsaken. ¹⁷ The Lord will bring upon you and your people and your father's house a day unlike any since Ephraim broke away from Judah—*the day of* the king of Assyria.

¹⁸ In that day the Lord will signal for the flies from the far rivers of Egypt and for the bees in the land of Assyria. ¹⁹ And they will come and settle with one accord in the riverbeds of the prairie and in rocky ravines, and by all ditches and water holes. ²⁰ In that day my Lord will use a **razor** hired at the **River**—the king of Assyria— to shave your head and the hair of your legs, and to cut off even your beard.

²¹ In that day a man will keep alive a young cow and a pair of sheep. ²² And because of their plentiful milk, men will eat the cream. All who remain in the land will feed on cream and honey.

²³ In that day every plot of ground with a thousand vines worth a thousand pieces of currency shall be briars and thorns. ²⁴ Men will go there with bows and arrows, for the whole land shall revert to wilderness. ²⁵ And on all hillsides cultivated by the hoe you will no longer go for fear of the briars and thorns, but they shall serve as a cattle range, a terrain for sheep to tread down.

8 The Lord said to me, Take a large scroll and write on it in common script: Hasten the plunder, hurry the spoil. ² And I called in reliable witnesses, Uriah the priest and Zechariah the son of Jeberechiah, to witness for me.

³ And when I had been with the prophetess, she conceived and gave birth to a son. And the Lord said to me, Name him Maher-Shalal-Hash-Baz.ᵈ ⁴ For before the child knows how to say, Father, or Mother, the wealth of Damascus and the plunder of Samaria will be brought before the king of Assyria.

ᶜ14   That is, *God is with us.*
ᵈ3   That is, *Hasten the plunder, hurry the spoil.*

⁵ The Lord addressed me again, and said,

> ⁶ Because these people have rejected
> the waters of Shiloah, which flow gently,

7:1, 4
> and rejoice in Rezin and the son of Remaliah,
> ⁷ therefore will my Lord
> cause to come up over them
> the great and mighty waters of the **River**—

7:17
> the king of Assyria in all his glory.
> He will rise up over all his channels
> and overflow all his banks.

28:2
> ⁸ He will sweep into Judea *like* a flood
> and, passing through, reach the very neck;
> his outspread wings will span

7:14
> the breadth of your land, O Immanuel.

> ⁹ Though nations form pacts,
> they shall be routed.
> Give heed, all you distant lands!

30:1
> You may take courage in one another,
> but shall be in fear;
> you may arm yourselves,
> but shall be terrorized.

> ¹⁰ Though you hold consultations,

28:15, 18
> they shall come to nought;
> though you make proposals,
> they shall not prove firm: God is with us!

¹¹ The Lord spoke to me, clasping my hand, and admonished me not to follow the ways of these people. For he said,

> ¹² Do not call a conspiracy all that these people
> call a conspiracy;

26:3–4
> be not afraid or awed
> by the thing they fear.
> ¹³ But sanctify the Lord of Hosts,
> making him your fear, him your awe.

4:5–6
> ¹⁴ And *to you* he will be a sanctuary,
> but to the two houses of Israel
> a stumbling block or obstructing rock,

28:13
> and a snare, catching unawares
> the inhabitants of Jerusalem.

¹⁵ Many will stumble into them,
24:17–18   and when they fall shall be broken,
and when they become ensnared
shall be taken captive.

29:11–12   ¹⁶ *For the Lord has said*, Bind up the testimony;
seal the law among my disciples.
¹⁷ I will wait for the Lord,
33:2   who hides his face from the house of Jacob,
and expect him.

¹⁸ As for me and the children the Lord has given me, we shall be signs and portents in Israel from the Lord of Hosts, who dwells in Mount Zion.

¹⁹ When men tell you to inquire of mediums and spiritists who huddle together and mutter, *say to them*, Should not a people inquire of their God? Should one inquire*ᵇ* of the dead on behalf of the living ²⁰ for doctrine and for a testimony? Surely, while they utter such words devoid of **light**, ²¹ they roam about embittered by hunger; and when they are hungry, they become enraged and, gazing upward, curse their king and their God. ²² They will look to the land, but there shall be a depressing scene of anguish and gloom; and thus are they banished into outer **darkness**.

9 But it shall not be gloomy to those who have been in anguish for her. In the past he humbled the land of Zebulon and Naphtali, but at the last he will exalt the **Sea** Route by the Jordan *in* Galilee of the nations.

² The people walking in **darkness**
60:1–2   have seen a bright **light**;
on the inhabitants of the land
of the shadow of **death**
has the **light** dawned.
26:2, 15   ³ Thou hast enlarged the nation
and increased its joy;
they rejoice at thy presence
as men rejoice at harvest time,
33:23   or as men are joyous when they divide spoil.

ᵇ19   So LXX; phrase not in MT.

289

4 For thou hast smashed the **yoke**
14:4-5   that burdened them,
    the **staff** of submission,
    the **rod** of those who subjected them,
10:26-27   as in the day of Midian's *defeat*.
5 And all boots used in battle
    and tunics rolled in blood
    have become fuel for bonfires.

7:14   6 For to us a child is born, a son appointed,
    who will shoulder the burden of government.
    He will be called
10:21   Wonderful Counsellor, one Mighty in Valor,
    a Father for Ever, a Prince of Peace—
7 that sovereignty may be extended
    and peace have no end;
16:5   that, on the throne of David
    and over his kingdom,
    his rule may be established and upheld
32:1   by justice and **righteousness**
    from this time forth and forever.
    The **zeal** of the Lord of Hosts will accomplish it.

8 This message my Lord sent to Jacob,
    and it shall befall Israel.
9 And the entire people—
    Ephraim and those who dwell in Samaria—
    shall know of it,
2:11-12   who say in pride and arrogance of heart,
10 The bricks have fallen down,
    but we will rebuild with hewn stone;
    the sycamores have been felled,
    but we will replace them with cedars!
11 But the Lord will strengthen
7:8   Rezin's enemies against them
    when he stirs up their adversaries:
12 Aramaeans from the east
    and Philistines from the west
    will devour Israel with open **mouth**.

5:25   Yet for all this his **anger** is not abated;
    his **hand** is upraised still.

¹³ But the people do not turn back

1:5   to him who smites them,

nor will they inquire of the Lord of Hosts.

¹⁴ Therefore the Lord will cut off from Israel

head and tail, palm top and reed, in a single day;

¹⁵ the elders or notables are the head,

the prophets who teach falsehoods, the tail.

3:12   ¹⁶ The leaders of these people have misled them,

and those who are led are confused.

¹⁷ My Lord is not pleased with their young men,

nor does he pity their fatherless and widows,

because all alike are godless malefactors,

52:5   and every mouth utters profanities.

Yet for all this his **anger** is not abated;

his **hand** is upraised still.

33:11–12 ¹⁸ Wickedness shall be set ablaze like a fire,

and briars and thorns shall it consume;

it shall ignite the jungle forests,

and they shall billow upward

in mushrooming clouds of smoke.

10:5–7   ¹⁹ At the **wrath** of the Lord of Hosts

the earth is scorched,

and people are but fuel for the **fire**.

Men will have no compassion for one another.

²⁰ They will snatch on the right, yet remain hungry;

8:21   they will devour on the left, but not be satisfied:

men will eat the flesh of their own offspring.

²¹ Manasseh *will turn* against Ephraim

and Ephraim against Manasseh,

and both will combine against Judah.

Yet for all this his **anger** is not abated;

14:26–27   his **hand** is upraised still.

10

Woe to those who enact unjust laws,

who draft oppressive legislation—

² denying justice to the needy,

29:21   depriving the poor of my people of their right,

making plunder of widows,

mere spoil of the fatherless!

³ What will you do in the day of reckoning
13:6–9   when the holocaust overtakes you from afar?
To whom will you flee for help?
Where will you leave your wealth?
⁴ There shall nothing remain
14:16–17   but to kneel among the captives
or fall among the slain.

Yet for all this his **anger** is not abated;
his **hand** is upraised still.

7:17, 20   ⁵ Hail the Assyrian, the **rod** of my **anger**!
He is a **staff**—my **wrath** in their **hand**.*
⁶ I will commission him against a godless nation,
appoint him over the people
deserving of my **vengeance**,
8:4   to pillage for plunder, to spoliate for spoil,
to tread underfoot like mud in the streets.

⁷ Nevertheless, it shall not seem so to him;
this shall not be what he has in mind.
His purpose shall be to annihilate
14:6   and to exterminate nations not a few.

⁸ He will say, Are not my commanders kings,
one and all?
⁹ Has not Calno fared like Carchemish?
36:19   Is not Hamath as Arpad,
Samaria no better than Damascus?
¹⁰ Since I could do this to the pagan states,
37:18–19   whose statues exceeded
those of Jerusalem and Samaria,
¹¹ shall I not do to Jerusalem and its images
even as I did to Samaria and its idols?

¹² But when my Lord has fully accomplished his work in Mount Zion and in Jerusalem, he will punish the king of Assyria for his notorious boasting and infamous conceit, ¹³ because he has said,

---

*5   Or, *My wrath is a staff in his hand.*

I have done it by my own ability
and shrewdness, for I am ingenious.

37:11   I have done away with the borders of nations,
I have ravaged their reserves,
I have vastly reduced the inhabitants.

33:4   ¹⁴ I have impounded the wealth of peoples like a nest,
and I have gathered up the whole world
as one gathers abandoned eggs;
not one flapped its wings,
or opened its mouth to utter a peep.

10:33–34   ¹⁵ Shall an **axe** exalt itself
above the one who hews with it,
or a **saw** vaunt itself
over him who handles it?

10:5   As though the **rod** wielded him who lifts it up!
As though the **staff** held up the one
who is not made of wood!

¹⁶ Therefore will the Lord, the Lord of Hosts,
send a consumption into his fertile lands,

30:30, 33   and cause a **fire** to flare up like a burning hearth,
to undermine his glory:
¹⁷ the **Light** of Israel will be the **fire**
and their Holy One the **flame**,
and it shall burn up and devour
his briars and thorns in a single day.

9:18   ¹⁸ His choice forests and productive fields
it will consume, both life and substance,
turning them into a rotting morass.
¹⁹ And the trees left of his forest shall be so few,
a child could record them.

1:9   ²⁰ In that day those who survive of Israel
and who escape of the house of Jacob
will no longer rely on him who struck them,
but will truly rely on the Lord,
the Holy One of Israel:

37:31–32   ²¹ of Jacob a remnant will return
to the one Mighty in Valor.

293

²² For though your people, O Israel,
48:18–19   be as the sands of the sea,
     only a remnant will return;
     although annihilation is decreed,
1:27–28   it shall overflow with **righteousness**.
²³ For my Lord, the Lord of Hosts,
     will carry out the utter destruction
28:22   decreed upon the whole earth.

²⁴ Therefore, thus says my Lord,
     the Lord of Hosts:
     O my people who inhabit Zion,
     be not afraid of the Assyrians,
     though they strike you with the **rod**
10:5, 15   or raise their **staff** over you,
     as did the Egyptians.
²⁵ For my **anger** will very soon come to an end;
     my **wrath** will become their undoing.

²⁶ The Lord of Hosts will raise the **whip** against them,
     as when he struck the Midianites
     at the rock of Oreb.
5:30   His **staff** is over the **Sea**,
     and he will lift it over them
     as he did to the Egyptians.
14:25 ²⁷ In that day their burdens shall be lifted
     from your shoulders,
     their **yoke** *removed* from your neck:
9:4   the **yoke** *that wore away your fatness*
     shall by fatness wear away.

²⁸ He advances on Aiath, passes through Migron;
36:1   at Micmash he marshals his weaponry.
²⁹ They cross over the pass,
     stopping overnight at Geba.
     Ramah is in a state of alarm,
5:26–29   Gibeah of Saul is fleeing.
³⁰ Cry out, O Daughter of Gallim!
     Hear her, Laishah; answer her, Anathoth!
³¹ Madmenah has moved out of the way,
     the inhabitants of Gebim are in full flight.

³² This same day he will but pause at Nob
and signal the advance

1:8   against the mountain of the Daughter of Zion,
the hill of Jerusalem.

³³ Then will the Lord, the Lord of Hosts,

2:13   shatter the towering *trees* with terrifying power;
the high in stature shall be hewn down,
the lofty ones leveled.

³⁴ The dense forests shall be battered down

32:19*   with *the force of* iron,
and Lebanon fall spectacularly.

11

A **shoot** will spring up from the **stock** of Jesse
and a **branch** from its graft bear fruit.

61:1-3   ² The Spirit of the Lord will rest upon him—
the spirit of wisdom and of understanding,

9:6   the spirit of counsel and of valor,
the spirit of knowledge
and of the fear of the Lord.

³ His intuition will be *guided*

8:13   by the fear of the Lord;
he will not judge by what his eyes see,
nor establish proof by what his ears hear.

2:4   ⁴ He will judge the poor with **righteousness**,
and with equity arbitrate for the lowly in the land;
he will smite the earth with the **rod** of his **mouth**

30:28   and with the **breath** of his **lips** slay the wicked.
⁵ **Righteousness** will be as a band about his waist,
faithfulness a girdle round his loins.

⁶ Then shall the wolf dwell among lambs
and the leopard lie down with young goats;
calves and young lions ᵃwill feedᵃ together,

49:9   and a youngster will lead them *to pasture.*
⁷ When a cow and bear browse,
their young will rest together;
the lion will eat straw like the ox.

ᵃ6   So 1QIsaᵃ; LXX. MT *and fatlings.*

295

⁸ A suckling infant will play near the adder's den,
and the toddler reach his hand
over the viper's nest.

65:25 ⁹ There shall be no harm or injury done
throughout my holy mountain,
for the earth shall be filled
2:3 with the knowledge of the Lord
as the oceans are overspread with waters.

¹⁰ In that day the **sprig** of Jesse,
who stands for an **ensign** to the peoples,
55:4-5 shall be sought by the nations,
and his residence shall be glorious.

¹¹ In that day my Lord will again *ᵇraiseᵇ* his **hand**
10:21-22 to reclaim the remnant of his people—
those who shall be left out of Assyria,
Egypt, Pathros, Cush, Elam, Shinar, Hamath,
and the isles of the sea.

49:22 ¹² He will raise the **ensign** to the nations
and assemble the exiled of Israel;
he will gather the scattered of Judah
43:5-6 from the four directions of the earth.

¹³ Ephraim's jealousy shall pass away
and the hostile ones of Judah be cut off;
Ephraim will not envy Judah,
nor Judah resent Ephraim.

¹⁴ But they will swoop on the Philistine flank
49:17 toward the west,
and together plunder those to the east;
they will take Edom and Moab at **hand**'s reach,
and the Ammonites will obey them.

¹⁵ The Lord will dry up the **tongue**
of the Egyptian **Sea** *ᶜby his mighty wind;ᶜ*
8:7 he will extend his **hand** over the **River**
and smite it into seven streams
to provide a way on foot.

ᵇ11 Hebrew *šēnît, a second time,* emended to *še'ēt;* compare Interpreter's Bible, 5:251.
ᶜ15 Phrase transposed; in text follows *and smite it.*

¹⁶ And there shall be a pathway out of Assyria

27:12-13   for the remnant of his people who shall be left,
            as there was for Israel
            when it came up from the land of Egypt.

12

            In that day you will say,
                I praise thee, O Lord.
            Although thou hast been angry with me,
10:25   thine **anger** is turned away
            and thou hast consoled me.
            ² In*ᵃ* the God of my **salvation** I will trust without fear;
28:5-6   for the Lord was my strength and *ᵇ*my song*ᵇ*
            when he became my **salvation**.
            ³ Then shall you rejoice in drawing water
58:11   from the fountains of **salvation**.

            ⁴ In that day you will say,
                Give thanks to the Lord; invoke his name.
            Make known his deeds among the nations;
                commemorate his exalted name.
            ⁵ Sing in praise of the Lord,
25:1   who has performed wonders;
                let it be acknowledged throughout the earth!
            ⁶ Shout and sing for joy, O inhabitants of Zion,
8:18   for renowned among you is the Holy One of Israel.

13

            An oracle concerning Babylon, which Isaiah the son of Amoz
            saw in vision:

5:26   ² Raise the **ensign** on a barren mountain;
                sound the **voice** among them!
            Beckon them with the **hand** to advance
                into the precincts of the elite.
4:3   ³ I have charged my holy ones,
                called out my valiant ones:
            *ᵃ*my **anger** is not upon*ᵃ* those who take pride in me.

ᵃ2   Hebrew *ʾel ʾēl;* so 1QIsaᵃ. A probable haplography in MT.
ᵇ2   Hebrew *zimrāt yâ,* a probable dittography, emended to *zimrātî.*
ᵃ3   Hebrew *lĕʾappî ʿallîzê,* exhibiting a double haplography, emended to *lōʾ ʾappî ʿal ʿallîzê.*

⁴ Hark! A tumult on the mountains,
  as of a vast multitude.

17:12 Hark! An uproar among kingdoms,
  as of nations assembling:
the Lord of Hosts is marshalling an army for war.
⁵ They come from a distant land beyond the horizon—
  the Lord and the instruments of his **wrath**—

10:23 to cause destruction throughout the earth.

⁶ Lament, for the day of the Lord is near;
  it shall come as a violent blow from the Almighty.
⁷ Then shall every hand grow weak
  and the hearts of all men melt.

2:19, 21 ⁸ They shall be terrified, in throes of agony,
  seized with trembling like a woman in labor.
Men will look at one another aghast,
  their faces set aflame.

63:4 ⁹ The day of the Lord shall come
  as a cruel outburst of **anger** and **wrath**
to make the earth a desolation,
  that sinners may be annihilated from it.

50:3 ¹⁰ The stars and constellations of the heavens
  will not shine.
When the sun rises, it shall be obscured;
  nor will the moon give its light.

3:11 ¹¹ I have decreed calamity for the world,
  punishment for the wicked;
I will put an end to the arrogance of insolent men

29:20 and humble the pride of tyrants.
¹² I will make mankind scarcer than fine gold,
  men *more rare* than gold of Ophir.

34:4 ¹³ I will cause disturbance in the heavens
  when the earth is jolted out of place
by the **anger** of the Lord of Hosts

9:19 in the day of his blazing **wrath**.

¹⁴ Then, like a deer that is chased,
  or a flock of sheep that no one rounds up,
each will return to his own people
  and everyone flee to his homeland.

¹⁵ Whoever is found shall be thrust through;

1:20   all who are caught shall fall by the **sword**.

¹⁶ Their infants shall be dashed in pieces before their eyes,
their homes plundered, their wives ravished.

21:2   ¹⁷ See, I stir up against them the Medes,
who do not value silver, nor covet gold.

¹⁸ Their bows shall tear apart the young.
They will show no mercy to the newborn;
their eye will not look with compassion on children.

21:9   ¹⁹ And Babylon, the most splendid of kingdoms,
the glory and pride of Chaldeans, shall be *thrown down*

1:9   as God overthrew Sodom and Gomorrah.

²⁰ Never shall it be reinhabited;
it shall not be resettled through all generations.
Nomads will not pitch their tents there,
nor will shepherds rest their flocks in it.

32:13–14   ²¹ But wild animals will infest it,
and its buildings overflow with weasels;
birds of prey will find lodging there
and demonic creatures prance about in it.

²² Jackals will cry out from its palaces,

34:13   howling creatures from its amusement halls.
Her time draws near;
Babylon's^b days shall not be prolonged.

14

The Lord will have compassion on Jacob
and once again choose Israel;
he will settle them in their own land,

5:17   and proselytes will adhere to them
and join the house of Jacob.

² The nations will take them

49:22   and bring them to their own place.
And the house of Israel will possess them
as menservants and maidservants

61:5   in the land of the Lord:
they will take captive their captors
and rule over their oppressors.

---

^b22 Hebrew *Her.*

³ In the day the Lord gives you relief from grief and anguish and from the arduous servitude imposed on you, ⁴ you will take up this taunt against the king of Babylon, and say,

How the tyrant has met his end
and tyranny*a* ceased!

9:4 ⁵ The Lord has broken the **staff** of the wicked,
the **rod** of those who ruled—
⁶ him who with unerring blows
10:6–7 struck down the nations in **anger**,
who subdued peoples in his **wrath**
by relentless oppression.
⁷ Now the whole earth is at rest and at peace;
there is jubilant celebration!
37:24 ⁸ The pine trees, too, rejoice over you,
as do the cedars of Lebanon:
Since you have been laid low,
10:15 no hewer has risen against us!

⁹ Sheol below was in commotion because of you,
anticipating your arrival;
on your account she roused all the spirits
of the world's leaders,
24:21–22 causing all who had ruled nations
to rise up from their thrones.
¹⁰ All alike were moved to say to you,
Even you have become powerless as we are!
You have become like us!

5:14 ¹¹ Your glory has been cast down to Sheol,
along with the music of your lyres.
Beneath you is a bed of maggots;
you are covered with worms.
54:15 ¹² How you have fallen from the heavens,
O morning star, son of the dawn!
You who commanded the nations
33:1 have been hewn down to earth!

¹³ You said in your heart, I will rise in the heavens
and set up my throne above the stars of God;

---

*a*4   Or, *rage;* so 1QIsaᵃ; LXX. MT rendering is unknown.

I will seat myself
in the mount of assembly *of the gods*,
in the utmost heights of Zaphon.
¹⁴ I will ascend above the altitude of the clouds;
37:23   I will make myself like the Most High!

¹⁵ But you have been brought down to Sheol,
38:18   to the utmost depths of the Pit.
¹⁶ Those who catch sight of you
stare at you, wondering,
5:25   Is this the man who made the earth shake
and kingdoms quake,
¹⁷ who turned the world into a wilderness,
37:26   demolishing its cities,
permitting not his captives to return home?

¹⁸ All rulers of nations lie in state,
each among his own kindred.
¹⁹ But you are cast away unburied
like a repugnant fetus,
31:8–9   exposed like the slain disfigured by the **sword**,
whose mangled remains are thrown in a gravel pit.

²⁰ You shall not share burial with them,
for you have destroyed your land
and murdered your people.
26:14   May the brood of miscreants
never more be mentioned!
30:31–32 ²¹ Prepare for the massacre of their sons,
in consequence of their fathers' deeds,
lest they rise up again
10:13–14   and take possession of the world,
and fill the face of the earth with cities.

²² I will rise up against them, says the Lord of Hosts.
I will cut off Babylon's name and remnant,
13:19   its offspring and descendants, says the Lord.
²³ I will turn it into swamplands, a haunt for ravens;
I will sweep it with the **broom** of destruction,
says the Lord of Hosts.

²⁴ The Lord of Hosts made an oath, saying,

As I foresaw it, so shall it happen;
as I planned it, so shall it be:
10:12 ²⁵ I will break Assyria in my own land,
trample them underfoot on my mountains;
their **yoke** shall be taken from them,
10:24–27 their burden removed from their shoulders.
²⁶ These are things determined upon the whole earth;
this is the **hand** upraised over all nations.
²⁷ For what the Lord of Hosts has determined,
who shall revoke?
43:13 When his **hand** is upraised, who can turn it away?

²⁸ In the year King Ahaz died, came this oracle:

²⁹ Rejoice not, all you Philistines,
now that the **rod** which struck you is broken.
From among the descendants of that **snake**
shall spring up a **viper**,
and his offspring shall be a **fiery flying serpent**.
40:11 ³⁰ The elect poor shall have pasture,
and the needy recline in safety.
But your descendants I will kill with famine,
14:22 and your survivors shall be slain.
³¹ Wail at the gates; howl in the city!
Utterly melt away, you Philistines!
9:18 From the North shall come *pillars of* smoke,
and no place he has designated shall evade it.
³² What shall then be told the envoys of the nation?
The Lord has founded Zion;
25:4 let his longsuffering people find refuge there.

15

An oracle concerning Moab:
When in one night Ar is devastated,
Moab shall be silenced;
25:12 when in one night Kir is razed,
Moab shall be destroyed.
² They will go up to the sanctuaries,
16:12 and in Dibon to the hill shrines, to weep;
they will wail in Moab over Nebo and Medeba.
Every head shall be bald, every beard cut off.

³ They will wear sackcloth openly;
  on the housetops and in the streets
  they will altogether wail and give way to weeping.

10:30 ⁴ Heshbon will cry for help, as will Elealeh;
  their appeal shall be heard as far as Jahaz.
  They will sound the alarm
    to summon the armed men of Moab,
  but their spirit shall be broken.
  ⁵ My heart will cry out for Moab;

21:15   its fugitives will reach Zoar
  and as far as Eglath Shelishiah.
  In tears they will ascend the slopes of Luhith;
  on the road to Horonaim

47:11 they will raise the cry of catastrophe.

  ⁶ For the waters of Nimrim shall be desolate;
  the grass shall dry up, vegetation disappear,

42:15   and no green foliage shall remain.
  ⁷ The surplus they have acquired,
  and their personal belongings,
  they will carry away
    over the Valley of the Willows.

13:11 ⁸ The cry of calamity
  shall encompass the land of Moab;
  the sound of it shall reach Eglaim
  and echo as far as Beer Elim.

  ⁹ Although the waters of Dibon shall flow with blood,
  yet will I impose more than this upon Dibon:

5:29 *I will bring* lions upon the fugitives of Moab
  and on those who remain in the land.

16 Send couriers to those who rule in the earth,
  from Sela in the desert
  to the mountain of the Daughter of Zion.
  ² Like fluttering birds forced out of the nest,

47:2   so are Moab's women at the fords of Arnon.
  ³ Provide a solution, *they say*; judge our case!

59:9–10   Overshadow us at high noon as though it were night!
  Shelter those dispossessed;
  betray not the refugees!

⁴ Let the exiles of Moab dwell with you;
be a refuge to them from the aggressors!

14:3-4   When oppressors are no more
and violence has ceased,
when tyrants are destroyed from the earth,
⁵ then, in loving kindness,

22:22-23   shall a throne be set up in the abode of David,
and in **faithfulness** a judge sit on it

9:7   who will maintain justice and expedite **righteousness**.

⁶ We have heard of the glories of Moab,
of its excessive pride and its boasting,
of its outbursts of false propaganda.

13:6   ⁷ For this shall the Moabites *be made to* lament,
and all *have cause to* bewail Moab:
they shall groan at the ruin of Kir Hareseth
in utter dejection.

24:7   ⁸ For the vineyards of Heshbon shall wither;
the ruling nations will smite Sibmah's vines.
Its runner vines reached Jazer,
trailing through the desert;

23:7   its branches spread abroad across the sea.
⁹ Therefore I will mourn as Jazer mourns
for the vines of Sibmah;
I will water you with my tears,

15:4   O Heshbon and Elealeh,
when your shouts of cheer
over the summer fruit and harvest are stilled.
¹⁰ The joyful festivity will be gone from the orchards;

32:12   no shouts of delight shall sound in the vineyards.
The wine treaders will tread no wine in the presses;
the vintage shout I will bring to an end.

¹¹ My breast will vibrate like a harp for Moab,

22:4   my inmost being for Kir Hareseth.
¹² For when the Moabites weary themselves
with petitioning on the hill shrines,
and enter their sanctuaries to pray,
it shall be to no avail.

¹³ These things the Lord spoke hitherto about Moab. ¹⁴ But now the Lord has said, Within three years, as the term of a lease, Moab's glory shall become ignominy. For all its large populace there shall be very few left, and those of no account.

17 An oracle concerning Damascus:
　　　Damascus shall cease to be a city
　　　　and become a heap of ruins.

27:10　² The cities of Aroer shall lie forsaken
　　　　and become places for herds to recline,
　　　　where no one will disturb them.
　　　³ When Ephraim's defense comes to an end,
8:4　　　so shall the sovereignty of Damascus:
　　　　as with the glory of the children of Israel,
　　　　so shall it be with Aram's remnant,
　　　says the Lord of Hosts.

　　　⁴ In that day Jacob's glory shall wane,
　　　　and his fatness of body become leanness.
27:12　⁵ After being like a harvest of ripe grain,
　　　　whose ears are reaped by the armful,
　　　　he will become like ears plucked
　　　　in the Valley of Rephaim
24:13　　⁶ when only the gleanings are left,
　　　　or when an olive tree is beaten,
　　　　having two or three berries in the topmost bough,
65:8　　or four or five in its most fruitful branch,
　　　　says the Lord, the God of Israel.

　　　⁷ In that day men will have regard to their Maker,
10:20　　and their eyes look to the Holy One of Israel,
　　　⁸ and regard not the altars,
　　　　the works of their hands,
　　　　nor look to things made by their fingers—
27:9　　　the idols of prosperity and the shining images.

⁹ In that day their mighty cities shall be like the deserted towns of the *Hivites and Amorites,* which they abandoned before the Israelites during the desolation.

---

*9　So LXX; MT *groves and treetops.*

10 For you have forgotten your God, your **salvation**,
26:1, 4   and not remembered the Rock, your fortress.
          Therefore, though you plant choice crops
          and sow hybrid seed,
       11 and though you make them thrive
          the day you plant them,
          causing them to sprout
          the very morning you sow them,
32:10   yet shall the harvest vanish
          in a day of diseases and incurable pain.

13:4   12 Woe to the many peoples in an uproar,
          who rage like the raging of the seas—
          tumultuous nations, in commotion
          like the turbulence of mighty waters!
28:2   13 Nations may roar like the roaring of great waters,
          but when he rebukes them they will flee far away;
          they will be driven before the wind
40:23–24   like chaff on the mountains,
          or as whirling *dust* in a storm.
       14 At evening time shall be the catastrophe,
          and before morning they shall be no more.
10:6   This is the lot of those who plunder us,
          the fate of those who despoil us.

18

          Woe to the land of buzzing wings
             beyond the rivers of Cush,
        2 which sends emissaries by sea,
          in swift craft across the water.
          They say, Go speedily, you messengers!
          Go to a people perpetually on the move,
51:13   a nation dreaded far and wide,
          a people continually infringing,
8:7   whose rivers have annexed their lands.

        3 All you who live in the world,
          you inhabitants of the earth,
          look to the **ensign**
             when it is lifted up in the mountains;
27:12–13 heed the **trumpet** when sounded!

306

⁴ For thus said the Lord to me:
    I will watch in silence over my dwelling place

25:4-5 when the searing heat overtakes the reapers,*
    and when the rainclouds *appear*

17:5 amid the fever of reaping.
⁵ For before the harvest,
    when the *time of* flowering is past
and the set blossoms are developing into young fruit,
    they will cut down the fruit-bearing twigs with knives

33:9 and remove the new branches by slashing.
⁶ All shall be left to the birds of prey
    of the mountains
and to the beasts of the land:
    the birds of prey will feed on them all summer
and the beasts of the land all winter.

60:12 ⁷ At that time shall tribute be brought
    to the Lord of Hosts
from a nation perpetually on the move,
    from a nation dreaded far and wide,
a people continually infringing,

37:11 whose rivers have annexed their lands,
to the place of the name of the Lord of Hosts:
    Mount Zion.

19

An oracle concerning Egypt:

When the Lord enters Egypt riding on swift clouds,
    the idols of Egypt will rock at his presence

13:6-7 and the Egyptians' hearts melt within them.

² I will stir up the Egyptians against the Egyptians;
    they will fight brother against brother

3:5 and neighbor against neighbor,
    city against city and state against state.
³ Egypt's spirit shall be drained from within;
    I will frustrate their plans,

44:17 and they will resort to the idols and to spiritists,
to mediums and witchcraft.

---

*4   Hebrew ʾôr, *light,* emended to ʾôreh.

⁴ Then will I deliver the Egyptians
  into the hand of a cruel master;
37:25   a harsh ruler will subject them,
  says my Lord, the Lord of Hosts.

⁵ The waters of the lakes shall ebb away
  as streambeds become desolate and dry.
42:15   ⁶ The rivers shall turn foul,
  and Egypt's waterways recede and dry up.
  Reeds and rushes shall wither;
  ⁷ vegetation adjoining canals and estuaries,
  and all things sown along irrigation channels,
15:6   shall shrivel and blow away and be no more.

⁸ Fishermen will deplore *their lot*
  and anglers in canals bemoan themselves;
  those who cast nets on water
50:2   will be in misery.
  ⁹ Manufacturers of combed linen
  and weavers of fine fabrics will be dismayed.
  ¹⁰ The textile workers will know despair,
  and all who work for wages *"suffer distress."*

¹¹ The ministers of Zoan are utter fools;
5:21   the wisest of Pharaoh's advisers give absurd counsel.
  How can you say to Pharaoh,
  We ourselves are as wise as the first rulers?
  ¹² Where are your wise men indeed?
44:25   Let them please tell you, if they can discern it,
  what the Lord of Hosts has in mind for Egypt!

¹³ The ministers of Zoan have been foolish,
  the officials of Noph deluded;
3:12   the heads of state have led Egypt astray.
  ¹⁴ The Lord has permeated them
  with a spirit of confusion;
  they have misled Egypt in all that she does,
29:9   causing her to stagger like a drunkard into his vomit.
  ¹⁵ And there shall be nothing the Egyptians
  can do about it,
36:6   neither head nor tail, palm top or reed.

ᵃ10 Hebrew ⟩*agmê nepeš*, *ponds for life*, emended to ⟨*agmê nepeš*.

¹⁶ In that day the Egyptians will be as women, fearful and afraid at the brandishing **hand** the Lord of Hosts wields over them. ¹⁷ The land of Judah shall become a source of terror to the Egyptians; all reminded of it shall dread what the Lord of Hosts has in store for them.

¹⁸ In that day five Hebrew-speaking cities in the land of Egypt will swear loyalty to the Lord of Hosts. One shall be known as the City of **Righteousness**.*ᵇ*

¹⁹ In that day there shall be an altar *erected* to the Lord in the midst of the land of Egypt and a monument to the Lord at its border. ²⁰ They shall serve as a sign and testimony of the Lord of Hosts in the land of Egypt: when they cry out to the Lord because of the oppressors, he will send them a savior, who will take up their cause and deliver them.

²¹ The Lord will make himself known to the Egyptians, and the Egyptians shall know the Lord in that day. They will worship by sacrifice and offerings, and make vows to the Lord and fulfill them. ²² The Lord will smite Egypt, and by smiting heal: they will turn back to the Lord, and he will respond to their pleas and heal them.

²³ In that day there shall be a highway from Egypt to Assyria. Assyrians shall come to Egypt and Egyptians go to Assyria, and the Egyptians shall labor with the Assyrians.

²⁴ In that day Israel shall be the third party to Egypt and to Assyria, a blessing in the midst of the earth. ²⁵ The Lord of Hosts will bless them, saying, Blessed be Egypt my people, Assyria the work of my **hands**, and Israel my inheritance.

20 In the year the general who was sent by Sargon king of Assyria came to Ashdod and took it by combat, ² the Lord had spoken through Isaiah the son of Amoz, saying, Go and ungird the sackcloth from your loins and remove the shoes from your feet. And he had done so, going naked and barefoot.

³ Then the Lord said, Just as my servant Isaiah has gone naked and barefoot for three years as a sign and portent against Egypt and Cush, ⁴ so shall the king of Assyria lead away the captives of Egypt and the exiles of Cush, both young and old, naked and barefoot,

---

*ᵇ*18   So LXX. MT *city of destruction;* 1QIsaᵃ *city of the sun.*

with buttocks uncovered—to Egypt's shame. ⁵ Men shall be appalled and perplexed at Cush, their hope, and at Egypt, their boast.

⁶ In that day shall the inhabitants of this isle say, See what has become of those we looked up to, on whom we relied*ᵃ* for help and deliverance from the king of Assyria! How shall we ourselves escape?

21 An oracle concerning the Wilderness of the West:

Like tornadoes sweeping through the South,
they come from the steppes, a land of terror.
² A grim vision has been revealed to me:

33:1
the traitor in the act of treachery,
the destroyer laying waste.

13:17
Attack, O Elamites! Lay siege, you Medes!
All the sighing that *Babylon*ᵃ has caused
I will bring to an end.

³ Therefore my whole frame is racked with trembling;

13:8
throes of agony have seized me like a woman in labor.
I am tormented beyond giving heed;
I am too distraught to see.
⁴ My mind reels, I am paralyzed with fear;
the nightfall I longed for has become a horror to me:

22:13
⁵ They prepare tables;
they deck them with candlesticks.
They are eating and drinking . . .

22:6–7
Mobilize, you commanders! Oil the armor!

⁶ Because of this my Lord said to me,
Go and appoint a watchman

52:8
who will report what he sees.
⁷ Let him watch for chariots with teams of horses,
riders on asses and riders on camels.
He must be most vigilant, fully alert.
⁸ Then the lookout*ᵇ* cried,

5:2
I have been standing on the watchtower
day in and day out, my Lord;
night after night I have stood guard.

---

*ᵃ*6   So 1QIsaᵃ; MT *to whom we fled.*
*ᵃ*2   Hebrew *she.*
*ᵇ*8   So 1QIsaᵃ; MT *a lion.*

310

9 Now they come: cavalry and teams of horses!
And he gave the reply,
13:1   She has fallen; Babylon has fallen.
All her idol gods he has razed to the ground.

10 ᶜTo you who know me, who are of my fold,
28:22   I have reported what I heard
from the Lord of Hosts, the God of Israel.

11 An oracle concerning Dumah:

Men call to me from Seir,
62:6   Watchman, what remains of the night?
Watchman, how much of the night is left?
12 The watchman replies,
Morning comes, though it is still night.
6:10   If you would ascertain it,
do so by repenting and coming back.

13 An oracle concerning those in Arabia:

You wandering bands of Dedanites,
22:8   who sojourn in the forests of Arabia,
14 bring water to greet the thirsty;
meet the fugitives with food,
O inhabitants of the land of Tema.
15 For they flee from destruction,
13:15,18   from the bared **sword**, the drawn **bow**
and the severity of war.

16 On account of this, my Lord said to me, Within a year, as the
term of a lease, Kedar's glory shall fully expire. 17 And the number
of valiant archers remaining of the sons of Kedar shall be few. The
Lord, the God of Israel, has spoken it.

22 An oracle concerning the Arena of Spectacles:

Whatever is the matter with you,
causing you all at once
to climb onto the housetops?
24:8   2 You resounded with loud cheers—
a tumultuous town, a city of revelry!

ᶜ10 So 1QIsaᵃ; MT *My threshed and winnowed ones.*

311

But your slain were not killed by the sword;
1:21   they did not die in battle!
³ Your chiefs, altogether in flight,
        are captured without using the bow;
        all of you left behind are caught easily
10:4   before you can get away.

⁴ Because of this I said,
Turn your attention from me,
        though I weep bitterly;
        hasten not to comfort me
51:19   at the ruin of the Daughter of my People.

⁵ For my Lord, the Lord of Hosts, has in store
a day of commotion and trampling and riot
        in the Arena of Spectacles,
5:5   *a day* of battering down walls,
        and of crying in distress, To the mountains!

21:2   ⁶ When Elam takes up the quiver,
        and horses are harnessed to the chariots of Aram,*ᵃ*
        and Kir uncovers the armor,
        ⁷ then shall your choice valleys fill with chariots,
21:7   and cavalry take up positions at your gateways.
        ⁸ And in the day Judea's defensive screen is removed,
        you will look to the forest home as protection.

29:1-3   ⁹ When you saw the city of David increasingly breached,
        you conserved water in the Lower Reservoir.
        ¹⁰ You took a census of the buildings in Jerusalem,
        tearing down buildings to fortify your wall.
        ¹¹ You built cisterns between the walls
7:3   for the water from the Old Reservoir,
        but you did not look to its Maker,
        nor have regard for the One who designed it long ago.

        ¹² In such a day my Lord, the Lord of Hosts,
20:1-2   calls for weeping and lamentation,
        for austerity and wearing sackcloth.

---

*ᵃ*6   Hebrew *ʾādām, man/men,* emended to *ʾărām.*

¹³ Instead, there is mirth and merrymaking,
the killing of cattle and slaughter of sheep,
21:5   eating meat and drinking wine:
Let us dine and drink, for tomorrow we die!

¹⁴ The Lord of Hosts revealed this to my ears: Such wickedness cannot be forgiven you till you die, says my Lord, the Lord of Hosts.

¹⁵ Thus said my Lord, the Lord of Hosts:
Go and see that steward, Shebna,
28:14   overseer of the palace.
¹⁶ *Say to him*, What are you up to?
Who do you think you are,
that you have hewn yourself a tomb here,
2:12–13   *like* those who hew their sepulchres up high,
carving out graves for themselves in the rock?

¹⁷ The Lord will hurl you away
as an athlete hurls a missile;
he will make you soar like a dart.
¹⁸ He will bind you tightly about
27:8   and send you spinning like a top
into an open country.
There shall you die,
and your *ing*lorious conveyance there
shall be a disgrace to your master's house.
22:25   ¹⁹ I will thrust you out of office;
you will be expelled from your post.

²⁰ In that day I will commission my servant Eliakim the son of Hilkiah: ²¹ I will clothe him with your robe and bind your girdle on him; I will appoint him your jurisdiction. And he will be a father to the inhabitants of Jerusalem and to the house of Judah. ²² I will invest him with the keys of the house of David: when he opens none shall shut, when he shuts none shall open. ²³ I will fasten him as a **nail** in a sure place, and he will be a throne of glory to the house of his father. ²⁴ Upon him shall be hung all the glory of his father's house: his descendants and posterity, including all the lesser vessels, from ordinary bowls to the most common containers.

²⁵ In that day, says the Lord of Hosts, the **nail** that was fastened in a sure place shall be removed. It shall be dislodged and fall, and the burden hanging on it cut off. The Lord has spoken it.

313

23 An oracle concerning Tyre:

Sound your sirens, O merchant ships!
For *Tyre*[a] is laid waste,

2:16   stripped of warehouse and wharf.
On their way from the land of Kittim
shall they be informed of it.

41:1   2 Be dumbfounded, you inhabitants of the isles,
who were amply replenished
by the traders of Sidon crossing the seas.
3 The grain of Shihor, the harvest of the Nile,
was her source of revenue upon the high seas

57:9   when she became the merchant of nations.

4 Be dismayed, O Sidon, because the **Sea**,
the mighty haven of the **Sea**, has declared,
I no longer labor and bear children!

47:9   I no longer rear young men or raise virgins!
5 When the news of Tyre reaches Egypt,
men will be in anguish at the report.

6 Move on to Tarshish lamenting,

41:5   you inhabitants of the isles.
7 Is this your festive *city* of ancient origin,
whose feet led her to settle far-off *lands*?
8 Who devised this stratagem against Tyre,
the imperial *city*,

24:2–4   whose traders were princes,
whose merchants the world's celebrities?
9 The Lord of Hosts devised it,
to make all glorying in excellence a profanity,

40:23   and the world's celebrities an utter execration.

10 Overflow your land like the Nile,
O Daughter of Tarshish: the harbor is no more.
11 The Lord will stretch out his **hand** over the **Sea**

14:26–27   and distress kingdoms;
he will give orders concerning the merchant *city*
that her ports of haven be destroyed.

---

[a]1   Hebrew *she*.

¹² He will say, You will frolic no more,

47:1–3
      O ravished virgin, Daughter of Sidon.
Get up and cross over to Kittim,
      though even there you will find no rest.

¹³ So too with the land of the Chaldeans,

43:14
      the people who founded *Tyre*^b for shipping.
Was it not the Assyrians who set up observatories,
      exposed its fortifications, and caused her downfall?
¹⁴ Sound your sirens, O merchant ships;
      your haven is desolate!

¹⁵ In that day Tyre shall be forgotten seventy years, the lifetime of a king. And at the end of seventy years, Tyre shall be as the harlot in the song:

¹⁶ Take a lyre and go about the town,
      O forgotten harlot.
Play skillfully; sing song after song,
      that you may be remembered.

¹⁷ For after seventy years, the Lord will revisit Tyre. And she will return to her trade and hire herself out to all the kingdoms of the world on the face of the earth. ¹⁸ Her merchandise and hire shall be consecrated to the Lord; it shall not be hoarded or stored up. Her commerce shall provide for those who dwell in the presence of the Lord, that they may eat their fill and be elegantly clothed.

24 Lo! The Lord will lay waste the earth and empty it;
he will disfigure its surface

6:11–12
      and scatter its inhabitants.
² And it shall be with priest as with people,
      with master as with servant,
      with mistress as with maid,

5:13–14
      with seller as with buyer,
      with lender as with borrower,
      with creditor as with debtor—
³ when the earth is sacked,

10:13
      it shall be utterly ravaged.
The Lord has given word concerning it.

---

^b13 Hebrew *her.*

⁴ The earth shall pine away,

34:1-2   the world miserably perish;
              the elite of the earth shall be made wretched.
⁵ The earth lies polluted under its inhabitants:
              they have transgressed the laws,
26:8-9   changed the ordinances,
              set at nought the ancient **covenant**.
⁶ The curse devours the earth,
              for those who dwell on it have incurred guilt;
              because of it the population of the earth
13:12   shall be diminished*
              and little of mankind remain.

⁷ The new wine withers on languishing vines,
              making all the lighthearted lament.
⁸ The rhythm of drums ceases,
5:11-12   the revelers' din stops;
              the pulsating of lyres comes to an end.
⁹ Men no longer drink wine amid song;
              liquor has turned bitter to drinkers.
32:12-14 ¹⁰ The towns of disorder are broken up;
              all houses are shuttered, that none may enter.
¹¹ Outside is *heard* the clamor for wine,
              though all joy has become gloom:
              the earth's vitality is gone.
¹² Havoc remains in the city;
3:26   the gates lie battered to ruin.

¹³ Then shall it happen in the earth among the nations
              as when an olive tree is beaten,
63:2-3   or as grapes are gleaned when the vintage is ended.
¹⁴ Then will these lift up their **voice** and shout for joy,
              and *those* from across the sea
              exult at the Lord's ingenuity.
42:10-12 ¹⁵ Because of it they will give glory to the Lord
              in the regions of sunrise,
              and in the isles of the sea
              to the name of the Lord, the God of Israel.

---

*6   So 1QIsaᵃ; MT *burned.*

30:29   **16** From a sector of the earth we hear singing:
Glorious are the righteous!
Whereas I thought, I am wasting away;
I am weakening:
66:5   woe is me; the traitors have been treacherous,
the turncoats have deceitfully betrayed!

17 Terrors and pitfalls and traps await you,
26:21   O inhabitants of the earth:
18 those who flee at the sound of terror
shall fall into a pit,
and those who get up from the pit
shall be caught in a trap.
For when the windows on high are opened,
54:10   the earth shall shake to its foundations.

19 The earth shall be crushed and rent;
the earth shall break up and cave in;
the earth shall convulse and lurch.
13:13   **20** The earth shall reel to and fro like a drunkard,
sway back and forth like a shanty;
its transgressions weigh it down,
and when it collapses it shall rise no more.

21 In that day will the Lord deal on high
with the hosts on high
26:13-14   and on earth with the rulers of the earth.
22 They shall be herded together
like prisoners to a dungeon
and shut in confinement many days, as punishment.
13:10   **23** The moon will blush and the sun be put to shame,
when the Lord of Hosts manifests his reign
in Mount Zion and in Jerusalem,
52:7-8   and *his* glory in the presence of his elders.

25 *In that day you will say,*
O Lord, thou art my God;
I will extol thee by praising thy name.
For with perfect **faithfulness**
thou hast performed wonders,
37:26   things planned of old.

² Thou hast made the city a heap of rubble,

26:5   fortified towns a ruin—

heathen mansions shall no more form cities,

nor ever be rebuilt!

³ For this will powerful peoples revere thee,

a community of tyrannous nations fear thee.

14:30, 32   ⁴ Thou wast a refuge for the poor,

a shelter for the needy in distress,

a covert from the downpour

4:5–6   and shade from the heat.

When the blasts of tyrants beat down

like torrents against a wall,

⁵ or like scorching heat in the desert,

thou didst quell the onslaughts of the heathen:

as burning heat by the shade of a cloud,

29:19–20   thou subduest the power of tyrants.

⁶ In this mountain will the Lord of Hosts prepare

a sumptuous feast for all peoples,

a feast of leavened cakes, succulent and delectable,

of matured wines well refined.

44:22   ⁷ In this mountain he will destroy

the veil that veils all peoples,

the shroud that shrouds all nations,

9:2   ⁸ by abolishing **Death** forever.

My Lord the Lord will wipe away

the tears from all faces;

54:8–9   he will remove the reproach of his people

from throughout the earth.

The Lord has spoken it.

12:1–2   ⁹ In that day you*ᵃ* will say, This is our God,

whom we expected would save us.

This is the Lord for whom we have waited;

33:2, 22   let us joyfully celebrate his **salvation**!

¹⁰ For in this mountain rests the **hand** of the Lord,

and under him Moab shall be trampled down

as straw is trampled in a dung pit.

ᵃ) So 1QIsaᵃ; MT *he*.

¹¹ For when he stretches his hands
into the midst of it,
as a swimmer spreads his hands to swim,

16:6–7   he will pull down his pride in the attempt.
¹² Your highly walled fortifications
he will lay low by razing them to the ground,

15:1   even with the dust.

26

In that day shall this song be sung in the land of Judah:

Our city is strong; **salvation** he has set up

60:18   as walls and barricades!
² Open the gates to let in the nation
righteous because it keeps faith.
³ Those whose minds are steadfast, *O Lord*,

31:5   thou preservest in perfect peace,
for in thee they are secure.

⁴ Ever trust in the Lord,

44:8   for the Lord Yah is an everlasting Rock.
⁵ He has put down the elite inhabitants
of the exalted city
by casting it to the ground,

47:1   laying it even with the dust.
⁶ It is trodden underfoot by the feet of the poor,
by the footsteps of those impoverished.

2:3   ⁷ The path of the righteous is straight;
thou pavest an undeviating course for the upright.
⁸ In the very passage of thine ordinances
we anticipate thee, O Lord;

52:6   the soul's desire is to contemplate thy name.
⁹ My soul yearns for thee in the night;
at daybreak my spirit within me seeks after thee.
For when thine ordinances are on the earth,
the inhabitants of the world learn **righteousness**.

¹⁰ Though **favor** be shown the wicked,

48:1, 18   they will not learn **righteousness**;
in a land of uprightness they remain perverse
and see not the glory of the Lord.

¹¹ O Lord, thy **hand** is lifted up,

9:17–18   but they perceive it not.

Let them perceive with dismay

thy **zeal** for thy people

33:14   when the **fire** prepared for thine enemies

consumes them.

57:1–2   ¹² O Lord, thou bringest about our peace;

even all that we have accomplished

thou hast done for us.

¹³ O Lord, our God, lords other than thou

have ruled over us,

34:12   but thee alone we recall by name.

¹⁴ They are dead, to live no more,

spirits who will not rise up;

thou appointest them to destruction,

wiping out all recollection of them.

9:3   ¹⁵ Thou hast enlarged the nation, O Lord,

and by enlarging it gained glory for thyself;

thou hast withdrawn all borders in the earth.

¹⁶ O Lord, in their distress they remembered thee;

they poured out silent prayers

64:5–7   when thy chastisements were upon them.

¹⁷ As a woman about to give birth

cries out from her pangs during labor,

64:1–2   so were we at thy presence, O Lord.

¹⁸ We were with child; we have been in labor,

but have brought forth only wind.

We have not wrought **salvation** in the earth,

37:3   that the inhabitants of the world might not fall.[a]

¹⁹ Yet shall thy dead live when their bodies[b] arise.

Thou wilt say to them,

Awake, and sing for joy,

52:1–2   you who abide in the dust:

your dew is the dew of sunrise!

For the earth shall cast up its dead.

---

[a]18 Or, *abort.*

[b]19 Hebrew *my body.* MT evidences incomplete third person pronoun suffix; compare LXX.

²⁰ Come, O my people, enter your chambers
and shut the doors behind you;
hide yourselves a little while
13:9   until the **wrath** is past.
²¹ For now will the Lord come out of his dwelling place
to punish the inhabitants of the earth
59:17–19   for their iniquities;
the earth will uncover the blood shed upon it
and no more conceal its slain.

27
In that day will the Lord,
with his great and powerful **sword**,
punish severely*a* Leviathan,
the evasive maritime serpent,
Leviathan, that devious sea monster,
66:16   when he slays the dragons of the **Sea**.

² In that day, sing *of the earth*ᵇ
as of a delightful vineyard
5:1   ³ of which I, the Lord, am keeper.
I water it constantly, watch over it night and day,
lest anything be amiss.
12:1   ⁴ I have no more **anger** *toward her.*
Should briars and thorns come up,
I will ruthlessly attack them
and altogether set them ablaze.
25:4   ⁵ But should they take hold of me for a refuge
and make peace with me,
they shall be reconciled to me.
⁶ For *in days* to come, when Jacob takes root
and Israel bursts into blossom,
4:2   the face of the earth shall fill with fruit.

⁷ Was he smitten as were his smiters?
Or was he slain as were they who slew him?
⁸ Thou hast dealt with them
by utterly banishing them, *O Lord.*
30:30   By his fierce blasts they were flung away
in the day of the burning east wind.

---

*a*1   Term modifies *sword,* an incongruity in translation.
*b*2   Hebrew *her;* compare 26:21; 27:6.

⁹ But by this shall Jacob's iniquity be expiated,

40:2   as a result of this his sins removed:

when he makes like crushed chalkstone

all altar stones,

2:8   leaving no idols of prosperity

and shining images standing.

¹⁰ Because *of them* the fortified cities lie forlorn,

17:9   deserted habitations, forsaken like a wilderness;

steers forage and recline there,

stripping bare the young branches *of trees.*

¹¹ A harvest of twigs dries, broken off by women

who come to light their fires with them.

1:3   They are not a discerning people.

Therefore their Maker shows them no mercy;

he who formed them favors them not.

¹² In that day the Lord will thresh out *his harvest* from the **torrent** of the **River** to the streams of Egypt. But you shall be gleaned one by one, O children of Israel.

¹³ In that day a loud **trumpet** shall sound, and they who were lost in the land of Assyria and they who were outcasts in the land of Egypt shall come and bow down to the Lord in the holy mountain at Jerusalem.

28

Woe to the garlands of glory

of the drunkards of Ephraim!

Their crowning splendor has become as fading wreaths

29:9   on the heads of ᵃthe opulentᵃ overcome with wine.

² My Lord has in store one mighty and strong:

as a ravaging hailstorm sweeping down,

8:7–8   or like an inundating deluge of mighty waters,

he will hurl them to the ground by his **hand**.

³ The proud garlands of the drunkards of Ephraim

63:6   shall be trodden underfoot.

⁴ And the fading wreaths, the crowns of glory

on the heads of ᵃthe opulent,ᵃ

shall be like the first-ripe fruit

18:5   before summer *harvest*:

ᵃ1, ᵃ4 Hebrew *gĕʾê šĕmānîm;* so 1QIsaᵃ. MT *gêʾ šĕmānîm, fat gully/ravine.*

he who sees it devours it
the moment he has hold of it.

⁵ In that day shall the Lord of Hosts
be as a crown of beauty and wreath of glory
10:21–22   to the remnant of his people:
⁶ a spirit of justice to him who sits in judgment,
a source of strength
to those who repulse the attack at the gates.

56:10–12   ⁷ These too have indulged in wine
and are giddy with strong drink:
priests and prophets have gone astray through liquor.
They are intoxicated with wine
19:14   and stagger because of strong drink;
they err as seers, they blunder in their decisions.
⁸ For all tables are filled with vomit;
no spot is without excrement.

⁹ Whom shall he give instruction?
53:1   Whom shall he enlighten with revelation?
Weanlings weaned from milk,
those just taken from the breast?
¹⁰ For it is but precept upon precept,
29:13   precept upon precept,
measure by measure, measure by measure;
a trifle here, a trifle there.

33:19   ¹¹ Therefore, by incomprehensible speech
and a strange **tongue**
must he speak to these people,
50:4   ¹² to whom he said, This is rest; let the weary rest!
This is a respite! But they would not listen.
¹³ So to them the word of the Lord remained:
Precept upon precept, precept upon precept,
measure by measure, measure by measure;
a trifle here, a trifle there, that,
8:14–15   persisting, they might lapse into stumbling
and break themselves,
become ensnared and be taken captive.

1:10   ¹⁴ Therefore hear the word of the Lord, you scoffers
who preside over these people in Jerusalem.

323

¹⁵ You have supposed, by taking refuge in deception
and hiding behind falsehoods,
to have covenanted with **Death**,
or reached an understanding with Sheol, that,
should a flooding **scourge** sweep through *the earth*,
it shall not reach you.

¹⁶ Therefore, thus says my Lord the Lord:
I lay in Zion a **stone**, a keystone,
a precious cornerstone, a sure foundation.
They who believe it will not do rashly.

¹⁷ I will make justice the measure,
righteousness the weight;
a hail shall sweep away your false refuge
and waters flood the hiding place.
¹⁸ Your covenant with **Death** shall prove void,^{*b*}
your understanding with Sheol have no effect:
when the flooding **scourge** sweeps through,
you shall be overrun by it.
¹⁹ As often as it sweeps through,
you shall be seized by it:
morning after morning it shall sweep through,
by day and by night *it shall seize you*;
it shall cause terror merely to hear word of it.
²⁰ *Then shall come to pass the proverb*:
The couch is too short to stretch out on,
the covering too narrow to wrap oneself in.

²¹ For the Lord will rise up
as he did on Mount Perazim,
and be stirred to anger, as in the Valley of Gibeon—
to perform his act, his unwonted act,
and do his work, his bizarre work.
²² Now therefore scoff not,
lest your bonds grow severe,
for I have heard utter destruction decreed
by my Lord, the Lord of Hosts,
upon the whole earth.

Margin references:
30:28
28:2
1:27
32:19*
21:1
8:9
33:10–13
10:12
13:5

---

*b*18 Hebrew *kŭppar, expiated,* emended to *hŭpar.*

324

²³ Give heed, and hear my **voice**!
50:10   Be attentive, and listen to what I say!
²⁴ Will the plowman be forever plowing to sow seed,
        disking and harrowing the same ground?
²⁵ When he has smoothed its surface,
        does he not sprinkle fennel and scatter cumin?
Does he not demarcate wheat from barley
        and *plant* buckwheat in its own plot?
28:9   ²⁶ His God instructs him,
        directing him in the proper procedure.

²⁷ Fennel is not threshed with a sharp-toothed sledge,
        nor is a cartwheel rolled over cumin:
fennel is beaten out with a stick
        and cumin with a rod.
²⁸ Domestic grain is ground;
59:8   one does not go on endlessly threshing it.
It cannot be ground
        by driving horse and threshing cart *over it*.
²⁹ These things originate with the Lord of Hosts,
40:13–14   whose counsel is wonderful,
        whose inspiration is surpassing.

29   Woe to Ariel—
        Ariel, the city where David lodged!
Though you add year to year,
        and the feastdays recur in succession,
² yet will I distress Ariel:
64:10–12   there shall be mourning and sorrow
        when she becomes as my ᵃaltar hearth.ᵃ
³ I will encamp against you round about,
        and beleaguer you with assault posts,
        and erect siege installations against you.
26:5   ⁴ And when you have been laid low,
        you will speak from the ground,
        your words uttering out of the dust:
your **voice** from the ground
        shall be like that of a medium;
29:18   your sayings shall whisper out of the dust.

ᵃ2   Or, *Ariel,* a wordplay.

⁵ Suddenly, in an instant,
      your crowds of evildoers*b* shall become as fine dust,
54:15   your violent mobs like flying chaff.
⁶ She shall be chastened by the Lord of Hosts
      with thunderous quakings,
resounding booms, tempestuous blasts
66:15   and conflagrations of devouring **flame**.

⁷ And the nations amassed to fight against Ariel,
      all who congregate at her stronghold
to distress her,
17:12–14   shall be as a dream seen in the night:
⁸ like a hungry man who dreams he eats,
      but awakens famished,
or like a thirsty man who dreams he drinks,
      but wakes up faint and craving.
So shall be all the nations
31:4   that amass to fight against Mount Zion.

⁹ Procrastinate, and become bewildered;
      preoccupy yourselves, until you cry for help.
Be drunk, but not with wine;
51:21   stagger, but not from strong drink.
¹⁰ The Lord has poured out on you
      a spirit of deep sleep:
he has shut your eyes, the prophets;
28:1   he has covered your heads, the seers.

¹¹ For you the sum of vision has become as the words of a sealed book that they give to one who is learned, saying, Please read this, and he answers, I cannot; it is sealed. ¹² Or if they give it to one who is unlearned, saying, Please read this, he answers, I am unlearned.

¹³ But my Lord says, Because these people
      approach me with the mouth
and pay me homage with their lips,
      while their heart remains far from me—
58:1–2   their piety toward me consisting of
      commandments of men learned by rote—

---

*b*5   So 1QIsaᵃ; LXX. MT *of strangers*.

¹⁴ therefore it is that I shall again astound these people
25:1   with wonder upon wonder,
      rendering void the knowledge of their sages,
      the intelligence of their wise men insignificant.

¹⁵ Woe to those who contrive
32:7   to hide their schemes from the Lord!
They work in the dark, thinking,
      Who will see us? Who will know?
¹⁶ What a contradiction you are!
45:9   Shall the potter be regarded as the clay?
Shall what is made say of its maker,
      He did not make me,
or a work of its designer, He doesn't understand?
¹⁷ In a very little while, shall not Lebanon
32:15   again become a fruitful land,
and lands now fruitful be considered backwoods?

¹⁸ In that day shall the deaf hear
      the words of the book
42:7   and the eyes of the blind see
      out of gross **darkness**.
¹⁹ The lowly shall obtain an increase of joy in the Lord,
61:1–3   and the poorest of men rejoice
      in the Holy One of Israel.

²⁰ For tyrants shall come to nought and scorners cease;
      all who persist in wickedness shall be cut off—
²¹ those who at a word adjudge a man to be guilty,
      who ensnare the defender at court,
59:15   who for nothing turn away him who is in the right.

²² Therefore thus says the Lord,
      who redeemed Abraham, to the house of Jacob:
No longer shall Jacob be dismayed;
      his face shall pale no more.
²³ For when he sees among him his children,
19:25   the work of my **hands**, hallowing my name,
      devoted to the Holy One of Jacob,
      reverencing the God of Israel,
²⁴ then will the erring in spirit gain understanding
28:9   and they who murmured accept instruction.

30 Woe to you, rebellious sons, says the Lord,
for drawing up plans, but not by me,
for making alliances without my approval,
only adding sin to sin!

31:1   ² They are bent on going down to Egypt—
but have not inquired at my **mouth**—
on seeking protection in Pharaoh's forces,

36:6   on taking shelter in Egypt's shadow.

³ But Pharaoh's protection shall turn to your shame,
shelter in Egypt's shadow to embarrassment.

19:13   ⁴ For all their officials at Zoan,
and their envoys' travels to Hanes,
⁵ they shall be utterly disgusted
with a people who will avail them nothing;
they shall be of no help or benefit,

20:3–4   but a humiliation and disgrace.

⁶ An oracle concerning the Beasts of Negeb:

Through a land of hardship and vicissitude,
of lions and the ᵃroaringᵃ king of beasts,
of vipers and the fiery flying serpent,

15:7   they carry their wealth
on the backs of young asses,
their riches on the humps of camels,
to a people who cannot profit them.
⁷ Egypt's help shall be futile and vain;

20:5   therefore I refer to her as an idle boast.

⁸ Go now, write on tablets concerning them;
record it in a book for the last day,

29:11, 18   as a testimony forever.
⁹ They are a rebellious people, sons who break faith,
children unwilling to obey the law of the Lord,
¹⁰ who say to the seers, See not!
and to those with visions,

29:10   Predict not what is right for us:
flatter us; foresee a farce!

ᵃ6   Hebrew *mēhem, of them,* emended to *nōhēm.*

¹¹ Get out of the way; move aside, off the path!

3:8

    Cease confronting us with the Holy One of Israel!

¹² Therefore, thus says the Holy One of Israel:

28:14

    Because you have rejected this word,

and rely on manipulation and double dealing,

and on them are dependent,

¹³ this iniquity will be to you as a perilous breach

exposed in a high wall

2:15

    which suddenly and unexpectedly collapses.

¹⁴ It shall shatter with a crash

like an earthenware vessel ruthlessly smashed,

among whose fragments shall not be found a shard

with which to scoop lit embers from a fireplace,

22:9–11

    or dip water from a tank.

¹⁵ For thus says my Lord the Lord,

the Holy One of Israel:

By a calm response triumph;

7:4

    with quiet confidence gain the victory.

But you would have none of it.

¹⁶ For you thought, Not so; we will flee on horses!

Therefore shall you flee indeed.

We will ride on swift mounts!

5:26

    Therefore shall your pursuers be swifter.

¹⁷ You will flee by the thousand at the threat of one,

by thousands at the threat of five,

till you are left as a **flagstaff** on a mountaintop,

18:3

    an **ensign** on a hill.

¹⁸ Then will the Lord delay *his coming*,

that he may favor you;

out of mercy toward you he will remain aloof.

For the Lord is the God of justice;

33:2

    blessed are all who wait for him.

¹⁹ O people of Zion, O inhabitants of Jerusalem,

you shall have no cause to weep.

He will graciously respond at the cry of your **voice**;

65:24

    he will answer you as soon as he hears it.

²⁰ Though my Lord give you the bread of adversity
and the water of affliction,
33:17   yet shall your Teacher remain hidden no longer,
but your eyes shall see the Master.
²¹ Your ears shall hear words from behind you
32:3   saying, This is the way; walk in it!
should you turn left or right.
²² You will discard as unclean
your graven idols plated with silver,
your cast idols gilded in gold;
31:7   you will eject them
as a menstruous woman *her impurity*
and say, Away with you!

²³ Then will he water with rain
55:10   the seed you sow in the ground,
that the land's increase of food
may be rich and abundant.
In that day your cattle shall graze
32:20   in ample pasture lands,
²⁴ and the oxen and asses that till the soil
eat grain silage winnowed with shovel and fork.

²⁵ On all mountain heights and prominent hills
shall appear streams of running water,
34:2–6   on the day of the great slaughter,
when the towers fall.
²⁶ The light of the moon
shall be as the light of the sun,
60:19–20   and the light of the sun increase sevenfold;
as the light of seven days shall it be,
in the day the Lord binds up
the fracture of his people
58:8   and heals their open wound.

²⁷ Behold, the Lord Omnipotent^b coming from afar!
His **wrath** is kindled, heavy is his **grievance**;
his **lips** flow with **indignation**,
66:15   his **tongue** is like a devouring **fire**.

---

*b*27   Literally, *the name of the Lord.*

330

28 His **breath** is like a raging **torrent**

8:8   that severs at the neck.

He comes to sift the nations

in the **sieve** of **falsehood**;

36:16–18   with an erring **bridle** on their jaws

he will try the peoples.

29 But for you there shall be singing,

51:11   as on the night when a festival commences,

and rejoicing of heart, as when men march

with flutes [and drums and lyres]*^c*

27:13   on their way to the mountain of the Lord,

to the Rock of Israel.

30 The Lord will cause his **voice** to resound,

51:9   and make visible his **arm** descending in furious **rage**,

with flashes of devouring **fire**,

explosive discharges and pounding hail.

31 At the **voice** of the Lord

31:9   the Assyrians will be terror-stricken,

they who used to strike with the **rod**.

32 At every sweep of the **staff** of authority,

when the Lord lowers it upon them,

14:25   they will be fought in mortal combat.

33 For Tophet has been prepared of old,

a hearth indeed, made ready for rulers;

66:24   broad and deep is its fire pit and ample its pyre;

the Lord's **breath** burns within it

like a **river** of lava.

31

Woe to those who go down to Egypt for help,

relying on horses,

putting their trust in immense numbers

43:17   of chariots and vast forces of horsemen,

but who do not look to the Holy One of Israel,

nor inquire of the Lord!

---

*c*29 Terms brought up from verse 32, where they follow *they will be fought*, a probable textual dislocation.

² Yet he too is shrewd
47:11   and will bring disaster *upon them*,
and not retract his words.
He will rise up against the brood of miscreants
30:1   and allies of evildoers.
³ The Egyptians are human, not divine;
their horses are flesh, not spirit:
14:26   when the Lord stretches out his **hand**,
those who help them will stumble
and those helped will fall;
20:6   both shall come to an end together.

⁴ For thus said the Lord to me:
As a lion or a young lion growls over the prey
when the shepherds muster in full force against him,
13:2, 4   and is not dismayed at the sound of their **voice**
nor daunted by their numbers,
so shall the Lord of Hosts be when he descends
64:1-2   to wage war upon Mount Zion and upon its heights.
⁵ As birds hover over [the nest],ᵃ
so will the Lord of Hosts guard Jerusalem;
37:35   by protecting it he will deliver it,
by passing over it, preserve it.

⁶ Return to him from whom you have contrived to go far astray,
O children of Israel. ⁷ For in that day every one of you will despise
your idolatrous silver and gold by which your hands have incurred
guilt.

⁸ And Assyria shall fall by a **sword** not of man;
49:2   a **sword** not of mortals shall devour them:
before that **sword** they shall waste away
and their young men melt;
⁹ their captainᵇ shall expire in terror
11:10   and their officers shrink from the **ensign**,
says the Lord, whose **fire** is in Zion,
whose furnace is in Jerusalem.

ᵃ5   Text emended to include Hebrew direct object *qēn* before the similar sounding adverb
kēn, so.
ᵇ9   Literally, *rock,* a possible military term.

32

A king shall reign in **righteousness**
and rulers rule with justice.

² And a man shall become as a shelter

38:2-6   from the wind or refuge from the storm,
like brooks of water in a desert place,
or the shade of a large rock in arid country.

30:20-21   ³ The eyes of those who see shall not be shut,
and the ears of those who hear shall listen.
⁴ The minds of the rash shall learn understanding,

35:5-6   and the tongues of the stammerers master eloquence.
⁵ The godless shall no longer be regarded as noble
nor rogues considered respectable.

⁶ For the godless utter blasphemy;
their heart ponders impiety:

29:13   how to practice hypocrisy and preach
perverse things concerning the Lord,
leaving the hungry soul empty,
depriving the thirsty *soul* of drink.

59:3-4   ⁷ And rogues scheme by malevolent means
and insidious devices to ruin the poor,
and with false slogans and accusations
to denounce the needy.
⁸ But the noble are of noble intent,

56:2   and stand up for what is virtuous.

⁹ Up, and listen to my **voice**, O complacent women;

3:16   you careless daughters, hear my words!
¹⁰ In little more than a year
you shall be in anguish, O carefree ones,
for when the harvest is over,

17:10-11   the produce shall fail to arrive.

¹¹ Be alarmed, you complacent women;
be perturbed, O careless daughters!
Strip yourselves bare;

22:12   put sackcloth around your waists.
¹² Beat your breasts for the choice fields
and flourishing vines.

¹³ For my people's land

5:6   shall be overgrown with briars and thorns.
     Mourn for all the amusement houses
         in the city of entertainment,

13:22   ¹⁴ for the palaces shall lie abandoned,
     the clamorous towns deserted.
     High rises and panoramic resorts
         shall become haunts for ever after,

34:13–14   the playground of wild animals,
     a browsing place for flocks.

^{19ᵃ} For by a hail shall forests be felled,

13:19   cities utterly leveled.
     ¹⁵ Then^b shall a Spirit from on high
         be poured out on us;

44:3   the desert shall become productive land
     and lands now productive
         be reckoned as brushwood.

¹⁶ So shall justice inhabit the desert,
     and **righteousness** abide in the farmland.

32:1   ¹⁷ And the effect of justice shall be peace,
     and the result of **righteousness**
         an assured calm forever.
¹⁸ My people shall dwell in peaceful settlements,

54:14   in safe neighborhoods, in comfortable dwellings.
²⁰ Blessed are you, who shall then sow by all waters,
     letting oxen and asses range free.

33

Woe to you, despoiler,
     who yourself was not despoiled;
O treacherous one,

21:2   with whom none have been treacherous:
when you have done with devastating,
     you shall be devastated;
when you are through betraying,

14:4   they shall betray you!

---

^a19   Verse appears out of sequence in text.
^b15   Hebrew ʿad, *until,* emended to ʾaz.

² O Lord, be favorable toward us;

25:9
    we have waited for thee.

Be our* strength of* arm from morning to morning,
    our **salvation in** troubled times.

³ The peoples fled from thy thunderous **voice**;

28:21
    at thine uprising the nations scattered.

⁴ Their spoil was harvested
    in the manner of caterpillars;
    like insatiable locusts they rushed upon it.

40:22
⁵ But the Lord is supreme, for he dwells on high;
    with justice and **righteousness** he will replenish Zion.

⁶ Your **faithfulness** in time *of trial*
    shall prove to be a strength,

11:2
    your wisdom and knowledge your **salvation**;
    your fear of the Lord shall be your riches.

⁷ See, their stalwarts sob in public;

48:18, 22
    the champions of peace weep bitterly.

⁸ The highways are desolate, travel is at an end.
    The treaties have been violated,
    their signatories** held in contempt;
    man is disregarded.

1:7
⁹ The Land lies withered and forlorn,
    Lebanon wilts shamefully;
    Sharon has been turned into a dry waste,
    Bashan and Carmel are denuded.

3:13
¹⁰ Now will I arise, says the Lord;
    I will now become prominent,
    now gain preeminence.

5:24
¹¹ You who conceived chaff and brought forth stubble,
    the **fire** of your own **breath** devours you!

¹² Whole nations have been burned like lime,

9:18-19
    mown down like thorns and set ablaze.

¹³ Take heed what I have done, you who are far off;
    you who are near, be apprised of my might!

**2   Hebrew *their*.
**8   So 1QIsaª; MT *cities*.

¹⁴ The sinners in Zion are struck with fear;
the godless are in the grip of trembling:

29:6 Who among us can live through the devouring **fire**?
Who among us can abide eternal burning?

¹⁵ They who conduct themselves righteously
and are honest in word,

32:8 who disdain extortion
and stay their hand from taking bribes,
who stop their ears at the mention of murder,
who shut their eyes at the sight of wickedness.

58:14 ¹⁶ They shall dwell on high;
the impregnable cliffs are their fortress.
Bread is provided them, their water is sure.

24:23 ¹⁷ Your eyes shall behold the King in his glory
and view the expanse of the earth.

¹⁸ You shall recount in your mind the terror:
Where are those who conducted the census?

14:24–25 Where are those who levied the tax?
Where are the ones who appraised the towers?

¹⁹ The insolent people are not to be seen,
a nation of incomprehensible speech,

28:11 whose babbling **tongue** was unintelligible.

²⁰ Behold Zion, the city of our solemn assemblies;
let your eyes rest upon Jerusalem,

54:13–14 the abode of peace—an immovable tent,
whose stakes shall never be uprooted,
nor any of its cords severed.

²⁴ᶜ None who reside there shall say, I am ill;
the people who inhabit it

43:25 shall be forgiven their iniquity.

²¹ May the Lord ᵈcause us to dwellᵈ there,
a country of rivers and broad streams,

27:1 where no warships sail
or majestic fleets pass by.

ᶜ24 Verse appears out of sequence in text.

ᵈ21 Hebrew ʾaddîr, *mighty one,* emended to yādîr.

23ᵉ Their riggings hang loose;
they hold not the **mast** in place
nor spread out the sail.

9:3 Now shall spoil in abundance be divided,
and even the lame take part in the plunder.

22 For the Lord is our Judge,
and the Lord our Lawgiver.

35:4 The Lord is our King; he himself will save us.

34 Come near, you nations, and hear!
Pay attention, you peoples!
Let the earth give heed, and all who are upon it,
the world, and all who spring from it.

63:6 2 The Lord's **rage** is upon all nations,
his **fury** upon all their hosts;
he has doomed them,

30:25 consigned them to the slaughter.

3 Their slain shall be flung out

5:25 and their corpses emit a stench;
ᵃtheir blood shall dissolve on the mountains,
4 their fat decompose [on the hills]ᵃ—

13:13 when the heavens are rolled up as a scroll,
and their starry hosts shed themselves with one accord,
like withered leaves from a vine,
or shrivelled fruit from a fig tree.

66:16 5 When my **sword** drinks its fill in the heavens,
it shall come down on Edom in judgment,
on the people I have sentenced to damnation.

63:3 6 The Lord has a **sword** that shall engorge with blood
and glut itself with fat—
the blood of lambs and he-goats,
the kidney fat of rams.

ᵉ23   Verse appears out of sequence in text.

ᵃ3, ᵃ4   A problematic couplet, whose literal translation of MT reads *the mountains shall dissolve with their blood, and all the host of heaven decompose*. Hebrew *kol ṣebāʾ haššamayîm*, emended to *gibʿôt mēḥelbām* and the sense of the passage rendered congruous with its context; compare the parallelism *blood/fat*, verses 6–7, and the reading *hills* for *host of heaven*, LXX.

For the Lord will hold a slaughter in Bozrah,
10:7   an immense massacre in the land of Edom;
     ⁷ among them shall fall bison, bulls, and steers.
     Their land shall be saturated with blood,
     their soil enriched with fat.

63:4   ⁸ For it is the Lord's day of **vengeance**,
     the year of **retribution** on behalf of Zion.

     ⁹ *Edom's*ᵇ streams shall turn into lava
     and her earth into brimstone;
13:19-20   her land shall become as burning pitch.
     ¹⁰ Night and day it shall not be quenched;
     its smoke shall ascend forever.
     It shall remain a wasteland
     from generation to generation;
     through endless ages none shall traverse it.
     ¹¹ But hawks and falcons shall possess it,
14:23   and owls and ravens inhabit it.
     It shall be surveyed with muddled measure
     and chaotic weight.

     ¹² Shall they summon its nobles when it is no kingdom,
26:13-14   when all its lords no longer exist?
     ¹³ For thorns shall overgrow its palaces,
     thistles and briars its strongholds;
32:14   it shall become the haunt of howling creatures,
     a reserveᶜ for birds of prey.
     ¹⁴ Prairie wolves shall greet jackals,
13:21-22   and wild goats call to one another.
     There too shall the night owl find repose
     and discover for herself a resting place.
     ¹⁵ There shall the hawk owl nest and lay eggs,
     hatch them and brood over her young.
     There too shall kites come together,
     each one accompanying her mate.

29:18   ¹⁶ Search, and read it in the book of the Lord:
     None is unaccounted for, not one lacks her mate.

ᵇ9   Hebrew *Her*.
ᶜ13   Hebrew *ḥāṣîr, grass,* emended to *ḥāṣēr*.

55:11   By his **mouth** he decreed it,
             by his Spirit he brings them together.
         ¹⁷ It is he who allots them an inheritance,
49:8   his **hand** that divides it by measure.
         They shall possess it forever,
             inhabit it from generation to generation.

35   Wilderness and arid land shall be jubilant;
             the desert shall rejoice
         when it blossoms like the crocus.
         ² Joyously it shall break out in flower,
             singing with delight;
60:13   it shall be endowed with the glory of Lebanon,
             the splendor of Carmel and Sharon.
         The glory of the Lord and the splendor of our God
4:5   they shall see *there*.

         ³ Strengthen the hands grown feeble,
             steady the failing knees.
         ⁴ Say to those with fearful hearts,
             Take courage, be unafraid!
59:18–20 See, your God is coming to avenge and to reward;
             God himself will come and deliver you.

42:6–7   ⁵ Then shall the eyes of the blind be opened
             and the ears of the deaf unstopped.
         ⁶ Then shall the lame leap like deer,
             and the **tongue** of the dumb shout for joy.
         Water shall break forth in the wilderness
41:17–18   and streams *flow* in the desert.
         ⁷ The land of mirages shall become one of lakes,
             the thirsty place springs of water;
         in the haunt of howling creatures
             [shall marshes break out],*ᵃ*
         in the reserves*ᵇ* shall come rushes and reeds.
43:19–20 ⁸ There shall be highways and roads
             which shall be called the Way of Holiness,
         *ᶜ*for they shall be for such*ᶜ* as are holy.

---

*ᵃ*7   Hebrew *ribṣâh, her resting place,* emended to *tiprōṣ biṣṣâ.*
*ᵇ*7   Hebrew *ḥaṣîr, grass,* emended to *ḥāṣēr;* compare 34:13.
*ᶜ*8   Phrase transposed; in text follows *traverse them.*

The unclean shall not traverse them;
on them shall no reprobates wander.
15:9 ⁹ No lions *shall be encountered there,*
nor shall wild beasts intrude.
But the redeemed shall walk them,
1:27 ¹⁰ the ransomed of the Lord shall return;
they shall come singing to Zion,
their heads crowned with everlasting joy.
30:29 They shall have won joy and gladness
when sorrow and sighing flee away.

36 In the fourteenth year of King Hezekiah *'s reign*, Sennacherib king of Assyria marched against all the fortified cities of Judea and seized them. ² And the king of Assyria sent Rabshakeh with a large army from Lachish to King Hezekiah at Jerusalem. And he took up a position by the aqueduct of the Upper Reservoir, on the road to the Laundry Plaza. ³ And Eliakim the son of Hilkiah, overseer of the palace, Shebna the secretary, and Joah the son of Asaph, the record keeper, went out to him.

⁴ And Rabshakeh said to them, Please tell Hezekiah, Thus says the great king, the king of Assyria: On what grounds do you behave with such confidence? ⁵ Do you suppose that in war mere words are *sufficient* tactics or *show of* strength? In whom have you put your trust, that you have rebelled against me? ⁶ It is clear you depend on the support of Egypt, that splintered reed which enters and pierces the palm of any man who leans on it. Such is Pharaoh king of Egypt to all who rely on him! ⁷ But if you tell me, We rely on the Lord our God, is he not the one whose shrines and altars Hezekiah abolished, telling Judea and Jerusalem to worship *only* at this altar? ⁸ Come now, wager with my lord the king of Assyria: I will give you two thousand horses, if you are able to put riders on them. ⁹ How then shall you repulse even one of the least of my lord's servants, depending as you do on Egypt for chariots and horsemen? ¹⁰ Moreover, could I have marched against this land and destroyed it without the Lord? For the Lord told me to come against this land and destroy it.

---

*d*9   Text emended to replace Hebrew *lōʾ yihyeh šām, shall not be there,* with *lōʾ yimmāṣēʾ šām*, which occurs as a duplication (fem.) following *intrude*.

¹¹ Then Eliakim, Shebna and Joah said to Rabshakeh, please speak to your servants in Aramaic, which we understand. Do not speak to us in Judean in the ears of the people who are on the wall.

¹² But Rabshakeh replied, Did my lord send me to say these things to you and to your lord and not to the men sitting on the wall, who with you are to eat their own dung and drink their own urine?

¹³ Then Rabshakeh stood and called out in a loud voice in Judean, Hear the words of the great king, the king of Assyria! ¹⁴ Thus says the king: Do not let Hezekiah delude you! He cannot deliver you. ¹⁵ Do not let Hezekiah make you trust in the Lord by saying, The Lord will surely save us; this city shall not be given into the **hand** of the king of Assyria.

¹⁶ Do not listen to Hezekiah! Thus says the king of Assyria: Make peace with me by coming out to me. Then every one of you will eat from his own vine and his own fig tree and drink water from his own cistern, ¹⁷ until I come back and take you to a land like your own, a land of grain and wine, a land of grain *fields* and vineyards.

¹⁸ *Beware*, lest Hezekiah mislead you by saying, The Lord will save us. Were any gods of the nations able to save their lands out of the **hand** of the king of Assyria? ¹⁹ Where are the gods of Hamath and Arpad? Where are the gods of Sepharvaim? Did they deliver Samaria out of my **hand**? ²⁰ Who of all the gods of those countries saved his land from my **hand**, that the Lord should save Jerusalem from my **hand**?

²¹ But they remained silent, replying nothing, for the king had commanded them not to answer him.

²² Then Eliakim the son of Hilkiah, overseer of the palace, Shebna the secretary, and Joah the son of Asaph, the record keeper, went to Hezekiah with their clothes rent and reported to him the things Rabshakeh had said.

37 When King Hezekiah heard it, he rent his clothes and put on sackcloth and entered the house of the Lord. ² And he sent Eliakim the overseer of the palace, Shebna the secretary, and the elders of the priests in sackcloth to the prophet Isaiah the son of Amoz.

⁵ᵃ And when King Hezekiah's servants came to Isaiah, ³ they said to him, Thus says Hezekiah: This is a woeful day, a day of reproof

---

ᵃ5   Verse appears out of sequence in text.

and disgrace. Children have reached the point of birth, but there is no strength to deliver them. ⁴ It may be that the Lord your God has heard the words of Rabshakeh, whom his lord the king of Assyria has sent to scorn the living God, and will rebuke him for the things the Lord your God has heard, were you to offer up prayer on behalf of the remnant that is left.

⁶ And Isaiah said to them, Tell your lord, Thus says the Lord: Be not afraid because of the words with which you have heard the king of Assyria's subordinates ridicule me. ⁷ See, I will give him a notion to return home upon hearing a rumor, and will cause him to fall by a **sword** in his own land.

⁸ And when Rabshakeh heard that the king of Assyria had left Lachish, he withdrew and found him fighting against Libnah.

⁹ Now *Sennacherib*ᵇ received a report that Tirhakah king of Cush had set out to fight against him. And when he heard it, he sent messengers to Hezekiah, telling them, ¹⁰ Speak thus to Hezekiah king of Judah: Let not your god in whom you trust delude you into thinking that Jerusalem shall not be given into the **hand** of the king of Assyria. ¹¹ You yourself have heard what the kings of Assyria have done, annexing all lands. Shall you then escape? ¹² Did the gods of the nations my fathers destroyed deliver them? *Did they deliver* Gozan and Haran, Rezeph and the Edenites in Tel Assar? ¹³ Where are the kings of Hamath and Arpad and the kings of the cities of Sepharvaim, Hena, and Ivvah?

¹⁴ And Hezekiah received the letter from the messengers and read it. Then Hezekiah went up to the house of the Lord and unrolled it before the Lord. ¹⁵ And Hezekiah prayed to the Lord and said,

¹⁶ O Lord of Hosts, God of Israel, who sittest enthroned between the cherubim, thou alone art God over all the kingdoms of the earth. It is thou who madest the heavens and the earth . . .

¹⁷ O Lord, give ear and hear; O Lord, open thine eyes and see. Listen to all the words Sennacherib has sent to mock the living God.

¹⁸ O Lord, the kings of Assyria have indeed destroyed all peoplesᶜ and their lands, ¹⁹ committing their gods to the **fire**. For they were no gods, but mere works of men's hands, of wood and of stone, and so they could destroy them. ²⁰ But now, O Lord our God, deliver us out of his **hand**, that all kingdoms on earth may know that thou alone art Lord.

ᵇ9   Hebrew *he*.
ᶜ18   Hebrew *hāʾărāṣôt, lands*, emended to *haggôyîm;* compare 2 Kings 19:17.

²¹ Then Isaiah the son of Amoz sent word to Hezekiah, saying, Thus says the Lord, the God of Israel: Because you have prayed to me concerning Sennacherib king of Assyria, ²² this is what the Lord has spoken against him:

62:11   The Virgin Daughter of Zion holds you in contempt;
         she laughs you to scorn.
     The Daughter of Jerusalem shakes her head at you.

37:6   ²³ Whom have you mocked and ridiculed?
     Against whom have you raised your **voice**,
         lifting your eyes to high heaven?
     Against the Holy One of Israel!
     ²⁴ By your servants you have blasphemed the Lord.
     You thought, On account of my vast chariotry
10:32-34   I have conquered the highest mountains,
         the farthest reaches of Lebanon.
     I have felled its tallest cedars, its choicest cypresses.
     I have reached its loftiest summit, its finest forest.
     ²⁵ I have dug wells and drunk of foreign^d waters.
     With the soles of my feet
20:4   I have dried up all Egypt's rivers!

     ²⁶ Have you not heard
         how I ordained this thing long ago,
25:1-2   how in days of old I planned it?
     Now I have brought it to pass.
     You were destined to demolish fortified cities,
         turning them into heaps of rubble,
     ²⁷ while their timorous inhabitants
42:17   shrank away in confusion,
     becoming as wild grass, transiently green,
         or like weeds on a roof
5:24   *that scorch*^{e} before they grow up.

     ²⁸ But I know where you dwell,
         and your comings and goings,
5:30   and how stirred up you are against me.

---

^{d}25   So 1QIsaᵃ; 2 Kings 19:24. Term not in MT.
^{e}27   So 1QIsaᵃ; MT reading obscure.

²⁹ And because of your snortings
10:12   and bellowings against me,
        which have mounted up to my ears,
        I will put my ring in your nose
        and my bit in your mouth
37:34   and turn you back by the way you came.

³⁰ But to you this shall be a sign:
        This year eat what grows wild,
7:21–22   and the following year what springs up of itself.
        But in the third year sow and harvest,
        plant vineyards and eat their fruit:
³¹ the remnant of the house of Judah that survives
27:6   shall once more take root below and bear fruit above.
³² For out of Jerusalem shall go a remnant,
4:2–3   and from Mount Zion a band of survivors.
        The **zeal** of the Lord of Hosts will accomplish it.

³³ Therefore, thus says the Lord
        concerning the king of Assyria:
1:8   He shall not enter this city or shoot an arrow here.
        He shall not advance against it with armor,
        nor erect siegeworks against it.
³⁴ By the way he came he shall return;
        he shall not enter this city, says the Lord.
38:6   ³⁵ I will protect this city and save it,
        for my own sake and for the sake of my servant David.

³⁶ Then the angel of the Lord went out and slew a hundred and eighty-five thousand in the Assyrian camp. And when men arose in the morning, there lay all their dead bodies!

³⁷ So Sennacherib king of Assyria broke camp and withdrew. And he returned to Nineveh, where he dwelt.

³⁸ And as he was worshiping in the temple of Nisroch his god, his sons Adrammelech and Sharezer slew him with a sword and fled to the land of Ararat. And his son Esarhaddon succeeded him as king.

38

In those days Hezekiah became gravely ill. And the prophet Isaiah the son of Amoz came to him and said, Thus says the Lord: Put your house in order. You will die; you will not recover.

² At this Hezekiah turned his face toward the wall and prayed to the Lord: ³ I beseech thee to remember, O Lord, how I have walked before thee faithfully and with full purpose of heart and have done what is good in thine eyes. . . . And Hezekiah wept disconsolately.

⁴ Then the word of the Lord came to Isaiah: ⁵ Go and tell Hezekiah, Thus says the Lord, the God of your father David: I have heard your prayer and seen your tears. I will add fifteen years to your life. ⁶ And I will deliver you and this city out of the **hand** of the king of Assyria; I will protect this city.

²¹ᵃ And Isaiah gave instructions to take fig packs and apply them to the swelling so that he could recover.

²²ᵃ But Hezekiah said, What of a sign that I shall *again* go up to the house of the Lord?

⁷ *And Isaiah replied*, This shall be a sign to you from the Lord, that the Lord will do the thing he has promised: ⁸ See, I make the shadow cast by the afternoon sun on the dial of Ahaz recede the ten degrees it has gone down. So the sun reversed its descent by ten degrees on the dial.

⁹ Hezekiah king of Judah's account of his illness, *written* upon his recovery:

	¹⁰ I said, in the prime of life
5:14	must I depart through Sheol's gates,
	deprived of the balance of my years?
	¹¹ I thought, I shall not see ᵇthe Lordᵇ
	in the land of the living;
30:20	I shall not now behold Man
	among those dwelling in mortality.
	¹² My tabernacle is being uprooted,
	carried away from me like a shepherd's tent.
38:1	My life is cut off like woven fabric;
	he is severing me from the loom.ᶜ
	¹³ Can I contain myself until morning,
	while like a lion he racks my whole frame?
21:11–12	*Surely*, as night has followed day,
	thou art bringing on my end!

ᵃ21, ᵃ22   Verse appears out of sequence in text.

ᵇ11   Hebrew *yāh yāh* emended to *YHWH*.

ᶜ12   MT adds *as night has followed day, thou art bringing on my end!* (so v. 13), a probable duplication. Compare LXX.

¹⁴ Like a mounting lark I twitter,
    like a dove I murmur.
My eyes are drawn looking heavenward;
    [I am utterly sleepless^d

26:16–17   from bitterness of soul. . . .]^e
O Lord, I am in straits; be my surety!

¹⁵ But what shall I say
    when he has *already* spoken for me,
    when he himself has brought it about?

33:6   ¹⁶ O my Lord, by means of such *trials*
    comes *a newness of* life,
    and throughout them all the renewal of my spirit.
¹⁷ Surely, for my own good I am in such dire distress;
    by its means thou drawest my soul

51:14   out of the Pit of dissolution.
For thou hast cast all my sins behind thee,
    [restoring and reviving me].^f

14:15   ¹⁸ For Sheol cannot praise thee, nor Death glorify thee;
    those who go down into the Pit
    have no *further* hope of thy **faithfulness**.

12:1–6   ¹⁹ But the living, only they bring thee praise,
    as I do this day; from father to sons
    they pass on the knowledge of thy **faithfulness**.
²⁰ O Lord, *may it please thee* to save me,
    and we will perform music

56:7   all the days of our lives in the house of the Lord.

39 At that time Merodach-Baladan the son of Baladan, king of Babylon, sent letters and gifts to Hezekiah, for he had heard of his illness and recovery. ² And Hezekiah was glad of them and showed *the envoys^a* his treasury—the silver and gold, the spices and fragrant oils, and his entire armory and all that was in his treasuries. There was nothing in his palace or in all his realm that Hezekiah did not show them.

---

^d14   Hebrew ^ʾ*eddaddeh kol šěnôtai, I will wander all my years,* emended to *nôddědâ kol šěnātî.*

^e14   Line brought up from verse 15, where it follows *brought it about.*

^f17   Phrase brought down from verse 16, where it follows *my spirit.*

^a2   Hebrew *them.*

3 Then the prophet Isaiah came to King Hezekiah and said, What did those men say to you, and where did they come from? And Hezekiah replied, They came from a distant land; *they came to me from Babylon.* 4 And *Isaiah*[b] asked, What did they see in your palace? And Hezekiah said, They saw everything there is in my palace. There is nothing in my treasuries that I did not show them.

5 Then Isaiah said to Hezekiah, Hear the word of the Lord of Hosts: 6 The time shall come when everything in your palace, and all that your forefathers have treasured up until now, shall be carried away to Babylon. Nothing shall be left, says the Lord. 7 And from among your own sons, your future offspring and descendants, they shall take *some* to serve as eunuchs in the palace of the king of Babylon.

8 But Hezekiah said to Isaiah, The word of the Lord you have spoken is good. For he thought, Then there shall be peace and loyalty during my reign.

40

Comfort and give solace to my people,
    says your God; 2 speak kindly to Jerusalem.
Announce to her that she has served her term,
    that her guilt has been expiated.

51:17
She has received from the Lord's **hand**
    double for all her sins.

3 A **voice** calls out,

62:10–11
In the desert prepare the way for the Lord;
in the wilderness
    pave a straight highway for our God:
4 every ravine must be raised up,
    every mountain and hill made low;

42:16
the uneven ground must become level
    and rough terrain a plain.

59:19–20
5 For the glory[a] of the Lord shall be revealed
    and all flesh see it at once.
By his **mouth** the Lord has spoken it.

---

b4   Hebrew *he*.
a5   Or, *presence*.

⁶ A **voice** said, Announce it.

48:20   And I asked, How shall I announce it?
All flesh is grass,
and at its best like a blossom of the field.

42:5   ⁷ ᵇThough the Spirit of the Lord breathe within it,
the people themselves are but herbage—
⁸ grass that withers, flowers that fade—
only the word of our God endures forever.

⁹ Scale the mountain heights,
52:7–10   O Zion, herald of good tidings.
Raise your **voice** mightily,
O Jerusalem, messenger of good news.
Make yourself heard, be not afraid;
proclaim to the cities of Judah: Behold your God!

¹⁰ See, my Lord the Lord comes with power;
his **arm** presides for him.
35:4   His reward is with him; his work precedes him.
¹¹ Like a shepherd he pastures his flock:
the lambs he gathers up with his **arm**
and carries in his bosom;
63:11–14   the ewes that give milk he leads gently along.

¹² Who measured out the waters
with the hollow of his **hand**
and gauged the heavens
by the span of his fingers?
45:12   Who compiled the earth's dust by measure,
weighing mountains in scales,
hills in a balance?
¹³ Who has comprehended the Spirit of the Lord,
46:11   that a man should let him know his plan?
¹⁴ Of whom was he counselled
that he might be enlightened,
by whom instructed in the path of discretion,
55:8–9   imparting to him knowledge,
acquainting him with the way of understanding?

ᵇ7   MT adds *Grass that withers, flowers that fade* (so v. 8), a probable duplication.
Compare 1QIsaᵃ; LXX.

¹⁵ The nations are but drops from a bucket,
counting no more than dust on a balance;
41:1–2 the isles he displaces as mere specks.
¹⁶ Lebanon would not suffice to kindle a fire,
nor *all* its beasts be adequate for sacrifice.
34:2 ¹⁷ Before him all nations are as nothing;
as less than the ether they are reckoned by him.

¹⁸ To whom then will you liken God?
What does he resemble in your estimation?
¹⁹ A figure cast by the artisan,
46:5–6 overlaid by the smith with gold,
fitted with a silver chain from the craftsman?
41:7^c The artisan encourages the smith,
and he who beats with a hammer
urges him who pounds the anvil.
44:12 They say of the welding, It is good,
though they fasten it with riveting
that it may not come loose.
²⁰ Those too poor for this *type of* sacrifice
44:13–15 select a wood that resists decay.
They seek an expert sculptor
to carve them an image that will not deteriorate.

²¹ Are you so unaware, that you have not heard?
Have you not been told before,
that you do not understand
by whom the earth was founded?
37:16 ²² By him who sits enthroned above the earth's sphere,
to whom its inhabitants are as grasshoppers,
who suspends the heavens like a canopy,
stretching them out as a tent to dwell in.
²³ By him who brings potentates to nought
41:25 and makes the authorities of the world null and void.
²⁴ When scarcely they are planted,
or scarcely they are sown,
when hardly their stalk has taken root in the earth,
17:13 he puffs at them and they wither,
and a storm sweeps them off as chaff.

---

^c41:7 Verse appears out of sequence in text.

²⁵ To whom then will you liken me,

46:9   to whom can I be compared? says the Holy One.

²⁶ Lift your eyes heavenward and see:
     Who formed these?
He who brings forth their hosts by number,

43:1   calling each one by name.
Because he is almighty and all powerful,
     not one is unaccounted for.

²⁷ Why then do you say, O Jacob,
     and speak thus, O Israel:
Our path has become obscured from the Lord;

51:22   our cause is overlooked by our God?

²⁸ Is it not known to you; have you not heard?
     The Lord is the God of eternity,

41:8–9   Creator of the ends of the earth.
He does not grow faint or weary;
     his intelligence cannot be fathomed.

²⁹ He supplies the weary with energy

58:11   and increases in vigor those who lack strength.

³⁰ Youths grow faint and weary,
     and young men slump down *of exhaustion.*

³¹ But they who hope in the Lord

49:4–5   shall be renewed in strength:
they shall ascend as on eagles' wings;
     they shall run without wearying,
     they shall walk and not faint.

41

Be silent before me, O isles;
     become still, you peoples!
Let them come forward and state their case;
     let us stand trial together.

46:11–13   ² Who has raised up **Righteousness** from the east,
     calling him to *the place of* his foot?
Who has delivered nations to him,
     toppled their rulers,

45:1   rendering them as dust to his **sword**,
     as driven stubble to his **bow**?

³ He puts them to flight, passing on unhindered
     by paths his feet have never trod.

⁴ Who is at work accomplishing *this*,
    foreordaining dynasties?

48:12   I, the Lord, first and last, am he.

⁵ The isles look on in fear;
    the ends of the earth are in trembling.

59:18   They flock together*ᵃ*
    and come ⁶ to one another's aid,
saying, each to his fellow, Courage!

44:1–2   ⁸ But you, O Israel, my servant,
    Jacob, whom I have chosen,
    offspring of Abraham my beloved friend,
    ⁹ you whom I have taken from the ends of the earth,

51:2   called from its farthest limits—
    to you I say, You are my servant;
    I have accepted you and not rejected you.

43:5–6   ¹⁰ Be not fearful, for I am with you;
    be not dismayed, for I am your God.
    I will strengthen you; I will also succor you

11:11–12   and uphold you with my righteous **right hand**.

¹¹ See, all who are enraged at you
    shall earn shame and disgrace;
    your adversaries shall come to nought, and perish.
¹² Should you look for those who contend with you,

17:13–14   you shall not find them;
    whoever wars against you
    shall be reduced to nothing.
¹³ For I, the Lord your God,

62:8   hold you by the **right hand** and say to you,
Have no fear; I will help you.

¹⁴ Be not afraid, you worms of Jacob;
    O men of Israel, [be not dismayed]:*ᵇ*
    I am your help, says the Lord;

49:26   your Redeemer is the Holy One of Israel.
    ¹⁵ I will make of you a sharp-toothed threshing sledge
    of new design, full of spikes:

---

*ᵃ*5   So 1QIsaᵃ; term not in MT.
*ᵇ*14   A reconstruction based on meter and parallelism; compare verse 10.

41:2	you shall thresh mountains to dust
	and make chaff of hills.

¹⁶ As you winnow them, a wind shall take them away,
a tempest dispel them.
Then will you rejoice in the Lord
and glory in the Holy One of Israel.

48:21   ¹⁷ When the poor and needy require water,
and there is none,
and their **tongue** becomes parched with thirst,
I the Lord will answer their want;
I, the God of Israel, will not forsake them.

35:6–7   ¹⁸ I will open up streams in barren hill country,
springs in the midst of the plains;
I will turn the desert into lakes,
parched lands into fountains of water.
¹⁹ I will bring cedars and acacias,
myrtles and oleasters in the wilderness;

55:13   I will place cypresses,
elms and box trees in the steppes—
²⁰ that all may see it and know, consider it,
and perceive that the Lord's **hand** did this,
that the Holy One of Israel created it.

45:21   ²¹ Present your case, says the Lord;
submit your evidence, says the King of Jacob.
²² Let them come forward and recount to us
their prophecies of events heretofore.
What were they? Tell us,

43:9   that we may examine them
and know whether they were fulfilled.
Or predict the future for us:
²³ Tell us of events to come hereafter,

47:13   so that we may know you are gods.
Perform something good or evil
at which we will be dazzled and all stand in awe.
²⁴ It is clear you are of no account,

44:9–10   that your works ^camount to nothing;^c
whoever accepts you is himself an abomination.

---

^c24 Hebrew *)āpa^c* (unknown) emended to *)āpes*.

352

45:13   ²⁵ I have raised up one from the north
       who calls on my name,
       who shall come from the direction of sunrise.
       He shall come upon dignitaries as on mud,
       tread them as clay like a potter.

48:14, 16   ²⁶ Who announced this beforehand, so we would know,
       declared it ahead of time,
       that we might say, *^d*He was right?*^d*
       Indeed, not one could foretell it,
44:25   not one make it known;
       no one has heard from you
       any [prophetic]*^e* utterance.
       ²⁷ But to Zion, he shall be her harbinger;*^f*
52:7   I will appoint him as a herald of tidings to Jerusalem.

       ²⁸ For when I looked there was no one,
       not one who could offer counsel,
       or when I questioned them,
       who could answer a word.
       ²⁹ Surely they are all iniquitous,
1:31   their works worthless;
       their outpourings are but wind and emptiness.

42

       My servant whom I sustain,
       my chosen one in whom I delight,
61:1   him I have endowed with my Spirit;
       he will dispense justice to the nations.*^a*
       ² He will not shout or raise his voice
52:15   to make himself heard in public.
       ³ Even a bruised reed he will not break;
       a dim wick he will not snuff out.
40:10   He will perform the work of justice
       in the cause of truth.

---

*^d*26   Literally, *The righteous one,* a pun on the subject of verses 2, 25.

*^e*26   Hebrew *riš'ôn,* a probable corruption (compare plural *ri'šonôt,* v. 22; *mēr'ōš,* v. 26), included in present verse; term commences verse 27 in MT.

*^f*27   Hebrew *hannōmeh* (compare Arabic); so 1QIsa^a. MT *hinnām, behold them/here they are.*

*^a*1   Hebrew *gôyim,* also *Gentiles.*

⁴ Neither shall he himself grow dim or be bruised
until he has brought about justice in the earth.

51:4–5   The isles await his law.

⁵ Thus says the Lord God,
who frames and suspends the heavens,

44:24   who gives form to the earth and its creatures,
the breath of life to the people upon it,
spirit to those who walk on it:

48:15   ⁶ I the Lord have rightfully called you
and will grasp you by the hand;
I have created you and appointed you
to be a **covenant** for the people,

49:6, 8   a **light** to the nations,ᵇ
⁷ to open eyes that are blind,
to free captives from confinement

9:2, 4   and from prison those who sit in **darkness**.

⁸ I am the Lord; that is my name.
I will not relinquish my glory to another,
nor my praise to wrought idols.
⁹ The prophecies of the former events
indeed came to pass,

48:6–7   but new things I yet foretell.
Before they spring up I declare them to you.

¹⁰ Sing to the Lord a new song;
sing his praise from the end of the earth.

24:14–15   ᶜLet the sea roar,ᶜ and all that lives in it,
the isles and they who inhabit them.
¹¹ Let the desert and its cities raise *their voice,*
and the villages where Kedar dwells;

16:1   let the inhabitants of Sela sing for joy
and cry out from the tops of the mountains.
¹² O let them give glory to the Lord,
and in the isles speak out in praise of him.

26:21   ¹³ The Lord will come forth like a warrior,
his passions aroused like a fighter;

ᵇ6   Hebrew *gôyîm,* also *Gentiles.*
ᶜ10   Hebrew *yôrdê hayyām, they who go down to the sea,* emended to *yirʿam hayyām.*

he will give the war cry,

31:4   raise the shout of victory over his enemies.

¹⁴ For a long time I have been silent,
    keeping still and restraining myself.
But now I will scream like a woman in labor
    and breathe hard and fast all at once.

54:10   ¹⁵ I will lay waste mountains and hills
    and make all their vegetation wither;
I will turn rivers into dry land and evaporate lakes.

49:9–10   ¹⁶ Then will I lead the blind by a way they did not know,
    and guide them in paths unfamiliar;
the **darkness** confronting them I will turn into **light**,

40:3–4   and the uneven ground make level.
These things I will not fail to perform.

¹⁷ But those who trust in idols
    and esteem their images as gods
shall retreat in utter confusion.

¹⁸ O you deaf, listen; O you blind, look and see!

43:10   ¹⁹ Who is blind but my own servant,
    or so deaf as the messenger I have sent?
Who is blind like those I have commissioned,
    as uncomprehending as the servant of the Lord—

6:9   ²⁰ seeing much but not giving heed,
    with open ears hearing nothing?

²¹ It is the will of the Lord, that,
    because of his **righteousness**,

42:4   they magnify the law and become illustrious.

²² Instead, they are a people plundered and sacked,
    all of them trapped in holes,
    hidden away in dungeons.

5:29   They have become a prey, yet no one rescues them,
    a spoil, yet none demands restitution.

²³ Who among you hearing this
    will take heed of it hereafter,
    and be mindful and obey?

²⁴ Who is it that hands Jacob over to plunder

10:6   and Israel to despoilers, if not the Lord,
    against whom we have sinned?

For they have no desire to walk in his ways
30:9   or obey his law.
        ²⁵ So in the heat of his **anger**
            he pours out on them the violence of war,
        till it envelopes them in flames—
            yet they remain unaware—
9:18–19   till it sets them on fire;
            yet they take it not to heart.

43 But now, thus says the Lord—
            he who formed you, O Jacob,
44:21–22   he who created you, O Israel:
        Do not fear, for I have redeemed you.
            I have called you by name; you are mine.
51:10–11   ² When you cross the waters, I will be with you;
            when you traverse the rivers,
            you shall not be overwhelmed.
        Though you walk through the **fire**,
33:14–15   you shall not be burned;
            its **flame** shall not consume you.

        ³ For I the Lord am your God,
            I, the Holy One of Israel, am your Savior;
        Egypt I have appointed as ransom for you,
20:4   Cush and Seba *I give* in place of you.
        ⁴ Because you are precious and revered in my eyes,
            and because I love you,
        I give men in return for you,
            peoples in exchange for your life.

        ⁵ Do not fear, for I am with you.
            I will bring your offspring from the east
41:8–9   and gather you from the west;
        ⁶ I will say to the north, Give up!
            to the south, Withhold not!
        Bring my sons from afar
49:22   and my daughters from the end of the earth—
        ⁷ all who are called by my name,
            whom I have formed, molded and wrought
            for my own glory.

42:7   ⁸ Let go the people who are blind, yet have eyes,
        who are deaf, yet have ears.

        ⁹ When all nations unitedly assembled,
        when the peoples were gathered together,
        who among them foretold these things,
45:21   or predicted events that have come to pass?
        Let them bring their witnesses
        and justify themselves,
        that those within hearing may say, It is true.
44:8   ¹⁰ But you are my witnesses, says the Lord,
        my servant whom I have chosen,
        to the end that you may recognize it and believe me,
        and perceive that I was the one *who foretold them*—
        before me no god was formed,
45:14   nor shall one exist after me.

        ¹¹ I myself am the Lord;
        apart from me there is no savior.
63:8-9 ¹² It is I who foretold and wrought **salvation**,
        making it known
        when there was no strange god among you.
        You are my witnesses, says the Lord,
        that I am divine,
46:4   ¹³ that from the first I have been present—
        from my **hand** none can deliver;
        when I work, who can thwart it?
        ¹⁴ Thus says the Lord, the Holy One of Israel,
        your Redeemer:
        For your sake I launch *an attack* on Babylon
        and bring down as fugitives all the Chaldeans,
23:13   they who sing the praises of shipping.
        ¹⁵ I the Lord, your Holy One,
        Creator of Israel, am your King.

        ¹⁶ Thus says the Lord—
11:15-16   who provides a way in the **Sea**,
        a path through the mighty waters,
        ¹⁷ who dispatches chariots and horses,
        armies of men in full strength;
37:36   they lie down as one, to rise no more,
        they flicker and die, snuffed out like a wick—

357

¹⁸ Never mind the prophecies of bygone events;
do not dwell on things of the past.

42:9   ¹⁹ See, I do a new thing; it is now springing up.
Surely, you are aware of it:
I am making roads through the desert,

35:6-8   streams in the wasteland.

²⁰ The wild beasts do me honor,
the jackals and birds of prey,
for bringing water to the wilderness,

41:17-18   streams to the dry land,
that I may give drink to my chosen people,
²¹ the people I formed for myself

42:12   to speak out in praise of me.

²² But you do not call upon me, O Jacob;
you have grown weary of me, O Israel.
²³ Yet *I required* not that you bring me
offerings from your flocks
or pay me homage by sacrificial slaughter;
I have not burdened you with oblations

66:3   or wearied you with burning incense.
²⁴ Nor *have I burdened you* to buy
me the fragrant calamus
or sate me with the fat of immolations.

53:5-6   Yet you have burdened me with your sins,
wearied me with your iniquities.
²⁵ But it is I myself, and for my own sake,
who blot out your offenses,

44:22   remembering your sins no more.

²⁶ Recount for me *the past*;
let us plead each our case.
Speak up and vindicate yourself.
²⁷ Your first father transgressed;
your spokesmen sinned against me.

64:10-11   ²⁸ Therefore I let *the holy cities* be profaned;
I gave Jacob to be ostracized, Israel to execration.

---

*a*28   Hebrew *śārê qōdeš, the princes of the sanctuary*, emended to *ʿārê qōdeš*; compare 47:6; 64:10.

44 Hear now, Jacob my servant,
and Israel whom I have chosen.
² Thus says the Lord, your Maker,
who formed you from the womb and succored you:
41:14   Be not afraid, O Jacob, my servant,
and Jeshurun whom I have chosen.

³ I will pour water on the thirsty *soil*,
showers upon the dry ground;
54:13   I will pour out my Spirit on your offspring,
my blessing upon your posterity.
⁴ They shall shoot up like grass
43:20   among streams*ᵃ* of water,
like willows by running brooks.
⁵ One will say, I am the Lord's,
and another name himself Jacob.
43:7   Yet others will inscribe on their arm, To the Lord,
and adopt the name Israel.

⁶ Thus says the Lord, the King of Israel,
the Lord of Hosts, their Redeemer:
I was at the first and I am at the last;
45:5   apart from me there is no God.
⁷ Who predicts *ᵇ*what happens*ᵇ* as do I,
and is the equal of me
in appointing a people from of old *ᶜ*as types,*ᶜ*
46:10   foretelling things to come?
⁸ Be not perturbed or shaken.
Have I not made it known to you from of old?
Did I not foretell it, you being my witnesses?
Is there a God, then, apart from me?
26:4   There is no Rock unknown to me.

⁹ All who manufacture idols are deranged;
the things they cherish profit nothing.
Those who promote them are themselves
42:17-20   sightless and mindless, to their own dismay.

---

*ᵃ*4   So LXX; term not in MT.
*ᵇ*7   Hebrew *yiqrāʾ*, *will call*, emended to *yiqrâ*.
*ᶜ*7   Hebrew *wěʾōtîyôt*, *the coming things*, emended to *kěʾōtôt*; compare 8:18; 1QIsaᵃ, 45:11.

359

¹⁰ Who would fashion a god or cast an idol
30:22   that cannot benefit them?
¹¹ Their whole society is confused;
          their fabricators are mere mortals.
          Were they all to assemble
          and take their stand *before me*,
41:5–6   they would at once cringe in fear.

¹² The smith with his tools works the iron over the coals
          and gives it shape by hammering;
46:6   he forges his *god* by the strength of his arm:
          when he becomes hungry, he no longer has strength;
          if he fails to drink water, he begins to grow faint.

¹³ The woodworker draws a diagram,
          sketching his *idol* with a marker.
          He creates it by chiselling to the outline of the dividers;
46:9   he gives it a human likeness, resembling man's beauty,
          fit to lodge in a house.

¹⁴ He is required to cut down cedars;
40:20   he must select holms and oaks
          and care for them among the trees of the forest.
          He plants firs, which the rain makes grow:
¹⁵ that which serves men as fuel,
          which they use to warm themselves
          or light fire with to bake bread,
2:8   of that they create gods which they adore,
          from it they make idols to which they stoop.

¹⁶ Half of it they burn in the fire.
          ^dOver it they broil a roast;^d
          they eat the meat and are satisfied.
          They also warm themselves and say,
47:14   Ah, it is warm ^ein front of^e the fire!
¹⁷ From the rest they make a god, their idol,
          to which they bow in adoration and pray,
46:7   Save us; you are our god!

---

^d16   Phrase transposed (compare v. 19); in text follows *eat the meat*.
^e16   So 1QIsaᵃ; MT *I see*.

¹⁸ They have become unaware and insensible;
their eyes are glazed so they cannot see,

6:10   their minds are incapable of discernment.
¹⁹ They reflect not,
nor have the sense or comprehension to say,
Part of this I burned in the fire;
I also baked bread in its embers,
roasted meat and ate it.
Am I not making an abomination of what is left?

46:8   Do I not stoop to a mere lump of wood?
²⁰ They are followers of ashes;
their deluded minds have distracted them.
They cannot liberate themselves *from them* or say,
Surely this thing in my hand is a fraud.

40:27   ²¹ Ponder these things, O Jacob, and you,ᶠ O Israel,
for you are my servant.
I have created you to be my servant, O Israel;
do not disregard me.

60:1–2 ²² I have removed your offenses like a thick fog,
your sins like a cloud of mist.

31:6–7 Return to me; I have redeemed you.
²³ Sing, O heavens, for what the Lord has done;
cause it to resound, O earth beneath!
Burst into song, O mountains,
forests, and all trees therein:
the Lord has redeemed Jacob;

60:21   he shall be glorified in Israel.

²⁴ Thus says the Lord, your Redeemer,
who formed you from the womb:
I am the Lord, the Maker of all things,

40:22   who alone suspends the heavens,
who himself gives form to the earth,
²⁵ who annuls the predictions of imposters
and makes fools of diviners,

29:14   who turns wise men about
and makes nonsense of their knowledge,

---

*f*21   Word transposed; in text follows *created you.*

50:10   ²⁶ who fulfills the word of his servant,
accomplishes the aims of his messengers,
who says of Jerusalem, It shall be reinhabited,
58:12   and of the cities of Judah, They shall be rebuilt,
their ruins I will restore,
²⁷ who says to the deep, Become dry;
I am drying up your currents,
63:11–13   ²⁸ who says of Cyrus, He is my shepherd;
he will do whatever I will.
He will say of Jerusalem that it must be rebuilt,
45:13   its temple foundations relaid.

45

Thus says the Lord to his anointed,
to Cyrus, whom I grasp by the right hand,
41:2   to subdue nations before him,
to ungird the loins of rulers,
opening doors ahead of him,
letting no gates remain shut:
57:14   ² I will go before you and level all obstacles;
I will break in pieces brazen doors
and cut through iron bars.
³ I will give you hidden treasures
60:17   and secret hoards of wealth—
that you may know that it is I the Lord,
the God of Israel, who calls you by name.

⁴ For the sake of my servant Jacob,
and Israel my chosen, I call you by name—
49:1–3   I named you when yet you knew me not.
⁵ I am the Lord, there is none other;
apart from me there is no God.
I girded you up when yet you knew me not—
⁶ that men from where the sun rises to where it sets
may know that without me there is nothing,
that I am the Lord, and that there is none other.

9:2   ⁷ I fashion **light** and form **darkness**;
I occasion peace and cause calamity.
I, the Lord, do all these things.
⁸ Rain down from above, O heavens;
let the skies overflow with **righteousness**.

Let the earth receive it and **salvation** ^ablossom;^a
46:13   let **righteousness** spring up forthwith.
I, the Lord, create it.

⁹ Woe to those in conflict with their Maker,
mere shards of earthenware pottery!
As though the clay were to say to him who molds it,
29:16   What are you doing?
Your **hands** have no skill for the work!
¹⁰ Woe to those who say to their Father,
What have you begotten?
66:7–9   or to the Woman, What have you borne?

¹¹ Thus says the Lord,
the Holy One of Israel, their Maker:
Will you ask me^b for signs^c concerning my children,
29:23   or dictate to me about the deeds of my **hands**?
¹² It is I who made the earth
and created man upon it;
I with my **hand**^d suspended the heavens,
appointing all their host.
42:6–7   ¹³ It is I who rightfully raise him up,
who facilitate his every step;
he will rebuild my city and set free my exiles
52:3, 5   without price or bribe, says the Lord of Hosts.

¹⁴ Thus says the Lord:
43:3   The wealth of Egypt and merchandise of Cush
^eshall pass on to you and become yours,^e
as shall the Sabeans, a people tall in stature.
They shall walk behind you in chains
60:14   and bow down to you, entreating you,
Surely God is in you; no other gods exist!

¹⁵ Truly thou art a God who dissembles himself,
O Savior, God of Israel.

---

^a8   So 1QIsa^a; LXX; MT *they bear fruit*.
^b11   Hebrew *šĕʾālûnî, Ask me*, emended to *tišʾālûnî*.
^c11   So 1QIsa^a; compare 7:11. MT *ʾōtiyôt, the coming things*.
^d12   So LXX; MT vocalization plural. Compare 48:13.
^e14   Phrase transposed; in text follows *tall in stature*.

¹⁶ As one, the makers of inventions retired in disgrace,
42:17   utterly dismayed and embarrassed.
¹⁷ But Israel is saved by the Lord
    with an everlasting **salvation**;
you shall not be dismayed or put to shame
worlds without end.

¹⁸ For thus says the Lord who created the heavens,
40:21–22   the God who formed the earth—
who made it secure and organized it,
    not to remain a chaotic waste,
but designed it to be inhabited:
    I am the Lord, there is none other.
48:16   ¹⁹ I speak not in secret
    from somewhere in a land of **darkness**;
I do not ask Jacob's offspring
    to seek me amid chaos.
51:1   I the Lord tell **righteousness**
and am forthright of speech.

²⁰ Gather yourselves and come;
    draw near, all you fugitives of the nations.
They who carried about their wooden idols
37:18–19   and prayed to gods that could not save them
were caught unawares.
²¹ Speak up and present your case;
    go ahead and consult one another.
Who foretold these things of old,
44:7   predicted them long ago?
Did not I, the Lord,
    apart from whom there is no God?
41:2   *Did not I*, the God of **righteousness**,
except for whom there is no Savior?

²² Turn to me and save yourselves,
    all you ends of the earth;
I am God, there is none other.
²³ By myself I swear it—
63:1   **righteousness** has issued from my **mouth**,
by a decree that cannot be revoked:
To me every knee shall bow
    and every tongue swear *allegiance*.

²⁴ It shall be said of me,

54:17
  By the Lord alone come **vindication**ᶠ and might.
  Before him must come in shame

66:5
  all who were incensed against him.
²⁵ In the Lord shall all Israel's offspring
  justify themselves and have cause to boast.

46   Bel slumps down, Nebo is stooped over:
  their idols are *loaded* upon beasts and cattle;
the images you bore aloft
  are piled as burdens on weary animals.
² *Such gods*ᵃ altogether sag and bow down,

45:20
  unable to rescue their burden;
they themselves go into captivity.

³ Hear me, O house of Jacob,

10:20–22
  and all you remnant of the house of Israel,
who have been a load on me since birth,
  borne up by me from the womb:
⁴ Even to your old age, I am present;
  till you turn grey, it is I who sustain you.

63:9
  It is I who made you, and I who bear you up;
it is I who carry and rescue you.

⁵ To whom will you compare me or count me equal?
  To whom will you liken me,

40:18, 25
  that we should appear similar?
⁶ They who squander gold from the purse
  and weigh out silver on the scales

41:7*
  hire a smith to make them a god
they bow down to and worship.
⁷ They bear it aloft, carrying it on their shoulders;
  when they set it in place, there it stands,
  unable to budge from its spot.
Though they cry to it for help, it does not answer;

36:19–20
  it cannot save them from trouble.

⁸ Put yourselves in mind of this
  and come to your senses;

48:5
  take it to heart, you offenders.

ᶠ24 Or, *righteousness*; compare verse 23.
ᵃ2 Hebrew *They*.

48:3   ⁹ Review the prophecies of the events of old!
       I am God, there is none other.
       I am divine; nothing resembles me.

44:7–8   ¹⁰ I foretell the end from the beginning,
       from ancient times things not yet done.
       I speak, and my purposes take effect;
       I accomplish all my will.

41:2, 25   ¹¹ I summon a **bird of prey** from the east,
       from a distant land
       the man [b]who performs my counsel.[b]

48:15   What I have spoken, I bring to pass;
       what I have planned, I do.
       ¹² Hear me, you stubborn-hearted,
       who are far from **righteousness**:

51:5   ¹³ I have brought near my **righteousness**;
       it is not now far off—
       my **salvation** shall no longer be delayed.

37:32–35   I will grant deliverance in Zion,
       and to Israel my glory.

47

       Get down and sit in the dust,
         O Virgin Daughter of Babylon;
       squat on the ground, dethroned,

21:2, 9   O Daughter of the Chaldeans.
       You shall no more be spoken of
       as delicate and refined.
       ² Take two grindstones and grind flour;
       unveil, disrobe, bare your legs,
       wade through streams:

57:12   ³ your nakedness shall be exposed
       and your shame uncovered.
       I will take vengeance
       and not be entreated of men,
       ⁴ *says* our Redeemer, the Holy One of Israel,

63:4   whose name is the Lord of Hosts.

       ⁵ Sit speechless; retire into obscurity,
         O Daughter of the Chaldeans.

---

[b]11   Or, *I have foreordained.*

No longer shall you be called,
Mistress of Kingdoms.
⁶ I was provoked by my people,

43:28   so I let my inheritance be defiled.
I gave them into your **hand**,
and you showed them no mercy;

10:27   even the aged you weighed down heavily with your **yoke**.
⁷ You thought, I, the Eternal Mistress, exist forever!
and did not consider these,ᵃ
or remember her final destiny.

⁸ Now therefore hear this, O pampered lady,
securely enthroned, thinking to herself,

45:6   I exist, and other than me there is nothing;
I shall not be widowed or bereaved of children:
⁹ Bereavement and widowhood

14:22   shall suddenly overtake you, both in one day.
They shall come upon you in full,
notwithstanding your many magical feats
and exceedingly strong combinations.

29:20   ¹⁰ Secure in your wickedness,
you thought, No one discerns me.
By your skill and science you were led astray,
thinking to yourself, I exist,
and there is none besides me!

9:18   ¹¹ Catastrophe shall overtake you,
which you shall not know how to avert by bribes;ᵇ
disaster shall befall you
from which you cannot ransom yourself:
there shall come upon you sudden ruin

13:9–13   such as you have not imagined.

¹² Persist, then, with your combinations
and with your many magical feats,

57:10   at which you have exerted yourself since your youth.
It may still be of use to you;
perhaps you can hinderᶜ it.

ᵃ7   For subject of term, see verse 6.
ᵇ11 Hebrew *šăḥrāh* (obscure) emended to *šăḥdāh;* contrast Israel to this verse, 43:3; 45:13.
ᶜ12 Hebrew *ta⟨ărôšî, cause terror,* emended to *ta⟨aṣôrî;* compare 66:9.

¹³ But you are powerless, despite all your tactics.
Now let those who unravel the heavens,
who observe the stars
41:22–24   and make predictions month by month,
stand by you and save you!

13:19   ¹⁴ See, as stubble they are burnt up in the **fire**,
unable themselves to escape the **hand** of the **flame**.
These are no embers to warm anyone;
44:16–19   such is no fire to sit by!
¹⁵ This is what your procurers*ᵈ* have profited you—
those for whom you have exerted yourself
since your youth—
each deviates his own way;
57:13   none is there to save you.

48 Hear this, O house of Jacob,
you who are named Israel—
though you*ᵃ* stem from the lineage*ᵇ* of Judah—
who take oaths in the name of the Lord
and invoke the God of Israel,
58:2   though not in truth or in **righteousness**,
² who call yourselves of the holy city,
upheld by the God of Israel,
whose name is the Lord of Hosts:
³ The prophecies of the events of the past
I made known long beforehand;
48:16   no sooner did they issue from my **mouth**,
than I caused them to be announced.
Then, suddenly, I acted and they came about.

46:12   ⁴ For I knew how stubborn you were—
your neck was an iron sinew, your brow brazen—
⁵ therefore I told you them beforehand;
I announced them to you before they transpired,
47:10   lest you should say, My idols did it;
my graven and wrought images caused it!

ᵈ15   Or, *merchants*. Noun transposed; in text follows *exerted yourself*. Compare verse 12.
ᵃ1   Hebrew *they*.
ᵇ1   Literally, *loins*. Hebrew *mimmê, from the waters*, emended to *mimmĕʿê*; compare the term in verse 19.

29:11 ⁶ But you have heard ᶜthe whole vision;ᶜ
how is it you do not proclaim it?
Yet as of now, I announce to you new things,
42:9 things withheld and unknown to you,
⁷ things now coming into being, not hitherto,
things you have not heard of before,
lest you should say, Indeed I knew them!
⁸ You have not heard them,
nor have you known them;
52:15 before this your ears have not been open to them.
For I knew you would turn treacherous;
you were called a transgressor from the womb.

13:5, 9, 13 ⁹ For my own name's sake I have bridled my **wrath**;
on account of my renown
I have shown restraint toward you
by not entirely destroying you.
¹⁰ See, I am refining you, though not as silver;
30:20 I am testing*ᵈ* you in the crucible of affliction.
¹¹ For my own sake, on my own account, I do it,
that my name*ᵉ* be not dishonored,
nor my glory, which I give to no other.

¹² Hear me, O Jacob, and Israel, my elect:
44:6 I am he who was at the first,
and I am he who is at the last.
¹³ It was my **hand** that founded the earth,
45:12 my **right hand** that stretched out the heavens;
when I call them, they arise at once.
¹⁴ All of you, assemble and hear:
41:26 Who among you*ᶠ* foretold these things?
It is him the Lord loves,
who shall perform his will in Babylon;
his **arm** shall be against the Chaldeans.
¹⁵ I myself have spoken it, and also called him;
46:11, 13 I have brought him, and I will prosper*ᵍ* his way.

---

*ᶜ*6 Hebrew *ḥazēh kullāh, See all of it!* emended to *ḥāzût kullāh;* compare 29:11.
*ᵈ*10 So 1QIsaᵃ; MT *choosing.*
*ᵉ*11 So LXX; term not in MT.
*ᶠ*14 Hebrew *bāhem, among them,* emended to *bākem.*
*ᵍ*15 So LXX; MT *and he shall prosper.*

369

¹⁶ Come near me and hear this:

45:19   I have not made predictions in secret;
        at their coming to pass, I have been present.
        Now my Lord the Lord has sent me;
42:1   his Spirit *is in me.*^b

¹⁷ Thus says the Lord, the Holy One of Israel,
        your Redeemer:
        I the Lord your God instruct you to your good,
        guiding you in the way you should go.
42:23 ¹⁸ Had you but obeyed my commandments,
        your peace would have been as a river,
        your **righteousness** like the waves of the sea;
     ¹⁹ your offspring would have been
10:22   as the sands in number,
        your descendants as many as their grains.
        Their names would not have been cut off
4:3   and obliterated from my presence.

²⁰ Go forth out of Babylon, flee from Chaldea!
        Make this announcement with resounding **voice**;
        broadcast it to the end of the earth.
        Say, The Lord has redeemed his servant Jacob.
49:10 ²¹ They thirsted not when he led them through arid places:
        he caused water to flow for them from the rock;
        he cleaved the rock and water gushed out.

57:21 ²² But there is no peace, says the Lord,
        for the wicked.

49   Hear me, O isles; listen, you distant peoples:
        The Lord called me before I was in the belly;
        before I was in my mother's womb,
45:4   he mentioned me by name.
     ² He has made my **mouth** like a sharp **sword**—
        in the shadow^a of his **hand** he hid me.
        He has made me into a polished **arrow**—
52:10*   in his quiver he kept me secret.

---

^b16   Compare 63:11.
^a2   Also, *guise.*

42:1

³ He said to me, You are my servant,
Israel, in whom I will be glorified.
⁴ I had thought, I have labored in vain,
I have spent my strength for nothing
and to no purpose!

50:8–9

Yet my cause rested with the Lord,
my recompense with my God.

⁵ For now the Lord has said—
he who formed me from the womb

43:1

to be his servant, to restore Jacob to him,
Israel having been gathered to him;
for I won honor in the eyes of the Lord

12:2

when my God became my strength—
⁶ he said: It is too small a thing
for you to be my servant
to raise up the tribes of Jacob
and to restore those preserved of Israel.
I will also appoint you to be a **light** to the nations,ᵇ

52:7, 10

that my **salvation** may be to the end of the earth.

⁷ Thus says the Lord,
the Redeemer and Holy One of Israel,
to him who is despised as a person,

52:14

who is abhorred by his nation,
a servant to those in authority:
Rulers shall rise up when they see you,
heads of state shall prostrate themselves,

52:13, 15

because the Lord keeps faith with you,
because the Holy One of Israel has chosen you.

⁸ Thus says the Lord:
At a favorable time I have answered you;
in the day of **salvation** I have come to your aid:
I have created you and appointed you

55:3–5

to be a **covenant** of the people,
to restore the Land and reapportion the desolate estates,
⁹ to say to the captives, Come forth!

42:6–7

and to those in **darkness**, Show yourselves!

ᵇ6   Also, *Gentiles;* compare verse 22; 42:1, 6.

They shall feed along the way
40:11   and find pasture on all barren heights;
10 they shall not hunger or thirst,
     nor be smitten by oppressive heat or by the sun:
     he who has mercy on them will guide them;
41:17–18   he will lead them by springs of water.

11 All my mountain ranges I will appoint as roads;
     my highways shall be on high.
12 See these, coming from afar, these, from the northwest,
43:5–6   and these, from the land of Sinim.
13 Shout for joy, O heavens; celebrate, O earth!
     Burst into song, O mountains!
     The Lord is comforting his people,
40:1–2   showing compassion for his afflicted.

14 But Zion said, The Lord has forsaken me,
     my Lord has forgotten me.
15 Can a woman forget her suckling infant,
     or feel no compassion for the child of her womb?
     Although these shall forget, I will not forget you.
53:5   16 See, I have engraved you on my palms;
     ʿI have sealed youᶜ to be continually before me.

17 Your sons shall hasten your ravagers away—
     those who ruined you shall depart from you.
18 Lift up your eyes and look around you;
60:4, 9   with one accord they gather and come to you.
     As surely as I live, says the Lord,
     you shall adorn yourself with them all as with jewels,
     bind them on you as does a bride.

1:7   19 For your ruins and ravaged places,
     and your land laid waste,
     shall now be too small for your inhabitants,
     despite the departure of your devourers.
54:1   20 The children born during the time of your bereavement
     shall yet say in your ears,
     This place is too cramped for us;
14:1–2   give us space in which to settle!

ᶜ16 Hebrew *ḥômōtayik, your walls,* emended to *ḥătamtîk.*

²¹ And you will say to yourself,
  Who bore me these while I was bereaved and barren?
  I was exiled, banished;
56:7–8   by whom were these reared?
  When I was left to myself, where were they?

²² Thus says my Lord the Lord:
  I will lift up my **hand** to the nations,
11:10–12   raise my **ensign** to the peoples;
  and they will bring your sons in their bosoms
  and carry your daughters on their shoulders.
60:10–11 ²³ Kings shall be your foster fathers,
  queens your nursing mothers.
  They will bow down before you,
45:14   their faces to the ground;
  they will lick the dust of your feet.
  Then shall you know that I am the Lord,
40:31   and that they who hope in me are not disappointed.

²⁴ Can the warrior's spoil be taken from him,
  or the tyrant's^d captives escape free?
10:5–6 ²⁵ Yet thus says the Lord: The warrior's spoil^e
  shall indeed be taken from him,
  and the tyrant's captives^f escape free:
  I myself will contend with your contenders,
9:4   and I will deliver your children.
²⁶ I will feed your oppressors with their own flesh;
  they shall be drunk with their own blood as with wine.
  And all flesh shall know that I the Lord am your Savior,
60:16   that your Redeemer is the Valiant One of Jacob.

50 Thus says the Lord:
  Where is your mother's bill of divorce
  with which I cast her out?
  Or to which of my creditors did I sell you?
55:7   Surely, by sinning you sold yourselves;
  because of your crimes was your mother an outcast.

---

^{d}24 So 1QIsaᵃ; LXX. MT *ṣaddîq, the righteous one's.*
^{e}25 So 1QIsaᵃ; MT *captives.*
^{f}25 So 1QIsaᵃ; MT *spoil.*

² Why was no one there when I came;
66:4   why did no one answer when I called?
Was my **hand** too short to redeem you;
have I no power to deliver?
51:10   By a mere rebuke I dry up the **Sea**;
rivers I turn into desert—
their fish become parched*ᵃ* for lack of water
and perish because of thirst.
³ I clothe the heavens with the blackness of mourning;
60:2   I put up sackcloth to cover them.

⁴ My Lord the Lord has endowed me with a learned **tongue**,
that I may know how to preach
43:22   to those grown weary a word to wake them up.
Morning by morning he wakens my ear to hear,
as at study;
⁵ my Lord the Lord has opened my ear,
and I rebel not, nor back away:
52:14   ⁶ I offered my back to smiters,
my cheeks to those who plucked out the beard;
I hid not my face from insult and spitting.

⁷ Because my Lord the Lord helps me,
I shall not be disgraced;
I have set my face like flint,
49:7   knowing I shall not be confounded.
⁸ He who vindicates me is near me.
Who has a dispute with me? Let us face one another!
Who will bring charges against me?
Let him confront me with them!
42:1   ⁹ See, my Lord the Lord sustains me.
Who then will incriminate me?
Surely all such shall wear out like a garment;
51:8   the moth shall consume them.

¹⁰ Who among you fears the Lord
and heeds the **voice** of his servant,
9:2   who, though he walk in **darkness** and have no **light**,
trusts in the name of the Lord and relies on his God?

---

*ᵃ*2   So 1QIsaᵃ; LXX. MT *turn foul.*

¹¹ But you are lighters of fires, all of you,
    who illuminate*ᵇ* with mere sparks.

59:9   Walk then by the light of your fires
    and by the sparks you have kindled.
    This shall you have from my **hand**:
    you shall lie down in agony.

51

Hear me, you followers of **righteousness**,
    seekers of the Lord:

17:10   Look to the rock from which you were cut,
    to the quarry out of which you were hewn;
    ² look to Abraham your father,
    to Sarah who bore you.

41:8–9   He was but one when I called him,
    but I blessed him by making him many.
    ³ For the Lord is comforting Zion,
    bringing solace to all her ruins;
    he is making her wilderness like Eden,

35:1–2   her desert as the garden of the Lord.
    Joyful rejoicing takes place there,
    thanksgiving with the **voice** of song.

⁴ Listen to me, my people;
    give heed to me, O my nation:

2:3, 5   The law shall go forth from me;
    my precepts shall be a light to the peoples.
    Then, suddenly, I will act:

46:12–13   ⁵ My **righteousness** shall be at hand
    and my **salvation** proceed;
    my **arms** shall judge the peoples—

42:4   the isles anticipate me, awaiting my **arm**.

⁶ Lift up your eyes to the heavens;
    look on the earth beneath:

50:3   the heavens shall vanish as by smoke,
    the earth wear out like a garment—
    its inhabitants shall die in the manner of vermin.

45:17   But my **salvation** shall be everlasting;
    my **righteousness** shall never fail.

---

*ᵇ*11   Hebrew *mě ʾazrê, gird up*, emended to *mě ʾîrê*.

21:10   ⁷ Hear me, you who know **righteousness**,
      O people in whose heart is my law:
      Do not fear the reproach of men;
      be undaunted by their ridicule.
      ⁸ For the moth shall consume them like a garment;
      moths shall devour them like wool.

62:1-2   But my **righteousness** shall endure forever,
      my **salvation** through endless generations.

      ⁹ Awake, arise; clothe yourself with power,
52:10*   O **arm** of the Lord!
      Bestir yourself, as in ancient times,
      as in generations of old.
      Was it not you who carved up Rahab,
      you who slew the **dragon**?

43:16   ¹⁰ Was it not you who dried up the **Sea**,
      the waters of the mighty deep,
      and made of ocean depths a way
      by which the redeemed might pass?

35:10   ¹¹ Let the ransomed of the Lord return!
      Let them come singing to Zion,
      their heads crowned with everlasting joy;
29:19   let them obtain joy and gladness,
      and sorrow and sighing flee away.

      ¹² I myself am your Comforter.
      Who are you that you fear mortal man,
      the children of men who shall be turned to grass?
      ¹³ Have you forgotten the Lord, your Maker—
51:16   who suspends the heavens,
      who sets the earth in place—
      that you go all day in constant dread
      of the oppressor's **rage**
      as he readies himself to wreak destruction?
14:6, 17   What is there to the **wrath** of the oppressor?
      ¹⁴ Soon now shall he who is bowed down be set free;
      he shall not die *as those destined* for the Pit,
      neither shall he want for food.
      ¹⁵ It is I the Lord your God,
      whose name is the Lord of Hosts,
5:30   who stir up the **Sea** so that its waves roar.

59:21   **16** I will put my words in your **mouth**
        and shelter you in the shadow of my **hand**,
        while I replant the heavens and set the earth in place,
        that I may say to Zion, You are my people.

52:1-2   **17** Rouse yourself; awaken and rise up, O Jerusalem,
        you who have drunk from the Lord's **hand**
        the cup of his **wrath**,
        drinking to the dregs the bowl of stupor.
      18 There was none to guide her
50:1   among all the children she bore,
        none to take her by the hand of all the sons she reared.

      19 Twofold *calamity* has befallen you:
        desolation, ruin—and who laments you?
3:25-26   famine, the **sword**—and who consoles*ᵃ* you?
      20 Your children lie in a faint at the corner of every street,
        taken in a net like bison.
      They have their fill of the **wrath** of the Lord,
        of your God's angry rebuke.

48:9-10   **21** Now therefore hear this, O wretched one,
        drunk, though not with wine.
      22 Thus says the Lord, your Lord and God,
        who defends the cause of his people:
      I am taking the cup of stupor from your **hand**;
        you shall drink no more from the bowl of my **wrath**.
60:14   **23** And I give it into the **hand** of your tormentors,
        those who said of your life,
      Lie prostrate that we may go over you—
        so that you made your back as the ground,
        a mere thoroughfare to passers-by.

52

Awake, arise; clothe yourself with power, O Zion!
      Put on your robes of glory, O Jerusalem, holy city.
      No more shall the uncircumcised and defiled enter you.
47:1-3   **2** Shake yourself free, rise from the dust;
        sit enthroned, O Jerusalem.
      Loose yourself from the bands around your neck,
61:1-3   O captive Daughter of Zion.

---

*ᵃ*19   So 1QIsaᵃ; LXX. MT *how can I console*.

³ Thus says the Lord: You were sold without price,
55:1-7   and you shall be redeemed without money.

⁴ For thus says my Lord the Lord:
At first my people went down to Egypt to sojourn there.
10:24   Then the Assyrians subjected them for nothing.
⁵ And now, what have I here? says the Lord.
My people are taken over without price;
those who govern them
3:12   ᵃact presumptuously,ᵃ says the Lord,
and my name is constantly abused all the day.

⁶ Therefore shall my people come to know my name;
in that day *they shall know*
26:8   that I, who speak, am at hand.
⁷ *Then shall they say,*
How comely upon the mountains
are the feet of the messenger announcing peace,
who brings tidings of good,
62:10-11   who heralds **salvation**,
saying to Zion, Your God reigns!

⁸ Hark! Your watchmen lift up their **voice**;
as one they cry out for joy,
40:9-10   for they shall see eye to eye
when the Lord returns *to* Zion.
10ᵇ The Lord has bared his holy **arm**
51:9-11   in the eyes of all nations,
that all ends of the earth may see
our God's **salvation**.
⁹ Break out all together into song,
you ruined places of Jerusalem:
51:3   the Lord has comforted his people;
he has redeemed Jerusalem.

¹¹ Turn away, depart;
48:20   touch nothing defiled as you leave *Babylon.*ᶜ
Come out of her and be pure,
you who bear the Lord's vessels.

ᵃ5   Also, *mock;* so 1QIsaᵃ. MT *wail.*
ᵇ10   Verse transposed; appears out of sequence in text.
ᶜ11   Hebrew *there.*

58:8   12 But you shall not leave in haste or go in flight:
the Lord will go before you,
the God of Israel behind you.

42:1, 4   13 My servant, being astute, shall be highly exalted;
he shall become exceedingly eminent:
14 just as he*d* appalled many—

57:17-19   his appearance was marred beyond human likeness,
his semblance unlike that of men—
15 So shall he yet astound*e* many nations,
rulers shutting their mouths at him—

48:6-8   what was not told them, they shall see;
what they had not heard, they shall consider.

53

Who has believed our revelation?
On whose account has the **arm** of the Lord
been revealed?

2 Like a **sapling** he grew up in his presence,
a stalk out of arid ground.
He had no distinguished appearance,

45:15   that we should notice him;
he had no *pleasing* aspect,
that we should find him attractive.

3 He was despised and disdained by men,
a man of grief, accustomed to suffering.

63:5   As one from whom men hide their faces
he was shunned, deemed by us of no merit.

4 Yet he bore our sufferings, endured our griefs,
though we thought him stricken,
smitten of God, and humbled.

43:25-27   5 But he was pierced for our transgressions,
crushed because of our iniquities;

26:12   the price of our peace he incurred,
and with his wounds we are healed.

6 We all like sheep had gone astray,
each of us headed his own way;

43:23-24   the Lord brought together upon him the iniquity of us all.

---

*d*14   Hebrew *you.*

*e*15   Or, *startle;* also *purge, sprinkle.*

⁷ He was harassed, yet submissive,
    and opened not his mouth—
43:12   like a **lamb** led to slaughter,
    like a sheep, dumb before its shearers,
    he opened not his mouth.
⁸ By arrest and trial he was taken away.
    Who can apprise his generation
    that he was cut off from the land of the living
63:8–9   for the crime of my people,
    to whom the blow was due?

⁹ He was appointed among the wicked in death,ᵃ
    among the rich was his burial;ᵇ
    yet he had done no violence,
    and deceit was not in his mouth.
¹⁰ But the Lord willed to crush him,
    causing him suffering,
24:5–6   that, if heᶜ made his life an offering for guilt,
    he might see his offspring and prolong his days,
    and that the purposes of the Lord
48:15   might prosper in his **hand**.

¹¹ He shall see the toil of his soul and be satisfied;
    because of his knowledge,
53:5–6   and by bearing their iniquities,
    shall my servant, the righteous one, vindicate many.
¹² I will assign him an inheritance among the great,
    and he shall divide the spoil with the mighty,
38:10–20   because he poured out his soul unto death,
    and was numbered with criminals—
    he bore the sins of many,
    and made intercession for the transgressors.

54 Sing, O barren woman who did not give birth;
    break into jubilant song, you who were not in labor.
    The children of the deserted wife
49:18–22   shall outnumber those of the espoused, says the Lord.

ᵃ9, ᵇ9   Terms transposed; appear reversed in text. Compare 14:20 and the lack of a burial
for the wicked and violent Tyrant.
ᶜ10   Hebrew *you*.

² Expand the site of your tent;
    extend the canopies of your dwellings.
33:20   Do not hold back; lengthen your cords
    and strengthen your stakes.
³ For you shall spread abroad
    to the right and to the left;
your offspring shall dispossess the nations
58:12   and resettle the desolate cities.

⁴ Be not fearful, for you shall not be confounded;
    be not ashamed, for you shall not be disgraced.
You shall forget the shame of your youth
    and remember no more
    the reproach of your widowhood.
62:4–5   ⁵ For he who espouses you is your Maker,
    whose name is the Lord of Hosts;
he who redeems you is the Holy One of Israel,
    who is called the God of all the earth.

49:13–14 ⁶ The Lord calls you back
    as a spouse forsaken and forlorn,
a wife married in youth only to be rejected,
    says your God.
2:6   ⁷ I forsook you indeed momentarily,
    but with loving compassion I will gather you up.
8:17   ⁸ In a fleeting surge of **anger** I hid my face from you,
    but with everlasting charity
I will have compassion on you,
    says the Lord, who redeems you.

⁹ This is to me as in the days*ᵃ* of Noah,
10:22–23   when I swore that the waters of Noah
    would no more flood the earth.
So I swear to have no more **anger** toward you,
    never again to rebuke you.
24:18–20 ¹⁰ For the mountains shall be removed
    and the hills collapse with shaking,
but my charity toward you shall never be removed,
61:8   nor my **covenant** of peace be shaken,
    says the Lord, who has compassion on you.

---

*ᵃ*9   So 1QIsaᵃ; MT *waters*.

51:21   11 Poor wretch, tempest-tossed and disconsolate!
I will lay antimony for your building stones
and sapphires for your foundations;
12 I will make your skylights of jacinth,
your gates of carbuncle,
and your entire boundary of precious stones.

59:21   13 All your children shall be taught by the Lord,
and great shall be the peace of your posterity.
14 You shall be firmly established through **righteousness**;
you will be far from oppression

41:10–13   and have no cause to fear,
far from ruin, for it shall not approach you.

15 Those who gather into mobs are not of me;

31:8–9   whoever masses against you shall fall because of you.
16 It is I who create the smith who fans the flaming coals,
forging weapons to suit his purpose;

21:2   it is I who create the ravager to destroy.
17 Whatever weapon is devised against you,
it shall not succeed;
every **tongue** that rises to accuse you,
you shall refute.
This is the heritage of the servants of the Lord,

45:24   and such is their **vindication**[b] by me, says the Lord.

55

Attention, all who thirst; come for water!
You who have no money,
come and buy food, that you may eat.

60:16   Come, buy wine and milk
with no money and at no cost.
2 Why do you spend money on what is not bread,
your labor on what does not satisfy?

1:19   Hear me well: Eat what is good,
and your souls shall enjoy abundance.

3 Give ear and come unto me;
pay heed, that your souls may live!
And I will make with you an everlasting **covenant**:

22:22–23   *my* loving fidelity toward David.

---

[b]17   Or, *righteousness;* compare verse 14.

⁴ See, I have appointed him a witness to the nations,
42:1–6   a prince and lawgiver of the peoples.
    ⁵ You will summon a nation that you did not know;
    a nation that did not know you will hasten to you—
    because of the Lord your God,
52:13   the Holy One of Israel, who gloriously endows you.

    ⁶ Inquire of the Lord while he is present;
    call upon him while he is near.
1:16   ⁷ Let the wicked forsake their ways
    and sinful men their thoughts.
    Let them return to the Lord,
    and he will have mercy on them;
44:22   to our God, who graciously pardons.

    ⁸ For my thoughts are not your thoughts,
    nor are your ways my ways, says the Lord.
    ⁹ But as the heavens are higher than the earth,
    so are my ways higher than your ways
    and my thoughts *higher* than your thoughts.
45:8   ¹⁰ And as the rains and snows descend from the sky
    and return not to it without watering the earth,
    to render it fertile and fruitful—
    providing seed for the sower and food for the eater—
44:26   ¹¹ so is the word that leaves my **mouth**:
    it does not return to me empty;
    it accomplishes what I desire,
    achieves the purpose for which I sent it.

49:9–11   ¹² You shall depart in joy and be led back in peace;
    the mountains and hills shall sing at your presence
    and the trees of the meadows all clap their hands.
    ¹³ In place of the thornbush shall come up the cypress,
41:19–20   in place of nettles, the myrtle.
    This shall serve as a testimony of the Lord,
    an everlasting sign that shall not be done away.

56

Thus says the Lord:
    Observe justice and perform righteousness,
    for soon my **salvation** will come
51:4–5   and my **righteousness** be revealed.

² Blessed is the man who does so—
the person who holds fast to them—
58:13   who keeps the Sabbath without profaning it,
who stays his hand from doing any evil.

14:1   ³ Let not the foreigner who adheres to the Lord say,
The Lord will surely exclude me from his people.
And let not the eunuch say, I am but a barren tree.
⁴ For thus says the Lord:
As for the eunuchs who keep my Sabbaths
and choose to do what I will—
42:6   holding fast to my **covenant**—
⁵ to them I will give a handclasp and a name
within the walls of my house
that is better than sons and daughters;
I will endow them with an everlasting name
66:22   that shall not be cut off.

⁶ And the foreigners who adhere to the Lord
to serve him,
26:13   who love the name of the Lord,
that they may be his servants—
all who keep the Sabbath without profaning it,
holding fast to my **covenant**—
⁷ these I will bring to my holy mountain
and gladden in my house of prayer.
Their offerings and sacrifices
19:19, 21   shall be accepted on my altar,
for my house shall be known
as a house of prayer for all nations.
⁸ Thus says my Lord the Lord,
27:13   who gathers up the outcasts of Israel:
I will gather others to those already gathered.

⁹ All you wild beasts, you animals of the forest,
come and devour!
42:18–20 ¹⁰ Their watchmen are altogether blind and unaware;
all of them are but dumb watchdogs unable to bark,
29:10   lolling seers fond of slumber.

¹¹ Gluttonous dogs, and insatiable,
such indeed are insensible shepherds.

53:6   They are all diverted to their own way,
            every one after his own advantage.
        12 Come, *they say*, let us get wine
28:7   and have our fill of liquor.
        For tomorrow will be like today, only far better!

57   The righteous*ᵃ* disappear,
            and no man gives it a thought;
        the godly are gathered out,
13:3   but no one perceives that from impending calamity
        the righteous are withdrawn.
        2 They who walk uprightly shall attain peace,
26:3   and rest in their beds.

        3 As for you, come here, you children of the sorceress,
            offspring of adulterer and harlot!
        4 At whose expense do you amuse yourselves?
            At whom do you open wide the **mouth**
3:8–9   and stick out the **tongue**?
        Surely you are born of sin, a spurious brood,
            5 who burn with lust among the oaks,
            under every burgeoning tree,
1:21   slayers of children in the gullies
            under the crags of rocks.
        6 Among the slippery stones of the ravines
            shall be your fate; they indeed are your lot.
        To them you pour out libations and make offerings.
65:6–7   How shall I be appeased of such things?

        7 On a lofty mountain
            you have made prominent your bed,
            and there you ascend to offer sacrifices.
        8 Behind doors and facades
            you have put up your emblems,
        and have exposed yourself to *others* than me:
39:1–4   mounting your bed, you have laid it wide open.
        And you bargain with those with whom you love to lie,
            your **hand** on their nakedness.*ᵇ*

---

*ᵃ*1   Or, *righteous one.*
*ᵇ*8   Literally, *foreparts.*

9 You bathe^c with oil for the king
and increase your perfumes;

47:5   you send your solicitors far abroad
and debase yourself to the depths.^d

10 Though wearied by your excessive ways,

23:16   you have not admitted despair;
you have found livelihood,
and therefore have not slackened.

11 Yet on whose account are you uneasy and apprehensive,

43:22   that you pretend and do not mention me,
nor even give me a thought?
Is it because I have so long kept silent
that you no longer fear me?

47:3   12 But I will expose your fornication
and the wantonness of your exploits.

13 When you cry out in distress,
let those who flock to you save you!

41:16   A wind shall carry all of them off;
a vapor shall take them away.

But they who seek refuge in me shall possess the earth
and receive an inheritance in my holy mountain.

62:10–11   14 It will be said: Excavate, pave a road!
Prepare the way;
remove the obstacles from the path of my people!

6:1   15 Thus says he who is highly exalted,
who abides forever, whose name is sacred:
I dwell on high in the holy place,

66:1–2   and with him who is humble and lowly in spirit—
refreshing the spirits of the lowly,
reviving the hearts of the humble.

16 I will not contend forever, nor always be angry;

12:1   the spirits and souls I have made would faint before me.

17 By his sin of covetousness I was provoked;
I struck him and hid *my face* in **anger**
when he strayed by following the ways of his heart.

---

^c9   From Hebrew root *śārâ*.
^d9   Hebrew *Sheol*.

386

38:9   ¹⁸ Yet I have seen his conduct and will recover him;
       I will guide him and amply console him
       and those who mourn for him,
      ¹⁹ who partake^e of the fruit of the lips:
53:5   Peace, well-being, to those far off
       and to those who are near,
       says the Lord who heals him.

17:12   ²⁰ But the wicked are like the raging **Sea**,
       unable to rest,
       whose waters heave up mire and mud:
48:21   ²¹ there is no peace, says my God, for the wicked.

58 Proclaim it aloud without restraint;
       raise your **voice** like a **trumpet**!
      Declare to my people their transgressions,
       to the house of Jacob their sins.
48:1   ² Yet they importune me daily,
       eager to learn my ways,
      like a nation practicing **righteousness**
      and not forsaking the precepts of their God.

      They inquire of me concerning correct ordinances,
29:13   desiring to draw nearer to God:
      ³ Why, when we fast, do you not notice?
       We afflict our bodies and you remain indifferent!
      It is because on your fast day you pursue your own ends
       and constrain all who toil for you.
3:5   ⁴ You fast amid strife and contention,
       striking out savagely with the fist.
      Your present fasts are not such
59:2   as to make your **voice** heard on high.

      ⁵ Is this the manner of fasting I have required,
       just a time for men to torment themselves?
      Is it only for bowing one's head like a reed
       and making one's bed of sackcloth and ashes?
24:5   Do you call that a fast,
       a day of the Lord's good graces?

---

^e19 Hebrew *bôrë⁾*, *create*, emended to *bôrê*.

⁶ Is not this the fast I require:
To release from wrongful bondage,
9:4   to untie the harness of the **yoke**,
to set the oppressed at liberty
and abolish all forms of subjection?
⁷ Is it not to share your food with the hungry,
25:4   to bring home the wretchedly poor,
and when you see men underclad to clothe them,
and not to neglect your own kin?

9:2   ⁸ Then shall your **light** break through like the dawn
and your healing speedily appear;
your **righteousness** will go before you,
and the glory of the Lord will be your rear guard.

⁹ Then, should you call, the Lord will respond;
30:19   should you cry, he will say, I am here.
Indeed, if you will banish servitude from among you,
and the pointing finger and offensive speech,
¹⁰ if you will give of your own to the hungry
and satisfy the needs of the oppressed,
60:1–2   then shall your **light** dawn amid **darkness**
and your twilight become as the noonday.

¹¹ The Lord will direct you continually;
he will satisfy your needs in the dearth
66:14   and bring vigor to your limbs.
And you will become like a well-watered garden,
like a spring of unfailing waters.
¹² They who came out of you will rebuild the ancient ruins;
61:4   you will restore the foundations of generations ago.
You shall be called a rebuilder of fallen walls,
a restorer of streets for resettlement.

¹³ If you will keep your feet from *trampling* the Sabbath—
from achieving your own ends on my holy day—
56:4, 6 and consider the Sabbath a delight,
the holy *day* of the Lord venerable,
and if you will honor it
by refraining from your everyday pursuits—
from occupying yourselves with your own affairs
1:13   and speaking of *business* matters—

14 then shall you delight in the Lord,

40:31   and I will make you traverse the heights of the earth
and nourish you with the heritage of Jacob your father.
By his **mouth** the Lord has spoken it.

59   Surely the Lord's **hand** has not become too short to save,
nor his ear dull of hearing!

2 It is your iniquities that separate you from your God;

1:15   your sins hide his face, so that he does not hear you.

3 For your palms are defiled with blood,
your fingers with iniquity;
your **lips** speak guile, your **tongue** utters duplicity.

46:12   4 None calls for **righteousness**;
no one sues for an honest cause.
They rely on empty words, deceitfully spoken;
they conceive misdeeds, they beget wickedness.

32:6–7   5 They hatch vipers' eggs and spin spiders' webs;
whoever eats of their eggs dies,
and if any is smashed, there emerges a serpent.

6 Their cobwebs are useless as clothing;
their fabrications are worthless for covering themselves.
Their works consist of wrongdoing;

30:12   they manipulate injurious dealings.

7 Their feet rush after evil;
they hasten to shed innocent blood.
Their thoughts are preoccupied with mischief;
havoc and disaster follow in their wake.

26:10   8 They are unacquainted with the way of perfection;
integrity is not within their bounds.
They have made crooked their paths;

57:21   none who treads them knows peace.

9 Therefore redress remains far from us
and **righteousness** is unable to reach us.
We look for **light**, but there prevails **darkness**;

50:10–11   for a glimmer *of hope*, but we walk amid gloom.

10 We grope along the borders like the blind;
we flounder like those without eyes.
We stumble at noon as in the dark of night;

8:22   in the prime of life we resemble the dead.

¹¹ We grumble like bears, all of us;
    we moan incessantly like doves.
    We expect justice when there is none;

17:10   *we look* for **salvation**, but it eludes us.

¹² For our transgressions before thee have multiplied;
    our sins testify against us.

64:6–7   Our offenses are evident; we perceive our iniquities:
¹³ willfully denying the Lord,
    backing away from following our God,
    perversely planning ways of extortion,
    conceiving in the mind and pondering
    illicit transactions.
¹⁴ And so redress is compelled to back away,

48:18   and **righteousness** to stand at a distance;
    truth stumbles in the public place
    and uprightness cannot enter.

¹⁵ When integrity is lacking,
    they who shun evil become a prey.

10:1–2   The Lord saw that there was no justice,
    and it displeased him.
¹⁶ When he saw it, he wondered
    why there was no one, not one who would intervene.

52:10*   So his own **arm** brought about **salvation** for him;
    his **righteousness** rallied to his cause.

41:2   ¹⁷ He put on **righteousness** as a breastplate
    and made **salvation** the helmet on his head;
    he clothed himself with **vengeance** for a garment
    and wrapped himself in **fury** as in a robe.
¹⁸ According to what they deserve, he will repay them:

63:2–4   **wrath** upon his adversaries,
    reprisals upon his enemies;
    to the isles he will render **retribution**.

40:5, 10   ¹⁹ From the West men will fear the Lord Omnipotent,[a]
    and from the rising of the sun his glory.

30:27–28   For he will come *upon them* like a hostile **torrent**
    impelled by the Spirit of the Lord.

---

[a]19 Literally, *the name of the Lord.*

²⁰ But he will come as Redeemer to Zion,
1:27   to those of Jacob who repent of transgression,
         says the Lord.

²¹ As for me, this is my **covenant** with them, says the Lord: My Spirit which is upon you and my words which I have placed in your **mouth** shall not depart from your **mouth**, nor from the **mouth** of your offspring, nor from the **mouth** of their offspring, says the Lord, from now on and forever.

60   Arise, shine, your **light** has dawned;
         the glory of the Lord has risen upon you!
² Although **darkness** covers the earth,
         and a thick mist the peoples,
4:5   upon you the Lord will shine;
         over you his glory shall be visible.
³ Nations will come to your **light**,
62:1–2   their rulers to the brightness of your dawn.
⁴ Lift up your eyes and look about you!
         They have all assembled to come to you:
         your sons shall arrive from afar;
49:18, 22 your daughters shall return to your side.

⁵ Then, when you see it, your face will light up,
         your heart swell with awe:
         the multitude of the **Sea** shall resort to you;
         a host of nations shall enter you.
66:20   ⁶ A myriad of camels shall cover *your land*,ᵃ
         the dromedaries of Midian and Ephah;
         all from Sheba will come,
         bearing gold and frankincense
42:10–12 and heralding the praises of the Lord.
⁷ All Kedar's flocks will gather to you,
         the rams of Nebaioth will serve you;
         they shall be accepted as offerings on my altar,
56:7   and thus I will make glorious my house of glory.
⁸ Who are these, aloft like clouds,
         flying as doves to their portals?

ᵃ6   Hebrew *you*.

⁹ From the isles they are gathering to me,
  the ships of Tarshish in the lead,

11:11–12 to bring back your children from afar,
  and with them their silver and gold,
  to the Lord Omnipotent,^b your God,
  to the Holy One of Israel,

42:21 who has made you illustrious.

¹⁰ Foreigners will rebuild your walls,
  and their rulers will minister to you.

14:6 Though I struck you in **anger**,
  I will gladly show you mercy.

¹¹ Your gates shall always remain open;
  they shall not be shut day or night,

2:2–5 that a host of nations may be brought to you
  and their rulers escorted in.

¹² And the nation or kingdom
  that will not serve you shall perish;
  such nations shall be utterly ruined.

35:2 ¹³ The splendor of Lebanon shall become yours—
  cypresses, pines, and firs together—
  to beautify the site of my sanctuary,
  to make glorious the place of my feet.

¹⁴ The sons of those who tormented you
  will come bowing before you;

49:7 all who reviled you will prostrate themselves at your feet.
  They will call you The City of the Lord,
  Zion of the Holy One of Israel.

54:6–7 ¹⁵ Although you had been forsaken and abhorred,
  with none passing through *your land*,
  yet I will make you an everlasting pride,
  the joy of generation after generation.

55:1 ¹⁶ You will suck the milk of the nations,
  suckling at the breasts of rulers.
  Then shall you know that I, the Lord,

43:3, 11 am your Savior,
  that your Redeemer is the Valiant One of Jacob.

---

*b*9 Literally, *the name of the Lord.*

¹⁷ In place of copper I will bring gold,
54:11–12   in place of iron, silver;
    in place of wood I will bring copper,
    in place of stones, iron.
    I will make peace your rulers
9:6–7   and **righteousness** your oppressors:
¹⁸ tyranny shall no more be heard of in your land,
    nor dispossession or disaster within your borders;
    you will regard **salvation** as your walls
26:1–2   and homage as your gates.

¹⁹ No longer shall the sun be your light by day,
    nor the brightness of the moon
    your illumination^c at night:
    the Lord will be your everlasting **light**
24:23   and your God your radiant glory.
²⁰ Your sun shall set no more,
    nor your moon wane:
    to you the Lord shall be an endless **light**
30:26   when your days of mourning are fulfilled.

²¹ Your entire people shall be righteous;
    they shall inherit the earth forever—
61:3   they are the branch I have planted,
    the work of my **hands**, in which I am glorified.
²² The least of them shall become a clan,
    the youngest a mighty nation.
    I the Lord will hasten it in its time.

61

    The Spirit of my Lord the Lord is upon me,
    for the Lord has anointed me
to announce good tidings to the lowly;
    he has sent me to bind up the brokenhearted,
42:1, 7   to proclaim liberty to the captives
    and the opening of the eyes to the bound,
² to herald the year of the Lord's **favor**
34:8   and the day of **vengeance** of our God,
    to comfort all who mourn:

---

^c19   So 1QIsa^a; LXX; term not in MT.

³ to endow those who mourn in Zion,
52:1   bestowing upon them a priestly headpiece
            in place of ashes,
        the festal anointing in place of mourning,
        a resplendent robe in place of a downcast spirit.
51:1, 7 They shall be called oaks of **righteousness**
        planted by the Lord for his glory.

⁴ They will rebuild the ancient ruins,
        raise up the old waste places;
54:3   they will renew the desolate cities
        demolished generations ago.
⁵ Aliens will tend and pasture your flocks;
        foreigners will be your farmhands and vinedressers.

66:21 ⁶ But you shall be called the priests of the Lord
        and referred to as the ministers of our God.
    You shall feed on the wealth of the nations
        and be gratified with their choicest provision.
66:5   ⁷ Because their*ᵃ* shame was twofold,
        and shouted insults were their lot,
    therefore in their land
        shall their inheritance be twofold
35:10   and everlasting joy be theirs.

⁸ For I the Lord love just dealings—
        but I abhor extortion in *those who* sacrifice—
    and I will appoint them a sure reward;
54:10   I will make with them an eternal **covenant.**
⁹ Their offspring shall be renowned among the nations,
        their posterity in the midst of the peoples;
    all who see them will acknowledge
        that they are of the lineage the Lord has blessed.

¹⁰ I rejoice exceedingly in the Lord;
        my soul delights in my God.
51:5–8 For he clothes me in garments of **salvation**,
        he arrays me in a robe of **righteousness**—
    like a bridegroom dressed in priestly attire,
49:18   or a bride adorned with her jewels.

ᵃ7   Hebrew *your.*

35:1 ¹¹ For as the earth brings forth its vegetation,
and as a garden causes what is sown to spring up in it,
so will my Lord the Lord

45:8 cause **righteousness** and praise to spring up
in the presence of all nations.

62 For Zion's sake I will not keep silent;
for Jerusalem's sake I will not remain still

49:6 till her **righteousness** shines like a **light**,
her **salvation** like a flaming torch.
² The nations shall behold your **righteousness**

60:1-3 and all their rulers your glory;
you shall be called by a new name
conferred by the **mouth** of the Lord.

³ Then shall you be a crown of glory
in the **hand** of the Lord,
a royal diadem in the palm of your God.

60:15 ⁴ You shall no more be called the forsaken one,
nor your land referred to as desolate;
you shall be known as she in whom I delight
and your land considered espoused.
For the Lord shall delight in you,
and your land shall be espoused.
⁵ As a young man weds a virgin,

49:22 so shall your sons wed you;
as the bridegroom rejoices over the bride,
so shall your God rejoice over you.

52:8 ⁶ I have appointed watchmen on your walls, O Jerusalem,
who shall not be silent day or night.
You who call upon the Lord, let not up
⁷ nor give him respite till he reestablishes Jerusalem
and makes it renowned in the earth.

52:10* ⁸ The Lord has sworn by his **right hand**, his mighty **arm**:
I will no more let your grain be food for your enemies,
nor shall foreigners drink the new wine you have toiled for.
⁹ Those who harvest it shall eat it,

37:30 giving praise to the Lord;
those who gather it shall drink it
within the environs of my sanctuary.

¹⁰ Pass on, go through gates;

40:3–5   prepare the way for the people!

Excavate, pave a highway cleared of stones;

11:10, 12   raise the **ensign** to the nations!

¹¹ The Lord has made proclamation to the end of the earth:

Tell the Daughter of Zion,

See, your **Salvation** comes,

40:10   his reward with him, his work preceding him.

¹² They shall be called the holy people,

the redeemed of the Lord;

and you shall be known as in demand,

52:9   a city never deserted.

63

Who is this coming from Edom in red-stained garments?

Who is this from Bozrah, arrayed in majesty,

pressing forward in the strength of his power?

It is I, who am mighty to save,

41:1–2   announcing **righteousness**!

² Why are you clothed in red, your garments

like those who tread *grapes* in the winepress?

³ Alone I have trodden out a vatful;

of the nations no one was with me.

I trod them down in my **anger**;

10:5–6   in my **wrath** I trampled them.

Their lifeblood spattered my garments,

and I have stained my whole attire.

⁴ For I had resolved on a day of **vengeance**,

and the year of my redeemed had come.

59:15–16   ⁵ I glanced around, but none would lend help;

I glared, but no one would assist.

So my own **arm** brought about **salvation** for me,

and my **wrath**, it assisted me.

⁶ I trod nations underfoot in my **anger**;

34:2, 8   I made them drunk by my **rage**

when I cast their glory to the ground.

⁷ I will recount in praise of the Lord

the Lord's loving favors,

26:12   according to all that the Lord has done for us,

according to the great kindness
he has mercifully and most graciously
38:19   rendered the house of Israel.

8 For he thought, Surely they are my people,
sons who will not play false;
and so he became their Savior:
9 with all their troubles he troubled himself,
37:36   the angel of his presence delivering them.
In his love and compassion
he himself redeemed them;
he lifted them up and carried them
46:3-4   all the days of old.
10 Yet they rebelled and grieved his holy Spirit,
till he became their enemy
1:2, 24   and himself fought against them.

11 Then his people*a* recalled the days of Moses of old:*b*
Where is he who brought them up out of the Sea
40:11   with the shepherd of his flock?
Where is he who put into him his holy Spirit,
12 who made his glorious **arm** proceed
at the **right hand** of Moses,
who divided the waters before them,
making an everlasting name for himself
51:9-10   13 when he led them through the deep?
Like the horse of the desert, they stumbled not;
14 like cattle descending *the slopes of* ravines,
it was the Spirit of the Lord that guided them.*c*
So thou didst lead thy people, O *Lord*,
12:4-6   acquiring illustrious renown.

15 O look down from heaven,
from thy holy and glorious celestial abode,
57:15   and behold!
Where now are thy **zeal** and thy might?
The yearnings of thy bosom and thy compassion
are withheld from us!

---

*a*11   Term transposed; in text follows *Moses.*
*b*11   Literally, *of old, of Moses.*
*c*14   So LXX; MT *gave them rest.*

¹⁶ Surely thou art our Father!

41:8–9   Though Abraham does not know us
or Israel recognize us,
thou, O Lord, art our Father;
Our Redeemer from Eternity is thy name.

65:2   ¹⁷ Why, O Lord, hast thou made us stray from thy ways,
hardening our hearts so that we do not fear thee?
Relent,*ᵈ* for the sake of thy servants,
the tribes that are thine inheritance.

¹⁸ But a little while had thy people possessed the holy place

64:10–11   when our enemies trod down thy sanctuary.

¹⁹ We have become as those
whom thou hast never ruled

43:26–28   and who have not been known by thy name.

64 O that thou wouldst rend the heavens and descend,
the mountains melting at thy presence—
² as when fire is lit for boiling water,
which bubbles over from the heat—
to make thyself known to thine adversaries,

2:19, 21   the nations trembling at thy presence—
³ as when thou didst perform awesome things
unexpected by us: thy descent *of old*,

31:4   when the mountains quaked before thee!
⁴ Never has it been heard or perceived by the ear,
nor has any eye seen a God besides thee,

33:2–3   who acts thus on behalf of those who wait for him.

⁵ But thou woundest those of us
who joyfully perform **righteousness**,
who remember thee by *following* thy ways—
*ᵃ*that in them we might ever be saved.*ᵃ*

42:24   Alas, thou wast roused to **anger** when we sinned,
⁶ and now we have altogether become as those defiled,
the sum of our righteousness as a menstruous rag.
We are decaying like leaves, all of us;

4:4   our sins, like a wind, sweep us away.

---

*ᵈ*17   Or, *Return.*

*ᵃ*5   Phrase transposed; in text follows *sinned.*

⁷ Yet none calls upon thy name,

59:1-2   or rouses himself to take hold of thee.
   For thou hast hidden thy face from us
   and enfeebled*ᵇ* us at the **hand** of our iniquities.

63:16   ⁸ Nevertheless, thou art our Father, O Lord;
   we are the clay and thou art the potter,
   and we are all alike the work of thy **hands.**ᶜ

   ⁹ Be not exceedingly angry, O Lord;

57:16   remember not iniquity forever.
   See, consider that we are all thy people!

   ¹⁰ Thy holy cities have become a wilderness;

6:11   Zion is a desert, Jerusalem a desolation.

   ¹¹ Our glorious holy temple
   where our fathers praised thee
   has been burned with **fire,**

1:7   and all places dear to us lie in ruins.

   ¹² At all this, O Lord, wilt thou restrain thyself,
   in silence letting us suffer so exceedingly?

65

I was available to those who did not inquire of me;ᵃ
I was accessible to those who did not seek me.
I said, Here am I; I am here,

55:6-7   to a nation that did not invoke my name.

   ² I held out my **hands** all the day to a defiant people,
   who walk in ways that are not good,
   following their own imagination—

   ³ a people who constantly provoke me to my face,

1:29   sacrificing in parks, making smoke upon bricks,

   ⁴ who sit in sepulchres, spend nights in hideouts,
   who eat swine's flesh,

66:17   their bowls full of polluted broth,

   ⁵ who think, Keep your distance,
   don't come near me; I am holier than thou!
   Such are a smoke to my nostrils,

66:24   a fire smoldering all day long.

ᵇ7   Literally, *melted.*
ᶜ8   So 1QIsaᵃ; LXX. Compare 60:21; *passim.* MT *hand.*
ᵃ1   So 1QIsaᵃ; LXX; term not in MT.

⁶ See, it is written before me that I will not be still

3:11   till I have paid back^b into their bosom

⁷ their^c own iniquities and their^c fathers' alike,
       says the Lord.
     To those who kindle sacrifice in the mountains,

57:5–6   who affront me on the hills, I will measure out
       in their laps the payment that has accrued.

⁸ Thus says the Lord:
     As when there is juice in a cluster of grapes
   and someone says, Don't destroy it, it is still good,
       so I will do on behalf of my servants

48:9   by not destroying everything:

⁹ I will extract offspring out of Jacob,
       and out of Judah heirs of my mountains;
   my chosen ones shall inherit them,
     my servants shall dwell there.

30:23   ¹⁰ Sharon shall become pasture for flocks,
       and the Valley of Achor a resting place
   for the herds of my people who seek me.

1:28   ¹¹ As for you who forsake the Lord
       and forget my holy mountain,
   who spread tables for Luck
       and pour mixed wines for Fortune,

34:6–7   ¹² I will destine you to the **sword**;
     all of you shall succumb to the slaughter.
   For when I called, you did not respond;

50:2   when I spoke, you would not give heed.
   You did what was evil in my eyes;
     you chose to do what was not my will.

¹³ Therefore thus says my Lord the Lord:

55:1–2   My servants shall eat indeed,
       while you shall hunger;
   my servants shall drink indeed,
       while you shall thirst;

65:18   my servants shall rejoice indeed,
       while you shall be dismayed.

---

^b6   Text adds *and paid back,* a probable duplication.
^c7, ^c7   So LXX; MT *your.*

66:14　　¹⁴ My servants shall shout indeed, for gladness of heart,
　　　　while you shall cry out with heartbreak,
　　　　howling from brokenness of spirit.
　　　¹⁵ Your name shall be left
1:10　　　to serve my chosen ones as a curse
　　　　when my Lord the Lord slays you.
　　　But his servants he will call by a different name.

　　　¹⁶ Those of them who invoke blessings
　　　　on themselves in the earth shall do so by the true God,
　　　and those of them who swear oaths in the earth
45:23　　shall do so by the God of truth.
　　　The troubles of the past shall be forgotten
　　　and hidden from my eyes.

66:22　　¹⁷ See, I create new heavens and a new earth;
　　　　former events shall not be remembered
　　　or recalled to mind.
　　　¹⁸ Rejoice, then, and be glad forever in what I create.
　　　See, I create Jerusalem to be a delight
60:15　　and its people a joy.

　　　¹⁹ I will delight in Jerusalem, rejoice in my people;
　　　no more shall be heard there
　　　the sound of weeping or the cry of distress.
　　　²⁰ No more shall there be infants alive but a few days,
13:15–16　or the aged who do not live out their years;
　　　those who die young shall be a hundred years old,
　　　and those who fail to reach a hundred shall be accursed.

　　　²¹ When men build houses, they will dwell in them;
　　　when they plant vineyards, they will eat their fruit.
　　　²² They shall not build so that others may dwell,
62:8–9　　or plant so that others may eat.
　　　The lifetime of my people shall be as the lifetime of a tree;
　　　my chosen ones shall outlast the work of their hands.

　　　²³ They shall not exert themselves in vain,
　　　or bear children doomed for calamity.
61:9　　For they are of the lineage of those blessed by the Lord,
　　　and their posterity with them.
58:9　　²⁴ Before they call I will reply;
　　　while they are yet speaking I will respond.

²⁵ The wolf and the lamb will graze alike,
11:6–9   and the lion will eat straw like the ox;
as for the serpent, dust shall be its food:
there shall be no harm or injury done
throughout my holy mountain, says the Lord.

66 Thus says the Lord:
The heavens are my throne
and the earth is my footstool.
What house would you build me?
What would serve me as a place of residence?
40:12, 22   ² These are all things my **hand** has made,
and thus all came into being, says the Lord.
And yet I have regard for those
57:15   who are of a humble and contrite spirit
and who are vigilant for my word.

³ But whoever slaughters an ox
is as one who kills a man,
43:23   and whoever sacrifices a lamb,
as one who breaks a dog's neck;
whoever presents a grain offering
is as one who offers swine's blood,
and whoever burns incense,
as one who venerates idols.
65:2   Just as they have preferred to go their own ways,
their souls delighting in their abominations,
⁴ so will I prescribe intrigues for them
51:13   and bring upon them the thing they dread.
For when I called, no one responded;
when I spoke, none gave heed.
They did what was evil in my eyes;
65:12   they chose to do what was not my will.

⁵ Hear the word of the Lord,
50:4   you who are vigilant for his word:
Your brethren who abhor you,
and exclude you because of my name, say,
Let the Lord manifest his glory,
that we may see cause for your joy!
41:11   But it is they who shall suffer shame.

⁶ Hark, a tumult from the city, a noise from the temple!

11:4   It is the **voice** of the Lord
paying his enemies what is due them.

⁷ Before she is in labor, she gives birth;

9:6   before her ordeal overtakes her, she delivers a son!
⁸ Who has heard the like,
or who has seen such things?
Can the earth labor but a day

55:5   and a nation be born at once?
For as soon as she was in labor,
Zion gave birth to her children.
⁹ Shall I bring to a crisis and not bring on birth?
says the Lord.

45:11   When it is I who cause the birth,
shall I hinder it? says your God.

¹⁰ Rejoice with Jerusalem and be glad for her,
all who love her;

65:18   join in her celebration, all who mourn for her.
¹¹ From now on nurse contentedly
at her consoling breasts;
draw at your pleasure

49:23   from the abundance of her bosom.ᵃ

¹² For thus says the Lord: See,
I will extend peace to her like a river,

60:5, 11   the bountyᵇ of the nations like a stream in flood.
Then shall you nurse and be carried upon the hip
and dandled on the knees.
¹³ As one who is comforted by his mother
I will comfort you;

49:13   for Jerusalem you shall be comforted.

¹⁴ Your heart shall rejoice to see it,
your limbs flourish like sprouting grass,
when the **hand** of the Lord

65:13–15   shall be manifest among his servants
and his **rage** among his enemies.

ᵃ11 Or, *glory*.
ᵇ12 Or, *glory*.

¹⁵ See, the Lord comes with **fire**,
19:1   his chariots like a whirlwind,
        to retaliate in furious **anger**,
        to rebuke with conflagrations of **fire**.
¹⁶ For with **fire** and with his **sword** shall the Lord
34:5, 9   execute judgment on all flesh,
        and those slain by the Lord shall be many.

¹⁷ As for the cultists who fornicate in the parks, following one in the center, who eat the flesh of swine and prawn and rodents— they with [their practices and ideas]^c shall be made an end of, says the Lord.

¹⁸ For I will come^d to gather all nations and tongues, that they may approach and behold my glory.

¹⁹ And I will set a mark upon them, sending those of them who survive to the nations that had not heard the news concerning me, nor seen my glory—to Tarshish, Pul, and Lud (the archers), to Tubal and Javan, and to the distant isles. And they shall declare my glory among the nations ²⁰ and shall bring back all your brethren from throughout the nations to Jerusalem my holy mountain, says the Lord, as offerings to the Lord—on horses, in chariots and wagons, and on mules and dromedaries—just as the Israelites brought offerings in pure vessels to the house of the Lord. ²¹ Of them likewise I will accept men to be priests and Levites, says the Lord.

²² And as the new heavens and the new earth which I make shall endure before me, says the Lord, so shall your offspring and name endure. ²³ And New Moon after New Moon, Sabbath after Sabbath, all flesh shall come to worship before me, says the Lord. ²⁴ And they shall go out and look upon the corpses of the people who transgressed against me, whose worms do not die and whose **fire** shall not be extinguished. They shall be a horror to all flesh.

---

^c17   Terms brought up from verse 18, where they follow *For I*.
^d18   Hebrew *bā'â, come* (fem. sing.), emended to *bā'*.

SELECTED REFERENCE WORKS

Alcalay, Reuben. *The Complete English—Hebrew, Hebrew—English Dictionary.* Jerusalem: Massada, 1970.

Biblia Hebraica. Ed. Rudolph Kittel. Stuttgart: Württembergische Bibelanstalt, 1973.

Botterweck, G. Johannes, and Helmer Ringgren. *Theological Dictionary of the Old Testament.* Grand Rapids, Mich.: Eerdmans, 1977.

Brown, Francis, S. R. Driver, and Charles A. Briggs. *A Hebrew and English Lexicon of the Old Testament.* Oxford: Clarendon Press, 1974.

Burrows, Millar. *The Dead Sea Scrolls of St. Mark's Monastery.* Vol. 1. New Haven, Conn.: American Schools of Oriental Research, 1950.

Even-Shoshan, Avraham. *Hamilon Hehadash.* 3 vols. Jerusalem: Sivan, 1975.

Guillaume, Alfred. "Some Readings in the Dead Sea Scroll of Isaiah." *Journal of Biblical Literature* 76 (1957): 40–43.

Hulst, A. R. *Old Testament Translation Problems.* Leiden, Netherlands: Brill, 1960.

Interpreter's Bible. Vol. 5. Nashville: Abingdon, 1956.

James, Forrest D. "A Critical Examination of the Text of Isaiah." Ph.D. diss., Boston University, 1959.

Mandelkern, Solomon. *Veteris Testamenti Concordantiae.* Tel Aviv: Schocken, 1974.

Rosenbloom, Joseph R. *The Dead Sea Isaiah Scroll: A Literary Analysis.* Grand Rapids, Mich.: Eerdmans, 1970.

Septuagint Version. Grand Rapids, Mich.: Zondervan, 1970.

Young, Robert. *Analytical Concordance to the Bible.* New York: Funk and Wagnall's, 1973.

A COMPREHENSIVE CONCORDANCE
OF THE BOOK OF ISAIAH

ABANDONED
10:14   as one gathers abandoned eggs;
17:9   which they abandoned before the
32:14   for the palaces shall lie abandoned,
ABASED
2:11   be lowered and man's pride abased;
2:17   haughtiness of men shall be abased,
ABATED
5:25   for all this his anger is not abated;
9:12   for all this his anger is not abated;
9:17   for all this his anger is not abated;
9:21   for all this his anger is not abated;
10:4   for all this his anger is not abated;
ABHOR
61:8   but I abhor extortion in those who
66:5   Your brethren who abhor you,
ABHORRED
49:7   who is abhorred by his nation,
60:15   you had been forsaken and abhorred,
ABIDE
26:19   you who abide in the dust:
32:16   righteousness abide in the farmland.
33:14   among us can abide eternal burning?
ABIDES
57:15   who abides forever, whose name is
ABILITY
10:13   I have done it by my own ability
ABLAZE
9:18   Wickedness shall be set ablaze like
27:4   and altogether set them ablaze.
33:12   down like thorns and set ablaze.
ABLE
36:8   if you are able to put riders on them.
36:18   nations able to save their lands out of
ABODE
1:21   righteousness made its abode in her,
16:5   be set up in the abode of David,
33:20   the abode of peace—an immovable
63:15   holy and glorious celestial abode,
ABOLISH
58:6   and abolish all forms of subjection?

ABOLISHED
36:7   and altars Hezekiah abolished,
ABOLISHING
3:12   abolishing your traditional ways.
25:8   by abolishing Death forever.
ABOMINATION
41:24   you is himself an abomination.
44:19   Am I not making an abomination of
ABOMINATIONS
66:3   delighting in their abominations,
ABRAHAM
29:22   who redeemed Abraham,
41:8   of Abraham my beloved friend,
51:2   look to Abraham your father,
63:16   Though Abraham does not know us
ABROAD
16:8   branches spread abroad across the
54:3   For you shall spread abroad
57:9   you send your solicitors far abroad
ABSURD
19:11   advisers give absurd counsel.
ABUNDANCE
33:23*   shall spoil in abundance be divided,
55:2   your souls shall enjoy abundance.
66:11   from the abundance of her bosom.
ABUNDANT
1:11   abundant sacrifices to me? says the
30:23   may be rich and abundant.
ABUSED
52:5   name is constantly abused all the day
ACACIAS
41:19   I will bring cedars and acacias,
ACCEPT
29:24   who murmured accept instruction.
66:21   Of them likewise I will accept men to
ACCEPTED
41:9   I have accepted you and not rejected
56:7   shall be accepted on my altar,
60:7   be accepted as offerings on my altar,
ACCEPTS
41:24   whoever accepts you is himself an

---

*Verses marked by an asterisk appear out of sequence in the text of Isaiah.

ACCESSIBLE
65:1 I was accessible to those who did not
ACCOMPANYING
34:15 each one accompanying her mate.
ACCOMPLICES
1:23 accomplices of robbers:
ACCOMPLISH
9:7 Lord of Hosts will accomplish it.
37:32 Lord of Hosts will accomplish it.
46:10 I accomplish all my will.
ACCOMPLISHED
10:12 accomplished his work in
26:12 even all that we have accomplished
ACCOMPLISHES
44:26 accomplishes the aims of his
55:11 it accomplishes what I desire,
ACCOMPLISHING
41:4 Who is at work accomplishing this,
ACCORD
1:23 with one accord they love bribes
7:19 settle with one accord
34:4 shed themselves with one accord,
49:18 with one accord they gather and come
ACCORDING
59:18 According to what they deserve,
63:7 according to all that the Lord has
63:7 according to the great kindness
ACCOUNT
14:9 on your account she roused all the
16:14 left, and those of no account.
21:16 On account of this, my Lord said
37:24 On account of my vast chariotry
38:9 Hezekiah king of Judah's account of
41:24 It is clear you are of no account,
48:9 on account of my renown
48:11 For my own sake, on my own account,
53:1 On whose account has the arm of the
57:11 Yet on whose account are you uneasy
ACCRUED
65:7 laps the payment that has accrued.
ACCURSED
65:20 to reach a hundred shall be accursed.
ACCUSATIONS
32:7 with false slogans and accusations
ACCUSE
54:17 every tongue that rises to accuse you,
ACCUSTOMED
53:3 man of grief, accustomed to suffering.
ACHIEVES
55:11 achieves the purpose for which I sent
ACHIEVING
58:13 achieving your own ends on my holy
ACHOR
65:10 and the Valley of Achor a resting
ACKNOWLEDGE
61:9 all who see them will acknowledge

ACKNOWLEDGED
12:5 let it be acknowledged throughout the
ACQUAINTING
40:14 acquainting him with the way of
ACQUIRED
15:7 The surplus they have acquired,
ACQUIRING
63:14 acquiring illustrious renown.
ACQUIT
5:23 who acquit the guilty for a bribe,
ACRE
5:10 A ten-acre vineyard shall yield
ACROSS
16:8 spread abroad across the sea.
18:2 in swift craft across the water.
24:14 and those from across the sea
ACT
21:2 the traitor in the act of treachery,
28:21 to perform his act, his unwonted act,
51:4 Then, suddenly, I will act:
52:5 act presumptuously, says the
ACTED
48:3 suddenly, I acted and they came
ACTIONS
3:8 their tongue and their actions
ACTS
64:4 who acts thus on behalf of those who
ADD
29:1 Though you add year to year,
38:5 I will add fifteen years to your life.
ADDER'S
11:8 infant will play near the adder's den,
ADDING
1:5 by adding to your waywardness?
30:1 only adding sin to sin!
ADDRESSED
7:10 Again the Lord addressed Ahaz, and
8:5 The Lord addressed me again, and
ADEQUATE
40:16 its beasts be adequate for sacrifice.
ADHERE
14:1 and proselytes will adhere to them
56:6 the foreigners who adhere to the Lord
ADHERES
56:3 foreigner who adheres to the Lord say
ADJOINING
19:7 vegetation adjoining canals and
ADJUDGE
29:21 at a word adjudge a man to be guilty,
ADMITTED
57:10 you have not admitted despair;
ADMONISHED
8:11 clasping my hand, and admonished
ADOLESCENTS
3:4 will make adolescents their rulers;
ADOPT
44:5 and adopt the name Israel.

ADORATION
44:17 they bow in adoration and pray
ADORE
 2:8 they adore the works of their hands,
 2:20 made for themselves to adore.
44:15 they create gods which they adore,
ADORN
49:18 you shall adorn yourself with them
ADORNED
61:10 or a bride adorned with her jewels.
ADRAMMELECH
37:38 Adrammelech and Sharezer slew him
ADULTERER
57:3 offspring of adulterer and harlot!
ADVANCE
10:32 and signal the advance
13:2 Beckon them to advance
37:33 He shall not advance against it with
ADVANCES
10:28 He advances on Aiath, passes through
ADVANTAGE
56:11 every one after his own advantage.
ADVERSARIES
 1:24 avenge me of my adversaries,
 9:11 when he stirs up their adversaries:
41:11 adversaries shall come to nought,
59:18 wrath upon his adversaries,
64:2 thyself known to thine adversaries,
ADVERSITY
30:20 Lord give you the bread of adversity
ADVISERS
 3:3 advisers, skilled craftsmen, and
19:11 Pharaoh's advisers give absurd
AFAR
10:3 holocaust overtakes you from afar?
30:27 Lord Omnipotent coming from afar!
43:6 Bring my sons from afar
49:12 See these, coming from afar, these,
60:4 your sons shall arrive from afar;
60:9 bring back your children from afar,
AFFAIRS
58:13 yourselves with your own affairs
AFFLICT
 3:17 the Lord will afflict the scalps
58:3 We afflict our bodies and you remain
AFFLICTED
49:13 showing compassion for his afflicted.
AFFLICTION
30:20 and the water of affliction,
48:10 you in the crucible of affliction.
AFFLUENT
 5:17 eat in the ruins of the affluent.
AFFRONT
 3:8 an affront to his glory before his very
65:7 who affront me on the hills, I will
AFLAME
13:8 aghast, their faces set aflame.

AFRAID
 8:12 be not afraid or awed by the
10:24 be not afraid of the Assyrians,
19:16 be as women, fearful and afraid
37:6 says the Lord: Be not afraid because
40:9 Make yourself heard, be not afraid;
41:14 Be not afraid, you worms of Jacob;
44:2 Be not afraid, O Jacob, my servant,
AGE
46:4 Even to your old age, I am present;
AGED
47:6 the aged you weighed down heavily
65:20 the aged who do not live out their
AGES
34:10 through endless ages none shall
AGGRESSORS
16:4 refuge to them from the aggressors!
AGHAST
13:8 Men will look at one another aghast,
AGONY
13:8 be terrified, in throes of agony,
21:3 throes of agony have seized me like a
50:11 you shall lie down in agony.
AHAZ
 1:1 Jotham, Ahaz, and Hezekiah, kings
 7:1 When Ahaz son of Jotham, the son
 7:3 Go out and meet Ahaz, you and
 7:10 Again the Lord addressed Ahaz, and
 7:12 But Ahaz said, I will not.
14:28 In the year King Ahaz died,
38:8 afternoon sun on the dial of Ahaz
AIATH
10:28 He advances on Aiath, passes through
AID
41:6 come to one another's aid,
49:8 I have come to your aid:
AIMS
44:26 accomplishes the aims of his
AIRS
 3:16 and put on airs, painting their eyes,
ALARM
10:29 Ramah is in a state of alarm,
15:4 They will sound the alarm
ALARMED
32:11 Be alarmed, you complacent women;
ALAS
 1:4 Alas, a nation astray, a people
64:5 Alas, thou wast roused to anger when
ALERT
21:7 He must be most vigilant, fully alert.
ALIENS
 1:7 native soil is devoured by aliens in
61:5 Aliens will tend and pasture your
ALIVE
 6:13 is felled, whose stump remains alive,
 7:21 will keep alive a young cow
65:20 no more shall there be infants alive

ALLEGIANCE
45:23   and every tongue swear allegiance.
ALLIANCES
30:1   making alliances without my approval
ALLIES
31:2   miscreants and allies of evildoers.
ALLOTS
34:17   who allots them an inheritance,
ALLOY
1:25   and remove all your alloy.
ALMIGHTY
13:6   as a violent blow from the Almighty.
40:26   Because he is almighty and all
ALOFT
46:1   the images you bore aloft
46:7   They bear it aloft, carrying it on
60:8   Who are these, aloft like clouds,
ALONE
2:11   the Lord alone shall be exalted in
2:17   the Lord alone shall be exalted in
26:13   but thee alone we recall by name.
37:16   alone art God over all the kingdoms
37:20   may know that thou alone art Lord.
44:24   who alone suspends the heavens,
45:24   By the Lord alone come vindication
63:3   Alone I have trodden out a vatful;
ALONG
14:11   along with the music of your lyres.
19:7   all things sown along irrigation
40:11   that give milk he leads gently along.
49:9   They shall feed along the way
59:10   We grope along the borders like the
ALOOF
30:18   toward you he will remain aloof.
ALOUD
58:1   Proclaim it aloud without restraint;
ALREADY
38:15   when he has already spoken for me,
56:8   others to those already gathered.
ALTAR
6:6   with tongs from the altar.
19:19   In that day there shall be an altar
27:9   chalkstone all altar stones,
29:2   she becomes as my altar hearth.
36:7   worship only at this altar?
56:7   shall be accepted on my altar,
60:7   be accepted as offerings on my altar,
ALTARS
17:8   and regard not the altars,
36:7   and altars Hezekiah abolished,
ALTITUDE
14:14   I will ascend above the altitude of
ALTOGETHER
1:28   shall be altogether shattered
15:3   they will altogether wail and give way
22:3   Your chiefs, altogether in flight,
27:4   and altogether set them ablaze.

46:2   Such gods altogether sag and bow
56:10   Their watchmen are altogether blind
64:6   we have altogether become as those
AMASS
29:8   amass to fight against Mount Zion.
AMASSED
29:7   amassed to fight against Ariel
AMID
18:4   amid the fever of reaping.
24:9   Men no longer drink wine amid song;
45:19   to seek me amid chaos.
58:4   You fast amid strife and contention,
58:10   shall your light dawn amid darkness
59:9   but we walk amid gloom.
AMISS
27:3   lest anything be amiss.
AMMONITES
11:14   and the Ammonites will obey them.
AMORITES
17:9   of the Hivites and Amorites
AMOUNT
41:24   your works amount to nothing.
AMOZ
1:1   The vision of Isaiah the son of Amoz
2:1   Isaiah the son of Amoz saw in vision:
13:1   Isaiah the son of Amoz saw in vision:
20:2   Isaiah the son of Amoz, saying,
37:2   the prophet Isaiah the son of Amoz.
37:21   Isaiah the son of Amoz sent word
38:1   the prophet Isaiah the son of Amoz
AMPLE
30:23   graze in ample pasture lands,
30:33   is its fire pit and ample its pyre;
AMPLY
23:2   who were amply replenished
57:18   will guide him and amply console him
AMULETS
3:20   zodiac signs and charm amulets,
AMUSE
57:4   expense do you amuse yourselves?
AMUSEMENT
13:22   creatures from its amusement halls.
32:13   Mourn for all the amusement houses
ANATHOTH
10:30   Laishah; answer her, Anathoth!
ANCIENT
23:7   your festive city of ancient origin,
24:5   set at nought the ancient covenant.
46:10   from ancient times things not yet
51:9   Bestir yourself, as in ancient times,
58:12   will rebuild the ancient ruins;
61:4   They will rebuild the ancient ruins,
ANGEL
37:36   Then the angel of the Lord went out
63:9   the angel of his presence delivering
ANGER
5:25   the anger of the Lord is kindled

5:25 for all this his anger is not abated;
7:4 the burning anger of Rezin and Aram
9:12 for all this his anger is not abated;
9:17 for all this his anger is not abated;
9:21 for all this his anger is not abated;
10:4 for all this his anger is not abated;
10:5 the Assyrian, the rod of my anger!
10:25 For my anger will very soon come to
12:1 thine anger is turned away
13:3 my anger is not upon those
13:9 a cruel outburst of anger and wrath
13:13 by the anger of the Lord of Hosts
14:6 struck down the nations in anger,
27:4 I have no more anger toward her.
28:21 stirred to anger, as in the Valley of
42:25 So in the heat of his anger
54:8 a fleeting surge of anger I hid my face
54:9 I swear to have no more anger toward
57:17 him and hid my face in anger
60:10 Though I struck you in anger,
63:3 I trod them down in my anger;
63:6 I trod nations underfoot in my anger;
64:5 thou wast roused to anger when we
66:15 to retaliate in furious anger,
ANGLERS
19:8 anglers in canals bemoan themselves;
ANGRY
12:1 thou hast been angry with me,
51:20 of your God's angry rebuke.
57:16 contend forever, nor always be angry;
64:9 Be not exceedingly angry, O Lord;
ANGUISH
8:22 scene of anguish and gloom;
9:1 who have been in anguish for her.
14:3 relief from grief and anguish
23:5 men will be in anguish at the report.
32:10 you shall be in anguish, O carefree
ANIMALS
13:21 But wild animals will infest it,
32:14 the playground of wild animals,
46:1 piled as burdens on weary animals.
56:9 All you wild beasts, you animals of
ANKLETS
3:18 the anklets, head ornaments and
ANNEXED
18:2 rivers have annexed their lands.
18:7 rivers have annexed their lands,
ANNEXING
37:11 have done, annexing all lands.
ANNIHILATE
10:7 His purpose shall be to annihilate
ANNIHILATED
1:28 who forsake the Lord are annihilated.
13:9 sinners may be annihilated from it.
ANNIHILATION
10:22 although annihilation is decreed,

ANNOUNCE
40:2 Announce to her that she has served
40:6 A voice said, Announce it,
40:6 I asked, How shall I announce it?
48:6 I announce to you new things,
61:1 to announce good tidings
ANNOUNCED
41:26 Who announced this beforehand, so
48:3 than I caused them to be announced.
48:5 I announced them to you before they
ANNOUNCEMENT
48:20 Make this announcement with
ANNOUNCING
52:7 the messenger announcing peace,
63:1 announcing righteousness!
ANNULS
44:25 who annuls the predictions of
ANOINTED
45:1 Thus says the Lord to his anointed,
61:1 for the Lord has anointed me
ANOINTING
61:3 festal anointing in place of mourning,
ANSWER
10:30 Hear her, Laishah; answer her,
30:19 he will answer you as soon as he
36:21 commanded them not to answer him.
41:17 I the Lord will answer their want;
41:28 who could answer a word.
46:7 it does not answer; it cannot
50:2 why did no one answer when I called?
ANSWERED
49:8 a favorable time I have answered you;
ANSWERS
29:11 Please read this, and he answers,
29:12 he answers, I am unlearned.
ANTICIPATE
26:8 we anticipate thee, O Lord;
51:5 isles anticipate me, awaiting my arm.
ANTICIPATING
14:9 anticipating your arrival;
ANTIMONY
54:11 I will lay antimony for your building
ANVIL
41:7* urges him who pounds the anvil.
APART
13:18 bows shall tear apart the young.
43:11 apart from me there is no savior.
44:6 apart from me there is no God.
44:8 Is there a God, then, apart from me?
45:5 apart from me there is no God.
45:21 apart from whom there is no God?
APOSTASY
1:4 they have lapsed into apostasy.
APPALLED
20:5 Men shall be appalled and perplexed
52:14 just as he appalled many—

APPEAL
1:17 appeal on behalf of the widow.
15:4 their appeal shall be heard as far as
APPEAR
18:4 and when the rainclouds appear
30:25 shall appear streams of running
46:5 that we should appear similar?
58:8 and your healing speedily appear;
APPEARANCE
52:14 his appearance was marred beyond
53:2 He had no distinguished appearance,
APPEASED
57:6 shall I be appeased of such things?
APPLY
38:21* packs and apply them to the swelling
APPOINT
10:6 appoint him over the people
21:6 Go and appoint a watchman
22:21 appoint him your jurisdiction.
41:27 I will appoint him as a herald of
49:6 I will also appoint to you to be a light
49:11 ranges I will appoint as roads;
61:8 I will appoint them a sure reward;
APPOINTED
9:6 to us a child is born, a son appointed,
42:6 I have created you and appointed you
43:3 Egypt I have appointed as ransom for
49:8 I have created you and appointed you
53:9 He was appointed among the wicked
55:4 I have appointed him a witness to the
62:6 I have appointed watchmen on your
APPOINTEST
26:14 thou appointest them to destruction,
APPOINTING
44:7 in appointing a people from of old
45:12 appointing all their host.
APPRAISED
33:18 Where are the ones who appraised the
APPREHEND
3:6 will a man apprehend a kinsman
APPREHENSIVE
57:11 are you uneasy and apprehensive,
APPRISE
53:8 Who can apprise his generation
APPRISED
33:13 be apprised of my might!
APPROACH
29:13 approach me with the mouth
54:14 for it shall not approach you.
66:18 approach and behold my glory.
APPROVAL
30:1 making alliances without my approval
APPROVE
1:13 I cannot approve.
AQUEDUCT
7:3 the aqueduct of the Upper Reservoir,
36:2 took up a position by the aqueduct

AR
15:1 When in one night Ar is devastated,
ARABIA
21:13 oracle concerning those in Arabia:
21:13 who sojourn in the forests of Arabia,
ARAM
7:1 Rezin king of Aram and Pekah son of
7:2 that Aram was leading Ephraim on,
7:4 the burning anger of Rezin and Aram
7:5 even though Aram has conceived
7:8 as Damascus is the capital of Aram.
22:6 harnessed to the chariots of Aram.
ARAMAIC
36:11 in Aramaic, which we understand.
ARAMENEANS
9:12 Aramaneans from the east
ARAM'S
17:3 so shall it be with Aram's remnant,
ARARAT
37:38 fled to the land of Ararat.
ARBITRATE
2:4 and arbitrate for many peoples,
11:4 with equity arbitrate for the lowly
ARCHERS
21:17 And the number of valiant archers
66:19 Tarshish, Pul, and Lud (the archers),
ARDUOUS
14:3 and from the arduous servitude
ARENA
22:1 concerning the Arena of Spectacles:
22:5 in the Arena of Spectacles,
ARID
32:2 shade of a large rock in arid country.
35:1 Wilderness and arid land shall be
48:21 he led them through arid places:
53:2 a stalk out of arid ground.
ARIEL
29:1 Woe to Ariel—
29:1 Ariel, the city where David lodged!
29:2 yet will I distress Ariel:
29:7 amassed to fight against Ariel,
ARISE
5:11 as soon as they arise in the morning,
26:19 dead live when their bodies arise.
33:10 Now will I arise, says the Lord;
48:13 when I call them, they arise at once.
51:9 Awake, arise; clothe yourself with
52:1 Awake, arise; clothe yourself with
60:1 Arise, shine, your light has dawned;
ARISEN
3:13 he has arisen to judge the nations.
ARISES
2:19 when he arises and strikes terror on
2:21 when he arises and strikes terror on
ARM
8:9 you may arm yourselves,
30:30 make visible his arm descending in

33:2   our strength of arm from morning
40:10   his arm presides for him.
40:11   the lambs he gathers up with his arm
44:5   Yet others will inscribe on their arm,
44:12   by the strength of his arm:
48:14   his arm shall be against the Chaldean
51:5   anticipate me, awaiting my arm.
51:9   O arm of the Lord!
52:10* The Lord has bared his holy arm
53:1   has the arm of the Lord
59:16   So his own arm brought about
62:8   by his right hand, his mighty arm:
63:5   So my own arm brought about
63:12   who made his glorious arm proceed
ARMED
15:4   to summon the armed men of Moab,
ARMFUL
17:5   whose ears are reaped by the armful,
ARMIES
43:17   armies of men in full strength;
ARMOR
21:5   Oil the armor!
22:6   and Kir uncovers the armor,
37:33   advance against it with armor,
ARMORY
39:2   and his entire armory
ARMS
51:5   my arms shall judge the peoples—
ARMY
13:4   Lord of Hosts is marshalling an army
36:2   with a large army from Lachish to
ARNON
16:2   Moab's women at the fords of Arnon.
AROER
17:2   The cities of Aroer shall lie forsaken
AROSE
37:36   And when men arose in the morning,
AROUND
32:11   put sackcloth around your waists.
49:18   Lift up your eyes and look around
52:2   from the bands around your neck,
63:5   I glanced around, but none would
AROUSED
5:29   they are aroused like young lions:
42:13   his passions aroused like a fighter;
ARPAD
10:9   Is not Hamath as Arpad,
36:19   are the gods of Hamath and Arpad?
37:12   are the kings of Hamath and Arpad
ARRAYED
63:1   this from Bozrah, arrayed in majesty,
ARRAYS
61:10   he arrays me in a robe of
ARREST
53:8   By arrest and trial he was taken
ARRIVAL
14:9   anticipating your arrival;

ARRIVE
32:10   the produce shall fail to arrive.
60:4   your sons shall arrive from afar;
ARROGANCE
9:9   say in pride and arrogance of heart,
13:11   end to the arrogance of insolent men
ARROGANT
2:12   for all the proud and arrogant
ARROW
37:33   this city or shoot an arrow here.
49:2   has made me into a polished arrow
ARROWS
5:28   Their arrows are sharp;
7:24   and arrows, for the whole land
ARTISAN
40:19   A figure cast by the artisan,
41:7*   The artisan encourages the smith,
ASAPH
36:3   of Asaph, the record keeper,
36:22   Joah the son of Asaph, the record
ASCEND
14:14   I will ascend above the altitude
15:5   they will ascend the slopes of Luhith;
34:10   its smoke shall ascend forever.
40:31   they shall ascend as on eagles' wings;
57:7   there you ascend to offer sacrifices.
ASCERTAIN
21:12   If you would ascertain it,
ASHAMED
1:29   And you will be ashamed of the oaks
54:4   be not ashamed, for you shall not be
ASHDOD
20:1   Assyria came to Ashdod and
ASHES
44:20   They are followers of ashes;
58:5   one's bed of sackcloth and ashes?
61:3   in place of ashes,
ASK
7:11   Ask a sign for yourself
45:11   you ask me for signs concerning
45:19   I do not ask Jacob's offspring
ASKED
39:4   And Isaiah asked, What did they see
40:6   And I asked, How shall I announce it?
ASLEEP
5:27   they do not drowse or fall asleep.
ASPECT
53:2   he had no pleasing aspect,
ASS
1:3   the ass its master's stall,
ASSAULT
29:3   and beleaguer you with assault posts,
ASSEMBLE
11:12   and assemble the exiled of Israel;
44:11   Were they all to assemble
48:14   All of you, assemble and hear:

ASSEMBLED
43:9   When all nations unitedly assembled,
60:4   They have all assembled to come to
ASSEMBLIES
33:20   the city of our solemn assemblies;
ASSEMBLING
13:4   as of nations assembling:
ASSEMBLY
4:5   and over its solemn assembly,
14:13   the mount of assembly of the gods,
ASSES
21:7   riders on asses and riders on camels.
30:6   on the backs of young asses,
30:24   the oxen and asses that till the soil
32:20   letting oxen and asses range free.
ASSIGN
53:12   I will assign him an inheritance
ASSIST
63:5   I glared, but no one would assist.
ASSISTED
63:5   and my wrath, it assisted me.
ASSURED
32:17   an assured calm forever.
ASSYRIA
7:17   the day of the king of Assyria.
7:18   bees in the land of Assyria.
7:20   the king of Assyria—to shave
8:4   brought before the king of Assyria.
8:7   the king of Assyria in all his glory.
10:12   Assyria for his notorious
11:11   who shall be left out of Assyria,
11:16   shall be a pathway out of Assyria
14:25   I will break Assyria in my own land,
19:23   highway from Egypt to Assyria.
19:23   and Egyptians go to Assyria,
19:24   third party to Egypt and to Assyria,
19:25   Assyria the work of my hands,
20:1   Assyria came to Ashdod and
20:4   so shall the king of Assyria
20:6   deliverance from the king of Assyria!
27:13   in the land of Assyria and they who
31:8   And Assyria shall fall by a sword not
36:1   reign, Sennacherib king of Assyria
36:2   And the king of Assyria sent
36:4   the great king, the king of Assyria:
36:8   king of Assyria: I will give you two
36:13   the great king, the king of Assyria!
36:15   into the hand of the king of Assyria.
36:16   the king of Assyria: Make peace with
36:18   the hand of the king of Assyria?
37:4   the king of Assyria has sent to scorn
37:8   King of Assyria had left Lachish,
37:10   the hand of the king of Assyria.
37:11   had heard what the kings of Assyria
37:18   O Lord, the kings of Assyria have
37:21   Sennacherib king of Assyria,
37:33   concerning the king of Assyria:

37:37   So Sennacherib king of Assyria broke
38:6   of the hand of the king of Assyria;
ASSYRIAN
10:5   Hail the Assyrian, the rod of my
37:36   in the Assyrian camp. And when
ASSYRIANS
10:24   be not afraid of the Assyrians,
19:23   Assyrians shall come to Egypt
19:23   shall labor with the Assyrians.
23:13   Assyrians who set up observatories,
30:31   Assyrians will be terror-stricken,
52:4   Then the Assyrians subjected them
ASSYRIA'S
37:6   Assyria's subordinates ridicule me.
ASTOUND
29:14   I shall again astound these people
52:15   So shall he yet astound many nations,
ASTRAY
1:4   Alas, a nation astray,
19:13   heads of state have led Egypt astray.
28:7   priests and prophets have gone astray
31:6   contrived to go far astray, O children
47:10   skill and science you were led astray,
53:6   We all like sheep had gone astray,
ASTUTE
52:13   My servant, being astute, shall be
ATE
44:19   roasted meat and ate it.
ATHLETE
22:17   as an athlete hurls a missile;
ATONED
6:7   your transgressions atoned for.
ATTACHMENTS
5:18   drawn to sin by vain attachments,
ATTACK
21:2   Attack, O Elamites! Lay siege,
27:4   I will ruthlessly attack them
28:6   who repulse the attack at the gates.
43:14   I launch an attack on Babylon
ATTAIN
57:2   walk uprightly shall attain to peace,
ATTEMPT
25:11   pull down his pride in the attempt.
ATTENTION
22:4   Turn your attention from me,
34:1   Pay attention, you peoples!
55:1   Attention, all who thirst; come for
ATTENTIVE
28:23   Be attentive, and listen to what I say!
ATTIRE
61:10   dressed in priestly attire,
63:3   and I have stained my whole attire.
ATTRACTIVE
53:2   that we should find him attractive.
AUGUR
3:2   and prophet, the augur and elder,

AUSTERITY
22:12 for austerity and wearing sackcloth.
AUTHORITIES
40:23 makes the authorities of the world
AUTHORITY
3:12 women wield authority over them.
30:32 every sweep of the staff of authority,
49:7 a servant to those in authority:
AVAIL
16:12 it shall be to no avail.
30:5 a people who will avail them nothing;
AVAILABLE
65:1 I was available to those who did not
AVENGE
1:24 avenge me of my enemies.
35:4 God is coming to avenge
AVERT
47:11 not know how to avert by bribes;
AWAIT
24:17 Terrors and pitfalls and traps await
42:4 The isles await his law.
AWAITING
51:5 isles anticipate me, awaiting my arm.
AWAKE
26:19 Awake, and sing for joy,
51:9 Awake, arise; clothe yourself with
52:1 Awake, arise; clothe yourself with
AWAKENS
29:8 but awakens famished,
AWE
8:13 making him your fear, him your awe.
41:23 will be dazzled and all stand in awe.
60:5 your heart swell with awe:
AWED
8:12 be not afraid or awed
AWESOME
2:10 the awesome presence of the Lord
2:19 the awesome presence of the Lord
2:21 the awesome presence of the Lord
64:3 thou didst perform awesome things
AXE
10:15 Shall an axe exalt itself
BABBLING
33:19 babbling tongue was unintelligible.
BABES
3:12 As for my people, babes subject them;
BABYLON
13:1 An oracle concerning Babylon,
13:19 And Babylon, the most splendid of
14:4 the king of Babylon, and say,
21:2 All the sighing that Babylon has
21:9 She has fallen; Babylon has fallen.
39:1 king of Babylon, sent letters and gifts
39:3 they came to me from Babylon.
39:6 shall be carried away to Babylon.
39:7 the palace of the king of Babylon.
43:14 I launch an attack on Babylon

47:1 O Virgin Daughter of Babylon;
48:14 shall perform his will in Babylon;
48:20 Go forth out of Babylon, flee from
52:11 defiled as you leave Babylon.
BABYLON'S
13:22 Babylon's days shall not be
14:22 I will cut off Babylon's name and
BACKING
59:13 backing away from following our God,
BACKS
30:6 on the backs of young asses,
BACKWOODS
29:17 fruitful be considered backwoods?
BAKE
44:15 or light fire with to bake bread,
BAKED
44:19 I also baked bread in its embers,
BALADAN
39:1 Merodach-Baladan the son of Baladan,
BALANCE
38:10 deprived of the balance of my years?
40:12 hills in a balance?
40:15 no more than dust on a balance;
BALD
15:2 Every head shall be bald, every beard
BALDNESS
3:17 of the women of Zion with baldness;
3:24 instead of the coiffure, baldness,
BAND
11:5 Righteousness will be as a band
37:32 from Mount Zion a band of survivors.
BANDS
21:13 You wandering bands of Dedanites
52:2 Loose yourself from the bands around
BANISH
58:9 Indeed, if you will banish servitude
BANISHED
8:22 and thus are they banished
49:21 I was exiled, banished;
BANISHING
27:8 by utterly banishing them, O Lord.
BANKS
8:7 and overflow all his banks.
BANQUETS
5:12 flutes, and wine at their banquets,
BARE
27:10 stripping bare the young branches
32:11 Strip yourselves bare;
47:2 unveil, disrobe, bare your legs,
BARED
21:15 from the bared sword, the drawn bow
52:10* The Lord has bared his holy arm
BAREFOOT
20:2 going naked and barefoot.
20:3 naked and barefoot for three
20:4 and old, naked and barefoot,

BARGAIN
57:8　And you bargain with those with
BARK
56:10　but dumb watchdogs unable to bark,
BARLEY
28:25　he not demarcate wheat from barley
BARREN
13:2　the ensign on a barren mountain;
41:18　I will open up streams in barren hill
49:9　find pasture on all barren heights;
49:21　while I was bereaved and barren?
54:1　Sing, O barren woman who did not
56:3　eunuch say, I am but a barren tree.
BARRICADES
26:1　as walls and barricades!
BARS
45:2　and cut through iron bars.
BASHAN
2:13　and against all the oaks of Bashan,
33:9　Bashan and Carmel are denuded.
BATH
5:10　vineyard shall yield but one bath,
BATHE
57:9　You bathe with oil for the king
BATS
2:20　to the moles and to the bats
BATTERED
10:34　dense forests shall be battered down
24:12　the gates lie battered to ruin.
BATTERING
22:5　a day of battering down walls,
BATTLE
9:5　And all boots used in battle
22:2　they did not die in battle!
BEAR
11:1　a branch from its graft bear fruit.
11:7　When a cow and bear browse,
23:4　I no longer labor and bear children!
37:31　take root below and bear fruit above.
46:4　and I who bear you up;
46:7　They bear it aloft, carrying it on
52:11　you who bear the Lord's vessels.
65:23　or bear children doomed for calamity.
BEARD
7:20　legs, and to cut off even your beard.
15:2　shall be bald, every beard cut off.
50:6　to those who plucked out the beard;
BEARING
18:5　will cut down the fruit-bearing twigs
53:11　and by bearing their iniquities,
60:6　bearing gold and frankincense
BEARS
59:11　We grumble like bears, all of us;
BEASTS
1:11　and fat of fatted beasts;
18:6　and to the beasts of the land:
18:6　and the beasts of the land all winter.

30:6　concerning the Beasts of Negeb:
30:6　and the roaring king of beasts,
35:9　nor shall wild beasts intrude.
40:16　its beasts be adequate for sacrifice.
43:20　The wild beasts do me honor,
46:1　Their idols are loaded upon beasts
56:9　All you wild beasts, you animals of
BEAT
2:4　They will beat their swords into,
25:4　When the blasts of tyrants beat down
32:12　Beat your breasts for the choice
BEATEN
17:6　or when an olive tree is beaten,
24:13　as when an olive tree is beaten,
28:27　fennel is beaten out with a stick
BEATS
41:7*　and he who beats with a hammer
BEAUTIFUL
4:2　shall be beautiful and glorious,
BEAUTIFY
60:13　to beautify the site of my sanctuary,
BEAUTY
3:24　for in place of beauty
28:5　be as a crown of beauty and wreath of
44:13　resembling man's beauty,
BECKON
13:2　Beckon them with the hand
BED
14:11　Beneath you is a bed of maggots;
57:7　you have made prominent your bed,
57:8　mounting your bed, you have laid it
58:5　making one's bed of sackcloth and
BEDS
19:5　stream beds become desolate and dry.
57:2　and rest in their beds.
BEER ELIM
15:8　and echo as far as Beer Elim.
BEES
7:18　and for the bees in the land
BEFOREHAND
41:26　Who announced this beforehand,
48:3　I made known long beforehand;
48:5　therefore I told you them beforehand;
BEGET
59:4　they beget wickedness.
BEGINNING
1:26　your counsellors as in the beginning.
46:10　I foretell the end from the beginning,
BEGINS
44:12　he begins to grow faint.
BEGOTTEN
45:10　What have you begotten?
BEHALF
1:17　appeal on behalf of the widow.
8:19　of the dead on behalf of the living
34:8　year of retribution on behalf of Zion.
37:4　offer up prayer on behalf of the

64:4 who acts thus on behalf of those who
65:8 so I will do on behalf of my servants
BEHAVE
36:4 On what grounds do you behave
BEHELD
1:1 which he beheld concerning Judea
BEHIND
22:3 all of you left behind are caught
26:20 and shut the doors behind you;
28:15 and hiding behind falsehoods,
30:21 ears shall hear words from behind
38:17 hast cast all my sins behind thee,
45:14 They shall walk behind you in chains
52:12 the God of Israel behind you.
57:8 Behind doors and facades
BEHOLD
30:27 Behold, the Lord Omnipotent coming
33:17 Your eyes shall behold the King in
33:20 Behold Zion, the city of our solemn
38:11 I shall not now behold Man
40:9 Judah: Behold your God!
62:2 shall behold your righteousness
63:15 glorious celestial abode, and behold!
66:18 may approach and behold my glory.
BEL
46:1 Bel slumps down, Nebo is stooped
BELEAGUER
29:3 and beleaguer you with assault posts,
BELIEVE
7:9 you will not believe it,
28:16 They who believe it will not do
43:10 you may recognize it and believe me,
BELIEVED
53:1 Who has believed our revelation?
BELLOWINGS
37:29 and bellowings against me,
BELLY
49:1 called me before I was in the belly;
BELONGINGS
15:7 and their personal belongings,
BELOVED
5:1 Let me sing for my beloved
5:1 My beloved had a vineyard
41:8 of Abraham my beloved friend,
BELTS
5:27 Their waist-belts come not loose
BEMOAN
19:8 anglers in canals bemoan themselves;
BENEFIT
30:5 shall be of no help or benefit,
44:10 that cannot benefit them?
BENT
30:2 are bent on going down to Egypt
BEREAVED
3:26 shall lie bereaved and forlorn;
47:8 be widowed or bereaved of children:
49:21 while I was bereaved and barren?

BEREAVEMENT
47:9 Bereavement and widowhood
49:20 during the time of your bereavement
BERRIES
17:6 two or three berries in the topmost
BESEECH
38:3 I beseech thee to remember, O Lord,
BESIDES
47:10 and there is none besides me!
64:4 has any eye seen a God besides thee,
BEST
5:13 their best men die of famine,
40:6 and at its best like a blossom of the
BESTIR
51:9 Bestir yourself, as in ancient times,
BESTOWING
61:3 bestowing upon them a priestly
BETRAY
16:3 betray not the refugees!
33:1 they shall betray you!
BETRAYED
24:16 turncoats have deceitfully betrayed!
BETRAYING
33:1 when you are through betraying,
BETRAYS
3:9 The look on their faces betrays them:
BEWAIL
16:7 and all have cause to bewail Moab:
BEWARE
36:18 Beware, lest Hezekiah mislead you
BEWILDERED
29:9 and become bewildered;
BILL
50:1 is your mother's bill of divorce
BILLOW
9:18 and they shall billow upward
BIND
8:16 has said, Bind up the testimony;
22:18 He will bind you tightly about
22:21 and bind your girdle on him; I will
49:18 bind them on you as does a bride.
61:1 to bind up the brokenhearted,
BINDS
30:26 in the day the Lord binds up
BIRD
46:11 I summon a bird of prey from the
BIRDS
13:21 birds of prey will find lodging there
16:2 Like fluttering birds forced out of
18:6 All shall be left to the birds of prey
18:6 the birds of prey will feed on them
31:5 As birds hover over [the nest],
34:13 a reserve for birds of prey.
43:20 the jackals and birds of prey,
BIRTH
7:14 with child shall give birth to a son
8:3 she conceived and gave birth to a son.

BIRTH *continued*
26:17 As a woman about to give birth
37:3 have reached the point of birth,
46:3 have been a load on me since birth,
54:1 barren woman who did not give birth;
66:7 she is in labor, she gives birth;
66:8 Zion gave birth to her children.
66:9 to a crisis and not bring on birth?
66:9 When it is I who cause the birth,
BISON
34:7 among them shall fall bison, bulls,
51:20 taken in a net like bison.
BIT
37:29 and my bit in your mouth
BITTER
5:20 bitterness sweet and the sweet bitter.
24:9 liquor has turned bitter to drinkers.
BITTERLY
22:4 though I weep bitterly;
33:7 the champions of peace weep bitterly.
BITTERNESS
5:20 bitterness sweet and the sweet bitter.
38:14 from bitterness of soul . . .
BIZARRE
28:21 and do this work, his bizarre work.
BLACKNESS
50:3 with the blackness of mourning;
BLASPHEMED
37:24 you have blasphemed the Lord.
BLASPHEMY
32:6 For the godless utter blasphemy;
BLASTS
25:4 When the blasts of tyrants beat down
27:8 By his fierce blasts they were flung
29:6 booms, tempestuous blasts
BLAZING
5:24 As a blazing fire consumes stubble,
13:13 in the day of his blazing wrath.
BLESS
19:25 The Lord of Hosts will bless them,
BLESSED
19:25 saying, Blessed be Egypt my people,
30:18 blessed are all who wait for him.
32:20 Blessed are you, who shall then sow
51:2 but I blessed him by making him
56:2 Blessed is the man who does so—
61:9 of the lineage the Lord has blessed.
65:23 lineage of those blessed by the Lord,
BLESSING
19:24 a blessing in the midst of the earth.
44:3 my blessing upon your posterity.
BLESSINGS
65:16 Those of them who invoke blessings
BLIND
29:18 and the eyes of the blind see
35:5 the eyes of the blind be opened
42:7 to open eyes that are blind,

42:16 Then will I lead the blind by a way
42:18 O you deaf, listen; O you blind, look
42:19 Who is blind but my own servant,
42:19 Who is blind like those I have
43:8 people who are blind, yet have eyes,
56:10 Their watchmen are altogether blind
59:10 along the borders like the blind;
BLOCK
8:14 a stumbling block or obstructing
BLOOD
1:11 the blood of bulls and sheep
1:15 your hands are filled with blood.
9:5 and tunics rolled in blood
15:9 waters of Dibon shall flow with blood,
26:21 earth will uncover the blood shed
34:3 their blood shall dissolve
34:6 sword that shall engorge with blood
34:6 the blood of lambs and he-goats,
34:7 land shall be saturated with blood,
49:26 drunk with their own blood as with
59:3 your palms are defiled with blood,
59:7 they hasten to shed innocent blood.
66:3 is as one who offers swine's blood,
BLOODSHED
4:4 Jerusalem of its bloodshed, in the
BLOSSOM
27:6 and Israel bursts into blossom,
40:6 and at its best like a blossom of the
45:8 receive it and salvation blossom;
BLOSSOMS
5:24 and their blossoms fly up like dust.
18:5 and the set blossoms are developing
35:1 when it blossoms like the crocus.
BLOT
43:25 who blot out your offenses,
BLOW
13:6 as a violent blow from the Almighty.
19:7 shrivel and blow away and be no
53:8 to whom the blow was due?
BLOWS
14:6 him who with unerring blows
BLUNDER
28:7 they blunder in their decisions.
BLUSH
1:29 and blush for the parks you were
24:23 The moon will blush and the sun be
BOAST
20:5 their hope,and at Egypt, their boast.
30:7 I refer to her as an idle boast.
45:25 justify . . . and have cause to boast.
BOASTING
10:12 boasting and infamous conceit,
16:6 its excessive pride and its boasting,
BODIES
26:19 dead live when their bodies arise.
37:36 there lay all their dead bodies!
58:3 We afflict our bodies and you remain

418

BOILING
64:2   as when fire is lit for boiling water,
BOISTEROUS
5:14   their boisterous ones and revelers.
BONDAGE
58:6   To release from wrongful bondage,
BONDS
28:22   lest your bonds grow severe,
BONFIRES
9:5   have become fuel for bonfires.
BOOK
29:11   as the words of a sealed book that
29:18   the deaf hear the words of the book
30:8   record it in a book for the last day,
34:16   read it in the book of the Lord:
BOOMS
29:6   resounding booms, tempestuous
BOOTS
9:5   And all boots used in battle
BORDER
19:19   to the Lord at its border.
BORDERS
10:13   away with the borders of nations,
26:15   hast withdrawn all borders in the
59:10   We grope along the borders like the
60:18   or disaster within your borders;
BORE
46:1   the images you bore aloft
49:21   bore me these while I was bereaved
51:2   to Sarah who bore you.
51:18   among all the children she bore,
53:4   Yet he bore our sufferings, endured
53:12   he bore the sins of many,
BORN
9:6   For to us a child is born, a son
49:20   The children born during the time of
57:4   Surely you are born of sin, a spurious
66:8   and a nation be born at once?
BORNE
45:10   to the Woman, What have you borne?
46:3   borne up by me from the womb:
BORROWER
24:2   with lender as with borrower,
BOSOM
40:11   and carries in his bosom;
63:15   The yearnings of thy bosom and thy
65:6   till I have paid back into their bosom
66:11   from the abundance of her bosom.
BOSOMS
49:22   will bring your sons in their bosoms
BOUGH
17:6   berries in the topmost bough,
BOUND
1:6   not been pressed out or bound up,
61:1   the opening of the eyes to the bound,

BOUNDARY
54:12   and your entire boundary of precious
BOUNDS
59:8   integrity is not within their bounds.
BOUNTY
66:12   the bounty of the nations like a
BOW
21:15   from the bared sword, the drawn bow
22:3   are captured without using the bow;
27:13   Egypt shall come and bow down
41:2   as driven stubble to his bow?
44:17   to which they bow in adoration and
45:14   and bow down to you, entreating you.
45:23   To me every knee shall bow
46:2   gods altogether sag and bow down,
46:6   they bow down to and worship.
49:23   They will bow down before you,
BOWED
51:14   shall he who is bowed down
BOWING
58:5   Is it only for bowing one's head
60:14   will come bowing before you;
BOWL
51:17   to the dregs the bowl of stupor.
51:22   no more from the bowl of my wrath.
BOWLS
22:24   from ordinary bowls to the most
65:4   their bowls full of polluted broth,
BOWS
5:28   all their bows are strung.
7:24   Men will go there with bows
13:18   Their bows shall tear apart the
BOX
41:19   elms and box trees in the steppes—
BOZRAH
34:6   Lord will hold a slaughter in Bozrah,
63:1   Who is this from Bozrah, arrayed in
BRACELETS
3:20   tiaras, bracelets and ribbons, zodiac
BRANCH
11:1   and a branch from its graft bear
17:6   or five in its most fruitful branch,
60:21   they are the branch I have planted,
BRANCHES
16:8   its branches spread abroad across the
18:5   remove the new branches by slashing.
27:10   stripping bare the young branches
BRANDISHING
19:16   at the brandishing hand the Lord
BRAZEN
45:2   I will break in pieces brazen doors
48:4   was an iron sinew, your brow brazen
BREACH
30:13   breach exposed in a high wall
BREACHED
22:9   city of David increasingly breached,

BREAD
30:20 Lord give you the bread of adversity
33:16 Bread is provided them, their water
44:15 or light fire with to bake bread,
44:19 I also baked bread in its embers,
55:2 spend money on what is not bread,
BREADTH
8:8 the breadth of your land,
BREAK
14:25 I will break Assyria in my own land,
24:19 the earth shall break up and cave in;
28:13 and break themselves,
30:9 people, sons who break faith,
35:2 Joyously it shall break out in flower,
35:6 Water shall break forth in the
35:7 shall marshes break out],
42:3 a bruised reed he will not break;
45:2 I will break in pieces brazen doors
52:9 Break out all together into song,
54:1 break into jubilant song, you who
58:8 your light break through like the
BREAKS
66:3 as one who breaks a dog's neck;
BREAST
16:11 My breast will vibrate like a harp for
28:9 those just taken from the breast?
BREASTPLATE
59:17 put on righteousness as a breastplate
BREASTS
32:12 Beat your breasts for the choice
60:16 suckling at the breasts of rulers.
66:11 at her consoling breasts;
BREATH
2:22 in whose nostrils is but breath!
11:4 and with the breath of his lips slay
30:28 His breath is like a raging torrent
30:33 the Lord's breath burns within it
33:11 fire of your own breath devours you!
42:5 breath of life to the people upon it,
BREATHE
40:7 Spirit of the Lord breathe within it,
42:14 and breathe hard and fast all at once.
BRETHREN
66:20 and shall bring back all your brethren
BRIARS
5:6 but briars and thorns shall overgrow
7:23 shall be briars and thorns.
7:25 go for fear of the briars and thorns,
9:18 and briars and thorns shall it
10:17 his briars and thorns in a single day.
27:4 Should briars and thorns come up,
32:13 be overgrown with briars and thorns.
34:13 thistles and briars its strongholds;
BRIBE
5:23 who acquit the guilty for a bribe,
45:13 without price or bribe, says the Lord

BRIBES
1:23 with one accord they love bribes
33:15 stay their hand from taking bribes,
47:11 not know how to avert by bribes;
BRICKS
9:10 The bricks have fallen down,
65:3 in parks, making smoke upon bricks,
BRIDE
49:18 bind them on you as does a bride.
61:10 or a bride adorned with her jewels.
62:5 a bridegroom rejoices over the bride,
BRIDEGROOM
61:10 like a bridegroom dressed in priestly
62:5 a bridegroom rejoices over the bride,
BRIDLE
30:28 with an erring bridle on their jaws
BRIDLED
48:9 I have bridled my wrath;
BRIGHT
9:2 have seen a bright light;
BRIGHTNESS
2:10 and from the brightness of his glory.
2:19 and from the brightness of his glory,
2:21 and from the brightness of his glory,
60:3 rulers to the brightness of your
60:19 nor the brightness of the moon
BRIMSTONE
34:9 and her earth into brimstone;
BRING
1:13 Bring no more worthless offerings;
3:14 He will bring to trial the elders of
7:17 The Lord will bring upon you
14:2 and bring them to their own place.
15:9 I will bring lions upon the
16:10 vintage shout I will bring to an end.
21:2 I will bring to an end.
21:14 bring water to greet the thirsty;
31:2 and will bring disaster upon them ,
38:19 living, only they bring thee praise,
41:19 I will bring cedars and acacias,
43:5 I will bring your offspring from the
43:6 Bring my sons from afar
43:9 Let them bring their witnesses
43:14 and bring down as fugitives all the,
43:23 I required not that you bring me
46:11 What I have spoken, I bring to pass:
49:22 they will bring your sons in their
50:8 Who will bring charges against me?
56:7 I will bring to my holy mountain
58:7 to bring home the wretchedly poor,
58:11 and bring vigor to your limbs.
60:9 to bring back your children from
60:17 In place of copper I will bring gold,
60:17 in place of wood I will bring copper,
66:4 and bring upon them the thing they
66:9 Shall I bring to a crisis and not bring
66:20 shall bring back all your brethren

BRINGEST
26:12 Lord, thou bringest about our peace;
BRINGING
38:13 thou art bringing on my end!
43:20 for bringing water to the wilderness,
51:3 bringing solace to all her ruins;
BRINGS
34:16 by his Spirit he brings them together.
40:23 By him who brings potentates to
40:26 He who brings forth their hosts by
52:7 who brings tidings of good,
61:11 the earth brings forth its vegetation,
BROAD
30:33 broad and deep is its fire pit and
33:21 country of rivers and broad streams,
BROADCAST
48:20 broadcast it to the end of the earth.
BROIL
44:16 Over it they broil a roast;
BROKE
7:17 Ephraim broke away from Judah—
37:37 So Sennacherib king of Assyria broke
BROKEN
5:5 I will have its wall broken through
8:15 and when they fall shall be broken,
14:5 Lord has broken the staff of the
14:29 the rod which struck you is broken.
15:4 but their spirit shall be broken.
24:10 The towns of disorder are broken up;
27:11 A harvest of twigs dries, broken off
BROKENHEARTED
61:1 me to bind up the brokenhearted,
BROKENNESS
65:14 howling from brokenness of spirit.
BROOD
14:20 May the brood of miscreants
31:2 up against the brood of miscreants
34:15 hatch them and brood over her young.
57:4 you are born of sin, a spurious brood,
BROOKS
32:2 like brooks of water in a desert place,
44:4 like willows by running brooks.
BROOM
14:23 it with the broom of destruction,
BROTH
65:4 their bowls full of polluted broth,
BROTHER
19:2 will fight brother against brother
BROUGHT
1:2 I have reared sons, brought them up,
2:9 Mankind is brought low
2:12 that they may be brought low.
2:17 and man's pride brought low;
3:9 brought disaster upon themselves!
5:15 Mankind is brought low
8:4 be brought before the king of
14:15 you have been brought down to Sheol

18:7 At that time shall tribute be brought
26:18 but have brought forth only wind.
33:11 conceived chaff and brought forth
37:26 Now I have brought it to pass.
38:15 he himself has brought it about?
42:4 brought about justice in the earth.
46:13 I have brought near my righteousness;
48:15 I have brought him, and I will
53:6 the Lord brought together upon him
59:16 his own arm brought about salvation
60:11 host of nations may be brought to you
63:5 my own arm brought about salvation
63:11 Where is he who brought them up
66:20 brought offerings in pure vessels
BROW
5:1 on the fertile brow of a hill.
48:4 was an iron sinew, your brow brazen
BROWSE
11:7 When a cow and bear browse,
BROWSING
32:14 a browsing place for flocks.
BRUISED
42:3 Even a bruised reed he will not
42:4 he himself grow dim or be bruised
BRUISES
1:6 wounds and bruises and festering
BRUSHWOOD
32:15 be reckoned as brushwood.
BUBBLES
64:2 which bubbles over from the heat—
BUCKET
40:15 nations are but drops from a bucket,
BUCKWHEAT
28:25 plant buckwheat in its own plot?
BUDGE
46:7 unable to budge from its spot.
BUILD
65:21 When men build houses,
65:22 not build so that others may dwell,
66:1 What house would you build me?
BUILDING
54:11 I will lay antimony for your building
BUILDINGS
5:9 many buildings shall lie desolate,
13:21 its buildings overflow with weasels;
22:10 You took a census of the buildings in
22:10 tearing down buildings to fortify
BUILT
5:2 He built a watchtower in its midst
22:11 You built cisterns between the walls
BULLS
1:11 the blood of bulls and sheep
34:7 shall fall bison, bulls, and steers.
BURDEN
1:14 They have become a burden on me;
9:6 shoulder the burden of government.
14:25 their burden removed from their

421

BURDEN *continued*
22:25 and the burden hanging on it cut off.
46:2 unable to rescue their burden;
BURDENED
9:4 the yoke that burdened them,
43:23 have not burdened you with oblations
43:24 Nor have I burdened you to buy
43:24 you have burdened me with your sins
BURDENS
10:27 In that day their burdens shall be
46:1 piled as burdens on weary animals.
BURGEONING
57:5 under every burgeoning tree,
BURIAL
14:20 You shall not share burial with them,
53:9 among the rich was his burial;
BURLAP
3:24 festive dress, a loincloth of burlap;
BURN
1:31 both shall burn up alike,
10:17 and it shall burn up and devour
44:16 Half of it they burn in the fire.
57:5 who burn with lust among the oaks,
BURNED
1:7 your cities burned with fire;
5:5 and let it be burned;
6:13 they shall be burned:
33:12 nations have been burned like lime,
43:2 you shall not be burned;
44:19 Part of this I burned in the fire;
64:11 has been burned with fire,
BURNING
4:4 spirit of justice, by a burning wind.
7:4 by the burning anger of Rezin and
10:16 fire to flare up like a burning hearth,
25:5 as burning heat by the shade of a
27:8 in the day of the burning east wind.
33:14 among us can abide eternal burning?
34:9 land shall become as burning pitch.
43:23 or wearied you with burning incense.
BURNS
30:33 the Lord's breath burns within it
66:3 and whoever burns incense,
BURNT
47:14 stubble they are burnt up in the fire,
BURST
44:23 Burst into song, O mountains,
49:13 Burst into song, O mountains!
BURSTS
27:6 and Israel bursts into blossom,
BUSINESS
58:13 and speaking of business matters—
BUTTOCKS
20:4 with buttocks uncovered—
BUY
43:24 Nor have I burdened you to buy
55:1 come and buy food, that you may eat.

55:1 Come, buy wine and milk
BUYER
24:2 with seller as with buyer,
BUZZING
18:1 Woe to the land of buzzing wings
BYGONE
43:18 the prophecies of bygone events;
CAKES
25:6 leavened cakes, succulent and
CALAMITY
3:11 when calamity overtakes them:
13:11 I have decreed calamity for the world,
15:8 The cry of calamity
45:7 I occasion peace and cause calamity.
51:19 Twofold calamity has befallen you:
57:1 that from impending calamity
65:23 or bear children doomed for calamity.
CALAMUS
43:24 me the fragrant calamus
CALL
8:12 Do not call a conspiracy all that these
8:12 call a conspiracy;
21:11 Men call to see me from Seir,
34:14 and wild goats call to one another.
43:22 But you do not call upon me,
45:4 Israel my chosen, I call you by name
48:2 who call yourselves of the holy city,
48:13 when I call them, they arise at once.
55:6 call upon him while he is near.
58:5 Do you call that a fast,
58:9 should you call, the Lord will
60:14 They will call you The City of the
62:6 You who call upon the Lord,
65:15 But his servants he will call by a
65:24 Before they call I will reply;
CALLED
1:26 After this you shall be called
4:1 only let us be called by your name—
4:3 in Jerusalem be called holy
6:3 They called out to one another,
6:4 at the sound of those who called
8:2 And I called in reliable witnesses,
9:6 He will be called
13:3 called out my valiant ones:
35:8 be called the Way of Holiness,
36:13 Then Rabshakeh stood and called out
41:9 called from its farthest limits—
42:6 I the Lord have rightfully called you
43:1 I have called you by name; you are
43:7 all who are called by my name,
47:5 No longer shall you be called,
48:8 called a transgressor from the womb.
48:15 myself have spoken it, and also called
49:1 Lord called me before I was in the
50:2 why did no one answer when I called?
51:2 He was but one when I called him,
54:5 who is called the God of all the earth.

58:12 You shall be called a rebuilder of
61:3 called oaks of righteousness
61:6 shall be called the priests of the Lord
62:2 you shall be called by a new name
62:4 shall no more be called the forsaken
62:12 They shall be called the holy people,
65:12 For when I called,you did not respond
66:4 For when I called, no one responded;
CALLING
40:26 calling each one by name.
41:2 calling him to the place of his
CALLS
22:12 calls for weeping and lamentation,
40:3 A voice calls out,
41:25 who calls on my name,
45:3 God of Israel, who calls you by name.
54:6 The Lord calls you back
59:4 None calls for righteousness;
64:7 Yet none calls upon thy name,
CALM
7:4 See to it that you remain calm
30:15 By a calm response triumph;
32:17 an assured calm forever.
CALNO
10:9 Has not Calno fared like Carchemish?
CALVES
11:6 calves and young lions will feed
CAMELS
21:7 riders on asses and riders on camels.
30:6 their riches on the humps of camels,
60:6 A myriad of camels shall cover your
CAMP
37:36 in the Assyrian camp. And when men
37:37 camp and withdrew. And he returned
CANALS
19:7 adjoining canals and estuaries,
19:8 anglers in canals bemoan themselves;
CANDLESTICKS
21:5 they deck them with candlesticks.
CANOPIES
54:2 extend the canopies of your
CANOPY
4:5 is glorious shall be a canopy.
40:22 suspends the heavens like a canopy,
CAPITAL
7:8 Damascus is the capital of Aram
7:9 Samaria is the capital of Ephraim
CAPTAIN
31:9 their captain shall expire in terror
CAPTIVE
5:13 my people become captive
8:15 shall be taken captive.
14:2 they will take captive their captors
28:13 ensnared and be taken captive.
52:2 O captive Daughter of Zion.
CAPTIVES
10:4 but to kneel among the captives

14:17 permitting not his captives to return
20:4 lead away the captives of Egypt
42:7 to free captives from confinement
49:9 to say to the captives, Come forth!
49:24 or the tyrant's captives escape free?
49:25 the tyrant's captives escape free:
61:1 to proclaim liberty to the captives
CAPTIVITY
46:2 they themselves go into captivity.
CAPTORS
14:2 they will take captive their captors
CAPTURED
22:3 are captured without using the bow;
CARBUNCLE
54:12 your gates of carbuncle,
CARCHEMISH
10:9 Has not Calno fared like Carchemish?
CARE
44:14 care for them among the trees of the
CAREFREE
32:10 shall be in anguish, O carefree ones,
CARELESS
32:9 you careless daughters, hear my
32:11 be perturbed, O careless daughters!
CARMEL
33:9 Bashan and Carmel are denuded.
35:2 the splendor of Carmel and Sharon,
CARRIED
38:12 carried away from me like a
39:6 up until now, shall be carried
45:20 They who carried about their wooden
63:9 he lifted them up and carried them
66:12 nurse and be carried upon the hip
CARRIES
40:11 and carries in his bosom;
CARRY
10:23 will carry out the utter destruction
15:7 they will carry away
30:6 they carry their wealth
46:4 it is I who carry and rescue you.
49:22 and carry your daughters on their
57:13 A wind shall carry all of them off;
CARRYING
6:6 carrying an ember which he had
46:7 They bear it aloft, carrying it on
CART
28:28 horse and threshing cart over it.
CARTWHEEL
28:27 nor is a cartwheel rolled over cumin:
CARVE
40:20 to carve them an image that will not
CARVED
51:9 Was it not you who carved up Rahab,
CARVING
22:16 carving out graves for themselves in
CASE
1:23 nor does the widow's case come before

CASE *continued*
16:3   they say; judge our case!
41:1   come forward and state their case;
41:21   Present your case, says the Lord;
43:26   let us plead each our case.
45:21   Speak up and present your case;
CAST
14:11   Your glory has been cast down to
14:19   But you are cast away unburied
19:8   those who cast nets on water
26:19   For the earth shall cast up its dead.
30:22   your cast idols gilded in gold;
38:8   See, I make the shadow cast by the
38:17   For thou hast cast all my sins behind
40:19   A figure cast by the artisan,
44:10   would fashion a god or cast an idol
50:1   with which I cast her out?
63:6   when I cast their glory to the ground.
CASTING
26:5   by casting it to the ground,
CATASTROPHE
15:5   they will raise the cry of catastrophe.
17:14   evening time shall be the catastrophe,
47:11   Catastrophe shall overtake you,
CATCH
14:16   Those who catch sight of you
CATCHING
8:14   and a snare, catching unawares
CATERPILLARS
33:4   in the manner of caterpillars;
CATTLE
7:25   but they shall serve as a cattle range,
22:13   the killing of cattle and slaughter of
30:23   In that day your cattle shall graze
46:1   are loaded upon beasts and cattle;
63:14   like cattle descending the slopes
CAUGHT
13:15   all who are caught shall fall by the
22:3   of you left behind are caught easily
24:18   shall be caught in a trap.
45:20   were caught unawares.
CAVALRY
21:9   Now they come: cavalry and teams of
22:7   and cavalry take up positions at your
CAVE
24:19   the earth shall break up and cave in;
CAVES
2:19   Men will go into caves in the rocks
CEASE
1:16   cease to do evil.
17:1   Damascus shall cease to be a city
29:20   come to nought and scorners cease;
30:11   Cease confronting us with the Holy
CEASED
14:4   his end and tyranny ceased!
16:4   and violence has ceased,

CEASES
24:8   The rhythm of drums ceases,
CEDARS
2:13   cedars of Lebanon that lift
9:10   but we will replace them with cedars!
14:8   as do the cedars of Lebanon:
37:24   I have felled its tallest cedars,
41:19   I will bring cedars and acacias,
44:14   He is required to cut down cedars;
CELEBRATE
25:9   us joyfully celebrate his salvation!
49:13   Shout for joy, O heavens; celebrate,
CELEBRATION
14:7   there is jubilant celebration!
66:10   join in her celebration, all who mourn
CELEBRITIES
23:8   merchants the world's celebrities?
23:9   world's celebrities an utter
CELESTIAL
63:15   thy holy and glorious celestial abode,
CENSUS
22:10   You took a census of the buildings in
33:18   those who conducted the census?
CENTER
66:17   devotees of those who are the center
CENTERS
5:8   in the centers of the land!
6:12   from the centers of the land.
CHAFF
17:13   like chaff on the mountains,
29:5   your violent mobs like flying chaff.
33:11   conceived chaff and brought forth
40:24   and a storm sweeps them off as chaff.
41:15   and make chaff of hills.
CHAIN
40:19   fitted with a silver chain from the
CHAINS
3:19   the pendants, chains and scarves,
45:14   They shall walk behind you in chains
CHALDEA
48:20   flee from Chaldea!
CHALDEANS
13:19   pride of Chaldeans, shall be thrown
23:13   So too with the land of the Chaldeans,
43:14   down as fugitives all the Chaldeans,
47:1   O Daughter of the Chaldeans.
47:5   O Daughter of the Chaldeans.
48:14   arm shall be against the Chaldeans.
CHALKSTONE
27:9   he makes like crushed chalkstone
CHAMBERS
26:20   O my people, enter your chambers
CHAMPIONS
5:22   and champions at mixing liquor!
33:7   the champions of peace weep bitterly.
CHANGED
24:5   changed the ordinances,

CHANNELS
8:7   He will rise up over all his channels
19:7   sown along irrigation channels,
CHAOS
45:19   to seek me amid chaos.
CHAOTIC
34:11   and chaotic weight.
45:18   not to remain a chaotic waste,
CHARGE
3:6   and take charge of this ruination!
CHARGED
13:3   I have charged my holy ones,
CHARGES
50:8   Who will bring charges against me?
CHARIOT
5:28   their chariot wheels revolve like a
CHARIOTS
2:7   and there is no end to their chariots.
21:7   Let him watch for chariots with teams
22:6   horses are harnessed to the chariots
22:7   choice valleys fill with chariots,
31:1   of chariots and vast forces of
36:9   chariots and horsemen?
43:17   who dispatches chariots and horses,
66:15   his chariots like a whirlwind,
66:20   in chariots and wagons, and on mules
CHARIOTRY
37:24   On account of my vast chariotry
CHARITY
54:8   but with everlasting charity
54:10   but my charity toward you shall
CHARM
3:20   zodiac signs and charm amulets,
CHASED
13:14   Then, like a deer that is chased,
CHASTENED
29:6   She shall be chastened by the Lord
CHASTISEMENTS
26:16   thy chastisements were upon them.
CHEEKS
50:6   my cheeks to those who plucked out
CHEER
16:9   when your shouts of cheer
CHEERS
22:2   You resounded with loud cheers—
CHERISH
44:9   things they cherish profit nothing.
CHERISHED
1:29   be ashamed of the oaks you cherished
5:7   people of Judah his cherished grove.
CHERUBIM
37:16   enthroned between the cherubim,
CHIEFS
22:3   Your chiefs, altogether in flight,
CHILD
7:14   with child shall give birth to a son
7:16   But before the child learns

8:4   For before the child knows
9:6   For to us a child is born, a son
10:19   a child could record them.
26:18   We were with child; we have been in
49:15   for the child of her womb?
CHILDREN
1:4   perverse children:
8:18   As for me and the children the
13:18   not look with compassion on children.
17:3   the glory of the children of Israel,
23:4   I no longer labor and bear children!
27:12   one, O children of Israel.
29:23   when he sees among him his children,
30:9   children unwilling to obey the law of
31:6   go far astray, O children of Israel.
37:3   Children have reached the point of
45:11   for signs concerning my children?
47:8   be widowed or bereaved of children:
49:20   The children born during the time of
49:25   and I will deliver your children.
51:12   the children of men who shall be
51:18   among all the children she bore,
51:20   Your children lie in a faint at the
54:1   The children of the deserted wife
54:13   All your children shall be taught by
57:3   you children of the sorceress,
57:5   slayers of children in the gullies
60:9   bring back your children from afar,
65:23   or bear children doomed for calamity.
66:8   Zion gave birth to her children.
CHISELLING
44:13   He creates it by chiselling to the
CHOICE
5:2   and planted it with choice vines,
10:18   His choice forests and productive
17:10   though you plant choice crops
22:7   then shall your choice valleys fill
32:12   your breasts for the choice fields
CHOICEST
37:24   tallest cedars, its choicest cypresses.
61:6   with their choicest provision.
CHOOSE
7:15   choose what is good.
7:16   to reject the evil and choose
14:1   and once again choose Israel;
56:4   and choose to do what I will—
CHOSE
65:12   you chose to do what was not my will
66:4   they chose to do what was not my will
CHOSEN
41:8   Jacob, whom I have chosen,
42:1   my chosen one in whom I delight,
43:10   my servant whom I have chosen,
43:20   may give drink to my chosen people,
44:1   and Israel whom I have chosen.
44:2   and Jeshurun whom I have chosen.
45:4   and Israel my chosen, I call you by

CHOSEN *continued*
49:7   Holy One of Israel has chosen you.
65:9   my chosen ones shall inherit them,
65:15 to serve my chosen ones as a curse
65:22 my chosen ones shall outlast the work
CISTERN
36:16 water from his own cistern,
CISTERNS
22:11 You built cisterns between the walls
CITIES
 1:7   your cities burned with fire;
 6:11 Until the cities lie desolate
14:17 demolishing its cities,
14:21 fill the face of the earth with cities.
17:2   The cities of Aroer shall lie forsaken
17:9   In that day their mighty cities
19:18 cities in the land of Egypt will
25:2   mansions shall no more form cities,
27:10 Because of them the fortified cities
32:19* cities utterly leveled.
36:1   against all the fortified cities
37:13 the kings of the cities of Sepharvaim,
37:26 destined to demolish fortified cities,
40:9   proclaim to the cities of Judah:
42:11 Let the desert and its cities raise
43:28 I let the holy cities be profaned;
44:26 the cities of Judah, They shall be
54:3   and resettle the desolate cities.
61:4   they will renew the desolate cities
64:10 Thy holy cities have become a
CITY
 1:8   a city under siege.
 1:21 How the faithful city
 1:26 City of Righteousness, a faithful city.
14:31 Wail at the gates; howl in the city!
17:1   Damascus shall cease to be a city
19:2   city against city and state against
19:18 as the City of Righteousness.
22:2   a tumultuous town, a city of revelry!
22:9   When you saw the city of David
23:7   your festive city of ancient origin,
23:8   the imperial city,
23:11 concerning the merchant city
24:12 Havoc remains in the city;
25:2   hast made the city a heap of rubble,
26:1   Our city is strong; salvation he has
26:5   of the exalted city
29:1   Ariel, the city where David lodged!
32:13 in the city of entertainment,
33:20 the city of our solemn assemblies;
36:15 save us; this city shall not be given
37:33 He shall not enter this city or shoot
37:34 he shall not enter this city, says the
37:35 I will protect this city and save it,
38:6   And I will deliver you and this city
38:6   I will protect this city.
45:13 rebuild my city and set free my

48:2   who call yourselves of the holy city,
52:1   O Jerusalem, Holy City
60:14 will call you The City of the Lord,
62:12 a city never deserted.
66:6   Hark, a tumult from the city, a noise
CLACKING
 3:16 and clacking with their feet,
CLAMOR
24:11 is heard the clamor for wine,
CLAMOROUS
32:14 the clamorous towns deserted.
CLAN
60:22 The least of them shall become a clan,
CLAP
55:12 of the meadows all clap their hands.
CLASPING
 8:11 clasping my hand, and admonished
CLAY
29:16 the potter be regarded as the clay?
41:25 tread them as clay like a potter.
45:9   As though the clay were to say to
64:8   we are the clay and thou art the
CLEAN
 1:16 Wash yourselves clean:
CLEANSED
 4:4   of the women of Zion and cleansed
CLEAR
36:6   It is clear you depend on the support
41:24 It is clear you are of no account,
CLEARED
62:10 pave a highway cleared of stones;
CLEARING
 5:2   He cultivated it, clearing it of stones,
CLEAVED
48:21 he cleaved the rock and water gushed
CLEVER
 5:21 and clever in their own view!
CLIFFS
 2:21 and fissures in the cliffs,
33:16 impregnable cliffs are their fortress.
CLIMB
22:1   to climb onto the housetops?
CLOAKS
 3:23 sheer linen, millinery, and cloaks.
CLOTHE
22:21 I will clothe him with your robe
50:3   I clothe the heavens with the
51:9   arise; clothe yourself with power,
52:1   arise; clothe yourself with power,
58:7   see men underclad to clothe them,
CLOTHED
23:18 their fill and be elegantly clothed.
59:17 he clothed himself with vengeance for
63:2   Why are you clothed in red,
CLOTHES
 4:1   wear our own clothes,
36:22 to Hezekiah with their clothes rent

426

COME *continued*
60:3 Nations will come to your light,
60:4 have all assembled to come to you:
60:6 all from Sheba will come,
60:14 will come bowing before you;
63:4 the year of my redeemed had come.
65:5 don't come near me; I am holier than
66:18 For I will come to gather all nations
66:23 all flesh shall come to worship
COMELY
52:7 How comely upon the mountains
COMES
5:29 and none comes to the rescue.
17:3 Ephraim's defense comes to an end,
21:12 Morning comes, though it is still
24:8 pulsating of lyres comes to an end.
30:28 He comes to sift the nations
38:16 comes a newness of life,
40:10 my Lord the Lord comes with power;
62:11 See, your Salvation comes,
66:15 See, the Lord comes with fire,
COMFORT
22:4 hasten not to comfort me
40:1 Comfort and give solace to my people,
61:2 to comfort all who mourn:
66:13 I will comfort you;
COMFORTABLE
32:18 in comfortable dwellings.
COMFORTED
52:9 the Lord has comforted his people;
66:13 one who is comforted by his mother
66:13 for Jerusalem you shall be comforted.
COMFORTER
51:12 I myself am your Comforter.
COMFORTING
49:13 The Lord is comforting his people,
51:3 For the Lord is comforting Zion,
COMING
21:12 do so by repenting and coming back.
30:18 will the Lord delay his coming ,
30:27 Lord Omnipotent coming from afar!
35:4 God is coming to avenge and to
36:16 me by coming out to me. Then every
48:7 things now coming into being, not
48:16 at their coming to pass, I have been
49:12 See these, coming from afar, these,
63:1 Who it this coming from Edom in red
COMINGS
37:28 and your comings and goings,
COMMANDED
14:12 You who commanded the nations
36:21 the king commanded them not to
COMMANDERS
10:8 He will say, Are not my commanders
21:5 Mobilize, you commanders! Oil the
COMMANDMENTS
29:13 commandments of men learned by

48:18 you but obeyed my commandments,
COMMEMORATE
12:4 commemorate his exalted name.
COMMENCES
30:29 the night when a festival commences,
COMMERCE
23:18 Her commerce shall provide for those
COMMISSION
10:6 I will commission him against a
22:20 In that day I will commission my
COMMISSIONED
42:19 blind like those I have commissioned,
COMMITTING
37:19 committing their gods to the fire.
COMMON
8:1 on it in common script:
22:24 bowls to the most common containers.
COMMOTION
14:9 Sheol below was in commotion
17:12 tumultuous nations, in commotion
22:5 a day of commotion and trampling
COMMUNITY
25:3 a community of tyrannous nations
COMPARE
46:5 you compare me or count me equal?
COMPARED
40:25 to whom can I be compared? says the
COMPASSION
9:19 Men will have no compassion for one
13:18 not look with compassion on children.
14:1 Lord will have compassion on Jacob
49:13 showing compassion for his afflicted.
49:15 feel no compassion for the child of
54:7 with loving compassion I will gather
54:8 I will have compassion on you,
54:10 the Lord, who has compassion on you.
63:9 In his love and compassion
63:15 of thy bosom and thy compassion
COMPELLED
59:14 redress is compelled to back away,
COMPILED
40:12 Who compiled the earth's dust by
COMPLACENT
32:9 to my voice, O complacent women;
32:11 Be alarmed, you complacent women;
COMPREHENDED
40:13 Who has comprehended the Spirit of
COMPREHENSION
44:19 nor have the sense or comprehension
CONCEAL
1:15 I will conceal my eyes from you;
6:2 with two conceal their location,
26:21 and no more conceal its slain.
CONCEIT
10:12 boasting and infamous conceit,
CONCEIVE
59:4 they conceive misdeeds, they beget

CONCEIVED
7:5 even though Aram has conceived
8:3 she conceived and gave birth to a son.
33:11 You who conceived chaff and brought
CONCEIVING
59:13 conceiving in the mind and pondering
CONDUCT
33:15 who conduct themselves righteously
57:18 I have seen his conduct and will
CONDUCTED
33:18 those who conducted the census?
CONFERRED
62:2 conferred by the mouth of the Lord.
CONFIDENCE
30:15 quiet confidence gain the victory.
36:4 with such confidence?
CONFINEMENT
24:22 and shut in confinement many days,
42:7 to free captives from confinement
CONFLAGRATIONS
29:6 conflagrations of devouring flame.
66:15 to rebuke with conflagrations of fire.
CONFLICT
45:9 to those in conflict with their Maker,
CONFOUNDED
50:7 knowing I shall not be confounded.
54:4 for you shall not be confounded;
CONFRONT
50:8 Let him confront me with them!
CONFRONTING
30:11 Cease confronting us with the Holy
42:16 the darkness confronting them I will
CONFUSED
9:16 and those who are led are confused.
44:11 Their whole society is confused;
CONFUSION
19:14 with a spirit of confusion;
37:27 shrank away in confusion,
42:17 shall retreat in utter confusion.
CONGREGATE
29:7 all who congregate at her stronghold
CONQUERED
37:24 I have conquered the highest
CONSECRATED
23:18 be consecrated to the Lord;
CONSEQUENCE
14:21 in consequence of their fathers'
CONSERVED
22:9 you conserved water in the Lower
CONSIDER
41:20 all may see it and know, consider it,
47:7 and did not consider these,
52:15 had not heard, they shall consider.
58:13 and consider the Sabbath a delight,
64:9 See, consider that we are all thy
CONSIDERATION
2:22 For of what consideration is he?

CONSIDERED
29:17 fruitful be considered backwoods?
32:5 nor rogues considered respectable.
62:4 and your land considered espoused.
CONSIGNED
34:2 consigned them to the slaughter.
CONSIST
59:6 Their works consist of wrongdoing;
CONSISTING
29:13 their piety toward me consisting of
CONSOLE
57:18 I will guide him and amply console
CONSOLED
12:1 and thou has consoled me.
CONSOLES
51:19 the sword—and who consoles you?
CONSOLING
66:11 at her consoling breasts;
CONSPIRACY
8:12 Do not call a conspiracy all that these
8:12 call a conspiracy;
CONSTANT
51:13 that you go all day in constant dread
CONSTANTLY
27:3 I water it constantly, watch over it
52:5 my name is constantly abused all the
65:3 a people who constantly provoke me
CONSTELLATIONS
13:10 The stars and constellations of the
CONSTRAIN
58:3 and constrain all who toil for you.
CONSULT
45:21 go ahead and consult one another.
CONSULTATIONS
8:10 Though you hold consultations,
CONSUME
9:18 briars and thorns shall it consume;
10:18 it will consume, both life and
43:2 its flame shall not consume you.
50:9 the moth shall consume them,
51:8 moth shall consume them like a
CONSUMES
5:24 As a blazing fire consumes stubble,
26:11 consumes them.
CONSUMMATION
6:3 the consummation of all the earth is
CONSUMPTION
10:16 send a consumption into his fertile
CONTAIN
38:13 Can I contain myself until morning,
CONTAINERS
22:24 bowls to the most common containers.
CONTEMPLATE
26:8 desire is to contemplate thy name.
CONTEMPT
33:8 their signatories held in contempt;
37:22 of Zion holds you in contempt;

CONTEND
3:13 Lord will take a stand and contend
41:12 look for those who contend with you,
49:25 I . . . will contend with your contenders
57:16 I will not contend forever, nor always
CONTENDERS
49:25 I . . . will contend with your contenders
CONTENT
2:6 content with the infantile heathen.
CONTENTEDLY
66:11 From now on nurse contentedly
CONTENTION
58:4 You fast amid strife and contention,
CONTINUALLY
18:2 a people continually infringing,
18:7 a people continually infringing,
49:16 have sealed you to be continually
58:11 The Lord will direct you continually;
CONTRADICTION
29:16 What a contradiction you are!
CONTRARY
3:8 are contrary to the Lord.
CONTRITE
66:2 are of a humble and contrite spirit
CONTRIVE
29:15 Woe to those who contrive
CONTRIVED
31:6 contrived to go far astray, O children
CONVENING
1:13 As for convening meetings at the New
CONVEYANCE
22:19 your inglorious conveyance there
CONVULSE
24:19 the earth shall convulse and lurch.
COPPER
60:17 In place of copper I will bring gold,
60:17 in place of wood I will bring copper,
CORDS
33:20 nor any of its cords severed.
54:2 Do not hold back; lengthen your cords
CORNER
51:20 lie in a faint at the corner of every
CORNERSTONE
28:16 a precious cornerstone, a sure
CORPSES
5:25 mountains quake, and their corpses
34:3 and their corpses emit a stench;
66:24 corpses of the people who
CORRECT
58:2 concerning correct ordinances,
COST
55:1 with no money and at no cost.
COUCH
28:20 The couch is too short to stretch out
COUNSEL
11:2 the spirit of counsel and of valor,
19:11 advisers give absurd counsel.

28:29 whose counsel is wonderful,
41:28 not one who could offer counsel,
46:11 man who performs my counsel.
COUNSELLED
40:14 Of whom was he counselled
COUNSELLOR
9:6 Wonderful Counsellor, one Mighty in
COUNSELLORS
1:26 your counsellors as in the beginning.
COUNT
46:5 you compare me or count me equal?
COUNTING
40:15 counting no more than dust on a
COUNTRIES
36:20 Who of all the gods of those countries
COUNTRY
22:18 into an open country.
32:2 shade of a large rock in arid country.
33:21 a country of rivers and broad
41:18 up streams in barren hill country,
COURAGE
8:9 You may take courage in one another,
35:4 Take courage, be unafraid!
41:6 saying, each to his fellow, Courage!
COURIERS
16:1 Send couriers to those who rule in the
COURSE
26:7 pavest an undeviating course for the
COURT
29:21 who ensnare the defender at court,
COURTS
1:12 requires you to trample my courts
COVENANT
24:5 set at nought the ancient covenant.
28:18 Your covenant with Death shall prove
42:6 to be a covenant for the people,
49:8 to be a covenant of the people,
54:10 nor my covenant of peace be shaken,
55:3 with you an everlasting covenant;
56:4 holding fast to my covenant—
56:6 holding fast to my covenant—
59:21 this is my covenant with them,
61:8 make with them an eternal covenant.
COVENANTED
28:15 to have covenanted with Death,
COVER
50:3 I put up sackcloth to cover them.
60:6 camels shall cover your land,
COVERED
14:11 you are covered with worms.
29:10 he has covered your heads, the seers.
COVERING
28:20 the covering too narrow to wrap
59:6 worthless for covering themselves.
COVERS
60:2 Although darkness covers the earth,

COVERT
25:4 a covert from the downpour
COVET
13:17 do not value silver, nor covet gold.
COVETOUSNESS
57:17 sin of covetousness I was provoked;
COW
7:21 alive a young cow and a pair of sheep.
11:7 When a cow and bear browse,
CRAFT
2:16 merchant ships and pleasure craft.
18:2 in swift craft across the water.
CRAFTSMAN
40:19 silver chain from the craftsman?
CRAFTSMEN
3:3 advisers, skilled craftsmen, and
CRAGS
57:5 under the crags of rocks.
CRAMPED
49:20 This place is too cramped for us;
CRASH
30:14 It shall shatter with a crash
CRAVING
29:8 but wakes up faint and craving.
CREAM
7:15 Cream and honey will he eat
7:22 men will eat the cream.
7:22 will feed on cream and honey.
CREATE
44:15 they create gods which they adore,
45:8 I, the Lord, create it.
54:16 It is I who create the smith who fans
54:16 I who create the ravager to destroy.
65:17 I create new heavens and a new earth;
65:18 and be glad forever in what I create.
65:18 See, I create Jerusalem to be a delight
CREATED
41:20 that the Holy One of Israel created it.
42:6 I have created you and appointed you
43:1 he who created you, O Israel:
44:21 I have created you to be my servant,
45:12 and created man upon it;
45:18 the Lord who created the heavens,
49:8 I have created you and appointed you
CREATES
44:13 He creates it by chiselling to the
CREATOR
40:28 Creator of the ends of the earth.
43:15 Creator of Israel, am your King.
CREATURES
13:21 demonic creatures prance about in it.
13:22 howling creatures from its
34:13 the haunt of howling creatures,
35:7 in the haunt of howling creatures
42:5 form to the earth and its creatures,
CREDITOR
24:2 with creditor as with debtor—

CREDITORS
50:1 which of my creditors did I sell you?
CRESCENTS
3:18 head ornaments and crescents,
CREVICES
2:21 Men will go into crevices in the rocks
CRIED
21:8 Then the lookout cried,
CRIES
26:17 cries out from her pangs during
CRIME
53:8 for the crime of my people,
CRIMES
50:1 of your crimes was your mother
CRIMINALS
1:28 But criminals and sinners
53:12 and was numbered with criminals—
CRIMSON
1:18 they have reddened as crimson,
CRINGE
44:11 they would at once cringe in fear.
CRISIS
66:9 I bring to a crisis and not bring on
CROCUS
35:1 when it blossoms like the crocus.
CROOKED
59:8 They have made crooked their paths;
CROPS
17:10 though you plant choice crops
CROSS
10:29 They cross over the pass,
23:12 Get up and cross over to Kittim,
43:2 When you cross the water, I will be
CROSSING
23:2 the traders of Sidon crossing the seas
CROWDS
29:5 your crowds of evildoers shall
CROWN
28:5 be as a crown of beauty and wreath of
62:3 Then shall you be a crown of glory
CROWNED
35:10 their heads crowned with everlasting
51:11 their heads crowned with everlasting
CROWNING
28:1 Their crowning splendor has become
CROWNS
28:4 fading wreaths, the crowns of glory
CRUCIBLE
1:25 away your dross as in a crucible,
48:10 testing you in the crucible of
CRUEL
13:9 a cruel outburst of anger and wrath
19:4 into the hand of a cruel master;
CRUSH
53:10 But the Lord willed to crush him,
CRUSHED
24:19 The earth shall be crushed and rent;

CRUSHED *continued*
27:9   he makes like crushed chalkstone
53:5   crushed because of our iniquities;
CRUTCH
3:1   of both staff and crutch—
CRY
10:30   Cry out, O Daughter of Gallim!
13:22   Jackals will cry out from its palaces,
15:4   Heshbon will cry for help, as will
15:5   My heart will cry out for Moab;
15:5   they will raise the cry of catastrophe.
15:8   The cry of calamity
19:20   cry out to the Lord because of
29:9   until you cry for help,
30:19   graciously respond at the cry of your
42:11   cry out from the tops of the mountain
42:13   he will give the war cry,
46:7   Though they cry to it for help, it does
52:8   as one they cry out for joy:
57:13   When you cry out in distress,
58:9   should you cry, he will say, I am
65:14   you shall cry out with heartbreak,
65:19   of weeping or the cry of distress.
CRYING
22:5   and of crying in distress,
CULTISTS
66:17   As for the cultists who fornicate in
CULTIVATED
5:2   He cultivated it, clearing it of stones,
7:25   And on all hillsides cultivated
CUMIN
28:25   sprinkle fennel and scatter cumin?
28:27   nor is a cartwheel rolled over cumin:
28:27   and cumin with a rod.
CUP
51:17   the cup of his wrath,
51:22   I am taking the cup of stupor from
CURRENCY
7:23   a thousand pieces of currency
CURRENTS
44:27   I am drying up your currents,
CURSE
8:21   gazing upward, curse their
24:6   The curse devours the earth,
65:15   to serve my chosen ones as a curse
CUSH
11:11   Egypt, Pathros, Cush, Elam, Shinar,
18:1   beyond the rivers of Cush,
20:3   against Egypt and Cush,
20:4   and the exiles of Cush, both young
20:5   at Cush, their hope, and at Egypt,
37:9   Tirhakah king of Cush had set out to
43:3   Cush and Seba I give in place of
45:14   of Egypt and merchandise of Cush
CUT
7:20   legs, and to cut off even your beard.
9:14   Therefore the Lord will cut off from

11:13   the hostile ones of Judah be cut off;
14:22   I will cut off Babylon's name and
15:2   head shall be bald, every beard cut
18:5   they will cut down the fruit-bearing
22:25   and the burden hanging on it cut off.
29:20   persist in wickedness shall be cut off
38:12   My life is cut off like woven fabric;
44:14   He is required to cut down cedars;
45:2   and cut through iron bars.
48:19   names would not have been cut off
51:1   to the rock from which you were cut,
53:8   cut off from the land of the living
56:5   that shall not be cut off.
CYPRESS
55:13   thornbush shall come up the cypress,
CYPRESSES
37:24   tallest cedars, its choicest cypresses.
41:19   I will place cypresses,
60:13   cypresses, pines, and firs together—
CYRUS
44:28   says of Cyrus, He is my shepherd;
45:1   to Cyrus, whom I grasp by the right
DAILY
58:2   Yet they importune me daily,
DAMASCUS
7:8   as Damascus is the capital of Aram
7:8   and Rezin the head of Damascus,
8:4   the wealth of Damascus and
10:9   Samaria no better than Damascus?
17:1   An oracle concerning Damascus:
17:1   Damascus shall cease to be a city
17:3   so shall the sovereignty of Damascus:
DAMNATION
34:5   people I have sentenced to damnation.
DANDLED
66:12   and dandled on the knees.
DARK
29:15   They work in the dark, thinking,
59:10   at noon as in the dark of night;
DARKENED
5:30   for the daylight shall be darkened
DARKNESS
5:20   They put darkness for light
5:20   and light for darkness;
8:22   into outer darkness.
9:2   The people walking in darkness
29:18   out of gross darkness.
42:7   prison those who sit in darkness.
42:16   darkness confronting them I will turn
45:7   I fashion light and form darkness;
45:19   somewhere in a land of darkness;
49:9   and to those in darkness, Show
50:10   though he walk in darkness and have
58:10   shall your light dawn amid darkness
59:9   light, but there prevails darkness;
60:2   Although darkness covers the earth,

DART
22:17 he will make you soar like a dart.
DASHED
13:16 infants shall be dashed to pieces
DAUGHTER
1:8 The Daughter of Zion is left
10:30 Cry out, O Daughter of Gallim!
10:32 the mountain of the Daughter of Zion
16:1 the mountain of the Daughter of Zion
22:4 ruin of the Daughter of my People.
23:10 O Daughter of Tarshish: the harbor
23:12 O ravished virgin, Daughter of Sidon.
37:22 The Virgin Daughter of Zion holds
37:22 The Daughter of Jerusalem shakes her
47:1 O Virgin Daughter of Babylon;
47:1 O Daughter of the Chaldeans.
47:5 O Daughter of the Chaldeans.
52:2 O captive Daughter of Zion.
62:11 Tell the Daughter of Zion,
DAUGHTERS
32:9 careless daughters, hear my words!
32:11 be perturbed, O careless daughters!
43:6 and my daughters from the end of the
49:22 carry your daughters on their
56:5 is better than sons and daughters;
60:4 daughters shall return to your side.
DAUNTED
31:4 nor daunted by their numbers,
DAVID
7:2 the house of David was informed
7:13 O house of David! Is it not enough
9:7 that, on the throne of David
16:5 be set up in the abode of David,
22:9 the city of David increasingly
22:22 of the house of David:
29:1 Ariel, the city where David lodged!
37:35 and for the sake of my servant David.
38:5 the God of your father David:
55:3 my loving fidelity toward David.
DAWN
14:12 O morning star, son of the dawn!
58:8 light break through like the dawn
58:10 shall your light dawn amid darkness
60:3 the brightness of your dawn.
DAWNED
9:2 has the light dawned.
60:1 Arise, shine, your light has dawned;
DAY
2:11 alone shall be exalted in that day.
2:12 The lord of Hosts has a day in store
2:17 alone shall be exalted in that day.
2:20 In that day men will throw away
3:7 he will raise his hand in that day
3:18 In that day the Lord will strip away
4:1 in that day, and say,
4:2 In that day the plant of the Lord
4:5 day and a mist glowing with

4:6 from the heat of the day,
5:30 stirred up against them in that day,
7:17 house a day unlike since
7:17 the day of the king of Assyria.
7:18 In that day the Lord will
7:20 In that day my Lord will use
7:21 In that day a man will keep
7:23 In that day every plot of ground
9:4 as in the day of Midian's defeat.
9:14 palm top and reed, in a single day;
10:3 will you do in the day of reckoning
10:17 his briars and thorns in a single day.
10:20 In that day those who survive of
10:27 In that day their burdens shall be
10:32 This same day he will but pause at
11:10 In that day the sprig of Jesse,
11:11 In that day my Lord will again raise
12:1 In that day you will say,
12:4 In that day you will say,
13:6 Lament, for the day of the Lord is
13:9 The day of the Lord shall come
13:13 in the day of his blazing wrath.
14:3 In the day the Lord gives you
17:4 In that day Jacob's glory shall wane,
17:7 In that day men will have regard to
17:9 In that day their mighty cities
17:11 the day you plant them,
17:11 in a day of diseases and incurable
19:16 In that day the Egyptians will
19:18 In that day five Hebrew-speaking
19:19 In that day there shall be an altar
19:21 Lord in that day. They will
19:23 In that day there shall be a
19:24 In that day Israel shall be the
20:6 In that day shall the inhabitants
21:8 day in and day out, my Lord;
22:5 a day of commotion and trampling
22:5 a day of battering down walls,
22:8 And in the day Judea's defensive
22:12 In such a day my Lord, the Lord of
22:20 In that day I will commission my
22:25 In that day, says the Lord of Hosts,
23:15 In that day Tyre shall be forgotten
24:21 In that day will the Lord deal on high
25:1 In that day you will say,
25:9 In that day you will say, This is our
26:1 In that day shall this song be sung in
27:1 In that day will the Lord,
27:2 In that day, sing of the earth
27:3 watch over it night and day,
27:8 in the day of the burning east wind.
27:12 In that day the Lord will thresh out
27:13 In that day a loud trumpet shall
28:5 In that day shall the Lord of Hosts
28:19 by day and by night it shall seize
29:18 In that day shall the deaf hear the
30:8 record it in a book for the last day,

DAY *continued*
30:23 In that day your cattle shall graze
30:25 on the day of the great slaughter,
30:26 in the day the Lord binds up
31:7 For in that day every one of you will
34:8 For it is the Lord's day of vengeance,
34:10 Night and day it shall not be
37:3 This is a woeful day, a day of reproof
38:13 Surely, as night has followed day,
38:19 as I do this day; from father to sons
47:9 overtake you, both in one day.
49:8 in the day of salvation I have come to
51:13 that you go all day in constant dread
52:5 is constantly abused all the day.
52:6 in that day they shall know
58:3 It is because on your fast day you
58:5 a day of the Lord's good graces?
58:13 your own ends on my holy day—
58:13 the holy day of the Lord venerable,
60:11 they shall not be shut day or night,
60:19 shall the sun be your light by day,
61:2 and the day of vengeance of our God,
62:6 who shall not be silent day or night.
63:4 I had resolved on a day of vengeance,
65:2 I held out my hands all the day to a
65:5 a fire smoldering all day long.
66:8 Can the earth labor but a day
DAYBREAK
26:9 at daybreak my spirit within me
DAYLIGHT
5:30 for the daylight shall be darkened
DAYS
2:2 In the latter days
13:22 Babylon's days shall not be
24:22 confinement many days,
27:6 For in days to come, when Jacob takes
30:26 as the light of seven days shall it be,
37:26 how in days of old I planned it?
38:1 days Hezekiah became gravely ill.
38:20 all the days of our lives in the house
53:10 see his offspring and prolong his days,
54:9 This is to me as in the days of Noah,
60:20 when your days of mourning are
63:9 all the days of old.
63:11 people recalled the days of Moses
65:20 infants alive but a few days,
DAZZLED
41:23 we will be dazzled and all stand in
DEAD
8:19 inquire of the dead on behalf of the
26:14 They are dead, to live no more,
26:19 Yet shall thy dead live when their
26:19 For the earth shall cast up its dead.
37:36 there lay all their dead bodies!
59:10 prime of life we resemble the dead.
DEAF
29:18 In that day shall the deaf hear the

35:5 and the ears of the deaf unstopped.
42:18 O you deaf, listen; O you blind, look
42:19 or so deaf as the messenger I have
43:8 who are deaf, yet have ears.
DEAL
24:21 In that day will the Lord deal on high
DEALING
30:12 manipulation and double dealing,
DEALINGS
59:6 they manipulate injurious dealings.
61:8 For I the Lord love just dealings—
DEALT
27:8 Thou hast dealt with them
DEAR
64:11 and all places dear to us lie in ruins.
DEARTH
58:11 will satisfy your needs in the dearth
DEATH
6:1 In the year of King Uzziah's death,
9:2 of the shadow of death
25:8 by abolishing Death forever.
28:15 to have covenanted with Death,
28:18 covenant with Death shall prove
38:18 nor Death glorify thee;
53:9 among the wicked in death,
53:12 he poured out his soul unto death,
DEBASE
2:9 when men thus debase themselves.
5:15 when men debase themselves,
57:9 and debase yourself to the depths.
DEBTOR
24:2 with creditor as with debtor—
DECAY
5:24 so shall their roots decay away
40:20 select a wood that resists decay.
DECAYING
64:6 We are decaying like leaves, all of us;
DECEIT
53:9 and deceit was not in his mouth.
DECEITFULLY
24:16 turncoats have deceitfully betrayed!
59:4 on empty words, deceitfully spoken;
DECEPTION
28:15 by taking refuge in deception
DECISIONS
28:7 they blunder in their decisions.
DECK
21:5 they deck them with candlesticks.
DECLARE
42:9 Before they spring up I declare them
58:1 Declare to my people their
66:19 And they shall declare my glory
DECLARED
23:4 mighty haven of the Sea, has declared,
41:26 declared it ahead of time,
DECOMPOSE
34:4 their fat decompose

DECREE
45:23 by a decree that cannot be revoked:
DECREED
10:22 although annihilation is decreed,
10:23 decreed upon the whole earth.
13:11 I have decreed calamity for the world,
28:22 have heard utter destruction decreed
34:16 By his mouth he decreed it,
DEDANITES
21:13 You wandering bands of Dedanites
DEEDS
 1:16 remove your wicked deeds
 3:11 for the deeds they have done!
12:4 Make known his deeds among the
14:21 consequence of their fathers' deeds,
45:11 about the deeds of my hands?
DEEMED
53:3 shunned, deemed by us of no merit.
DEEP
29:10 a spirit of deep sleep:
30:33 broad and deep is its fire pit and
44:27 who says to the deep, Become dry;
51:10 the waters of the mighty deep,
63:13 when he led them through the deep?
DEER
13:14 Then, like a deer that is chased,
35:6 Then shall the lame leap like deer,
DEFEAT
 9:4 as in the day of Midian's defeat.
DEFENDER
29:21 who ensnare the defender at court,
DEFENDS
51:22 who defends the cause of his people:
DEFENSE
17:3 Ephraim's defense comes to an end,
DEFENSIVE
22:8 in that day Judea's defensive screen
DEFIANT
65:2 hands all the day to a defiant people,
DEFILED
47:6 so I let my inheritance be defiled.
52:1 uncircumcised and defiled enter you.
52:11 touch nothing defiled as you leave
59:3 your palms are defiled with blood,
64:6 altogether become as those defiled,
DEGREES
38:8 the ten degrees it has gone down.
38:8 descent by ten degrees on the dial.
DEJECTION
16:7 groan . . . in utter dejection.
DELAY
30:18 will the Lord delay his coming,
DELAYED
46:13 salvation shall no longer be delayed.
DELECTABLE
25:6 cakes, succulent and delectable,

DELICATE
47:1 as delicate and refined.
DELIGHT
16:10 no shouts of delight shall sound in
35:2 singing with delight;
42:1 my chosen one in whom I delight,
58:13 and consider the Sabbath a delight,
58:14 then shall you delight in the Lord,
62:4 be known as she in whom I delight
62:4 For the Lord shall delight in you,
65:18 See, I create Jerusalem to be a delight
65:19 I will delight in Jerusalem, rejoice in
DELIGHTFUL
27:2 as of a delightful vineyard
DELIGHTING
66:3 delighting in their abominations,
DELIGHTS
61:10 my soul delights in my God.
DELINQUENTS
 3:4 delinquents will lord it over them.
DELIVER
19:4 Then will I deliver the Egyptians
19:20 up their cause and deliver them.
31:5 by protecting it he will deliver it,
35:4 God himself will come and deliver
36:14 delude you! He cannot deliver you.
36:19 Did they deliver Samaria out of my
37:3 there is no strength to deliver them.
37:12 destroyed deliver them?
37:12 Did they deliver Gozan
37:20 now, O Lord our God, deliver us out
38:6 And I will deliver you and this city
43:13 from my hand none can deliver;
49:25 and I will deliver your children.
50:2 have I no power to deliver?
DELIVERANCE
20:6 deliverance from the king of Assyria!
46:12 I will grant deliverance in Zion,
DELIVERED
41:2 Who has delivered nations to him,
DELIVERING
63:9 angel of his presence delivering them
DELIVERS
66:7 overtakes her, she delivers a son!
DELUDE
36:14 delude you! He cannot deliver you.
37:10 delude you into thinking that
DELUDED
19:13 the officials of Noph deluded;
44:20 their deluded minds have distracted
DELUGE
28:2 like an inundating deluge of mighty
DEMAND
 1:17 Learn to do good: demand justice,
62:12 and you shall be known as in demand,
DEMANDS
42:22 a spoil, yet none demands restitution.

DEMARCATE
28:25 Does he not demarcate wheat from
DEMOLISH
37:26 destined to demolish fortified cities,
DEMOLISHED
61:4 demolished generations ago.
DEMOLISHING
14:17 demolishing its cities,
DEMONIC
13:21 and demonic creatures prance about
DEN
11:8 infant will play near the adder's den,
DENOUNCE
32:7 to denounce the needy.
DENSE
10:34 The dense forests shall be battered
DENUDED
33:9 Bashan and Carmel are denuded.
DENY
5:23 but deny justice to the innocent!
DENYING
10:2 denying justice to the needy,
59:13 willfully denying the Lord,
DEPART
38:10 must I depart through Sheol's gates,
49:17 ruined you shall depart from you,
52:11 Turn away, depart;
55:12 You shall depart in joy and be led
59:21 shall not depart from your mouth,
DEPARTURE
49:19 the departure of your devourers.
DEPEND
36:6 It is clear you depend on the support
DEPENDENT
30:12 and on them are dependent,
DEPENDING
36:9 depending as you do on Egypt for
DEPLORE
19:8 Fishermen will deplore their lot
DEPRESSING
8:22 but there shall be a depressing
DEPRIVED
38:10 deprived of the balance of my years?
DEPRIVES
3:1 deprives Judea and Jerusalem
DEPRIVING
3:14 your houses by depriving the needy.
10:2 depriving the poor of my people of
32:6 depriving the thirsty soul of drink.
DEPTHS
7:11 whether in the depths below
14:15 to the utmost depths of the Pit.
51:10 and made of ocean depths a way
57:9 and debase yourself to the depths.
DERANGED
44:9 who manufacture idols are deranged;

DESCEND
5:14 into it descend their elite with the
55:10 rains and snows descend from the sky
64:1 rend the heavens and descend,
DESCENDANTS
14:22 offspring and descendants, says the
14:29 From among the descendants of that
14:30 your descendants I will kill with
22:24 his descendants and posterity,
39:7 offspring and descendants, they shall
48:19 your descendants as many as their
DESCENDING
30:30 his arm descending in furious rage,
63:14 like cattle descending the slopes
DESCENDS
31:4 Lord of Hosts be when he descends
DESCENT
38:8 sun reversed its descent by ten
64:3 unexpected by us: thy descent of
DESERT
16:1 from Sela in the desert
16:8 trailing through the desert;
25:5 or like scorching heat in the desert,
32:2 like brooks of water in a desert place,
32:15 the desert shall become productive
32:16 So shall justice inhabit the desert,
35:1 the desert shall rejoice
35:6 and streams flow in the desert.
40:3 In the desert prepare the way for the
41:18 I will turn the desert into lakes,
42:11 Let the desert and its cities
43:19 I am making roads through the desert,
50:2 rivers I turn into desert—
51:3 her desert as the garden of the Lord.
63:13 Like the horse of the desert, they
64:10 Zion is a desert, Jerusalem a
DESERTED
17:9 shall be like the deserted towns
27:10 deserted habitations, forsaken like a
32:14 the clamorous towns deserted.
54:1 The children of the deserted wife
62:12 a city never deserted.
DESERVE
59:18 According to what they deserve, he
DESERVING
10:6 deserving of my vengeance,
DESIGN
41:15 of new design, full of spikes:
DESIGNATED
14:31 he has designated shall evade it.
DESIGNED
22:11 the One who designed it long ago.
45:18 but designed it to be inhabited:
DESIGNER
29:16 or a work of its designer, He doesn't
DESIRE
26:8 the soul's desire is to contemplate

42:24 For they have no desire to walk in his
55:11 it accomplishes what I desire,
DESIRING
58:2 desiring to draw nearer to God:
DESIST
2:22 Desist from the things of man,
DESOLATE
5:9 many buildings shall lie desolate,
6:11 Until the cities lie desolate
15:6 waters of Nimrim shall be desolate;
19:5 streambeds become desolate and dry.
23:14 your haven is desolate!
33:8 highways are desolate, travel is at an
49:8 reapportion the desolate estates,
54:3 and resettle the desolate cities.
61:4 they will renew the desolate cities
62:4 nor your land referred to as desolate;
DESOLATION
5:6 I will make it a desolation:
13:9 to make the earth a desolation,
17:9 Israelites during the desolation.
51:19 desolation, ruin—and who laments
64:10 is a desert, Jerusalem a desolation.
DESPAIR
19:10 textile workers will know despair,
57:10 you have not admitted despair;
DESPISE
31:7 despise your idolatrous silver and
DESPISED
5:24 For they have despised the law of the
49:7 to him who is despised as a person,
53:3 He was despised and disdained by
DESPITE
47:13 powerless, despite all your tactics.
49:19 despite the departure of your
DESPOIL
17:14 the fate of those who despoil us.
DESPOILED
33:1 who yourself was not despoiled;
DESPOILER
33:1 Woe to you, despoiler,
DESPOILERS
42:24 and Israel to despoilers, if not the
DESTINE
65:12 I will destine you to the sword;
DESTINED
37:26 You were destined to demolish
51:14 he shall not die as those destined
DESTINY
47:7 or remember her final destiny.
DESTITUTE
3:26 she shall sit on the ground destitute.
DESTROY
25:7 In this mountain he will destroy
36:10 this land and destroy it.
37:19 and so they could destroy them.
54:16 is I who create the ravager to destroy.

65:8 Don't destroy it, it is still good,
DESTROYED
14:20 for you have destroyed your land
15:1 Moab shall be destroyed.
16:4 tyrants are destroyed from the earth,
23:11 that her ports of haven be destroyed.
36:10 this land and destroyed it without
37:12 my fathers destroyed deliver them?
37:18 destroyed all peoples and their
DESTROYER
21:2 the destroyer laying waste.
DESTROYING
48:9 by not entirely destroying you.
65:8 by not destroying everything:
DESTRUCTION
10:23 will carry out the utter destruction
13:5 to cause destruction throughout the
14:23 it with the broom of destruction,
21:15 For they flee from destruction,
26:14 thou appointest them to destruction,
28:22 for I have heard utter destruction
51:13 readies himself to wreak destruction?
DETERIORATE
40:20 an image that will not deteriorate.
DETERMINED
14:26 These are things determined upon the
14:27 the Lord of Hosts has determined,
DETESTS
1:14 my soul detests.
DETHRONED
47:1 squat on the ground, dethroned,
DEVASTATED
15:1 When in one night Ar is devastated,
33:1 you shall be devastated;
DEVASTATING
33:1 when you have done with devastating,
DEVELOPING
18:5 blossoms are developing into young
DEVIATES
47:15 each deviates his own way;
DEVICES
32:7 insidious devices to ruin the poor,
DEVIOUS
27:1 Leviathan, that devious sea monster,
DEVISED
23:8 Who devised this stratagem against
23:9 The Lord of Hosts devised it,
54:17 Whatever weapon is devised against
DEVOID
8:20 words devoid of light,
DEVOTED
29:23 devoted to the Holy One of Jacob,
DEVOUR
9:12 will devour Israel with open mouth.
9:20 they will devour on the left, but not
10:17 and it shall burn up and devour
31:8 sword not of mortals shall devour

DEVOUR *continued*
51:8   moths shall devour them like wool.
56:9   come and devour!
DEVOURED
1:7   your native soil is devoured by aliens
3:14   It is you who have devoured the
DEVOURERS
49:19   the departure of your devourers.
DEVOURING
29:6   conflagrations of devouring flame.
30:27   his tongue is like a devouring fire.
30:30   with flashes of devouring fire
33:14   can live through the devouring fire?
DEVOURS
24:6   The curse devours the earth,
28:4   he who sees it devours it
33:11   fire of your own breath devours you!
DEW
26:19   your dew is the dew of sunrise!
DIADEM
62:3   royal diadem in the palm of your God
DIAGRAM
44:13   The woodworker draws a diagram,
DIAL
38:8   afternoon sun on the dial of Ahaz
38:8   descent by ten degrees on the dial.
DIBON
15:2   and to Dibon to the hill shrines, to
15:9   Although the water of Dibon shall
15:9   I impose more than this upon Dibon:
DICTATE
45:11   or dictate to me about the deeds
DIDST
25:5   thou didst quell the onslaughts of the
63:14   So thou didst lead thy people, O
64:3   as when thou didst perform awesome
DIE
5:13   their best men die of famine,
22:2   they did not die in battle!
22:13   dine and drink, for tomorrow we die!
22:14   till you die, says my Lord,
22:18   There shall you die,
38:1   You will die; you will not recover.
43:17   they flicker and die, snuffed out
51:6   shall die in the manner of vermin.
51:14   he shall not die as those destined
65:20   those who die young shall be a
66:24   against me, whose worms do not die
DIED
14:28   In the year King Ahaz died, came this
DIES
59:5   whoever eats of their eggs dies,
DIFFERENT
65:15   he will call by a different name.
DIGNITARIES
41:25   He shall come upon dignitaries as on

DIGNITARY
3:3   the officer and dignitary,
DILUTED
1:22   your wine diluted with water.
DIM
42:3   a dim wick he will not snuff out.
42:4   Neither shall he himself grow dim or
DIMINISHED
24:6   shall be diminished
DIN
24:8   the revelers' din stops;
DINE
22:13   Let us dine and drink, for tomorrow
DIP
30:14   or dip water from a tank.
DIRE
38:17   own good I am in such dire distress;
DIRECT
58:11   The Lord will direct you continually;
DIRECTING
28:26   directing him in the proper
DIRECTION
41:25   come from the direction of sunrise.
DIRECTIONS
11:12   from the four directions of the earth.
DISAPPEAR
15:6   shall dry up, vegetation disappear,
57:1   The righteous disappear,
DISAPPOINTED
49:23   who hope in me are not disappointed.
DISASTER
3:9   brought disaster upon themselves!
31:2   and will bring disaster upon them ,
47:11   disaster shall befall you
59:7   havoc and disaster follow in their
60:18   nor dispossession or disaster within
DISCARD
30:22   You will discard as unclean
DISCERN
19:12   please tell you, if they can discern it,
DISCERNING
27:11   They are not a discerning people.
DISCERNMENT
44:18   minds are incapable of discernment.
DISCERNS
47:10   you thought, No one discerns me.
DISCHARGES
30:30   explosive discharges and pounding
DISCIPLES
8:16   seal the law among my disciples.
DISCONSOLATE
54:11   tempest-tossed and disconsolate!
DISCONSOLATELY
38:3   And Hezekiah wept disconsolately.
DISCOVER
34:14   discover for herself a resting place.

DISCRETION
40:14 instructed in the path of discretion,
DISDAIN
33:15 who disdain extortion
DISDAINED
53:3 He was despised and disdained by
DISEASED
1:5 the whole heart diseased.
DISEASES
17:11 a day of diseases and incurable pain.
DISFIGURE
24:1 he will disfigure its surface
DISFIGURED
14:19 the slain disfigured by the sword,
DISGRACE
22:18 shall be a disgrace to your master's
30:5 but a humiliation and disgrace.
37:3 a day of reproof and disgrace.
41:11 shall earn shame and disgrace;
45:16 of inventions retired in disgrace,
DISGRACED
50:7 I shall not be disgraced;
54:4 for you shall not be disgraced.
DISGUSTED
30:5 they shall be utterly disgusted
DISHONORED
48:11 that my name be not dishonored,
DISKING
28:24 disking and harrowing the same
DISLODGED
22:25 It shall be dislodged and fall,
DISMAY
26:11 Let them perceive with dismay
44:9 and mindless, to their own dismay.
DISMAYED
19:9 of fine fabrics will be dismayed,
23:4 Be dismayed, O Sidon, because the
29:22 No longer shall Jacob be dismayed;
31:4 not dismayed at the sound of their
41:10 be not dismayed, for I am your God.
41:14 O men of Israel, [be not dismayed]:
45:16 utterly dismayed and embarrassed.
45:17 you shall not be dismayed or put to
65:13 while you shall be dismayed.
DISOBEY
1:20 But if you are unwilling and disobey,
DISORDER
24:10 The towns of disorder are broken up;
DISPATCHES
43:17 who dispatches chariots and horses,
DISPEL
41:16 a tempest dispel them.
DISPENSE
1:23 they do not dispense justice to the
42:1 he will dispense justice to the
DISPLACES
40:15 the isles he displaces as mere specks.

DISPLEASED
59:15 and it displeased him.
DISPOSSESS
54:3 shall dispossess the nations
DISPOSSESSED
16:3 Shelter those dispossessed;
DISPOSSESSION
60:18 nor dispossession or disaster within
DISPUTE
50:8 Who has a dispute with me?
DISREGARD
44:21 do not disregard me.
DISREGARDED
33:8 man is disregarded.
DISROBE
47:2 unveil, disrobe, bare your legs,
DISSEMBLES
45:15 art a God who dissembles himself,
DISSOLUTION
38:17 out of the Pit of dissolution.
DISSOLVE
34:3 their blood shall dissolve on
DISTANCE
59:14 righteousness to stand at a distance;
65:5 who think, Keep your distance,
DISTANT
5:26 He raises an ensign to distant nations
8:9 Give heed, all you distant lands!
13:5 They come from a distant land beyond
39:3 They came from a distant land;
46:11 from a distant land and the man who
49:1 O isles; listen, you distant peoples:
66:19 and Javan, and to the distant isles.
DISTINGUISHED
53:2 He had no distinguished appearance,
DISTRACTED
44:20 deluded minds have distracted them.
DISTRAUGHT
21:3 I am too distraught to see.
DISTRESS
19:10 work for wages suffer distress.
22:5 crying in distress, To the mountains!
23:11 and distress kingdoms;
25:4 a shelter for the needy in distress.
26:16 O Lord, in their distress they
29:2 yet will I distress Ariel:
29:7 at her stronghold to distress her,
38:17 I am in such dire distress;
57:13 When you cry out in distress,
65:19 of weeping or the cry of distress.
DISTRESSING
5:30 too shall be a distressing gloom,
DISTURB
17:2 where no one will disturb them.
DISTURBANCE
13:13 I will cause disturbance in the

DITCHES
7:19 and by all ditches and water holes.
DIVERTED
56:11 They are all diverted to their own
DIVIDE
9:3 are joyous when they divide spoil.
53:12 he shall divide the spoil with the
DIVIDED
33:23* shall spoil in abundance be divided,
63:12 who divided the waters before them,
DIVIDERS
44:13 to the outline of the dividers;
DIVIDES
34:17 his hand that divides it by measure.
DIVINE
31:3 The Egyptians are human, not divine;
43:12 that I am divine,
46:9 I am divine; nothing resembles me.
DIVINERS
44:25 and makes fools of diviners,
DIVORCE
50:1 is your mother's bill of divorce
DOCTRINE
8:20 for doctrine and for a testimony?
DOGS
56:11 Gluttonous dogs, and insatiable,
DOG'S
66:3 as one who breaks a dog's neck;
DOING
45:9 What are you doing?
56:2 stays his hand from doing any evil.
DOMESTIC
28:28 Domestic grain is ground;
DOOMED
34:2 he has doomed them,
65:23 or bear children doomed for calamity.
DOORS
26:20 and shut the doors behind you;
45:1 opening doors ahead of him,
45:2 I will break in pieces brazen doors
57:8 Behind doors and facades
DOUBLE
30:12 on manipulation and double dealing,
40:2 double for all her sins.
DOVE
38:14 like a dove I murmur.
DOVES
59:11 we moan incessantly like doves.
60:8 flying as doves to their portals?
DOWNCAST
5:15 of the high-minded to be downcast.
61:3 robe in place of a downcast
DOWNFALL
23:13 and caused her downfall?
DOWNPOUR
4:6 downpour and from rain.
25:4 a covert from the downpour

DRAFT
10:1 who draft oppressive legislation—
DRAGON
51:9 you who slew the dragon?
DRAGONS
27:1 when he slays the dragons of the Sea.
DRAINED
19:3 Egypt's spirit shall be drained from
DRAW
45:20 draw near, all you fugitives of the
58:2 desiring to draw nearer to God:
66:11 draw at your pleasure
DRAWEST
38:17 by its means thou drawest my soul
DRAWING
12:3 shall you rejoice in drawing water
30:1 for drawing up plans, but not by me,
DRAWN
5:18 Woe to those drawn to sin by vain
21:15 from the bared sword, the drawn bow
38:14 eyes are drawn looking heavenward;
DRAWS
5:25 he draws back his hand against them
13:23 Her time draws near;
44:13 The woodworker draws a diagram,
DREAD
19:17 all reminded of it shall dread what
51:13 that you go all day in constant dread
66:4 upon them the thing they dread.
DREADED
18:2 a nation dreaded far and wide,
18:7 from a nation dreaded far and wide,
DREAM
29:7 shall be as a dream in the night.
DREAMS
29:8 a hungry man who dreams he eats,
29:8 a thirsty man who dreams he drinks,
DREGS
51:17 drinking to the dregs the bowl of
DRESS
3:22 the elegant dress, the shawl, the
3:24 instead of the festive dress, a
DRESSED
61:10 a bridegroom dressed in priestly
DRIED
37:25 I have dried up all Egypt's rivers!
51:10 Was it not you who dried up the Sea,
DRIES
27:11 A harvest of twigs dries, broken off
DRINK
22:13 Let us dine and drink, for tomorrow
24:9 Men no longer drink wine amid song;
28:7 and are giddy with strong drink:
28:7 and stagger because of strong drink;
29:9 stagger, but not from strong drink.
32:6 depriving the thirsty soul of drink.
36:12 drink their own urine?

440

36:16 and his own fig tree and drink
43:20 I may give drink to my chosen people,
44:12 if he fails to drink water, he begins
51:22 you shall drink no more from the
62:8 shall foreigners drink the new wine
62:9 those who gather it shall drink it
65:13 my servants shall drink indeed,
DRINKERS
24:9 liquor has turned bitter to drinkers.
DRINKING
5:22 to those who are valiant at drinking
21:5 They are eating and drinking . . .
22:13 eating meat and drinking wine:
51:17 drinking to the dregs the bowl of
DRINKS
29:8 a thirsty man who dreams he drinks,
34:5 When my sword drinks its fill in the
DRIVE
6:12 For the Lord will drive men away,
DRIVEN
17:13 they will be driven before the wind
41:2 as driven stubble to his bow?
DRIVING
28:28 by driving horse and threshing cart
DROMEDARIES
60:6 the dromedaries of Midian and Ephah;
66:20 on mules and dromedaries
DROPS
40:15 nations are but drops from a bucket,
DROSS
1:22 Your silver has become dross,
1:25 smelt away your dross as in a
DROWSE
5:27 they do not drowse or fall asleep.
DRUMS
5:12 drums, flutes, and wine at their
24:8 The rhythm of drums ceases,
30:29 [and drums and lyres]
DRUNK
29:9 Be drunk, but not with wine;
37:24 have dug wells and drunk of foreign
49:26 shall be drunk with their own blood
51:17 you who have drunk from the Lord's
51:21 drunk, though not with wine.
63:6 I made them drunk by my rage
DRUNKARD
19:14 her to stagger like a drunkard
24:20 shall reel to and fro like a drunkard,
DRUNKARDS
28:1 of the drunkards of Ephraim!
28:3 The proud garlands of the drunkards
DRY
5:24 and as dry weeds wane before the
11:15 The Lord will dry up the tongue
15:6 the grass shall dry up,
19:5 streambeds become desolate and dry.
19:6 Egypt's waterways recede and dry up.

33:9 has been turned into a dry waste,
42:15 I will turn rivers into dry land and
43:20 streams to the dry land,
44:3 showers upon the dry ground;
44:27 who says to the deep, Become dry;
50:2 By a mere rebuke I dry up the Sea;
DRYING
44:27 I am drying up your currents,
DUE
53:8 to whom the blow was due?
66:6 paying his enemies what is due them.
DUG
37:25 I have dug wells and drunk of
DULL
6:10 dull their ears and shut their eyes,
59:1 nor his ear dull of hearing!
DUMAH
21:11 An oracle concerning Dumah:
DUMB
6:5 I have been struck dumb,
35:6 the tongue of the dumb shout for joy.
53:7 a sheep, dumb before its shearers,
56:10 all of them are but dumb watchdogs
DUMBFOUNDED
23:2 Be dumbfounded, you inhabitants of
DUNG
25:10 as straw is trampled in a dung pit.
36:12 with you are to eat their own dung
DUNGEON
24:22 like prisoners to a dungeon
DUNGEONS
42:22 hidden away in dungeons.
DUPLICITY
59:3 your tongue utters duplicity.
DUST
2:10 Go into the rocks; hide in the dust
5:24 and their blossoms fly up like dust.
17:13 or as whirling dust in a storm.
25:12 even with the dust.
26:5 laying it even with the dust.
26:19 you who abide in the dust:
29:4 your words uttering out of the dust:
29:4 sayings shall whisper out of the dust.
29:5 evildoers shall become as fine dust,
40:12 compiled the earth's dust by measure
40:15 counting no more than dust on a
41:2 rendering them as dust to his sword,
41:15 you shall thresh mountains to dust
47:1 Get down and sit in the dust,
49:23 they will lick the dust of your feet,
52:2 yourself free, rise from the dust;
65:25 the serpent, dust shall be its food:
DWELL
5:8 and you are restricted to dwell
9:9 and those who dwell in Samaria—
11:6 shall the wolf dwell among lambs
16:4 Let the exiles of Moab dwell with you;

DWELL *continued*
23:18 dwell in the presence of the Lord,
24:6 who dwell on it have incurred guilt;
32:18 My people shall dwell in peaceful
33:16 They shall dwell on high;
33:21 the Lord cause us to dwell there,
37:28 But I know where you dwell,
40:22 them out as a tent to dwell in.
43:18 do not dwell on things of the past.
57:15 I dwell on high in the holy place,
65:9 my servants shall dwell there.
65:21 they will dwell in them;
65:22 not build so that others may dwell,
DWELLING
18:4 watch in silence over my dwelling
26:21 Lord come out of his dwelling place
38:11 among those dwelling in mortality.
DWELLINGS
32:18 in comfortable dwellings.
54:2 the canopies of your dwellings.
DWELLS
8:18 who dwells in Mount Zion.
33:5 is supreme, for he dwells on high;
42:11 and the villages where Kedar dwells;
DWELT
37:37 to Nineveh, where he dwelt.
DYNASTIES
41:4 foreordaining dynasties?
EAGER
58:2 eager to learn my ways,
EAGLES
40:31 they shall ascend as on eagles' wings;
EAR
37:17 O Lord, give ear and hear; O Lord,
50:4 by morning he wakens my ear to hear,
50:5 my Lord the Lord has opened my ear,
55:3 Give ear and come unto me;
59:1 nor his ear dull of hearing!
64:4 been heard or perceived by the ear,
EARN
41:11 shall earn shame and disgrace;
EARS
3:21 rings for the fingers and for the ears,
6:10 dull their ears and shut their eyes,
6:10 and hear with their ears,
11:3 establish proof by what his ears hear.
17:5 whose ears are reaped by the armful,
17:5 he will become like ears plucked
22:14 of Hosts revealed this to my ears:
30:21 Your ears shall hear words from
32:3 ears of those who hear shall listen.
33:15 who stop their ears at the mention of
35:5 and the ears of the deaf unstopped.
36:11 ears of the people who are on the
37:29 which have mounted up to my ears,
42:20 with open ears hearing nothing?
43:8 who are deaf, yet have ears.

48:8 before this your ears have not been
49:20 shall yet say in your ears,
EARTH
1:2 Hear, O heavens!, Give heed, O earth!
2:19 he arises and strikes terror on earth.
2:21 he arises and strikes terror on earth.
6:3 the consummation of all the earth is
9:19 the earth is scorched,
10:23 decreed upon the whole earth.
11:4 he will smite the earth with the rod
11:9 for the earth shall be filled
11:12 from the four directions of the earth.
12:5 acknowledged throughout the earth!
13:5 destruction throughout the earth.
13:9 to make the earth a desolation,
13:13 when the earth is jolted out of place
14:7 Now the whole earth is at rest and at
14:12 have been hewn down to earth!
14:16 the man who made the earth shake
14:21 fill the face of the earth with cities.
14:26 determined upon the whole earth;
16:1 to those who rule in the earth,
16:4 tyrants are destroyed from the earth,
18:3 you inhabitants of the earth,
19:24 a blessing in the midst of the earth.
23:17 on the face of the earth.
24:1 Lord will lay waste the earth and
24:3 when the earth is sacked,
24:4 The earth shall pine away,
24:4 elite of the earth shall be made
24:5 The earth lies polluted under its
24:6 The curse devours the earth,
24:6 the population of the earth shall be
24:13 in the earth among the nations
24:16 From a sector of the earth we hear
24:17 O inhabitants of the earth:
24:18 the earth shall shake to its
24:19 The earth shall be crushed and rent;
24:19 the earth shall convulse and lurch.
24:20 The earth shall reel to and fro like a
24:21 on earth with the rulers of the earth.
25:8 from throughout the earth.
26:9 thine ordinances are on the earth,
26:15 withdrawn all borders in the earth.
26:18 not wrought salvation in the earth,
26:19 For the earth shall cast up its dead.
26:21 to punish the inhabitants of the earth
26:21 the earth will uncover the blood shed
27:2 In that day, sing of the earth
27:6 face of the earth shall fill with fruit.
28:15 scourge sweep through the earth,
28:22 upon the whole earth.
33:17 and view the expanse of the earth.
34:1 Let the earth give heed,
34:9 and her earth into brimstone;
37:16 over all the kingdoms of the earth.
37:16 madest the heavens and the earth . . .

37:20 his hand, that all kingdoms on earth
40:21 by whom the earth was founded?
40:24 stalk has taken root in the earth,
40:28 Creator of the ends of the earth.
41:5 ends of the earth are in trembling.
41:9 have taken from the ends of the earth,
42:4 brought about justice in the earth.
42:5 who gives form to the earth and its
42:10 his praise from the end of the earth.
43:6 daughters from the end of the earth—
44:23 cause it to resound, O earth beneath!
44:24 who himself gives form to the earth,
45:8 Let the earth receive it and salvation
45:12 It is I who made the earth
45:18 the God who formed the earth—
45:22 all you ends of the earth;
48:13 was my hand that founded the earth,
48:20 broadcast it to the end of the earth.
49:6 may be to the end of the earth.
49:13 O heavens; celebrate, O earth!
51:6 look on the earth beneath:
51:6 the earth wear out like a garment—
51:13 who sets the earth in place—
51:16 heavens and set the earth in place,
52:10* that all ends of the earth may see
54:5 who is called the God of all the earth.
54:9 would no more flood the earth.
55:9 the heavens are higher than the earth,
55:10 not to it without watering the earth,
57:13 refuge in me shall possess the earth
58:14 you traverse the heights of the earth
60:2 Although darkness covers the earth,
60:21 they shall inherit the earth forever—
61:11 For as the earth brings forth its
62:7 and makes it renowned in the earth.
62:11 proclamation to the end of the earth:
65:16 themselves in the earth shall do so by
65:16 them who swear oaths in the earth
65:17 I create new heavens and a new earth;
66:1 and the earth is my footstool.
66:8 Can the earth labor but a day
66:22 as the new heavens and the new earth

EARTHENWARE
30:14 like an earthenware vessel ruthlessly
45:9 mere shards of earthenware pottery!

EARTH'S
4:2 and the earth's fruit the pride and
24:11 the earth's vitality is gone.
40:12 Who compiled the earth's dust by
40:22 enthroned above the earth's sphere,

EAST
2:6 mystics from the East
9:12 Arameneans from the east
11:14 together plunder those to the east;
27:8 in the day of the burning east wind.
41:2 up Righteousness from the east,
43:5 bring your offspring from the east

46:11 summon a bird of prey from the east,

EAT
1:19 you shall eat the good of the land.
3:10 they shall eat the fruits of their own
4:1 We will eat our own food,
5:17 proselytes eat in the ruins of the
7:15 Cream and honey will he eat
7:22 men will eat the cream.
9:20 men will eat the flesh of their own
11:7 the lion will eat straw like the ox.
23:18 that they may eat their fill and be
30:24 eat grain silage winnowed with shovel
36:12 with you are to eat their own dung
36:16 one of you will eat from his own vine
37:30 This year eat what grows wild,
37:30 plant vineyards and eat their fruit:
44:16 they eat the meat and are satisfied.
55:1 come and buy food, that you may eat.
55:2 Hear me well: Eat what is good,
62:9 Those who harvest it shall eat it,
65:4 who eat swine's flesh,
65:13 My servants shall eat indeed,
65:21 vineyards, they will eat their fruit.
65:22 or plant so that others may eat.
65:25 the lion will eat straw like the ox;
66:17 who eat the flesh of swine

EATEN
1:20 you shall be eaten by the sword.

EATER
55:10 for the sower and food for the eater—

EATING
21:5 They are eating and drinking . . .
22:13 eating meat and drinking wine:

EATS
29:8 a hungry man who dreams he eats,
59:5 whoever eats of their eggs dies,

EBB
19:5 waters of the lakes shall ebb away

ECHO
15:8 and echo as far as Beer Elim.

EDEN
51:3 is making her wilderness like Eden,

EDENITES
37:12 and the Edenites in Tel Assar?

EDOM
11:14 they will take Edom and Moab at
34:5 come down on Edom in judgment,
34:6 massacre in the land of Edom;
63:1 Who it this coming from Edom in red

EDOM'S
34:9 Edom's streams shall turn into lava

EGGS
10:14 as one gathers abandoned eggs;
34:15 shall the hawk owl nest and lay eggs,
59:5 hatch vipers' eggs and spin spiders'
59:5 whoever eats of their eggs dies,

EGLAIM
15:8 the sound of it shall reach Eglaim
EGLATH SHELISHIAH
15:5 and as far as Eglath Shelishiah.
EGYPT
7:18 the far rivers of Egypt
11:11 Egypt, Pathros, Cush, Elam, Shinar,
11:16 it came up from the land of Egypt.
19:1 An oracle concerning Egypt:
19:1 When the Lord enters Egypt riding on
19:1 the idols of Egypt will rock at his
19:12 Lord of Hosts has in mind for Egypt!
19:13 heads of state have led Egypt astray.
19:14 they have misled Egypt in all that she
19:18 cities in the land of Egypt will
19:19 of the land of Egypt and a monument
19:20 in the land of Egypt: when they
19:22 The Lord will smite Egypt,
19:23 highway from Egypt to Assyria.
19:23 Assyrians shall come to Egypt
19:24 third party to Egypt and to Assyria,
19:25 saying, Blessed by Egypt my people,
20:3 against Egypt and Cush,
20:4 lead away the captives of Egypt
20:5 their hope, and at Egypt, their boast.
23:5 When the news of Tyre reaches Egypt,
27:12 River to the streams of Egypt.
27:13 Egypt shall come and bow down
30:2 They are bent on going down to Egypt
31:1 Woe . . . who go down to Egypt
36:6 of Egypt, that splintered reed which
36:6 of Egypt to all who rely on him!
36:9 depending as you do on Egypt for
43:3 Egypt I have appointed as ransom for
45:14 The wealth of Egypt and merchandise
52:4 people went down to Egypt to sojourn
EGYPT'S
19:3 Egypt's spirit shall be drained
19:6 Egypt's waterways recede and dry up.
20:4 buttocks uncovered—to Egypt's shame.
30:2 on taking shelter in Egypt's shadow.
30:3 in Egypt's shadow to embarrassment.
30:7 Egypt's help shall be futile and vain;
37:25 I have dried up all Egypt's rivers!
EGYPTIAN
11:15 the tongue of the Egyptian Sea
EGYPTIANS
10:24 as did the Egyptians.
10:26 as he did to the Egyptians.
19:2 up the Egyptians against the Egyptians
19:4 Then will I deliver the Egyptians
19:15 there shall be nothing the Egyptians
19:16 In that day the Egyptians will
19:17 a source of terror to the Egyptians;
19:21 known to the Egyptians, and
19:21 the Egyptians shall know the
19:23 and Egyptians go to Assyria,

19:23 and the Egyptians shall labor
31:3 The Egyptians are human, not divine;
EGYPTIAN'S
19:1 Egyptians' hearts melt within them.
EIGHTY-FIVE
37:36 a hundred and eighty-five thousand
EJECT
30:22 you will eject them as a menstruous
ELAM
11:11 Egypt, Pathros, Cush, Elam, Shinar,
22:6 When Elam takes up the quiver,
ELAMITES
21:2 Attack, O Elamites! Lay siege, you
ELDER
3:2 and prophet, the augur and elder,
ELDERLY
3:5 young will be insolent to the elderly,
ELDERS
3:14 He will bring to trial the elders of
9:15 the elders or notables are the head,
24:23 glory in the presence of his elders.
37:2 and the elders of the priests in
ELEALEH
15:4 will cry for help, as will Elealeh
16:9 O Heshbon and Elealeh,
ELECT
14:30 The elect poor shall have pasture,
48:12 O Jacob, and Israel, my elect:
ELEGANT
3:22 the elegant dress, the shawl, the
ELEGANTLY
23:18 their fill and be elegantly clothed.
ELEVATED
2:14 all high mountains and elevated hills,
ELIAKIM
22:20 servant Eliakim the son of Hilkiah:
36:3 And Eliakim the son of Hilkiah,
36:11 Then Eliakim, Shebna and Joah said
36:22 Then Eliakim the son of Hilkiah,
37:2 And he sent Eliakim the overseer of
ELIM
15:8 and echo as far as Beer Elim.
ELITE
5:14 into it descend their elite with the
13:2 into the precincts of the elite.
24:4 elite of the earth shall be made
26:5 He has put down the elite inhabitants
ELMS
41:19 elms and box trees in the steppes—
ELOQUENCE
32:4 the stammerers master eloquence.
ELUDES
59:11 look for salvation, but it eludes us.
EMBARRASSED
45:16 utterly dismayed and embarrassed.
EMBARRASSMENT
30:3 in Egypt's shadow to embarrassment.

EMBER
6:6　carrying an ember which he had
EMBERS
30:14　to scoop lit embers from a fireplace,
44:19　I also baked bread in its embers,
47:14　These are no embers to warm anyone;
EMBITTERED
8:21　they roam about embittered
EMBLEMS
57:8　you have put up your emblems,
EMERGES
59:5　there emerges a serpent.
EMINENT
52:13　he shall become exceedingly eminent:
EMISSARIES
18:2　which sends emissaries by sea,
EMIT
34:3　and their corpses emit a stench;
EMPTINESS
41:29　are but wind and emptiness.
EMPTY
24:1　lay waste the earth and empty it;
32:6　leaving the hungry soul empty,
55:11　it does not return to me empty;
59:4　They rely on empty words,
ENACT
10:1　Woe to those who enact unjust laws,
ENCAMP
29:3　I will encamp against you round
ENCOMPASS
15:8　shall encompass the land of Moab;
ENCOUNTERED
35:9　No lions shall be encountered
ENCOURAGES
41:7*　The artisan encourages the smith,
END
2:7　and there is no end to their wealth;
2:7　and there is no end to their chariots.
7:3　the end of the aqueduct of the Upper
9:7　and peace have no end;
10:25　anger will very soon come to an end;
13:11　I will put an end to the arrogance of
14:4　his end and tyranny ceased!
16:10　vintage shout I will bring to an end.
17:3　Ephraim's defense comes to an end,
21:2　I will bring to an end.
23:15　And at the end of seventy years, Tyre
24:8　pulsating of lyres comes to an end.
31:3　both shall come to an end together.
33:8　are desolate, travel is at an end.
38:13　thou art bringing on my end!
42:10　his praise from the end of the earth.
43:6　daughters from the end of the earth
43:10　to the end that you may recognize it
45:17　worlds without end.
46:10　I foretell the end from the beginning,
48:20　broadcast it to the end of the earth.

49:6　may be to the end of the earth.
62:11　proclamation to the end of the earth
66:17　made an end of, says the Lord.
ENDED
24:13　gleaned when the vintage is ended.
ENDLESS
34:10　through endless ages none shall
51:8　through endless generations.
60:20　you the Lord shall be an endless light
ENDLESSLY
28:28　does not go on endlessly threshing it.
ENDOW
56:5　I will endow them with an everlasting
61:3　to endow those who mourn in Zion,
ENDOWED
35:2　be endowed with the glory of
42:1　him I have endowed with my Spirit;
50:4　Lord has endowed me with a learned
ENDOWS
55:5　of Israel, who gloriously endows you.
ENDS
7:4　two smoking tail ends of kindling,
40:28　Creator of the ends of the earth.
41:5　the ends of the earth are in
41:9　have taken from the ends of the earth,
45:22　all you ends of the earth;
52:10*　that all ends of the earth may see
58:3　fast day you pursue your own ends
58:13　achieving your own ends on my holy
ENDURE
51:8　righteousness shall endure forever,
ENDURED
53:4　our sufferings, endured our griefs,
ENDURES
40:8　the word of our God endures forever.
ENEMIES
1:24　avenge me of my enemies.
9:11　Rezin's enemies against them
26:11　the fire prepared for thine enemies
42:13　the shout of victory over his enemies.
59:18　reprisals upon his enemies;
62:8　your grain be food for your enemies,
63:18　our enemies trod down thy sanctuary.
66:6　paying his enemies what is due them.
66:14　and his rage among his enemies.
ENERGY
40:29　He supplies the weary with energy
ENFEEBLED
64:7　and enfeebled us at the hand of our
ENGORGE
34:6　a sword that shall engorge with blood
ENGRAVED
49:16　See, I have engraved you on my palms
ENJOY
55:2　your souls shall enjoy abundance.
ENLARGED
9:3　Thou hast enlarged the nation

ENLARGED *continued*
26:15 Thou hast enlarged the nation,
ENLARGING
26:15 by enlarging it gained glory for
ENLIGHTEN
28:9 shall he enlighten with revelation?
ENLIGHTENED
40:14 that he might be enlightened,
ENRAGED
 8:21 they become enraged and,
41:11 See, all who are enraged at you
ENRICHED
34:7 their soil enriched with fat.
ENSIGN
 5:26 He raises an ensign to distant nations
11:10 stands for an ensign to the peoples,
11:12 will raise the ensign to the nations
13:2 Raise the ensign on a barren
18:3 look to the ensign
30:17 an ensign on a hill.
31:9 their officers shrink from the ensign,
49:22 raise my ensign to the peoples;
62:10 raise the ensign to the nations!
ENSNARE
29:21 who ensnare the defender at court,
ENSNARED
 8:15 and when they become ensnared
28:13 ensnared and be taken captive.
ENTER
16:12 and enter their sanctuaries to pray,
24:10 are shuttered, that none may enter.
26:20 O my people, enter your chambers
37:33 He shall not enter this city or shoot
37:34 he shall not enter this city, says the
52:1 uncircumcised and defiled enter you.
59:14 and uprightness cannot enter.
60:5 a host of nations shall enter you.
ENTERED
37:1 entered the house of the Lord.
ENTERS
19:1 When the Lord enters Egypt riding on
36:6 enters and pierces the palm of any
ENTERTAINMENT
32:13 in the city of entertainment,
ENTHRONED
37:16 sittest enthroned between the
40:22 By him who sits enthroned above the
47:8 securely enthroned, thinking to
52:2 sit enthroned, O Jerusalem.
ENTIRE
 9:9 And the entire people—
39:2 fragrant oils, and his entire armory
54:12 your entire boundary of precious
60:21 Your entire people shall be righteous;
ENTIRELY
48:9 by not entirely destroying you.

ENTREATED
47:3 and not be entreated of men,
ENTREATING
45:14 and bow down to you, entreating you.
ENVELOPES
42:25 till it envelopes them in flames—
ENVIRONS
62:9 within the environs of my sanctuary.
ENVOYS
14:32 then be told the envoys of the nation?
39:2 showed the envoys his treasuries
ENVOYS'
30:4 and their envoys' travels to Hanes,
ENVY
11:13 Ephraim will not envy Judah,
EPHAH
 5:10 a homer of seed but an ephah.
60:6 the dromedaries of Midian and Ephah;
EPHRAIM
 7:2 that Aram was leading Ephraim on,
 7:5 has Ephraim and the son of Remaliah,
 7:8 sixty-five years shall Ephraim
 7:9 as Samaria is the capital of Ephraim
 7:17 Ephraim broke away from Judah—
 9:9 Ephraim and those who dwell in
 9:21 Manasseh will turn against Ephraim
 9:21 and Ephraim against Manasseh,
11:13 Ephraim will not envy Judah,
11:13 nor Judah resent Ephraim.
28:1 of the drunkards of Ephraim!
28:3 garlands of the drunkards of Ephraim
EPHRAIM'S
11:13 Ephraim's jealousy shall pass away
17:3 When Ephraim's defense comes to an
EQUAL
44:7 and is equal of me
46:5 you compare me or count me equal?
EQUITY
11:4 with equity arbitrate for the lowly
ERECT
29:3 erect siege installations against you.
37:33 nor erect siegeworks against it.
ERECTED
19:19 erected to the Lord in the midst
ERR
28:7 they err as seers, they blunder in
ERRING
29:24 erring in spirit gain understanding
30:28 with an erring bridle on their jaws
ESARHADDON
37:38 And his son Esarhaddon succeeded
ESCAPE
 5:29 they seize the prey, and escape,
10:20 and who escape of the house of Jacob
20:6 How shall we ourselves escape?
37:11 Shall you then escape?
47:14 unable themselves to escape the hand

49:24 or the tyrant's captives escape free?
49:25 the tyrant's captives escape free:
ESCORTED
60:11 and their rulers escorted in.
ESPOUSED
54:1 outnumber those of the espoused,
62:4 and your land considered espoused.
62:4 and your land shall be espoused.
ESPOUSES
54:5 For he who espouses you is your Maker
ESTABLISH
11:3 nor establish proof by what his ears
ESTABLISHED
2:2 shall become established
9:7 rule may be established and upheld
54:14 established through righteousness
ESTATES
49:8 and reapportion the desolate estates,
ESTEEM
42:17 and esteem their images as gods
ESTIMATION
40:18 he resemble in your estimation?
ESTUARIES
19:7 adjoining canals and estuaries,
ETERNAL
33:14 among us can abide eternal burning?
47:7 you thought, I, the Eternal Mistress,
61:8 make with them an eternal covenant.
ETERNITY
40:28 The Lord is the God of eternity,
63:16 Redeemer from Eternity is thy name.
ETHER
40:17 less than ether they are reckoned by
EUNUCH
56:3 And let not the eunuch say, I am
EUNUCHS
39:7 some to serve as eunuchs in
56:4 the eunuchs who keep my Sabbaths
EVADE
14:31 he has designated shall evade it.
EVAPORATE
42:15 into dry land and evaporate lakes.
EVASIVE
27:1 the evasive maritime serpent,
EVENING
17:14 evening time shall be the catastrophe
EVENTS
41:22 their prophecies of events heretofore.
41:23 Tell us of events to come hereafter,
42:9 The prophecies of the former events
43:9 predicted events that have come to
43:18 the prophecies of bygone events;
46:9 prophecies of the events of old!
48:3 prophecies of the events of the past
65:17 former events shall not be
EVER
3:16 ever flirting when they walk

9:6 a Father for Ever, a Prince of Peace—
25:2 nor ever be rebuilt!
26:4 Ever trust in the Lord,
32:14 shall become haunts for ever after,
64:5 that in them we might ever be saved.
EVERLASTING
26:4 the Lord Yah is an everlasting Rock.
35:10 heads crowned with everlasting joy.
45:17 with an everlasting salvation;
51:6 But my salvation shall be everlasting;
51:11 heads crowned with everlasting joy;
54:8 but with everlasting charity
55:3 with you an everlasting covenant;
55:13 an everlasting sign that shall not be
56:5 endow them with an everlasting name
60:15 I will make you an everlasting pride,
60:19 Lord will be your everlasting light
61:7 and everlasting joy be theirs.
63:12 an everlasting name for himself
EVIDENCE
41:21 submit your evidence, says the King
EVIDENT
59:12 Our offenses are evident;
EVIL
1:16 cease to do evil.
5:20 Woe to those who suppose what is evil
5:20 and what is good, evil!
7:5 an evil plot against you,
7:15 to reject what is evil and
7:16 to reject the evil and choose
41:23 Perform something good or evil
56:2 stays his hand from doing any evil.
59:7 Their feet rush after evil;
59:15 they who shun evil become a prey.
65:12 You did what was evil in my eyes;
66:4 They did what was evil in my eyes;
EVILDOERS
29:5 evildoers shall become as fine dust,
31:2 and allies of evildoers.
EWES
40:11 ewes that give milk he leads gently
EXALT
9:1 the last he will exalt the Sea Route
10:15 Shall an axe exalt itself
EXALTED
2:11 Lord alone shall be exalted in that
2:12 and for all who are exalted,
2:17 Lord alone shall be exalted in that
5:16 But the Lord of Hosts will be exalted
6:1 highly exalted, the skirt of his robe
12:4 commemorate his exalted name.
26:5 of the exalted city
52:13 being astute, shall be highly exalted;
57:15 Thus says he who is highly exalted,
EXAMINE
41:22 that we may examine them

EXCAVATE
57:14 It will be said: Excavate, pave a road!
62:10 Excavate, pave a highway cleared of
EXCEEDED
10:10 whose statues exceeded
EXCEEDINGLY
47:9 and exceedingly strong combinations.
52:13 he shall become exceedingly eminent:
61:10 I rejoice exceedingly in the Lord;
64:9 Be not exceedingly angry, O Lord;
64:12 letting us suffer so exceedingly?
EXCELLENCE
23:9 to make all glorying in excellence a
EXCEPT
45:21 except for whom there is no Savior?
EXCESSIVE
16:6 its excessive pride and its boasting,
57:10 wearied by your excessive ways,
EXCHANGE
43:4 peoples in exchange for your life.
EXCLUDE
56:3 Lord will surely exclude me from his
66:5 and exclude you because of my name,
EXCREMENT
4:4 has washed away the excrement
28:8 no spot with without excrement.
EXECRATION
23:9 celebrities an utter execration.
43:28 to be ostracized, Israel to execration.
EXERT
65:23 They shall not exert themselves in
EXERTED
47:12 at which you have exerted yourself
47:15 for whom you have exerted yourself
EXHAUSTION
40:30 men slump down of exhaustion.
EXILED
11:12 and assemble the exiled of Israel;
49:21 I was exiled, banished;
EXILES
16:4 Let the exiles of Moab dwell with you;
20:4 and the exiles of Cush, both young
45:13 my city and set free my exiles
EXIST
34:12 when all its lords no longer exist?
43:10 nor shall one exist after me.
45:14 God is in you; no other gods exist!
47:7 I, the Eternal Mistress, exist forever!
47:8 I exist, and other than me there is
47:10 thinking to yourself, I exist,
EXODUS
6:12 and great shall be the exodus
EXPAND
54:2 Expand the site of your tent;
EXPANSE
33:17 and view the expanse of the earth.

EXPECT
8:17 and expect him.
59:11 We expect justice when there is none;
EXPECTED
5:2 Then he expected it to yield grapes,
5:4 When I expected it to yield grapes,
5:7 He expected justice,
25:9 whom we expected would save us.
EXPEDITE
16:5 justice and expedite righteousness.
EXPELLED
22:19 you will be expelled from you post.
EXPENSE
57:4 At whose expense do you amuse
EXPERT
40:20 They seek an expert sculptor
EXPIATED
27:9 shall Jacob's iniquity be expiated,
40:2 that her guilt has been expiated.
EXPIRE
21:16 Kedar's glory shall fully expire.
31:9 their captain shall expire in terror
EXPLOITS
57:12 and the wantonness of your exploits.
EXPLOSIVE
30:30 explosive discharges and pounding
EXPOSE
3:17 the Lord will expose their private
57:12 But I will expose your fornication
EXPOSED
14:19 exposed like the slain disfigured by
23:13 exposed its fortifications, and caused
30:13 breach exposed in a high wall
47:3 your nakedness shall be exposed
57:8 and have exposed yourself to others
EXTEND
11:15 he will extend his hand over the
54:2 extend the canopies of your
66:12 I will extend peace to her like a
EXTENDED
9:7 that sovereignty may be extended
EXTERMINATE
10:7 and to exterminate nations not a few.
EXTINGUISH
1:31 and there shall be none to extinguish.
EXTINGUISHED
66:24 whose fire shall not be extinguished.
EXTOL
25:1 I will extol thee by praising thy
EXTORTION
33:15 who disdain extortion
59:13 planning ways of extortion,
61:8 I abhor extortion in those who
EXTRACT
65:9 I will extract offspring out of Jacob,
EXULT
24:14 exult at the Lord's ingenuity.

EYE
13:18 their eye will not look with
52:8 they shall see eye to eye
64:4 nor has any eye seen a God besides
EYES
 1:15 I will conceal my eyes from you;
 1:16 from before my eyes;
 2:11 The haughty eyes of men shall be
 3:8 to his glory before his very eyes.
 3:16 and put on airs, painting their eyes,
 5:15 causing the eyes of the high-minded
 5:21 who are wise in their own eyes
 6:5 the Lord of Hosts, with my own eyes!
 6:10 dull their ears and shut their eyes,
 6:10 lest they see with their eyes
11:3 will not judge by what his eyes see,
13:16 be dashed to pieces before their eyes,
17:7 their eyes look to the Holy One of
29:10 he has shut your eyes, the prophets;
29:18 and the eyes of the blind see
30:20 but your eyes shall see the Master.
32:3 The eyes of those who see shall not be
33:15 who shut their eyes at the sight of
33:17 Your eyes shall behold the King in
33:20 let your eyes rest upon Jerusalem,
35:5 Then shall the eyes of the blind be
37:17 open thine eyes and see.
37:23 lifting your eyes to high heaven?
38:3 have done what is good in thine eyes.
38:14 My eyes are drawn looking
40:26 Lift your eyes heavenward and see:
42:7 to open eyes that are blind,
43:4 are precious and revered in my eyes,
43:8 people who are blind, yet have eyes,
44:18 their eyes are glazed so they cannot
49:5 I won honor in the eyes of the Lord
49:18 Lift up your eyes and look around
51:6 Lift up your eyes to the heavens;
52:10* in the eyes of all nations,
59:10 we flounder like those without eyes.
60:4 Lift up your eyes and look about you!
61:1 the opening of the eyes to the bound,
65:12 You did what was evil in my eyes;
65:16 and hidden from my eyes.
66:4 They did what was evil in my eyes;
FABRIC
38:12 My life is cut off like woven fabric;
FABRICATIONS
59:6 their fabrications are worthless for
FABRICATORS
44:11 their fabricators are mere mortals.
FABRICS
19:9 of fine fabrics will be dismayed,
FACADES
57:8 Behind doors and facades
FACE
 8:17 hides his face from the house of

14:21 fill the face of the earth with cities.
23:17 on the face of the earth.
27:6 face of the earth shall fill with fruit.
29:22 his face shall pale no more.
38:2 At this Hezekiah turned his face
50:6 I hid not my face from insult and
50:7 I have set my face like flint,
50:8 Let us face one another!
54:8 a fleeting surge of anger I hid my face
57:17 him and hid my face in anger
59:2 your sins hide his face, so that he
60:5 you see it, your face will light up,
64:7 For thou hast hidden thy face from us
65:3 constantly provoke me to my face,
FACES
 3:9 The look on their faces betrays them:
 3:15 humbling the faces of the poor?
13:8 their faces set aflame.
25:8 the tears from all faces;
49:23 their faces to the ground;
53:3 one from whom men hide their faces
FACILITATE
45:13 who facilitate his every step
FADE
40:8 grass that withers, flowers that fade—
FADING
28:1 has become as fading wreaths
28:4 And the fading wreaths, the crowns of
FAIL
32:10 the produce shall fail to arrive.
42:16 things I will not fail to perform.
51:6 my righteousness shall never fail.
65:20 and those who fail to reach a hundred
FAILING
35:3 steady the failing knees.
FAILS
44:12 if he fails to drink water, he begins
FAINT
29:8 but wakes up faint and craving.
40:28 He does not grow faint or weary;
40:30 Youths grow faint and weary,
40:31 they shall walk and not faint.
44:12 drink water, he begins to grow faint.
51:20 children lie in a faint at the corner
57:16 I have made would faint before me.
FAITH
26:2 righteous because it keeps the faith.
30:9 people, sons who break faith,
49:7 the Lord keeps faith with you,
FAITHFUL
 1:21 How the faithful city
 1:26 City of Righteousness, a faithful city.
FAITHFULLY
38:3 I have walked before thee faithfully
FAITHFULNESS
11:5 faithfulness a girdle round his loins.
16:5 and in faithfulness a judge sit on it

FAITHFULNESS *continued*
25:1   For with perfect faithfulness
33:6   Your faithfulness in time of trial
38:18 no further hope of thy faithfulness.
38:19 the knowledge of thy faithfulness.
FALCONS
34:11 But hawks and falcons shall posses it,
FALL
3:8   Jerusalem will falter and Judea fall
5:27 they do not drowse or fall asleep.
8:15 and when they fall shall be broken,
10:4 or fall among the slain.
10:34 and Lebanon fall spectacularly.
13:15 are caught shall fall by the sword.
22:25 It shall be dislodged and fall,
24:18 shall fall into a pit,
26:18 of the world might not fall.
30:25 when the towers fall.
31:3 and those helped will fall:
31:8 Assyria shall fall by a sword not of
34:7 among them shall fall bison, bulls,
37:7 fall by the sword in his own land.
54:15 whoever masses against you shall fall
FALLEN
9:10 The bricks have fallen down,
14:12 How you have fallen from the heavens
21:9 She has fallen; Babylon has fallen.
58:12 called a rebuilder of fallen walls,
FALSE
2:18 will utterly supplant the false gods.
16:6 of its outburst of false propaganda.
28:17 shall sweep away your false refuge
32:7 with false slogans and accusations
63:8 sons who will not play false;
FALSEHOOD
30:28 in the sieve of falsehood;
FALSEHOODS
9:15 the prophets who teach falsehoods,
28:15 and hiding behind falsehoods,
FALTER
3:8 Jerusalem will falter and Judea fall
FAMINE
5:13 their best men die of famine,
14:30 descendants I will kill with famine,
51:19 famine, the sword—and who consoles
FAMISHED
29:8 but awakens famished,
FANS
54:16 the smith who fans the flaming coals,
FAR
7:18 the far rivers of Egypt
15:4 appeal shall be heard as far as Jahaz.
15:5 and as far as Eglath Shelishiah.
15:8 and echo as far as Beer Elim.
17:13 rebukes them they will flee far away;
18:2 a nation dreaded far and wide,
18:7 from a nation dreaded far and wide,

23:7 feet led her to settle far-off lands
29:13 while their heart remains far from me
31:6 contrived to go far astray, O children
33:13 what I have done, you who are far off;
46:12 who are far from righteousness;
46:12 it is not now far off—
54:14 you will be far from oppression
54:14 far from ruin, for it shall not
56:12 will be like today, only far better!
57:9 you send your solicitors far abroad
57:19 Peace, well-being, to those far off
59:9 redress remains far from us
FARCE
30:10 flatter us; foresee a farce!
FARED
10:9 Has not Calno fared like Carchemish?
FARM
32:16 righteousness abide in the farm land.
FARMHANDS
61:5 foreigners will be your farmhands
FARTHEST
37:24 the farthest reaches of Lebanon.
41:9 called from its farthest limits—
FASHION
44:10 Who would fashion a god
45:7 I fashion light and form darkness;
FAST
42:14 and breathe hard and fast all at once.
56:2 the person who holds fast to them—
56:4 holding fast to my covenant—
56:6 holding fast to my covenant—
58:3 when we fast, do you not notice?
58:4 You fast amid strife and contention,
58:5 Do you call that a fast,
58:6 Is not this the fast I require:
FASTDAY
58:3 your fastday you pursue your own ends
FASTEN
22:23 I will fasten him as a nail in the sure
41:7* though they fasten it with riveting
FASTENED
22:25 the nail that was fastened in a
FASTING
58:5 the manner of fasting I have required,
FASTS
58:4 Your present fasts are not such
FAT
1:11 and fat of fatted beasts;
6:10 the heart of these people grow fat;
34:4 their fat decompose [on the hills]
34:6 and glut itself with fat—
34:6 the kidney fat of rams.
34:7 their soil enriched with fat.
43:24 sate me with the fat of immolations.
FATE
17:14 the fate of those who despoil us.
57:6 of the ravines shall be your fate;

FATHER
8:4 how to say, Father, or Mother,
9:6 a Father for Ever, a Prince of Peace—
22:21 And he will be a father to the
22:23 of glory to the house of his father.
38:5 the God of your father David:
38:19 as I do this day; from father to sons
43:27 Your first father transgressed;
45:10 Woe to those who say to their Father,
51:2 look to Abraham your father,
58:14 the heritage of Jacob your father.
63:16 Surely thou art our Father!
63:16 thou, O Lord, art our Father;
64:8 Nevertheless, thou art our Father,
FATHERLESS
1:17 plead the cause of the fatherless,
1:23 dispense justice to the fatherless,
9:17 nor does he pity their fatherless and
10:2 mere spoil of the fatherless!
FATHER'S
3:6 of his father's house, and say,
7:17 and your people and your father's
22:24 glory of his father's house:
FATHERS
37:12 Did the gods of the nations my fathers
49:23 Kings shall be your foster fathers,
64:11 where our fathers praised thee
FATHERS'
65:7 own iniquities and their fathers' alike,
FATHOMED
40:28 his intelligence cannot be fathomed.
FATNESS
10:27 that wore away your fatness
10:27 shall by fatness wear away.
17:4 his fatness of body become leanness.
FATTED
1:11 and fat of fatted beasts;
FAVOR
26:10 Though favor be shown the wicked,
30:18 that he may favor you;
61:2 to herald the year of the Lord's favor
FAVORABLE
33:2 O Lord, be favorable toward us;
49:8 At a favorable time I have answered
FAVORS
27:11 he who formed them favors them not.
63:7 the Lord's loving favors,
FEAR
7:25 go for fear of the briars and thorns,
8:9 but shall be in fear;
8:12 by the thing they fear.
8:13 making him your fear, him your awe.
11:2 and of the fear of the Lord.
11:3 by the fear of the Lord;
12:2 my salvation I will trust without fear;
21:4 mind reels, I am paralyzed with fear;
25:3 community of tyrannous nations fear

33:6 fear of the Lord shall be your riches.
33:14 sinners in Zion are struck with fear;
41:5 The isles look on in fear;
41:13 Have no fear; I will help you.
43:1 Do not fear, for I have redeemed you.
43:5 Do not fear, for I am with you.
44:11 they would at once cringe in fear.
51:7 Do not fear the reproach of men;
51:12 are you that you fear mortal man,
54:14 and have no cause to fear,
57:11 that you no longer fear me?
59:19 From the West men will fear the Lord
63:17 so that we do not fear thee?
FEARFUL
19:16 be as women, fearful and afraid
35:4 Say to those with fearful hearts,
41:10 Be not fearful, for I am with you;
54:4 Be not fearful, for you shall not be
FEARS
50:10 Who among you fears the Lord
FEAST
25:6 a sumptuous feast for all peoples,
25:6 a feast of leavened cakes, succulent
FEASTDAYS
29:1 the feastdays recur in succession,
FEATS
47:9 your many magical feats
47:12 and with your many magical feats,
FEEBLE
35:3 Strengthen the hands grown feeble,
FEED
5:17 Then shall his sheep feed in their
7:22 will feed on cream and honey.
11:6 and young lions will feed together,
18:6 birds of prey will feed on them all
49:9 They shall feed along the way
49:26 I will feed your oppressors with their
61:6 You shall feed on the wealth of the
FEEL
49:15 feel no compassion for the child of
FEET
1:6 the soles of the feet even to the head
3:16 and clacking with their feet,
20:2 the shoes from your feet.
23:7 whose feet led her to settle far-off
26:6 underfoot by the feet of the poor,
37:25 With the soles of my feet
41:3 by paths his feet have never trod.
49:23 they will lick the dust of your feet,
52:7 feet of the messenger announcing
58:13 If you will keep your feet from
59:7 Their feet rush after evil;
60:13 to make glorious the place of my feet.
60:14 prostrate themselves at your feet.
FELLED
3:25 men shall be felled by the sword,
6:13 when it is felled, whose stump

FELLED *continued*
9:10 the sycamores have been felled,
32:19* For by hail shall forests be felled,
37:24 I have felled its tallest cedars,
FELLOW
41:6 saying, each to his fellow, Courage!
FENNEL
28:25 does he not sprinkle fennel and
28:27 Fennel is not threshed with a sharp
28:27 fennel is beaten out with a stick
FERTILE
5:1 on the fertile brow of a hill.
10:16 a consumption into his fertile lands,
55:10 to render it fertile and fruitful—
FESTAL
61:3 the festal anointing in place of
FESTERING
1:6 and bruises and festering sores;
FESTIVAL
30:29 the night when a festival commences,
FESTIVE
3:24 instead of the festive dress,
23:7 Is this your festive city of ancient
FESTIVITY
16:10 The joyful festivity will be gone
FETUS
14:19 like a repugnant fetus,
FEVER
18:4 amid the fever of reaping.
FEW
1:9 Lord of Hosts left us a few survivors,
10:7 and to exterminate nations not a few.
10:19 left of his forest shall be so few,
16:14 populace there shall be very few
21:17 shall be few. The Lord, the God
65:20 tbe infants alive but a few days,
FIDELITY
55:3 my loving fidelity toward David.
FIELD
1:8 a hut in a melon field,
5:8 link field to field till no place is left.
40:6 at its best like a blossom of the field.
FIELDS
10:18 choice forests and productive fields
32:12 your breasts for the choice fields
36:17 land of grain fields and vineyards.
FIERCE
27:8 By his fierce blasts they were flung
FIERY
14:29 shall be a fiery flying serpent.
30:6 vipers and the fiery flying serpent,
FIFTEEN
38:5 I will add fifteen years to your life.
FIG
34:4 or shrivelled fruit from a fig tree.
36:16 and his own fig tree and drink
38:21* Isaiah gave instructions to take fig

FIGHT
19:2 will fight brother against brother
29:7 amassed to fight against Ariel,
29:8 amass to fight against Mount Zion.
37:9 king of Cush had set out to fight
FIGHTER
42:13 his passions aroused like a fighter;
FIGHTING
37:8 found him fighting against Libnah.
FIGURE
40:19 A figure cast by the artisan,
FILL
1:11 I have had my fill of offerings of rams
3:14 fill your houses by depriving the
14:21 and fill the face of the earth with
22:7 your choice valleys fill with chariots,
23:18 that they may eat their fill
27:6 face of the earth shall fill with fruit.
34:5 sword drinks its fill in the heavens,
51:20 They have their fill of the wrath of
56:12 and have our fill of liquor.
FILLED
1:15 your hands are filled with blood.
1:21 She was filled with justice;
6:4 and a mist filled the temple
11:9 for the earth shall be filled
28:8 For all tables are filled with vomit;
FILLING
6:1 filling the sanctuary.
FINAL
47:7 or remember her final destiny.
FIND
13:21 birds of prey will find lodging there
14:32 longsuffering people find refuge
23:12 even there you will find no rest.
34:14 too shall the night owl find repose
41:12 you shall not find them;
49:9 find pasture on all barren heights;
53:2 that we should find him attractive.
FINE
5:9 large and fine houses unoccupied.
13:12 make mankind scarcer than fine gold,
19:9 weavers of fine fabrics will be
29:5 evildoers shall become as fine dust,
FINERY
3:18 the Lord will strip away their finery
FINEST
37:24 its loftiest summit, its finest forest.
FINGER
58:9 pointing finger and offensive speech,
FINGERS
2:8 things their own fingers have made.
3:21 rings for the fingers and for the ears,
17:8 look to things made by their fingers
40:12 by the span of his fingers?
59:3 your fingers with iniquity;

FIRE
1:7   your cities burned with fire;
4:5   fire by night: above all that
5:24   As a blazing fire consumes stubble,
9:18   shall be set ablaze like a fire,
9:19   and people are but fuel for the fire.
10:16 a fire to flare up like a burning
10:17 the Light of Israel will be the fire
26:11 the fire prepared for thine enemies
30:27 his tongue is like a devouring fire.
30:30 with flashes of devouring fire
30:33 broad and deep is its fire pit and
31:9   says the Lord, whose fire is in Zion,
33:11 the fire of your own breath devours
33:14 live through the devouring fire?
37:19 committing their gods to the fire.
40:16 would not suffice to kindle a fire,
42:25 till it sets them on fire;
43:2   Though you walk through the fire,
44:15 or light fire with to bake bread,
44:16 Half of it they burn in the fire.
44:16 Ah, it is warm in front of the fire!
44:19 Part of this I burned in the fire;
47:14 stubble they are burnt up in the fire,
47:14 such is no fire to sit by!
64:2   as when fire is lit for boiling water,
64:11 has been burned with fire,
65:5   a fire smoldering all day long.
66:15 See, the Lord comes with fire,
66:15 to rebuke with conflagrations of fire.
66:16 For with fire and with his sword
66:24 whose fire shall not be extinguished.
FIREPLACE
30:14 to scoop lit embers from a fireplace,
FIRES
27:11 come to light their fires with them.
50:11 you are lighters of fires, all of you,
50:11 Walk then by the light of your fires
FIRM
8:10   they shall not prove firm:
FIRMLY
54:14 You shall be firmly established
FIRS
44:14 He plants firs, which the rain makes
60:13 cypresses, pines, and firs together—
FIRST
1:26   restore your judges as at the first,
19:11 are as wise as the first rulers?
28:4   shall be like the first-ripe fruit
41:4   I, the Lord, first and last, am he.
43:13 from the first I have been present—
43:27 Your first father transgressed;
44:6   I was at the first and I am at the last;
48:12 I am he who was at the first,
52:4   At first my people went down to
FIRST-RIPE
28:4   shall be like the first-ripe fruit

FISH
50:2   their fish become parched for lack
FISHERMEN
19:8   Fishermen will deplore their lot
FISSURES
2:21   and fissures in the cliffs,
FIST
58:4   striking out savagely with the fist.
FIT
44:13 fit to lodge in a house.
FITTED
40:19 fitted with a silver chain from the
FIVE
17:6   or four or five in its most fruitful
19:18 In that day five Hebrew-speaking
30:17 by thousands at the threat of five,
37:36 a hundred and eighty-five thousand
FLAGSTAFF
30:17 are left as a flagstaff on a mountain
FLAME
5:24   as dry weeds wane before the flame,
10:17 and their Holy One the flame,
29:6   conflagrations of devouring flame.
43:2   its flame shall not consume you.
47:14 to escape the hand of the flame.
FLAMES
42:25 till it envelopes them in flames—
FLAMING
54:16 the smith who fans the flaming coals,
62:1   her salvation like a flaming torch.
FLANK
11:14 the Philistine flank toward the West,
FLAPPED
10:14 not one flapped its wings,
FLARE
10:16 cause a fire to flare up like a burning
FLASHES
30:30 with flashes of devouring fire
FLATTER
30:10 flatter us; foresee a farce!
FLAUNT
3:9   they flaunt their sin like Sodom;
FLED
33:3   The peoples fled from thy thunderous
37:38 sword and fled to the land of Ararat.
FLEE
10:3   To whom will you flee for help?
13:14 and everyone flee to his homeland.
17:13 rebukes them they will flee far away;
21:15 For they flee from destruction,
24:18 those who flee at the sound of terror
30:16 Not so; we will flee on horses!
30:16 Therefore shall you flee indeed.
30:17 You will flee by the thousand at the
35:10 when sorrow and sighing flee away.
48:20 Go forth out of Babylon, flee from
51:11 and sorrow and sighing flee away.

FLEEING
10:29 Gibeah of Saul is fleeing.
FLEETING
54:8 In a fleeting surge of anger I hid my
FLEETS
33:21 or majestic fleets pass by.
FLESH
 9:20 men will eat the flesh of their own
31:3 their horses are flesh, not spirit:
40:5 and all flesh see it at once.
40:6 All flesh is grass,
49:26 your oppressors with their own flesh;
49:26 And all flesh shall know that I the
65:4 who eat swine's flesh,
66:16 execute judgments on all flesh,
66:17 who eat the flesh of swine
66:23 all flesh shall come to worship
66:24 They shall be a horror to all flesh.
FLEW
 6:6 Then one of the seraphs flew to me
FLICKER
43:17 they flicker and die, snuffed out like
FLIES
 7:18 signal for the flies from
FLIGHT
10:31 of Gebim are in full flight.
22:3 Your chiefs, altogether in flight,
41:3 He puts them to flight, passing on
52:12 shall not leave in haste or go in flight
FLINT
 5:28 of their warhorses resembles flint;
50:7 I have set my face like flint,
FLIRTING
 3:16 ever flirting when they walk
FLOCK
13:14 a flock of sheep that no one rounds
40:11 a shepherd he pastures his flock:
41:5 They flock together and come
57:13 let those who flock to you save you!
63:11 with the shepherd of his flock?
FLOCKS
13:20 will shepherds rest their flocks in it.
32:14 a browsing place for flocks.
43:23 offerings from your flocks
60:7 All Kedar's flocks will gather to you,
61:5 will tend and pasture your flocks;
65:10 shall become pasture for flocks,
FLOOD
 8:8 will sweep into Judea like a flood
28:17 and waters flood the hiding place.
54:9 would no more flood the earth.
66:12 the nations like a stream in flood.
FLOODING
28:15 should a flooding scourge sweep
28:18 when the flooding scourge sweeps
FLOUNDER
59:10 we flounder like those without eyes.

FLOUR
47:2 Take two grindstones and grind flour;
FLOURISH
66:14 limbs flourish like sprouting grass,
FLOURISHING
32:12 and flourishing vines.
FLOW
 2:2 and all nations will flow to it.
 8:6 waters of Shiloah, which flow gently,
15:9 water of Dibon shall flow with blood,
30:27 his lips flow with indignation,
35:6 and streams flow in the desert.
48:21 he caused water to flow for them
FLOWER
35:2 Joyously it shall break out in flower,
FLOWERING
18:5 when the time of flowering is past
FLOWERS
40:8 grass that withers, flowers that fade—
FLUNG
27:8 fierce blasts they were flung away
34:3 Their slain shall be flung out
FLUTES
 5:12 drums, flutes, and wine at their ,
30:29 with flutes [and drums and lyres;]
FLUTTERING
16:2 Like fluttering birds forced out of
FLY
 5:24 and their blossoms fly up like dust.
 6:2 and with two fly about.
FLYING
14:29 shall be a fiery flying serpent.
29:5 your violent mobs like flying chaff.
30:6 vipers and the fiery flying serpent,
60:8 flying as doves to their portals?
FOG
44:22 your offenses like a thick fog,
FOLD
21:10 know me, who are of my fold,
FOLIAGE
15:6 and no green foliage shall remain.
FOLLOW
 2:3 that we may follow in his paths.
 2:5 let us follow the light of the Lord.
 8:11 me not to follow the ways of
59:7 and disaster follow in their wake.
FOLLOWED
38:13 Surely, as night has followed day,
FOLLOWERS
44:20 They are followers of ashes;
51:1 you followers of righteousness,
FOLLOWING
37:30 and the following year what springs
57:17 he strayed by following the ways of
59:13 backing away from following our God,
64:5 remember thee by following thy
65:2 following their own imagination—

66:17 following one in the center
FOND
1:29 blush for the parks you were fond of;
56:10 lolling seers fond of slumber.
FOOD
3:1 all food supply and water supply,
3:7 There is neither food nor clothing in
4:1 We will eat our own food,
21:14 meet the fugitives with food,
30:23 that the land's increase of food
51:14 neither shall he want for food.
55:1 come and buy food, that you may eat.
55:10 for the sower and food for the eater—
58:7 is it not to share your food with the
62:8 I will no more let your grain be food
65:25 the serpent, dust shall be its food:
FOOLISH
19:13 ministers of Zoan have been foolish,
FOOLS
19:11 The ministers of Zoan are utter fools;
44:25 and makes fools of diviners,
FOOT
11:15 to provide a way on foot.
41:2 him to the place of his foot?
FOOTSTEPS
26:6 the footsteps of those impoverished.
FOOTSTOOL
66:1 and the earth is my footstool.
FORAGE
27:10 steers forage and recline there,
FORBEAR
2:9 Forbear them not!
FORBID
5:6 I will forbid the rainclouds to rain on
FORCE
7:6 We will take it for ourselves by force
10:34 with the force of iron,
31:4 muster in full force against him,
FORCED
16:2 birds forced out of the nest,
FORCES
30:2 protection in Pharaoh's forces,
31:1 of chariots and vast forces of
FORDS
16:2 Moab's women at the fords of Arnon.
FOREFATHERS
39:6 and all that your forefathers
FOREIGN
37:25 wells and drunk of foreign waters.
FOREIGNER
56:3 Let not the foreigner who adheres to
FOREIGNERS
1:7 waste at its takeover by foreigners.
56:6 And the foreigners who adhere to the
60:10 Foreigners will rebuild your walls,
61:5 foreigners will be your farmhands
62:8 nor shall foreigners drink the new

FOREORDAINING
41:4 foreordaining dynasties?
FORESAW
14:24 As I foresaw it, so shall it happen;
FORESEE
30:10 flatter us; foresee a farce!
FOREST
7:2 trees in a forest are shaken by a gale.
10:19 trees left of his forest shall be so few
22:8 look to the forest home as protection.
37:24 its loftiest summit, its finest forest.
44:14 them among the trees of the forest.
56:9 beasts, you animals of the forest,
FORESTS
9:18 it shall ignite the jungle forests,
10:18 His choice forests and productive
10:34 The dense forests shall be battered
21:13 who sojourn in the forests of Arabia,
32:19* For by hail shall forests be felled,
44:23 forests, and all trees therein:
FORETELL
41:26 Indeed, not one could foretell it,
42:9 but new things I yet foretell.
44:8 Did I not foretell it, you being my
46:10 I foretell the end from the beginning,
FORETELLING
44:7 foretelling things to come?
FORETOLD
43:9 among them foretold these things,
43:10 I was the one who foretold them—
43:12 I who foretold and wrought salvation,
45:21 Who foretold these things of old,
48:14 among you foretold these things?
FOREVER
9:7 from this time forth and forever.
25:8 by abolishing Death forever.
28:24 Will the plowman be forever plowing
30:8 as a testimony forever.
32:17 an assured calm forever.
34:10 its smoke shall ascend forever.
34:17 They shall possess it forever,
40:8 the word of our God endures forever.
47:7 I, the Eternal Mistress, exist forever!
51:8 righteousness shall endure forever,
57:15 who abides forever, whose name is
57:16 I will not contend forever, nor always
59:21 the Lord, from now on and forever.
60:21 they shall inherit the earth forever—
64:9 remember not iniquity forever.
65:18 and be glad forever in what I create.
FORGES
44:12 he forges his god by the strength of
FORGET
49:15 Can a woman forget her suckling
49:15 shall forget, I will not forget you.
54:4 You shall forget the shame of your
65:11 and forget my holy mountain,

FORGING
54:16 forging weapons to suit his purpose;
FORGIVEN
22:14 wickedness cannot be forgiven you
33:24* shall be forgiven their iniquity.
FORGOTTEN
17:10 For you have forgotten your God,
23:15 In that day Tyre shall be forgotten
23:16 O forgotten harlot.
49:14 my Lord has forgotten me.
51:13 you forgotten the Lord, you Maker—
65:16 troubles of the past shall be forgotten
FORK
30:24 silage winnowed with shovel and fork.
FORLORN
3:26 shall lie bereaved and forlorn;
27:10 the fortified cities lie forlorn,
33:9 The Land lies withered and forlorn,
54:6 as a spouse forsaken and forlorn,
FORM
4:5 the Lord will form a cloud by
8:9 Though nations form pacts,
25:2 mansions shall no more form cities,
42:5 who gives form to the earth and its
44:24 who himself gives form to the earth,
45:7 I fashion light and form darkness;
FORMED
27:11 he who formed them favors them not.
40:26 Who formed these?
43:1 he who formed you, O Jacob,
43:7 whom I have formed, molded and
43:10 before me no god was formed,
43:21 the people I formed for myself
44:2 who formed you from the womb and
44:24 who formed you from the womb:
45:18 the God who formed the earth—
49:5 he who formed me from the womb
FORMER
42:9 The prophecies of the former events
65:17 former events shall not be
FORMS
58:6 and abolish all forms of subjection?
FORNICATE
66:17 the cultists who fornicate in the parks,
FORNICATION
57:12 But I will expose your fornication
FORSAKE
1:28 who forsake the Lord are annihilated.
41:17 God of Israel, will not forsake them.
55:7 Let the wicked forsake their ways
65:11 As for you who forsake the Lord
FORSAKEN
1:4 they have forsaken the Lord,
2:6 O Lord, hast forsaken thy people,
7:16 rulers you loathe shall lie forsaken.
17:2 The cities of Aroer shall lie forsaken
27:10 forsaken like a wilderness;

49:14 The Lord has forsaken me,
54:6 as a spouse forsaken and forlorn,
60:15 you had been forsaken and abhorred,
62:4 no more be called the forsaken one,
FORSAKING
58:2 not forsaking the precepts of their God
FORSOOK
54:7 I forsook you indeed momentarily,
FORTH
1:15 When you spread forth your hands,
2:3 For out of Zion shall go forth the law,
9:7 from this time forth and forever.
24:20 sway back and forth like a shanty,
26:18 but have brought forth only wind.
33:11 chaff and brought forth stubble
35:6 Water shall break forth in the
40:26 who brings forth their hosts by
42:13 Lord will come forth like a warrior,
48:20 Go forth out of Babylon, flee from
49:9 to say to the captives, Come forth!
51:4 The law shall go forth from me;
61:11 the earth brings forth its vegetation,
FORTHRIGHT
45:19 and am forthright of speech.
FORTHWITH
5:26 Forthwith they come, swiftly and
45:8 righteousness spring up forthwith.
FORTIFICATIONS
23:13 exposed its fortifications, and caused
25:12 Your highly walled fortifications
FORTIFIED
25:2 fortified towns a ruin—
27:10 Because of them the fortified cities
36:1 marched against all the fortified cities
37:26 destined to demolish fortified cities,
FORTIFY
22:10 tearing down buildings to fortify
FORTRESS
17:10 remembered the Rock, your fortress.
33:16 impregnable cliffs are their fortress.
FORTUNE
65:11 and pour mixed wines for Fortune,
FORWARD
41:1 Let them come forward and state their
41:22 Let them come forward and recount to
63:1 pressing forward in the strength of
FOSTER
49:23 Kings shall be your foster fathers,
FOUGHT
30:32 they will be fought in mortal combat.
63:10 and himself fought against them.
FOUL
19:6 The rivers shall turn foul,
FOUND
13:15 Whoever is found shall be thrust
30:14 fragments shall not be found a shard
37:8 found him fighting against Libnah.

57:10 you have found livelihood,
FOUNDATION
6:4 The threshold shook to its foundation
28:16 cornerstone, a sure foundation.
FOUNDATIONS
24:18 earth shall shake to its foundations.
44:28 its temple foundations relaid.
54:11 and sapphires for your foundations;
58:12 restore the foundations of generation
FOUNDED
14:32 The Lord has founded Zion;
23:13 who founded Tyre for shipping.
40:21 by whom the earth was founded?
48:13 was my hand that founded the earth,
FOUNTAINS
12:3 from the fountains of salvation.
41:18 lands into fountains of water.
FOUR
11:12 from the four directions of the earth.
17:6 or four or five in its most fruitful
FOURTEENTH
36:1 In the fourteenth year of King
FRACTURE
30:26 the fracture of his people
FRAGMENTS
30:14 whose fragments shall not be found
FRAGRANT
39:2 the spices and fragrant oils,
43:24 me the fragrant calamus
FRAME
21:3 Therefore my whole frame is racked
38:13 a lion he racks my whole frame?
FRAMES
42:5 who frames and suspends the
FRANKINCENSE
60:6 bearing gold and frankincense
FRAUD
44:20 this thing in my hand is a fraud.
FREE
32:20 letting oxen and asses range free.
42:7 to free captives from confinement
45:13 my city and set free my exiles
49:24 or the tyrant's captives escape free?
49:25 the tyrant's captives escape free:
51:14 he who is bowed down be set free;
52:2 Shake yourself free, rise from the
FRIEND
41:8 of Abraham my beloved friend,
FRO
24:20 shall reel to and fro like a drunkard,
FROLIC
23:12 He will say, You will frolic no more,
FRUIT
4:2 and the earth's fruit the pride and
11:1 a branch from its graft bear fruit.
16:9 summer fruit and harvest are stilled.
18:5 are developing into young fruit,

18:5 cut down the fruit-bearing twigs with
27:6 face of the earth shall fill with fruit.
28:4 shall be like the first-ripe fruit
34:4 or shrivelled fruit from a fig tree.
37:30 plant vineyards and eat their fruit:
37:31 take root below and bear fruit above.
57:19 who partake of the fruit of the lips:
65:21 vineyards, they will eat their fruit.
FRUITFUL
17:6 or five in its most fruitful branch,
29:17 again become a fruitful land,
29:17 and lands now fruitful be considered
55:10 to render it fertile and fruitful—
FRUITS
3:10 they shall eat the fruits of their own
FRUSTRATE
19:3 I will frustrate their plans,
FUEL
9:5 have become fuel for bonfires.
9:19 and people are but fuel for the fire.
44:15 that which serves men as fuel,
FUGITIVES
15:5 its fugitives will reach Zoar
15:9 bring lions upon the fugitives of
21:14 meet the fugitives with food,
43:14 down as fugitives all the Chaldeans,
45:20 all you fugitives of the nations.
FULFILL
19:21 to the Lord and fulfill them.
FULFILLED
41:22 know whether they were fulfilled.
60:20 your days of mourning are fulfilled.
FULFILLS
44:26 who fulfills the word of his servant,
FURIOUS
30:30 his arm descending in furious rage,
66:15 to retaliate in furious anger,
FURNACE
31:9 whose furnace is in Jerusalem.
FURTHER
1:5 Why be smitten further
38:18 have no further hope of thy
FURY
34:2 his fury upon all their hosts;
59:17 wrapped himself in fury as in a robe.
FUTILE
30:7 Egypt's help shall be futile and vain;
FUTURE
39:7 among your own sons, your future
41:22 Or predict the future for us:
GAIN
29:24 erring in spirit gain understanding
30:15 quiet confidence gain the victory.
33:10 now gain preeminence.
GAINED
26:15 enlarging it gained glory for thyself;

GALE
7:2   trees in a forest are shaken by a gale.
GALILEE
9:1   the Jordan in Galilee of the nations.
GALLIM
10:30 Cry out, O Daughter of Gallim!
GARDEN
1:30   and as a garden that has no water.
51:3   her desert as the garden of the Lord.
58:11 become like a well-watered garden,
61:11 and as a garden causes what is sown
GARLANDS
28:1   Woe to the garlands of glory
28:3   The proud garlands of the drunkards
GARMENT
50:9   such shall wear out like a garment;
51:6   the earth wear out like a garment—
51:8   shall consume them like a garment;
59:17 with vengeance for a garment
GARMENTS
61:10 clothes me in garments of salvation,
63:1   from Edom in red-stained garments?
63:2   you clothed in red, your garments
63:3   lifeblood spattered my garments,
GATES
14:31 Wail at the gates; howl in the city!
24:12 the gates lie battered to ruin.
26:2   Open the gates to let in the nation
28:6   who repulse the attack at the gates.
38:10 must I depart through Sheol's gates,
45:1   letting no gates remain shut:
54:12 your gates of carbuncle,
60:11 Your gates shall always remain open;
60:18 and homage as your gates.
62:10 Pass on, go through gates;
GATEWAYS
3:26   Her gateways shall lie bereaved and
22:7   take up positions at your gateways.
GATHER
11:12 he will gather the scattered of Judah
43:5   and gather you from the west;
45:20 Gather yourselves and come;
49:18 with one accord they gather and come
54:7   I will gather you up.
54:15 Those who gather into mobs are not of
56:8   I will gather others to those already
60:7   All Kedar's flocks will gather to you,
62:9   those who gather it shall drink it
66:18 For I will come to gather all nations
GATHERED
10:14 I have gathered up the whole world
43:9   the peoples were gathered together,
49:5   Israel having been gathered to him;
56:8   others to those already gathered.
57:1   the godly are gathered out,
GATHERING
1:13   wickedness with the solemn gathering

60:9   the isles they are gathering to me,
GATHERS
10:14 as one gathers abandoned eggs;
40:11 the lambs he gathers up with his arm
56:8   who gathers up the outcasts of Israel:
GAUGED
40:12 and gauged the heavens
GAVE
8:3   she conceived and gave birth to a son.
21:9   and he gave the reply,
38:21* Isaiah gave instructions to take fig
43:28 I gave Jacob to be ostracized,
47:6   I gave them into your hand,
66:4   when I spoke, none gave heed.
66:8   Zion gave birth to her children.
GAZING
8:21   gazing upward, curse their
GEBA
10:29 stopping overnight at Geba.
GEBIM
10:31 inhabitants of Gebim are in full
GENERAL
20:1   In the year the general who
GENERATION
34:10 from generation to generation;
34:17 inhabit it from generation to generation
53:8   Who can apprise his generation
60:15 the joy of generation after generation.
GENERATIONS
13:20 be resettled through all generations.
51:8   through endless generations.
51:9   as in generations of old.
58:12 the foundations of generations ago.
61:4   demolished generations ago.
GENTLY
8:6   waters of Shiloah, which flow gently,
40:11 that give milk he leads gently along.
GIBEAH
10:29 Gibeah of Saul is fleeing.
GIBEON
28:21 as in the Valley of Gibeon—
GIDDY
28:7   and are giddy with strong drink:
GIFTS
39:1   sent letters and gifts to Hezekiah,
GILDED
30:22 your cast idols gilded in gold;
GIRDED
45:5   I girded you up when yet you knew
GIRDLE
3:24   instead of the girdle, a piece of twine,
11:5   faithfulness a girdle round his loins.
22:21 and bind your girdle on him; I will
GIVE
1:2   Hear, O heavens!, Give head, O earth!
1:10   give heed to the law of our God,
7:14   give you a sign: the young woman

7:14 with child shall give birth to a son
8:9 Give heed, in all you distant lands!
12:4 Give thanks to the Lord; invoke his
13:10 nor will the moon give its light.
15:3 altogether wail and give way to the
19:11 Pharaoh's advisers give absurd
23:11 give orders concerning the merchant
24:15 they will give glory to the Lord
26:17 As a woman about to give birth
28:9 Whom shall he give instruction?
28:23 Give heed, and hear my voice!
29:11 they give to one who is learned,
29:12 Or if they give it to one who is
30:20 Lord give you the bread of adversity
34:1 Let the earth give heed, and all who
36:8 king of Assyria: I will give you two
37:7 I will give him a notion to return
37:17 O Lord, give ear and hear; O Lord,
40:1 Comfort and give solace to my people,
40:11 the ewes that give milk he leads
42:12 O let them give glory to the Lord,
42:13 he will give the war cry,
43:3 Cush and Seba I give in place of you.
43:4 I give men in return for you,
43:6 I will say to the north, Give up!
43:20 I may give drink to my chosen people,
45:3 I will give you hidden treasures
48:11 my glory, which I give to no other.
49:20 give us space in which to settle!
51:4 give heed to me, O my nation:
51:23 I give it into the hand of your
54:1 barren woman who did not give birth;
55:3 Give ear and come unto me;
56:5 I will give a handclasp and a name
57:11 nor even give me a thought?
58:10 will give of your own to the hungry
62:7 nor give him respite till he
65:12 I spoke, you would not give heed.
GIVEN
8:18 Lord has given me, we shall be
24:3 Lord has given word concerning it.
36:15 save us; this city shall not be given
37:10 shall not be given into the hand of
GIVES
14:3 In the day the Lord gives you
42:5 who gives form to the earth and its
44:12 and gives it shape by hammering;
44:13 he gives it a human likeness,
44:24 who himself gives form to the earth,
57:1 and no man gives it a thought;
66:7 she is in labor, she gives birth;
GIVING
21:3 I am tormented beyond giving heed;
42:20 seeing much but not giving heed,
62:9 giving praise to the Lord;
GLAD
39:2 And Hezekiah was glad of them and

65:18 be glad forever in what I create.
66:10 Rejoice with Jerusalem and be glad
GLADDEN
56:7 and gladden in my house of prayer.
GLADLY
60:10 I will gladly show you mercy.
GLADNESS
35:10 They shall have won joy and gladness
51:11 let them obtain joy and gladness,
65:14 shout indeed, for gladness of heart,
GLANCED
63:5 I glanced around, but none would
GLARED
63:5 I glared, but no one would assist.
GLAZED
44:18 eyes are glazed so they cannot see,
GLEANED
24:13 grapes are gleaned when the vintage
27:12 But you shall be gleaned one by
GLEANINGS
17:6 when only the gleanings are left,
GLIMMER
59:9 for a glimmer of hope, but we walk
GLOOM
5:30 too shall be a distressing gloom,
8:22 scene of anguish and gloom;
24:11 though all joy has become gloom:
59:9 but we walk amid gloom.
GLOOMY
9:1 But it shall be gloomy to those
GLORIES
16:6 We have heard of the glories of Moab,
GLORIFIED
44:23 he shall be glorified in Israel.
49:3 Israel, in whom I will be glorified.
60:21 in which I am glorified.
GLORIFY
38:18 praise thee, nor Death glorify thee;
GLORIOUS
4:2 shall be beautiful and glorious,
4:5 is glorious shall be a canopy.
11:10 and his residence shall be glorious.
24:16 Glorious are the righteous!
60:7 I will make glorious my house of
60:13 to make glorious the place of my feet.
63:12 who made his glorious arm proceed
63:15 thy holy and glorious celestial abode,
64:11 Our glorious holy temple
GLORIOUSLY
55:5 who gloriously endows you.
GLORY
2:10 and from the brightness of his glory.
2:19 and from the brightness of his glory,
2:21 and from the brightness of his glory,
3:8 affront to his glory before his very
4:2 glory of the survivors of Israel.
6:3 of all the earth is his glory

GLORY *continued*
8:7   the king of Assyria in all his glory.
10:16 to undermine his glory:
13:19 the glory and pride of Chaldeans,
14:11 Your glory has been cast down to
16:14 of a lease, Moab's glory shall
17:3   the glory of the children of Israel,
17:4   In that day Jacob's glory shall wane,
21:16 Kedar's glory shall fully expire.
22:23 of glory to the house of his father.
22:24 glory of his father's house:
24:15 they will give glory to the Lord
24:23 glory in the presence of his elders.
26:10 and see not the glory of the Lord.
26:15 enlarging it gained glory for thyself;
28:1   Woe to the garlands of glory
28:4   fading wreaths, the crowns of glory
28:5   a crown of beauty and wreath of glory
33:17 shall behold the King in his glory
35:2   endowed with the glory of Lebanon,
35:2   The glory of the Lord and the
40:5   For the glory of the Lord shall be
41:16 and glory in the Holy One of Israel.
42:8   not relinquish my glory to another,
42:12 O let them give glory to the Lord,
43:7   wrought for my own glory.
46:12 and to Israel my glory.
48:11 Nor my glory, which I give to no
52:1   Put on your robes of glory, O
58:8   glory of the Lord will be your rear
59:19 from the rising of the sun his glory.
60:1   glory of the Lord has risen upon you!
60:2   over you his glory shall be visible.
60:7   will make glorious my house of glory.
60:19 and your God your radiant glory.
61:3   planted by the Lord for his glory.
62:2   and all their rulers your glory;
62:3   Then shall you be a crown of glory
63:6   when I cast their glory to the ground.
66:5   Let the Lord manifest his glory,
66:18 may approach and behold my glory.
66:19 concerning me, nor seen my glory—
66:19 declare my glory among the nations
GLORYING
23:9   glorying in excellence a profanity,
GLOWING
4:5   day and a mist glowing with
GLUT
34:6   and glut itself with fat—
GLUTTONOUS
56:11 Gluttonous dogs, and insatiable,
GO
2:3   Many peoples shall go, saying,
2:3   Come, let us go up
2:3   For out of Zion shall go forth the law,
2:10   Go into the rocks; hide in the dust
2:19   Men will go into caves in the rocks

2:21   Men will go into crevices in the rocks
5:11   Woe to those who go after liquor
6:8   Whom shall I send? Who will go for
6:9   And he said, Go, and say to these
6:9   Go on hearing, but not understanding
6:9   Go on seeing, but not perceiving.
7:3   Go out and meet Ahaz,
7:24   Men will go there with bows
7:25   go for fear of the briars and thorns,
15:2   They will go up to the sanctuaries,
18:2   They say, Go speedily, you
18:2   Go to a people perpetually on the
19:23 and Egyptians go to Assyria,
20:2   Go and ungird the sackcloth
21:6   Go and appoint a watchman
22:15 Go and see that steward, Shebna,
23:16 Take a lyre and go about the town,
28:28 one does not go on endlessly
30:8   Go now, write on tablets concerning
31:1   Woe to those who go down to Egypt
31:6   contrived to go far astray, O children
37:32 out of Jerusalem shall go a remnant,
38:5   Go and tell Hezekiah, Thus says the
38:22* again go up to the house of the Lord?
38:18 those who go down into the Pit
43:8   Let go the people who are blind,
45:2   I will go before you and level all
45:21 go ahead and consult one another.
46:2   they themselves go into captivity.
48:17 guiding you in the way you should go.
48:20 Go forth out of Babylon, flee
51:4   The law shall go forth from me;
51:13 that you go all day in constant dread
51:23 Lie prostrate that we may go over you
52:12 shall not leave in haste or go in flight
52:12 the Lord will go before you
58:8   righteousness will go before you,
62:10 Pass on, go through gates;
66:3   have preferred to go their own ways,
66:24 And they shall go out and look upon
GOATS
11:6   leopard lie down with young goats;
34:6   the blood of lambs and he-goats,
34:14 and wild goats call to one another.
GOD
1:10   give heed to the law of our God,
2:3   to the house of the God of Jacob,
5:16   the holy God show himself holy
7:11   from the Lord your God,
7:13   you also try the patience of my God?
8:10   shall not prove firm: God is with us!
8:19   inquire of their God? Should one
8:21   curse their king and their God.
12:2   In the God of my salvation I will
13:19 as God overthrew Sodom and
14:13 up my throne above the stars of God;
17:6   says the Lord, the God of Israel.

17:10	For you have forgotten your God,	48:2	upheld by the God of Israel,
21:10	the Lord of Hosts, the God of Israel.	48:17	I the Lord your God instruct you to
21:17	The Lord, the God of Israel	49:4	my recompense with my God.
24:15	name of the Lord, the God of Israel.	49:5	when my God became my strength—
25:1	O Lord, thou art my God;	50:10	of the Lord and relies on his God?
25:9	day you will say, This is our God,	51:15	It is I the Lord your God,
26:13	O Lord, our God, lords other than	51:22	says the Lord, your Lord and God,
28:26	His God instructs him,	52:7	saying to Zion, Your God reigns!
29:23	reverencing the God of Israel,	52:12	the God of Israel behind you.
30:18	For the Lord is the God of justice;	53:4	smitten of God, and humbled.
35:2	the Lord and the splendor of our God	54:5	who is called the God of all the earth.
35:4	See, your God is coming to avenge	54:6	to be rejected, says your God.
35:4	God himself will come and deliver	55:5	because of the Lord your God,
36:7	Lord our God, is he not the one	55:7	to our God, who graciously pardons.
37:4	the Lord your God has heard	57:21	no peace, says my God, for the wicked
37:4	living God, and will rebuke him for	58:2	forsaking the precepts of their God.
37:4	the Lord your God has heard,	58:2	desiring to draw nearer to God:
37:10	Let not your god in whom you trust	59:2	that separate you from your God;
37:16	O Lord of Hosts, God of Israel,	59:13	backing away from following our God,
37:16	alone art God over all the kingdoms	60:9	to the Lord Omnipotent, your God,
37:17	has sent to mock the living God.	60:19	and your God your radiant glory.
37:20	But now, O Lord our God, deliver us	61:2	and the day of vengeance of our God,
37:21	God of Israel: Because you have	61:6	to as the ministers of our God.
37:38	temple of Nisroch his god, his sons	61:10	my soul delights in my God.
38:5	the God of your father David: I have	62:3	royal diadem in the palm of your God
40:1	says your God; speak kindly	62:5	so shall your God rejoice over you.
40:3	pave a straight highway for our God:	64:4	has any eye seen a God besides thee,
40:8	the word of our God endures forever.	65:16	the earth shall do so by the true God,
40:9	the cities of Judah: Behold your God!	65:16	shall do so by the God of truth.
40:18	To whom then will you liken God?	66:9	shall I hinder it? says your God.
40:27	our cause is overlooked by our God?		**GODLESS**
40:28	The Lord is the God of eternity,	9:17	all alike are godless malefactors,
41:10	be not dismayed, for I am your God.	10:6	him against a godless nation,
41:13	For I, the Lord your God,	32:5	The godless shall no longer be
41:17	I, the God of Israel, will not forsake	32:6	For the godless utter blasphemy;
42:5	Thus says the Lord God,	33:14	godless are in the grip of trembling:
43:3	For I the Lord am your God,		**GODLY**
43:10	before me no god was formed,	57:1	the godly are gathered out,
43:12	there was no strange god among you.		**GODS**
44:6	apart from me there is no God.	2:18	will utterly supplant the false gods.
44:8	Is there a God, then, apart from me?	2:20	their idols of silver and gods of gold
44:10	would fashion a god or cast an idol	14:13	the mount of assembly of the gods,
44:12	he forges his god by the strength of	21:9	All her idol gods he has razed to the
44:17	the rest they make a god, their idol,	36:18	Lord will save us. Were any gods of
44:17	Save us; you are our god!	36:19	Where are the gods of Hamath and
45:3	God of Israel, who calls you by name.	36:19	Where are the gods of Sepharvaim?
45:5	apart from me there is no God.	36:20	Who of all the gods of those countries
45:14	God is in you; no other gods exist!	37:12	Did the gods of the nations my
45:15	art a God who dissembles himself,	37:19	committing their gods to the fire.
45:15	O Savior, God of Israel.	37:19	For they were no gods, but mere
45:18	the God who formed the earth—	41:23	so that we may know you are gods.
45:21	Did not I, the God of righteousness,	42:17	and esteem their images as gods
45:21	apart from whom there is no God?	44:15	they create gods which they adore,
45:22	I am God, there is none other.	45:14	God is in you; no other gods exist!
46:6	hire a smith to make them a god	45:20	prayed to gods that could not save
46:9	I am God, there is none other.	46:2	Such gods altogether sag and bow
48:1	and invoke the God of Israel,		

GOD'S
51:20 of your God's angry rebuke.
52:10* our God's salvation.
GOING
20:2 And he had done so, going
30:2 They are bent on going down to Egypt
GOINGS
37:28 and your comings and goings,
GOLD
2:7 Their land is full of silver and gold
2:20 their idols of silver and gods of gold
13:12 make mankind scarcer than fine gold,
13:12 men more rare than gold of Ophir.
13:17 do not value silver, nor covet gold.
30:22 your cast idols gilded in gold;
31:7 your idolatrous silver and gold
39:2 this treasuries—the silver and gold,
40:19 overlaid by the smith with gold,
46:6 who squander gold from the purse
60:6 bearing gold and frankincense
60:9 and with them their silver and gold,
60:17 In place of copper I will bring gold,
GOMORRAH
1:9 or become like Gomorrah.
1:10 you people of Gomorrah!
13:19 God overthrew Sodom and Gomorrah.
GONE
16:10 will be gone from the orchards;
20:3 my servant Isaiah has gone
24:11 the earth's vitality is gone.
28:7 priests and prophets have gone astray
38:8 the ten degrees it has gone down.
53:6 We all like sheep had gone astray,
GOOD
1:17 Learn to do good: demand justice,
1:19 you shall eat the good of the land.
5:20 who suppose what is evil to be good
5:20 and what is good, evil!
7:15 choose what is good.
7:16 the good, the land whose two
38:3 have done what is good in thine eyes
38:17 Surely, for my own good I am in such
39:8 Lord you have spoken is good.
40:9 O Zion, herald of good tidings.
40:9 O Jerusalem, messenger of good news.
41:7* They say of the welding, It is good,
41:23 Perform something good or evil
48:17 your God instruct you to your good,
52:7 who brings tidings of good,
55:2 Hear me well: Eat what is good,
58:5 a day of the Lord's good graces?
61:1 to announce good tidings to the lowly;
65:2 who walk in ways that are not good,
65:8 Don't destroy it, it is still good,
GOVERN
52:5 those who govern them

GOVERNMENT
9:6 shoulder the burden of government.
GOZAN
37:12 Gozan and Haran, Rezeph and the
GRACES
58:5 a day of the Lord's good graces?
GRACIOUSLY
30:19 He will graciously respond at the cry
55:7 to our God, who graciously pardons.
63:7 has mercifully and most graciously
GRAFT
11:1 a branch from its graft bear fruit.
GRAIN
17:5 being like a harvest of ripe grain,
23:3 The grain of Shihor,the harvest of the
28:28 Domestic grain is ground;
30:24 eat grain silage winnowed with shovel
36:17 a land like your own, a land of grain
36:17 a land of grain fields and vineyards
62:8 I will no more let your grain be food
66:3 whoever presents a grain offering
GRAINS
48:19 descendants as many as their grains.
GRANT
46:12 I will grant deliverance in Zion,
GRAPES
5:2 Then he expected it to yield grapes,
5:2 but it produced wild grapes.
5:4 When I expected it to yield grapes,
5:4 why did it produce wild grapes?
24:13 or as grapes are gleaned when the
63:2 who tread grapes in the winepress
65:8 there is juice in a cluster of grapes
GRASP
42:6 and will grasp you by the hand;
45:1 whom I grasp by the right hand,
GRASS
15:6 the grass shall dry up, vegetation
37:27 becoming as wild grass, transiently
40:6 All flesh is grass,
40:8 grass that withers, flowers that fade—
44:4 They shall shoot up like grass
51:12 men who shall be turned to grass?
66:14 limbs flourish like sprouting grass,
GRASSHOPPERS
40:22 its inhabitants are as grasshoppers,
GRATIFIED
61:6 gratified with their choicest
GRAVEL
14:19 remains are thrown in a gravel pit.
GRAVELY
38:1 Hezekiah became gravely ill.
GRAVEN
30:22 your graven idols plated with silver,
48:5 my graven and wrought images caused
GRAVES
22:16 graves for themselves in the rock?

GRAZE
30:23 In that day your cattle shall graze
65:25 wolf and the lamb will graze alike,
GREAT
6:12 and great shall be the exodus
8:7 great and mighty waters of the River—
17:13 roar like the roaring of great water,
27:1 with his great and powerful sword,
30:25 on the day of the great slaughter,
36:4 the great king, the king of Assyria:
36:13 the great king, the king of Assyria!
53:12 an inheritance among the great,
54:13 and great shall be the peace of your
63:7 according to the great kindness
GREEN
15:6 and no green foliage shall remain.
37:27 as wild grass, transiently green,
GREET
21:14 bring water to greet the thirsty;
34:14 Prairie wolves shall greet jackals,
GREW
53:2 Like a sapling he grew up in his
GREY
46:4 till you turn grey, it is I who sustain
GRIEF
14:3 relief from grief and anguish
53:3 a man of grief, accustomed to
GRIEFS
53:4 our sufferings, endured our griefs,
GRIEVANCE
30:27 is kindled, heavy is his grievance;
GRIEVED
63:10 rebelled and grieved his holy Spirit,
GRIM
21:2 A grim vision has been revealed to
GRIND
47:2 Take two grindstones and grind flour;
GRINDSTONES
47:2 Take two grindstones and grind flour;
GRIP
33:14 godless are in the grip of trembling:
GROAN
16:7 they shall groan at the ruin of Kir
GROPE
59:10 We grope along the borders like the
GROSS
29:18 out of gross darkness.
GROUND
2:19 and holes in the ground,
3:26 she shall sit on the ground destitute.
7:23 In that day every plot of ground
21:9 idol gods he has razed to the ground.
25:12 lay low by razing them to the ground,
26:5 by casting it to the ground,
28:2 hurl them to the ground by his hand.
28:24 and harrowing the same ground?
28:28 Domestic grain is ground;

28:28 It cannot be ground
29:4 you will speak from the ground,
29:4 your voice from the ground
30:23 the seed you sow in the ground,
40:4 the uneven ground must become level
42:16 and the uneven ground make level.
44:3 showers upon the dry ground;
47:1 squat on the ground, dethroned,
49:23 their faces to the ground;
51:23 you made your back as the ground,
53:2 a stalk out of arid ground.
63:6 when I cast their glory to the ground.
GROUNDS
36:4 On what grounds do you behave
GROVE
5:7 people of Judah his cherished grove.
GROW
6:10 the heart of these people grow fat;
13:7 Then shall every hand grow weak
28:22 lest your bonds grow severe.
37:27 that scorch before they grow up.
40:28 He does not grow faint or weary;
40:30 Youths grow faint and weary,
42:4 Neither shall he himself grow dim or
44:12 he begins to grow faint.
44:14 plants firs, which the rain makes grow:
GROWLING
5:29 growling, they seize the prey, and
GROWLS
31:4 or a young lion growls over the prey
GROWN
35:3 Strengthen the hands grown feeble,
43:22 you have grown weary of me, O Israel.
50:4 to those grown weary a word to wake
GROWS
5:27 Not one of them grows weary,
37:30 This year eat what grows wild,
GRUMBLE
59:11 We grumble like bears, all of us;
GUARD
21:8 night after night I have stood guard.
31:5 the Lord of Hosts guard Jerusalem;
58:8 the Lord will be your rear guard.
GUIDE
42:16 and guide them in paths unfamiliar;
49:10 has mercy on them will guide them;
51:18 There was none to guide her home
57:18 I will guide him and amply console
GUIDED
11:3 His intuition will be guided
63:14 Spirit of the lord that guided them.
GUIDING
48:17 guiding you in the way you should go.
GUILE
59:3 your lips speak guile, your tongue
GUILT
24:6 who dwell on it have incurred guilt;

GUILT *continued*
31:7 your hands have incurred guilt.
40:2 that her guilt has been expiated.
53:10 he made his life an offering for guilt,
GUILTY
5:23 who acquit the guilty for a bribe,
29:21 at a word adjudge a man to be guilty,
GULLIES
57:5 slayers of children in the gullies
GUSHED
48:21 cleaved the rock and water gushed out
HABITATIONS
27:10 deserted habitations, forsaken like a
HAIL
10:5 Hail the Assyrian, the rod of my
28:17 a hail shall sweep away your false
30:30 discharges and pounding hail.
32:19* For by hail shall forests be felled,
HAILSTORM
28:2 a ravaging hailstorm sweeping down,
HAIR
7:20 your head and the hair of your
HALF
44:16 Half of it they burn in the fire.
HALLOWING
29:23 work of my hands, hallowing my name
HALLS
13:22 creatures from its amusement halls.
HAMATH
10:9 Is not Hamath as Arpad,
11:11 Pathros, Cush, Elam, Shinar, Hamath,
36:19 Where are the gods of Hamath and
37:13 Where are the kings of Hamath and
HAMMER
41:7* and he who beats with a hammer
HAMMERING
44:12 and gives it shape by hammering;
HAND
1:25 I will restore my hand over you
3:7 But he will raise his hand in that
5:25 he draws back his hand against them
5:25 his hand is upraised still.
8:11 clasping my hand, and admonished
9:12 his hand is upraised still.
9:17 his hand is upraised still.
9:21 his hand is upraised still.
10:4 his hand is upraised still.
10:5 is a staff—my wrath in their hand.
11:8 and the toddler reach his hand
11:11 my Lord will again raise his hand
11:15 will extend his hand over the River
13:2 Beckon them with the hand to advance
13:7 Then shall every hand grow weak
14:26 this is the hand upraised over all
14:27 When his hand is upraised, who can
19:4 into the hand of a cruel master;
19:16 at the brandishing hand the Lord

23:11 will stretch out his hand over the Sea
25:10 mountain rests the hand of the Lord,
26:11 O Lord, thy hand is lifted up,
28:2 hurl them to the ground by his hand.
31:3 when the Lord stretches out his hand,
33:15 stay their hand from taking bribes,
34:17 his hand that divides it by measure.
36:15 into the hand of the king of Assyria.
36:18 the hand of the king of Assyria?
36:19 they deliver Samaria out of my hand?
36:20 saved his land from my hand, that the
36:20 should save Jerusalem from my hand?
37:10 not be given into the hand of the king
37:20 of his hand, that all kingdoms on
38:6 out of the hand of the king of Assyria
40:2 She has received from the Lord's hand
40:12 with the hollow of his hand
41:10 you with my righteous right hand.
41:13 hold you by the right hand and say to
41:20 that the Lord's hand did this,
42:6 and will grasp you by the hand;
43:13 from my hand none can deliver;
44:20 this thing in my hand is a fraud.
45:1 whom I grasp by the right hand,
45:12 my hand suspended the heavens,
47:6 I gave them into your hand,
47:14 to escape the hand of the flame.
48:13 It was my hand that founded the
48:13 my right hand that stretched out the
49:2 in the shadow of his hand he hid me.
49:22 I will lift up my hand to the nations,
50:2 Was my hand too short to redeem you
50:11 This shall you have from my hand:
51:5 My righteousness shall be at hand
51:16 shelter you in the shadow of my hand,
51:17 who have drunk from the Lord's hand
51:18 none to take her by the hand of all
51:22 the cup of stupor from your hand;
51:23 it into the hand of your tormentors,
52:6 that I, who speak, am at hand.
53:10 might prosper in his hand.
56:2 who stays his hand from doing any
57:8 your hand on their nakedness.
59:1 Lord's hand has not become too
62:3 in the hand of the Lord,
62:8 Lord has sworn by his right hand,
63:12 at the right hand of Moses,
64:7 and enfeebled us at the hand of our
66:2 are all things my hand has made,
66:14 when the hand of the Lord
HANDS
1:15 When you spread forth your hands,
1:15 your hands are filled with blood.
2:8 they adore the works of their hands,
5:12 nor perceive his hands at work.
17:8 the works of their hands,
19:25 Assyria the work of my hands,

25:11 For when he stretches his hands
25:11 swimmer spreads his hands to swim,
29:23 the work of my hands, hallowing my
31:7 which your hands have incurred guilt
35:3 Strengthen the hands grown feeble,
37:19 of men's hands, or wood and of stone,
42:24 Who is it that hands Jacob over to
45:9 Your hands have no skill for the work
45:11 me about the deeds of my hands?
55:12 the meadows all clap their hands.
60:21 the work of my hands, in which I am
64:8 are all alike the work of thy hands.
65:2 I held out my hands all the day to a
65:22 shall outlast the work of their hands.
HANDCLASP
56:5 I will give a handclasp and a name
HAND'S
11:14 Edom and Moab at hand's reach,
HANDLES
10:15 over him who handles it?
HANES
30:4 and their envoys' travels to Hanes,
HANG
33:23* Their riggings hang loose;
HANGING
22:25 and the burden hanging on it cut off.
HAPPEN
14:24 As I foresaw it, so shall it happen;
24:13 Then shall it happen in the earth
HAPPENS
44:7 Who predicts what happens as do I,
HARAN
37:12 Gozan and Haran, Rezeph and the
HARASSED
53:7 He was harassed, yet submissive,
HARBINGER
41:27 to Zion, he shall be her harbinger;
HARBOR
23:10 Tarshish: the harbor is no
HARD
42:14 and breathe hard and fast all at once.
HARDENING
63:17 hardening our hearts so that we do
HARDLY
40:24 when hardly their stalk has taken
HARDSHIP
30:6 land of hardship and vicissitude,
HARK
13:4 Hark! A tumult on the mountains,
13:4 Hark! An uproar among kingdoms,
52:8 Hark! Your watchmen lift up their
66:6 Hark, a tumult from the city, a noise
HARLOT
1:21 has become a harlot!
23:15 shall be as the harlot in the song:
23:16 O forgotten harlot.
57:3 offspring of adulterer and harlot!

HARM
11:9 There shall be no harm or injury done
65:25 there shall be no harm or injury done
HARNESS
58:6 to untie the harness of the yoke,
HARNESSED
22:6 horses are harnessed to the chariots
HARP
16:11 My breast will vibrate like a harp for
HARPS
5:12 There are harps and lyres,
HARROWING
28:24 and harrowing the same ground?
HARSH
19:4 a harsh ruler will subject them,
HARVEST
9:3 as men rejoice at harvest time,
16:9 summer fruit and harvest are stilled.
17:5 being like a harvest of ripe grain,
17:11 yet shall the harvest vanish
18:5 For before the harvest,
23:3 of Shihor, the harvest of the Nile,
27:11 A harvest of twigs dries, broken off
27:12 his harvest from the torrent of the
28:4 before the summer harvest :
32:10 for when the harvest is over,
37:30 But in the third year sow and harvest,
62:9 Those who harvest it shall eat it,
HARVESTED
33:4 Their spoil was harvested
HASTE
52:12 shall not leave in haste or go in
HASTEN
8:1 Hasten the plunder, hurry the spoil.
22:4 hasten not to comfort me
49:17 Your sons shall hasten your ravagers
55:5 nor know you will hasten to you—
59:7 they hasten to shed innocent blood.
60:22 I the Lord will hasten it in its time.
HATCH
34:15 hatch them and brood over her young.
59:5 They hatch vipers' eggs and spin
HAUGHTINESS
2:17 The haughtiness of men shall be
HAUGHTY
2:11 The haughty eyes of men shall be
3:16 the women of Zion are haughty
HAUNT
14:23 swamplands, a haunt for ravens;
34:13 the haunt of howling creatures,
35:7 in the haunt of howling creatures
HAUNTS
32:14 shall become haunts for ever after,
HAVEN
23:4 mighty haven of the Sea, has declared,
23:11 that her ports of haven be destroyed.
23:14 your haven is desolate!

HAVOC
24:12 Havoc remains in the city;
59:7 havoc and disaster follow in their
HAWK
34:15 There shall the hawk owl nest and lay
HAWKS
34:11 But hawks and falcons shall posses it,
HEAD
1:5 The whole head is sick
1:6 the soles of the feet even to the head
2:2 as the head of the mountains;
3:18 head ornaments and crescents,
7:8 and Rezin the head of Damascus,
7:9 son of Remaliah the head of Samaria,
7:20 your head and the hair of your
9:14 head and tail, palm top and reed,
9:15 the elders or notables are the head,
15:2 Every head shall be bald, every beard
19:15 neither head nor tail, palm top or
37:22 Jerusalem shakes her head at you.
58:5 only for bowing one's head like a reed
59:17 salvation the helmet on his head;
HEADED
53:6 each of us headed his own way;
HEADPIECE
61:3 upon them a priestly headpiece
HEADS
19:13 heads of state have led Egypt astray.
28:1 the heads of the opulent overcome
28:4 on the heads of the opulent
29:10 he has covered your heads, the seers.
35:10 their heads crowned with everlasting
49:7 heads of state shall prostrate
51:11 their heads crowned with everlasting
HEAL
19:22 and by smiting heal it: they
19:22 their pleas and heal them.
HEALED
6:10 and repent, and be healed.
53:5 and with his wounds we are healed.
HEALING
58:8 and your healing speedily appear;
HEALS
30:26 and heals their open wound.
57:19 says the Lord who heals him.
HEAP
17:1 and become a heap of ruins.
25:2 hast made the city a heap of rubble,
HEAPS
37:26 turning them into heaps of rubble,
HEAR
1:2 Hear, O heavens!, Give heed, O earth!
1:10 Hear the word of the Lord,
1:15 you pray at length, I will not hear
6:10 and hear with their ears,
10:30 Hear her, Laishah; answer her,
11:3 establish proof by what his ears hear.

24:16 sector of the earth we hear singing:
28:14 Therefore hear the word of the Lord,
28:19 terror merely to hear word of it.
28:23 Give heed, and hear my voice!
29:18 that day shall the deaf hear the words
30:21 ears shall hear words from behind
32:3 ears of those who hear shall listen.
32:9 careless daughters, hear my words!
34:1 Come near, you nations, and hear!
36:13 loud voice in Judean, Hear the words
37:17 O Lord, give ear and hear; O Lord,
39:5 Hear the word of the Lord of Hosts:
44:1 Hear now, Jacob my servant,
46:3 Hear me, O house of Jacob,
46:12 Hear me, you stubborn-hearted,
47:8 Now therefore hear this, O pampered
48:1 Hear this, O house of Jacob,
48:12 Hear me, O Jacob, and Israel, my elect
48:14 All of you, assemble and hear:
48:16 Come near and hear this:
49:1 Hear me, O isles; listen, you distant
50:4 by morning he wakens my ear to hear,
51:1 Hear me, you followers of
51:7 Hear me, you who know
51:21 Now therefore hear this, O wretched
55:2 Hear me well: Eat what is good,
59:2 so that he does not hear you.
66:5 Hear the word of the Lord,
HEARD
6:8 Then I heard the voice of my Lord
15:4 appeal shall be heard as far as Jahaz.
16:6 We have heard of the glories of Moab,
21:10 I have reported what I heard
24:11 Outside is heard the clamor for wine
28:22 I . . . heard utter destruction decreed
37:1 When King Hezekiah heard it, he rent
37:4 the Lord your God has heard,
37:6 the words with which you have heard
37:8 when Rabshakeh heard that the king
37:9 And when he heard it,
37:11 You yourself had heard what the
37:26 Have you not heard how I ordained
38:5 of your father David: I have heard
39:1 had heard of his illness and recovery.
40:9 Make yourself heard, be not afraid;
40:21 so unaware, that you have not heard?
40:28 not known to you; have you not heard?
41:26 no one has heard from you
42:2 to make himself heard in public.
48:6 you have heard the whole vision;
48:7 things you have not heard of before,
48:8 You have not heard them
52:15 what they had not heard, they shall
58:4 as to make your voice heard on high.
60:18 tyranny shall no more be heard of
64:4 Never has it been heard or perceived
65:19 no more shall be heard there

66:8 Who has heard the like,
66:19 to the nations that had not heard the
HEARING
5:9 of Hosts spoke this in my hearing:
6:9 Go on hearing, but not understanding
37:7 upon hearing a rumor, and will cause
42:20 with open ears hearing nothing?
42:23 Who among you hearing this
43:9 that those within hearing may say,
59:1 nor his ear dull of hearing!
HEARS
30:19 answer you as soon as he hears it.
HEART
1:5 the whole heart diseased.
6:10 the heart of these people grow fat;
6:10 understand in their heart,
9:9 say in pride and arrogance of heart,
14:13 You said in your heart, I will rise in
15:5 My heart will cry out for Moab;
29:13 while their heart remains far from me
30:29 and rejoicing of heart, as when men
32:6 their heart ponders impiety:
38:3 and with full purpose of heart and
42:25 yet they take it not to heart.
46:8 take it to heart, you offenders.
51:7 O people in whose heart is my law:
57:17 by following the ways of his heart
60:5 your heart swell with awe:
65:14 shout indeed, for gladness of heart,
66:14 Your heart shall rejoice to see it,
HEARTBREAK
65:14 you shall cry out with heartbreak,
HEARTH
10:16 fire to flare up like a burning hearth,
29:2 she becomes as my altar hearth.
30:33 a hearth indeed, made ready for
HEARTS
13:7 and the hearts of all men melt.
19:1 and the Egyptians' hearts melt within
35:4 Say to those with fearful hearts,
57:15 reviving the hearts of the humble.
63:17 hardening our hearts so that we do
HEAT
4:6 from the heat of the day,
18:4 when the searing heat overtakes the
25:4 and shade from the heat.
25:5 or like scorching heat in the desert,
25:5 burning heat by the shade of a cloud,
42:25 So in the heat of his anger
49:10 by oppressive heat or by the sun;
64:2 which bubbles over from the heat—
HEATHEN
2:6 content with the infantile heathen.
25:2 heathen mansions shall no more form
25:5 quell the onslaughts of the heathen:
HEAVE
57:20 whose waters heave up mire and mud:

HEAVEN
37:23 lifting your eyes to high heaven?
63:15 O look down from heaven,
HEAVENS
1:2 Hear, O heavens!, Give head, O earth!
13:10 and constellations of the heavens
13:13 will cause disturbance in the heavens
14:12 How you have fallen from the heavens
14:13 your heart, I will rise in the heavens
34:4 when the heavens are rolled up as a
34:5 sword drinks its fill in the heavens,
37:16 who madest the heavens and the earth
40:12 and gauged the heavens
40:22 suspends the heavens like a canopy,
42:5 frames and suspends the heavens,
44:23 Sing, O heavens, for what the Lord
44:24 who alone suspends the heavens,
45:8 Rain down from above, O heavens;
45:12 with my hand suspended the heavens,
45:18 the Lord who created the heavens,
47:13 let those who unravel the heavens,
48:13 hand that stretched out the heavens;
49:13 Shout for joy, O heavens; celebrate,
50:3 clothe the heavens with the blackness
51:6 Lift up your eyes to the heavens;
51:6 the heavens shall vanish as by smoke,
51:13 who suspends the heavens,
51:16 while I replant the heavens and set
55:9 But as the heavens are higher than
64:1 rend the heavens and descend,
65:17 I create new heavens and a new earth;
66:1 The heavens are my throne
66:22 as the new heavens and the new earth
HEAVENWARD
38:14 eyes are drawn looking heavenward;
40:26 Lift your eyes heavenward and see:
HEAVILY
47:6 weighed down heavily with your yoke.
HEAVY
30:27 is kindled, heavy is his grievance;
HEBREW
19:18 In that day five Hebrew-speaking
HEDGE
5:5 I will have its hedge removed
HEED
1:2 Hear, O heavens!, Give heed, O earth!
1:10 give heed to the law of our God,
7:13 Then Isaiah said, Take heed,
8:9 Give heed, in all your distant lands!
18:3 heed the trumpet when sounded!
21:3 I am tormented beyond giving heed;
28:23 Give heed, and hear my voice!
33:13 Take heed what I have done,
34:1 Let the earth give heed,
42:20 seeing much but not giving heed,
42:23 will take heed of it hereafter,
51:4 give heed to me, O my nation:

HEED *continued*
55:3   pay heed, that your souls may live!
65:12   I spoke, you would not give heed.
66:4   when I spoke, none gave heed.
HEEDS
50:10   and heeds the voice of his servant,
HE-GOATS
1:11   blood of bulls and sheep and he-goats
34:6   the blood of lambs and he-goats,
HEIGHTS
7:11   or in the heights above.
14:13   in the utmost heights of Zaphon.
30:25   all mountain heights and prominent
31:4   Mount Zion and upon its heights.
40:9   Scale the mountain heights,
49:9   find pasture on all barren heights;
58:14   you traverse the heights of the earth
HEIRS
65:9   out of Judah heirs of my mountains;
HELD
10:15   As though the staff held up the one
33:8   their signatories held in contempt;
65:2   I held out my hands all the day to a
HELMET
59:17   salvation the helmet on his head;
HELP
10:3   To whom will you flee for help?
15:4   Heshbon will cry for help, as will
20:6   on whom we relied for help and
29:9   until you cry for help,
30:5   shall be of no help or benefit,
30:7   Egypt's help shall be futile and vain;
31:1   those who go down to Egypt for help,
31:3   those who help them will stumble
41:13   Have no fear; I will help you.
41:14   I am your help, says the Lord;
46:7   Though they cry to it for help,
63:5   but none would lend help;
HELPED
31:3   and those helped will fall:
HELPS
50:7   Because my Lord the Lord helps me,
HENA
37:13   of the cities of Sepharvaim, Hena,
HERALD
40:9   O Zion, herald of good tidings.
41:27   appoint him as a herald of tidings
61:2   to herald the year of the Lord's favor
HERALDING
60:6   and heralding the praises of the Lord.
HERALDS
52:7   who heralds salvation,
HERBAGE
40:7   people themselves are but herbage—
HERDED
24:22   They shall be herded together

HERDS
17:2   become places for herds to recline,
65:10   the herds of my people who seek me.
HERITAGE
54:17   heritage of the servants of the Lord,
58:14   you with the heritage of Jacob
HESHBON
15:4   Heshbon will cry for help, as will
16:8   vineyards of Heshbon shall wither;
16:9   O Heshbon and Elealeh,
HEW
22:16   who hew their sepulchres up high,
HEWED
5:2   and hewed for it a winepress as well.
HEWER
14:8   no hewer has risen against us!
HEWN
9:10   but we will rebuild with hewn stone;
10:33   high in stature shall be hewn down,
14:12   have been hewn down to earth!
22:16   you have hewn yourself a tomb here,
51:1   quarry out of which you were hewn;
HEWS
10:15   above the one who hews with it,
HEZEKIAH
1:1   Ahaz, and Hezekiah, kings of Judah:
36:2   King Hezekiah at Jerusalem.
36:4   Please tell Hezekiah, Thus says
36:7   and altars Hezekiah abolished,
36:14   says the king: Do not let Hezekiah
36:15   Do not let Hezekiah make you trust in
36:16   Do not listen to Hezekiah! Thus says
36:18   Beware, lest Hezekiah mislead you
36:22   went to Hezekiah with their clothes
37:1   When King Hezekiah heard it, he rent
37:3   they said to him, Thus says Hezekiah:
37:9   messengers to Hezekiah, telling them
37:10   Speak thus to Hezekiah king of Judah:
37:14   Hezekiah received the letter from the
37:14   Then Hezekiah went up to the house
37:15   And Hezekiah prayed to the Lord and
37:21   to Hezekiah, saying, Thus says the
38:1   days Hezekiah became gravely ill.
38:2   this Hezekiah turned his face toward
38:3   And Hezekiah wept disconsolately.
38:5   Go and tell Hezekiah, Thus says the
38:22* But Hezekiah said, What of a sign
38:9   Hezekiah king of Judah's account of
39:1   sent letters and gifts to Hezekiah,
39:2   Hezekiah was glad of them and
39:2   that Hezekiah did not show them.
39:3   prophet Isaiah came to King Hezekiah
39:3   And Hezekiah replied,
39:4   And Hezekiah said, They saw
39:5   Then Isaiah said to Hezekiah,
39:8   But Hezekiah said to Isaiah,

HEZEKIAH'S
36:1   fourteenth year of King Hezekiah's
37:5*   when King Hezekiah's servants came
HID
49:2   in the shadow of his hand he hid me.
50:6   I hid not my face from insult and
54:8   a fleeting surge of anger I hid my face
57:17   I struck him and hid my face in
HIDDEN
30:20   Teacher remain hidden no longer,
42:22   hidden away in dungeons.
45:3   I will give you hidden treasures
64:7   For thou hast hidden thy face from us
65:16   and hidden from my eyes.
HIDE
2:10   Go into the rocks; hide in the dust
3:9   they cannot hide it.
26:20   hide yourselves a little while
29:15   to hide their schemes from the Lord!
53:3   one from whom men hide their faces
59:2   your sins hide his face, so that he
HIDEOUTS
65:4   sepulchres, spend nights in hideouts,
HIDES
8:17   who hides his face from the house of
HIDING
28:15   and hiding behind falsehoods,
28:17   and waters flood the hiding place.
HIGH
2:13   Lebanon that lift themselves up high,
2:14   all high mountains and elevated hills,
5:15   causing the eyes of the high-minded
10:33   high in stature shall be hewn down,
14:14   will make myself like the Most High!
16:3   Overshadow us at high noon
22:16   who hew their sepulchres up high,
23:3   source of revenue upon the high seas
24:18   when the windows on high are opened
24:21   In that day will the Lord deal on high
24:21   with the hosts on high
30:13   breach exposed in a high wall
32:14   High rises and panoramic resorts
32:15   Then shall a Spirit from on high
33:5   is supreme, for he dwells on high;
33:16   They shall dwell on high;
37:23   lifting your eyes to high heaven?
49:11   my highways shall be on high.
57:15   I dwell on high in the holy place,
58:4   as to make your voice heard on high.
HIGHER
55:9   the heavens are higher than the earth,
55:9   so are my ways higher than your ways
55:9   thoughts higher than your thoughts.
HIGHEST
37:24   conquered the highest mountains,
HIGHLY
6:1   highly exalted, the skirt of his robe

25:12   Your highly walled fortifications
52:13   being astute, shall be highly exalted;
57:15   Thus says he who is highly exalted,
HIGH-MINDED
5:15   eyes of the high-minded to be
HIGHWAY
19:23   highway from Egypt to Assyria.
40:3   pave a straight highway for our God:
62:10   pave a highway cleared of stones;
HIGHWAYS
33:8   highways are desolate, travel is at an
35:8   There shall be highways and roads
49:11   my highways shall be on high.
HILKIAH
22:20   servant Eliakim the son of Hilkiah:
36:3   And Eliakim the son of Hilkiah,
36:22   Then Eliakim the son of Hilkiah,
HILL
5:1   on the fertile brow of a hill.
10:32   the hill of Jerusalem.
15:2   to Dibon to the hill shrines, to weep;
16:12   with petitioning on the hill shrines,
30:17   an ensign on a hill.
40:4   every mountain and hill made low;
41:18   up streams in barren hill country,
HILLS
2:2   shall be preeminent among the hills,
2:14   all high mountains and elevated hills,
30:25   mountain heights and prominent hills
34:4   fat decompose [on the hills]
40:12   hills in a balance?
41:15   and make chaff of hills.
42:15   I will lay waste mountains and hills
54:10   and the hills collapse with shaking,
55:12   the mountains and hills shall sing
65:7   who affront me on the hills,
HILLSIDES
7:25   And on all hillsides cultivated
HINDER
47:12   perhaps you can hinder it.
66:9   shall I hinder it? says your God.
HIRE
23:17   return to her trade and hire herself
23:18   Her merchandise and hire shall
46:6   hire a smith to make them a god
HIRED
7:20   a razor hired at the River—
HITCHED
5:18   hitched to transgression like a
HIVITES
17:9   of the Hivites and Amorites
HOARDED
23:18   it shall not be hoarded or stored up.
HOARDS
45:3   and secret hoards of wealth—
HOE
7:25   by the hoe you will no longer

HOED
5:6 it shall neither be pruned nor hoed,
HOLD
4:1 women will take hold of one man
8:10 Though you hold consultations,
27:5 But should they take hold of me for a
28:4 the moment he has hold of it.
33:23* they hold not the mast in place
34:6 For the Lord will hold a slaughter in
41:13 hold you by the right hand and say to
54:2 Do not hold back; lengthen your cords
64:7 or rouses himself to take hold of thee.
HOLDING
56:4 holding fast to my covenant—
56:6 holding fast to my covenant—
HOLDS
37:22 of Zion holds you in contempt;
56:2 the person who holds fast to them—
HOLES
2:19 and holes in the ground,
7:19 and by all ditches and water holes.
42:22 all of them trapped in holes,
HOLIER
65:5 come near me; I am holier than you!
HOLINESS
35:8 shall be called the Way of Holiness,
HOLLOW
40:12 with the hollow of his hand
HOLMS
44:14 he must select holms and oaks
HOLOCAUST
10:3 when the holocaust overtakes you
HOLY
1:4 have spurned the Holy One of Israel,
4:3 in Jerusalem be called holy
5:16 the holy God show himself holy
5:19 Let the plan of the Holy One of Israel
5:24 the words of the Holy One of Israel.
6:3 Most holy is the Lord of Hosts;
6:13 the holy offspring be what is left
10:17 and their Holy One the flame,
10:20 the Holy One of Israel:
11:9 throughout my holy mountain,
12:6 among you is the Holy One of Israel.
13:3 I have charged my holy ones,
17:7 eyes look to the Holy One of Israel,
27:13 to the Lord in the holy mountain at
29:19 in the Holy One of Israel.
29:23 devoted to the Holy One of Jacob,
30:15 the Holy One of Israel:
31:1 do not look to the Holy One of Israel,
35:8 they shall be for such as are holy.
37:23 Against the Holy One of Israel?
40:25 I be compared? says the Holy One.
41:14 Redeemer is the Holy One of Israel.
41:16 and glory in the Holy One of Israel.

41:20 that the Holy One of Israel created it.
43:3 the Holy One of Israel, am your Savior
43:14 the Lord, the Holy One of Israel,
43:15 I the Lord, your Holy One,
43:28 I let the holy cities be profaned;
45:11 the Holy One of Israel, their Maker:
47:4 our Redeemer, the Holy One of Israel,
48:2 who call yourselves of the holy city,
48:17 says the Lord, the Holy One of Israel,
49:7 the Redeemer and Holy One of Israel,
49:7 Holy One of Israel has chosen you.
52:1 O Jerusalem, holy city.
52:10* The Lord has bared his holy arm
54:5 redeems you is the Holy One of Israel
55:5 the Holy One of Israel, who gloriously
56:7 I will bring to my holy mountain
57:13 an inheritance in my holy mountain.
57:15 I dwell on high in the holy place,
58:13 your own ends on my holy day—
58:13 the holy day of the Lord venerable,
60:9 to the Holy One of Israel,
60:14 Zion of the Holy One of Israel.
62:12 They shall be called the holy people,
63:10 rebelled and grieved his holy Spirit,
63:11 he who put into him his holy Spirit,
63:15 thy holy and glorious celestial abode,
63:18 thy people possessed the holy place
64:10 Thy holy cities have become a
64:11 Our glorious holy temple
65:11 and forget my holy mountain,
65:25 throughout my holy mountain, says
66:20 Jerusalem my holy mountain, says
HOMAGE
29:13 and pay me homage with their lips,
43:23 or pay me homage by sacrificial
60:18 and homage as your gates.
HOME
22:8 look to the forest home as protection.
37:7 will give him a notion to return home
58:7 to bring home the wretchedly poor,
HOMELAND
13:14 and everyone flee to his homeland.
HOMER
5:10 a homer of seed but an ephah.
HOMES
13:16 their homes plundered, their wives
HONEST
33:15 and are honest in word,
59:4 no one sues for an honest cause.
HONEY
7:15 Cream and honey will he eat
7:22 will feed on cream and honey.
HONOR
43:20 The wild beasts do me honor,
49:5 I won honor in the eyes of the Lord
58:13 and if you will honor it

HONORABLE
3:5   the vile to the honorable.
HOOKS
2:4   Their spears into pruning hooks:
HOPE
20:5   at Cush, their hope, and at Egypt,
38:18   no further hope of thy faithfulness.
40:31   But they who hope in the Lord
49:23   who hope in me are not disappointed.
59:9   for a glimmer of hope, but we walk
HORIZON
5:26   them from beyond the horizon.
13:5   a distant land beyond the horizon—
HORONAIM
15:5   on the road to Horonaim
HORROR
21:4   I longed for has become a horror
66:24   They shall be a horror to all flesh.
HORSE
28:28   by driving horse and threshing
63:13   Like the horse of the desert,
HORSEMEN
31:1   chariots and vast forces of horsemen,
36:9   chariots and horsemen?
HORSES
2:7   their land is full of horses
21:7   for chariots with teams of horses,
21:9   come: cavalry and teams of horses!
22:6   horses are harnessed to the chariots
30:16   Not so; we will flee on horses!
31:1   relying on horses,
31:3   their horses are flesh, not spirit:
36:8   thousand horses, if you are able to
43:17   who dispatches chariots and horses,
66:20   as offerings to the Lord—on horses,
HOSIERY
3:23   hosiery, sheer linen, millinery, and
HOST
45:12   appointing all their host.
60:5   a host of nations shall enter you.
60:11   a host of nations may be brought
HOSTILE
11:13   the hostile ones of Judah be cut off;
59:19   upon them like a hostile torrent
HOSTS
1:9   Had not the Lord of Hosts left us a
1:24   Therefore the Lord, the Lord of Hosts,
2:12   The Lord of Hosts has a day in store
3:1   Even now, the Lord, the Lord of Hosts
3:15   says Lord of Hosts.
5:7   The vineyard of the Lord of Hosts is
5:9   The Lord of Hosts spoke this in my
5:16   But the Lord of Hosts will be exalted
5:24   despised the law of the Lord of Hosts
6:3   Most holy is the Lord of Hosts;
6:5   have seen the King, the Lord of Hosts,
8:13   But sanctify the Lord of Hosts,

8:18   from the Lord of Hosts,
9:7   The zeal of the Lord of Hosts will
9:13   will they inquire of the Lord of Hosts
9:19   At the wrath of the Lord of Hosts
10:16   the Lord, the Lord of Hosts,
10:23   For my Lord, the Lord of Hosts,
10:24   says my Lord, the Lord of Hosts:
10:26   The Lord of Hosts will raise the whip
10:33   Then will the Lord, the Lord of Hosts,
13:4   Lord of Hosts is marshalling an army
13:13   by the anger of the Lord of Hosts
14:22   against them, says the Lord of Hosts.
14:23   says the Lord of Hosts.
14:24   The Lord of Hosts made an oath,
14:27   For what the Lord of Hosts has
17:3   says the Lord of Hosts.
18:7   brought to the Lord of Hosts
18:7   of the name of the Lord of Hosts:
19:4   says my Lord, the Lord of Hosts.
19:4   says my Lord, the Lord of Hosts.
19:12   Lord of Hosts has in mind for Egypt!
19:16   the Lord of Hosts wields over them.
19:17   Lord of Hosts has in store for them.
19:18   swear loyalty to the Lord of Hosts.
19:20   testimony of the Lord of Hosts
19:25   The Lord of Hosts will bless them,
21:10   the Lord of Hosts, the God of Israel.
22:5   For my Lord, the Lord of Hosts,
22:12   such a day my Lord, the Lord of Hosts
22:14   The Lord of Hosts revealed this to my
22:14   says my Lord, the Lord of Hosts.
22:15   thus said my Lord, the Lord of Hosts:
22:25   In that day, says the Lord of Hosts,
23:9   The Lord of Hosts devised it,
24:21   with the hosts on high
24:23   the Lord of Hosts manifests his reign
25:6   this mountain will the Lord of Hosts
28:5   In that day shall the Lord of Hosts
28:22   by my Lord, the Lord of Hosts,
28:29   originate with the Lord of Hosts,
29:6   be chastened by the Lord of Hosts
31:4   Lord of Hosts be when he descends
31:5   so will the Lord of Hosts guard
34:2   his fury upon all their hosts;
34:4   their starry hosts shed themselves
37:16   O Lord of Hosts, God of Israel,
37:32   The zeal of the Lord of Hosts will
39:5   Hear the word of the Lord of Hosts:
40:26   He who brings forth their hosts by
44:6   the Lord of Hosts, their Redeemer:
45:13   or bribe, says the Lord of Hosts.
47:4   whose name is the Lord of Hosts.
48:2   whose name is the Lord of Hosts:
51:15   whose name is the Lord of Hosts,
HOUSE
2:2   the mountain of the Lord's house
2:3   to the house of the God of Jacob,

471

HOUSE *continued*
2:5   O house of Jacob, come,
2:6   the house of Jacob, because,
3:6   of his father's house, and say,
3:7   food nor clothing in my house;
5:7   of the Lord of Hosts is the house
5:8   Woe to those who join house to house
7:2   And when the house of David was
7:13 O house of David! Is it not enough
7:17 house a day unlike any since
8:17 his face from the house of Jacob,
10:20 and who escape of the house of Jacob
14:1 and join the house of Jacob.
14:2 And the house of Israel will possess
22:18 be a disgrace to your master's house.
22:21 to the house of Judah.
22:22 of the house of David:
22:23 of glory to the house of his father.
22:24 glory of his father's house:
29:22 Abraham, to the house of Jacob:
37:1 entered the house of the Lord.
37:14 went up to the house of the Lord and
37:31 the remnant of the house of Judah
38:1 your house in order. You will die;
38:22* again go up to the house of the Lord
38:20 of our lives in the house of the Lord.
44:13 fit to lodge in a house.
46:3 Hear me, O house of Jacob,
46:3 you remnant of the house of Israel,
48:1 Hear this, O house of Jacob,
56:5 within the walls of my house
56:7 and gladden in my house of prayer.
56:7 for my house shall be known
56:7 as a house of prayer for all nations.
58:1 to the house of Jacob their sins.
60:7 will make glorious my house of glory.
63:7 rendered the house of Israel.
66:1 What house would you build me?
66:20 to the house of the Lord.
HOUSES
3:14 your houses by depriving the needy.
5:9 large and fine houses unoccupied.
6:11 the houses without a man,
8:14 but to the two houses of Israel
24:10 houses are shuttered, that none may
32:13 Mourn for all the amusement houses
65:21 When men build houses, they will
HOUSETOPS
15:3 on the housetops and in the streets
22:1 to climb onto the housetops?
HOVER
31:5 As birds hover over [the nest],
HOW
1:21 How the faithful city
6:11 I replied, For how long, my Lord?
8:4 how to say, Father, or Mother,
14:4 How the tyrant has met

14:12 How you have fallen from the heavens
19:11 How can you say to Pharaoh,
20:6 How shall we ourselves escape?
21:11 Watchman, how much of the night is
32:6 how to practice hypocrisy and preach
36:9 How then shall you repulse even
37:26 how I ordained this thing long ago,
37:26 how in days of old I planned it?
37:28 how stirred up you are against me.
38:3 how I have walked before thee
40:6 And I asked, How shall I announce it?
47:11 not know how to avert by bribes
48:4 For I knew how stubborn you were—
48:6 how is it you do not proclaim it?
50:4 that I may know how to preach
52:7 How comely upon the mountains
57:6 How shall I be appeased of such
HOWL
14:31 Wail at the gates; howl in the city!
HOWLING
13:22 howling creatures from its
34:13 the haunt of howling creatures,
35:7 in the haunt of howling creatures
65:14 howling from brokenness of spirit.
HUDDLE
8:19 who huddle together and mutter,
HUMAN
31:3 The Egyptians are human, not divine;
44:13 he gives it a human likeness,
52:14 was marred beyond human likeness,
HUMBLE
13:11 and humble the pride of tyrants.
57:15 who is humble and lowly in spirit—
57:15 reviving the hearts of the humble.
66:2 are of a humble and contrite spirit
HUMBLED
9:1 the past he humbled the land
53:4 smitten of God, and humbled.
HUMBLING
3:15 humbling the faces of the poor?
HUMILIATION
30:5 but a humiliation and disgrace.
HUMPS
30:6 their riches on the humps of camels,
HUNDRED
37:36 a hundred and eighty-five thousand
65:20 young shall be a hundred years old,
65:20 fail to reach a hundred shall be
HUNG
22:24 Upon him shall be hung all the
HUNGER
8:21 by hunger; and when they are hungry,
49:10 they shall not hunger or thirst,
65:13 while you shall hunger;
HUNGRY
8:21 by hunger; and when they are hungry,
9:20 on the right, yet remain hungry;

29:8   like a hungry man who dreams he eats
32:6   leaving the hungry soul empty,
44:12   when he becomes hungry, he no
58:7   to share your food with the hungry,
58:10   will give of your own to the hungry
HURL
22:17   The Lord will hurl you away
28:2   he will hurl them to the ground by
HURLS
22:17   as an athlete hurls a missile;
HURRY
8:1   Hasten the plunder, hurry the spoil.
HUT
1:8   a hut in a melon field,
HYBRID
17:10   and sow hybrid seed,
HYPOCRISY
32:6   how to practice hypocrisy and preach
IDEAS
66:17   [their practices and ideas] shall
IDLE
30:7   I refer to her as an idle boast.
IDOL
21:9   All her idol gods he has razed to the
44:10   would fashion a god or cast an idol
44:13   sketching his idol with a marker.
44:17   the rest they make a god, their idol,
IDOLATROUS
31:7   despise your idolatrous silver and
IDOLS
2:8   Their land is full of idols:
2:20   their idols of silver and gods of gold
10:11   even as I did to Samaria and its idols?
17:8   the idols of prosperity and the
19:1   the idols of Egypt will rock at his
19:3   resort to the idols and to spiritists,
27:9   leaving no idols of prosperity
30:22   your graven idols plated with silver,
30:22   your cast idols gilded in gold;
42:8   nor my praise to wrought idols.
42:17   But those who trust in idols
44:9   who manufacture idols are deranged;
44:15   from it they make idols to which they
45:20   who carried about their wooden idols
46:1   Their idols are loaded upon beasts
48:5   lest you should say, My idols did it;
66:3   as one who venerates idols.
IGNITE
9:18   it shall ignite the jungle forests,
IGNOMINY
3:24   there shall be ignominy.
16:14   become ignominy. For all its
ILL
33:24*   who reside there shall say, I am ill;
38:1   Hezekiah became gravely ill.
ILLICIT
59:13   pondering illicit transactions.

ILLNESS
38:9   illness, written upon his recovery:
39:1   heard of his illness and recovery.
ILLUMINATE
50:11   who illuminate with mere sparks.
ILLUMINATION
60:19   your illumination at night:
ILLUSTRIOUS
42:21   the law and become illustrious.
60:9   who has made you illustrious.
63:14   acquiring illustrious renown.
IMAGE
40:20   to carve them an image that will not
IMAGES
10:11   I not do to Jerusalem and its images
17:8   of prosperity and the shining images.
27:9   and shining images standing.
42:17   and esteem their images as gods
46:1   the images you bore aloft
48:5   graven and wrought images caused it!
IMAGINATION
65:2   following their own imagination—
IMAGINED
47:11   such as you have not imagined.
IMMANUEL
7:14   and name him Immanuel.
8:8   of your land, O Immanuel.
IMMENSE
31:1   their trust in immense numbers
34:6   an immense massacre in the land of
IMMOLATIONS
43:24   with the fat of immolations.
IMMOVABLE
33:20   abode of peace—an immovable tent,
IMPARTING
40:14   imparting to him knowledge,
IMPELLED
59:19   impelled by the Spirit of the Lord.
IMPENDING
57:1   that from impending calamity
IMPERIAL
23:8   the imperial city,
IMPIETY
32:6   their heart ponders impiety:
IMPORTUNE
58:2   Yet they importune me daily,
IMPOSE
15:9   yet will I impose more than this upon
IMPOSED
14:3   servitude imposed on you,
IMPOSTERS
44:25   annuls the predictions of imposters
IMPOUNDED
10:14   I have impounded the wealth of
IMPOVERISHED
26:6   the footsteps of those impoverished.

IMPREGNABLE
33:16 the impregnable cliffs are their
IMPURITY
30:22 menstruous woman her impurity
INCAPABLE
44:18 minds are incapable of discernment.
INCENSE
1:13 they are as a loathsome incense to me.
43:23 or wearied you with burning incense.
66:3 and whoever burns incense,
INCENSED
45:24 all who were incensed against him.
INCESSANTLY
59:11 we moan incessantly like doves.
INCLUDING
22:24 including all the lesser vessels,
INCOMPREHENSIBLE
28:11 by incomprehensible speech
33:19 a nation of incomprehensible speech,
INCREASE
29:19 obtain an increase of joy in the Lord,
30:23 that the land's increase of food
30:26 light of the sun increase sevenfold;
57:9 and increase your perfumes;
INCREASED
9:3 and increased its joy;
INCREASES
40:29 and increases in vigor those who lack
INCREASINGLY
22:9 city of David increasingly breached,
INCRIMINATE
50:9 Who then will incriminate me?
INCURABLE
17:11 a day of diseases and incurable pain.
INCURRED
24:6 who dwell on it have incurred guilt;
31:7 your hands have incurred guilt.
53:5 the price of our peace he incurred,
INDIFFERENT
58:3 and you remain indifferent!
INDIGNATION
30:27 his lips flow with indignation,
INDULGED
28:7 These too have indulged in wine
INFAMOUS
10:12 boasting and infamous conceit,
INFANT
11:8 A suckling infant will play near the
49:15 a woman forget her suckling infant,
INFANTILE
2:6 content with the infantile heathen.
INFANTS
13:16 Their infants shall be dashed to
65:20 there be infants alive but a few days,
INFEST
13:21 But wild animals will infest it,

INFLAMED
5:11 at night parties, inflamed by wine!
INFORM
5:5 Let me now inform you
INFORMED
7:2 the house of David was informed
23:1 shall they be informed of it.
INFRINGING
18:2 a people continually infringing,
18:7 a people continually infringing,
INGENIOUS
10:13 and shrewdness, for I am ingenious.
INGENUITY
24:14 exult at the Lord's ingenuity.
INGLORIOUS
22:18 your inglorious conveyance there
INHABIT
10:24 O my people who inhabit Zion,
32:16 So shall justice inhabit the desert,
33:24* the people who inhabit it
34:11 and owls and ravens inhabit it.
34:17 inhabit it from generation to
42:10 the isles and they who inhabit them.
INHABITANT
6:11 and without inhabitant,
INHABITANTS
5:3 Now, O inhabitants of Jerusalem and
8:14 the inhabitants of Jerusalem.
9:2 on the inhabitants of the land
10:13 I have vastly reduced the inhabitants.
10:31 The inhabitants of Gebim are in full
12:6 sing for joy, O inhabitants of Zion,
18:3 you inhabitants of the earth,
20:6 In that day shall the inhabitants
21:14 O inhabitants of the land of Tema.
22:21 inhabitants of Jerusalem and
23:2 Be dumbfounded, you inhabitants of
23:6 you inhabitants of the isles.
24:1 and scatter its inhabitants.
24:5 lies polluted under its inhabitants:
24:17 O inhabitants of the earth:
26:5 He has put down the elite inhabitants
26:9 the inhabitants of the world learn
26:18 that the inhabitants of the world
26:21 to punish the inhabitants of the earth
30:19 Zion, O inhabitants of Zion,
37:27 while their timorous inhabitants
40:22 its inhabitants are as grasshoppers,
42:11 let the inhabitants of Sela sing for joy
49:19 be too small for your inhabitants,
51:6 its inhabitants shall die in the
INHERIT
60:21 they shall inherit the earth forever—
65:9 my chosen ones shall inherit them,
INHERITANCE
19:25 and Israel my inheritance.
34:17 he who allots them an inheritance,

47:6   so I let my inheritance be defiled.
53:12   assign him an inheritance among the
57:13   an inheritance in my holy mountain.
61:7   shall their inheritance be twofold
63:17   the tribes that are thine inheritance.
INIQUITIES
26:21   for their iniquities;
43:24   wearied me with your iniquities.
53:5   crushed because of our iniquities;
53:11   and by bearing their iniquities,
59:2   It is your iniquities that separate
59:12   we perceive our iniquities:
64:7   us at the hand of our iniquities.
65:7   own iniquities and their fathers'
INIQUITY
27:9   shall Jacob's iniquity be expiated,
30:13   iniquity will be to you as a perilous
33:24* shall be forgiven their iniquity.
53:6   upon him the iniquity of us all.
59:3   your fingers with iniquity;
64:9   remember not iniquity forever.
INJURIOUS
59:6   they manipulate injurious dealings.
INJURY
11:9   There shall be no harm or injury done
65:25   there shall be no harm or injury done
INJUSTICE
5:7   but there was injustice;
INMOST
16:11   my inmost being for Kir Hareseth.
INNOCENT
5:23   but deny justice to the innocent!
59:7   they hasten to shed innocent blood.
INQUIRE
8:19   When men tell you to inquire
8:19   inquire of their God? Should one
8:19   inquire of the dead on behalf of the
9:13   nor will they inquire of the Lord of
31:1   nor inquire of the Lord!
55:6   Inquire of the Lord while he is
58:2   They inquire of me concerning
65:1   to those who did not inquire of me;
INQUIRED
30:2   but have not inquired at my mouth—
INSATIABLE
33:4   like insatiable locusts they rushed
56:11   Gluttonous dogs, and insatiable,
INSATIABLY
5:14   opening her mouth insatiably;
INSCRIBE
44:5   Yet others will inscribe on their arm,
INSCRIBED
4:3   all who were inscribed to be
INSENSIBLE
1:3   my people are insensible.
44:18   have become unaware and insensible;
56:11   indeed are insensible shepherds.

INSIDIOUS
32:7   insidious devices to ruin the poor,
INSIGNIFICANT
29:14   intelligence . . . wise men insignificant
INSOLENT
3:5   young will be insolent to the elderly,
13:11   end to the arrogance of insolent men
33:19   insolent people are not to be seen,
INSPIRATION
28:29   whose inspiration is surpassing.
INSTALLATIONS
29:3   erect siege installations against you.
INSTANT
29:5   Suddenly, in an instant,
INSTRUCT
2:3   that he may instruct us in his ways,
48:17   I the Lord your God instruct you to
INSTRUCTED
40:14   instructed in the path of discretion,
INSTRUCTION
28:9   Whom shall he give instruction?
29:24   who murmured accept instruction.
INSTRUCTIONS
38:21* Isaiah gave instructions to take fig
INSTRUCTS
28:26   His God instructs him,
INSTRUMENTS
13:5   the Lord and the instruments of his
INSULT
50:6   I hid not my face from insult and
INSULTS
61:7   and shouted insults were their lot,
INTEGRITY
59:8   integrity is not within their bounds.
59:15   When integrity is lacking,
INTELLIGENCE
29:14   the intelligence of their wise men
40:28   his intelligence cannot be fathomed.
INTENT
32:8   But the noble are of noble intent,
INTERCESSION
53:12   and made intercession for the
INTERVENE
59:16   no one, not one who would intervene.
INTIMIDATED
7:4   and unafraid. Be not intimidated
INTOXICATED
28:7   They are intoxicated with wine
INTRIGUES
66:4   so will I prescribe intrigues for them
INTRUDE
35:9   nor shall wild beasts intrude.
INTUITION
11:3   His intuition will be guided
INUNDATING
28:2   an inundating deluge of mighty

INVADE
7:6 Let us invade Judea and stir up
INVENTIONS
45:16 makers of inventions retired in
INVEST
22:22 I will invest him with the keys
INVOKE
12:4 thanks to the Lord; invoke his name.
48:1 and invoke the God of Israel,
65:1 a nation that did not invoke my name
65:16 Those of them who invoke blessings
IRON
10:34 with the force of iron,
44:12 tools works the iron over the coals
45:2 and cut through iron bars.
48:4 your neck was an iron sinew, your
60:17 in place of iron, silver;
60:17 in place of stones, iron.
IRRIGATION
19:7 sown along irrigation channels,
ISAIAH
1:1 The vision of Isaiah the son of Amoz
2:1 which Isaiah the son of Amoz saw in
7:3 Then the Lord said to Isaiah,
7:13 Then Isaiah said, Take heed,
13:1 which Isaiah the son of
20:2 Isaiah the son of Amoz, saying,
20:3 my servant Isaiah has gone
36:2 to the prophet Isaiah the son of Amoz
37:5* Hezekiah's servants came to Isaiah,
37:6 And Isaiah said to them, Tell your
37:21 Isaiah the son of Amoz sent word
38:1 And the prophet Isaiah the son of
38:4 the word of the Lord came to Isaiah:
38:21* Isaiah gave instructions to take fig
38:7 And Isaiah replied, This shall be
39:3 Then the prophet Isaiah came to King
39:4 And Isaiah asked, What did they
39:5 Then Isaiah said to Hezekiah,
39:8 But Hezekiah said to Isaiah, The word
ISLE
20:6 of this isle say, See what has
ISLES
11:11 and the isles of the sea.
23:2 you inhabitants of the isles,
23:6 you inhabitants of the isles.
24:15 and in the isles of the sea
40:15 the isles he displaces as mere specks.
41:1 Be silent before me, O isles;
41:5 The isles look on in fear;
42:4 The isles await his law.
42:10 the isles and they who inhabit them.
42:12 and in the isles speak out praise of
49:1 Hear me, O isles; listen, you distant
51:5 the isles anticipate me, awaiting my
59:18 to the isles he will render
60:9 From the isles they are gathering to

66:19 and to the distant isles.
ISRAEL
1:3 but Israel does not know;
1:4 have spurned the Holy One of Israel,
1:24 the Valiant One of Israel, declares,
4:2 glory of the survivors of Israel.
5:7 Lord of Hosts is the house of Israel
5:19 Let the plan of the Holy One of Israel
5:24 the words of the Holy One of Israel.
7:1 Remaliah king of Israel came up to
8:14 but to the two houses of Israel
8:18 signs and portents in Israel
9:8 and it shall befall Israel.
9:12 will devour Israel with open mouth.
9:14 the Lord will cut off from Israel
10:17 the Light of Israel will be the fire
10:20 that day those who survive of Israel
10:20 the Holy One of Israel:
10:22 For though your people, O Israel,
11:12 and assemble the exiled of Israel;
11:16 as there was for Israel
12:6 among you is the Holy One of Israel.
14:1 and once again choose Israel;
14:2 And the house of Israel will possess
17:3 the glory of the children of Israel,
17:6 says the Lord, the God of Israel.
17:7 eyes look to the Holy One of Israel,
19:24 In that day Israel shall be the
19:25 and Israel my inheritance.
21:10 the Lord of Hosts, the God of Israel.
21:17 of Israel, has spoken it.
24:15 name of the Lord, the God of Israel.
27:6 and Israel bursts into blossom,
27:12 one, O children of Israel.
29:19 in the Holy One of Israel.
29:23 reverencing the God of Israel,
30:11 us with the Holy One of Israel!
30:12 thus says the Holy One of Israel:
30:15 the Holy One of Israel:
30:29 to the Rock of Israel.
31:1 do not look to the Holy One of Israel,
31:6 to go far astray, O children of Israel.
37:16 O Lord of Hosts, God of Israel,
37:21 God of Israel: Because you have
37:23 Against the Holy One of Israel?
40:27 and speak thus, O Israel:
41:8 But you, O Israel, my servant,
41:14 O men of Israel, [be not dismayed]:
41:14 Redeemer is the Holy One of Israel.
41:16 and glory in the Holy One of Israel.
41:17 I, the God of Israel, will not forsake
41:20 that the Holy One of Israel created it.
42:24 Israel to despoilers, if not the Lord,
43:1 he who created you, O Israel:
43:3 Holy One of Israel, am your Savior;
43:14 says the Lord, the Holy One of Israel,
43:15 Creator of Israel, am your King.

43:22 you have grown weary of me, O Israel.
43:28 to be ostracized, Israel to execration.
44:1 and Israel whom I have chosen.
44:5 and adopt the name Israel.
44:6 says the Lord, the King of Israel,
44:21 O Jacob, and you, O Israel,
44:23 he shall be glorified in Israel.
45:3 God of Israel, who calls you by name.
45:4 Israel my chosen, I call you by name
45:11 the Holy One of Israel, their Maker:
45:15 O Savior, God of Israel.
45:17 But Israel is saved by the Lord
45:25 In the Lord shall all Israel's
46:3 you remnant of the house of Israel,
46:12 and to Israel my glory.
47:4 our Redeemer, the Holy One of Israel,
48:1 you who are named Israel—
48:1 and invoke the God of Israel,
48:2 upheld by the God of Israel,
48:12 Hear me, O Jacob, and Israel, my
48:17 says the Lord, the Holy One of Israel,
49:3 Israel, in whom I will be glorified.
49:5 Israel having been gathered to him;
49:6 to restore those preserved of Israel.
49:7 the Redeemer and Holy One of Israel,
49:7 because the Holy One of Israel has
52:12 the God of Israel behind you.
54:5 redeems you is the Holy One of Israel
55:5 the Holy One of Israel, who gloriously
56:8 who gathers up the outcasts of Israel:
60:9 to the Holy One of Israel,
60:14 Zion of the Holy One of Israel.
63:7 rendered the house of Israel.
63:16 or Israel recognize us,
ISRAELITES
17:9 Israelites during the desolation.
66:20 just as the Israelites
ISRAEL'S
45:25 shall all Israel's offspring
ISSUE
48:3 did they issue from my mouth,
ISSUED
45:23 righteousness has issued from my
ITSELF
10:15 Shall an axe exalt itself
10:15 or a saw vaunt itself
34:6 and glut itself with fat—
37:30 year what springs up of itself.
IVVAH
37:13 Sepharvaim, Hena, and Ivvah?
JACINTH
54:12 I will make your skylights of jacinth,
JACKALS
13:22 Jackals will cry out from its palaces,
34:14 Prairie wolves shall greet jackals,
43:20 the jackals and birds of prey,

JACOB
2:3 to the house of the God of Jacob,
2:5 O house of Jacob, come,
2:6 the house of Jacob, because,
8:17 hides his face from the house of Jacob
9:8 This message my Lord sent to Jacob,
10:20 and who escape of the house of Jacob
10:21 of Jacob a remnant will return
14:1 Lord will have compassion on Jacob
14:1 and join the house of Jacob.
27:6 days to come, when Jacob takes root
29:22 Abraham, to the house of Jacob:
29:22 No longer shall Jacob be dismayed;
29:23 devoted to the Holy One of Jacob,
40:27 Why then do you say, O Jacob,
41:8 Jacob, whom I have chosen,
41:14 Be not afraid, you worms of Jacob;
41:21 your evidence, says the King of Jacob.
42:24 that hands Jacob over to plunder
43:1 he who formed you, O Jacob,
43:22 But you do not call upon me, O Jacob
43:28 I gave Jacob to be ostracized, Israel to
44:1 Hear now, Jacob my servant,
44:2 Be not afraid, O Jacob, my servant,
44:5 and another name himself Jacob.
44:21 Ponder these things, O Jacob, and
44:23 the Lord has redeemed Jacob;
45:4 For the sake of my servant Jacob,
46:3 Hear me, O house of Jacob,
48:1 Hear this, O house of Jacob,
48:12 Hear me, O Jacob, and Israel,
48:20 has redeemed his servant Jacob.
49:5 to restore Jacob to him,
49:6 to raise up the tribes of Jacob
49:26 Redeemer is the Valiant One of Jacob.
58:1 to the house of Jacob their sins.
58:14 you with the heritage of Jacob your
59:20 of Jacob who repent of transgression,
60:16 Redeemer is the Valiant One of Jacob.
65:9 I will extract offspring out of Jacob,
JACOB'S
17:4 In that day Jacob's glory shall wane,
27:9 But by this shall Jacob's iniquity be
45:19 I do not ask Jacob's offspring
JACINTH
54:12 I will make your skylights of jacinth,
JAHAZ
15:4 appeal shall be heard as far as Jahaz.
JAVAN
66:19 Tubal and Javan, and to the distant
JAWS
30:28 with an erring bridle on their jaws
JAZER
16:8 Its runner vines reached Jazer,
16:9 I will mourn as Jazer mourns
JEALOUSY
11:13 Ephraim's jealousy shall pass away

JEBERECHIAH
8:2   son of Jeberechiah, to witness for me.

JERUSALEM
1:1   Jerusalem during the reigns of
2:1   A prophecy concerning . . . Jerusalem
2:3   from Jerusalem the word of the Lord.
3:1   deprives Judea and Jerusalem
3:8   Jerusalem will falter and Judea fall
4:3   in Jerusalem be called holy
4:3   among the living at Jerusalem.
4:4   Jerusalem of its bloodshed, in the
5:3   Now, O inhabitants of Jerusalem and
7:1   king of Israel came up to Jerusalem
8:14   the inhabitants of Jerusalem.
10:10   those of Jerusalem and Samaria,
10:11   shall I not do to Jerusalem and its
10:12   Mount Zion and in Jerusalem,
10:32   the hill of Jerusalem.
22:10   census of the buildings in Jerusalem,
22:21   inhabitants of Jerusalem and
24:23   in Mount Zion and in Jerusalem,
27:13   in the holy mountain at Jerusalem.
28:14   over these people in Jerusalem.
30:19   O inhabitants of Jerusalem,
31:5   the Lord of Hosts guard Jerusalem;
31:9   whose furnace is in Jerusalem.
33:20   let your eyes rest upon Jerusalem,
36:2   King Hezekiah at Jerusalem.
36:7   Judea and Jerusalem to worship
36:20   should save Jerusalem from my hand?
37:10   thinking that Jerusalem
37:22   The Daughter of Jerusalem shakes her
37:32   out of Jerusalem shall go a remnant,
40:2   speak kindly to Jerusalem.
40:9   O Jerusalem, messenger of good news.
41:27   as a herald of tidings to Jerusalem.
44:26   of Jerusalem, It shall be reinhabited,
44:28   of Jerusalem that it must be rebuilt,
51:17   awaken and rise up, O Jerusalem,
52:1   robes of glory, O Jerusalem,
52:2   sit enthroned, O Jerusalem.
52:9   you ruined places of Jerusalem:
52:9   he has redeemed Jerusalem.
62:6   watchmen on your walls, O Jerusalem,
62:7   till he reestablishes Jerusalem
64:10   a desert, Jerusalem a desolation.
65:18   See, I create Jerusalem to be a delight
65:19   I will delight in Jerusalem, rejoice in
66:10   Rejoice with Jerusalem and be glad
66:13   for Jerusalem you shall be comforted.
66:20   Jerusalem my holy mountain,

JERUSALEM'S
62:1   for Jerusalem's sake I will not remain

JESHURUN
44:2   and Jeshurun whom I have chosen.

JESSE
11:1   will spring up from the stock of Jesse

11:10   In that day the sprig of Jesse,

JEWELS
49:18   yourself with them all as with jewels,
61:10   or a bride adorned with her jewels.

JOAH
36:3   the secretary, and Joah the son
36:11   Then Eliakim, Shebna and Joah said
36:22   Joah the son of Asaph,

JOIN
5:8   Woe to those who join house to house
14:1   and join the house of Jacob.
66:10   join in her celebration,

JOLTED
13:13   when the earth is jolted out of place

JORDAN
9:1   by the Jordan in Galilee of the

JOTHAM
1:1   Jotham, Ahaz, and Hezekiah, kings of
7:1   When Ahaz son of Jotham, the son of

JOY
9:3   and increased its joy;
12:6   Shout and sing for joy, O inhabitants
24:11   though all joy has become gloom:
24:14   lift up their voice and shout for joy,
26:19   Awake, and sing for joy,
29:19   obtain an increase of joy in the Lord,
35:6   the tongue of the dumb shout for joy.
35:10   heads crowned with everlasting joy.
35:10   They shall have won joy and gladness
42:11   let the inhabitants of Sela sing for joy
49:13   Shout for joy, O heavens; celebrate, O
51:11   heads crowned with everlasting joy;
51:11   let them obtain joy and gladness,
52:8   as one they cry out for joy:
55:12   You shall depart in joy and be led
60:15   the joy of generation after generation.
61:7   and everlasting joy be theirs.
65:18   and its people a joy.
66:5   that we may see cause for your joy!

JOYFUL
16:10   The joyful festivity will be gone from
51:3   Joyful rejoicing takes place there,

JOYFULLY
25:9   joyfully celebrate his salvation!
64:5   who joyfully perform righteousness,

JOYOUS
9:3   are joyous when they divide spoil

JOYOUSLY
35:2   Joyously it shall break out in flower,

JUBILANT
14:7   there is jubilant celebration!
35:1   and arid land shall be jubilant;
54:1   break into jubilant song, you who

JUDAH
1:1   Ahaz, and Hezekiah, kings of Judah:
7:1   was king of Judah,
7:17   Ephraim broke away from Judah—

478

9:21 and both will combine against Judah.
11:12 he will gather the scattered of Judah
11:13 the hostile ones of Judah be cut off;
11:13 Ephraim will not envy Judah,
11:13 nor Judah resent Ephraim.
19:17 The land of Judah shall become
22:21 to the house of Judah.
26:1 song be sung in the land of Judah:
37:10 Speak thus to Hezekiah king of Judah:
37:31 remnant of the house of Judah that
38:9 Hezekiah king of Judah's account of
40:9 proclaim to the cities of Judah:
44:26 cities of Judah, They shall be rebuilt,
48:1 you stem from the lineage of Judah
65:9 out of Judah heirs of my mountains;
JUDAH'S
38:9 Hezekiah king of Judah's account of
JUDEA
1:1 which he beheld concerning Judea
2:1 A prophecy concerning Judea and
3:1 deprives Judea and Jerusalem
3:8 Jerusalem will falter and Judea fall
5:3 Jerusalem and you men of Judea,
7:6 Let us invade Judea and stir up
8:8 will sweep into Judea like a flood
36:1 of Judea and seized them.
36:7 Judea and Jerusalem to worship
JUDEAN
36:11 Do not speak to us in Judean in the
36:13 loud voice in Judean, Hear the words
JUDEA'S
22:8 the day Judea's defensive screen is
JUDGE
2:4 He will judge between the nations
3:13 he has arisen to judge the nations.
5:3 judge between me and my vineyard!
11:3 will not judge by what his eyes see,
11:4 He will judge the poor with
16:3 Provide a solution . . . judge our case!
16:5 and in faithfulness a judge sit on it
33:22 For the Lord is our Judge,
51:5 my arms shall judge the peoples—
JUDGES
1:26 I will restore your judges as at the
JUDGMENT
5:16 by a just judgment,
28:6 justice to him who sits in judgment,
34:5 down on Edom in judgment,
66:16 execute judgment on all flesh,
JUICE
65:8 there is juice in a cluster of grapes
JUNGLE
9:18 it shall ignite the jungle forests,
JURISDICTION
22:21 appoint him your jurisdiction.
JUST
5:16 by a just judgment,

20:3 Then the Lord said, Just as
28:9 those just taken from the breast?
52:14 just as he appalled many—
58:5 just a time for men to torment
61:8 For I the Lord love just dealings—
66:3 Just as they have preferred to go
66:20 dromedaries—just as the Israelites
JUSTICE
1:17 Learn to do good: demand justice,
1:21 She was filled with justice;
1:23 not dispense justice to the fatherless,
1:27 Zion shall be ransomed by justice,
4:4 spirit of justice, by a burning wind.
5:7 He expected justice,
5:23 but deny justice to the innocent!
9:7 by justice and righteousness
10:2 denying justice to the needy,
16:5 maintain justice and expedite
28:6 a spirit of justice to him who sits in
28:17 I will make justice the measure,
30:18 For the Lord is the God of justice;
32:1 and rulers rule with justice
32:16 So shall justice inhabit the desert,
32:17 the effect of justice shall be peace,
33:5 with justice and righteousness he
42:1 dispense justice to the nations.
42:3 He will perform the work of justice
42:4 brought about justice in the earth.
56:1 Observe justice and perform
59:11 We expect justice when there is none;
59:15 Lord saw that there was no justice,
JUSTIFY
43:9 and justify themselves,
45:25 justify themselves and have cause to.
KEDAR
21:17 remaining of the sons of Kedar
42:11 and the villages where Kedar dwells;
KEDAR'S
21:16 Kedar's glory shall fully expire.
60:7 All Kedar's flocks will gather to you,
KEEP
7:21 In that day a man will keep
56:4 the eunuchs who keep my Sabbaths
56:6 keep the Sabbath without profaning
58:13 feet from trampling the Sabbath—
62:1 For Zion's sake I will not keep silent;
65:5 who think, Keep your distance,
KEEPER
27:3 of which I, the Lord, am keeper.
36:3 Asaph, the record keeper, went out
36:22 the son of Asaph, the record keeper,
KEEPING
42:14 keeping still and restraining myself.
KEEPS
26:2 righteous because it keeps the faith.
49:7 the Lord keeps faith with you,
56:2 keeps the Sabbath without profaning

KERCHIEF
3:22 the shawl, the kerchief and the purse,
KEYS
22:22 I will invest him with the keys
KEYSTONE
28:16 I lay in Zion a stone, a keystone,
KIDNEY
34:6 the kidney fat of rams.
KILL
14:30 descendants I will kill with famine,
KILLED
22:2 slain were not killed by the sword;
KILLING
22:13 the killing of cattle and slaughter of
KILLS
66:3 is as one who kills a man,
KIN
58:7 and not to neglect your own kin?
KINDLE
40:16 would not suffice to kindle a fire,
65:7 To those who kindle sacrifice in the
KINDLED
5:25 the anger of the Lord is kindled
30:27 His wrath is kindled, heavy is his
50:11 and by the sparks you have kindled.
KINDLING
7:4 two smoking tail ends of kindling,
KINDLY
40:2 speak kindly to Jerusalem.
KINDNESS
16:5 then, in loving kindness,
63:7 according to the great kindness
KINDRED
14:18 each among his own kindred.
KING
6:1 In the year of King Uzziah's death,
6:5 I have seen the King, the Lord of
7:1 was king of Judah,
7:1 Rezin king of Aram and Pekah son of
7:1 Remaliah king of Israel came up to
7:17 the day of the king of Assyria.
7:20 the king of Assyria—to shave
8:4 brought before the king of Assyria.
8:7 the king of Assyria in all his glory.
8:21 curse this king and their God.
10:12 he will punish the king of
14:4 taunt against the king of Babylon
14:28 in the year King Ahaz died, came this
20:1 was sent by Sargon king of
20:4 so shall the king of Assyria
20:6 deliverance from the king of Assyria!
23:15 seventy years, the lifetime of a king.
30:6 and the roaring king of beasts,
32:1 A king shall reign in righteousness
33:17 shall behold the King in his glory
33:22 The Lord is our King; he himself will
36:1 fourteenth year of King Hezekiah's

36:1 Sennacherib king of Assyria
36:2 And the king of Assyria sent
36:2 King Hezekiah at Jerusalem.
36:4 the great king, the king of Assyria:
36:6 who leans on it. Such is Pharaoh king
36:8 king of Assyria: I will give you two
36:13 the great king, the king of Assyria!
36:14 Thus says the king: Do not let
36:15 into the hand of the king of Assyria.
36:16 the king of Assyria: Make peace with
36:18 the hand of the king of Assyria?
36:21 for the king commanded them not to
37:1 When King Hezekiah heard it,
37:5* And when King Hezekiah's servants
37:4 the king of Assyria has sent to scorn
37:6 king of Assyria's subordinates
37:8 Rabshakeh heard that the king
37:9 Tirhakah king of Cush had set out to
37:10 Speak thus to Hezekiah king of Judah:
37:10 into the hand of the king of Assyria.
37:21 Sennacherib king of Assyria,
37:33 concerning the king of Assyria:
37:37 So Sennacherib king of Assyria broke
37:38 Esarhaddon succeeded him as king.
38:6 the hand of the king of Assyria;
38:9 Hezekiah king of Judah's account of
39:1 king of Babylon, sent letters and gifts
39:3 prophet Isaiah came to King Hezekiah
39:7 the palace of the king of Babylon.
41:21 your evidence, says the King of Jacob.
43:15 Creator of Israel, am your King.
44:6 says the Lord, the King of Israel,
57:9 You bathe with oil for the king
KINGDOM
9:7 and over his kingdom,
34:12 its nobles when it is no kingdom,
60:12 And the nation or kingdom
KINGDOMS
13:4 Hark! An uproar among kingdoms,
13:19 Babylon...most splendid of kingdoms
14:16 and kingdoms quake,
23:11 and distress kingdoms;
23:17 out to all the kingdoms of the world
37:16 God over all the kingdoms of the
37:20 his hand, that all kingdoms on earth
47:5 Mistress of Kingdoms.
KINGS
1:1 Ahaz, and Hezekiah, kings of Judah:
10:8 Are not my commanders kings,
37:11 had heard what the kings of Assyria
37:13 Where are the kings of Hamath and
37:13 the kings of the cities of Sepharvaim,
37:18 O Lord, the kings of Assyria have
49:23 Kings shall be your foster fathers,
KING'S
7:2 the king's mind and the minds of

KINSMAN
3:6 Then will a man apprehend a kinsman
KIR
15:1 when in one night Kir is razed,
22:6 and Kir uncovers the armor,
KIR HARESETH
16:7 groan at the ruin of Kir Hareseth
16:11 my inmost being for Kir Hareseth.
KITES
34:15 There too shall kites come together,
KITTIM
23:1 way from the land of Kittim
23:12 Get up and cross over to Kittim,
KNEE
45:23 To me every knee shall bow
KNEEL
10:4 but to kneel among the captives
KNEES
35:3 steady the failing knees.
66:12 and dandled on the knees.
KNEW
45:4 I named you . . . you knew me not.
45:5 I girded you up . . . you knew me
48:4 For I knew how stubborn you were—
48:7 you should say, Indeed I knew them!
48:8 For I knew you would turn treacherous
KNIVES
18:5 the fruit-bearing twigs with knives
KNOW
1:3 but Israel does not know;
5:19 soon come to pass, and we will know!
9:9 shall know of it,
19:10 textile workers will know despair,
19:21 the Egyptians shall know the
21:10 To you who know me,
29:15 Who will see us? Who will know?
37:20 may know that thou alone art Lord.
37:28 But I know where you dwell,
40:13 a man should let him know his plan?
41:20 that all may see it and know, consider
41:22 and know whether they were
41:23 so that we may know you are gods.
41:26 this beforehand, so we would know,
42:16 blind by a way they did not know,
45:3 you may know that it is I the Lord,
45:6 may know that without me there is
47:11 not know how to avert by bribes;
49:23 shall you know that I am the Lord,
49:26 know that I the Lord am your Savior,
50:4 that I may know how to preach
51:7 you who know righteousness,
52:6 my people come to know my name;
52:6 in that day they shall know
55:5 a nation that you did not know;
55:5 a nation that did not know you will
60:16 Then shall you know that I, the Lord,
63:16 Though Abraham does not know us

KNOWING
50:7 knowing I shall not be confounded.
KNOWLEDGE
5:13 for lack of knowledge
11:2 the spirit of knowledge
11:9 with the knowledge of the Lord
29:14 void the knowledge of their sages,
33:6 and knowledge your salvation;
38:19 on the knowledge of thy faithfulness.
40:14 imparting to him knowledge,
44:25 makes nonsense of their knowledge,
53:11 because of his knowledge,
KNOWN
12:4 Make known his deeds among the
19:18 One shall be known as the City of
19:21 known to the Egyptians, and
40:28 Is it not known to you; have you not
41:26 not one make it known;
43:12 making it known
44:8 Have I not made it known to you
48:3 I made known long beforehand;
48:8 nor have you known them;
56:7 for my house shall be known
62:4 be known as she in whom I delight
62:12 and you shall be known as in demand,
63:19 have not been known by thy name.
64:2 to make thyself known to thine
KNOWS
1:3 The ox knows its owner,
8:4 For before the child knows
59:8 none who treads them knows peace.
LABOR
13:8 trembling like a woman in labor.
19:23 and the Egyptians shall labor
21:3 seized me like a woman in labor.
23:4 I no longer labor and bear children!
26:17 from her pangs during labor,
26:18 with child; we have been in labor,
42:14 I will scream like a woman in labor
54:1 you who were not in labor.
55:2 your labor on what does not satisfy?
66:7 Before she is in labor, she gives
66:8 Can the earth labor but a day
66:8 For as soon as she was in labor,
LABORED
49:4 I had thought, I have labored in vain,
LABORS
3:10 eat the fruits of their own labors.
LACHISH
36:2 with a large army from Lachish to
37:8 of Assyria had left Lachish,
LACK
5:13 for lack of knowledge
40:29 in vigor those who lack strength.
50:2 fish become parched for lack of
LACKING
59:15 When integrity is lacking,

481

LACKS
34:16 not one lacks her mate.
LADY
47:8 hear this, O pampered lady,
LAID
1:7 laid waste at its takeover by
14:8 Since you have been laid low,
23:1 For Tyre is laid waste,
29:4 And when you have been laid low,
49:19 and your land laid waste,
57:8 your bed, you have laid it wide open,
LAISHAH
10:30 Hear her, Laishah; answer her,
LAKES
19:5 waters of the lakes shall ebb away
35:7 of mirages shall become one of lakes,
41:18 I will turn the desert into lakes,
42:15 into dry land and evaporate lakes.
LAMB
53:7 like a lamb led to slaughter,
65:25 The wolf and the lamb will graze alike
66:3 and whoever sacrifices a lamb,
LAMBS
11:6 shall the wolf dwell among lambs
34:6 the blood of lambs and he-goats,
40:11 the lambs he gathers up with his arm
LAME
33:23* the lame take part in the plunder.
35:6 Then shall the lame leap like deer,
LAMENT
13:6 Lament, for the day of the Lord is
16:7 the Moabites be made to to lament,
24:7 making all the lighthearted lament.
LAMENTATION
22:12 calls for weeping and lamentation,
LAMENTING
23:6 Move on to Tarshish lamenting,
LAMENTS
51:19 desolation, ruin—and who laments
LAND
1:19 you shall eat the good of the land.
2:7 Their land is full of silver and gold
2:7 their land is full of horses
2:8 Their land is full of idols:
5:8 in the centers of the land!
5:30 And should one look to the land,
6:11 and the land ravaged to ruin.
6:12 from the centers of the land.
7:16 the good, the land whose two
7:18 the land of Assyria.
7:22 All who remain in the land
7:24 land shall revert to wilderness.
8:8 the breadth of your land,
8:22 They will look to the land,
9:1 the past he humbled the land
9:2 on the inhabitants of the land
11:4 arbitrate for the lowly in the land;

11:16 came up from the land of Egypt.
13:5 a distant land beyond the horizon—
14:1 he will settle them in their own land,
14:2 in the land of the Lord:
14:20 for you have destroyed your land
14:25 I will break Assyria in my own land,
15:8 shall encompass the land of Moab;
15:9 and on those who remain in the land.
18:1 Woe to the land of buzzing wings
18:6 and to the beasts of the land:
18:6 and the beasts of the land all winter.
19:17 The land of Judah shall become
19:18 cities in the land of Egypt will
19:19 of the land of Egypt and a monument
19:20 in the land of Egypt: when they
21:1 steppes, a land of terror.
21:14 O inhabitants of the land of Tema.
23:1 their way from the land of Kittim
23:10 Overflow your land like the Nile,
23:13 So too with the land of the Chaldeans,
26:1 song be sung in the land of Judah:
26:10 in a land of uprightness they remain
27:13 in the land of Assyria and they who
27:13 were outcasts in the land of
29:17 again become a fruitful land,
30:6 Through a land of hardship and
32:13 For my people's land
32:15 desert shall become productive land
33:9 The Land lies withered and forlorn,
32:16 righteousness abide in the farm land.
34:6 massacre in the land of Edom;
34:7 Their land shall be saturated with
34:9 her land shall become as burning
35:1 Wilderness and arid land shall be
35:7 The land of mirages shall become one
36:10 this land and destroyed it without
36:10 this land and destroy it.
36:17 a land like your own, a land of grain
36:17 a land of grain fields and vineyards
36:20 saved his land from my hand,
37:7 fall by the sword in his own land.
37:38 sword and fled to the land of Ararat.
38:11 in the land of the living;
39:3 They came from a distant land;
42:15 I will turn rivers into dry land
43:20 streams to the dry land,
45:19 somewhere in a land of darkness;
46:11 from a distant land
49:8 to restore the Land and reapportion
49:12 and these, from the land of Sinim.
49:19 and your land laid waste,
53:8 was cut off from the land of the living
60:6 camels shall cover your land,
60:15 none passing through your land,
60:18 no more be heard of in your land,
61:7 therefore in their land
62:4 nor your land referred to as desolate;

62:4   and your land considered espoused.
62:4   and your land shall be espoused.
LANDS
8:9   Give heed, in all you distant lands!
10:16   consumption into his fertile lands,
18:2   rivers have annexed their lands.
18:7   rivers have annexed their lands,
23:7   feet led her to settle far-off lands?
29:17   now fruitful be considered
30:23   in ample pasture lands,
32:15   and lands now productive
36:18   nations able to save their lands out of
37:11   have done, annexing all lands.
37:18   all peoples and their lands,
41:18   parched lands into fountains of
LAND'S
30:23   that the land's increase of food
LANGUISHING
24:7   wine withers on languishing vines,
LAPS
65:7   in their laps the payment that has
LAPSE
28:13   they might lapse into stumbling
LAPSED
1:4   they have lapsed into apostasy.
LARGE
5:9   large and fine houses unoccupied.
8:1   Take a large scroll and write
16:14   large populace there shall be very few
32:2   shade of a large rock in arid country.
36:2   with a large army from Lachish to
LARK
38:14   Like a mounting lark I twitter,
LAST
9:1   the last he will exalt the Sea Route
30:8   record it in a book for the last day,
41:4   I, the Lord, first and last, am he.
44:6   I was at the first and I am at the last;
48:12   and I am he who is at the last.
LATTER
2:2   In the latter days
LAUGHS
37:22   she laughs you to scorn.
LAUNCH
43:14   For your sake I launch an attack on
LAUNDRY
7:3   on the road to the Laundry Plaza.
36:2   the Laundry Plaza.
LAVA
30:33   like a river of lava.
34:9   Edom's streams shall turn into lava
LAW
1:10   give heed to the law of our God,
2:3   For out of Zion shall go forth the law,
5:24   despised the law of the Lord of Hosts
8:16   seal the law among my disciples.

30:9   unwilling to obey the law of the Lord,
42:4   The isles await his law.
42:21   they magnify the law and become
42:24   or obey his law.
51:4   The law shall go forth from me;
51:7   O people in whose heart is my law:
LAWGIVER
33:22   and the Lord our Lawgiver.
55:4   a prince and lawgiver of the peoples.
LAWS
10:1   Woe to those who enact unjust laws,
24:5   they have transgressed the laws,
LAY
21:2   Attack, O Elamites! Lay siege, you
24:1   Lo! The Lord will lay waste the earth
25:12   he will lay low by razing them to the
28:16   I lay in Zion a stone, a keystone,
34:15   shall the hawk owl nest and lay eggs,
37:36   there lay all their dead bodies!
42:15   I will lay waste mountains and hills
54:11   I will lay antimony for your building
LAYING
21:2   the destroyer laying waste.
26:5   laying it even with the dust.
LEAD
11:6   youngster will lead them to
20:4   lead away the captives of Egypt
42:16   Then will I lead the blind by a way
49:10   he will lead them by springs of water.
60:9   the ships of Tarshish in the lead,
63:14   So thou didst lead thy people,
LEADER
3:6   You have a tunic: be our leader
3:7   make me a leader of the people.
LEADERS
1:10   O leaders of Sodom;
3:12   your leaders mislead you,
9:16   The leaders of these people have
14:9   of the world's leaders,
LEADING
7:2   that Aram was leading Ephraim on,
LEADS
40:11   that give milk he leads gently along.
LEANNESS
17:4   his fatness of body become leanness.
LEANS
36:6   who leans on it. Such is Pharaoh king
LEAP
35:6   Then shall the lame leap like deer,
LEARN
1:17   Learn to do good: demand justice,
2:4   nor will they learn warfare any more.
26:9   inhabitants of the world learn
26:10   they will not learn righteousness;
32:4   the rash shall learn understanding,
58:2   eager to learn my ways,

LEARNED
7:15 by the time he has learned
29:11 they give to one who is learned,
29:13 commandments of men learned by
50:4 endowed me with a learned tongue,
LEARNS
7:16 But before the child learns
LEASE
16:14 of a lease, Moab's glory shall
21:16 of a lease, Kedar's glory shall fully
LEAST
36:9 one of the least of my lord's servants,
60:22 The least of them shall become a clan,
LEAVE
10:3 Where will you leave your wealth?
52:11 defiled as you leave Babylon.
52:12 But you shall not leave in haste or go
LEAVENED
25:6 a feast of leavened cakes, succulent
LEAVES
1:30 like an oak whose leaves wither,
34:4 like withered leaves from a vine,
55:11 so is the word that leaves my mouth:
64:6 We are decaying like leaves, all of us;
LEAVING
27:9 leaving no idols of prosperity
32:6 leaving the hungry soul empty,
LEBANON
2:13 cedars of Lebanon that lift
10:34 and Lebanon fall spectacularly.
14:8 as do the cedars of Lebanon:
29:17 little while, shall not Lebanon
33:9 Lebanon wilts shamefully;
35:2 endowed with the glory of Lebanon,
37:24 the farthest reaches of Lebanon.
40:16 Lebanon would not suffice to kindle a
60:13 The splendor of Lebanon shall become
LED
9:16 and those who are led are confused.
19:13 heads of state have led Egypt astray.
23:7 whose feet led her to settle far-off
47:10 skill and science you were led astray,
48:21 They thirsted not when he led them
53:7 like a lamb led to slaughter,
55:12 depart in joy and be led back in
63:13 when he led them through the deep?
LEFT
1:8 The Daughter of Zion is left
1:9 Had not the Lord of Hosts left
4:3 Then shall they who are left
5:8 link field to field till no place is left.
6:13 holy offspring be what is left
9:20 they will devour on the left,
10:19 And the trees left of his forest shall
11:11 who shall be left out of Assyria,
11:16 of his people who shall be left,
16:14 very few left, and those of no account.

17:6 when only the gleanings are left,
18:6 All shall be left to the birds of prey
21:11 how much of the night is left?
22:3 you left behind are caught easily
30:17 till you are left as a flagstaff on a
30:21 should you turn left or right.
37:4 on behalf of the remnant that is left.
37:8 of Assyria had left Lachish,
39:6 Nothing shall be left, says the Lord.
44:19 an abomination of what is left?
49:21 When I was left to myself, where were
54:3 to the right and to the left;
65:15 Your name shall be left
LEGISLATION
10:1 who draft oppressive legislation—
LEGS
7:20 legs, and to cut off even your beard.
47:2 unveil, disrobe, bare your legs,
LEND
63:5 but none would lend help;
LENDER
24:2 with lender as with borrower,
LENGTH
1:15 though you pray at length, I will not
LENGTHEN
54:2 Do not hold back; lengthen your cords
LEOPARD
11:6 the leopard lie down with young goats
LET
1:18 Come now, let us put it to the test,
2:3 Come, let us go up
2:5 let us follow the light of the Lord.
4:1 only let us be called by your name—
5:1 Let me sing for my beloved
5:5 Let me now inform you
5:5 and let it be burned;
5:5 and let it be trampled.
5:19 Let him quickly speed up his work
5:19 Let the plan of the Holy One of Israel
7:6 Let us invade Judea and stir up
12:5 let it be acknowledged throughout the
14:32 let his longsuffering people find
16:4 Let the exiles of Moab dwell with you;
19:12 Let them please tell you, if they can
21:7 Let him watch for chariots with teams
22:13 Let us dine and drink, for tomorrow
25:9 let us joyfully celebrate his
26:2 Open the gates to let in the nation
26:11 Let them perceive with dismay
28:12 This is rest; let the weary rest!
33:20 let your eyes rest upon Jerusalem,
34:1 Let the earth give heed, and all who
33:20 let your eyes rest upon Jerusalem,
36:14 says the king: Do not let Hezekiah
36:15 Do not let Hezekiah make you trust in
37:10 Let not your god in whom you trust
40:13 a man should let him know his plan?

41:1 Let them come forward and state their
41:1 let us stand trial together.
41:22 Let them come forward and recount to
42:10 Let the sea roar, and all that lives
42:11 Let the desert and its cities raise
42:11 let the inhabitants of Sela sing for joy
42:12 O let them give glory to the Lord,
43:8 Let go the people who are blind, yet
43:9 Let them bring their witnesses
43:26 let us plead each our case.
43:28 I let the holy cities be profaned;
45:8 let the skies overflow with
45:8 let the earth receive it and salvation
45:8 let righteousness spring up
47:6 so I let my inheritance be defiled.
47:13 let those who unravel the heavens,
50:8 Let us face one another!
50:8 Let him confront me with them!
51:11 Let the ransomed of the Lord return!
51:11 Let them come singing to Zion,
51:11 let them obtain joy and gladness,
55:7 Let the wicked forsake their ways
55:7 Let them return to the Lord,
56:3 Let not the foreigner who adheres to
56:3 And let not the eunuch say, I am but
56:12 Come, they say, let us get wine
57:13 let those who flock to you save you!
62:6 who call upon the Lord, let not up
62:8 I will no more let your grain be food
66:5 Let the Lord manifest his glory,
LETTER
37:14 And Hezekiah received the letter
LETTERS
39:1 king of Babylon, sent letters and gifts
LETTING
32:20 letting oxen and asses range free.
45:1 letting no gates remain shut:
64:12 in silence letting us suffer so
LEVEL
40:4 the uneven ground must become level
42:16 and the uneven ground make level.
45:2 go before you and level all obstacles;
LEVELED
10:33 the lofty ones leveled.
32:19* cities utterly leveled.
LEVIATHAN
27:1 punish severely Leviathan,
27:1 Leviathan, that devious sea monster,
LEVIED
33:18 Where are those who levied the tax?
LEVITES
66:21 be priests and Levites, says the Lord.
LIBATIONS
57:6 pour out libations and make offerings
LIBERATE
44:20 They cannot liberate themselves

LIBERTY
58:6 to set the oppressed at liberty
61:1 to proclaim liberty to the captives
LIBNAH
37:8 found him fighting against Libnah.
LICK
49:23 they will lick the dust of your feet,
LIE
3:26 Her gateways shall lie bereaved and
5:9 many buildings shall lie desolate,
5:25 lie like litter about the streets.
6:11 Until the cities lie desolate
7:16 rulers you loathe shall lie forsaken.
11:6 leopard lie down with young goats;
14:18 All rulers of nations lie in state,
17:2 The cities of Aroer shall lie forsaken
24:12 the gates lie battered to ruin.
27:10 the fortified cities lie forlorn,
32:14 for the palaces shall lie abandoned,
43:17 they lie down as one, to rise no more,
50:11 you shall lie down in agony.
51:20 Your children lie in a faint at the
51:23 Lie prostrate that we may go over you
57:8 those with whom you love to lie,
64:11 and all places dear to us lie in ruins.
LIES
24:5 The earth lies polluted under its
33:9 The Land lies withered and forlorn,
LIFE
10:18 will consume, both life and substance
38:5 I will add fifteen years to your life.
38:10 I said, in the prime of life
38:12 My life is cut off like woven fabric;
38:16 comes a newness of life,
42:5 the breath of life to the people upon
43:4 peoples in exchange for your life.
51:23 those who said of your life,
53:10 that, if he made his life an offering
59:10 in the prime of life we resemble the
LIFEBLOOD
63:3 Their lifeblood spattered my garment
LIFETIME
23:15 seventy years, the lifetime of a king.
65:22 The lifetime of my people shall be
65:22 shall be as the lifetime of a tree;
LIFT
2:4 nation will not lift the sword against
2:13 Lebanon that lift themselves up high,
10:26 and he will lift it over them
24:14 Then will these lift up their voice
40:26 Lift your eyes heavenward and see:
49:18 Lift up your eyes and look around
49:22 I will lift up my hand to the nations,
51:6 Lift up your eyes to the heavens;
52:8 Your watchmen lift up their voice;
60:4 Lift up your eyes and look about you!

LIFTED
10:27 that day their burdens shall be lifted
18:3 when it is lifted up in the mountains;
26:11 O Lord, thy hand is lifted up,
63:9 he lifted them up and carried them
LIFTING
37:23 lifting your eyes to high heaven?
LIFTS
10:15 the rod wielded him who lifts it up!
LIGHT
2:5 let us follow the light of the Lord.
5:20 They put darkness for light
5:20 and light for darkness;
8:20 words devoid of light,
9:2 have seen a bright light;
9:2 has the light dawned.
10:17 the Light of Israel will be the fire
13:10 nor will the moon give its light.
27:11 who come to light their fires with
30:26 The light of the moon
30:26 shall be as the light of the sun,
30:26 and the light of the sun increase
30:26 as the light of seven days shall it be,
42:6 a light to the nations,
42:16 I will turn into light,
44:15 or light fire with to bake bread,
45:7 I fashion light and form darkness;
49:6 to you to be a light to the nations,
50:10 walk in darkness and have no light,
50:11 Walk then by the light of your fires
51:4 precepts shall be a light to the people
58:8 Then shall your light break through
58:10 shall your light dawn amid darkness
59:9 We look for light, but there prevails
60:1 Arise, shine, your light has dawned;
60:3 Nations will come to your light,
60:5 you see it, your face will light up,
60:19 shall the sun be your light by day,
60:19 Lord will be your everlasting light
60:20 tthe Lord shall be an endless light
62:1 her righteousness shines like a light,
LIGHTERS
50:11 But you are lighters of fires, all of
LIGHTHEARTED
24:7 making all the lighthearted lament.
LIKEN
40:18 To whom then will you liken God?
40:25 To whom then will you liken me,
46:5 To whom will you liken me,
LIKENESS
44:13 he gives it a human likeness,
52:14 was marred beyond human likeness,
LIKEWISE
66:21 Of them likewise I will accept men to
LIMBS
58:11 and bring vigor to your limbs.
66:14 your limbs flourish like sprouting

LIME
33:12 nations have been burned like lime,
LIMITS
41:9 called from its farthest limits—
LINEAGE
48:1 you stem from the lineage of Judah
61:9 the lineage the Lord has blessed
65:23 lineage of those blessed by the Lord,
LINEN
3:23 hosiery, sheer linen, millinery, and
19:9 Manufacturers of combed linen
LINGER
5:11 who linger at night parties, inflamed
LINK
5:8 and link field to field till no place is
LION
5:29 They have the roar of a lion;
11:7 the lion will eat straw like the ox.
31:4 As a lion or a young lion growls over
38:13 like a lion he racks my whole frame?
65:25 and the lion will eat straw like the
LIONS
5:29 they are aroused like young lions:
11:6 calves and young lions will feed
15:9 I will bring lions upon the
30:6 of lions and the roaring king of
35:9 No lions shall be encountered
LIPS
6:7 See, this has touched your lips:
11:4 breath of his lips slay the wicked.
29:13 and pay me homage with their lips,
30:27 his lips flow with indignation,
57:19 who partake of the fruit of the lips:
59:3 your lips speak guile, your tongue
LIQUOR
5:11 Woe to those who go after liquor
5:22 and champions at mixing liquor!
24:9 liquor has turned bitter to drinkers.
28:7 have gone astray through liquor.
56:12 and have our fill of liquor.
LISTEN
28:12 But they would not listen.
28:23 Be attentive, and listen to what I say!
32:3 ears of those who hear shall listen.
32:9 Up, and listen to my voice,
36:16 Do not listen to Hezekiah! Thus says
37:17 Listen to all the words
42:18 O you deaf, listen; O you blind, look
49:1 Hear me, O isles; listen, you distant
51:4 Listen to me, my people;
LIT
30:14 with which to scoop lit embers from a
64:2 as when fire is lit for boiling water,
LITTER
5:25 lie like litter about the streets.
LITTLE
24:6 and little of mankind remain.

26:20 hide yourselves a little while
29:17 In a very little while, shall not
32:10 In little more than a year
63:18 But a little while had thy people
LIVE
6:5 I live among a people of unclean
18:3 All you who live in the world,
26:14 They are dead, to live no more,
26:19 thy dead live when their bodies
33:14 Who among us can live through the
49:18 As surely as I live, says the Lord,
55:3 pay heed, that your souls may live!
65:20 aged who do not live out their years;
LIVELIHOOD
57:10 you have found livelihood,
LIVES
38:20 all the days of our lives in the house
42:10 sea roar, and all that lives in it,
LIVING
4:3 among the living at Jerusalem.
8:19 of the dead on behalf of the living
37:4 living God, and will rebuke him for
37:17 has sent to mock the living God.
38:11 in the land of the living;
38:19 But the living, only they bring thee
53:8 cut off from the land of the living
LO
24:1 Lo! The Lord will lay waste the earth
LOAD
46:3 who have been a load on me since
LOADED
46:1 Their idols are loaded upon beasts
LOATHE
7:16 rulers you loathe shall lie forsaken.
LOATHSOME
1:13 they are as a loathsome incense to me.
LOCATION
6:2 with two conceal their location,
LOCUSTS
33:4 like insatiable locusts they rushed
LODGE
44:13 fit to lodge in a house.
LODGED
29:1 Ariel, the city where David lodged!
LODGING
13:21 birds of prey will find lodging there
LOFTIEST
37:24 I have reached its loftiest summit,
LOFTY
2:13 It shall come against all the lofty
10:33 the lofty ones leveled.
57:7 On a lofty mountain
LOINCLOTH
3:24 instead . . . a loincloth of burlap;
LOINS
11:5 faithfulness a girdle round his loins.
20:2 from your loins and remove

45:1 to ungird the loins of rulers,
LOLLING
56:10 lolling seers fond of slumber.
LONG
6:11 And I replied, For how long, my
22:11 the One who designed it long ago.
37:26 how I ordained this thing long ago,
42:14 For a long time I have been silent,
45:21 predicted them long ago?
48:3 I made known long beforehand;
57:11 because I have so long kept silent
65:5 a fire smoldering all day long.
LONGED
21:4 the nightfall I longed for has become
LONGER
7:25 by the hoe you will no longer
10:20 will no longer rely on him who struck
23:4 I no longer labor and bear children!
23:4 I no longer rear young men or raise
24:9 Men no longer drink wine amid song;
29:22 No longer shall Jacob be dismayed;
30:20 Teacher remain hidden no longer,
32:5 The godless shall no longer be
34:12 when all its lords no longer exist?
44:12 he no longer has strength;
46:12 salvation shall no longer be delayed.
47:5 No longer shall you be called,
57:11 that you no longer fear me?
60:19 No longer shall the sun be your light
LONGSUFFERING
14:32 let his longsuffering people find
LOOK
3:9 The look on their faces betrays them:
5:30 And should one look to the land,
8:22 They will look to the land,
13:8 Men will look at one another aghast,
13:18 will not look with compassion on
17:7 eyes look to the Holy One of Israel,
17:8 nor look to things made by their
18:3 look to the ensign
22:8 you will look to the forest home as
22:11 but you did not look to its Maker,
31:1 but who do not look to the Holy One
41:5 The isles look on in fear;
41:12 Should you look for those who
42:18 deaf, listen; O you blind, look and see
49:18 Lift up your eyes and look around
51:1 Look to the rock from which you were
51:2 look to Abraham your father,
51:6 look on the earth beneath:
59:9 We look for light, but there prevails
59:11 we look for salvation, but it eludes
60:4 Lift up your eyes and look about you!
63:15 O look down from heaven,
66:24 And they shall go out and look upon
LOOKED
20:6 become of those we looked up to,

LOOKED *continued*
41:28 For when I looked there was no one,
LOOKING
38:14 eyes are drawn looking heavenward;
LOOKOUT
21:8 Then the lookout cried,
LOOM
38:12 he is severing me from the loom.
LOOSE
5:27 Their waist-belts come not loose
33:23* Their riggings hang loose;
41:7* that it may not come loose.
52:2 Loose yourself from the bands around
LORD
1:2 The Lord has spoken:
1:4 they have forsaken the Lord,
1:9 Had not the Lord of Hosts left us a
1:10 Hear the word of the Lord,
1:11 sacrifices to me? says the Lord.
1:18 put it to the test, says the Lord:
1:20 By his mouth the Lord has spoken it.
1:24 Therefore the Lord, the Lord of Hosts,
1:28 who forsake the Lord are annihilated.
2:3 to the mountain of the Lord,
2:3 from Jerusalem the word of the Lord.
2:5 let us follow the light of the Lord.
2:6 For thou, O Lord, hast forsaken thy
2:10 the awesome presence of the Lord
2:11 the Lord alone shall be exalted in
2:12 The lord of Hosts has a day in store
2:17 the Lord alone shall be exalted in
2:19 the awesome presence of the Lord
2:21 the awesome presence of the Lord
3:1 Even now, the Lord, the Lord of Hosts
3:4 I, the Lord, will make adolescents
3:4 delinquents will lord it over them.
3:8 are contrary to the Lord.
3:13 The Lord will take a stand and
3:15 says the Lord of Hosts.
3:16 The Lord says, moreover,
3:17 the Lord will afflict the scalps
3:17 the Lord will expose their private
3:18 In that day the Lord will strip away
4:2 In that day the plant of the Lord
4:4 This shall be when my Lord
4:5 the Lord will form a cloud by
5:7 The vineyard of the Lord of Hosts is
5:9 The Lord of Hosts spoke this in
5:12 they regard not what the Lord does,
5:16 But the Lord of Hosts will be exalted
5:24 despised the law of the Lord of Hosts
5:25 the anger of the Lord is kindled
6:1 I saw my Lord seated on a throne,
6:3 Most holy is the Lord of Hosts;
6:5 I have seen the King, the Lord of
6:8 I heard the voice of my Lord saying,
6:11 I replied, For how long, my Lord?

6:12 For the Lord will drive men away,
7:3 Then the Lord said to Isaiah,
7:7 Thus says my Lord the Lord:
7:10 Again the Lord addressed Ahaz, and
7:11 from the Lord your God,
7:12 I will not put the Lord to the test.
7:14 Therefore will my Lord of himself
7:17 The Lord will bring upon you
7:18 In that day the Lord will
7:20 In that day my Lord will use
8:1 The Lord said to me,
8:3 And the Lord said to me,
8:5 The Lord addressed me again, and
8:7 therefore will my Lord
8:11 The Lord spoke to me,
8:13 But sanctify the Lord of Hosts,
8:16 For the Lord has said, Bind up
8:17 I will wait for the Lord,
8:18 the children the Lord has given me,
8:18 from the Lord of Hosts,
9:7 The zeal of the Lord of Hosts will
9:8 This message my Lord sent to Jacob,
9:11 But the Lord will strengthen
9:13 they inquire of the Lord of Hosts.
9:14 Therefore the Lord will cut off from
9:17 My Lord is not pleased with their
9:19 At the wrath of the Lord of Hosts
10:12 But when my Lord has fully
10:16 will the Lord, the Lord of Hosts,
10:20 but will truly rely on the Lord,
10:23 For my Lord, the Lord of Hosts,
10:24 Therefore, thus says my Lord,
10:24 the Lord of Hosts:
10:26 The Lord of Hosts will raise the whip
10:33 Then will the Lord, the Lord of Hosts,
11:2 The Spirit of the Lord will rest upon
11:2 and of the fear of the Lord.
11:3 by the fear of the Lord;
11:9 with the knowledge of the Lord
11:11 In that day my Lord will again raise
11:15 The Lord will dry up the tongue
12:1 I praise thee, O Lord.
12:2 for the Lord was my strength and my
12:4 Give thanks to the Lord; invoke his
12:5 Sing in praise of the Lord,
13:4 the Lord of Hosts is marshalling an
13:5 the Lord and the instruments of his
13:6 for the day of the Lord is near;
13:9 The day of the Lord shall come
13:13 by the anger of the Lord of Hosts
14:1 The Lord will have compassion on
14:2 in the land of the Lord:
14:3 In the day the Lord gives you
14:5 The Lord has broken the staff of the
14:22 says the Lord of Hosts.
14:22 and descendants, says the Lord.
14:23 says the Lord of Hosts.

14:24	The Lord of Hosts made an oath,
14:27	the Lord of Hosts has determined,
14:32	The Lord has founded Zion;
16:13	These things the Lord spoke hitherto
16:14	But now the Lord has said,
17:3	says the Lord of Hosts.
17:6	says the Lord, the God of Israel.
18:4	For thus said the Lord to me:
18:7	to the Lord of Hosts
18:7	place of the name of the Lord of Hosts
19:1	When the Lord enters Egypt riding on
19:4	says my Lord, the Lord of Hosts.
19:12	what the Lord of Hosts has in mind
19:14	The Lord has permeated them
19:16	at the brandishing hand the Lord
19:17	the Lord of Hosts has in store for
19:18	swear loyalty to the Lord of Hosts.
19:19	erected to the Lord in the midst
19:19	to the Lord at its border.
19:20	testimony of the Lord of Hosts
19:20	cry out to the Lord because of
19:21	The Lord will make himself
19:21	Lord in that day. They will
19:21	to the Lord and fulfill them.
19:22	The Lord will smite Egypt,
19:22	will turn back to the Lord,
19:25	The Lord of Hosts will bless them,
20:2	the Lord had spoken through
20:3	Then the Lord said, Just as
21:6	Because of this my Lord said to me,
21:8	day in and day out, my Lord;
21:10	from the Lord of Hosts, the God of
21:16	On account of this, my Lord said
21:17	shall be few. The Lord, the God
22:5	For my Lord, the Lord of Hosts,
22:12	such a day my Lord, the Lord of Hosts
22:14	The Lord of Hosts revealed this to my
22:14	till you die, says my Lord, the Lord
22:15	Thus said my Lord, the Lord of Hosts:
22:17	The Lord will hurl you away
22:25	In that day, says the Lord of Hosts,
22:25	The Lord has spoken it.
23:9	The Lord of Hosts devised it,
23:11	The Lord will stretch out his hand
23:17	for after seventy years, the Lord
23:18	be consecrated to the Lord;
23:18	dwell in the presence of the Lord,
24:1	Lo! The Lord will lay waste the earth
24:3	The Lord has given word concerning
24:15	they will give glory to the Lord
24:15	the name of the Lord, the God of
24:21	In that day will the Lord deal on high
24:23	when the Lord of Hosts manifests his
25:1	O Lord, thou art my God;
25:6	In this mountain will the Lord of
25:8	My Lord the Lord will wipe away
25:8	The Lord has spoken it.

25:9	This is the Lord for whom we have
25:10	mountain rests the hand of the Lord,
26:3	whose minds are steadfast, O Lord ,
26:4	Ever trust in the Lord,
26:4	the Lord Yah is an everlasting Rock.
26:8	we anticipate thee, O Lord;
26:10	and see not the glory of the Lord.
26:11	O Lord, thy hand is lifted up,
26:12	O Lord, thou bringest about our
26:13	O Lord, our God, lords other than
26:15	hast enlarged the nation, O Lord,
26:16	O Lord, in their distress they
26:17	so were we at thy presence, O Lord.
26:21	For now will the Lord come out of his
27:1	In that day will the Lord,
27:3	of which I, the Lord, am keeper.
27:8	by utterly banishing them, O Lord.
27:12	In that day the Lord will thresh out
27:13	to the Lord in the holy mountain at
28:2	My Lord has in store one mighty and
28:5	In that day shall the Lord of Hosts
28:13	the word of the Lord remained:
28:14	Therefore hear the word of the Lord,
28:16	thus says my Lord the Lord
28:21	For the Lord will rise up
28:22	by my Lord, the Lord of Hosts,
28:29	originate with the Lord of Hosts,
29:6	be chastened by the Lord of Hosts
29:10	The Lord has poured out on you
29:13	But my Lord says, Because these
29:15	to hide their schemes from the Lord!
29:19	obtain an increase of joy in the Lord,
29:22	Therefore thus says the Lord,
30:1	rebellious sons, says the Lord,
30:9	unwilling to obey the law of the Lord,
30:15	For thus says my Lord the Lord,
30:18	the Lord delay his coming ,
30:18	For the Lord is the God of justice;
30:20	Though my Lord give you the bread
30:26	in the day the Lord binds up
30:27	Behold, the Lord Omnipotent coming
30:29	to the mountain of the Lord,
30:30	The Lord will cause his voice to
30:31	At the voice of the Lord
30:32	when the Lord lowers it upon them,
31:1	nor inquire of the Lord!
31:3	when the Lord stretches out his hand,
31:4	For thus said the Lord to me:
31:4	so shall the Lord of Hosts be when he
31:5	the Lord of Hosts guard Jerusalem;
31:9	says the Lord, whose fire is in Zion;
32:6	perverse things concerning the Lord,
33:2	O Lord, be favorable toward us;
33:5	But the Lord is supreme, for he
33:6	your fear of the Lord shall be your
33:10	Now will I arise, says the Lord;
33:21	May the Lord cause us to dwell

LORD *continued*

33:22	For the Lord is our Judge,
33:22	and the Lord our Lawgiver.
33:22	The Lord is our King; he himself will
34:6	The Lord has a sword that shall
34:6	the Lord will hold a slaughter
34:16	and read it in the book of the Lord:
35:2	The glory of the Lord and the
35:10	ransomed of the Lord shall return;
36:7	Lord our God, is he not the one
36:8	Come now, wager with my lord the
36:10	destroyed it without the Lord?
36:10	For the Lord told me to come against
36:12	Did my lord send me
36:12	these things to you and to your lord
36:15	the Lord by saying, The Lord will
36:18	The Lord will save us. Were any gods
36:20	his land from my hand, that the Lord
37:1	entered the house of the Lord.
37:4	It may be that the Lord your God has
37:4	words of of Rabshakeh, whom his lord
37:4	the Lord your God has heard, were
37:6	Isaiah said to them, Tell your lord,
37:6	Thus says the Lord: Be not afraid
37:14	went up to the house of the Lord and
37:14	unrolled it before the Lord.
37:15	Hezekiah prayed to the Lord and said,
37:16	O Lord of Hosts, God of Israel,
37:17	O Lord, give ear and hear; O Lord,
37:18	O Lord, the kings of Assyria have
37:20	But now, O Lord our God, deliver us
37:20	may know that thou alone art Lord.
37:21	saying, Thus says the Lord,
37:22	this is what the Lord has spoken
37:24	you have blasphemed the Lord.
37:32	The zeal of the Lord of Hosts will
37:33	Therefore, thus says the Lord
37:34	not enter this city, says the Lord.
37:36	Then the angel of the Lord went out
38:1	him and said, Thus says the Lord:
38:2	the wall and prayed to the Lord:
38:3	I beseech thee to remember, O Lord,
38:4	the word of the Lord came to Isaiah:
38:5	tell Hezekiah, Thus says the Lord,
38:22*	go up to the house of the Lord?
38:7	to you from the Lord, that the Lord
38:11	I thought, I shall not see the Lord
38:14	O Lord, I am in straits; be my surety!
38:16	O my Lord, by means of such trials
38:20	O Lord, may it please thee to save
38:20	of our lives in the house of the Lord.
39:5	Hear the word of the Lord of Hosts:
39:6	Nothing shall be left, says the Lord.
39:8	Lord you have spoken is good.
40:3	desert prepare the way for the Lord;
40:5	glory of the Lord shall be revealed
40:5	By his mouth the Lord has spoken it.

40:7	Spirit of the Lord breathe within it,
40:10	Lord the Lord comes with power;
40:13	comprehended the Spirit of the Lord,
40:27	has become obscured from the Lord;
40:28	The Lord is the God of eternity,
40:31	But they who hope in the Lord
41:4	I, the Lord, first and last, am he.
41:13	For I, the Lord your God,
41:14	I am your help, says the Lord;
41:16	Then will you rejoice in the Lord
41:17	I the Lord will answer their want;
41:21	Present your case, says the Lord;
42:5	Thus says the Lord God,
42:6	I the Lord have rightfully called you
42:8	I am the Lord; that is my name.
42:10	Sing to the Lord a new song;
42:12	O let them give glory to the Lord,
42:13	The Lord will come forth like a
42:19	as the servant of the Lord
42:21	It is the will of the Lord,
42:24	to despoilers, if not the Lord,
43:1	But now, thus says the Lord—
43:3	For I the Lord am your God,
43:10	you are my witnesses, says the Lord,
43:11	I myself am the Lord;
43:12	You are my witnesses, says the Lord,
43:14	Thus says the Lord, the Holy One of
43:15	I the Lord, your Holy One,
43:16	Thus says the Lord—
44:2	Thus says the Lord, your Maker,
44:5	inscribe on their arm, To the Lord,
44:6	Thus says the Lord, the King of
44:6	the Lord of Hosts, their Redeemer:
44:23	Sing . . . for what the Lord has
44:23	the Lord has redeemed Jacob;
44:24	Thus says the Lord, your Redeemer,
44:24	I am the Lord, the Maker of all things
45:1	Thus says the Lord to his anointed,
45:3	you may know that it is I the Lord,
45:5	I am the Lord, there is none other;
45:6	I am the Lord, and that there is none
45:7	I, the Lord, do all these things.
45:8	I, the Lord, create it.
45:11	Thus says the Lord,
45:13	without price or bribe, says the Lord
45:14	Thus says the Lord:
45:17	But Israel is saved by the Lord
45:18	For thus says the Lord who created
45:18	I am the Lord, there is none other.
45:19	I the Lord tell righteousness
45:21	Did not I, the Lord,
45:24	By the Lord alone come vindication
45:25	In the Lord shall all Israel's
47:4	whose name is the Lord of Hosts.
48:1	take oaths in the name of the Lord
48:2	whose name is the Lord of Hosts:
48:14	It is him the Lord loves,

48:16 Now my Lord the Lord has sent me;
48:17 Thus says the Lord, the Holy One of
48:17 I the Lord your God instruct you to
48:20 Say, The Lord has redeemed his
48:22 But there is no peace, says the Lord,
49:1 The Lord called me before I was in
49:4 Yet my cause rested with the Lord,
49:5 For now the Lord has said—
49:5 won honor in the eyes of the Lord
49:7 Thus says the Lord,
49:7 the Lord keeps faith with you,
49:8 Thus says the Lord:
49:13 The Lord is comforting his people,
49:14 But Zion said, The Lord has forsaken
49:14 my Lord has forgotten me.
49:18 As surely as I live, says the Lord,
49:22 Thus says my Lord the Lord:
49:23 shall you know that I am the Lord,
49:25 Yet thus says the Lord: The warrior's
49:26 know that I the Lord am your Savior,
50:1 Thus says the Lord:
50:4 My Lord the Lord has endowed me
50:5 my Lord the Lord has opened my ear,
50:7 Because my Lord the Lord helps me,
50:9 See, my Lord the Lord sustains me.
50:10 Who among you fears the Lord
50:10 trusts in the name of the Lord and
51:1 seekers of the Lord:
51:3 For the Lord is comforting Zion,
51:3 her desert as the garden of the Lord.
51:9 O arm of the Lord!
51:11 Let the ransomed of the Lord return!
51:13 Have you forgotten the Lord,
51:15 It is I the Lord your God,
51:15 whose name is the Lord of Hosts,
51:20 their fill of the wrath of the Lord,
51:22 Thus says the Lord, your Lord and
52:3 Thus says the Lord: you were sold
52:4 For thus says the Lord the Lord:
52:5 what have I here? says the Lord.
52:5 presumptuously, says the Lord,
52:8 when the Lord returns to Zion
52:9 the Lord has comforted his people;
52:10* The Lord has bared his holy arm
52:12 the Lord will go before you
53:1 whose account has the arm of the Lord
53:6 the Lord brought together upon him
53:10 But the Lord willed to crush him,
53:10 and that the purposes of the Lord
54:1 those of the espoused, says the Lord.
54:5 whose name is the Lord of Hosts;
54:6 The Lord calls you back
54:8 says the Lord, who redeems you.
54:10 says the Lord, who has compassion on
54:13 children shall be taught by the Lord,
54:17 heritage of the servants of the Lord,
54:17 vindication by me, says the Lord.

55:5 because of the Lord your God,
55:6 Inquire of the Lord while he is
55:7 Let them return to the Lord,
55:8 your ways my ways, says the Lord.
55:13 serve as a testimony of the Lord,
56:1 Thus says the Lord:
56:3 foreigner who adheres to the Lord
56:3 The Lord will surely exclude me from
56:4 For thus says the Lord:
56:6 the foreigners who adhere to the Lord
56:6 who love the name of the Lord,
56:8 Thus says my Lord the Lord,
57:19 says the Lord who heals him.
58:8 and the glory of the Lord will be your
58:9 you call, the Lord will respond;
58:11 The Lord will direct you continually;
58:13 the holy day of the Lord venerable,
58:14 then shall you delight in the Lord,
58:14 By his mouth the Lord has spoken it.
59:13 willfully denying the Lord,
59:15 The Lord saw that there was no
59:19 men will fear the Lord Omnipotent,
59:19 impelled by the Spirit of the Lord.
59:20 of transgression, says the Lord.
59:21 says the Lord: My Spirit which is
59:21 says the Lord, from now on and
60:1 the glory of the Lord has risen upon
60:2 upon you the Lord will shine;
60:6 and heralding the praises of the Lord.
60:9 to the Lord Omnipotent, your God,
60:14 will call you The City of the Lord,
60:16 Then shall you know that I, the Lord,
60:19 the Lord will be your everlasting
60:20 to you the Lord shall be an endless
60:22 I the Lord will hasten it in its time.
61:1 The Spirit of my Lord the Lord is
61:1 for the Lord has anointed me
61:3 planted by the Lord for his glory.
61:6 shall be called the priests of the Lord
61:8 For I the Lord love just dealings—
61:9 of the lineage the Lord has blessed.
61:10 I rejoice exceedingly in the Lord;
61:11 so will my Lord the Lord
62:2 conferred by the mouth of the Lord.
62:3 in the hand of the Lord,
62:4 For the Lord shall delight in you,
62:6 You who call upon the Lord,
62:8 The Lord has sworn by his right
62:9 giving praise to the Lord;
62:11 The Lord has made proclamation to
62:12 the redeemed of the Lord;
63:7 I will recount in praise of the Lord
63:7 to all that the Lord has done for us,
63:14 Spirit of the lord that guided them.
63:14 thou didst lead thy people, O Lord,
63:16 thou, O Lord, art our Father;
63:17 Why, O Lord, hast thou made us stray

LORD *continued*

64:8   thou art our Father, O Lord;
64:9   Be not exceedingly angry, O Lord;
64:12   At all this, O Lord, wilt thou restrain
65:7   their fathers' alike, says the Lord.
65:8   Thus says the Lord: As when
65:11   As for you who forsake the Lord
65:13   thus says my Lord the Lord:
65:15   when my Lord the Lord slays you.
65:23   lineage of those blessed by the Lord,
65:25   my holy mountain, says the Lord.
66:1   Thus, says the Lord: The heavens
66:2   all came into being, says the Lord.
66:5   Hear the word of the Lord,
66:5   Let the Lord manifest his glory,
66:6   It is the voice of the Lord
66:9   not bring on birth? says the Lord.
66:12   For thus says the Lord: See,
66:14   when the hand of the Lord
66:15   See, the Lord comes with fire,
66:16   with his sword shall the Lord
66:16   slain by the Lord shall be many.
66:17   made an end of, says the Lord.
66:20   my holy mountain, says the Lord,
66:20   as offerings to the Lord—on horses,
66:20   to the house of the Lord.
66:21   be priests and Levites, says the Lord.
66:22   says the Lord, so shall your offspring
66:23   before me, says the Lord.

LORDS

26:13   O Lord, our God, lords other than
34:12   when all its lords no longer exist?

LORD'S

2:2   the mountain of the Lord's house
24:14   exult at the Lord's ingenuity.
30:33   the Lord's breath burns within it
34:2   The Lord's rage is upon all nations,
34:8   For it is the Lord's day of vengeance,
36:9   one of the least of my lord's servants,
40:2   She has received from the Lord's hand
41:20   perceive that the Lord's hand did this
44:5   One will say, I am the Lord's,
51:17   who have drunk from the Lord's hand
52:11   you who bear the Lord's vessels.
58:5   a day of the Lord's good graces?
59:1   Surely the Lord's hand has not
61:2   to herald the year of the Lord's favor
63:7   the Lord's loving favors,

LOST

27:13   sound, and they who were lost

LOT

17:14   This is the lot of those who plunder
19:8   Fishermen will deplore their lot
57:6   your fate; they indeed are your lot.
61:7   and shouted insults were their lot,

LOUD

22:2   You resounded with loud cheers—

27:13   In that day a loud trumpet shall
36:13   loud voice in Judean, Hear the words

LOVE

1:23   with one accord they love bribes
5:1   a love song about his vineyard:
43:4   and because I love you,
56:6   who love the name of the Lord,
57:8   those with whom you love to lie,
61:8   For I the Lord love just dealings—
63:9   In his love and compassion
66:10   be glad for her, all who love her;

LOVES

48:14   It is him the Lord loves,

LOVING

16:5   then, in loving kindness,
54:7   but with loving compassion I will
55:3   my loving fidelity toward David.
63:7   the Lord's loving favors,

LOW

2:9   Mankind is brought low
2:12   that they may be brought low.
2:17   and man's pride brought low;
5:15   Mankind is brought low
14:8   Since you have been laid low,
25:12   he will lay low by razing them to the
29:4   And when you have been laid low,
40:4   every mountain and hill made low;

LOWER

22:9   water in the Lower Reservoir.

LOWERED

2:11   haughty eyes of men shall be lowered

LOWERS

30:32   when the Lord lowers it upon them,

LOWLY

11:4   arbitrate for the lowly in the land;
29:19   The lowly shall obtain an increase of
57:15   who is humble and lowly in spirit—
57:15   refreshing the spirits of the lowly,
61:1   to announce good tidings to the lowly

LOYAL

7:9   because you are not loyal.

LOYALTY

19:18   swear loyalty to the Lord of Hosts.
39:8   be peace and loyalty during my reign.

LUCK

65:11   who spread tables for Luck

LUD

66:19   Tarshish, Pul, and Lud (the archers),

LUHITH

15:5   they will ascend the slopes of Luhith;

LUMP

44:19   I not stoop to a mere lump of wood?

LURCH

24:19   the earth shall convulse and lurch.

LUST

57:5   who burn with lust among the oaks,

LYRE
23:16 Take a lyre and go about the town,
LYRES
5:12 There are harps and lyres,
14:11 along with the music of your lyres.
24:8 the pulsating of lyres comes to an
30:29 with flutes [and drums and lyres;]
MADE
1:18 they can be made white as snow;
1:21 righteousness made its abode in her,
2:8 things their own fingers have made.
2:20 which they have made for themselves
10:15 who is not made of wood!
14:16 Is this the man who made the earth
14:24 The Lord of Hosts made an oath,
16:7 the Moabites be made to to lament,
17:8 look to things made by their finger—
24:4 of the earth shall be made wretched.
25:2 Thou hast made the city a heap of
29:16 Shall what is made say of its maker,
30:33 a hearth indeed, made ready for
40:4 every mountain and hill made low;
44:8 Have I not made it known to you
45:12 It is I who made the earth
45:18 who made it secure and organized it,
46:4 It is I who made you, and I who bear
48:3 I made known long beforehand;
48:16 I have not made predictions in secret;
49:2 He has made my mouth like a sharp
49:2 He has made me into a polished arrow
51:10 and made of ocean depths a way
51:23 so that you made your back as the
53:10 that, if he made his life an offering
53:12 and made intercession for the
57:7 you have made prominent your bed,
57:16 souls I have made would faint before
59:8 They have made crooked their paths;
59:17 and made salvation the helmet on his
60:9 who has made you illustrious.
62:11 The Lord has made proclamation to
63:6 I made them drunk by my rage
63:12 who made his glorious arm proceed
63:17 Why, O Lord, hast thou made us stray
66:2 are all things my hand has made,
66:17 made an end of, says the Lord.
MADEST
37:16 It is thou who madest the heavens and
MADMENAH
10:31 Madmenah has moved out of the way,
MAGGOTS
14:11 Beneath you is a bed of maggots;
MAGICAL
47:9 your many magical feats
47:12 and with your many magical feats,
MAGISTRATE
3:2 the magistrate and prophet, the augur

MAGNIFY
42:21 they magnify the law and become
MAHER-SHALAL-HASH-BAZ
8:3 Name him Maher-Shalal-Hash-Baz
MAID
24:2 with mistress as with maid,
MAIDSERVANTS
14:2 as menservants and maidservants
MAINTAIN
16:5 who will maintain justice and
MAJESTIC
33:21 or majestic fleets pass by.
MAJESTY
63:1 this from Bozrah, arrayed in majesty,
MAKE
3:4 will make adolescents their rulers;
3:7 you cannot make me a leader of the
5:6 I will make it a desolation;
5:20 they make bitterness sweet and the
6:10 Make the heart of these people grow
8:10 though you make proposals,
12:4 Make known his deeds among the
13:9 to make the earth a desolation,
13:12 I will make mankind scarcer than
14:14 I will make myself like the Most
17:11 and though you make them thrive
19:21 The Lord will make himself
19:21 offerings, and make vows
22:17 he will make you soar like a dart.
23:9 to make all glorying in excellence a
27:5 and make peace with me,
28:17 I will make justice the measure,
29:16 He did not make me,
30:30 and make visible his arm descending
36:15 Do not let Hezekiah make you trust in
36:16 the king of Assyria: Make peace with
38:8 See, I make the shadow cast by the
40:9 Make yourself heard, be not afraid;
41:15 I will make of you a sharp-toothed
41:15 and make chaff of hills.
41:26 not one make it known;
42:2 to make himself heard in public.
42:15 and make all their vegetation wither;
42:16 and the uneven ground make level.
44:15 from it they make idols to which they
44:17 From the rest they make a god, their
46:6 hire a smith to make them a god
47:13 and make predictions month by
48:20 Make this announcement with
54:12 I will make your skylights of jacinth,
55:3 I will make with you an everlasting
57:6 pour out libations and make offerings
58:4 as to make your voice heard on high.
58:14 I will make you traverse the heights
60:7 I will make glorious my house of
60:13 to make glorious the place of my feet.
60:15 I will make you an everlasting pride,

MAKE *continued*
60:17 I will make peace your rulers
61:8 I will make with them an eternal
64:2 to make thyself known to thine
66:22 which I make shall endure before me,
MAKER
17:7 men will have regard to their Maker,
22:11 but you did not look to its Maker,
27:11 their Maker shows them no mercy;
29:16 Shall what is made say of its maker,
44:2 Thus says the Lord, your Maker,
44:24 I am the Lord, the Maker of all
45:9 those in conflict with their Maker,
45:11 the Holy One of Israel, their Maker:
51:13 you forgotten the Lord, your Maker—
54:5 he who espouses you is your Maker,
MAKERS
45:16 the makers of inventions retired in
MAKES
27:9 he makes like crushed chalkstone
40:23 and makes the authorities of the
44:14 firs, which the rain makes grow:
44:25 and makes fools of diviners,
44:25 and makes nonsense of their
62:7 and makes it renowned in the earth.
MAKING
8:13 making him your fear, him your awe.
10:2 making plunder of widows,
24:7 making all the lighthearted lament.
30:1 for making alliances without my
43:12 salvation, making it known
43:19 I am making roads through the desert,
44:19 Am I not making an abomination of
51:2 I blessed him by making him many.
51:3 he is making her wilderness like
58:5 and making one's bed of sackcloth
63:12 making an everlasting name for
65:3 in parks, making smoke upon bricks,
MALEFACTORS
9:17 all alike are godless malefactors,
MALEVOLENT
32:7 rogues scheme by malevolent means
MAN
2:22 Desist from the things of man,
3:2 the valiant man and soldier,
3:5 every man his neighbor.
3:6 Then will a man apprehend a kinsman
4:1 women will take hold of one man
6:5 for I am a man of unclean speech,
6:11 the houses without a man,
7:21 In that day a man will keep'
14:16 Is this the man who made the earth
29:8 like a hungry man who dreams he
29:8 a thirsty man who dreams he drinks,
29:21 at a word adjudge a man to be guilty,
31:8 shall fall by a sword not of man;
32:2 And a man shall become as a shelter

33:8 man is disregarded.
36:6 pierces the palm of any man
38:11 I shall not now behold Man
40:13 that a man should let him know his
45:12 and created man upon it;
46:11 the man who performs my
51:12 you that you fear mortal man,
53:3 a man of grief, accustomed to
56:2 Blessed is the man who does so—
57:1 and no man gives it a thought;
62:5 As a young man weds a virgin,
66:3 is as one who kills a man,
MAN'S
2:11 and man's pride abased;
2:17 and man's pride brought low;
44:13 human likeness, resembling man's
MANASSEH
9:21 Manasseh will turn against Ephraim
9:21 and Ephraim against Manasseh,
MANGLED
14:19 whose mangled remains are thrown in
MANIFEST
66:5 Let the Lord manifest his glory,
66:14 shall be manifest among his servants
MANIFESTS
24:23 the Lord of Hosts manifests his reign
MANIPULATE
59:6 they manipulate injurious dealings.
MANIPULATION
30:12 rely on manipulation and double
MANKIND
2:9 Mankind is brought low
5:15 Mankind is brought low
13:12 make mankind scarcer than fine gold,
24:6 and little of mankind remain.
MANNER
33:4 in the manner of caterpillars;
51:6 shall die in the manner of vermin.
58:5 Is this the manner of fasting I have
MANSIONS
25:2 heathen mansions shall no more form
MANUFACTURE
44:9 who manufacture idols are deranged;
MANUFACTURERS
19:9 Manufacturers of combed linen
MANY
2:3 Many peoples shall go, saying,
2:4 and arbitrate for many peoples,
5:9 many buildings shall lie desolate,
8:15 Many will stumble into them,
17:12 Woe to the many peoples in an
24:22 and shut in confinement many days,
47:9 notwithstanding your many magical
47:12 and with your many magical feats,
48:19 descendants as many as their grains.
51:2 I blessed him by making him many.
52:14 just as he appalled many—

52:15 So shall he yet astound many nations,
53:11 the righteous one, vindicate many,
53:12 he bore the sins of many,
66:16 slain by the Lord shall be many.
MARCH
30:29 rejoicing of heart, as when men march
MARCHED
36:1 marched against all the fortified
36:10 could I have marched against
MARITIME
27:1 the evasive maritime serpent,
MARK
66:19 And I will set a mark upon them,
MARKER
44:13 sketching his idol with a marker.
MARRED
52:14 his appearance was marred beyond
MARRIED
54:6 a wife married in youth only to be
MARSHALLING
13:4 Lord of Hosts is marshalling an army
MARSHALLS
10:28 Micmash he marshals his weaponry.
MARSHES
35:7 [shall marshes break out],
MASSACRE
14:21 Prepare for the massacre of their
34:6 an immense massacre in the land of
MASSES
5:13 their masses perish with thirst.
5:14 descend their elite with the masses,
54:15 whoever masses against you shall fall
MAST
33:23* they hold not the mast in place
MASTER
19:4 into the hand of a cruel master;
24:2 with master as with servant,
30:20 but your eyes shall see the Master.
32:4 the stammerers master eloquence.
MASTER'S
1:3 the ass its master's stall,
22:19 be a disgrace to your master's house.
MATE
34:15 each one accompanying her mate.
34:16 for, not one lacks her mate.
MATTER
22:1 Whatever is the matter with you,
MATTERS
58:13 and speaking of business matters—
MATURED
25:6 of matured wines well refined.
MEADOWS
55:12 trees of the meadows all clap their
MEAN
3:15 What do you mean by oppressing my
MEANS
32:7 rogues scheme by malevolent means

38:16 O my Lord, by means of such trials
38:17 by its means thou drawest my soul
MEASURE
28:10 measure by measure,
28:10 measure by measure,
28:13 measure by measure,
28:13 measure by measure,
28:17 I will make justice the measure,
34:11 be surveyed with muddled measure
34:17 his hand that divides it by measure.
40:12 the earth's dust by measure,
65:7 on the hills, I will measure out
MEASURED
40:12 Who measured out the waters
MEAT
22:13 eating meat and drinking wine:
44:16 they eat the meat and are satisfied.
44:19 roasted meat and ate it.
MEDEBA
15:2 wail in Moab over Nebo and Medeba.
MEDES
13:17 See, I stir up against them the Medes,
21:2 O Elamites! Lay siege, you Medes!
MEDIUM
29:4 shall be like that of a medium;
MEDIUMS
8:19 of mediums and spiritists
19:3 to mediums and witchcraft.
MEET
7:3 Go out and meet Ahaz,
21:14 meet the fugitives with food,
MEETINGS
1:13 convening meetings at the New Month
1:14 Your monthly and regular meetings
MELON
1:8 a hut in a melon field,
MELT
13:7 and the hearts of all men melt.
14:31 Utterly melt away, you Philistines!
19:1 Egyptians' hearts melt within them.
31:8 and their young men melt;
MELTING
64:1 mountains melting at thy presence—
MEN
2:9 when men thus debase themselves.
2:11 haughty eyes of men shall be lowered
2:17 haughtiness of men shall be abased,
2:19 Men will go into caves in the rocks
2:20 In that day men will throw away
2:21 Men will go into crevices in the rocks
3:25 Your men shall be felled by the
5:3 Jerusalem and you men of Judea,
5:13 their best men die of famine,
5:15 when men debase themselves,
6:12 For the Lord will drive men away,
7:13 for you to try the patience of men?
7:22 men will eat the cream.

495

MEN *continued*
7:24 Men will go there with bows
8:19 When men tell you to inquire
9:3 as men rejoice at harvest time,
9:3 or as men are joyous when they divide
9:17 not pleased with their young men,
9:19 Men will have no compassion for one
9:20 men will eat the flesh of their own
13:7 and the hearts of all men melt.
13:8 Men will look at one another aghast,
13:11 end to the arrogance of insolent men
13:12 men more rare than gold of Ophir.
15:4 to summon the armed men of Moab,
17:7 In that day men will have regard to
19:12 Where are your wise men indeed?
20:5 Men shall be appalled and perplexed
21:11 Men call to see me from Seir,
23:4 I no longer rear young men or raise
23:5 men will be in anguish at the report.
24:9 Men no longer drink wine amid song;
29:13 commandments of men learned by
29:14 the intelligence of their wise men
29:19 and the poorest of men rejoice
30:29 rejoicing of heart, as when men march
31:8 and their young men melt;
36:12 and not to the men sitting on the wall
37:36 in the Assyrian camp. And when men
39:3 What did those men say to you
40:30 men slump down of exhaustion.
41:14 O men of Israel, [be not dismayed]:
43:4 I give men in return for you,
43:17 armies of men in full strength,
44:15 that which serves men as fuel,
44:25 who turns wise men about
45:6 that men from where the sun rises to
47:3 and not be entreated of men,
51:7 Do not fear the reproach of men;
51:12 men who shall be turned to grass?
52:14 his semblance unlike that of men—
53:3 was despised and disdained by men,
53:3 one from whom men hide their faces
55:7 and the sinful men their thoughts.
58:5 just a time for men to torment
58:7 when you see men underclad to clothe
59:19 From the West men will fear the Lord
65:21 When men build houses, they will
66:21 Of them likewise I will accept men to
MEN'S
37:19 of men's hands, of wood and of stone,
MENSERVANTS
14:2 as menservants and maidservants
MENSTRUOUS
30:22 as a menstruous woman her
64:6 righteousness as a menstruous rag.
MENTION
33:15 their ears at the mention of murder,
57:11 you pretend and do not mention me,

MENTIONED
14:20 never more be mentioned!
49:1 he mentioned me by name.
MERCHANDISE
23:18 Her merchandise and hire shall
45:14 Egypt and merchandise of Cush
MERCHANT
2:16 both merchant ships and pleasure
23:1 Sound your sirens, O merchant ships!
23:3 she became the merchant of nations.
23:11 orders concerning the merchant city
23:14 Sound your sirens, O merchant ships;
MERCHANTS
23:8 whose merchants the world's
MERCIFULLY
63:7 he has mercifully and most
MERCY
13:18 will show no mercy to the newborn;
27:11 their Maker shows them no mercy;
30:18 out of mercy toward you he will
47:6 and you showed them no mercy;
49:10 he who has mercy on them will guide
55:7 and he will have mercy on them;
60:10 I will gladly show you mercy.
MERIT
53:3 shunned, deemed by us of no merit.
MERODACH-BALADAN
39:1 Merodach-Baladan the son of Baladan,
MERRYMAKING
22:13 there is mirth and merrymaking,
MESSAGE
9:8 This message my Lord sent to Jacob,
MESSENGER
40:9 O Jerusalem, messenger of good news.
42:19 so deaf as the messenger I have sent?
52:7 the messenger announcing peace,
MESSENGERS
18:2 Go speedily, you messengers!
37:9 messengers to Hezekiah, telling
37:14 messengers and read it. Then
44:26 the aims of his messengers,
MET
14:4 How the tyrant has met his end
MICMASH
10:28 at Micmash he marshals his
MIDIAN
60:6 the dromedaries of Midian and Ephah;
MIDIANITES
10:26 as when he struck the Midianites
MIDIAN'S
9:4 as in the day of Midian's defeat.
MIDST
5:2 He built a watchtower in its midst
19:19 erected to the Lord in the midst
19:24 a blessing in the midst of the earth.
25:11 his hands into the midst of it,
41:18 springs in the midst of the plains;

61:9   posterity in the midst of the peoples;
MIGHT
3:25   your might overthrown in war.
26:18   inhabitants of the world might not
28:13   they might lapse into stumbling
33:13   be apprised of my might!
40:14   that he might be enlightened,
41:26   that we might say, He was right?
45:24   come vindication and might.
51:10   by which the redeemed might pass?
53:10   he might see his offspring and
53:10   might prosper in his hand.
63:15   now are thy zeal and thy might?
64:5   that in them we might ever be saved.
MIGHTILY
40:9   Raise your voice mightily,
MIGHTY
1:31   The mighty shall be as refuse,
8:7   great and mighty waters of the River—
9:6   Counsellor, one Mighty in Valor,
10:21   to the one Mighty in Valor.
11:15   Egyptian Sea by his mighty wind;
17:9   In that day their mighty cities
17:12   like the turbulence of mighty waters!
23:4   the mighty haven of the Sea, has
28:2   Lord has in store one mighty and
28:2   inundating deluge of mighty waters,
43:16   a path through the mighty waters,
51:10   the waters of the mighty deep,
53:12   divide the spoil with the mighty,
60:22   the youngest a mighty nation.
62:8   by his right hand, his mighty arm:
63:1   It is I, who am mighty to save,
MIGRON
10:28   He advances . . . passes through Migron
MILK
7:22   And because of their plentiful milk,
28:9   Weanlings weaned from milk,
40:11   the ewes that give milk he leads
55:1   Come, buy wine and milk
60:16   You will suck the milk of the nations,
MILLINERY
3:23   hosiery, sheer linen, millinery, and
MIND
7:2   the king's mind and the minds of
10:7   this shall not be what he has in mind.
19:12   Lord of Hosts has in mind for Egypt!
21:4   My mind reels, I am paralyzed with
33:18   recount in your mind the terror:
43:18   Never mind the prophecies of bygone
46:8   Put yourselves in mind of this
59:13   conceiving in the mind and pondering
65:17   or recalled to mind.
MINDFUL
42:23   and be mindful and obey?
MINDLESS
44:9   sightless and mindless, to their own

MINDS
7:2   the king's mind and the minds of
26:3   Those whose minds are steadfast,
32:4   The minds of the rash shall learn
44:18   their minds are incapable of
44:20   their deluded minds have distracted
MINISTER
60:10   and their rulers will minister to you.
MINISTERS
19:11   The ministers of Zoan are utter fools;
19:13   The ministers of Zoan have been
61:6   as the ministers of our God.
MIRAGES
35:7   The land of mirages shall become one
MIRE
57:20   whose waters heave up mire and mud:
MIRTH
22:13   there is mirth and merrymaking,
MISCHIEF
59:7   are preoccupied with mischief;
MISCREANTS
14:20   May the brood of miscreants
31:2   against the brood of miscreants
MISDEEDS
59:4   they conceive misdeeds, they beget
MISERABLY
24:4   the world miserably perish;
MISERY
19:8   will be in misery.
MISLEAD
3:12   O my people, your leaders mislead
36:18   Beware, lest Hezekiah mislead you
MISLED
19:14   they have misled Egypt in all that she
MISSILE
22:17   as an athlete hurls a missile;
MIST
4:5   day and a mist glowing with
5:30   by an overhanging mist.
6:4   and a mist filled the temple
44:22   your sins like a cloud of mist.
60:2   and a thick mist the peoples,
MISTRESS
24:2   with mistress as with maid,
47:5   Mistress of Kingdoms.
47:7   You thought, I, the Eternal Mistress,
MIXED
65:11   and pour mixed wines for Fortune,
MIXING
5:22   and champions at mixing liquor!
MOAB
11:14   they will take Edom and Moab at
15:1   An oracle concerning Moab:
15:1   Moab shall be silenced;
15:1   Moab shall be destroyed.
15:2   they will wail in Moab over Nebo and
15:4   to summon the armed men of Moab,

MOAB *continued*
15:5 My heart will cry out for Moab;
15:8 shall encompass the land of Moab;
15:9 lions upon the fugitives of Moab
16:4 Let the exiles of Moab dwell with you;
16:6 We have heard of the glories of Moab,
16:7 and all have cause to bewail Moab:
16:11 will vibrate like a harp for Moab,
16:13 the Lord spoke hitherto about Moab.
25:10 under him Moab shall be trampled
MOABITES
16:7 For this shall the Moabites be made
16:12 For when the Moabites weary
MOAB'S
16:2 so are Moab's women at the fords of
16:14 of a lease, Moab's glory shall
MOAN
59:11 we moan incessantly like doves.
MOBILIZE
21:5 Mobilize, you commanders! Oil the
MOBS
29:5 your violent mobs like flying chaff.
54:15 who gather into mobs are not of me;
MOCK
37:17 has sent to mock the living God.
MOCKED
37:23 Whom have you mocked and
MOLDED
43:7 whom I have formed, molded and
MOLDS
45:9 clay were to say to him who molds it,
MOLES
2:20 to the moles and to the bats
MOMENT
28:4 the moment he has hold of it.
MOMENTARILY
54:7 I forsook you indeed momentarily,
MONEY
52:3 shall be redeemed without money.
55:1 You who have no money,
55:1 with no money and at no cost.
55:2 Why do you spend money on what is
MONSTER
27:1 Leviathan, that devious sea monster,
MONTH
1:13 convening meetings at the New Month
47:13 make predictions month by month,
MONTHLY
1:14 Your monthly and regular meetings
MONUMENT
19:19 of the land of Egypt and a monument
MOON
13:10 nor will the moon give its light.
24:23 The moon will blush and the sun be
30:26 The light of the moon
60:19 nor the brightness of the moon
60:20 nor your moon wane:

66:23 And New Moon after New Moon,
MORASS
10:18 turning them into a rotting morass.
MORE
1:13 Bring no more worthless offerings;
5:4 What more could have been done
13:12 men more rare than gold of Ophir.
14:20 never more be mentioned!
15:9 I impose more than this upon Dibon:
16:4 When oppressors are no more
17:14 before morning they shall be no more.
19:7 and blow away and be no more.
23:10 Tarshish: the harbor is no more.
23:12 He will say, You will frolic no more,
24:20 it collapses it shall rise no more.
25:2 mansions shall no more form cities,
26:14 They are dead, to live no more,
26:21 and no more conceal its slain.
27:4 I have no more anger toward her.
29:22 his face shall pale no more.
32:10 In little more than a year
37:31 shall once more take root below and
40:15 counting no more than dust on a
43:17 they lie down as one, to rise no more,
43:25 remembering your sins no more.
47:1 You shall no more be spoken of
51:22 you shall drink no more from the
52:1 No more shall the uncircumcised and
54:4 and remember no more
54:9 would no more flood the earth.
54:9 So I swear to have no more anger
60:18 tyranny shall no more be heard of in
60:20 Your sun shall set no more,
62:4 You shall no more be called the
62:8 I will no more let your grain be food
65:19 no more shall be heard there
65:20 No more shall there be infants alive
MORNING
5:11 as soon as they arise in the morning,
14:12 O morning star, son of the dawn!
17:11 the very morning you sow them,
17:14 before morning they shall be no more.
21:12 Morning comes, though it is still
28:19 morning after morning it shall sweep
33:2 arm from morning to morning,
37:36 arose in the morning, there lay all
38:13 Can I contain myself until morning,
50:4 Morning by morning he wakens my
MORTAL
30:32 they will be fought in mortal combat.
51:12 are you that you fear mortal man,
MORTALITY
38:11 among those dwelling in mortality.
MORTALS
31:8 a sword not of mortals shall devour
44:11 their fabricators are mere mortals.

MOSES
63:11 recalled the days of Moses of old:
63:12 at the right hand of Moses,
MOST
6:3 Most holy is the Lord of Hosts;
13:19 the most splendid of kingdoms,
14:14 make myself like the Most High!
17:6 or five in its most fruitful branch,
21:7 He must be most vigilant, fully alert.
22:24 bowls to the most common containers.
63:7 mercifully and most graciously
MOTH
50:9 the moth shall consume them,
51:8 For the moth shall consume them like
MOTHER
8:4 how to say, Father, or Mother,
50:1 of your crimes was your mother an
66:13 who is comforted by his mother
MOTHERS
49:23 queens your nursing mothers.
MOTHER'S
49:1 before I was in my mother's womb,
50:1 Where is your mother's bill of
MOTHS
51:8 moths shall devour them like wool.
MOUNT
4:5 Over the whole site of Mount Zion,
8:18 who dwells in Mount Zion.
10:12 Mount Zion and in Jerusalem,
14:13 the mount of assembly of the gods,
18:7 to the place . . . Mount Zion.
24:23 in Mount Zion and in Jerusalem,
28:21 as he did on Mount Perazim,
29:8 amass to fight against Mount Zion.
31:4 to wage war upon Mount Zion and
37:32 from Mount Zion a band of survivors.
MOUNTAIN
2:2 the mountain of the Lord's house
2:3 to the mountain of the Lord,
10:32 against the mountain of the Daughter
11:9 throughout my holy mountain,
13:2 the ensign on a barren mountain;
16:1 mountain of the Daughter of Zion.
25:6 In this mountain will the Lord of
25:7 In this mountain he will destroy
25:10 For in this mountain rests the hand
27:13 in the holy mountain at Jerusalem.
30:25 On all mountain heights and
30:29 their way to the mountain of the Lord,
40:4 every mountain and hill made low;
40:9 Scale the mountain heights,
49:11 All my mountain ranges I will
56:7 I will bring to my holy mountain
57:7 On a lofty mountain
57:13 an inheritance in my holy mountain.
65:11 and forget my holy mountain,
65:25 throughout my holy mountain, says

66:20 Jerusalem my holy mountain, says
MOUNTAINS
2:2 as the head of the mountains;
2:14 against all high mountains and
5:25 the mountains quake, and their
13:4 Hark! A tumult on the mountains,
14:25 them underfoot on my mountains;
17:13 like chaff on the mountains,
18:3 when it is lifted up in the mountains;
18:6 birds of prey of the mountains
22:5 crying in distress, To the mountains!
34:3 dissolve on the mountains,
37:24 conquered the highest mountains,
40:12 weighing mountains in scales,
41:15 you shall thresh mountains to dust
42:11 from the tops of the mountains.
42:15 I will lay waste mountains and hills
44:23 Burst into song, O mountains,
49:13 Burst into song, O mountains!
52:7 How comely upon the mountains
54:10 For the mountains shall be removed
55:12 the mountains and hills shall sing at
64:1 the mountains melting at thy
64:3 when the mountains quaked before
65:7 kindle sacrifice in the mountains,
65:9 out of Judah heirs of my mountains;
MOUNTAINTOP
30:17 left as a flagstaff on a mountaintop,
MOUNTED
37:29 which have mounted up to my ears,
MOUNTING
38:14 Like a mounting lark I twitter,
57:8 mounting your bed, you have laid it
MOUNTS
30:16 We will ride on swift mounts!
MOURN
16:9 Therefore I will mourn as Jazer
32:13 Mourn for all the amusement houses
57:18 and those who mourn for him,
61:2 to comfort all who mourn:
61:3 to endow those who mourn in Zion,
66:10 join in her celebration, all who mourn
MOURNING
29:2 there shall be mourning and sorrow
50:3 with the blackness of mourning;
60:20 when your days of mourning are
61:3 festal anointing in place of mourning,
MOURNS
16:9 I will mourn as Jazer mourns
MOUTH
1:20 By his mouth the Lord has spoken it.
5:14 opening her mouth insatiably;
6:7 Touching it to my mouth, he said,
9:12 will devour Israel with open mouth.
9:17 and every mouth utters profanities.
10:14 or opened its mouth to utter a peep.
11:4 the earth with the rod of his mouth

MOUTH *continued*

29:13 approach me with the mouth
30:2 but have not inquired at my mouth—
34:16 By his mouth he decreed it,
37:29 and my bit in your mouth
40:5 By his mouth the Lord has spoken it.
45:23 has issued from my mouth,
48:3 sooner did they issue from my mouth,
49:2 made my mouth like a sharp sword—
51:16 I will put my words in your mouth
53:7 and opened not his mouth—
53:7 he opened not his mouth.
53:9 and deceit was not in his mouth.
55:11 so is the word that leaves my mouth:
57:4 At whom do you open wide the mouth
58:14 By his mouth the Lord has spoken it.
59:21 mouth shall not depart from your
59:21 shall not depart from your mouth,
59:21 nor from the mouth of your offspring,
59:21 nor from the mouth of their offspring,
62:2 conferred by the mouth of the Lord.

MOUTHS

52:15 rulers shutting their mouths at him—

MOVE

18:2 a people perpetually on the move,
18:7 a nation perpetually on the move,
23:6 Move on to Tarshish lamenting,
30:11 Get out of the way; move aside,

MOVED

10:31 Madmenah has moved out of the way,
14:10 All alike were moved to say to you,

MOWN

33:12 mown down like thorns and set

MUCH

21:11 Watchman, how much of the night is
42:20 seeing much but not giving heed,

MUD

10:6 tread underfoot like mud in the
41:25 come upon dignitaries as on mud,
57:20 whose waters heave up mire and mud:

MUDDLED

34:11 be surveyed with muddled measure

MULES

66:20 in chariots and wagons, and on mules

MULTIPLIED

59:12 before thee have multiplied;

MULTITUDE

13:4 as of a vast multitude.
60:5 the multitude of the Sea shall resort

MURDER

33:15 Stop . . . ears at the mention of murder

MURDERED

14:20 and murdered your people.

MURDERERS

1:21 but now murderers.

MURMUR

38:14 like a dove I murmur.

MURMURED

29:24 and they who murmured accept

MUSHROOMING

9:18 in mushrooming clouds of smoke.

MUSIC

14:11 along with the music of your lyres.
38:20 and we will perform music

MUSTER

31:4 shepherds muster in full force

MUTTER

8:19 who huddle together and mutter,

MYRIAD

60:6 A myriad of camels shall cover your

MYRTLE

55:13 in place of nettles, the myrtle.

MYRTLES

41:19 myrtles and oleasters in the

MYSTICS

2:6 mystics from the East

NAIL

22:23 fasten him as a nail in the sure place
22:25 nail that was fastened in a sure place

NAKED

20:2 naked and barefoot.
20:3 naked and barefoot for three
20:4 and old, naked and barefoot,

NAKEDNESS

47:3 your nakedness shall be exposed
57:8 your hand on their nakedness.

NAME

4:1 only let us be called by your name—
7:14 and name him Immanuel (God is with
8:3 Name him Maher-Shalal-Hash-Baz
12:4 thanks to the Lord; invoke his name.
12:4 commemorate his exalted name.
14:22 I will cut off Babylon's name and
18:7 to the place of the name of the Lord
24:15 to the name of the Lord, the God of
25:1 extol thee by praising thy name.
26:8 desire is to contemplate thy name.
26:13 but thee alone we recall by name.
29:23 work of my hands, hallowing my name
40:26 calling each one by name.
41:25 who calls on my name,
42:8 I am the Lord; that is my name.
43:1 I have called you by name; you are
43:7 all who are called by my name,
44:5 and another name himself Jacob.
44:5 and adopt the name Israel.
45:3 God of Israel, who calls you by name.
45:4 Israel my chosen, I call you by name
47:4 whose name is the Lord of Hosts.
48:1 take oaths in the name of the Lord
48:2 whose name is the Lord of Hosts:
48:11 that my name be not dishonored,
49:1 he mentioned me by name.
50:10 trusts in the name of the Lord and

51:15	whose name is the Lord of Hosts,	10:7	and to exterminate nations not a few.
52:5	and my name is constantly abused all	10:13	done away with the borders of nations
52:6	my people come to know my name;	11:10	shall be sought by the nations,
54:5	whose name is the Lord of Hosts;	11:12	raise the ensign to the nations
56:5	I will give a handclasp and a name	12:4	known his deeds among the nations;
56:5	endow them with an everlasting name	13:4	as of nations assembling:
56:6	who love the name of the Lord,	14:2	The nations will take them
57:15	abides forever, whose name is sacred:	14:6	struck down the nations in anger,
62:2	you shall be called by a new name	14:9	causing all who had ruled nations
63:12	an everlasting name for himself	14:12	You who commanded the nations
63:16	Redeemer from Eternity is thy name.	14:18	All rulers of nations lie in state,
63:19	have not been known by thy name.	14:26	is the hand upraised over all nations.
64:7	Yet none calls upon thy name,	16:8	the ruling nations will smite Sibmah
65:1	nation that did not invoke my name.	17:12	tumultuous nations, in commotion
65:15	Your name shall be left	17:13	Nations may roar like the roaring of
65:15	he will call by a different name.	23:3	she became the merchant of nations.
66:5	and exclude you because of my name,	24:13	in the earth among the nations
66:22	your offspring and name endure.	25:3	a community of tyrannous nations

NAMED

45:4	I named you . . . you knew me not.	25:7	the shroud that shrouds all nations,
48:1	you who are named Israel—	29:7	And the nations amassed to fight

NAME'S

48:9	For my own name's sake I have	29:8	So shall be all the nations
		30:28	He comes to sift the nations

NAPHTALI

9:1	of Zebulon and Naphtali, but at	33:3	at thine uprising the nations
		33:12	Whole nations have been burned like

NARROW

28:20	the covering too narrow to wrap	34:1	Come near, you nations, and hear!

NATION

1:4	Alas, a nation astray,	34:2	The Lord's rage is upon all nations,
2:4	nation will not lift the sword against	36:18	nations able to save their lands out of
2:4	not lift the sword against nation,	37:12	Did the gods of the nations my
7:8	be shattered as a nation.	40:15	The nations are but drops from a
9:3	Thou hast enlarged the nation	40:17	Before him all nations are as nothing;
10:6	him against a godless nation,	41:2	Who has delivered nations to him
14:32	then be told the envoys of the nation?	42:1	dispense justice to the nations.
18:2	a nation dreaded far and wide,	42:6	a light to the nations,
18:7	from a nation dreaded far and wide,	43:9	When all nations unitedly assembled,
18:7	from a nation perpetually on the	45:1	to subdue nations before him,
26:2	Open the gates to let in the nation	45:20	all you fugitives of the nations.
26:15	Thou hast enlarged the nation, O	49:6	to you to be a light to the nations,
33:19	a nation of incomprehensible speech,	49:22	I will lift up my hand to the nations,
49:7	who is abhorred by his nation,	52:10*	in the eyes of all nations,
51:4	give heed to me, O my nation:	52:15	So shall he yet astound many nations,
55:5	You will summon a nation that you	54:3	shall dispossess the nations
55:5	a nation that did not know you will	55:4	him a witness to the nations
58:2	nation practicing righteousness	56:7	as a house of prayer for all nations.
60:22	the youngest a mighty nation.	60:3	Nations will come to your light,
60:12	And the nation or kingdom	60:5	a host of nations shall enter you.
65:1	nation that did not invoke my name.	60:11	that a host of nations may be brought
66:8	and a nation be born at once?	60:12	such nations shall be utterly ruined.

NATIONS

2:2	and all nations will flow to it.	60:16	You will suck the milk of the nations,
2:4	He will judge between the nations	60:22	the youngest a mighty nations.
3:13	he has arisen to judge the nations.	61:6	feed on the wealth of the nations
5:26	He raises an ensign to distant nations	61:9	shall be renowned among the nations,
8:9	Though nations form pacts,	61:11	in the presence of all nations.
9:1	Jordan in Galilee of the nations.	62:2	The nations shall behold your
		62:10	raise the ensign to the nations!
		63:3	of the nations no one was with me.
		63:6	I trod nations underfoot in my anger;
		64:2	the nations trembling at thy presence

NATIONS *continued*
66:12 the bounty of the nations like a
66:18 For I will come to gather all nations
66:19 to the nations that had not heard the
66:19 declare my glory among the nations
66:20 from throughout the nations to
NATIVE
 1:7 your native soil is devoured by aliens
NEAR
11:8 infant will play near the adder's den,
13:6 the day of the Lord is near;
13:22 Her time draws near;
33:13 you who are near, be apprised of my
34:1 Come near, you nations, and hear!
45:20 draw near, all you fugitives of the
46:13 I have brought near my righteousness;
48:16 Come near me and hear this:
50:8 He who vindicates me is near me.
55:6 call upon him while he is near.
57:19 and to those who are near,
65:5 don't come near me; I am holier than
NEARER
58:2 desiring to draw nearer to God:
NEBAIOTH
60:7 the rams of Nebaioth will serve you;
NEBO
15:2 they will wail in Moab over Nebo and
46:1 Bel slumps down, Nebo is stooped
NECK
 8:8 passing through, reach the very neck;
10:27 their yoke removed from your neck:
30:28 that severs at the neck.
48:4 your neck was an iron sinew, your
52:2 from the bands around your neck,
66:3 as one who breaks a dog's neck;
NEEDS
58:10 satisfy the needs of the oppressed,
58:11 he will satisfy your needs in the
NEEDY
 3:14 your houses by depriving the needy.
10:2 denying justice to the needy,
14:30 and the needy recline in safety.
25:4 a shelter for the needy in distress.
32:7 to denounce the needy.
41:17 the poor and needy require water,
NEGEB
30:6 oracle concerning the Beasts of Negeb
NEGLECT
58:7 and not to neglect your own kin?
NEIGHBOR
 3:5 every man his neighbor.
19:2 and neighbor against neighbor,
NEIGHBORHOODS
32:18 in safe neighborhoods, in comfortable
NEITHER
 3:7 There is neither food nor clothing in
 5:6 it shall neither be pruned nor hoed,

19:15 neither head nor tail, palm top or
42:4 Neither shall he himself grow dim or
51:14 neither shall he want for food.
NEST
10:14 the wealth of peoples like a nest,
11:8 over the viper's nest.
16:2 birds forced out of the nest,
31:5 As birds hover over [the nest],
34:15 shall the hawk owl nest and lay eggs,
NET
51:20 taken in a net like bison.
NETS
19:8 those who cast nets on water
NETTLES
55:13 in place of nettles, the myrtle.
NEVER
13:20 Never shall it be reinhabited;
14:20 never more be mentioned!
33:20 whose stakes shall never be uprooted
41:3 by paths his feet have never trod.
43:18 Never mind the prophecies of bygone
51:6 my righteousness shall never fail.
54:9 never again to rebuke you.
54:10 charity toward you shall never be
62:12 a city never deserted.
63:19 whom thou hast never ruled
64:4 Never has it been heard or perceived
NEVERTHELESS
10:7 Nevertheless, it shall not seem so to
64:8 Nevertheless, thou art our Father, O
NEW
 1:13 convening meetings at the New Month
18:5 remove the new branches by slashing.
24:7 The new wine withers on languishing
41:15 of new design, full of spikes:
42:9 but new things I yet foretell.
42:10 Sing to the Lord a new song;
43:19 See, I do a new thing; it is now
48:6 I announce to you new things,
62:2 you shall be called by a new name
62:8 drink the new wine you have toiled
65:17 See, I create new heavens and a new
66:22 as the new heavens and the new earth
66:23 And New Moon after New Moon,
NEWBORN
13:18 show no mercy to the newborn;
NEWNESS
38:16 comes a newness of life,
NEWS
23:5 When the news of Tyre reaches Egypt,
40:9 O Jerusalem, messenger of good news.
66:19 news concerning me, nor seen my
NIGHT
 4:5 fire by night: above all that
 5:11 who linger at night parties, inflamed
15:1 When in one night Ar is devastated,
15:1 when in one night Kir is razed,

16:3   at high noon as though it were night!
21:8   night after night I have stood guard.
21:11   Watchman, what remains of the night?
21:11   how much of the night is left?
21:12   though it is still night.
26:9   My soul yearns for thee in the night;
27:3   watch over it night and day,
28:19   by day and by night it shall seize
29:7   shall be as a dream in the night.
30:29   as on the night when a festival
34:10   Night and day it shall not be
34:14   There too shall the night owl find
38:13   Surely, as night has followed day,
59:10   at noon as in the dark of night;
60:11   they shall not be shut day or night,
60:19   your illumination at night:
62:6   who shall not be silent day or night.
NIGHTFALL
21:4   the nightfall I longed for has become
NIGHTS
65:4   spend nights in hideouts,
NILE
23:3   Shihor, the harvest of the Nile,
23:10   Overflow your land like the Nile,
NIMRIM
15:6   waters of Nimrim shall be desolate;
NINEVEH
37:37   to Nineveh, where he dwelt.
NISROCH
37:38   temple of Nisroch his god, his sons
NOAH
54:9   This is to me as in the days of Noah,
54:9   when I swore that the water of Noah
NOB
10:32   same day he will but pause at Nob
NOBLE
32:5   shall no longer be regarded as noble
32:8   But the noble are of noble intent,
NOBLES
34:12   Shall they summon its nobles when it
NOISE
66:6   from the city, a noise from the
NOMADS
13:20   Nomads will not pitch their tents
NONE
1:31   and there shall be none to extinguish.
5:29   and none comes to the rescue.
22:22   when he opens none shall shut,
22:22   when he shuts none shall open.
24:10   shuttered, that none may enter.
30:15   But you would have none of it.
33:1   whom none have been treacherous:
33:24*   None who reside there shall say,
34:10   endless ages none shall traverse it.
34:16   None is unaccounted for, not one
41:17   and there is none,
42:22   a spoil, yet none demands restitution.

43:13   from my hand none can deliver;
45:5   I am the Lord, there is none other;
45:6   Lord, and that there is none other.
45:18   I am the Lord, there is none other.
45:22   I am God, there is none other.
46:9   I am God, there is none other.
47:10   and there is none besides me!
47:15   none is there to save you.
51:18   There was none to guide her home
51:18   none to take her by the hand of all
59:4   None calls for righteousness;
59:8   none who treads them knows peace.
59:11   We expect justice when there is none;
60:15   with none passing through your
63:5   but none would lend help;
64:7   Yet none calls upon thy name,
66:4   when I spoke, none gave heed.
NONSENSE
44:25   and makes nonsense of their
NOON
16:3   Overshadow us at high noon as though
59:10   We stumble at noon as in the dark of
NOONDAY
58:10   twilight become as the noonday.
NOPH
19:13   the officials of Noph deluded;
NORTH
14:31   From the North shall come pillars of
41:25   I have raised up one from the north
43:6   I will say to the north, Give up!
NORTHWEST
49:12   from afar, these, from the northwest,
NOSE
37:29   I will put my ring in your nose
NOSTRILS
2:22   in whose nostrils is but breath!
65:5   Such are a smoke to my nostrils,
NOTABLES
9:15   the elders or notables are the head,
NOTHING
1:6   there is nothing sound,
10:4   There shall nothing remain
19:15   there shall be nothing the Egyptians
29:21   who for nothing turn away him who is
30:5   a people who will avail them nothing;
36:21   remained silent, replying nothing,
39:2   nothing in his palace or in all his
39:4   There is nothing in my treasuries
39:6   Nothing shall be left, says the Lord.
40:17   Before him all nations are as nothing;
41:12   shall be reduced to nothing.
41:24   your works amount to nothing.
42:20   with open ears hearing nothing?
44:9   things they cherish profit nothing.
45:6   that without me there is nothing,
46:9   I am divine; nothing resembles me.
47:8   and other than me there is nothing;

NOTHING *continued*
49:4   I have spent my strength for nothing
52:4   Assyrians subjected them for nothing
52:11 touch nothing defiled as you leave
NOTICE
53:2   that we should notice him;
58:3   when we fast, do you not notice?
NOTION
37:7   will give him a notion to return home
NOTORIOUS
10:12 Assyria for his notorious
NOTWITHSTANDING
47:9   notwithstanding your many magical
NOUGHT
 8:10 they shall come to nought;
24:5   set at nought the ancient covenant.
29:20 shall come to nought and scorners
40:23 him who brings potentates to nought
41:11 adversaries shall come to nought, and
NOURISH
58:14 and nourish you with the heritage of
NULL
40:23 authorities of the world null and void
NUMBER
21:17 And the number of valiant archers
40:26 brings forth their hosts by number,
48:19 have been as the sands in number,
NUMBERED
53:12 and was numbered with criminals—
NUMBERS
31:1   their trust in immense numbers
31:4   nor daunted by their numbers,
NURSE
66:11 From now on nurse contentedly
66:12 Then shall you nurse and be carried
NURSING
49:23 queens your nursing mothers.
OAK
 1:30 like an oak whose leaves wither,
 6:13 But like the terebinth or the oak
OAKS
 1:29 be ashamed of the oaks you cherished
 2:13 and against all the oaks of Bashan,
44:14 he must select holms and oaks
57:5   who burn with lust among the oaks,
61:3   shall be called oaks of righteousness
OATH
14:24 The Lord of Hosts made an oath,
OATHS
48:1   take oaths in the name of the Lord
65:16 them who swear oaths in the earth
OBEY
 1:19 If you are willing and obey,
11:14 and the Ammonites will obey them.
30:9   children unwilling to obey the law of
42:23 and be mindful and obey?
42:24 or obey his law.

OBEYED
48:18 Had you but obeyed my
OBLATIONS
43:23 not burdened you with oblations
OBLITERATED
48:19 and obliterated from my presence.
OBSCURED
13:10 the sun rises, it shall be obscured;
40:27 Our path has become obscured from
OBSCURITY
47:5   Sit speechless; retire into obscurity,
OBSERVATORIES
23:13 Assyrians who set up observatories,
OBSERVE
47:13 who observe the stars
56:1   Observe justice and perform
OBSTACLES
45:2   before you and level all obstacles;
57:14 remove the obstacles from the path of
OBSTRUCTING
 8:14 stumbling block or obstructing rock,
OBTAIN
29:19 lowly shall obtain an increase of joy
51:11 let them obtain joy and gladness,
OCCASION
45:7   I occasion peace and cause calamity.
OCCUPYING
58:13 from occupying yourselves with your
OCCUR
 7:7   It shall not occur or transpire.
OCEAN
51:10 and made of ocean depths a way
OCEANS
11:9   as the oceans are overspread with
OFFENDERS
46:8   take it to heart, you offenders.
OFFENSES
43:25 who blot out your offenses,
44:22 I have removed your offenses like a
59:12 Our offenses are evident; we perceive
OFFENSIVE
58:9   pointing finger and offensive speech,
OFFER
37:4   your God has heard, were you to offer
41:28 not one who could offer counsel,
57:7   there you ascend to offer sacrifices.
OFFERED
50:6   I offered my back to smiters,
OFFERING
53:10 he made his life an offering for guilt,
66:3   whoever presents a grain offering
OFFERINGS
 1:11 I have had my fill of offerings of rams
 1:13 Bring no more worthless offerings;
19:21 offerings, and make vows
43:23 offerings from your flocks
56:7   Their offerings and sacrifices

57:6   out libations and make offerings.
60:7   they shall be accepted as offerings on
66:20 as offerings to the Lord—on horses,
66:20 brought offerings in pure vessels
OFFICE
22:19 I will thrust you out of office;
OFFICER
3:3   the officer and dignitary,
OFFICERS
31:9   and their officers shrink from the
OFFICIALS
19:13 the officials of Noph deluded;
30:4   For all their officials at Zoan,
OFFSPRING
1:4   the offspring of wrongdoers,
6:13   the holy offspring be what is left
9:20   eat the flesh of their own offspring.
14:22 its offspring and descendants, says
14:29 and his offspring shall be a fiery
39:7   offspring and descendants, they shall
41:8   offspring of Abraham my beloved
43:5   bring your offspring from the east
44:3   pour out my Spirit on your offspring,
45:19 I do not ask Jacob's offspring
45:25 the Lord shall all Israel's offspring
48:19 your offspring would have been as the
53:10 he might see his offspring and
54:3   your offspring shall dispossess the
57:3   offspring of adulterer and harlot!
59:21 nor from the mouth of your offspring,
59:21 nor from the mouth of their offspring,
61:9   Their offspring shall be renowned
65:9   I will extract offspring out of Jacob,
66:22 so shall your offspring and name
OIL
21:5   Oil the armor!
57:9   You bathe with oil for the king
OILS
39:2   the spices and fragrant oils, and his
OINTMENT
1:6   nor soothed with ointment.
OLD
20:4   and old, naked and barefoot,
22:11 for the water from the Old Reservoir,
25:1   things planned of old.
30:33 For Tophet has been prepared of Old,
37:26 how in days of old I planned it?
44:7   appointing people from old as types
44:8   made it known to you from of old?
45:21 Who foretold these things of old,
46:4   Even to your old age, I am present;
46:9   the prophecies of the events of old!
51:9   as in generations of old.
61:4   raise up the old waste places;
63:9   all the days of old.
63:11 recalled the days of Moses of old:
64:3   thy descent of old,

65:20 young shall be a hundred years old,
OLEASTERS
41:19 and oleasters in the wilderness;
OLIVE
17:6   or when an olive tree is beaten,
24:13 as when an olive tree is beaten,
OMNIPOTENT
30:27 Lord Omnipotent coming from afar!
59:19 men will fear the Lord Omnipotent,
60:9   to the Lord Omnipotent, your God,
ONSLAUGHTS
25:5   quell the onslaughts of the heathen:
OPEN
9:12   will devour Israel with open mouth.
22:18 into an open country.
22:22 when he shuts none shall open.
26:2   Open the gates to let in the nation
30:26 and heals their open wound.
37:17 give ear and hear; O Lord, open
41:18 I will open up streams in barren hill
42:7   to open eyes that are blind,
42:20 with open ears hearing nothing?
48:8   your ears have not been open to them.
57:4   whom do you open wide the mouth
57:8   your bed, you have laid it wide open,
60:11 Your gates shall always remain open;
OPENED
10:14 or opened its mouth to utter a peep.
24:18 when the windows on high are opened
35:5   shall the eyes of the blind be opened
50:5   my Lord the Lord has opened my ear,
53:7   and opened not his mouth—
53:7   he opened not his mouth.
OPENING
5:14   opening her mouth insatiably;
45:1   opening doors ahead of him,
61:1   the opening of the eyes to the bound,
OPENLY
15:3   They will wear sackcloth openly;
OPENS
22:22 when he opens none shall shut,
OPHIR
13:12 men more rare than gold of Ophir.
OPPRESS
3:5   People will oppress one another,
OPPRESSED
1:17   stand up for the oppressed;
58:6   to set the oppressed at liberty
58:10 satisfy the needs of the oppressed,
OPPRESSING
3:15   you mean by oppressing my people,
OPPRESSION
14:6   by relentless oppression.
54:14 you will be far from oppression
OPPRESSIVE
10:1   who draft oppressive legislation—
49:10 nor be smitten by oppressive heat or

OPPRESSOR
51:13 there to the wrath of the oppressor?
OPPRESSORS
14:2 and rule over their oppressors.
16:4 When oppressors are no more
19:20 the oppressors, he will send
49:26 I will feed your oppressors with their
60:17 and righteousness your oppressors:
OPPRESSOR'S
51:13 of the oppressor's rage
OPULENT
28:1 on the heads of the opulent
28:4 on the heads of the opulent,
ORACLE
13:1 An oracle concerning Babylon,
14:28 King Ahaz died, came this oracle:
15:1 An oracle concerning Moab:
17:1 An oracle concerning Damascus:
19:1 An oracle concerning Egypt:
21:1 An oracle concerning the Wilderness
21:11 An oracle concerning Dumah:
21:13 An oracle concerning those in
22:1 An oracle concerning the Arena of
23:1 An oracle concerning Tyre:
30:6 An oracle concerning the Beasts of
ORATORS
3:3 skilled craftsmen, and orators.
ORCHARDS
16:10 will be gone from the orchards;
ORDAINED
37:26 how I ordained this thing long ago,
ORDEAL
66:7 before her ordeal overtakes her, she
ORDER
38:1 Put your house in order. You will
ORDERS
23:11 he will give orders concerning the
ORDINANCES
24:5 changed the ordinances,
26:8 very passage of thine ordinances
26:9 thine ordinances are on the earth.
58:2 of me concerning correct ordinances,
ORDINARY
22:24 from ordinary bowls to the most
OREB
10:26 at the rock of Oreb.
ORGANIZED
45:18 who made it secure and organized it,
ORIGIN
23:7 your festive city of ancient origin,
ORIGINATE
28:29 These things originate with the Lord
ORNAMENTS
3:18 head ornaments and crescents,
OSTRACIZED
43:28 I gave Jacob to be ostracized, Israel to

OTHER
26:13 our God, lords other than thou
45:5 I am the Lord, there is none other;
45:6 the Lord, and that there is none other
45:14 God is in you; no other gods exist!
45:18 I am the Lord, there is none other.
45:22 I am God, there is none other.
46:9 I am God, there is none other.
47:8 and other than me there is nothing;
48:11 my glory, which I give to no other.
OTHERS
44:5 Yet others will inscribe on their arm,
56:8 I will gather others to those already
57:8 exposed yourself to others than me:
65:22 not build so that others may dwell,
65:22 or plant so that others may eat.
OURSELVES
7:6 We will take it for ourselves by force
19:11 We ourselves are as wise as the first
20:6 How shall we ourselves escape?
OUTBURST
13:9 as a cruel outburst of anger and
16:6 of its outburst of false propaganda.
OUTBURSTS
16:6 of its outbursts of false propaganda.
OUTCAST
50:1 crimes was your mother an outcast.
OUTCASTS
27:13 were outcasts in the land of
56:8 who gathers up the outcasts of Israel:
OUTCRY
5:7 but there was an outcry.
OUTER
8:22 into outer darkness.
OUTLAST
65:22 my chosen ones shall outlast the work
OUTLINE
44:13 by chiselling to the outline of the
OUTNUMBER
54:1 shall outnumber those of the
OUTPOURINGS
41:29 their outpourings are but wind and
OUTSIDE
24:11 Outside is heard the clamor for
OUTSPREAD
8:8 his outspread wings will span
OVERCOME
28:1 the opulent overcome with wine.
OVERFLOW
8:7 and overflow all his banks.
10:22 it shall overflow with righteousness.
13:21 its buildings overflow with weasels;
23:10 Overflow your land like the Nile,
45:8 skies overflow with righteousness.
OVERGROW
5:6 briars and thorns shall overgrow it.
34:13 For thorns shall overgrow its palaces,

OVERGROWN
32:13 shall be overgrown with briars and
OVERHANGING
5:30 by an overhanging mist.
OVERHEAD
6:2 Seraphs stood by him overhead,
OVERLAID
40:19 overlaid by the smith with gold,
OVERLOOKED
40:27 our cause is overlooked by our God?
OVERNIGHT
10:29 stopping overnight at Geba.
OVERPOWER
7:1 against it, but could not overpower it:
OVERRUN
28:18 you shall be overrun by it.
OVERSEER
22:15 overseer of the palace.
36:3 overseer of the palace,
36:22 the son Hilkiah, overseer of
37:2 And he sent Eliakim the overseer of
OVERSHADOW
16:3 Overshadow us at high noon
OVERSPREAD
11:9 oceans are overspread with waters.
OVERTAKE
47:9 overtake you, both in one day.
47:11 Catastrophe shall overtake you,
OVERTAKES
3:11 when calamity overtakes them :
10:3 when the holocaust overtakes you
18:4 when the searing heat overtakes the
66:7 before her ordeal overtakes her, she
OVERTHREW
13:19 as God overthrew Sodom and
OVERTHROWN
3:25 your might overthrown in war.
OVERWHELMED
43:2 you shall not be overwhelmed.
OWL
34:14 shall the night owl find repose
34:15 There shall the hawk owl nest and lay
OWLS
34:11 and owls and ravens inhabit it.
OWNER
1:3 The ox knows its owner,
OX
1:3 The ox knows its owner,
11:7 the lion will eat straw like the ox.
65:25 the lion will eat straw like the ox;
66:3 But whoever slaughters an ox
OXEN
30:24 and the oxen and asses that till the
32:20 letting oxen and asses range free.
PACKS
38:21* packs and apply them to the swelling

PACTS
8:9 Though nations form pacts,
PAGAN
10:10 I could do this to the pagan states,
PAID
3:11 they shall be paid back
65:6 till I have paid back into their bosom
PAIN
17:11 a day of diseases and incurable pain.
PAINTING
3:16 and put on airs, painting their eyes,
PAIR
7:21 alive a young cow and a pair of sheep.
PALACE
22:15 overseer of the palace.
36:3 overseer of the palace,
36:22 the palace, Shebna the secretary, and
37:2 the palace, Shebna the secretary,
39:2 nothing in his palace or in all his
39:4 What did they see in your palace?
39:4 in my palace. There is nothing in my
39:6 in your palace, and all that your
39:7 the palace of the king of Babylon.
PALACES
13:22 Jackals will cry out from its palaces,
32:14 for the palaces shall lie abandoned,
34:13 For thorns shall overgrow its palaces,
PALE
29:22 his face shall pale no more.
PALM
9:14 head and tail, palm top and reed,
19:15 neither head nor tail, palm top or
36:6 and pierces the palm of any man
62:3 royal diadem in the palm of your God
PALMS
49:16 See, I have engraved you on my palms
59:3 For your palms are defiled with
PAMPERED
47:8 therefore hear this, O pampered lady,
PANGS
26:17 cries out from her pangs during
PANORAMIC
32:14 High rises and panoramic resorts
PARALYZED
21:4 mind reels, I am paralyzed with fear;
PARCHED
41:17 and their tongue becomes parched
41:18 parched lands into fountains of
50:2 become parched for lack of water
PARDONS
55:7 to our God, who graciously pardons.
PARKS
1:29 and blush for the parks you were
65:3 sacrificing in parks, making smoke
66:17 cultists who fornicate in the parks,
PART
33:23* the lame take part in the plunder.

PART *continued*
44:19 Part of this I burned in the fire;
PARTAKE
57:19 who partake of the fruit of the lips:
PARTIES
5:11 who linger at night parties, inflamed
PARTS
3:17 Lord will expose their private parts.
PARTY
19:24 third party to Egypt and to Assyria,
PASS
5:19 soon come to pass, and we will know!
10:29 They cross over the pass,
11:13 Ephraim's jealousy shall pass away
28:20 Then shall come to pass the
33:21 or majestic fleets pass by.
37:26 Now I have brought it to pass.
38:19 they pass on the knowledge of thy
42:9 indeed came to pass,
43:9 events that have come to pass?
45:14 shall pass on to you and
46:11 What I have spoken, I bring to pass:
48:16 at their coming to pass, I have been
51:10 by which the redeemed might pass?
62:10 Pass on, go through gates;
PASSAGE
26:8 the very passage of thine ordinances
PASSERS-BY
51:23 a mere thoroughfare to passers-by.
PASSES
10:28 advances on Aiath, passes through
PASSING
8:8 passing through, reach the very neck;
31:5 by passing over it, preserve it.
41:3 them to flight, passing on unhindered
60:15 with none passing through your
PASSIONS
42:13 his passions aroused like a fighter;
PAST
9:1 the past he humbled the land
18:5 when the time of flowering is past
26:20 until the wrath is past.
43:18 do not dwell on things of the past.
43:26 Recount for me the past;
48:3 prophecies of the events of the past
65:16 troubles of the past shall be forgotten
PASTURE
5:17 his sheep feed in their pasture,
11:6 will lead them to pasture.
14:30 The elect poor shall have pasture,
30:23 in ample pasture lands,
49:9 and find pasture on all barren
61:5 Aliens will tend and pasture your
65:10 shall become pasture for flocks,
PASTURES
40:11 Like a shepherd he pastures his

PATH
26:7 The path of the righteous is straight;
30:11 move aside, off the path!
40:14 instructed in the path of discretion,
40:27 Our path has become obscured from
43:16 a path through the mighty waters,
57:14 obstacles from the path of my people!
PATHROS
11:11 Egypt, Pathros, Cush, Elam, Shinar,
PATHS
2:3 that we may follow in his paths.
41:3 by paths his feet have never trod.
42:16 and guide them in paths unfamiliar;
59:8 They have made crooked their paths;
PATHWAY
11:16 shall be a pathway out of Assyria
PATIENCE
7:13 for you to try the patience of men?
7:13 you also try the patience of my God?
PAUSE
10:32 same day he will but pause at Nob
PAVE
40:3 pave a straight highway for our God:
57:14 It will be said: Excavate, pave a road!
62:10 Excavate, pave a highway cleared of
PAVEST
26:7 thou pavest an undeviating course for
PAY
29:13 and pay me homage with their lips,
34:1 Pay attention, you peoples!
43:23 or pay me homage by sacrificial
55:3 pay heed, that your souls may live!
PAYING
66:6 paying his enemies what is due them.
PAYMENT
65:7 the payment that has accrued.
PEACE
9:6 a Father for Ever, a Prince of Peace—
9:7 and peace have no end;
14:7 whole earth is at rest and at peace;
26:3 thou preservest in perfect peace,
26:12 thou bringest about our peace;
27:5 and make peace with me,
32:17 the effect of justice shall be peace,
33:7 the champions of peace weep bitterly.
33:20 the abode of peace—an immovable
36:16 the king of Assyria: Make peace with
39:8 be peace and loyalty during my reign.
45:7 I occasion peace and cause calamity.
48:18 your peace would have been as a
48:22 But there is no peace, says the Lord,
52:7 the messenger announcing peace,
53:5 the price of our peace he incurred,
54:10 nor my covenant of peace be shaken,
54:13 shall be the peace of your posterity.
55:12 in joy and be led back in peace;
57:2 walk uprightly shall attain to peace,

57:19 Peace, well-being, to those far off
57:21 there is no peace, says my God, for
59:8 none who treads them knows peace.
60:17 I will make peace your rulers
66:12 I will extend peace to her like a
PEACEFUL
32:18 shall dwell in peaceful settlements,
PEEP
10:14 or opened its mouth to utter a peep.
PEKAH
7:1 Rezin king of Aram and Pekah son of
PENDANTS
3:19 the pendants, chains and scarves,
PEOPLE
1:3 my people are insensible.
1:4 a people weighed down by sin,
1:10 you people of Gomorrah!
2:6 O Lord, hast forsaken thy people,
3:5 People will oppress one another,
3:7 make me a leader of the people.
3:12 As for my people, babes subject them;
3:12 O my people, your leaders mislead
3:14 to trial the elders of his people
3:15 you mean by oppressing my people,
5:7 and the people of Judah his cherished
5:13 Therefore are my people exiled
5:25 against his people:
6:5 and I live among a people of unclean
6:9 Go, and say to these people,
6:10 Make the heart of these people grow
6:13 And while yet a tenth of the people
7:2 his people were shaken,
7:17 and your people and your
8:6 Because these people have rejected
8:11 these people. For he said,
8:12 a conspiracy all that these people
8:19 say to them, Should not a people
9:2 The people walking in darkness
9:9 And the entire people—
9:13 But the people do not turn back
9:16 The leaders of these people have
9:19 and people are but fuel for the fire.
10:2 depriving the poor of my people of
10:6 appoint him over the people
10:22 For though your people, O Israel,
10:24 O my people who inhabit Zion,
11:11 to reclaim the remnant of his people—
11:16 for the remnant of his people who
13:14 each will return to his own people
14:20 and murdered your people.
14:32 let his longsuffering people find
18:2 Go to a people perpetually on the
18:2 a people continually infringing,
18:7 a people continually infringing,
19:25 saying, Blessed by Egypt my people,
22:4 ruin of the Daughter of my People.
23:13 the people who founded Tyre for

24:2 it shall be with priest as with people,
25:8 remove the reproach of his people
26:11 thy zeal for thy people
26:20 Come, O my people, enter your
27:11 They are not a discerning people.
28:5 to the remnant of his people:
28:11 must he speak to these people,
28:14 who preside over these people in
29:13 my Lord says, Because these people
29:14 I shall again astound these people
30:5 with a people who will avail them
30:6 to a people who cannot profit them.
30:9 They are a rebellious people, sons
30:19 O people of Zion, O inhabitants of
30:26 the fracture of his people
32:18 My people shall dwell in peaceful
33:19 The insolent people are not to be
33:24* the people who inhabit it
34:5 on the people I have sentenced to
36:11 ears of the people who are on the
40:1 Comfort and give solace to my people,
40:7 the people themselves are but
42:5 the breath of life to the people upon
42:6 to be a covenant for the people,
42:22 Instead, they are a people plundered
43:8 Let go the people who are blind, yet
43:20 I may give drink to my chosen people,
43:21 the people I formed for myself
44:7 in appointing a people from of old as
45:14 the Sabeans, a people tall in stature.
47:6 I was provoked by my people,
49:8 to be a covenant of the people,
49:13 The Lord is comforting his people,
51:4 Listen to me, my people;
51:7 O people in whose heart is my law:
51:16 I may say to Zion, You are my people
51:22 who defends the cause of his people:
52:4 At first my people went down to
52:5 My people are taken over without
52:6 my people come to know my name;
52:9 the Lord has comforted his people;
53:8 for the crime of my people,
56:3 surely exclude me from his people.
57:14 obstacles from the path of my people!
58:1 Declare to my people their
60:21 Your entire people shall be righteous;
62:10 prepare the way for the people!
62:12 They shall be called the holy people,
63:8 Surely they are my people,
63:11 Then his people recalled the days of
63:14 So thou didst lead thy people, O
63:18 a little while had thy people
64:9 consider that we are all thy people!
65:2 all the day to a defiant people,
65:3 a people who constantly provoke me
65:10 for the herds of my people who seek
65:18 and its people a joy.

PEOPLE *continued*
65:19   rejoice in my people;
65:22   The lifetime of my people shall be as
66:24   corpses of the people who
PEOPLES
  2:3   Many peoples shall go, saying,
  2:4   and arbitrate for many peoples,
10:14   the wealth of peoples like a nest,
11:10   stands for an ensign to the peoples,
14:6   who subdued peoples in his wrath
17:12   to the many peoples in an uproar,
25:3   For this will powerful peoples revere
25:6   a sumptuous feast for all peoples,
25:7   the veil that veils all peoples,
30:28   he will try the peoples.
33:3   The peoples fled from thy thunderous
34:1   Pay attention, you peoples!
37:18   destroyed all peoples and their
41:1   become still, you peoples!
43:4   peoples in exchange for your life.
43:9   when the peoples were gathered
49:1   O isles; listen, you distant peoples:
49:22   raise my ensign to the peoples;
51:4   shall be a light to the peoples.
51:5   my arms shall judge the peoples—
55:4   a prince and lawgiver of the peoples.
60:2   and a thick mist the peoples,
61:9   posterity in the midst of the peoples;
PEOPLE'S
32:13   For my people's land
PERAZIM
28:21   as he did on Mount Perazim,
PERCEIVE
  5:12   nor perceive his hands at work.
26:11   but they perceive it not.
26:11   Let them perceive with dismay
41:20   and perceive that the Lord's hand did
43:10   and perceive that I was the one who
59:12   we perceive our iniquities:
PERCEIVED
64:4   it been heard or perceived by the ear,
PERCEIVES
57:1   but no one perceives that from
PERCEIVING
  6:9   Go on seeing, but not perceiving.
PERFECT
25:1   For with perfect faithfulness
26:3   thou preservest in perfect peace,
PERFECTION
59:8   with the way of perfection;
PERFORM
28:21   to perform his act, his unwonted act,
38:20   and we will perform music
41:23   Perform something good or evil
42:3   He will perform the work of justice
42:16   things I will not fail to perform.
48:14   who shall perform his will in

56:1   justice and perform righteousness,
64:3   thou didst perform awesome things
64:5   who joyfully perform righteousness,
PERFORMED
12:5   who has performed wonders;
25:1   thou hast performed wonders,
PERFORMS
46:11   man who performs my counsel.
PERFUME
  3:24   instead of perfume there shall be a
PERFUMES
57:9   and increase your perfumes;
PERHAPS
47:12   perhaps you can hinder it.
PERILOUS
30:13   iniquity will be to you as a perilous
PERISH
  5:13   their masses perish with thirst.
24:4   the world miserably perish;
41:11   shall come to nought, and perish.
50:2   and perish because of thirst.
60:12   that will not serve you shall perish;
PERMEATED
19:14   The Lord has permeated them
PERMITTING
14:17   permitting not his captives to return
PERPETUALLY
18:2   a people perpetually on the move,
18:7   a nation perpetually on the move,
PERPLEXED
20:5   Men shall be appalled and perplexed
PERSIST
29:20   all who persist in wickedness shall
47:12   Persist, then, with your combinations
PERSISTING
28:13   persisting, they might lapse into
PERSON
49:7   to him who is despised as a person,
56:2   the person who holds fast to them—
PERSONAL
15:7   and their personal belongings,
PERTURBED
32:11   be perturbed, O careless daughters!
44:8   Be not perturbed or shaken.
PERVERSE
  1:4   perverse children:
26:10   of uprightness they remain perverse
32:6   perverse things concerning the Lord,
PERVERSELY
59:13   perversely planning ways of
PETITIONING
16:12   with petitioning on the hill shrines,
PHARAOH
19:11   How can you say to Pharaoh,
36:6   who leans on it. Such is Pharaoh king
PHARAOH'S
19:11   the wisest of Pharaoh's advisers give

30:2 protection in Pharaoh's forces,
30:3 But Pharaoh's protection shall turn to
PHILISTINE
11:14 swoop on the Philistine flank toward
PHILISTINES
2:6 like the Philistines,
9:12 and Philistines from the west
14:29 Rejoice not, all you Philistines,
14:31 Utterly melt away, you Philistines!
PHYSICIAN
3:7 and swear, I am no physician.
PIECE
3:24 instead of the girdle, a piece of twine,
PIECES
7:23 a thousand pieces of currency
13:16 be dashed to pieces before their eyes,
45:2 I will break in pieces brazen doors
PIERCED
53:5 But he was pierced for our
PIERCES
36:6 and pierces the palm of any man
PIETY
29:13 their piety toward me consisting of
PILED
46:1 are piled as burdens on weary
PILLAGE
10:6 to pillage for plunder, to spoliate for
PILLARS
14:31 North shall come pillars of smoke,
PINE
14:8 The pine trees, too, rejoice over you,
24:4 The earth shall pine away,
PINES
60:13 cypresses, pines, and firs together—
PIT
14:15 to the utmost depths of the Pit.
14:19 remains are thrown in a gravel pit.
24:18 shall fall into a pit,
24:18 and those who get up from the pit
25:10 as straw is trampled in a dung pit.
30:33 broad and deep is its fire pit and
38:17 out of the Pit of dissolution.
38:18 those who go down into the Pit
51:14 as those destined for the Pit,
PITCH
13:20 Nomads will not pitch their tents
34:9 land shall become as burning pitch.
PITFALLS
24:17 Terrors and pitfalls and traps await
PITY
9:17 nor does he pity their fatherless and
PLACE
3:24 for in place of beauty
5:8 link field to field till no place is left.
13:13 when the earth is jolted out of place
14:2 and bring them to their own place.
14:31 and no place he has designated shall

18:4 in silence over my dwelling place
18:7 to the place of the name of the Lord
22:23 the sure place, and he will be a
22:25 sure place shall be removed.
26:21 Lord come out of his dwelling place
28:17 and waters flood the hiding place.
32:2 like brooks of water in a desert place,
32:14 a browsing place for flocks.
33:23* they hold not the mast in place
34:14 discover for herself a resting place.
35:7 the thirsty place springs of water;
41:2 calling him to the place of his
41:19 I will place cypresses,
43:3 Seba I give in place of you.
46:7 when they set it in place, there it
49:20 This place is too cramped for us;
51:3 Joyful rejoicing takes place there,
51:13 who sets the earth in place—
51:16 heavens and set the earth in place,
55:13 In place of the thornbush shall come
55:13 in place of nettles, the myrtle,
57:15 I dwell on high in the holy place,
59:14 truth stumbles in the public place
60:13 to make glorious the place of my feet.
60:17 In place of copper I will bring gold,
60:17 in place of iron, silver;
60:17 in place of wood I will bring copper,
60:17 in place of stones, iron.
61:3 in place of ashes,
61:3 festal anointing in place of mourning,
61:3 a resplendent robe in place of a
63:18 thy people possessed the holy place
65:10 Valley of Achor a resting place
66:1 What would serve me as a place of
PLACED
59:21 my words which I have placed in your
PLACES
17:2 and become places for herds to
48:21 he led them through arid places:
49:19 For your ruins and ravaged places,
52:9 you ruined places of Jerusalem:
61:4 raise up the old waste places;
64:11 and all places dear to us lie in ruins.
PLAIN
40:4 and rough terrain a plain.
PLAINS
41:18 springs in the midst of the plains;
PLAN
5:19 Let the plan of the Holy One of Israel
40:13 a man should let him know his plan?
PLANNED
14:24 as I planned it, so shall it be:
25:1 things planned of old.
37:26 how in days of old I planned it?
46:11 what I have planned, I do.
PLANNING
59:13 perversely planning ways of

PLANS
19:3   I will frustrate their plans,
30:1   for drawing up plans, but not by me,
PLANT
4:2   In that day the plant of the Lord
17:10   though you plant choice crops
17:11   the day you plant them,
28:25   and plant buckwheat in its own plot?
37:30   plant vineyards and eat their fruit:
65:21   when they plant vineyards, they will
65:22   or plant so that others may eat.
PLANTED
5:2   and planted it with choice vines,
40:24   When scarcely they are planted,
60:21   they are the branch I have planted,
61:3   planted by the Lord for his glory.
PLATED
30:22   your graven idols plated with silver,
PLAY
11:8   A suckling infant will play near the
23:16   Play skillfully; sing song after song,
63:8   sons who will not play false;
PLAYGROUND
32:14   the playground of wild animals,
PLAZA
7:3   on the road to the Laundry Plaza.
36:2   the Laundry Plaza.
PLEAD
1:17   plead the cause of the fatherless,
43:26   let us plead each our case.
PLEAS
19:22   their pleas and heal them.
PLEASE
5:3   please judge between me and my
19:12   Let them please tell you, if they can
29:11   Please read this, and he answers,
29:12   saying, Please read this, he answers,
36:4   Please tell Hezekiah, Thus says
36:11   Rabshakeh, please speak to your
38:20   O Lord, may it please thee to save
PLEASED
9:17   My Lord is not pleased with their
PLEASING
53:2   he had no pleasing aspect,
PLEASURE
2:16   merchant ships and pleasure craft.
66:11   draw at your pleasure
PLENTIFUL
7:22   And because of their plentiful milk,
PLOT
7:5   an evil plot against you,
7:23   In that day every plot of ground
28:25   plant buckwheat in its own plot?
PLOWING
28:24   plowman be forever plowing to sow
PLOWMAN
28:24   Will the plowman be forever plowing

PLOWSHARES
2:4   beat their swords into plowshares,
PLUCKED
17:5   he will become like ears plucked
50:6   to those who plucked out the beard;
PLUNDER
8:1   Hasten the plunder, hurry the spoil.
8:4   the plunder of Samaria will
10:2   making plunder of widows,
10:6   for plunder, to spoliate for spoil,
11:14   together plunder those to the east;
17:14   This is the lot of those who plunder
33:23*   the lame take part in the plunder.
42:24   is it that hands Jacob over to plunder
PLUNDERED
13:16   their homes plundered, their wives
42:22   they are a people plundered and
POINT
37:3   have reached the point of birth,
POINTING
58:9   the pointing finger and offensive
POLISHED
49:2   He has made me into a polished arrow
POLLUTED
24:5   The earth lies polluted under its
65:4   their bowls full of polluted broth,
PONDER
44:21   Ponder these things, O Jacob, and
PONDERING
59:13   and pondering illicit transactions.
PONDERS
32:6   their heart ponders impiety:
POOR
3:15   humbling the faces of the poor?
10:2   depriving the poor of my people of
11:4   He will judge the poor with
14:30   The elect poor shall have pasture,
25:4   Thou wast a refuge for the poor,
26:6   underfoot by the feet of the poor,
32:7   insidious devices to ruin the poor,
40:20   Those too poor for this type of
41:17   When the poor and needy require
54:11   Poor wretch, tempest-tossed and
58:7   to bring home the wretchedly poor,
POOREST
29:19   and the poorest of men rejoice
POPULACE
16:14   populace there shall be very few
POPULATION
24:6   of it the population of the earth
PORTALS
60:8   flying as doves to their portals?
PORTENTS
8:18   signs and portents in Israel
PORTS
23:11   that her ports of haven be destroyed.

POSITION
36:2   he took up a position by the aqueduct
POSITIONS
22:7   take up positions at your gateways.
POSSESS
14:2   the house of Israel will possess them
34:11   But hawks and falcons shall posses it,
34:17   They shall possess it forever,
57:13   refuge in me shall possess the earth
POSSESSED
63:18   thy people possessed the holy place
POSSESSION
14:21   and take possession of the world,
POST
22:19   you will be expelled from your post.
POSTERITY
22:24   his descendants and posterity,
44:3   my blessing upon your posterity.
54:13   shall be the peace of your posterity.
61:9   their posterity in the midst of the
65:23   and their posterity with them.
POSTS
29:3   and beleaguer you with assault posts,
POTENTATES
40:23   By him who brings potentates to
POTTER
29:16   shall the potter be regarded as the
41:25   tread them as clay like a potter.
64:8   are the clay and thou art the potter,
POTTERY
45:9   mere shards of earthenware pottery!
POUNDING
30:30   discharges and pounding hail.
POUNDS
41:7*   urges him who pounds the anvil.
POUR
44:3   I will pour water on the thirsty soil,
44:3   I will pour out my Spirit on your
57:6   To them you pour out libations and
65:11   and pour mixed wines for Fortune,
POURED
26:16   they poured out silent prayers
29:10   The Lord has poured out on you
32:15   be poured out on us;
53:12   because he poured out his soul unto
POURS
42:25   he pours out on them the violence of
POWER
10:33   trees with terrifying power;
25:5   thou subduest the power of tyrants.
40:10   my Lord the Lord comes with power;
50:2   have I no power to deliver?
51:9   arise; clothe yourself with power,
52:1   clothe yourself with power, O Zion!
63:1   forward in the strength of his power?
POWERFUL
25:3   For this will powerful peoples revere

27:1   with his great and powerful sword,
40:26   he is almighty and all powerful,
POWERLESS
14:10   you have become powerless as we are!
47:13   But you are powerless, despite all
PRACTICE
32:6   how to practice hypocrisy and preach
PRACTICES
66:17   [their practices and ideas] shall
PRACTICING
58:2   a nation practicing righteousness
PRAIRIE
7:19   prairie and in rocky ravines,
34:14   Prairie wolves shall greet jackals,
PRAISE
12:1   I praise thee, O Lord.
12:5   Sing in praise of the Lord,
38:18   For Sheol cannot praise thee, nor
38:19   only they bring thee praise,
42:8   nor my praise to wrought idols.
42:10   sing his praise from the end of the
42:12   in the isles speak out praise of him.
43:21   to speak out in praise of me.
61:11   righteousness and praise to spring up
62:9   giving praise to the Lord;
63:7   I will recount in praise of the Lord
PRAISED
64:11   where our fathers praised thee
PRAISES
43:14   who sing the praises of shipping.
60:6   and heralding the praises of the Lord.
PRAISING
25:1   extol thee by praising thy name.
PRANCE
13:21   demonic creatures prance about in it.
PRAWN
66:17   and prawn and rodents—they with
PRAY
1:15   though you pray at length, I will not
16:12   and enter their sanctuaries to pray,
44:17   they bow in adoration and pray,
PRAYED
37:15   And Hezekiah prayed to the Lord and
37:21   Because you have prayed
38:2   the wall and prayed to the Lord:
45:20   and prayed to gods that could not
PRAYER
37:4   up prayer on behalf of the remnant
38:5   your prayer and seen your tears.
56:7   and gladden in my house of prayer.
56:7   as a house of prayer for all nations.
PRAYERS
26:16   they poured out silent prayers
PREACH
32:6   how to practice hypocrisy and preach
50:4   that I may know how to preach

513

PRECEDING
62:11 with him; his work preceding him.
PRECEDES
40:10 with him; his work precedes him.
PRECEPT
28:10 For it is but precept upon precept,
28:10 precept upon precept,
28:13 Precept upon precept,
28:13 precept upon precept,
PRECEPTS
51:4   my precepts shall be a light to the
58:2   not forsaking the precepts of their
PRECINTS
13:2   into the precincts of the elite.
PRECIOUS
28:16 a precious cornerstone, a sure
43:4   Because you are precious and revered
54:12 entire boundary of precious stones.
PREDICT
30:10 Predict not what is right for us:
41:22 Or predict the future for us:
PREDICTED
43:9   or predicted events that have come to
45:21 predicted them long ago?
PREDICTIONS
44:25 annuls the predictions of imposters
47:13 and make predictions month by
48:16 I have not made predictions in secret;
PREDICTS
44:7   Who predicts what happens as do I,
PREEMINENCE
33:10 now gain preeminence.
PREEMINENT
 2:2   shall be preeminent among the hills,
PREFERRED
66:3   have preferred to go their own ways,
PREOCCUPIED
59:7   are preoccupied with mischief;
PREOCCUPY
29:9   preoccupy yourselves, until you cry
PREPARE
14:21 Prepare for the massacre of their sons,
21:5   They prepare tables;
25:6   will the Lord of Hosts prepare
40:3   In the desert prepare the way for the
57:14 Prepare the way;
62:10 prepare the way for the people!
PREPARED
26:11 the fire prepared for thine enemies
30:33 For Tophet has been prepared of Old,
PRESCRIBE
66:4   so will I prescribe intrigues for them
PRESENCE
 1:7   devoured by aliens in your presence,
 2:10 the awesome presence of the Lord
 2:19 the awesome presence of the Lord
 2:21 the awesome presence of the Lord

 6:2   two they could veil their presence,
 9:3   they rejoice at thy presence
19:1   of Egypt will rock at his presence
23:18 dwell in the presence of the Lord,
24:23 glory in the presence of his elders.
26:17 so were we at thy presence, O Lord.
48:19 and obliterated from my presence.
53:2   a sapling he grew up in his presence,
55:12 hills shall sing at your presence
61:11 in the presence of all nations.
63:9   the angel of his presence delivering
64:1   mountains melting at thy presence—
64:2   the nations trembling at thy presence
PRESENT
41:21 Present your case, says the Lord;
43:13 from the first I have been present—
45:21 Speak up and present your case;
46:4   Even to your old age, I am present;
48:16 coming to pass, I have been present.
55:6   the Lord while he is present;
58:4   Your present fasts are not such
PRESENTS
66:3   whoever presents a grain offering
PRESERVE
31:5   by passing over it, preserve it.
PRESERVED
49:6   to restore those preserved of Israel.
PRESERVEST
26:3   thou preservest in perfect peace,
PRESIDE
28:14 who preside over these people in
PRESIDES
40:10 his arm presides for him.
PRESSED
 1:6   not been pressed out or bound up,
PRESSES
16:10 will tread no wine in the presses;
PRESSING
63:1   pressing forward in the strength of
PRESUMPTUOUSLY
52:5   act presumptuously, says the
PRETEND
57:11 you pretend and do not mention me,
PREVAILS
59:9   light, but there prevails darkness;
PREY
 5:29 growling, they seize the prey, and
13:21 birds of prey will find lodging there
18:6   All shall be left to the birds of prey
18:6   the birds of prey will feed on them
31:4   a young lion growls over the prey
34:13 a reserve for birds of prey.
42:22 They have become a prey, yet no one
43:20 the jackals and birds of prey,
46:11 I summon a bird of prey from the
59:15 they who shun evil become a prey.

PRICE
45:13 without price or bribe, says the Lord
52:3 you were sold without price,
52:5 people are taken over without price;
53:5 the price of our peace he incurred,
PRIDE
2:11 and man's pride abased;
2:17 and man's pride brought low;
4:2 and the earth's fruit the pride and
9:9 who say in pride and arrogance of
13:3 who take pride in me.
13:11 and humble the pride of tyrants.
13:19 the glory and pride of Chaldeans,
16:6 of its excessive pride and its
25:11 pull down his pride in the attempt.
60:15 I will make you an everlasting pride,
PRIEST
8:2 Uriah the Priest and Zechariah
24:2 And it shall be with priest as with
PRIESTLY
61:3 upon them a priestly headpiece
61:10 bridegroom dressed in priestly attire
PRIESTS
28:7 priests and prophets have gone astray
37:2 the elders of the priests in sackcloth
61:6 shall be called the priests of the Lord
66:21 be priests and Levites, says the Lord.
PRIME
38:10 I said, in the prime of life
59:10 in the prime of life we resemble the
PRINCE
9:6 a Father for Ever, a Prince of Peace—
55:4 a prince and lawgiver of the peoples.
PRINCES
23:8 whose traders were princes,
PRISON
42:7 and from prison those who sit in
PRISONERS
24:22 like prisoners to a dungeon
PRIVATE
3:17 Lord will expose their private parts.
PROCEDURE
28:26 him in the proper procedure.
PROCEED
51:5 and my salvation proceed;
63:12 who made his glorious arm proceed
PROCLAIM
40:9 proclaim to the cities of Judah:
48:6 how is it you do not proclaim it?
58:1 Proclaim it aloud without restraint;
61:1 to proclaim liberty to the captives
PROCLAMATION
62:11 The Lord has made proclamation to
PROCRASTINATE
29:9 Procrastinate, and become bewildered
PROCURERS
47:15 This is what your procurers have

PRODUCE
5:4 why did it produce wild grapes?
32:10 the produce shall fail to arrive.
PRODUCED
5:2 but it produced wild grapes.
PRODUCTIVE
10:18 choice forests and productive fields
32:15 desert shall become productive land
32:15 and lands now productive
PROFANED
43:28 I let the holy cities be profaned;
PROFANING
56:2 keeps the Sabbath without profaning
56:6 keep the Sabbath without profaning
PROFANITIES
9:17 and every mouth utters profanities.
PROFANITY
23:9 glorying in excellence a profanity,
PROFIT
30:6 to a people who cannot profit them.
44:9 things they cherish profit nothing.
PROFITED
47:15 your procurers have profited you—
PROLONG
53:10 his offspring and prolong his days,
PROLONGED
13:23 days shall not be prolonged.
PROMINENT
30:25 mountain heights and prominent hills
33:10 I will now become prominent,
57:7 you have made prominent your bed,
PROMISED
38:7 do the thing he has promised:
PROMOTE
44:9 Those who promote them are
PROOF
11:3 nor establish proof by what his ears
PROPAGANDA
16:6 of its outburst of false propaganda.
PROPER
28:26 directing him in the proper
PROPHECIES
41:22 their prophecies of events heretofore.
42:9 The prophecies of the former events
43:18 Never mind the prophecies of bygone
46:9 Review the prophecies of the events
48:3 The prophecies of the events of the
PROPHECY
2:1 A prophecy concerning Judea and
PROPHET
3:2 the magistrate and prophet, the augur
37:2 to the prophet Isaiah the son of Amoz
38:1 And the prophet Isaiah the son of
39:3 Then the prophet Isaiah came to King
PROPHETESS
8:3 when I had been with the prophetess,

PROPHETIC
41:26 any [prophetic] utterance.
PROPHETS
9:15 the prophets who teach falsehoods,
28:7 priests and prophets have gone astray
29:10 he has shut your eyes, the prophets;
PROPOSALS
8:10 though you make proposals,
PROSELYTES
5:17 and proselytes eat in the ruins of the
14:1 and proselytes will adhere to them
PROSPER
48:15 and I will prosper his way.
53:10 might prosper in his hand.
PROSPERITY
17:8 the idols of prosperity and the
27:9 leaving no idols of prosperity
PROSTRATE
49:7 heads of state shall prostrate
51:23 Lie prostrate that we may go over you
60:14 all who reviled you will prostrate
PROTECT
37:35 I will protect this city and save it,
38:6 I will protect this city.
PROTECTING
31:5 by protecting it he will deliver it,
PROTECTION
22:8 look to the forest home as protection.
30:2 on seeking protection in Pharaoh's
30:3 But Pharaoh's protection shall turn to
PROUD
2:12 for all the proud and arrogant
28:3 The proud garlands of the drunkards
PROVE
8:10 they shall not prove firm: God is
28:18 covenant with Death shall prove void
33:6 shall prove to be a strength,
PROVERB
28:20 come to pass the proverb:
PROVIDE
2:6 they provide themselves with
11:15 to provide a way on foot.
16:3 Provide a solution, they say; judge
23:18 Her commerce shall provide for those
PROVIDED
33:16 Bread is provided them, their water
PROVIDES
43:16 who provides a way in the Sea,
PROVIDING
55:10 providing seed for the sower and food
PROVISION
61:6 with their choicest provision.
PROVOKE
65:3 a people who constantly provoke me
PROVOKED
47:6 I was provoked by my people,
57:17 sin of covetousness I was provoked;

PRUNED
5:6 it shall neither be pruned nor hoed,
PRUNING
2:4 Their spears into pruning hooks:
PUBLIC
33:7 See, their stalwarts sob in public;
42:2 to make himself heard in public.
59:14 truth stumbles in the public place
PUFFS
40:24 he puffs at them and they wither,
PUL
66:19 to Tarshish, Pul, and Lud (the
PULL
25:11 he will pull down his pride in the
PULSATING
24:8 the pulsating of lyres comes to an
PUNISH
10:12 he will punish the king of
26:21 to punish the inhabitants of the earth
27:1 punish severely Leviathan,
PUNISHMENT
13:11 punishment for the wicked;
24:22 many days, as punishment.
PURE
52:11 Come out of her and be pure,
66:20 brought offerings in pure vessels
PURPOSE
1:11 For what purpose are your
10:7 His purpose shall be to annihilate
38:3 and with full purpose of heart and
49:4 and to no purpose!
54:16 forging weapons to suit his purpose;
55:11 achieves the purpose for which I sent
PURPOSES
46:10 I speak, and my purposes take effect;
53:10 and that the purposes of the Lord
PURSE
3:22 the shawl, the kerchief and the purse,
46:6 who squander gold from the purse
PURSUE
58:3 fast day you pursue your own ends
PURSUERS
30:16 shall your pursuers be swifter.
PURSUITS
58:13 from your everyday pursuits
PYRE
30:33 is its fire pit and ample its pyre;
QUAKE
5:25 the mountains quake, and their
14:16 and kingdoms quake,
QUAKED
64:3 the mountains quaked before thee!
QUAKINGS
29:6 with thunderous quakings,
QUARRY
51:1 to the quarry out of which you were

QUEENS
49:23   queens your nursing mothers.
QUELL
25:5   thou didst quell the onslaughts of the
QUENCHED
34:10   and day it shall not be quenched;
QUESTIONED
41:28   or when I questioned them,
QUICKLY
5:19   Let him quickly speed up his work
QUIET
30:15   with quiet confidence gain the
QUIVER
22:6   When Elam takes up the quiver,
49:2   in his quiver he kept me secret.
RABSHAKEH
36:2   the king of Assyria sent Rabshakeh
36:4   And Rabshakeh said to them,
36:11   Rabshakeh, please speak to your
36:12   But Rabshakeh replied, Did my lord
36:13   Then Rabshakeh stood and called out
36:22   him the things Rabshakeh had said.
37:4   words of of Rabshakeh, whom his lord
37:8   when Rabshakeh heard that the king
RACKED
21:3   my whole frame is racked with
RACKS
38:13   like a lion he racks my whole frame?
RADIANT
60:19   and your God your radiant glory.
RAG
64:6   righteousness as a menstruous rag.
RAGE
17:12   who rage like the raging of the seas—
30:30   his arm descending in furious rage,
34:2   The Lord's rage is upon all nations,
51:13   of the oppressor's rage
63:6   I made them drunk by my rage
66:14   and his rage among his enemies.
RAGING
17:12   who rage like the raging of the seas—
30:28   His breath is like a raging torrent
57:20   the wicked are like the raging Sea,
RAHAB
51:9   Was it not you who carved up Rahab,
RAIN
4:6   downpour and from rain.
5:6   forbid the rainclouds to rain on it.
30:23   Then will he water with rain
44:14   firs, which the rain makes grow:
45:8   Rain down from above, O heavens;
RAINCLOUDS
5:6   I will forbid the rainclouds to rain on
18:4   and when the rainclouds appear
RAINS
55:10   And as the rains and snows descend

RAISE
3:7   But he will raise his hand in that
10:24   or raise their staff over you,
10:26   The Lord of Hosts will raise the whip
11:11   my Lord will again raise his hand
11:12   He will raise the ensign to the
13:2   Raise the ensign on a barren
15:5   they will raise the cry of catastrophe.
23:4   rear young men or raise virgins!
40:9   Raise your voice mightily,
42:2   He will not shout or raise his voice
42:11   and its cities raise their voice,
42:13   raise the shout of victory over his
45:13   It is I who rightfully raise him up,
49:6   to raise up the tribes of Jacob
49:22   raise my ensign to the peoples;
58:1   raise your voice like a trumpet!
61:4   raise up the old waste places;
62:10   raise the ensign to the nations!
RAISED
37:23   Against whom have you raised your
40:4   every ravine must be raised up,
41:2   Who has raised up Righteousness
41:25   I have raised up one from the north
RAISES
5:26   He raises an ensign to distant nations
RALLIED
59:16   righteousness rallied to his cause.
RAMAH
10:29   Ramah is in a state of alarm,
RAMS
1:11   I have had my fill of offerings of rams
34:6   the kidney fat of rams.
60:7   the rams of Nebaioth will serve you;
RANGE
7:25   but they shall serve as a cattle range,
32:20   letting oxen and asses range free.
RANGES
49:11   All my mountain ranges I will
RANSOM
43:3   Egypt I have appointed as ransom for
47:11   which you cannot ransom yourself:
RANSOMED
1:27   For Zion shall be ransomed by
35:10   the ransomed of the Lord shall
51:11   Let the ransomed of the Lord return!
RARE
13:12   men more rare than gold of Ophir.
RASH
32:4   The minds of the rash shall learn
RASHLY
28:16   who believe it will not do rashly.
RAVAGED
6:11   and the land ravaged to ruin.
10:13   I have ravaged their reserves,
24:3   it shall be utterly ravaged.
49:19   For your ruins and ravaged places,

RAVAGER
54:16 is I who create the ravager to destroy.
RAVAGERS
49:17 sons shall hasten your ravagers away
RAVAGING
28:2 as a ravaging hailstorm sweeping
RAVENOUS
  5:14 Sheol becomes ravenous,
RAVENS
14:23 into swamplands, a haunt for ravens;
34:11 and owls and ravens inhabit it.
RAVINE
40:4 every ravine must be raised up,
RAVINES
  7:19 prairie and in rocky ravines,
57:6 the slippery stones of the ravines
63:14 descending the slopes of ravines,
RAVISHED
13:16 plundered, their wives ravished.
23:12 O ravished virgin, Daughter of Sidon.
RAZED
15:1 when in one night Kir is razed,
21:9 idol gods he has razed to the ground.
RAZING
25:12 lay low by razing them to the ground,
RAZOR
  7:20 a razor hired at the River—
REACH
  8:8 passing through, reach the very neck;
11:8 and the toddler reach his hand
11:14 Edom and Moab at hand's reach,
15:5 its fugitives will reach Zoar
15:8 the sound of it shall reach Eglaim
28:15 it shall not reach you.
59:9 righteousness is unable to reach us.
65:20 those who fail to reach a hundred
REACHED
16:8 Its runner vines reached Jazer,
28:15 or reached an understanding with
37:3 Children have reached the point of
37:24 I have reached it loftiest summit,
REACHES
23:5 When the news of Tyre reaches Egypt,
37:24 the farthest reaches of Lebanon.
READ
29:11 Please read this, and he answers,
29:12 saying, Please read this, he answers,
34:16 Search, and read it in the book of the
37:14 messengers and read it.
READIES
51:13 as he readies himself to wreak
READY
30:33 hearth indeed, made ready for rulers
REALM
39:2 in his palace or in all his realm
REAPED
17:5 whose ears are reaped by the armful,

REAPERS
18:4 searing heat overtakes the reapers,
REAPING
18:4 amid the fever of reaping.
REAPPORTION
49:8 and reapportion the desolate estates,
REAR
23:4 I no longer rear young men or raise
58:8 of the Lord will be your rear guard.
REARED
  1:2 I have reared sons, brought them up,
49:21 by whom were these reared?
51:18 the hand of all the sons she reared.
REBEL
50:5 and I rebel not, nor back away:
REBELLED
36:5 that you have rebelled against me?
63:10 Yet they rebelled and grieved his
REBELLIOUS
30:1 Woe to you, rebellious sons, says the
30:9 They are a rebellious people, sons
REBUILD
  9:10 but we will rebuild with hewn stone;
45:13 he will rebuild my city and set free
58:12 who came out of you will rebuild the
60:10 Foreigners will rebuild your walls,
61:4 They will rebuild the ancient ruins,
REBUILDER
58:12 be called a rebuilder of fallen walls,
REBUILT
25:2 nor ever be rebuilt!
44:26 cities of Judah, They shall be rebuilt,
44:28 Jerusalem that it must be rebuilt,
REBUKE
37:4 living God, and will rebuke him for
50:2 By a mere rebuke I dry up the Sea;
51:20 of your God's angry rebuke.
54:9 never again to rebuke you.
66:15 to rebuke with conflagrations of fire.
REBUKES
17:13 when he rebukes them they will flee
RECALL
26:13 but thee alone we recall by name.
RECALLED
63:11 Then his people recalled the days of
65:17 or recalled to mind.
RECEDE
19:6 Egypt's waterways recede and dry up.
38:8 sun on the dial of Ahaz recede
RECEIVE
45:8 Let the earth receive it and salvation
57:13 and receive an inheritance in my holy
RECEIVED
37:9 Now Sennacherib received a report
37:14 And Hezekiah received the letter
40:2 She has received from the Lord's hand

RECKONED
32:15 be reckoned as brushwood.
40:17 less than the ether they are reckoned
RECKONING
10:3 will you do in the day of reckoning
RECLAIM
11:11 to reclaim the remnant of his people—
RECLINE
14:30 and the needy recline in safety.
17:2 become places for herds to recline,
27:10 steers forage and recline there,
RECOGNIZE
43:10 you may recognize it and believe me,
63:16 or Israel recognize us,
RECOLLECTION
26:14 wiping out all recollection of them.
RECOMPENSE
49:4 my recompense with my God.
RECONCILED
27:5 they shall be reconciled to me.
RECORD
10:19 a child could record them.
30:8 record it in a book for the last day,
36:3 of Asaph, the record keeper, went out
36:22 the son of Asaph, the record keeper,
RECOUNT
33:18 recount in your mind the terror:
41:22 Let them come forward and recount to
43:26 Recount for me the past ;
63:7 I will recount in praise of the Lord
RECOVER
38:1 You will die; you will not recover.
38:21* so that he could recover.
57:18 seen his conduct and will recover him
RECOVERY
38:9 illness, written upon his recovery:
39:1 had heard of his illness and recovery.
RECUR
29:1 the feastdays recur in succession,
RED
63:1 coming from Edom in red-stained
63:2 Why are you clothed in red, your
REDDENED
1:18 they have reddened as crimson,
REDEEM
50:2 Was my hand too short to redeem you
REDEEMED
29:22 who redeemed Abraham, to the house
35:9 But the redeemed shall walk them
43:1 Do not fear, for I have redeemed you.
44:22 Return to me; I have redeemed you.
44:23 the Lord has redeemed Jacob;
48:20 The Lord has redeemed his servant
51:10 by which the redeemed might pass?
52:3 shall be redeemed without money.
52:9 he has redeemed Jerusalem.
62:12 the redeemed of the Lord;

63:4 the year of my redeemed had come.
63:9 he himself redeemed them;
REDEEMER
41:14 your Redeemer is the Holy One
43:14 Holy One of Israel, your Redeemer:
44:6 the Lord of Hosts, their Redeemer:
44:24 Thus says the Lord, your Redeemer,
47:4 our Redeemer, the Holy One of Israel,
48:17 Holy One of Israel, your Redeemer:
49:7 the Redeemer and Holy One of Israel,
49:26 Redeemer is the Valiant One of Jacob.
59:20 But he will come as Redeemer to Zion
60:16 Redeemer is the Valiant One of Jacob.
63:16 Redeemer from Eternity is thy name.
REDEEMS
54:5 he who redeems you is the Holy One
54:8 says the Lord, who redeems you.
REDRESS
59:9 Therefore redress remains far from
59:14 And so redress is compelled to back
RED-STAINED
63:1 from Edom in red-stained garments?
REDUCED
10:13 I have vastly reduced the inhabitants.
41:12 shall be reduced to nothing.
REED
9:14 head and tail, palm top and reed,
19:15 head nor tail, palm top or reed.
36:6 of Egypt, that splintered reed which
42:3 Even a bruised reed he will not
58:5 only for bowing one's head like a reed
REEDS
19:6 Reeds and rushes shall wither;
35:7 shall come rushes and reeds.
REEL
24:20 The earth shall reel to and fro like a
REELS
21:4 My mind reels, I am paralyzed with
REESTABLISHES
62:7 till he reestablishes Jerusalem
REFER
30:7 I refer to her as an idle boast.
REFERRED
61:6 and referred to as the ministers of
62:4 nor your land referred to as desolate;
REFINED
25:6 of matured wines well refined.
47:1 as delicate and refined.
REFINING
48:10 See, I am refining you, though not as
REFLECT
44:19 They reflect not,
REFRAINING
58:13 by refraining from your everyday
REFRESHING
57:15 refreshing the spirits of the lowly,

REFUGE
4:6   a secret refuge from the
14:32   his longsuffering people find refuge
16:4   be a refuge to them from the
25:4   Thou wast a refuge for the poor,
27:5   they take hold of me for a refuge
28:15   by taking refuge in deception
28:17   shall sweep away your false refuge
32:2   the wind or refuge from the storm,
57:13   But they who seek refuge in me shall
REFUGEES
16:3   betray not the refugees!
REFUSE
1:31   The mighty shall be as refuse,
REFUTE
54:17   every tongue . . . you shall refute.
REGARD
5:12   but they regard not what the Lord
17:7   men will have regard to their Maker,
17:8   and regard not the altars,
22:11   nor have regard for the One who
60:18   you will regard salvation as your
66:2   And yet I have regard for those
REGARDED
29:16   the potter be regarded as the clay?
32:5   shall no longer be regarded as noble
REGIONS
24:15   in the regions of sunrise,
REGULAR
1:14   Your monthly and regular meetings
REIGN
24:23   the Lord of Hosts manifests his reign
32:1   A king shall reign in righteousness
36:1   of King Hezekiah's reign
39:8   be peace and loyalty during my reign.
REIGNS
1:1   during the reigns of Uzziah,
52:7   saying to Zion, Your God reigns!
REINFORCED
2:15   every tall tower and reinforced wall,
REINHABITED
13:20   Never shall it be reinhabited;
44:26   of Jerusalem, It shall be reinhabited,
REJECT
7:15   to reject what is evil and
7:16   to reject the evil and choose
REJECTED
8:6   Because these people have rejected
30:12   Because you have rejected this word,
41:9   I have accepted you and not rejected
54:6   married in youth only to be rejected,
REJOICE
8:6   rejoice in Rezin and the son of
9:3   they rejoice at thy presence
9:3   as men rejoice at harvest time,
12:3   Then shall you rejoice in drawing
14:8   The pine trees, too, rejoice over you,

14:29   Rejoice not, all you Philistines,
29:19   and the poorest of men rejoice
35:1   the desert shall rejoice
41:16   Then will you rejoice in the Lord
61:10   I rejoice exceedingly in the Lord;
62:5   so shall your God rejoice over you.
65:13   my servants shall rejoice indeed,
65:18   Rejoice, then, and be glad forever in.
65:19   in Jerusalem, rejoice in my people;
66:10   Rejoice with Jerusalem and be glad
66:14   Your heart shall rejoice to see it,
REJOICES
62:5   a bridegroom rejoices over the bride,
REJOICING
30:29   and rejoicing of heart, as when men
51:3   Joyful rejoicing takes place there,
RELAID
44:28   its temple foundations relaid.
RELEASE
58:6   To release from wrongful bondage,
RELENT
63:17   Relent, for the sake of thy servants,
RELENTLESS
14:6   by relentless oppression.
RELIABLE
8:2   And I called in reliable witnesses,
RELIED
20:6   on whom we relied for help and
RELIEF
14:3   relief from grief and anguish
RELIES
50:10   of the Lord and relies on his God?
RELIEVE
1:24   Woe to them! I will relieve me
RELINQUISH
42:8   I will not relinquish my glory to
RELY
10:20   will no longer rely on him who struck
10:20   but will truly rely on the Lord,
30:12   and rely on manipulation and double
36:6   of Egypt to all who rely on him!
36:7   But if you tell me, We rely on the
59:4   They rely on empty words,
RELYING
31:1   relying on horses,
REMAIN
4:3   in Zion and they who remain
6:13   remain in it, or return,
7:4   See to it that you remain calm
7:22   All who remain in the land
9:20   yet remain hungry;
10:4   There shall nothing remain
15:6   and no green foliage shall remain.
15:9   and on those who remain in the land.
24:6   and little of mankind remain.
26:10   uprightness they remain perverse
30:18   toward you he will remain aloof.

30:20 Teacher remain hidden no longer,
34:10 It shall remain a wasteland
42:25 yet they remain unaware—
45:1 letting no gates remain shut:
45:18 not to remain a chaotic waste,
58:3 bodies and you remain indifferent!
60:11 Your gates shall always remain open;
62:1 I will not remain still
REMAINED
28:13 the word of the Lord remained:
36:21 But they remained silent,
REMAINING
21:17 remaining of the sons of Kedar
REMAINS
6:13 whose stump remains alive,
14:19 whose mangled remains are thrown in
21:11 Watchman, what remains of the night?
24:12 Havoc remains in the city;
29:13 while their heart remains far from me
59:9 Therefore redress remains far from
REMALIAH
7:1 Remaliah king of Israel came up to
7:4 and the son of Remaliah,
7:5 Ephraim and the son of Remaliah,
7:9 son of Remaliah the head of Samaria,
8:6 in Rezin and the son of Remaliah,
REMEMBER
38:3 I beseech thee to remember, O Lord,
47:7 or remember her final destiny.
54:4 and remember no more
64:5 who remember thee by following
64:9 remember not iniquity forever.
REMEMBERED
17:10 and not remembered the Rock, your
23:16 that you may be remembered.
26:16 their distress they remembered thee;
65:17 events shall not be remembered
REMEMBERING
43:25 remembering your sins no more.
REMINDED
19:17 all reminded of it shall dread what
REMNANT
10:21 of Jacob a remnant will return
10:22 only a remnant will return;
11:11 to reclaim the remnant of his people—
11:16 for the remnant of his people who
14:22 cut off Babylon's name and remnant,
17:3 so shall it be with Aram's remnant,
28:5 to the remnant of his people:
37:4 on behalf of the remnant that is left.
37:31 the remnant of the house of Judah
37:32 out of Jerusalem shall go a remnant,
46:3 you remnant of the house of Israel,
REMOVE
1:16 remove your wicked deeds
1:25 and remove all your alloy.
18:5 and remove the new branches by

20:2 from your loins and remove
25:8 he will remove the reproach of his
57:14 remove the obstacles from the path of
REMOVED
5:5 I will have its hedge removed
10:27 their yoke removed from your neck:
14:25 their burden removed from their
22:8 Judea's defensive screen is removed,
22:25 sure place shall be removed.
27:9 as a result of this his sins removed:
44:22 I have removed your offenses like a
54:10 For the mountains shall be removed
54:10 toward you shall never be removed,
REND
64:1 O that thou wouldst rend the heavens
RENDER
55:10 to render it fertile and fruitful—
59:18 the isles he will render retribution.
RENDERED
63:7 rendered the house of Israel.
RENDERING
29:14 rendering void the knowledge of their
41:2 rendering them as dust to his sword,
RENEGADES
1:23 Your rulers are renegades,
RENEW
61:4 they will renew the desolate cities
RENEWAL
38:16 them all the renewal of my spirit.
RENEWED
40:31 shall be renewed in strength:
RENOWN
48:9 on account of my renown
63:14 acquiring illustrious renown.
RENOWNED
12:6 for renowned among you is the Holy
61:9 offspring shall be renowned among
62:7 and makes it renowned in the earth.
RENT
24:19 The earth shall be crushed and rent;
36:22 to Hezekiah with their clothes rent
37:1 Hezekiah heard it, he rent his clothes
REPAY
59:18 they deserve, he will repay them:
REPENT
1:27 those of her who repent by
6:10 and repent, and be healed.
59:20 Jacob who repent of transgression,
REPENTING
21:12 do so by repenting and coming back.
REPHAIM
17:5 in the Valley of Rephaim
REPLACE
9:10 but we will replace them with cedars!
REPLANT
51:16 while I replant the heavens and set

REPLENISH
33:5   righteousness he will replenish Zion.
REPLENISHED
23:2   who were amply replenished
REPLIED
  6:8   And I replied, Here am I; send me!
  6:11   And I replied, For how long, my
36:12   But Rabshakeh replied, Did my lord
38:7   And Isaiah replied, This shall be
39:3   And Hezekiah replied,
REPLIES
21:12   The watchman replies,
REPLY
21:9   and he gave the reply,
65:24   Before they call I will reply;
REPLYING
36:21   remained silent, replying nothing,
REPORT
21:6   who will report what he sees.
23:5   men will be in anguish at the report.
37:9   Sennacherib received a report that
REPORTED
21:10   I have reported what I heard
36:22   and reported to him the things
REPOSE
34:14   too shall the night owl find repose
REPRISALS
59:18   reprisals upon his enemies;
REPROACH
  4:1   take away our reproach!
25:8   remove the reproach of his people
51:7   Do not fear the reproach of men;
54:4   the reproach of your widowhood.
REPROBATES
35:8   on them shall no reprobates wander.
REPROOF
37:3   a woeful day, a day of reproof and
REPUGNANT
14:19   like a repugnant fetus,
REPULSE
28:6   to those who repulse the attack at the
36:9   How then shall you repulse even
REQUIRE
41:17   the poor and needy require water,
58:6   Is not this the fast I require:
REQUIRED
43:23   Yet I required not that you bring
44:14   He is required to cut down cedars;
58:5   the manner of fasting I have required,
REQUIRES
  1:12   who requires you to trample my
RESCUE
  5:29   and none comes to the rescue.
46:2   unable to rescue their burden;
46:4   it is I who carry and rescue you.
RESCUES
42:22   become a prey, yet no one rescues

RESEMBLE
40:18   What does he resemble in your
59:10   prime of life we resemble the dead.
RESEMBLES
  5:28   tread of their warhorses resembles
46:9   I am divine; nothing resembles me.
RESEMBLING
44:13   human likeness, resembling man's
RESENT
11:13   nor Judah resent Ephraim.
RESERVE
34:13   a reserve for birds of prey.
RESERVES
10:13   I have ravaged their reserves,
35:7   in the reserves shall come rushes
RESERVOIR
  7:3   the aqueduct of the Upper Reservoir,
22:9   water in the Lower Reservoir.
22:11   for the water from the Old Reservoir,
36:2   of the Upper Reservoir, on the road to
RESETTLE
54:3   and resettle the desolate cities.
RESETTLED
13:20   it shall not be resettled through all
RESETTLEMENT
58:12   a restorer of streets for resettlement.
RESIDE
33:24* None who reside there shall say, I am
RESIDENCE
11:10   and his residence shall be glorious.
66:1   serve me as a place of residence?
RESISTS
40:20   select a wood that resists decay.
RESOLVED
63:4   For I had resolved on a day of
RESORT
19:3   resort to the idols and to spiritists,
60:5   multitude of the Sea shall resort to
RESORTS
32:14   High rises and panoramic resorts
RESOUND
30:30   Lord will cause his voice to resound,
44:23   cause it to resound, O earth beneath!
RESOUNDED
22:2   You resounded with loud cheers—
RESOUNDING
29:6   resounding booms, tempestuous
48:20   announcement with resounding voice;
RESPECTABLE
32:5   nor rogues considered respectable.
RESPITE
28:12   This is a respite! But they would not
62:7   nor give him respite till he
RESPLENDENT
61:3   a resplendent robe in place of a
RESPOND
19:22   and he will respond to

30:19 He will graciously respond at the cry
58:9 you call, the Lord will respond;
65:12 when I called, you did not respond;
65:24 they are yet speaking I will respond.
RESPONDED
66:4 For when I called, no one responded;
RESPONSE
30:15 By a calm response triumph;
REST
11:2 Spirit of the Lord will rest upon him
11:7 their young will rest together;
13:20 nor will shepherds rest their flocks
14:7 Now the whole earth is at rest and at
23:12 even there you will find no rest.
28:12 This is rest; let the weary rest!
33:20 let your eyes rest upon Jerusalem,
44:17 From the rest they make a god, their
57:2 and rest in their beds.
57:20 unable to rest,
RESTED
49:4 Yet my cause rested with the Lord,
RESTING
34:14 discover for herself a resting place.
65:10 the Valley of Achor a resting place
RESTITUTION
42:22 a spoil, yet none demands restitution.
RESTORE
1:25 I will restore my hand over you
1:26 I will restore your judges as at the
44:26 their ruins I will restore,
49:5 to be his servant, to restore Jacob to
49:6 to restore those preserved of Israel.
49:8 to restore the Land and reapportion
58:12 you will restore the foundations of
RESTORER
58:12 a restorer of streets for resettlement.
RESTORING
38:17 [restoring and reviving me].
RESTRAIN
64:12 O Lord, wilt thou restrain thyself,
RESTRAINING
42:14 keeping still and restraining myself.
RESTRAINT
48:9 I have shown restraint toward you
58:1 Proclaim it aloud without restraint;
RESTRICTED
5:8 and you are restricted to dwell
RESTS
25:10 For in this mountain rests the hand
RESULT
27:9 as a result of this his sins removed:
32:17 and the result of righteousness
RETALIATE
66:15 to retaliate in furious anger,
RETIRE
47:5 Sit speechless; retire into obscurity,

RETIRED
45:16 the makers of inventions retired in
RETRACT
31:2 and not retract his words.
RETREAT
42:17 shall retreat in utter confusion.
RETRIBUTION
34:8 year of retribution on behalf of Zion.
59:18 the isles he will render retribution.
RETURN
6:13 remain in it, or return,
10:21 of Jacob a remnant will return
10:22 only a remnant will return;
13:14 each will return to his own people
14:17 not his captives to return home?
23:17 return to her trade and hire herself
31:6 Return to him from whom you have
35:10 ransomed of the Lord shall return;
37:7 I will give him a notion to return
37:34 By the way he came he shall return;
43:4 I give men in return for you,
44:22 Return to me; I have redeemed you.
51:11 Let the ransomed of the Lord return!
55:7 Let them return to the Lord,
55:10 and return not to it without watering
55:11 it does not return to me empty;
60:4 your daughters shall return to your
RETURNED/RETURNS
37:37 And he returned to Nineveh,
52:8 when the Lord returns to Zion
REVEALED
21:2 A grim vision has been revealed to
22:14 Lord of Hosts revealed this to my ears
40:5 glory of the Lord shall be revealed
53:1 the arm of the Lord been revealed?
56:1 and my righteousness be revealed.
REVELATION
28:9 shall he enlighten with revelation?
53:1 Who has believed our revelation?
REVELERS
5:14 their boisterous ones and revelers.
REVELERS'
24:8 the revelers' din stops;
REVELRY
22:2 a tumultuous town, a city of revelry!
REVENUE
23:3 source of revenue upon the high seas
REVERE
25:3 will powerful peoples revere thee,
REVERED
43:4 are precious and revered in my eyes,
REVERENCING
29:23 reverencing the God of Israel,
REVERSED
38:8 sun reversed its descent by ten
REVERT
7:24 land shall revert to wilderness.

REVIEW
46:9   Review the prophecies of the events
REVILED
  5:24   and reviled the words of the Holy One
60:14   all who reviled you will prostrate
REVISIT
23:17   will revisit Tyre. And she will
REVIVING
38:17   [restoring and reviving me].
57:15   reviving the hearts of the humble.
REVOKE
14:27   who shall revoke?
REVOKED
45:23   by a decree that cannot be revoked:
REVOLTED
  1:2   but they have revolted against me.
REVOLVE
  5:28   their chariot wheels revolve like a
REWARD
35:4   God is coming to avenge and to reward
40:10   His reward is with him; his work
61:8   I will appoint them a sure reward;
62:11   his reward with him, his work
REWARDS
  1:23   and run after rewards;
REZEPH
37:12   Rezeph and the Edenites in Tel
REZIN
  7:1   Rezin king of Aram and Pekah son of
  7:4   the burning anger of Rezin and Aram
  7:8   and Rezin the head of Damascus,
  8:6   rejoice in Rezin and the son of
REZIN'S
  9:11   Rezin's enemies against them
RHYTHM
24:8   The rhythm of drums ceases,
RIBBONS
  3:20   tiaras, bracelets and ribbons, zodiac
RICH
30:23   may be rich and abundant.
53:9   among the rich was his burial;
RICHES
30:6   their riches on the humps of camels,
33:6   fear of the Lord shall be your riches.
RIDE
30:16   We will ride on swift mounts!
RIDERS
21:7   riders on asses and riders on camels.
36:8   put riders on them.
RIDICULE
37:6   Assyria's subordinates ridicule me.
51:7   be undaunted by their ridicule.
RIDICULED
37:23   have you mocked and ridiculed?
RIDING
19:1   Lord enters Egypt riding on swift

RIGGINGS
33:23* Their riggings hang loose;
RIGHT
  9:20   They will snatch on the right, yet
10:2   the poor of my people of their right,
29:21   turn away him who is in the right.
30:10   Predict not what is right for us:
30:21   should you turn left or right.
41:10   you with my righteous right hand.
41:13   hold you by the right hand and say to
41:26   that we might say, He was right?
45:1   whom I grasp by the right hand,
48:13   my right hand that stretched out the
54:3   to the right and to the left;
62:8   The Lord has sworn by his right hand,
63:12   at the right hand of Moses,
RIGHTEOUS
  3:10   Tell the righteous it shall be well
24:16   Glorious are the righteous!
26:2   righteous because it keeps the faith.
26:7   The path of the righteous is straight;
41:10   uphold you with my righteous right
53:11   shall my servant, the righteous one,
57:1   The righteous disappear,
57:1   the righteous are withdrawn.
60:21   Your entire people shall be righteous;
RIGHTEOUSLY
33:15   who conduct themselves righteously
RIGHTEOUSNESS
  1:21   righteousness made its abode in her,
  1:26   the City of Righteousness, a faithful
  1:27   of her who repent by righteousness.
  5:16   by his righteousness.
  9:7   by justice and righteousness
10:22   it shall overflow with righteousness.
11:4   judge the poor with righteousness,
11:5   Righteousness will be as a band about
16:5   justice and expedite righteousness.
19:18   as the City of Righteousness.
26:9   of the world learn righteousness.
26:10   they will not learn righteousness;
28:17   righteousness the weight;
32:1   A king shall reign in righteousness
32:16   and righteousness abide in the
32:17   and the result of righteousness
33:5   with justice and righteousness he
41:2   Who has raised up Righteousness
42:21   because of his righteousness,
45:8   overflow with righteousness.
45:8   let righteousness spring up
45:19   I the Lord tell righteousness
45:21   Did not I, the God of righteousness,
45:23   righteousness has issued from my
46:12   who are far from righteousness;
46:13   I have brought near my righteousness;
48:1   not in truth or in righteousness,
48:18   your righteousness like the waves of

51:1 you followers of righteousness,
51:5 My righteousness shall be at hand
51:6 my righteousness shall never fail.
51:7 you who know righteousness,
51:8 But my righteousness shall endure
54:14 established through righteousness;
56:1 justice and perform righteousness,
56:1 and my righteousness be revealed.
58:2 a nation practicing righteousness
58:8 your righteousness will go before
59:4 None calls for righteousness;
59:9 and righteousness is unable to reach
59:14 and righteousness to stand at a
59:16 his righteousness rallied to his
59:17 He put on righteousness as a
60:17 and righteousness your oppressors:
61:3 shall be called oaks of righteousness
61:10 me in a robe of righteousness—
61:11 cause righteousness and praise to
62:1 till her righteousness shines like a
62:2 shall behold your righteousness
63:1 announcing righteousness!
64:5 who joyfully perform righteousness,
64:6 the sum of our righteousness as a
RIGHTFULLY
42:6 I the Lord have rightfully called you
45:13 It is I who rightfully raise him up,
RING
37:29 I will put my ring in your nose
RINGS
3:21 rings for the fingers and for the ears,
RIOT
22:5 of commotion and trampling and riot
RIPE
17:5 being like a harvest of ripe grain,
28:4 shall be like the first-ripe fruit
RISE
8:7 He will rise up over all his channels
14:9 to rise up from their thrones,
14:13 I will rise in the heavens
14:21 lest they rise up again
14:22 I will rise up against them, says the
24:20 it collapses it shall rise no more.
26:14 spirits who will not rise up;
28:21 For the Lord will rise up
31:2 He will rise up against the brood of
43:17 they lie down as one, to rise no more,
49:7 Rulers shall rise up when they see
51:17 Rouse yourself; awaken and rise up,
52:2 Shake yourself free, rise from the
RISEN
14:8 no hewer has risen against us!
60:1 glory of the Lord has risen upon you!
RISES
13:10 When the sun rises, it shall be
32:14 High rises and panoramic resorts
45:6 that men from where the sun rises to

54:17 every tongue that rises to accuse you,
RISING
59:19 and from the rising of the sun his
RIVER
7:20 a razor hired at the River—
8:7 and mighty waters of the River—
11:15 will extend his hand over the River
27:12 River to the streams of Egypt.
30:33 like a river of lava.
48:18 peace would have been as a river,
66:12 extend peace to her like a river,
RIVERBEDS
7:19 in the riverbeds of the
RIVERS
7:18 the far rivers of Egypt
18:1 beyond the rivers of Cush,
18:2 whose rivers have annexed their
18:7 whose rivers have annexed their
19:6 The rivers shall turn foul,
33:21 a country of rivers and broad
37:25 I have dried up all Egypt's rivers!
42:15 I will turn rivers into dry land and
43:2 when you traverse the rivers,
50:2 rivers I turn into desert—
RIVETING
41:7* though they fasten it with riveting
ROAD
7:3 on the road to the Laundry Plaza.
15:5 on the road to Horonaim
36:2 of the Upper Reservoir, on the road to
57:14 It will be said: Excavate, pave a road!
ROADS
35:8 There shall be highways and roads
43:19 I am making roads through the desert,
49:11 ranges I will appoint as roads;
ROAM
8:21 they roam about embittered
ROAR
5:29 They have the roar of a lion;
17:13 may roar like the roaring of great
42:10 Let the sea roar, and all that lives
51:15 stir up the Sea so that its waves roar.
ROARING
17:13 roar like the roaring of great water,
30:6 lions and the roaring king of beasts
ROAST
44:16 Over it they broil a roast;
ROASTED
44:19 roasted meat and ate it.
ROBBERS
1:23 accomplices of robbers:
ROBE
6:1 highly exalted, the skirt of his robe
22:21 I will clothe him with your robe
59:17 wrapped himself in fury as in a robe.
61:3 a resplendent robe in place of a
61:10 he arrays me in a robe of

ROBES
52:1   Put on your robes of glory, O
ROCK
8:14   stumbling block or obstructing rock,
10:26 at the rock of Oreb.
17:10 and not remembered the Rock, your
19:1   Egypt will rock at his presence
22:16 out graves for themselves in the rock?
26:4   the Lord Yah is an everlasting Rock.
30:29 to the Rock of Israel.
32:2   shade of a large rock in arid country.
44:8   There is no Rock unknown to me.
48:21 water to flow for them from the rock;
48:21 he cleaved the rock and water gushed
51:1   Look to the rock from which you were
ROCKS
2:10   Go into the rocks; hide in the dust
2:19   Men will go into caves in the rocks
2:21   Men will go into crevices in the rocks
57:5   under the crags of rocks.
ROCKY
7:19   prairie and in rocky ravines,
ROD
9:4   the rod of those who subjected them,
10:5   the Assyrian, the rod of my anger!
10:15 As though the rod wielded him who
10:24 though they strike you with the rod
11:4   smite the earth with the rod of his
14:5   the rod of those who ruled—
14:29 now that the rod which struck you is
28:27 and cumin with a rod.
30:31 they who used to strike with the rod.
RODENTS
66:17 and prawn and rodents—they with
ROGUES
32:5   nor rogues considered respectable.
32:7   And rogues scheme by malevolent
ROLLED
9:5   and tunics rolled in blood
28:27 nor is a cartwheel rolled over cumin:
34:4   the heavens are rolled up as a scroll,
ROOF
37:27 or like weeds on a roof
ROOT
27:6   days to come, when Jacob takes root
37:31 shall once more take root below and.
40:24 hardly their stalk has taken root in
ROOTS
5:24   so shall their roots decay away
ROTE
29:13 of men learned by rote—
ROTTING
10:18 turning them into a rotting morass.
ROUGH
40:4   and rough terrain a plain.
ROUND
11:5   faithfulness a girdle round his loins.

29:3   I will encamp against you round
ROUNDS
13:14 a flock of sheep that no one rounds up
ROUSE
51:17 Rouse yourself; awaken and rise up,
ROUSED
14:9   account she roused all the spirits
64:5   Alas, thou wast roused to anger when
ROUSES
64:7   or rouses himself to take hold of thee.
ROUTE
9:1   the last he will exalt the Sea Route
ROUTED
8:9   they shall be routed,
ROYAL
62:3   a royal diadem in the palm of your
RUBBLE
25:2   hast made the city a heap of rubble,
37:26 turning them into heaps of rubble,
RUIN
6:11   and the land ravaged to ruin.
16:7   groan at the ruin of Kir Hareseth
22:4   at the ruin of the Daughter of my
24:12 the gates lie battered to ruin.
25:2   fortified towns a ruin—
32:7   insidious devices to ruin the poor,
47:11 shall come upon you sudden ruin
51:19 desolation, ruin—and who laments
54:14 far from ruin, for it shall not
RUINATION
3:6   and take charge of this ruination!
RUINED
1:7   Your land is ruined,
49:17 those who ruined you shall depart
52:9   you ruined places of Jerusalem:
60:12 such nations shall be utterly ruined.
RUINS
5:17   proselytes eat . . . ruins of the affluent.
17:1   and become a heap of ruins.
44:26 their ruins I will restore,
49:19 For your ruins and ravaged places,
51:3   bringing solace to all her ruins;
58:12 you will rebuild the ancient ruins;
61:4   They will rebuild the ancient ruins,
64:11 and all places dear to us lie in ruins.
RULE
9:7   his rule may be established and
14:2   and rule over their oppressors.
16:1   to those who rule in the earth,
32:1   and rulers rule with justice
RULED
14:5   the rod of those who ruled—
14:9   causing all who had ruled nations
26:13 have ruled over us,
63:19 whom thou hast never ruled
RULER
7:6   set a ruler over it—the son of Tabeal.

19:4   a harsh ruler will subject them,
RULERS
1:23   Your rulers are renegades,
3:4   will make adolescents their rulers;
3:14   and their rulers, and say to them ,
7:16   rulers you loathe shall lie forsaken.
14:18   All rulers of nations lie in state,
19:11   are as wise as the first rulers?
24:21   on earth with the rulers of the earth.
30:33   a hearth . . . , made ready for rulers;
32:1   and rulers rule with justice
41:2   toppled their rulers,
45:1   to ungird the loins of rulers,
49:7   Rulers shall rise up when they see
52:15   rulers shutting their mouths at him—
60:3   their rulers to the brightness of your
60:10   and their rulers will minister to you.
60:11   and their rulers escorted in.
60:16   suckling at the breasts of rulers.
60:17   I will make peace your rulers
62:2   and all their rulers your glory;
RULING
16:8   the ruling nations will smite
RUMOR
37:7   upon hearing a rumor, and will cause
RUN
1:23   and run after rewards;
40:31   they shall run without wearying,
RUNNER
16:8   Its runner vines reached Jazer,
RUNNING
30:25   appear streams of running water,
44:4   like willows by running brooks.
RUSH
59:7   Their feet rush after evil;
RUSHED
33:4   insatiable locusts they rushed upon
RUSHES
19:6   Reeds and rushes shall wither;
35:7   reserves shall come rushes and
RUTHLESSLY
27:4   I will ruthlessly attack them
30:14   like an earthenware vessel ruthlessly
SABBATH
1:13   and on the Sabbath,
56:2   who keeps the Sabbath without
56:6   all who keep the Sabbath without
58:13   feet from trampling the Sabbath—
58:13   and consider the Sabbath a delight,
66:23   after New Moon, Sabbath after
66:23   Sabbath, all flesh shall come to
SABBATHS
56:4   the eunuchs who keep my Sabbaths
SABEANS
45:14   the Sabeans, a people tall in stature.
SACKCLOTH
15:3   They will wear sackcloth openly;

20:2   Go and ungird the sackcloth
32:11   put sackcloth around your waists.
22:12   for austerity and wearing sackcloth.
37:1   clothes and put on sackcloth and
37:2   the elders of the priests in sackcloth
50:3   I put up sackcloth to cover them.
58:5   one's bed of sackcloth and ashes?
SACKED
24:3   when the earth is sacked,
42:22   are a people plundered and sacked,
SACRED
57:15   forever, whose name is sacred:
SACRIFICE
19:21   worship by sacrifice and
40:16   its beasts be adequate for sacrifice.
40:20   too poor for this type of sacrifice
61:8   extortion in those who sacrifice—
65:7   To those who kindle sacrifice in the
SACRIFICES
1:11   abundant sacrifices to me? says the
56:7   Their offerings and sacrifices
57:7   there you ascend to offer sacrifices.
66:3   and whoever sacrifices a lamb,
SACRIFICIAL
43:23   me homage by sacrificial slaughter;
SACRIFICING
65:3   sacrificing in parks, making smoke
SAFE
32:18   in safe neighborhoods, in comfortable
SAFETY
14:30   and the needy recline in safety.
SAG
46:2   Such gods altogether sag and bow
SAGES
29:14   void the knowledge of their sages,
SAIL
33:21   where no warships sail
33:23* nor spread out the sail.
SAKE
37:35   my own sake and for the sake of my.
43:14   For your sake I launch an attack on
43:25   it is I myself, and for my own sake,
45:4   For the sake of my servant Jacob,
48:9   For my own name's sake I have
48:11   For my own sake, on my own account,
62:1   For Zion's sake I will not keep silent;
62:1   for Jerusalem's sake I will not remain
63:17   Relent, for the sake of thy servants,
SALVATION
12:2   In the God of my salvation I will
12:2   when he became my salvation.
12:3   from the fountains of salvation.
17:10   forgotten your God, your salvation,
25:9   us joyfully celebrate his salvation!
26:1   Our city is strong; salvation he has
26:18   We have not wrought salvation in the
33:2   our salvation in troubled times.

SALVATION *continued*
33:6   and knowledge your salvation;
43:12 I who foretold and wrought salvation,
45:8   Let the earth receive it and salvation
45:17 with an everlasting salvation;
46:12 my salvation shall no longer be
49:6   that my salvation may be to the end
49:8   in the day of salvation I have come to
51:5   and my salvation proceed;
51:6   But my salvation shall be everlasting;
51:8   my salvation through endless
52:7   who heralds salvation,
52:10* our God's salvation.
56:1   for soon my salvation will come
59:11 we look for salvation, but it eludes
59:16 arm brought about salvation for him;
59:17 and made salvation the helmet on his
60:18 you will regard salvation as your
61:10 clothes me in garments of salvation,
62:1   her salvation like a flaming torch.
62:11 See, your Salvation comes,
63:5   own arm brought about salvation for
SAMARIA
7:9   But as surely as Samaria is the
7:9   son of Remaliah the head of Samaria,
8:4   the plunder of Samaria will
9:9   and those who dwell in Samaria—
10:9   Samaria no better than Damascus?
10:10 those of Jerusalem and Samaria,
10:11 even as I did to Samaria and its idols?
36:19 Did they deliver Samaria out of my
SAME
10:32 This same day he will but pause at
28:24 and harrowing the same ground?
SANCTIFY
8:13   But sanctify the Lord of Hosts,
SANCTUARIES
15:2   They will go up to the sanctuaries,
16:12 and enter their sanctuaries to pray,
SANCTUARY
6:1   filling the sanctuary.
8:14   And to you he will be a sanctuary,
60:13 to beautify the site of my sanctuary,
62:9   within the environs of my sanctuary.
63:18 our enemies trod down thy sanctuary.
SANDAL
5:27   nor their sandal thongs undone.
SANDS
10:22 be as the sands of the sea,
48:19 have been as the sands in number,
SAPLING
53:2   Like a sapling he grew up in his
SAPPHIRES
54:11 and sapphires for your foundations;
SARAH
51:2   to Sarah who bore you.

SARGON
20:1   was sent by Sargon king of
SATE
43:24 or sate me with the fat of
SATISFIED
9:20   on the left, but not be satisfied:
44:16 they eat the meat and are satisfied.
53:11 the toil of his soul and be satisfied;
SATISFY
55:2   your labor on what does not satisfy?
58:10 satisfy the needs of the oppressed,
58:11 he will satisfy your needs in the
SATURATED
34:7   land shall be saturated with blood,
SAUL
10:29 Gibeah of Saul is fleeing.
SAVAGELY
58:4   striking out savagely with the fist.
SAVE
25:9   whom we expected would save us.
33:22 is our King; he himself will save us.
36:15 save us; this city shall not be given
36:18 The Lord will save us. Were any gods
36:18 nations able to save their lands out of
36:20 should save Jerusalem from my hand?
37:35 I will protect this city and save it,
38:20 O Lord, may it please thee to save
44:17 Save us; you are our god!
45:20 prayed to gods that could not save
45:22 Turn to me and save yourselves,
46:7   it cannot save them from trouble.
47:13 stand by you and save you!
47:15 none is there to save you.
57:13 let those who flock to you save you!
59:1   has not become too short to save,
63:1   It is I, who am mighty to save,
SAVED
36:20 saved his land from my hand, that the
45:17 But Israel is saved by the Lord
64:5   that in them we might ever be saved.
SAVIOR
19:20 them a savior, who will take
43:3   Holy One of Israel, am your Savior;
43:11 apart from me there is no savior.
45:15 O Savior, God of Israel.
45:21 except for whom there is no Savior?
49:26 know that I the Lord am your Savior,
60:16 I, the Lord, am your Savior,
63:8   and so he became their Savior:
SAW
2:1   Isaiah the son of Amoz saw in vision:
6:1   I saw my Lord seated on a throne,
10:15 or a saw vaunt itself
13:1   Isaiah the son of Amoz saw in vision:
22:9   When you saw the city of David
39:4   They saw everything there is

59:15 The Lord saw that there was no
59:16 When he saw it, he wondered
SAYINGS
29:4 your sayings shall whisper out of the
SCALE
40:9 Scale the mountain heights,
SCALES
40:12 weighing mountains in scales,
46:6 and weigh out silver on the scales
SCALPS
3:17 the Lord will afflict the scalps
SCARCELY
40:24 When scarcely they are planted,
40:24 or scarcely they are sown,
SCARCER
13:12 I will make mankind scarcer than
SCARLET
1:18 though your sins are as scarlet,
SCARVES
3:19 the pendants, chains and scarves,
SCATTER
24:1 and scatter its inhabitants.
28:25 sprinkle fennel and scatter cumin?
SCATTERED
11:12 he will gather the scattered of Judah
33:3 thine uprising the nations scattered.
SCENE
8:22 scene of anguish and gloom;
SCHEME
32:7 And rogues scheme by malevolent
SCHEMES
29:15 to hide their schemes from the Lord!
SCIENCE
47:10 By your skill and science you were
SCOFF
28:22 Now therefore scoff not,
SCOFFERS
28:14 the word of the Lord, you scoffers
SCOOP
30:14 with which to scoop lit embers from a
SCORCH
37:27 that scorch before they grow up.
SCORCHED
9:19 the earth is scorched,
SCORCHING
25:5 or like scorching heat in the desert,
SCORN
37:4 the king of Assyria has sent to scorn
37:22 she laughs you to scorn.
SCORNERS
29:20 come to nought and scorners cease;
SCOURGE
28:15 should a flooding scourge sweep
28:18 when the flooding scourge sweeps
SCREAM
42:14 But now I will scream like a woman in

SCREEN
22:8 in the day Judea's defensive screen is
SCRIPT
8:1 write on it in common script:
SCROLL
8:1 Take a large scroll and write
34:4 the heavens are rolled up as a scroll,
SCULPTOR
40:20 They seek an expert sculptor
SEA
2:16 against [all vessels at sea,]
5:30 even as the Sea is stirred up.
9:1 the last he will exalt the Sea Route
10:22 be as the sands of the sea,
10:26 His staff is over the Sea,
11:11 and the islands of the sea.
11:15 of the Egyptian Sea by his mighty
16:8 spread abroad across the sea.
18:2 which sends emissaries by sea,
23:4 dismayed, O Sidon, because the Sea,
23:4 the mighty haven of the Sea, has
23:11 will stretch out his hand over the Sea
24:14 and those from across the sea
24:15 and in the isles of the sea
27:1 Leviathan, that devious sea monster,
27:1 when he slays the dragons of the Sea.
42:10 Let the sea roar, and all that lives
43:16 who provides a way in the Sea,
48:18 like the waves of the sea;
50:2 By a mere rebuke I dry up the Sea;
51:10 Was it not you who dried up the Sea,
51:15 stir up the Sea so that its waves roar.
57:20 the wicked are like the raging Sea,
60:5 the multitude of the Sea shall resort
63:11 who brought them up out of the Sea
SEAL
8:16 seal the law among my disciples.
SEALED
29:11 as the words of a sealed book that
29:11 I cannot; it is sealed.
49:16 I have sealed you to be
SEARCH
34:16 Search, and read it in the book of the
SEARING
18:4 when the searing heat overtakes the
SEAS
17:12 who rage like the raging of the seas—
23:2 traders of Sidon crossing the seas.
23:3 source of revenue upon the high seas
SEAT
14:13 I will seat myself
SEATED
6:1 I saw my Lord seated on a throne,
SEBA
43:3 Cush and Seba I give in place of
SECRET
4:6 a secret refuge from the

SECRET *continued*
45:3   and secret hoards of wealth—
45:19   I speak not in secret
48:16   I have not made predictions in secret;
49:2   in his quiver he kept me secret.
SECRETARY
36:3   Shebna the secretary, and Joah the
36:22   the palace, Shebna the secretary, and
37:2   the palace, Shebna the secretary,
SECTOR
24:16   From a sector of the earth we hear
SECURE
26:3   for in thee they are secure.
45:18   who made it secure and organized it,
47:10   Secure in your wickedness,
SECURELY
47:8   securely enthroned, thinking to
SEE
1:12   When you come to see me,
5:19   so we may see it!
6:7   See, this has touched your lips:
6:10   lest they see with their eyes
7:4   Say to him, See to it that you remain
11:3   will not judge by what his eyes see,
13:17   See, I stir up against them the Medes,
20:6   of this isle say, See what has
21:3   I am too distraught to see.
22:15   Go and see that steward, Shebna,
26:10   and see not the glory of the Lord.
29:15   Who will see us? Who will know?
29:18   and the eyes of the blind see
30:10   who say to the seers, See not!
30:20   but your eyes shall see the Master.
32:3   eyes of those who see shall not be
33:7   See, their stalwarts sob in public;
35:2   the glory . . . they shall see there.
35:4   See, your God is coming to avenge
37:7   See, I will give him a notion to return
37:17   open thine eyes and see. Listen to all
38:8   See, I make the shadow cast by the
38:11   I thought, I shall not see the Lord
39:4   What did they see in your palace?
40:5   and all flesh see it at once.
40:10   See, my Lord the Lord comes with
40:26   Lift your eyes heavenward and see:
41:11   See, all who are enraged at you
41:20   that all may see it and know, consider
42:18   listen; O you blind, look and see!
43:19   See, I do a new thing; it is now
44:18   eyes are glazed so they cannot see,
47:14   See, as stubble they are burnt up in
48:10   See, I am refining you, though not as
49:7   Rulers shall rise up when they see
49:12   See these, coming from afar, these,
49:16   See, I have engraved you on my
50:9   See, my Lord the Lord sustains me.
52:8   before their very eyes they see

52:10* that all ends of the earth may see
52:15   was not told them, they shall see;
53:10   he might see his offspring and
53:11   He shall see the toil of his soul and
55:4   See, I have appointed him a witness
58:7   and when you see men underclad to
60:5   Then, when you see it, your face will
61:9   all who see them will acknowledge
62:11   See, your Salvation comes,
64:9   See, consider that we are all thy
65:6   See, it is written before me that I will
65:17   See, I create new heavens and a new
65:18   See, I create Jerusalem to be a
66:5   that we may see cause for your joy!
66:12   For thus says the Lord: See,
66:14   Your heart shall rejoice to see it,
66:15   See, the Lord comes with fire,
SEED
5:10   a homer of seed but an ephah.
17:10   and sow hybrid seed,
28:24   be forever plowing to sow seed,
30:23   the seed you sow in the ground,
55:10   providing seed for the sower and
SEEING
6:9   Go on seeing, but not perceiving.
42:20   seeing much but not giving heed,
SEEK
40:20   They seek an expert sculptor
45:19   to seek me amid chaos.
57:13   But they who seek refuge in me shall
65:1   to those who did not seek me.
65:10   the herds of my people who seek me.
SEEKERS
51:1   seekers of the Lord:
SEEKING
30:2   on seeking protection in Pharaoh's
SEEKS
26:9   my spirit within me seeks after thee.
SEEM
10:7   it shall not seem so to him;
SEEN
6:5   I have seen the King, the Lord of
9:2   have seen a bright light;
29:7   shall be as a dream seen in the night.
33:19   insolent people are not to be seen,
38:5   your prayer and seen your tears.
57:18   Yet I have seen his conduct and will
64:4   nor has any eye seen a God besides
66:8   or who has seen such things?
66:19   concerning me, nor seen my glory—
SEERS
28:7   they err as seers, they blunder in
29:10   he has covered your heads, the seers.
30:10   who say to the seers, See not!
56:10   lolling seers fond of slumber.
SEES
21:6   who will report what he sees.

28:4 he who sees it devours it
29:23 For when he sees among him his
SEIR
21:11 Men call to see me from Seir,
SEIZE
5:29 growling, they seize the prey, and
28:19 and by night it shall seize you
SEIZED
13:8 seized with trembling like a woman
21:3 throes of agony have seized me like a
28:19 you shall be seized by it:
36:1 of Judea and seized them.
SELA
16:1 from Sela in the desert
42:11 let the inhabitants of Sela sing for joy
SELECT
40:20 select a wood that resists decay.
44:14 he must select holms and oaks
SELL
50:1 which of my creditors did I sell you?
SELLER
24:2 with seller as with buyer,
SEMBLANCE
52:14 his semblance unlike that of men—
SEND
6:8 Whom shall I send? Who will go for
6:8 And I replied, Here am I; send me!
10:16 send a consumption into his fertile
16:1 Send couriers to those who rule in the
19:20 the oppressors, he will send
22:18 and send you spinning like a top
36:12 Did my lord send me to say these
57:9 you send your solicitors far abroad
SENDING
66:19 sending those of them who survive
SENDS
18:2 which sends emissaries by sea,
SENNACHERIB
36:1 Sennacherib king of Assyria
37:9 Sennacherib received a report that
37:17 Sennacherib has sent to mock the
37:21 to me concerning Sennacherib king of
37:37 So Sennacherib king of Assyria broke
SENSE
44:19 nor have the sense or comprehension
SENSES
46:8 and come to your senses;
SENT
9:8 This message my Lord sent to Jacob,
20:1 was sent by Sargon king of
36:2 the king of Assyria sent Rabshakeh
37:2 And he sent Eliakim the overseer of
37:4 king of Assyria has sent to scorn
37:9 And when he heard it, he sent
37:16 Sennacherib has sent to mock the
37:20 Isaiah the son of Amoz sent word
39:1 king of Babylon, sent letters

42:19 the messenger I have sent?
48:16 Now my Lord the Lord has sent me;
55:11 the purpose for which I sent it.
61:1 he has sent me to bind up the
SENTENCED
34:5 I have sentenced to damnation.
SEPARATE
59:2 that separate you from your God;
SEPHARVAIM
36:19 Where are the gods of Sepharvaim?
37:13 cities of Sepharvaim, Hena, and Ivvah
SEPULCHRES
22:16 who hew their sepulchres up high,
65:4 who sit in sepulchres, spend nights
SERAPHS
6:2 Seraphs stood by him overhead,
6:6 Then one of the seraphs flew to me
SERPENT
14:29 shall be a fiery flying serpent.
27:1 the evasive maritime serpent,
30:6 vipers and the fiery flying serpent,
59:5 is smashed, there emerges a serpent.
65:25 as for the serpent, dust shall be its
SERVANT
20:3 my servant Isaiah has gone
22:20 my servant Eliakim the son of
24:2 with master as with servant,
37:35 and for the sake of my servant David.
41:8 But you, O Israel, my servant,
41:9 to you I say, You are my servant;
42:1 My servant whom I sustain,
42:19 Who is blind but my own servant,
42:19 uncomprehending as the servant of
43:10 my servant whom I have chosen,
44:1 Hear now, Jacob my servant,
44:2 Be not afraid, O Jacob, my servant,
44:21 for you are my servant.
44:21 I have created you to be my servant,
44:26 who fulfills the word of his servant,
45:4 For the sake of my servant Jacob,
48:20 Lord has redeemed his servant Jacob.
49:3 He said to me, You are my servant,
49:5 to be his servant, to restore Jacob to
49:6 for you to be my servant
49:7 a servant to those in authority:
50:10 and heeds the voice of his servant,
52:13 My servant, being astute, shall be
53:11 shall my servant, the righteous one,
SERVANTS
36:9 of the least of my lord's servants,
36:11 please speak to your servants
37:5* And when King Hezekiah's servants
37:24 By your servants you have
54:17 heritage of the servants of the Lord,
56:6 that they may be his servants—
63:17 Relent, for the sake of thy servants,
65:8 so I will do on behalf of my servants

531

SERVANTS *continued*
65:9   my servants shall dwell there.
65:13 My servants shall eat indeed,
65:13 my servants shall drink indeed,
65:13 my servants shall rejoice indeed,
65:14 My servants shall shout indeed, for
65:15 But his servants he will call by a
66:14 shall be manifest among his servants
SERVE
7:25   but they shall serve as a cattle range,
19:20 They shall serve as a sign and
39:7   some to serve as eunuchs in
55:13 This shall serve as a testimony of the
56:6   who adhere to the Lord to serve him,
60:7   the rams of Nebaioth will serve you;
60:12 that will not serve you shall perish;
65:15 to serve my chosen ones as a curse
66:1   would serve me as a place of residence
SERVED
40:2   to her that she has served her term,
SERVITUDE
14:3   servitude imposed on you,
58:9   Indeed, if you will banish servitude
SET
7:6   and set a ruler over it—the son of
9:18   Wickedness shall be set ablaze like a
13:8   their faces set aflame.
14:13 and set up my throne above the stars
16:5   shall a throne be set up in the abode
18:5   and the set blossoms are developing
23:13 Assyrians who set up observatories,
24:5   set at nought the ancient covenant.
26:1   city is strong; salvation he has set up
27:4   and altogether set them ablaze.
33:12 down like thorns and set ablaze.
37:9   king of Cush had set out to fight
45:13 he will settle my city and set free
46:7   when they set it in place, there it
50:7   I have set my face like flint,
51:14 he who is bowed down be set free;
51:16 heavens and set the earth in place,
58:6   to set the oppressed at liberty
60:20 Your sun shall set no more,
66:19 And I will set a mark upon them,
SETS
42:25 till it sets them on fire;
45:6   where the sun rises to where it sets
51:13 who sets the earth in place—
SETTLE
7:19   settle with one accord
14:1   he will settle them in their own land,
23:7   feet led her to settle far-off lands?
49:20 give us space in which to settle!
SETTLEMENTS
32:18 shall dwell in peaceful settlements,
SEVEN
4:1   Seven women will take hold of one

11:15 and smite it into seven streams
30:26 as the light of seven days shall it be,
SEVENFOLD
30:26 light of the sun increase sevenfold;
SEVENTY
23:15 seventy years, the lifetime of a king.
23:15 And at the end of seventy years, Tyre
23:17 for after seventy years, the Lord
SEVERE
28:22 lest your bonds grow severe,
SEVERED
33:20 nor any of its cords severed.
SEVERELY
27:1   punish severely Leviathan,
SEVERING
38:12 he is severing me from the loom.
SEVERITY
21:15 and the severity of war.
SEVERS
30:28 that severs at the neck.
SHADE
4:6   It shall be a shelter and shade
25:4   and shade from the heat.
25:5   burning heat by the shade of a cloud,
32:2   shade of a large rock in arid country.
SHADOW
9:2   of the shadow of death
30:2   on taking shelter in Egypt's shadow.
30:3   shelter in Egypt's shadow to
38:8   See, I make the shadow cast by the
49:2   in the shadow of his hand he hid me.
51:16 shelter you in the shadow of my hand,
SHAKE
14:16 the man who made the earth shake
24:18 the earth shall shake to its
52:2   Shake yourself free, rise from the
SHAKEN
7:2   his people were shaken,
7:2   trees in a forest are shaken by a gale.
44:8   Be not perturbed or shaken.
54:10 nor my covenant of peace be shaken,
SHAKES
37:22 Jerusalem shakes her head at you.
SHAKING
54:10 and the hills collapse with shaking,
SHAME
20:4   to Egypt's shame.
24:23 blush and the sun be put to shame,
30:3   protection shall turn to your shame,
41:11 shall earn shame and disgrace;
45:17 not be dismayed or put to shame
45:24 Before him must come in shame
47:3   and your shame uncovered.
54:4   shall forget the shame of your youth
61:7   Because their shame was twofold,
66:5   But it is they who shall suffer shame.

SHAMEFULLY
33:9   Lebanon wilts shamefully;
SHANTY
24:20   sway back and forth like a shanty;
SHAPE
44:12   and gives it shape by hammering;
SHARD
30:14   fragments shall not be found a shard
SHARDS
45:9   mere shards of earthenware pottery!
SHARE
14:20   You shall not share burial with them,
58:7   to share your food with the hungry,
SHAREZER
37:38   Adrammelech and Sharezer slew him
SHARON
33:9   Sharon has been turned into a dry
35:2   the splendor of Carmel and Sharon,
65:10   Sharon shall become pasture for
SHARP
5:28   Their arrows are sharp;
28:27   with a sharp-toothed sledge,
41:15   I will make of you a sharp-toothed
49:2   made my mouth like a sharp sword—
SHATTER
10:33   shatter the towering trees with
30:14   It shall shatter with a crash
SHATTERED
1:28   shall be altogether shattered
7:8   be shattered as a nation.
SHAVE
7:20   the king of Assyria—to shave
SHAWL
3:22   the elegant dress, the shawl,
SHEARERS
53:7   a sheep, dumb before its shearers,
SHEAR-JASHUB
7:3   you and your son Shear-Jashub,
SHEBA
60:6   all from Sheba will come,
SHEBNA
22:15   Go and see that steward, Shebna,
36:3   Shebna the secretary, and Joah the
36:11   Then Eliakim, Shebna and Joah said
36:22   the palace, Shebna the secretary, and
37:2   the palace, Shebna the secretary,
SHED
26:21   earth will uncover the blood shed
34:4   their starry hosts shed themselves
59:7   they hasten to shed innocent blood.
SHEEP
1:11   blood of bulls and sheep and he-goats
5:17   Then shall his sheep feed in their
7:21   alive a young cow and a pair of sheep.
7:25   a terrain for sheep to tread down.
13:14   or a flock of sheep that no one rounds
22:13   of cattle and slaughter of sheep,

53:6   We all like sheep had gone astray,
53:7   like a sheep, dumb before its
SHEER
3:23   hosiery, sheer linen, millinery, and
SHELISHIAH
15:5   and as far as Eglath Shelishiah.
SHELTER
1:8   like a shelter in a vineyard,
4:6   It shall be a shelter and shade
16:3   Shelter those dispossessed;
25:4   a shelter for the needy in distress.
30:2   on taking shelter in Egypt's shadow.
30:3   shelter in Egypt's shadow to
32:2   And a man shall become as a shelter
51:16   and shelter you in the shadow of my
SHEOL
5:14   Sheol becomes ravenous,
14:9   Sheol below was in commotion
14:11   glory has been cast down to Sheol,
14:15   you have been brought down to Sheol,
28:15   reached an understanding with Sheol,
28:18   understanding with Sheol have no
38:18   For Sheol cannot praise thee, nor
SHEOL'S
38:10   must I depart through Sheol's gates,
SHEPHERD
40:11   Like a shepherd he pastures his
44:28   says of Cyrus, He is my shepherd;
63:11   with the shepherd of his flock?
SHEPHERDS
13:20   nor will shepherds rest their flocks
31:4   the shepherds muster in full force
56:11   indeed are insensible shepherds.
SHEPHERD'S
38:12   away from me like a shepherd's tent.
SHIHOR
23:3   The grain of Shihor, the harvest of the
SHILOAH
8:6   the waters of Shiloah, which flow
SHINAR
11:11   Egypt, Pathros, Cush, Elam, Shinar,
SHINE
13:10   the stars . . . will not shine.
60:1   Arise, shine, your light has dawned;
60:2   upon you the Lord will shine;
SHINES
62:1   her righteousness shines like a light,
SHINING
17:8   of prosperity and the shining images.
27:9   and shining images standing.
SHIPPING
23:13   who founded Tyre for shipping.
43:14   who sing the praises of shipping.
SHIPS
2:16   both merchant ships and pleasure
23:1   Sound your sirens, O merchant ships!
23:14   Sound your sirens, O merchant ships;

SHIPS *continued*
60:9   the ships of Tarshish in the lead,
SHOES
20:2   the shoes from your feet.
SHOOK
 6:4   The threshold shook to its foundation
SHOOT
11:1   A shoot will spring up from the stock
37:33 not enter this city or shoot an arrow
44:4   They shall shoot up like grass
SHORT
28:20 The couch is too short to stretch out
50:2   Was my hand too short to redeem
59:1   hand . . . become too short to save,
SHOULDER
 9:6   who will shoulder the burden of
SHOULDERS
10:27 lifted from your shoulders,
14:25 removed from their shoulders.
46:7   carrying it on their shoulders;
49:22 your daughters on their shoulders.
SHOUT
12:6   Shout and sing for joy, O inhabitants
16:10 the vintage shout I will bring to an
24:14 lift up their voice and shout for joy,
35:6   the tongue of the dumb shout for joy.
42:2   He will not shout or raise his voice
42:13 raise the shout of victory over his
49:13 Shout for joy, O heavens; celebrate, O
65:14 My servants shall shout indeed, for
SHOUTED
61:7   and shouted insults were their lot,
SHOUTS
16:9   when your shouts of cheer
16:10 no shouts of delight shall sound in
SHOVEL
30:24 eat grain silage winnowed with shovel
SHOW
 5:16 the holy God show himself holy
13:18 They will show no mercy to the
36:5   show of strength? In whom have
39:2   that Hezekiah did not show them.
39:4   that I did not show them.
49:9   in darkness, Show yourselves!
60:10 I will gladly show you mercy.
SHOWED
39:2   was glad of them and showed
47:6   and you showed them no mercy;
SHOWERS
44:3   showers upon the dry ground;
SHOWING
49:13 showing compassion for his afflicted.
SHOWN
26:10 Though favor be shown the wicked,
48:9   I have shown restraint toward you
SHOWS
27:11 Therefore their Maker shows them no

SHRANK
37:27 shrank away in confusion,
SHREWD
31:2   Yet he too is shrewd
SHREWDNESS
10:13 and shrewdness, for I am ingenious.
SHRINES
15:2   to Dibon to the hill shrines, to weep;
16:12 with petitioning on the hill shrines,
36:7   shrines and altars Hezekiah
SHRINK
31:9   their officers shrink from the ensign,
SHRIVEL
19:7   shrivel and blow away and be no more
SHRIVELLED
34:4   or shrivelled fruit from a fig tree.
SHROUD
25:7   the shroud that shrouds all nations,
SHROUDS
25:7   the shroud that shrouds all nations,
SHUN
59:15 they who shun evil become a prey.
SHUNNED
53:3   he was shunned, deemed by us of no
SHUT
 6:10 dull their ears and shut their eyes,
22:22 when he opens none shall shut,
24:22 and shut in confinement many days,
26:20 and shut the doors behind you;
29:10 he has shut your eyes, the prophets;
32:3   of those who see shall not be shut,
33:15 who shut their eyes at the sight of
45:1   letting no gates remain shut:
60:11 they shall not be shut day or night,
SHUTS
22:22 when he shuts none shall open.
SHUTTERED
24:10 all houses are shuttered, that none
SHUTTING
52:15 rulers shutting their mouths at him—
SIBMAH
16:9   for the vines of Sibmah;
SIBMAH'S
16:8   nations will smite Sibmah's vines.
SICK
 1:5   The whole head is sick
SIDE
60:4   daughters shall return to your side.
SIDON
23:2   traders of Sidon crossing the seas.
23:4   be dismayed, O Sidon, because the
23:12 O ravished virgin, Daughter of Sidon.
SIEGE
 1:8   a city under siege.
21:2   O Elamites! Lay siege, you Medes!
29:3   erect siege installations against you.

SIEGEWORKS
37:33 nor erect siegeworks against it.
SIEVE
30:28 in the sieve of falsehood;
SIFT
30:28 He comes to sift the nations
SIGHING
21:2 All the sighing that Babylon has
35:10 when sorrow and sighing flee away.
51:11 and sorrow and sighing flee away.
SIGHT
14:16 Those who catch sight of you
33:15 their eyes at the sight of wickedness.
SIGHTLESS
44:9 sightless and mindless, to their own
SIGN
7:11 Ask a sign for yourself
7:14 give you a sign: the young woman
19:20 They shall serve as a sign and
20:3 three years as a sign and portent
37:30 But to you this shall be a sign:
38:22* But Hezekiah said, What of a sign
38.7 This shall be a sign
55:13 an everlasting sign that shall not be
SIGNAL
7:18 signal for the flies from
10:32 and signal the advance
SIGNATORIES
33:8 their signatories held in contempt;
SIGNS
3:20 zodiac signs and charm amulets,
8:18 signs and portents in Israel
45:11 Will you ask me for signs
SILAGE
30:24 eat grain silage winnowed with shovel
SILENCE
18:4 I will watch in silence over my
64:12 in silence letting us suffer so
SILENCED
15:1 Moab shall be silenced;
SILENT
26:16 they poured out silent prayers
36:21 But they remained silent, replying
41:1 Be silent before me, O isles;
42:14 For a long time I have been silent,
57:11 because I have so long kept silent
62:1 For Zion's sake I will not keep silent;
62:6 who shall not be silent day or night.
SILVER
1:22 Your silver has become dross,
2:7 Their land is full of silver and gold
2:20 their idols of silver and gods of gold
13:17 who do not value silver, nor covet
30:22 your graven idols plated with silver,
31:7 despise your idolatrous silver and
39:2 envoys his treasures—the silver
40:19 fitted with a silver chain from the

46:6 and weigh out silver on the scales
48:10 am refining you, though not as silver
60:9 and with them their silver and gold,
60:17 in place of iron, silver;
SIMILAR
46:5 that we should appear similar?
SIN
1:4 a people weighed down by sin,
3:9 they flaunt their sin like Sodom;
5:18 Woe to those drawn to sin by vain
30:1 only adding sin to sin!
57:4 Surely you are born of sin, a spurious
57:17 By his sin of covetousness I was
SINCE
7:17 house a day unlike any since
10:10 Since I could do this to the pagan
14:8 Since you have been laid low,
46:3 have been a load on me since birth,
47:12 exerted yourself since your youth.
47:15 exerted yourself since your youth
SINEW
48:4 your neck was an iron sinew, your
SINFUL
55:7 and the sinful men their thoughts.
SING
5:1 Let me sing for my beloved
12:5 Sing in praise of the Lord,
12:6 Shout and sing for joy, O inhabitants
23:16 Play skillfully; sing song after song,
26:19 Awake, and sing for joy,
27:2 In that day, sing of the earth
42:10 Sing to the Lord a new song;
42:10 sing his praise from the end of the
42:11 let the inhabitants of Sela sing for joy
43:14 they who sing the praises of
44:23 Sing, O heavens, for what the Lord
54:1 Sing, O barren woman who did not
55:12 hills shall sing at your presence
SINGING
24:16 a sector of the earth we hear singing:
30:29 But for you there shall be singing,
35:2 singing with delight;
35:10 they shall come singing to Zion,
51:11 Let them come singing to Zion,
SINGLE
9:14 palm top and reed, in a single day;
10:17 his briars and thorns in a single day.
SINIM
49:12 and these, from the land of Sinim.
SINNED
42:24 against whom we have sinned?
43:27 your spokesmen sinned against me.
64:5 wast roused to anger when we sinned,
SINNERS
1:28 But criminals and sinners
13:9 sinners may be annihilated from it.
33:14 The sinners in Zion are struck with

SINNING
50:1 Surely, by sinning you sold yourselves;
SINS
1:18 though your sins are as scarlet,
6:7 your sins are taken away,
27:9 as a result of this his sins removed:
38:17 hast cast all my sins behind thee,
40:2 double for all her sins.
43:24 you have burdened me with your sins,
43:25 remembering your sins no more.
44:22 your sins like a cloud of mist.
53:12 he bore the sins of many,
58:1 to the house of Jacob their sins.
59:2 your sins hide his face, so that he
59:12 our sins testify against us.
64:6 our sins, like a wind, sweep us away.
SIRENS
23:1 Sound your sirens, O merchant ships!
23:14 Sound your sirens, O merchant ships;
SIT
3:26 she shall sit on the ground destitute.
16:5 and in faithfulness a judge sit on it
42:7 prison those who sit in darkness.
47:1 Get down and sit in the dust,
47:5 Sit speechless; retire into obscurity,
47:14 such is no fire to sit by!
52:2 sit enthroned, O Jerusalem.
65:4 who sit in sepulchres, spend nights
SITE
4:5 Over the whole site of Mount Zion,
54:2 Expand the site of your tent;
60:13 to beautify the site of my sanctuary,
SITS
28:6 justice to him who sits in judgment,
40:22 By him who sits enthroned above the
SITTEST
37:16 who sittest enthroned between the
SITTING
36:12 and not to the men sitting on the wall
SIX
6:2 each having six wings—
SIXTY-FIVE
7:8 within sixty-five years shall
SKETCHING
44:13 sketching his idol with a marker.
SKIES
45:8 skies overflow with righteousness.
SKILL
45:9 Your hands have no skill for the
47:10 By your skill and science you were
SKILLED
3:3 skilled craftsmen, and orators.
SKILLFULLY
23:16 Play skillfully; sing song after song,
SKIRT
6:1 highly exalted, the skirt of his robe

SKY
55:10 rains and snows descend from the sky
SKYLIGHTS
54:12 I will make your skylights of jacinth,
SLACKENED
57:10 and therefore have not slackened.
SLAIN
10:4 or fall among the slain.
14:19 exposed like the slain disfigured by
14:30 and your survivors shall be slain.
22:2 But your slain were not killed by the
26:21 and no more conceal its slain.
27:7 Or was he slain as were they who slew
34:3 Their slain shall be flung out
66:16 slain by the Lord shall be many.
SLASHING
18:5 remove the new branches by slashing.
SLAUGHTER
22:13 killing of cattle and slaughter of sheep
30:25 on the day of the great slaughter,
34:2 consigned them to the slaughter.
34:6 Lord will hold a slaughter in Bozrah,
43:23 homage by sacrificial slaughter;
53:7 like a lamb led to slaughter,
65:12 you shall succumb to the slaughter.
SLAUGHTERS
66:3 But whoever slaughters an ox
SLAY
11:4 breath of his lips slay the wicked.
SLAYERS
57:5 slayers of children in the gullies
SLAYS
27:1 when he slays the dragons of the Sea.
65:15 when my Lord the Lord slays you.
SLEDGE
28:27 with a sharp-toothed sledge,
41:15 you a sharp-toothed threshing sledge
SLEEP
29:10 a spirit of deep sleep:
SLEEPLESS
38:14 [I am utterly sleepless
SLEW
27:7 he slain as were they who slew him?
37:36 slew a hundred and eighty-five
37:38 Adrammelech and Sharezer slew him
51:9 you who slew the dragon?
SLIPPERY
57:6 Among the slippery stones of the
SLOGANS
32:7 false slogans and accusations
SLOPES
15:5 In tears they will ascend the slopes
63:14 descending the slopes of ravines,
SLUMBER
56:10 lolling seers fond of slumber.
SLUMP
40:30 men slump down of exhaustion.

SLUMPS
46:1   Bel slumps down, Nebo is stooped
SMALL
49:6   he said: It is too small a thing
49:19   now be too small for your inhabitants
SMASHED
9:4   For thou hast smashed the yoke
30:14   vessel ruthlessly smashed,
59:5   and if any is smashed, there emerges
SMELT
1:25   and smelt away your dross as in a
SMITE
11:4   he will smite the earth with the rod
11:15   and smite it into seven streams
16:8   nations will smite Sibmah's vines.
19:22   The Lord will smite Egypt,
SMITERS
27:7   Was he smitten as were his smiters?
50:6   I offered my back to smiters,
SMITES
9:13   to him who smites them,
SMITH
40:19   overlaid by the smith with gold,
41:7*   The artisan encourages the smith,
44:12   The smith with his tools works the
46:6   hire a smith to make them a god
54:16   the smith who fans the flaming coals,
SMITING
19:22   and by smiting heal it: they
SMITTEN
1:5   Why be smitten further
27:7   Was he smitten as were his smiters?
49:10   nor be smitten by oppressive heat or
53:4   smitten of God, and humbled.
SMOKE
9:18   in mushrooming clouds of smoke.
14:31   North shall come pillars of smoke,
34:10   its smoke shall ascend forever.
51:6   the heavens shall vanish as by smoke,
65:3   making smoke upon bricks,
65:5   Such are a smoke to my nostrils,
SMOKING
7:4   by these two smoking tail ends of
SMOLDERING
65:5   a fire smoldering all day long.
SMOOTHED
28:25   When he has smoothed its surface,
SNAKE
14:29   among the descendants of that snake
SNARE
8:14   and a snare, catching unawares
SNATCH
9:20   They will snatch on the right, yet
SNORTINGS
37:29   And because of your snortings
SNOW
1:18   they can be made white as snow;

SNOWS
55:10   And as the rains and snows descend
SNUFF
42:3   a dim wick he will not snuff out.
SNUFFED
43:17   they flicker and die, snuffed out like
SOAR
22:17   he will make you soar like a dart.
SOB
33:7   See, their stalwarts sob in public;
SOCIETY
44:11   Their whole society is confused;
SODOM
1:9   we should have been as Sodom,
1:10   O leaders of Sodom;
3:9   they flaunt their sin like Sodom;
13:19   as God overthrew Sodom and
SOIL
1:7   your native soil is devoured by aliens
30:24   oxen and asses that till the soil
34:7   their soil enriched with fat.
44:3   I will pour water on the thirsty soil,
SOJOURN
21:13   who sojourn in the forests of Arabia,
52:4   went down to Egypt to sojourn there.
SOLACE
40:1   Comfort and give solace to my
51:3   bringing solace to all her ruins;
SOLD
50:1   Surely, by sinning you sold yourselves;
52:3   you were sold without price,
SOLDIER
3:2   the valiant man and soldier,
SOLEMN
1:13   with the solemn gathering
4:5   and over its solemn assembly,
33:20   the city of our solemn assemblies;
SOLES
1:6   From the soles of the feet even to
37:25   With the soles of my feet
SOLICITORS
57:9   you send your solicitors far abroad
SOLUTION
16:3   Provide a solution, they say; judge
SOMEONE
65:8   and someone says, Don't destroy it, it
SOMETHING
41:23   Perform something good or evil
SOMEWHERE
45:19   somewhere in a land of darkness;
SON
1:1   The vision of Isaiah the son of Amoz
2:1   Isaiah the son of Amoz saw in vision:
7:1   Ahaz son of Jotham, the son of Uzziah
7:1   Rezin king of Aram and Pekah son of
7:3   you and your son Shear-Jashub,
7:4   and the son of Remaliah,

SON *continued*

7:5	Ephraim and the son of Remaliah,
7:6	set a ruler over it—the son of Tabeal.
7:9	son of Remaliah the head of Samaria,
7:14	with child shall give birth to a son
8:2	the son of Jeberechiah, to witness for
8:3	she conceived and gave birth to a son.
8:6	in Rezin and the son of Remaliah,
9:6	to us a child is born, a son appointed,
13:1	which Isaiah the son of Amoz
14:12	O morning star, son of the dawn!
20:2	Isaiah the son of Amoz, saying,
22:20	servant Eliakim the son of Hilkiah:
36:3	the son of Hilkiah, overseer of the
36:3	the secretary, and Joah the son
36:22	Then Eliakim the son of Hilkiah,
36:22	Joah the son of Asaph,
37:2	the prophet Isaiah the son of Amoz.
37:21	The Isaiah the son of Amoz sent word
37:38	And his son Esarhaddon succeeded
38:1	the prophet Isaiah the son of Amoz
39:1	Merodach-Baladan the son of Baladan,
66:7	she delivers a son!

SONG

5:1	a love song about his vineyard:
12:2	Lord was my strength and my song
23:15	shall be as the harlot in the song:
23:16	Play skillfully; sing song after song,
24:9	Men no longer drink wine amid song;
26:1	In that day shall this song be sung in
42:10	Sing to the Lord a new song;
44:23	Burst into song, O mountains,
49:13	Burst into song, O mountains!
51:3	thanksgiving with the voice of song.
52:9	Break out all together into song,
54:1	break into jubilant song, you who

SONS

1:2	I have reared sons, brought them up,
14:21	for the massacre of their sons,
21:17	remaining of the sons of Kedar
30:1	Woe to you, rebellious sons, says the
30:9	rebellious people, sons who break
37:38	temple of Nisroch his god, his sons
38:19	as I do this day; from father to sons
39:7	And from among your own sons, your
43:6	Bring my sons from afar
49:17	Your sons shall hasten your ravagers
49:22	will bring your sons in their bosoms
51:18	the hand of all the sons she reared.
56:5	is better than sons and daughters;
60:4	your sons shall arrive from afar;
60:14	The sons of those who tormented you
62:5	so shall your sons wed you;
63:8	sons who will not play false;

SOON

5:11	as soon as they arise in the morning,
5:19	soon come to pass, and we will know!

10:25	anger will very soon come to an end;
30:19	answer you as soon as he hears it.
51:14	Soon now shall he who is bowed down
56:1	for soon my salvation will come
66:8	For as soon as she was in labor,

SOONER

48:3	no sooner did they issue from my

SOOTHED

1:6	nor soothed with ointment.

SORCERESS

57:3	you children of the sorceress,

SORES

1:6	bruises and festering sores;

SORROW

29:2	there shall be mourning and sorrow
35:10	when sorrow and sighing flee away.
51:11	and sorrow and sighing flee away.

SOUGHT

11:10	shall be sought by the nations,

SOUL

1:14	meetings my soul detests.
26:9	My soul yearns for thee in the night;
32:6	leaving the hungry soul empty,
32:6	depriving the thirsty soul of drink.
38:14	from bitterness of soul . . .
38:17	by its means thou drawest my soul
53:11	the toil of his soul and be satisfied;
53:12	he poured out his soul unto death,
61:10	my soul delights in my God.

SOULS

3:9	Woe to their souls;
55:2	your souls shall enjoy abundance.
55:3	pay heed, that your souls may live!
57:16	the spirits and souls I have made
66:3	their souls delighting in their

SOUL'S

26:8	the soul's desire is to contemplate

SOUND

1:6	there is nothing sound,
6:4	at the sound of those who called
13:2	sound the voice among them!
15:4	They will sound the alarm
15:8	the sound of it shall reach Eglaim
16:10	delight shall sound in the vineyards.
23:1	Sound your sirens, O merchant ships!
23:14	Sound your sirens, O merchant ships;
24:18	those who flee at the sound of terror
27:13	a loud trumpet shall sound
31:4	dismayed at the sound of their voice
65:19	the sound of weeping or the cry of

SOUNDED

18:3	heed the trumpet when sounded!

SOURCE

19:17	a source of terror to the Egyptians;
23:3	was her source of revenue upon the
28:6	a source of strength to those who

SOUTH
21:1   through the South, they come from
43:6   to the south, Withhold not!
SOVEREIGNTY
9:7   that sovereignty may be extended
17:3   so shall the sovereignty of Damascus:
SOW
17:10 and sow hybrid seed,
17:11 the very morning you sow them,
28:24 be forever plowing to sow seed,
30:23 the seed you sow in the ground,
32:20 who shall then sow by all waters,
37:30 But in the third year sow and harvest,
SOWER
55:10 providing seed for the sower and
SOWN
19:7   and all things sown along irrigation
40:24 or scarcely they are sown,
61:11 garden causes what is sown to spring
SPACE
49:20 give us space in which to settle!
SPAN
8:8   his outspread wings will span
40:12 by the span of his fingers?
SPARK
1:31   their works a spark;
SPARKS
50:11 who illuminate with mere sparks.
50:11 and by the sparks you have kindled.
SPATTERED
63:3   Their lifeblood spattered my
SPEAK
28:11 must he speak to these people,
29:4   you will speak from the ground,
36:11 please speak to your servants
36:11 Do not speak to us in Judean in the
37:10 Speak thus to Hezekiah king of Judah:
40:2   speak kindly to Jerusalem.
40:27 and speak thus, O Israel:
42:12 in the isles speak out praise of him.
43:21 to speak out in praise of me.
43:26 Speak up and vindicate yourself.
45:19 I speak not in secret
45:21 Speak up and present your case;
46:10 I speak, and my purposes take effect;
52:6   that I, who speak, am at hand.
59:3   your lips speak guile, your tongue
SPEAKING
19:18 In that day five Hebrew-speaking
58:13 and speaking of business matters—
65:24 they are yet speaking I will respond.
SPEARS
2:4   Their spears into pruning hooks:
SPECKS
40:15 isles he displaces as mere specks.
SPECTACLES
22:1   concerning the Arena of Spectacles:

22:5   in the Arena of Spectacles,
SPECTACULARLY
10:34 and Lebanon fall spectacularly.
SPEECH
6:5   for I am a man of unclean speech,
6:5   among a people of unclean speech:
28:11 by incomprehensible speech
33:19 a nation of incomprehensible speech,
45:19 and am forthright of speech.
58:9   pointing finger and offensive speech,
SPEECHLESS
47:5   Sit speechless; retire into obscurity,
SPEED
5:19   Let him quickly speed up his work
SPEEDILY
5:26   they come, swiftly and speedily.
18:2   Go speedily, you messengers!
58:8   and your healing speedily appear;
SPEND
55:2   Why do you spend money on what is
65:4   spend nights in hideouts,
SPENT
49:4   I have spent my strength for nothing
SPHERE
40:22 enthroned above the earth's sphere,
SPICES
39:2   the spices and fragrant oils, and his
SPIDERS'
59:5   vipers' eggs and spin spiders' webs;
SPIKES
41:15 of new design, full of spikes:
SPIN
59:5   vipers' eggs and spin spiders' webs;
SPINNING
22:18 and send you spinning like a top
SPIRIT
4:4   spirit of justice, by a burning wind.
11:2   The Spirit of the Lord will rest upon
11:2   the spirit of wisdom and of
11:2   the spirit of counsel and of valor,
11:2   the spirit of knowledge
15:4   but their spirit shall be broken.
19:3   Egypt's spirit shall be drained from
19:14 with a spirit of confusion;
26:9   my spirit within me seeks after thee.
28:6   a spirit of justice to him who sits in
29:10 a spirit of deep sleep:
29:24 erring in spirit gain understanding
31:3   their horses are flesh, not spirit:
32:15 Then shall a Spirit from on high
34:16 by his Spirit he brings them together.
38:16 them all the renewal of my spirit.
40:7   Though the Spirit of the Lord
40:13 comprehended the Spirit of the Lord,
42:1   him I have endowed with my Spirit;
42:5   spirit to those who walk on it:
44:3   I will pour out my Spirit on your

SPIRIT *continued*
48:16 his Spirit is in me.
57:15 who is humble and lowly in spirit—
59:19 impelled by the Spirit of the Lord.
59:21 My Spirit which is upon you
61:1   The Spirit of my Lord the Lord is
61:3   robe in place of a downcast spirit.
63:10 rebelled and grieved his holy Spirit,
63:11 he who put into him his holy Spirit,
63:14 it was the Spirit of the lord that
65:14 howling from brokenness of spirit.
66:2   of a humble and contrite spirit
SPIRITISTS
 8:19 of mediums and spiritists
19:3   resort to the idols and to spiritists,
SPIRITS
14:9   account she roused all the spirits
26:14 spirits who will not rise up;
57:15 refreshing the spirits of the lowly,
57:16 the spirits and souls I have made
SPITTING
50:6   my face from insult and spitting.
SPLENDID
13:19 the most splendid of kingdoms,
SPLENDOR
28:1   Their crowning splendor has become
35:2   the splendor of Carmel and Sharon,
35:2   the Lord and the splendor of our God
60:13 The splendor of Lebanon shall become
SPLINTERED
36:6   of Egypt, that splintered reed which
SPOIL
 8:1   Hasten the plunder, hurry the spoil.
 9:3   are joyous when they divide spoil.
10:2   mere spoil of the fatherless!
10:6   for plunder, to spoliate for spoil,
33:4   Their spoil was harvested
33:23* Now shall spoil in abundance be
42:22 a spoil, yet none demands restitution.
49:24 Can the warrior's spoil be taken from
49:25 says the Lord: The warrior's spoil
53:12 shall divide the spoil with the mighty
SPOKE
 5:9   The Lord of Hosts spoke this in
 8:11 The Lord spoke to me,
16:13 These things the Lord spoke hitherto
65:12 when I spoke, you would not give
66:4   when I spoke, none gave heed.
SPOKEN
 1:2   The Lord has spoken:
 1:20 By his mouth the Lord has spoken it.
20:2   the Lord had spoken through
21:17 the God of Israel, has spoken it.
22:25 The Lord has spoken it.
25:8   The Lord has spoken it.
37:22 the Lord has spoken against him:
38:15 when he has already spoken for me,

39:8   Lord you have spoken is good.
40:5   By his mouth the Lord has spoken it.
46:11 What I have spoken, I bring to pass:
47:1   You shall no more be spoken of
48:15 I myself have spoken it, and also
58:14 By his mouth the Lord has spoken it.
59:4   empty words, deceitfully spoken;
SPOKESMEN
43:27 your spokesmen sinned against me.
SPOLIATE
10:6   for plunder, to spoliate for spoil,
SPOT
28:8   no spot is without excrement.
46:7   unable to budge from its spot.
SPOUSE
54:6   as a spouse forsaken and forlorn,
SPREAD
 1:15 When you spread forth your hands,
16:8   branches spread abroad across the
33:23* nor spread out the sail.
54:3   For you shall spread abroad
65:11 who spread tables for Luck
SPREADS
25:11 as a swimmer spreads his hands to
SPRIG
11:10 In that day the sprig of Jesse,
SPRING
11:1   A shoot will spring up from the stock
14:29 shall spring up a viper,
34:1   the world, and all who spring from it.
42:9   Before they spring up I declare them
45:8   righteousness spring up forthwith.
58:11 like a spring of unfailing waters.
61:11 garden causes what is sown to spring
61:11 righteousness and praise to spring up
SPRINGING
43:19 a new thing; it is now springing up.
SPRINGS
35:7   the thirsty place springs of water;
37:30 following year what springs up of
41:18 springs in the midst of the plains;
49:10 he will lead them by springs of water.
SPRINKLE
28:25 does he not sprinkle fennel and
SPROUT
17:11 causing them to sprout
SPROUTING
66:14 limbs flourish like sprouting grass,
SPURIOUS
57:4   you are born of sin, a spurious brood,
SPURNED
 1:4   they have spurned the Holy One of
SQUANDER
46:6   They who squander gold from the
SQUAT
47:1   squat on the ground, dethroned,

STAFF
3:1   of both staff and crutch—
9:4   the staff of submission,
10:5   He is a staff—my wrath in their
10:15 As though the staff held up the one
10:24 or raise their staff over you,
10:26 His staff is over the Sea,
14:5   has broken the staff of the wicked,
30:32 every sweep of the staff of authority,
STAGGER
19:14 causing her to stagger like a
28:7   and stagger because of strong drink;
29:9   stagger, but not from strong drink.
STAINED
63:1   from Edom in red-stained garments?
63:3   and I have stained my whole attire.
STAKES
33:20 whose stakes shall never be uprooted
54:2   and strengthen your stakes.
STALK
40:24 hardly their stalk has taken root in
53:2   a stalk out of arid ground.
STALL
1:3   the ass its master's stall,
STALWARTS
33:7   See, their stalwarts sob in public;
STAMMERERS
32:4   tongues of the stammerers master
STAND
1:17   stand up for the oppressed;
3:13   Lord will take a stand and contend
32:8   and stand up for what is virtuous.
41:1   let us stand trial together.
41:23 will be dazzled and all stand in awe.
44:11 and take their stand before me ,
47:13 stand by you and save you!
59:14 and righteousness to stand at a
STANDING
6:13   offspring be what is left standing:
21:8   been standing on the watchtower
27:9   and shining images standing.
STANDS
11:10 who stands for an ensign to the
46:7   they set it in place, there it stands,
STAR
14:12 O morning star, son of the dawn!
STARE
14:16 stare at you, wondering,
STARRY
34:4   and their starry hosts shed
STARS
13:10 The stars and constellations of the
14:13 my throne above the stars of God;
47:13 who observe the stars
STATE
10:29 Ramah is in a state of alarm,
14:18 All rulers of nations lie in state,

19:2   against city and state against state.
19:13 the heads of state have led Egypt
41:1   come forward and state their case;
49:7   heads of state shall prostrate
STATES
10:10 I could do this to the pagan states,
STATUES
10:10 whose statues exceeded
STATURE
10:33 the high in stature shall be hewn
45:14 the Sabeans, a people tall in stature.
STAY
33:15 stay their hand from taking bribes,
STAYS
56:2   stays his hand from doing any evil.
STEADFAST
26:3   Those whose minds are steadfast,
STEADY
35:3   steady the failing knees.
STEERS
27:10 steers forage and recline there,
34:7   shall fall bison, bulls, and steers.
STEM
48:1   you stem from the lineage of Judah
STENCH
3:24   of perfume there shall be a stench,
34:3   and their corpses emit a stench;
STEP
45:13 who facilitate his every step
STEPPES
21:1   steppes, a land of terror.
41:19 elms and box trees in the steppes—
STEWARD
22:15 Go and see that steward, Shebna,
STICK
28:27 fennel is beaten out with a stick
57:4   and stick out the tongue?
STILLED
16:9   summer fruit and harvest are stilled.
STIR
7:6   Let us invade Judea and stir up
13:17 See, I stir up against them the Medes,
19:2   I will stir up the Egyptians against
51:15 who stir up the Sea so that its waves
STIRRED
5:30   He shall be stirred up against them
5:30   even as the Sea is stirred up.
28:21 and be stirred to anger, as in the
37:28 and how stirred up you are against
STIRS
9:11   when he stirs up their adversaries:
STOCK
11:1   will spring up from the stock of Jesse
STONE
9:10   but we will rebuild with hewn stone;
28:16 I lay in Zion a stone, a keystone,
37:19 of men's hands, of wood and of stone,

STONES
5:2 He cultivated it, clearing it of stones,
27:9 all altar stones,
54:11 antimony for your building stones
54:12 entire boundary of precious stones.
57:6 Among the slippery stones of the
60:17 in place of stones, iron.
62:10 pave a highway cleared of stones;
STOOD
6:2 Seraphs stood by him overhead,
21:8 night after night I have stood guard.
36:13 Then Rabshakeh stood and called out
STOOP
44:15 they make idols to which they stoop.
44:19 Do I not stoop to a mere lump of
STOOPED
46:1 Nebo is stooped over:
STOP
33:15 who stop their ears at the mention of
STOPPING
10:29 stopping overnight at Geba.
STOPS
24:8 the revelers' din stops;
STORE
2:12 The lord of Hosts has a day in store
19:17 Lord of Hosts has in store for them.
22:5 the Lord of Hosts, has in store a day
28:2 My Lord has in store one mighty and
STORED
23:18 it shall not be hoarded or stored up.
STORM
17:13 or as whirling dust in a storm.
32:2 the wind or refuge from the storm,
40:24 and a storm sweeps them off as chaff.
STRAIGHT
26:7 The path of the righteous is straight;
40:3 pave a straight highway for our God:
STRAITS
38:14 O Lord, I am in straits; be my surety!
STRANGE
28:11 and a strange tongue
43:12 there was no strange god among you.
STRATAGEM
23:8 Who devised this stratagem against
STRAW
11:7 the lion will eat straw like the ox.
25:10 as straw is trampled in a dung pit.
65:25 the lion will eat straw like the ox;
STRAY
63:17 thou made us stray from thy ways,
STRAYED
57:17 when he strayed by following the
STREAM
19:5 as stream beds become desolate
66:12 the nations like a stream in flood.
STREAMS
11:15 and smite it into seven streams

27:12 River to the streams of Egypt.
30:25 shall appear streams of running
33:21 of rivers and broad streams,
34:9 Edom's streams shall turn into lava
35:6 and streams flow in the desert.
41:18 I will open up streams in barren hill
43:19 streams in the wasteland.
43:20 streams to the dry land,
44:4 among streams of water,
47:2 wade through streams:
STREET
51:20 faint at the corner of every street,
STREETS
5:25 lie like litter about the streets.
10:6 underfoot like mud in the streets.
15:3 on the housetops and in the streets
58:12 restorer of streets for resettlement
STRENGTH
12:2 Lord was my strength and my song
28:6 a source of strength
33:2 Be our strength of arm from
33:6 shall prove to be a strength,
36:5 show of strength? In whom have
37:3 there is no strength to deliver them.
40:29 in vigor those who lack strength.
40:31 shall be renewed in strength:
43:17 armies of men in full strength;
44:12 his god by the strength of his arm:
44:12 hungry, he no longer has strength;
49:4 I have spent my strength for nothing
49:5 when my God became my strength—
63:1 pressing forward in the strength of
STRENGTHEN
9:11 But the Lord will strengthen
35:3 Strengthen the hands grown feeble,
41:10 I will strengthen you; I will also
54:2 and strengthen your stakes.
STRETCH
23:11 The Lord will stretch out his hand
28:20 The couch is too short to stretch out
STRETCHED
48:13 my right hand that stretched out the
STRETCHES
25:11 For when he stretches his hands
31:3 when the Lord stretches out his hand,
STRETCHING
40:22 stretching them out as a tent to dwell
STRICKEN
30:31 Assyrians will be terror-stricken,
53:4 though we thought him stricken,
STRIFE
58:4 You fast amid strife and contention,
STRIKE
10:24 though they strike you with the rod
30:31 they who used to strike with the rod.
STRIKES
2:19 he arises and strikes terror on earth.

2:21 he arises and strikes terror on earth.
5:25 and strikes them;
STRIKING
58:4 striking out savagely with the fist.
STRIP
3:18 the Lord will strip away their finery
32:11 Strip yourselves bare;
STRIPPED
23:1 stripped of warehouse and wharf.
STRIPPING
27:10 stripping bare the young branches
STRONG
26:1 Our city is strong; salvation he has
28:2 has in store one mighty and strong:
28:7 and are giddy with strong drink:
28:7 and stagger because of strong drink;
29:9 stagger, but not from strong drink.
47:9 and exceedingly strong combinations.
STRONGHOLD
29:7 all who congregate at her stronghold
STRONGHOLDS
34:13 thistles and briars its strongholds;
STRUCK
6:5 I have been struck dumb,
10:20 longer rely on him who struck them,
10:26 as when he struck the Midianites
14:6 struck down the nations in anger,
14:29 the rod which struck you is broken.
33:14 sinners in Zion are struck with fear;
57:17 I struck him and hid my face in
60:10 Though I struck you in anger,
STRUNG
5:28 all their bows are strung.
STUBBLE
5:24 As a blazing fire consumes stubble,
33:11 chaff and brought forth stubble,
41:2 as driven stubble to his bow?
47:14 See, as stubble they are burnt up in
STUBBORN
48:4 For I knew how stubborn you were—
STUBBORN-HEARTED
46:12 Hear me, you stubborn-hearted,
STUDY
50:4 my ear to hear, as at study;
STUMBLE
5:27 nor does any stumble;
8:15 Many will stumble into them,
31:3 those who help them will stumble
59:10 We stumble at noon as in the dark of
STUMBLED
63:13 horse of the desert, they stumbled
STUMBLES
59:14 truth stumbles in the public place
STUMBLING
8:14 a stumbling block or obstructing
28:13 they might lapse into stumbling

STUMP
6:13 whose stump remains alive,
STUPOR
51:17 to the dregs the bowl of stupor.
51:22 I am taking the cup of stupor from
SUBDUE
45:1 to subdue nations before him,
SUBDUED
14:6 who subdued peoples in his wrath
SUBDUEST
25:5 thou subduest the power of tyrants.
SUBJECT
3:12 for my people, babes subject them;
19:4 a harsh ruler will subject them,
SUBJECTED
9:4 the rod of those who subjected them,
52:4 subjected them for nothing.
SUBJECTION
58:6 and abolish all forms of subjection?
SUBMISSION
9:4 the staff of submission,
SUBMISSIVE
53:7 He was harassed, yet submissive,
SUBMIT
41:21 submit your evidence, says the King
SUBORDINATES
37:6 Assyria's subordinates ridicule me.
SUBSTANCE
10:18 consume, both life and substance,
SUCCEED
54:17 it shall not succeed;
SUCCEEDED
37:38 Esarhaddon succeeded him as king.
SUCCESSION
29:1 the feastdays recur in succession,
SUCCOR
41:10 I will also succor you
SUCCORED
44:2 from the womb and succored you:
SUCCULENT
25:6 cakes, succulent and delectable,
SUCCUMB
65:12 you shall succumb to the slaughter.
SUCK
60:16 You will suck the milk of the nations,
SUCKLING
11:8 A suckling infant will play near the
49:15 a woman forget her suckling infant,
60:16 suckling at the breasts of rulers.
SUDDEN
47:11 shall come upon you sudden ruin
SUDDENLY
29:5 Suddenly, in an instant,
30:13 which suddenly and unexpectedly
47:9 shall suddenly overtake you, both in
48:3 Then, suddenly, I acted and they
51:4 Then, suddenly, I will act:

SUES
59:4   no one sues for an honest cause.
SUFFER
19:10   work for wages suffer distress.
64:12   letting us suffer so exceedingly?
66:5   But it is they who shall suffer shame.
SUFFERING
53:3   accustomed to suffering.
53:10   causing him suffering,
SUFFERINGS
53:4   Yet he bore our sufferings, endured
SUFFICE
40:16   Lebanon would not suffice to kindle a
SUFFICIENT
36:5   words are sufficient tactics or
SUIT
54:16   forging weapons to suit his purpose;
SUM
29:11   For you the sum of vision has become
64:6   the sum of our righteousness as a
SUMMER
16:9   over the summer fruit and harvest
18:6   prey will feed on them all summer
28:4   before the summer harvest:
SUMMIT
37:24   I have reached its loftiest summit,
SUMMON
15:4   to summon the armed men of Moab,
34:12   Shall they summon its nobles when it
46:11   I summon a bird of prey from the
55:5   You will summon a nation that you
SUMMONS
5:26   and summons them from beyond the
SUMPTUOUS
25:6   a sumptuous feast for all peoples,
SUN
13:10   When the sun rises, it shall be
24:23   blush and the sun be put to shame,
30:26   shall be as the light of the sun,
30:26   light of the sun increase sevenfold;
38:8   afternoon sun on the dial of Ahaz
38:8   sun reversed its descent by ten
45:6   where the sun rises to where it sets
49:10   by oppressive heat or by the sun;
59:19   from the rising of the sun his glory.
60:19   No longer shall the sun be your light
60:20   Your sun shall set no more,
SUNG
26:1   In that day shall this song be sung in
SUNRISE
24:15   in the regions of sunrise,
26:19   your dew is the dew of sunrise!
41:25   come from the direction of sunrise.
SUPPLANT
2:18   He will utterly supplant the false
SUPPLIES
40:29   He supplies the weary with energy

SUPPLY
3:1   all food supply and water supply,
SUPPORT
36:6   It is clear you depend on the support
SUPPOSE
5:20   who suppose what is evil to be good
36:5   Do you suppose that in war mere
SUPPOSED
28:15   You have supposed, by taking refuge
SUPREME
33:5   But the Lord is supreme, for he
SURE
22:23   fasten him as a nail in the sure place
22:25   sure place shall be removed.
28:16   cornerstone, a sure foundation.
33:16   provided them, their water is sure.
61:8   I will appoint them a sure reward;
SURELY
5:9   Surely many buildings shall lie
7:8   For as surely as Damascus is the
7:9   But as surely as Samaria is the
8:20   Surely, while they utter such
36:15   Lord by saying, The Lord will surely
38:13   Surely, as night has followed day,
38:17   Surely, for my own good I am in such
41:29   Surely they are all iniquitous,
43:19   Surely, you are aware of it:
44:20   Surely this thing in my hand is a
45:14   Surely God is in you; no other gods
49:18   As surely as I live, says the Lord,
50:1   Surely, by sinning you sold
50:9   Surely all such shall wear out like a
56:3   The Lord will surely exclude me from
57:4   Surely you are born of sin, a spurious
59:1   Surely the Lord's hand has not
63:8   thought, Surely they are my people
63:16   Surely thou art our Father!
SURETY
38:14   O Lord, I am in straits; be my surety!
SURFACE
24:1   he will disfigure its surface
28:25   When he has smoothed its surface,
SURGE
54:8   In a fleeting surge of anger I hid my
SURPASSING
28:29   whose inspiration is surpassing.
SURPLUS
15:7   The surplus they have acquired,
SURVEYED
34:11   It shall be surveyed with muddled
SURVIVE
10:20   In that day those who survive of
66:19   sending those of them who survive
SURVIVES
37:31   remnant . . . Judah that survives
SURVIVORS
1:9   Lord of Hosts left us a few survivors,

4:2   glory of the survivors of Israel.
14:30 and your survivors shall be slain.
37:32 from Mount Zion a band of survivors.
SUSPENDED
45:12 my hand suspended the heavens,
SUSPENDS
40:22 who suspends the heavens like a
42:5   who frames and suspends the
44:24 who alone suspends the heavens,
51:13 who suspends the heavens,
SUSTAIN
42:1   My servant whom I sustain,
46:4   you turn grey, it is I who sustain you.
SUSTAINS
50:9   See, my Lord the Lord sustains me.
SWAMPLANDS
14:23 I will turn it into swamplands, a
SWAY
24:20 sway back and forth like a shanty;
SWEAR
3:7   and swear, I am no physician.
19:18 swear loyalty to the Lord of Hosts.
45:23 By myself I swear it—
45:23 and every tongue swear allegiance.
54:9   So I swear to have no more anger
65:16 of them who swear oaths in the earth
SWEEP
8:8   He will sweep into Judea like a
14:23 I will sweep it with the broom of
28:15 should a flooding scourge sweep
28:17 a hail shall sweep away your false
28:19 after morning it shall sweep through
30:32 At every sweep of the staff of
64:6   our sins, like a wind, sweep us away.
SWEEPING
21:1   Like tornadoes sweeping
28:2   ravaging hailstorm sweeping down,
SWEEPS
28:18 the flooding scourge sweeps through,
28:19 As often as it sweeps through,
40:24 and a storm sweeps them off as chaff.
SWEET
5:20   bitterness sweet and the sweet bitter.
SWELL
60:5   your heart swell with awe:
SWELLING
38:21* packs and apply them to the swelling
SWIFT
18:2   in swift craft across the water.
19:1   enters Egypt riding on swift clouds,
30:16 We will ride on swift mounts!
SWIFTER
30:16 shall your pursuers be swifter.
SWIFTLY
5:26   they come, swiftly and speedily.
SWIM
25:11 swimmer spreads his hands to swim,

SWIMMER
25:11 swimmer spreads his hands to swim,
SWINE
66:17 who eat the flesh of swine
SWINE'S
65:4   who eat swine's flesh,
66:3   is as one who offers swine's blood,
SWOOP
11:14 But they will swoop on the Philistine
SWORD
1:20   you shall be eaten by the sword.
2:4   will not lift the sword against nation,
3:25   men shall be felled by the sword,
13:15 are caught shall fall by the sword.
14:19 the slain disfigured by the sword,
21:15 from the bared sword, the drawn bow
22:2   slain were not killed by the sword;
27:1   with his great and powerful sword,
31:8   Assyria shall fall by a sword not of
31:8   a sword not of mortals shall devour
31:8   that sword they shall waste away
34:5   When my sword drinks its fill in the
34:6   The Lord has a sword that shall
37:7   fall by the sword in his own land.
37:38 with a sword and fled to the land of
41:2   rendering them as dust to his sword,
49:2   made my mouth like a sharp sword—
51:19 famine, the sword—and who
65:12 I will destine you to the sword;
66:16 with fire and with his sword shall the
SWORDS
2:4   They will beat their swords into
SWORE
54:9   when I swore that the water of Noah
SWORN
62:8   The Lord has sworn by his right
SYCAMORES
9:10   the sycamores have been felled,
TABEAL
7:6   set a ruler over it—the son of Tabeal.
TABERNACLE
38:12 My tabernacle is being uprooted,
TABLES
21:5   They prepare tables;
28:8   For all tables are filled with vomit;
65:11 who spread tables for Luck
TABLETS
30:8   Go now, write on tablets concerning
TACTICS
36:5   words are sufficient tactics or
47:13 powerless, despite all your tactics.
TAIL
7:4   two smoking tail ends of kindling,
9:14   head and tail, palm top and reed,
9:15   who teach falsehoods, the tail.
19:15 neither head nor tail, palm top or

TAKE

3:6 and take charge of this ruination!
3:13 The Lord will take a stand and
4:1 Seven women will take hold of one
4:1 take away our reproach!
7:6 We will take it for ourselves by force
7:13 Then Isaiah said, Take heed,
8:1 Take a large scroll and write
8:9 You may take courage in one another,
11:14 they will take Edom and Moab at
13:3 who take pride in me.
14:2 The nations will take them
14:2 they will take captive their captors
14:4 you will take up this
14:21 and take possession of the world,
19:20 them a savior, who will take
22:7 and calvary take up positions at your
23:16 Take a lyre and go about the town,
27:5 But should they take hold of me for a
33:13 Take heed what I have done, you who
33:23* the lame take part in the plunder.
35:4 Take courage, be unafraid!
36:17 until I come back and take you to
37:31 shall once more take root below and
38:21* Isaiah gave instructions to take fig
39:7 and descendants, they shall take
41:16 a wind shall take them away,
42:23 will take heed of it hereafter,
42:25 yet they take it not to heart.
44:11 and take their stand before me ,
46:8 take it to heart, you offenders.
46:10 I speak, and my purposes take effect;
47:2 Take two grindstones and grind flour;
47:3 I will take vengeance
48:1 who take oaths in the name of the
51:18 none to take her by the hand of all
57:13 a vapor shall take them away.
64:7 rouses himself to take hold of thee.

TAKEN

6:6 an ember which he had taken
6:7 your sins are taken away,
8:15 shall be taken captive.
14:25 their yoke shall be taken from them,
28:9 those just taken from the breast?
28:13 ensnared and be taken captive.
40:24 stalk has taken root in the earth,
41:9 I have taken from the ends of the
49:24 Can the warrior's spoil be taken from
49:25 shall indeed be taken from him,
51:20 taken in a net like bison.
52:5 My people are taken over without
53:8 By arrest and trial he was taken

TAKEOVER

1:7 laid waste at its takeover by

TAKES

22:6 When Elam takes up the quiver,
27:6 days to come, when Jacob takes root

51:3 Joyful rejoicing takes place there,

TAKING

28:15 by taking refuge in deception
30:2 on taking shelter in Egypt's shadow.
33:15 stay their hand from taking bribes,
51:22 I am taking the cup of stupor from

TALL

2:15 against every tall tower and
45:14 the Sabeans, a people tall in stature.

TALLEST

37:24 I have felled its tallest cedars, its

TANK

30:14 or dip water from a tank.

TARSHISH

23:6 Move on to Tarshish lamenting,
23:10 O Daughter of Tarshish: the harbor
60:9 the ships of Tarshish in the lead,
66:19 to Tarshish, Pul, and Lud

TAUGHT

54:13 children shall be taught by the Lord,

TAUNT

14:4 taunt against the king of Babylon

TAX

33:18 Where are those who levied the tax?

TEACH

9:15 the prophets who teach falsehoods,

TEACHER

30:20 yet shall your Teacher remain hidden

TEAMS

21:7 for chariots with teams of horses,
21:9 cavalry and teams of horses!

TEARING

22:10 tearing down buildings to fortify

TEAR

13:18 bows shall tear apart the young.

TEARS

15:5 In tears they will ascend the slopes
16:9 I will water you with my tears,
25:8 the tears from all faces;
38:5 your prayer and seen your tears.

TEL ASSAR

37:12 the Edenites in Tel Assar?

TELL

3:10 Tell the righteous it shall be well
8:19 When men tell you to inquire
19:12 Let them please tell you, if they can
36:4 Please tell Hezekiah, Thus says
36:7 But if you tell me, We rely on the
37:6 Isaiah said to them, Tell your lord,
38:5 Go and tell Hezekiah, Thus says the
41:22 What were they? Tell us,
41:23 Tell us of events to come hereafter,
45:19 I the Lord tell righteousness
62:11 Tell the Daughter of Zion,

TELLING

36:7 telling Judea and Jerusalem to
37:9 to Hezekiah, telling them,

TEMA
21:14 O inhabitants of the land of Tema.
TEMPEST
41:16 a tempest dispel them.
TEMPEST-TOSSED
54:11 tempest-tossed and disconsolate!
TEMPESTUOUS
29:6 booms, tempestuous blasts
TEMPLE
6:4 and a mist filled the temple
37:38 temple of Nisroch his god, his sons
44:28 its temple foundations relaid.
64:11 Our glorious holy temple
66:6 the city, a noise from the temple!
TEN
5:10 A ten-acre vineyard shall yield but
38:8 the ten degrees it has gone down.
38:8 reversed its descent by ten degrees
TEND
61:5 Aliens will tend and pasture your
TENT
33:20 abode of peace—an immovable tent,
38:12 away from me like a shepherd's tent.
40:22 stretching them out as a tent to dwell
54:2 Expand the site of your tent;
TENTH
6:13 And while yet a tenth of the people
TENTS
13:20 Nomads will not pitch their tents
TEREBINTH
6:13 But like the terebinth or the oak
TERM
16:14 Within three years, as the term
21:16 to me, Within a year, as the term
40:2 to her that she has served her term,
TERRAIN
7:25 a terrain for sheep to tread down.
40:4 and rough terrain a plain.
TERRIFIED
13:8 They shall be terrified, in throes of
TERRIFYING
10:33 trees with terrifying power;
TERROR
2:19 he arises and strikes terror on earth.
2:21 he arises and strikes terror on earth.
19:17 a source of terror to the Egyptians;
21:1 steppes, a land of terror.
24:18 those who flee at the sound of terror
28:19 it shall cause terror merely to hear
30:31 Assyrians will be terror-stricken,
31:9 captain shall expire in terror
33:18 recount in your mind the terror:
TERRORIZED
8:9 but shall be terrorized.
TERRORS
24:17 Terrors and pitfalls and traps await

TERROR-STRICKEN
30:31 Assyrians will be terror-stricken,
TEST
1:18 Come now, let us put it to the test,
7:12 I will not put the Lord to the test.
TESTIFY
59:12 our sins testify against us.
TESTIMONY
8:16 has said, Bind up the testimony;
8:20 for doctrine and for a testimony?
19:20 testimony of the Lord of Hosts
30:8 as a testimony forever.
55:13 serve as a testimony of the Lord,
TESTING
48:10 I am testing you in the crucible of
TEXTILE
19:10 The textile workers will know
THAN
5:4 for my vineyard than I have done for
10:9 Samaria no better than Damascus?
13:12 mankind scarcer than fine gold,
13:12 men more rare than gold of Ophir.
15:9 I impose more than this upon Dibon:
26:13 our God, lords other than thou
32:10 In little more than a year
40:15 no more than dust on a balance;
40:17 as less than ether they are reckoned
47:8 I exist, and other than me there is
48:3 than I caused them to be announced.
55:9 the heavens are higher than the earth,
55:9 so are my ways higher than your ways
55:9 thoughts higher than your thoughts.
56:5 is better than sons and daughters;
57:8 exposed yourself to others than me:
65:5 come near me; I am holier than you!
THANKS
12:4 Give thanks to the Lord; invoke his
THANKSGIVING
51:3 thanksgiving with the voice of song.
THESE
6:9 he said, Go, and say to these people,
6:10 Make the heart of these people grow
7:4 by these two smoking tail ends of
8:6 Because these people have rejected
8:11 these people. For he said,
8:12 a conspiracy all that these people
9:16 leaders of these people have misled
14:26 These are things determined upon the
16:13 These things the Lord spoke hitherto
24:14 Then will these lift up their voice
28:7 These too have indulged in wine
28:11 must he speak to these people,
28:14 who preside over these people in
28:29 These things originate with the Lord
29:13 Lord says, Because these people
29:14 I shall again astound these people
36:12 to say these things to you and to your

THESE *continued*

40:26 Who formed these?
42:16 These things I will not fail to
43:9 among them foretold these things,
44:21 Ponder these things, O Jacob, and
45:7 I, the Lord, do all these things.
45:21 Who foretold these things of old,
47:7 and did not consider these,
47:14 These are no embers to warm anyone;
48:14 among you foretold these things?
49:12 See these, coming from afar, these,
49:12 and these, from the land of Sinim.
49:15 Although these shall forget, I will not
49:21 Who bore me these while I was
49:21 by whom were these reared?
56:7 these I will bring to my holy
60:8 Who are these, aloft like clouds,
66:2 These are all things my hand has

THICK

44:22 your offenses like a thick fog,
60:2 and a thick mist the peoples,

THING

8:12 by the thing they fear.
37:26 how I ordained this thing long ago,
38:7 do the thing he has promised:
43:19 See, I do a new thing; it is now
44:20 Surely this thing in my hand is a
49:6 he said: It is too small a thing
66:4 upon them the thing they dread.

THINGS

2:8 things their own fingers have made.
2:22 Desist from the things of man,
14:26 These are things determined upon the
16:13 These things the Lord spoke hitherto
17:8 nor look to things made by their
19:7 and all things sown along irrigation
25:1 things planned of old.
28:29 These things originate with the Lord
32:6 perverse things concerning the Lord,
36:12 to say these things to you and to your
36:22 him the things Rabshakeh had said.
37:4 and will rebuke him for the things
42:9 but new things I yet foretell.
42:16 These things I will not fail to
43:9 them foretold these things,
43:18 do not dwell on things of the past.
44:7 foretelling things to come?
44:9 the things they cherish profit
44:21 Ponder these things, O Jacob, and
44:24 the Lord, the Maker of all things,
45:7 I, the Lord, do all these things.
45:21 Who foretold these things of old,
46:10 ancient times things not yet done.
48:6 of now, I announce to you new things
48:6 things withheld and unknown to you,
48:7 things now coming into being, not
48:7 things you have not heard of before,

48:14 among you foretold these things?
57:6 shall I be appeased of such things?
64:3 thou didst perform awesome things
66:2 These are all things my hand has
66:8 or who has seen such things?

THINK

5:19 who think, Let him quickly speed up
22:16 Who do you think you are,
65:5 who think, Keep your distance,

THINKING

29:15 They work in the dark, thinking,
37:10 delude you into thinking that
47:8 enthroned, thinking to herself,
47:10 thinking to yourself, I exist,

THIRD

19:24 third party to Egypt and to Assyria,
37:30 But in the third year sow and harvest,

THIRST

5:13 their masses perish with thirst.
41:17 tongue becomes parched with thirst,
49:10 they shall not hunger or thirst,
50:2 and perish because of thirst.
55:1 Attention, all who thirst; come for
65:13 while you shall thirst;

THIRSTED

48:21 They thirsted not when he led them

THIRSTY

21:14 bring water to greet the thirsty;
29:8 or like a thirsty man who dreams he
32:6 depriving the thirsty soul of drink.
35:7 the thirsty place springs of water;
44:3 I will pour water on the thirsty soil,

THISTLES

34:13 thistles and briars its strongholds;

THONGS

5:27 nor their sandal thongs undone.

THORNBUSH

55:13 In place of the thornbush shall come

THORNS

5:6 but briars and thorns shall overgrow
7:23 shall be briars and thorns.
7:25 go for fear of the briars and thorns,
9:18 and briars and thorns shall it
10:17 his briars and thorns in a single day.
27:4 Should briars and thorns come up,
32:13 be overgrown with briars and thorns.
33:12 down like thorns and set ablaze.
34:13 For thorns shall overgrow its palaces,

THOROUGHFARE

51:23 a mere thoroughfare to passers-by.

THOUGHT

6:5 Then I thought, Woe is me:
24:16 Whereas I thought, I am wasting away
30:16 For you thought, Not so; we will flee
37:24 You thought, On account of my vast
38:11 I thought, I shall not see the Lord
39:8 For he thought, Then there shall

47:7 You thought, I, the Eternal Mistress,
47:10 you thought, No one discerns me.
49:4 I had thought, I have labored in vain,
53:4 though we thought him stricken,
57:1 and no man gives it a thought;
57:11 nor even give me a thought?
63:8 For he thought, Surely they are my
THOUGHTS
55:7 and the sinful men their thoughts.
55:8 my thoughts are not your thoughts,
55:9 thoughts higher than your thoughts.
59:7 Their thoughts are preoccupied with
THOUSAND
7:23 with a thousand vines worth
7:23 a thousand pieces of currency
30:17 You will flee by the thousand at the
36:8 thousand horses, if you are able to
37:36 a hundred and eighty-five thousand
THOUSANDS
30:17 by thousands at the threat of five,
THREAT
30:17 by the thousand at the threat of one,
30:17 by thousands at the threat of five,
THREE
16:14 Within three years, as the term
17:6 having two or three berries in the
20:3 naked and barefoot for three
THRESH
27:12 In that day the Lord will thresh out
41:15 you shall thresh mountains to dust
THRESHED
28:27 Fennel is not threshed with a sharp-
THRESHING
28:28 does not go on endlessly threshing it.
28:28 by driving horse and threshing cart
41:15 you a sharp-toothed threshing sledge
THRESHOLD
6:4 The threshold shook to its foundation
THRIVE
17:11 and though you make them thrive
THROES
13:8 shall be terrified, in throes of agony,
21:3 throes of agony have seized me like a
THRONE
6:1 I saw my Lord seated on a throne,
9:7 that, on the throne of David
14:13 and set up my throne above the stars
16:5 shall a throne be set up in the abode
22:23 sure place, and he will be a throne
66:1 The heavens are my throne
THRONES
14:9 to rise up from their thrones,
THROW
2:20 In that day men will throw away
THROWN
13:19 Chaldeans, shall be thrown down
14:19 remains are thrown in a gravel pit.

THRUST
13:15 is found shall be thrust through;
22:19 I will thrust you out of office;
THUNDEROUS
29:6 with thunderous quakings,
33:3 fled from thy thunderous voice;
THWART
43:13 when I work, who can thwart it?
THYSELF
26:15 enlarging it gained glory for thyself,
64:2 to make thyself known to thine
64:12 O Lord, wilt thou restrain thyself,
TIARAS
3:20 tiaras, bracelets and ribbons, zodiac
TIDINGS
40:9 O Zion, herald of good tidings.
41:27 him as a herald of tidings to
52:7 who brings tidings of good,
61:1 announce good tidings to the lowly;
TIGHTLY
22:18 He will bind you tightly about
TILL
5:8 link field to field till no place is left.
22:14 till you die, says my Lord, the Lord
30:17 till you are left as a flagstaff on a
30:24 the oxen and asses that till the soil
42:25 till it envelopes them in flames—
42:25 till it sets them on fire;
46:4 till you turn grey, it is I who sustain
62:1 till her righteousness shines like a
62:7 till he reestablishes Jerusalem
63:10 till he became their enemy
65:6 till I have paid back into their bosom
TIME
7:15 by the time he has learned
9:3 as men rejoice at harvest time,
9:7 from this time forth and forever.
13:23 Her time draws near;
17:14 At evening time shall be the
18:5 when the time of flowering is past
18:7 At that time shall tribute be brought
33:6 Your faithfulness in time of trial
39:1 At that time Merodach-Baladan the
39:6 The time shall come when everything
41:26 declared it ahead of time,
42:14 For a long time I have been silent,
49:8 At a favorable time I have answered
49:20 during the time of your bereavement
58:5 just a time for men to torment
60:22 I the Lord will hasten it in its time.
TIMES
33:2 our salvation in troubled times.
46:10 from ancient times things not yet
51:9 Bestir yourself, as in ancient times,
TIMOROUS
37:27 while their timorous inhabitants

TIRHAKAH
37:9 Tirhakah king of Cush had set out to
TODAY
56:12 For tomorrow will be like today, only
TODDLER
11:8 and the toddler reach his hand
TOGETHER
 8:19 who huddle together and mutter,
11:6 and young lions will feed together,
11:7 their young will rest together;
11:14 and together plunder those to the
24:22 They shall be herded together
31:3 both shall come to an end together.
34:15 There too shall kites come together,
34:16 by his Spirit he brings them together.
41:1 let us stand trial together.
41:5 They flock together and come
43:9 the peoples were gathered together,
52:9 Break out all together into song,
53:6 the Lord brought together upon him
60:13 cypresses, pines, and firs together—
TOIL
53:11 He shall see the toil of his soul and
58:3 and constrain all who toil for you.
TOILED
62:8 the new wine you have toiled for.
TOLD
14:32 What shall then be told the envoys of
36:10 For the Lord told me to come against
40:21 Have you not been told before,
48:5 therefore I told you them beforehand;
52:15 what was not told them, they shall
TOMB
22:16 that you have hewn yourself a tomb
TOMORROW
22:13 dine and drink, for tomorrow we die!
56:12 tomorrow will be like today, only far
TONGS
 6:6 with tongs from the altar.
TONGUE
 3:8 because their tongue and their
11:15 The Lord will dry up the tongue
28:11 and a strange tongue
30:27 his tongue is like a devouring fire.
33:19 babbling tongue was unintelligible.
35:6 the tongue of the dumb shout for joy.
41:17 and their tongue becomes parched
45:23 and every tongue swear allegiance.
50:4 endowed me with a learned tongue,
54:17 every tongue that rises to accuse
57:4 and stick out the tongue?
59:3 speak guile, your tongue utters
TONGUES
32:4 and the tongues of the stammerers
66:18 to gather all nations and tongues,
TOOK
20:1 took it by combat,

22:10 You took a census of the buildings in
36:2 And he took up a position by the
TOOLS
44:12 The smith with his tools works the
TOOTHED
28:27 with a sharp-toothed sledge,
41:15 I will make of you a sharp-toothed
TOP
 9:14 head and tail, palm top and reed,
19:15 neither head nor tail, palm top or
22:18 and send you spinning like a top
TOPHET
30:33 For Tophet has been prepared of Old,
TOPMOST
17:6 three berries in the topmost bough,
TOPPLED
41:2 toppled their rulers,
TOPS
42:11 out from the tops of the mountains.
TORCH
62:1 her salvation like a flaming torch.
TORMENT
58:5 for men to torment themselves?
TORMENTED
21:3 I am tormented beyond giving heed;
60:14 The sons of those who tormented you
TORMENTORS
51:23 it into the hand of your tormentors,
TORNADOES
21:1 Like tornadoes sweeping
TORRENT
27:12 his harvest from the torrent of the
30:28 His breath is like a raging torrent
59:19 upon them like a hostile torrent
TORRENTS
25:4 like torrents against a wall,
TOUCH
52:11 touch nothing defiled as you leave
TOUCHED
 6:7 See, this has touched your lips:
TOUCHING
 6:7 Touching it to my mouth, he said,
TOWARD
11:14 the Philistine flank toward the West
27:4 I have no more anger toward her.
29:13 their piety toward me consisting of
30:18 out of mercy toward you he will
33:2 O Lord, be favorable toward us;
38:2 turned his face toward the wall
48:9 I have shown restraint toward you
54:9 have no more anger toward you,
54:10 but my charity toward you shall
55:3 my loving fidelity toward David.
TOWER
 2:15 against every tall tower and
TOWERING
10:33 shatter the towering trees with

TOWERS
30:25 when the towers fall.
33:18 the ones who appraised the towers?
TOWN
22:2 a tumultuous town, a city of revelry!
23:16 Take a lyre and go about the town,
TOWNS
17:9 shall be like the deserted towns
24:10 The towns of disorder are broken up;
25:2 fortified towns a ruin—
32:14 the clamorous towns deserted.
TRADE
23:17 return to her trade and hire herself
TRADERS
23:2 traders of Sidon crossing the seas.
23:8 whose traders were princes,
TRADITIONAL
3:12 abolishing your traditional ways.
TRAILER
5:18 to transgression like a trailer,
TRAILING
16:8 trailing through the desert;
TRAITOR
21:2 the traitor in the act of treachery,
TRAITORS
24:16 the traitors have been treacherous,
TRAMPLE
1:12 you to trample my courts so?
14:25 trample them underfoot on my
TRAMPLED
5:5 and let it be trampled.
25:10 Moab shall be trampled down
25:10 as straw is trampled in a dung pit.
63:3 in my wrath I trampled them.
TRAMPLING
22:5 commotion and trampling and riot
58:13 feet from trampling the Sabbath—
TRANSACTIONS
59:13 and pondering illicit transactions.
TRANSGRESSED
24:5 they have transgressed the laws,
43:27 Your first father transgressed;
66:24 of the people who transgressed
TRANSGRESSION
5:18 hitched to transgression like a
59:20 Jacob who repent of transgression,
TRANSGRESSIONS
6:7 your transgressions atoned for.
24:20 its transgressions weigh it down,
53:5 was pierced for our transgressions,
58:1 to my people their transgressions,
59:12 For our transgressions before thee
TRANSGRESSOR
48:8 called a transgressor from the womb.
TRANSGRESSORS
53:12 intercession for the transgressors.

TRANSIENTLY
37:27 as wild grass, transiently green,
TRANSPIRE
7:7 It shall not occur or transpire.
TRANSPIRED
48:5 them to you before they transpired,
TRAP
24:18 shall be caught in a trap.
TRAPPED
42:22 all of them trapped in holes,
TRAPS
24:17 Terrors and pitfalls and traps await
TRAVEL
33:8 travel is at an end.
TRAVELS
30:4 and their envoys' travels to Hanes,
TRAVERSE
34:10 endless ages none shall traverse it.
35:8 The unclean shall not traverse them;
43:2 when you traverse the rivers,
58:14 I will make you traverse the heights
TREACHEROUS
24:16 the traitors have been treacherous,
33:1 O treacherous one,
33:1 whom none have been treacherous:
48:8 I knew you would turn treacherous;
TREACHERY
21:2 the traitor in the act of treachery,
TREAD
5:28 The tread of their warhorses
7:25 a terrain for sheep to tread down.
10:6 to tread underfoot like mud in the
16:10 The wine treaders will tread no wine
41:25 tread them as clay like a potter.
63:2 like those who tread grapes in the
TREADERS
16:10 The wine treaders will tread no wine
TREADS
59:8 none who treads them knows peace.
TREASURED
39:6 have treasured up until now,
TREASURES
45:3 I will give you hidden treasures
TREASURIES
39:2 and all that was in his treasuries.
39:4 There is nothing in my treasuries
TREASURY
39:2 the envoys his treasury—the silver
TREATIES
33:8 The treaties have been violated,
TREE
17:6 or when an olive tree is beaten,
24:13 as when an olive tree is beaten,
34:4 or shrivelled fruit from a fig tree.
36:16 and his own fig tree and drink
56:3 eunuch say, I am but a barren tree.

TREE *continued*
57:5   under every burgeoning tree,
65:22   shall be as the lifetime of a tree;
TREES
7:2   as trees in a forest are shaken by a
10:19   And the trees left of his forest shall
10:33   the towering trees with terrifying
14:8   The pine trees, too, rejoice over you,
27:10   bare the young branches of trees.
41:19   elms and box trees in the steppes—
44:14   them among the trees of the forest.
44:23   forests, and all trees therein:
55:12   and the trees of the meadows all clap
TREMBLING
13:8   seized with trembling like a woman
21:3   frame is racked with trembling;
33:14   godless are in the grip of trembling:
41:5   ends of the earth are in trembling.
64:2   the nations trembling at thy presence
TRIAL
3:14   He will bring to trial the elders of
33:6   Your faithfulness in time of trial
41:1   let us stand trial together.
53:8   By arrest and trial he was taken
TRIALS
38:16   O my Lord, by means of such trials
TRIBES
49:6   to raise up the tribes of Jacob
63:17   the tribes that are thine inheritance.
TRIBUTE
18:7   At that time shall tribute be brought
TRIFLE
28:10   a trifle here, a trifle there.
28:13   a trifle here, a trifle there, that,
TRIUMPH
30:15   By a calm response triumph;
TROD
41:3   by paths his feet have never trod.
63:3   I trod them down in my anger;
63:6   I trod nations underfoot in my anger;
63:18   our enemies trod down thy sanctuary.
TRODDEN
26:6   It is trodden underfoot by the feet of
28:3   shall be trodden underfoot.
63:3   Alone I have trodden out a vatful;
TROUBLE
7:6   invade Judah and stir up trouble
46:7   it cannot save them from trouble.
65:16   troubles of the past shall be forgotten
TROUBLED
33:2   our salvation in troubled times.
63:9   their troubles he troubled himself,
TROUBLES
63:9   their troubles he troubled himself,
TRUE
43:9   within hearing may say, It is true.
65:16   the earth shall do so by the true God,

TRULY
10:20   but will truly rely on the Lord,
45:15   Truly thou art a God who dissembles
TRUMPET
18:3   heed the trumpet when sounded!
27:13   In that day a loud trumpet shall
58:1   raise your voice like a trumpet!
TRUST
12:2   my salvation I will trust without fear;
26:4   Ever trust in the Lord,
31:1   their trust in immense numbers
36:5   you put your trust, that you have
36:15   Do not let Hezekiah make you trust in
37:10   Let not your god in whom you trust
42:17   But those who trust in idols
TRUSTS
50:10   trusts in the name of the Lord and
TRUTH
42:3   in the cause of truth.
48:1   though not in truth or in
59:14   truth stumbles in the public place
65:16   shall do so by the God of truth.
TRY
7:13   for you to try the patience of men?
7:13   you also try the patience of my God?
30:28   he will try the peoples.
TUBAL
66:19   to Tubal and Javan, and to the distant
TUMULT
13:4   Hark! A tumult on the mountains,
66:6   Hark, a tumult from the city, a noise
TUMULTUOUS
17:12   tumultuous nations, in commotion
22:2   a tumultuous town, a city of revelry!
TUNIC
3:6   You have a tunic: be our leader
TUNICS
9:5   and tunics rolled in blood
TURBULENCE
17:12   like the turbulence of mighty waters!
TURN
9:13   But the people do not turn back
9:21   Manasseh will turn against Ephraim
14:23   I will turn it into swamplands, a
14:27   is upraised, who can turn it away?
19:6   The rivers shall turn foul,
19:22   will turn back to the Lord,
22:4   Turn your attention from me,
29:21   who for nothing turn away him who is
30:3   protection shall turn to your shame,
30:21   should you turn left or right.
34:9   Edom's streams shall turn into lava
37:29   turn you back by the way you came.
41:18   I will turn the desert into lakes,
42:15   I will turn rivers into dry land and
42:16   them I will turn into light,
45:22   Turn to me and save yourselves,

46:4   till you turn grey, it is I who sustain
48:8   I knew you would turn treacherous;
50:2   rivers I turn into desert—
52:11   Turn away, depart;
TURNCOATS
24:16   the turncoats have deceitfully
TURNED
12:1   thine anger is turned away
14:17   who turned the world into a
24:9   liquor has turned bitter to drinkers.
33:9   Sharon has been turned into a dry
38:2   Hezekiah turned his face toward
51:12   men who shall be turned to grass?
TURNING
10:18   turning them into a rotting morass.
37:26   turning them into heaps of rubble,
TURNS
44:25   who turns wise men about
TWIGS
18:5   will cut down the fruit-bearing twigs
27:11   A harvest of twigs dries, broken off
TWILIGHT
58:10   your twilight become as the noonday.
TWINE
3:24   instead of the girdle, a piece of twine,
TWITTER
38:14   Like a mounting lark I twitter,
TWO
6:2   with two they could veil their
6:2   with two conceal their location,
6:2   and with two fly about.
7:4   by these two smoking tail ends of
7:16   the good, the land whose two
8:14   but to the two houses of Israel
17:6   having two or three berries in the
36:8   king of Assyria: I will give you two
47:2   Take two grindstones and grind flour;
TWOFOLD
51:19   Twofold calamity has befallen you:
61:7   Because their shame was twofold,
61:7   shall their inheritance be twofold
TYPE
40:20   too poor for this type of sacrifice
TYPES
44:7   a people from of old as types,
TYRANNOUS
25:3   a community of tyrannous nations
TYRANNY
14:4   his end and tyranny ceased!
60:18   tyranny shall no more be heard of in
TYRANT
14:4   How the tyrant has met
TYRANTS
13:11   and humble the pride of tyrants.
16:4   when tyrants are destroyed from the
25:4   When the blasts of tyrants beat down
25:5   thou subduest the power of tyrants.

29:20   For tyrants shall come to nought and
TYRANT'S
49:24   or the tyrant's captives escape free?
49:25   and the tyrant's captives escape
TYRE
23:1   An oracle concerning Tyre:
23:1   For Tyre is laid waste,
23:5   When the news of Tyre reaches Egypt,
23:8   devised this stratagem against Tyre,
23:13   the people who founded Tyre for
23:15   In that day Tyre shall be forgotten
23:15   And at the end of seventy years, Tyre
23:17   will revisit Tyre. And she will
UNABLE
46:2   unable to rescue their burden;
46:7   unable to budge from its spot.
47:14   unable themselves to escape the hand
56:10   but dumb watchdogs unable to bark,
57:20   unable to rest,
59:9   righteousness is unable to reach us.
UNACCOUNTED
34:16   None is unaccounted for, not one
40:26   not one is unaccounted for.
UNACQUAINTED
59:8   They are unacquainted with the way
UNAFRAID
7:4   and unafraid. Be not intimidated
35:4   Take courage, be unafraid!
UNAWARE
40:21   Are you so unaware, that you have not
42:25   yet they remain unaware—
44:18   They have become unaware and
56:10   altogether blind and unaware;
UNAWARES
8:14   and a snare, catching unawares
45:20   were caught unawares.
UNBURIED
14:19   But you are cast away unburied
UNCIRCUMCISED
52:1   No more shall the uncircumcised and
UNCLEAN
6:5   for I am a man of unclean speech,
6:5   among a people of unclean speech:
30:22   You will discard as unclean
35:8   The unclean shall not traverse them;
UNCOMPREHENDING
42:19   as uncomprehending as the servant of
UNCOVER
26:21   uncover the blood shed upon it
UNCOVERED
20:4   with buttocks uncovered—
47:3   and your shame uncovered.
UNCOVERS
22:6   and Kir uncovers the armor,
UNDAUNTED
51:7   be undaunted by their ridicule.

UNDERCLAD
58:7   see men underclad to clothe them,
UNDERFOOT
10:6   to tread underfoot like mud in the
14:25   trample them underfoot on my
26:6   It is trodden underfoot by the feet of
28:3   shall be trodden underfoot.
63:6   I trod nations underfoot in my anger;
UNDERMINE
10:16   to undermine his glory:
UNDERSTAND
6:10   understand in their heart,
29:16   He doesn't understand?
36:11   in Aramaic, which we understand.
40:21   that you do not understand
UNDERSTANDING
6:9   Go on hearing, but not understanding
11:2   wisdom and of understanding,
28:15   or reached an understanding with
28:18   your understanding with Sheol have
29:24   erring in spirit gain understanding
32:4   the rash shall learn understanding,
40:14   with the way of understanding?
UNDEVIATING
26:7   thou pavest an undeviating course for
UNDONE
5:27   nor their sandal thongs undone.
UNDOING
10:25   my wrath will become their undoing.
UNEASY
57:11   are you uneasy and apprehensive,
UNERRING
14:6   him who with unerring blows
UNEVEN
40:4   the uneven ground must become level
42:16   and the uneven ground make level.
UNEXPECTED
64:3   unexpected by us: thy descent of old,
UNEXPECTEDLY
30:13   and unexpectedly collapses.
UNFAILING
58:11   like a spring of unfailing waters.
UNFAMILIAR
42:16   and guide them in paths unfamiliar;
UNGIRD
20:2   Go and ungird the sackcloth
45:1   to ungird the loins of rulers,
UNHINDERED
41:3   them to flight, passing on unhindered
UNINTELLIGIBLE
33:19   babbling tongue was unintelligible.
UNITEDLY
43:9   When all nations unitedly assembled,
UNJUST
10:1   Woe to those who enact unjust laws,
UNKNOWN
44:8   There is no Rock unknown to me.

48:6   things withheld and unknown to you,
UNLEARNED
29:12   they give it to one who is unlearned,
29:12   he answers, I am unlearned.
UNLIKE
7:17   house a day unlike any since
52:14   his semblance unlike that of men—
UNOCCUPIED
5:9   large and fine houses unoccupied.
UNRAVEL
47:13   let those who unravel the heavens,
UNROLLED
37:14   the house of the Lord and unrolled it
UNSTOPPED
35:5   and the ears of the deaf unstopped.
UNTIE
58:6   to untie the harness of the yoke,
UNVEIL
47:2   unveil, disrobe, bare your legs,
UNWILLING
1:20   But if you are unwilling and disobey,
30:9   children unwilling to obey the law of
UNWONTED
28:21   to perform his act, his unwonted act,
UPHELD
9:7   rule may be established and upheld
48:2   upheld by the God of Israel,
UPHOLD
41:10   uphold you with my righteous right
UPPER
7:3   the aqueduct of the Upper Reservoir,
36:2   of the Upper Reservoir, on the road to
UPRAISED
5:25   his hand is upraised still.
9:12   his hand is upraised still.
9:17   his hand is upraised still.
9:21   his hand is upraised still.
10:4   his hand is upraised still.
14:26   is the hand upraised over all nations.
14:27   When his hand is upraised, who can
UPRIGHT
26:7   undeviating course for the upright.
UPRIGHTLY
57:2   They who walk uprightly shall attain
UPRIGHTNESS
26:10   in a land of uprightness they remain
59:14   and uprightness cannot enter.
UPRISING
33:3   at thine uprising the nations scatter
UPROAR
13:4   Hark! An uproar among kingdoms,
17:12   to the many peoples in an uproar,
UPROOTED
33:20   whose stakes shall never be uprooted
38:12   My tabernacle is being uprooted,
UPWARD
8:21   gazing upward, curse their

9:18 and they shall billow upward
URGES
41:7* urges him who pounds the anvil.
URIAH
8:2 Uriah the Priest and Zechariah
URINE
36:12 drink their own urine?
USE
7:20 In that day my Lord will use
44:15 which they use to warm themselves
47:12 It may still be of use to you;
USED
9:5 And all boots used in battle
30:31 they who used to strike with the rod.
USELESS
59:6 cobwebs are useless as clothing;
USING
22:3 are captured without using the bow;
UTMOST
14:13 in the utmost heights of Zaphon.
14:15 to the utmost depths of the Pit.
UTTER
8:20 Surely, while they utter such
10:14 or opened its mouth to utter a peep.
10:23 will carry out the utter destruction
16:7 in utter dejection.
19:11 The ministers of Zoan are utter fools;
23:9 celebrities an utter execration.
28:22 have heard utter destruction decreed
32:6 For the godless utter blasphemy;
42:17 shall retreat in utter confusion.
UTTERANCE
41:26 any [prophetic] utterance.
UTTERING
29:4 your words uttering out of the dust:
UTTERLY
2:18 He will utterly supplant the false
14:31 Utterly melt away, you Philistines!
24:3 it shall be utterly ravaged.
27:8 by utterly banishing them, O Lord.
30:5 they shall be utterly disgusted
32:19* cities utterly leveled.
38:14 [I am utterly sleepless
45:16 utterly dismayed and embarrassed.
60:12 such nations shall be utterly ruined.
UTTERS
9:17 and every mouth utters profanities.
59:3 guile, your tongue utters duplicity.
UZZIAH
1:1 during the reigns of Uzziah,
7:1 son of Jotham, the son of Uzziah,
UZZIAH'S
6:1 In the year of King Uzziah's death,
VAIN
5:18 drawn to sin by vain attachments,
30:7 Egypt's help shall be futile and vain;
49:4 I had thought, I have labored in vain,

65:23 shall not exert themselves in vain,
VALIANT
1:24 the Valiant One of Israel, declares,
3:2 the valiant man and soldier,
5:22 who are valiant at drinking wine
13:3 called out my valiant ones:
21:17 And the number of valiant archers
49:26 Redeemer is the Valiant One of Jacob.
60:16 Redeemer is the Valiant One of Jacob.
VALLEY
15:7 over the Valley of the Willows.
17:5 in the Valley of Rephaim
28:21 to anger, as in the Valley of Gibeon
65:10 and the Valley of Achor a resting
VALLEYS
22:7 your choice valleys fill with chariots,
VALOR
9:6 Counsellor, one Mighty in Valor,
10:21 to the one Mighty in Valor.
11:2 the spirit of counsel and of valor,
VALUE
13:17 who do not value silver, nor covet
VANISH
17:11 yet shall the harvest vanish
51:6 the heavens shall vanish as by smoke,
VAPOR
57:13 a vapor shall take them away.
VAST
13:4 as of a vast multitude.
31:1 and vast forces of horsemen,
37:24 On account of my vast chariotry
VASTLY
10:13 I have vastly reduced the inhabitants.
VATFUL
63:3 Alone I have trodden out a vatful;
VAUNT
10:15 or a saw vaunt itself
VEGETATION
15:6 shall dry up, vegetation disappear,
19:7 vegetation adjoining canals and
42:15 and make all their vegetation wither;
61:11 the earth brings forth its vegetation,
VEIL
6:2 two they could veil their presence,
25:7 the veil that veils all peoples,
VEILS
25:7 the veil that veils all peoples,
VENERABLE
58:13 the holy day of the Lord venerable,
VENERATES
66:3 as one who venerates idols.
VENGEANCE
10:6 deserving of my vengeance,
34:8 For it is the Lord's day of vengeance,
47:3 I will take vengeance
59:17 he clothed himself with vengeance for
61:2 and the day of vengeance of our God,

VENGEANCE *continued*
63:4   I had resolved on a day of vengeance,
VERMIN
51:6   shall die in the manner of vermin.
VESSEL
30:14 like an earthenware vessel ruthlessly
VESSELS
2:16   against [all vessels at sea,]
22:24 including all the lesser vessels,
52:11 you who bear the Lord's vessels.
66:20 brought offerings in pure vessels
VIBRATE
16:11 My breast will vibrate like a harp for
VICISSITUDE
30:6   a land of hardship and vicissitude,
VICTORY
30:15 quiet confidence gain the victory.
42:13 the shout of victory over his enemies.
VIEW
5:21   and clever in their own view!
33:17 and view the expanse of the earth.
VIGILANT
21:7   He must be most vigilant, fully alert.
66:2   and who are vigilant for my word.
66:5   you who are vigilant for his word:
VIGOR
40:29 and increases in vigor those who lack
58:11 and bring vigor to your limbs.
VILE
3:5   the vile to the honorable.
VILLAGES
42:11 and the villages where Kedar dwells;
VINDICATE
43:26 Speak up and vindicate yourself.
53:11 the righteous one, vindicate many,
VINDICATES
50:8   He who vindicates me is near me.
VINDICATION
45:24 By the Lord alone come vindication
54:17 such is their vindication by me,
VINE
34:4   like withered leaves from a vine,
36:16 one of you will eat from his own vine
VINEDRESSERS
61:5   be your farmhands and vinedressers.
VINES
5:2   and planted it with choice vines,
7:23   with a thousand vines worth
16:8   nations will smite Sibmah's vines.
16:8   Its runner vines reached Jazer,
16:9   for the vines of Sibmah;
24:7   wine withers on languishing vines,
32:12 and flourishing vines.
VINEYARD
1:8   like a shelter in a vineyard,
3:14   who have devoured the vineyard;
5:1   a love song about his vineyard:

5:1   My beloved had a vineyard
5:3   judge between me and my vineyard!
5:4   my vineyard than I have done for it?
5:5   what I will do to my vineyard:
5:7   The vineyard of the Lord of Hosts is
5:10   A ten-acre vineyard shall yield but
27:2   as of a delightful vineyard
VINEYARDS
16:8   For the vineyards of Heshbon shall
16:10 delight shall sound in the vineyards.
36:17 land of grain fields and vineyards.
37:30 plant vineyards and eat their fruit:
65:21 when they plant vineyards, they will
VINTAGE
16:10 the vintage shout I will bring to an
24:13 gleaned when the vintage is ended.
VIOLATED
33:8   The treaties have been violated,
VIOLENCE
16:4   and violence has ceased,
42:25 pours out on them the violence of war
53:9   yet he had done no violence,
VIOLENT
13:6   it shall come as a violent blow from
29:5   your violent mobs like flying chaff.
VIPER
14:29 shall spring up a viper,
VIPER'S
11:8   over the viper's nest.
59:5   They hatch vipers' eggs and spin
VIRGIN
23:12 O ravished virgin, Daughter of Sidon.
37:22 The Virgin Daughter of Zion holds
47:1   O Virgin Daughter of Babylon;
62:5   As a young man weds a virgin,
VIRGINS
23:4   rear young men or raise virgins!
VIRTUOUS
32:8   and stand up for what is virtuous.
VISIBLE
30:30 and make visible his arm descending
60:2   over you his glory shall be visible.
VISION
1:1   The vision of Isaiah the son of Amoz
2:1   Isaiah the son of Amoz saw in vision:
13:1   Isaiah the son of Amoz saw in vision:
21:2   A grim vision has been revealed to
29:11 For you the sum of vision has become
48:6   you have heard the whole vision;
VISIONS
30:10 and to those with visions,
VITALITY
24:11 the earth's vitality is gone.
VOICE
6:8   Then I heard the voice of my Lord
13:2   sound the voice among them!
24:14 Then will these lift up their voice

28:23 Give heed, and hear my voice!
29:4 your voice from the ground
30:19 respond at the cry of your voice;
30:30 The Lord will cause his voice to
30:31 At the voice of the Lord
31:4 dismayed at the sound of their voice
32:9 Up, and listen to my voice,
33:3 fled from thy thunderous voice;
36:13 loud voice in Judean, Hear the words
37:23 whom have you raised your voice,
40:3 A voice calls out,
40:6 A voice said, Announce it,
40:9 Raise your voice mightily,
42:2 He will not shout or raise his voice
42:11 and its cities raise their voice,
48:20 with resounding voice;
50:10 and heeds the voice of his servant,
51:3 thanksgiving with the voice of song.
52:8 Your watchmen lift up their voice;
58:1 raise your voice like a trumpet!
58:4 as to make your voice heard on high.
66:6 It is the voice of the Lord

VOID
28:18 covenant with Death shall prove void
29:14 rendering void the knowledge of their
40:23 of the world null and void.

VOMIT
19:14 drunkard into his vomit.
28:8 For all tables are filled with vomit;

VOWS
19:21 offerings, and make vows

WADE
47:2 wade through streams:

WAGE
7:1 to wage war against it, but could not
31:4 to wage war upon Mount Zion and

WAGER
36:8 Come now, wager with my lord the

WAGES
19:10 and all who work for wages suffer

WAGONS
66:20 in chariots and wagons, and on mules

WAIL
14:31 Wail at the gates; howl in the city!
15:2 they will wail in Moab over Nebo and
15:3 they will altogether wail and give way

WAIST
5:27 Their waist-belts come not loose
11:5 will be as a band about his waist,

WAISTS
32:11 put sackcloth around your waists.

WAIT
8:17 I will wait for the Lord,
30:18 blessed are all who wait for him.
64:4 on behalf of those who wait for him.

WAITED
25:9 the Lord for whom we have waited;
33:2 we have waited for thee.

WAKE
50:4 grown weary a word to wake them up.
59:7 and disaster follow in their wake.

WAKENS
50:4 by morning he wakens my ear to hear,

WAKES
29:8 but wakes up faint and craving.

WALK
3:16 ever flirting when they walk
30:21 saying, This is the way; walk in it!
35:9 But the redeemed shall walk them
40:31 they shall walk and not faint.
42:5 spirit to those who walk on it:
42:24 have no desire to walk in his ways
43:2 Though you walk through the fire,
45:14 They shall walk behind you in chains
50:10 who, though he walk in darkness and
50:11 Walk then by the light of your fires
57:2 They who walk uprightly shall attain
59:9 but we walk amid gloom.
65:2 who walk in ways that are not good,

WALKED
38:3 I have walked before thee faithfully

WALKING
9:2 The people walking in darkness

WALL
2:15 tall tower and reinforced wall,
5:5 I will have its wall broken through
22:10 down buildings to fortify your wall.
25:4 like torrents against a wall,
30:13 breach exposed in a high wall
36:11 of the people who are on the wall.
36:12 and not to the men sitting on the wall
38:2 the wall and prayed to the Lord:

WALLED
25:12 Your highly walled fortifications

WALLS
22:5 a day of battering down walls
22:11 You built cisterns between the walls,
26:1 as walls and barricades!
56:5 within the walls of my house
58:12 be called a rebuilder of fallen walls,
60:10 Foreigners will rebuild your walls,
60:18 will regard salvation as your walls
62:6 appointed watchmen on your walls,

WANDER
35:8 on them shall no reprobates wander.

WANDERING
21:13 You wandering bands of Dedanites

WANE
5:24 as dry weeds wane before the flame,
17:4 In that day Jacob's glory shall wane,
60:20 nor your moon wane:

WANT
1:11 I do not want.
41:17 I the Lord will answer their want;
51:14 neither shall he want for food.
WANTONNESS
57:12 and the wantonness of your exploits.
WAR
3:25 your might overthrown in war.
7:1 to wage war against it, but could not
13:4 Hosts is marshalling an army for war.
21:15 and the severity of war.
31:4 to wage war upon Mount Zion and
36:5 Do you suppose that in war mere
42:13 he will give the war cry,
42:25 pours out on them the violence of war
WAREHOUSE
23:1 stripped of warehouse and wharf.
WARFARE
2:4 nor will they learn warfare any more.
WARHORSES
5:28 The tread of their warhorses
WARM
44:15 which they use to warm themselves
44:16 They also warm themselves and say,
44:16 Ah, it is warm in front of the fire!
47:14 These are no embers to warm anyone;
WARRIOR
42:13 Lord will come forth like a warrior,
WARRIOR'S
49:24 Can the warrior's spoil be taken from
49:25 The warrior's spoil
WARS
41:12 whoever wars against you
WARSHIPS
33:21 where no warships sail
WASH
1:16 Wash yourselves clean:
WASHED
4:4 has washed away the excrement
WASTE
1:7 laid waste at its takeover by
21:2 the destroyer laying waste.
23:1 For Tyre is laid waste,
24:1 Lo! The Lord will lay waste the earth
31:8 that sword they shall waste away
33:9 has been turned into a dry waste,
42:15 I will lay waste mountains and hills
45:18 not to remain a chaotic waste,
49:19 and your land laid waste,
61:4 raise up the old waste places;
WASTELAND
34:10 It shall remain a wasteland
43:19 streams in the wasteland.
WASTING
24:16 Whereas I thought, I am wasting away
WATCH
18:4 I will watch in silence over my

21:7 Let him watch for chariots with teams
27:3 watch over it night and day,
WATCHDOGS
56:10 but dumb watchdogs unable to bark,
WATCHMAN
21:6 Go and appoint a watchman
21:11 Watchman, what remains of the night?
21:11 Watchman, how much of the night is
21:12 The watchman replies,
WATCHMEN
52:8 Your watchmen lift up their voice;
56:10 Their watchmen are altogether blind
62:6 I have appointed watchmen on your
WATCHTOWER
5:2 He built a watchtower in its midst
21:8 been standing on the watchtower
WATER
1:22 your wine diluted with water.
1:30 and as a garden that has no water.
3:1 all food supply and water supply,
7:19 and by all ditches and water holes.
12:3 shall you rejoice in drawing water
16:9 I will water you with my tears,
18:2 in swift craft across the water.
19:8 those who cast nets on water
21:14 bring water to greet the thirsty;
22:9 you conserved water in the Lower
22:11 for the water from the Old Reservoir,
27:3 I water it constantly, watch over it
30:14 or dip water from a tank.
30:20 and the water of affliction,
30:23 Then will he water with rain
30:25 appear streams of running water,
32:2 like brooks of water in a desert place,
33:16 Bread is provided them, their water
35:6 Water shall break forth in the
35:7 the thirsty place springs of water;
36:16 water from his own cistern,
41:17 the poor and needy require water,
41:18 lands into fountains of water.
43:20 for bringing water to the wilderness,
44:3 I will pour water on the thirsty soil,
44:4 among streams of water,
44:12 if he fails to drink water, he begins
48:21 he caused water to flow for them from
48:21 the rock and water gushed out.
49:10 he will lead them by springs of water.
50:2 become parched for lack of water
55:1 all who thirst; come for water!
64:2 as when fire is lit for boiling water,
WATERING
55:10 not to it without watering the earth,
WATERS
8:6 the waters of Shiloah, which flow
8:7 great and mighty waters of the River
11:9 oceans are overspread with waters.
15:6 For the waters of Nimrim shall be

15:9 Although the waters of Dibon shall
17:12 like the turbulence of mighty waters!
17:13 roar like the roaring of great waters,
19:5 The waters of the lakes shall ebb away
28:2 inundating deluge of mighty waters,
28:17 and waters flood the hiding place.
32:20 who shall then sow by all waters,
37:25 wells and drunk of foreign waters.
40:12 Who measured out the waters
43:2 When you cross the waters, I will be
43:16 a path through the mighty waters,
51:10 the waters of the mighty deep,
54:9 when I swore that the waters of Noah
57:20 whose waters heave up mire and mud:
58:11 like a spring of unfailing waters.
63:12 who divided the waters before them,
WATERWAYS
19:6 Egypt's waterways recede and dry up.
WAVES
48:18 righteousness like the waves of the
51:15 stir up the Sea so that its waves roar.
WAY
10:31 Madmenah has moved out of the way,
11:15 to provide a way on foot.
15:3 wail and give way to weeping.
23:1 On their way from the land of
30:11 Get out of the way; move aside,
30:21 saying, This is the way; walk in it!
30:29 on their way to the mountain of the
35:8 shall be called the Way of Holiness,
37:29 turn you back by the way you came.
37:34 By the way he came he shall return;
40:3 In the desert prepare the way for the
40:14 him with the way of understanding?
42:16 I lead the blind by a way they did not
43:16 who provides a way in the Sea,
47:15 each deviates his own way;
48:15 and I will prosper his way.
48:17 guiding you in the way you should go.
49:9 They shall feed along the way
51:10 and made of ocean depths a way
53:6 each of us headed his own way;
56:11 are all diverted to their own way,
57:14 Prepare the way;
59:8 unacquainted with the way of
62:10 prepare the way for the people!
WAYS
2:3 that he may instruct us in his ways,
3:12 abolishing your traditional ways.
8:11 me not to follow the ways of
42:24 have no desire to walk in his ways
55:7 Let the wicked forsake their ways
55:8 nor are your ways my ways, says the
55:9 so are my ways higher than your ways
57:10 wearied by your excessive ways,
57:17 by following the ways of his heart,
58:2 eager to learn my ways,

59:13 planning ways of extortion,
63:17 thou made us stray from thy ways,
64:5 thee by following thy ways—
65:2 who walk in ways that are not good,
66:3 have preferred to go their own ways,
WAYWARDNESS
1:5 by adding to your waywardness?
WEAK
13:7 Then shall every hand grow weak
WEAKENING
24:16 I am weakening:
WEALTH
2:7 and there is no end to their wealth;
8:4 the wealth of Damascus and
10:3 Where will you leave your wealth?
10:14 I have impounded the wealth of
30:6 they carry their wealth
45:3 and secret hoards of wealth—
45:14 The wealth of Egypt and merchandise
61:6 feed on the wealth of the nations
WEANED
28:9 Weanlings weaned from milk,
WEANLINGS
28:9 Weanlings weaned from milk,
WEAPON
54:17 Whatever weapon is devised against
WEAPONRY
10:28 Micmash he marshals his weaponry.
WEAPONS
54:16 forging weapons to suit his purpose;
WEAR
4:1 wear our own clothes,
10:27 shall by fatness wear away.
15:3 They will wear sackcloth openly;
50:9 such shall wear out like a garment;
51:6 the earth wear out like a garment—
WEARIED
43:23 or wearied you with burning incense.
43:24 wearied me with your iniquities.
57:10 wearied by your excessive ways,
WEARING
22:12 for austerity and wearing sackcloth.
WEARY
1:14 I am weary of putting up with them.
5:27 Not one of them grows weary,
16:12 For when the Moabites weary
28:12 This is rest; let the weary rest!
40:28 He does not grow faint or weary;
40:29 He supplies the weary with energy
40:30 Youths grow faint and weary,
43:22 you have grown weary of me, O Israel.
46:1 piled as burdens on weary animals.
50:4 to those grown weary a word to wake
WEARYING
40:31 they shall run without wearying,
WEASELS
13:21 buildings overflow with weasels;

WEAVERS
19:9 and weavers of fine fabrics will be
WEBS
59:5 vipers' eggs and spin spiders' webs;
WED
62:5 so shall your sons wed you;
WEDS
62:5 As a young man weds a virgin,
WEEDS
5:24 as dry weeds wane before the flame,
37:27 or like weeds on a roof
WEEP
15:2 to Dibon to the hill shrines, to weep;
22:4 though I weep bitterly;
30:19 you shall have no cause to weep.
33:7 the champions of peace weep bitterly.
WEEPING
15:3 wail and give way to weeping.
22:12 calls for weeping and lamentation,
65:19 the sound of weeping or the cry of
WEIGH
24:20 its transgressions weigh it down,
46:6 and weigh out silver on the scales
WEIGHED
1:4 a people weighed down by sin,
47:6 even the aged you weighed down
WEIGHING
40:12 weighing mountains in scales,
WEIGHT
28:17 righteousness the weight;
34:11 and chaotic weight.
WELDING
41:7* They say of the welding, It is good,
WELL
3:10 Tell the righteous it shall be well
5:2 and hewed for it a winepress as well.
25:6 of matured wines well refined.
55:2 Hear me well: Eat what is good,
58:11 become like a well-watered garden,
WELL-BEING
57:19 Peace, well-being, to those far off
WELLS
37:24 I have dug wells and drunk of
WEPT
38:3 And Hezekiah wept disconsolately.
WEST
9:12 and Philistines from the west
11:14 the Philistine flank toward the West,
21:1 of the West: Like tornadoes sweeping
43:5 and gather you from the west;
59:19 From the West men will fear the Lord
WHARF
23:1 stripped of warehouse and wharf.
WHEAT
28:25 Does he not demarcate wheat from
WHEELS
5:28 their chariot wheels revolve like a

WHILE
6:13 And while yet a tenth of the people
8:20 Surely, while they utter such
26:20 hide yourselves a little while
29:13 while their heart remains far from me
29:17 In a very little while, shall not
37:27 while their timorous inhabitants
38:13 while like a lion he racks my whole
49:21 Who bore me these while I was
51:16 while I replant the heavens and set
55:6 Inquire of the Lord while he is
55:6 call upon him while he is near.
63:18 But a little while had thy people
65:13 while you shall hunger;
65:13 while you shall thirst;
65:13 while you shall be dismayed.
65:14 while you shall cry out with
65:24 while they are yet speaking I will
WHIP
10:26 Hosts will raise the whip against
WHIRLING
17:13 or as whirling dust in a storm.
WHIRLWIND
5:28 wheels revolve like a whirlwind.
66:15 his chariots like a whirlwind,
WHISPER
29:4 sayings shall whisper out of the dust.
WHITE
1:18 they can be made white as snow;
1:18 they may become white as wool.
WHOLE
1:5 The whole head is sick
1:5 the whole heart diseased.
4:5 Over the whole site of Mount Zion,
7:24 and arrows, for the whole land
10:14 I have gathered up the whole world
10:23 decreed upon the whole earth.
14:7 Now the whole earth is at rest and at
14:26 determined upon the whole earth;
21:3 Therefore my whole frame is racked
28:22 destruction . . . upon the whole earth.
33:12 Whole nations have been burned like
38:13 like a lion he racks my whole frame?
44:11 Their whole society is confused;
48:6 you have heard the whole vision;
63:3 and I have stained my whole attire.
WICK
42:3 a dim wick he will not snuff out.
43:17 and die, snuffed out like a wick—
WICKED
1:16 remove your wicked deeds
3:11 But woe to the wicked
11:4 breath of his lips slay the wicked.
13:11 punishment for the wicked;
14:5 has broken the staff of the wicked,
26:10 Though favor be shown the wicked,
48:22 no peace, says my Lord, for the wicked

53:9   among the wicked in death,
55:7   Let the wicked forsake their ways
57:20 But the wicked are like the raging
57:21 no peace, says my God, for the wicked

WICKEDNESS
1:13   wickedness with the solemn gathering
9:18   Wickedness shall be set ablaze like a
22:14 Such wickedness cannot be forgiven
29:20 persist in wickedness shall be cut off
33:15 their eyes at the sight of wickedness.
47:10 Secure in your wickedness,
59:4   misdeeds, they beget wickedness.

WIDE
18:7   from a nation dreaded far and wide,
57:4   At whom do you open wide the mouth
57:8   your bed, you have laid it wide open,

WIDOW
1:17   appeal on behalf of the widow.

WIDOW'S
1:23 nor does the widow's case come before

WIDOWED
47:8   I shall not be widowed or bereaved of

WIDOWHOOD
47:9   Bereavement and widowhood
54:4   the reproach of your widowhood.

WIDOWS
9:17   he pity their fatherless and widows,
10:2   making plunder of widows,

WIELD
3:12   women wield authority over them.

WIELDED
10:15 the rod wielded him who lifts it up!

WIELDS
19:16 of Hosts wields over them.

WIFE
54:1   The children of the deserted wife
54:6   a wife married in youth only to be

WILD
5:2   but it produced wild grapes.
5:4   why did it produce wild grapes?
13:21 But wild animals will infest it,
32:14 the playground of wild animals,
34:14 and wild goats call to one another.
35:9   nor shall wild beasts intrude.
37:27 becoming as wild grass, transiently
37:30 This year eat what grows wild,
43:20 The wild beasts do me honor,
56:9   All you wild beasts, you animals of

WILDERNESS
7:24   land shall revert to wilderness.
14:17 turned the world into a wilderness,
21:1   An oracle concerning the Wilderness
27:10 forsaken like a wilderness;
35:1   Wilderness and arid land shall be
35:6   shall break forth in the wilderness
40:3   in the wilderness pave a straight
41:19 and oleasters in the wilderness;

43:20 for bringing water to the wilderness,
51:3   is making her wilderness like Eden,
64:10 holy cities have become a wilderness;

WILLFULLY
59:13 willfully denying the Lord,

WILLING
1:19   If you are willing and obey,

WILLOWS
15:7   over the Valley of the Willows.
44:4   like willows by running brooks.

WILTS
33:9   Lebanon wilts shamefully;

WIND
4:4   spirit of justice, by a burning wind.
11:15 Egyptian Sea by his mighty wind;
17:13 they will be driven before the wind
26:18 but have brought forth only wind.
27:8   in the day of the burning east wind.
32:2   from the wind or refuge from the
41:16 As you winnow them, a wind shall
41:29 their outpourings are but wind and
57:13 A wind shall carry all of them off;
64:6   our sins, like a wind, sweep us away.

WINDOWS
24:18 For when the windows on high are

WINE
1:22   your wine diluted with water.
5:11   at night parties, inflamed by wine!
5:12   flutes, and wine at their banquets,
5:22   who are valiant at drinking wine
16:10 The wine treaders will tread no wine
22:13 eating meat and drinking wine:
24:7   The new wine withers on languishing
24:9   Men no longer drink wine amid song;
24:11 is heard the clamor for wine,
28:1   of the opulent overcome with wine.
28:7   These too have indulged in wine
28:7   They are intoxicated with wine
29:9   Be drunk, but not with wine;
36:17 and wine, a land of grain fields and
49:26 with their own blood as with wine.
51:21 drunk, though not with wine.
55:1   Come, buy wine and milk
56:12 Come, they say, let us get wine
62:8   foreigners drink the new wine you

WINEPRESS
5:2   and hewed for it a winepress as well.
63:2   who tread grapes in the winepress?

WINES
25:6   of matured wines well refined.
65:11 and pour mixed wines for Fortune,

WINGS
6:2   each having six wings—
8:8   his outspread wings will span
10:14 not one flapped its wings,
18:1   Woe to the land of buzzing wings
40:31 they shall ascend as on eagles' wings;

WINNOW
41:16 As you winnow them, a wind shall
WINNOWED
30:24 eat grain silage winnowed with shovel
WINTER
18:6 and the beasts of the land all winter.
WIPE
25:8 My Lord the Lord will wipe away
WIPING
26:14 wiping out all recollection of them.
WISDOM
11:2 the spirit of wisdom and of
33:6 your wisdom and knowledge your
WISE
5:21 Woe to those who are wise in their
19:11 We ourselves are as wise as the first
19:12 Where are your wise men indeed?
29:14 the intelligence of their wise men
44:25 who turns wise men about
WISEST
19:11 the wisest of Pharaoh's advisers give
WITCHCRAFT
19:3 to mediums and witchcraft.
WITHDRAWN
26:15 thou hast withdrawn all borders in
57:1 the righteous are withdrawn.
WITHDREW
37:8 had left Lachish, he withdrew
37:37 camp and withdrew. And he returned
WITHER
1:30 like an oak whose leaves wither,
16:8 vineyards of Heshbon shall wither;
19:6 Reeds and rushes shall wither;
40:24 he puffs at them and they wither,
42:15 and make all their vegetation wither;
WITHERED
33:9 The Land lies withered and forlorn,
34:4 like withered leaves from a vine,
WITHERS
24:7 The new wine withers on languishing
40:8 grass that withers, flowers that fade—
WITHHELD
48:6 things withheld and unknown to you,
63:15 are withheld from us!
WITHHOLD
43:6 to the south, Withhold not!
WITNESS
8:2 son of Jeberechiah, to witness for me.
55:4 See, I have appointed him a witness to
WITNESSES
8:2 And I called in reliable witnesses,
43:9 Let them bring their witnesses
43:10 But you are my witnesses, says the
43:12 You are my witnesses, says the Lord,
44:8 foretell it, you being my witnesses?
WIVES
13:16 plundered, their wives ravished.

WOE
1:24 Woe to them! I will relieve me
3:9 Woe to their souls;
3:11 But woe to the wicked
5:8 Woe to those who join house to house
5:11 Woe to those who go after liquor
5:18 Woe to those drawn to sin by vain
5:20 Woe to those who suppose what is evil
5:21 Woe to those who are wise in their
5:22 Woe to those who are valiant at
5:23 Woe to those who acquit the guilty
6:5 Then I thought, Woe is me:
10:1 Woe to those who enact unjust laws,
17:12 Woe to the many peoples in an
18:1 Woe to the land of buzzing wings
24:16 woe is me; the traitors have been
28:1 Woe to the garlands of glory
29:1 Woe to Ariel—
29:15 Woe to those contrive
30:1 Woe to you, rebellious sons, says the
31:1 Woe to those who go down to Egypt
33:1 Woe to you, despoiler,
45:9 Woe to those in conflict with their
45:10 Woe to those who say to their Father,
WOEFUL
37:3 This is a woeful day, a day of reproof
WOLF
11:6 Then shall the wolf dwell among
65:25 The wolf and the lamb will graze
WOLVES
34:14 Prairie wolves shall greet jackals,
WOMAN
7:14 give you a sign: the young woman
13:8 with trembling like a woman in labor.
21:3 have seized me like a woman in labor.
26:17 As a woman about to give birth
30:22 as a menstruous woman her
42:14 I will scream like a woman in labor
45:10 the Woman, What have you borne?
49:15 Can a woman forget her suckling
54:1 Sing, O barren woman who did not
WOMB
44:2 who formed you from the womb
44:24 who formed you from the womb:
46:3 borne up by me from the womb:
48:8 called a transgressor from the womb.
49:1 before I was in my mother's womb,
49:5 he who formed me from the womb
49:15 for the child of her womb?
WOMEN
3:12 women wield authority over them.
3:16 the women of Zion are haughty
3:17 of the women of Zion with baldness;
4:1 Seven women will take hold of one
4:4 of the women of Zion and cleansed
16:2 Moab's women at the fords of Arnon.
19:16 be as women, fearful and afraid

27:11 twigs dries, broken off by women
32:9 O complacent women;
32:11 Be alarmed, you complacent women;
WON
35:10 They shall have won joy and gladness
49:5 I won honor in the eyes of the Lord
WONDER
29:14 with wonder upon wonder,
WONDERED
59:16 When he saw it, he wondered
WONDERFUL
9:6 Wonderful Counsellor, one Mighty in
28:29 whose counsel is wonderful,
WONDERING
14:16 stare at you, wondering,
WONDERS
12:5 who has performed wonders;
25:1 thou hast performed wonders,
WOOD
10:15 who is not made of wood!
37:19 of men's hands, of wood and of stone,
40:20 select a wood that resists decay.
44:19 I not stoop to a mere lump of wood?
60:17 in place of wood I will bring copper,
WOODEN
45:20 who carried about their wooden idols
WOODWORKER
44:13 The woodworker draws a diagram,
WOOL
1:18 they may become white as wool.
51:8 moths shall devour them like wool.
WORD
1:10 Hear the word of the Lord,
2:3 from Jerusalem the word of the Lord.
24:3 Lord has given word concerning it.
28:13 So to them the word of the Lord
28:14 Therefore hear the word of the Lord,
28:19 terror merely to hear word of it.
29:21 those who at a word adjudge a man to
30:12 Because you have rejected this word,
33:15 and are honest in word,
37:21 Isaiah the son of Amoz sent word
38:4 Then the word of the Lord came to
39:5 Hear the word of the Lord of Hosts:
39:8 said to Isaiah, The word of the
40:8 only the word of our God endures
41:28 who could answer a word.
44:26 who fulfills the word of his servant,
50:4 grown weary a word to wake them up.
55:11 so is the word that leaves my mouth:
66:2 and who are vigilant for my word.
66:5 Hear the word of the Lord,
66:5 you who are vigilant for his word:
WORDS
5:24 and reviled the words of the Holy One
8:20 words devoid of light,
29:4 your words uttering out of the dust:

29:11 as the words of a sealed book that
29:18 the deaf hear the words of the book
30:21 Your ears shall hear words from
31:2 and not retract his words.
32:9 careless daughters, hear my words!
36:5 words are sufficient tactics or
36:13 loud voice in Judean, Hear the words
37:4 the words of of Rabshakeh, whom his
37:6 of the words with which you have
37:17 eyes and see. Listen to all the words
51:16 I will put my words in your mouth
59:4 They rely on empty words,
59:21 and my words which I have placed in
WORE
10:27 the yoke that wore away your
WORK
5:12 nor perceive his hands at work.
5:19 Let him quickly speed up his work
10:12 accomplished his work in
19:10 and all who work for wages suffer
19:25 Assyria the work of my hands,
28:21 and do this work, his bizarre work.
29:15 They work in the dark, thinking,
29:16 or a work of its designer, He doesn't
29:23 the work of my hands, hallowing my
40:10 his work precedes him.
41:4 Who is at work accomplishing this
42:3 He will perform the work of justice
43:13 when I work, who can thwart it?
45:9 hands have no skill for the work!
60:21 the work of my hands, in which I am
62:11 his work preceding him.
64:8 are all alike the work of thy hands.
65:22 shall outlast the work of their hands.
WORKERS
19:10 textile workers will know despair,
WORKS
1:31 their works a spark;
2:8 they adore the works of their hands,
17:8 the works of their hands,
37:19 they were no gods, but mere works
41:24 your works amount to nothing.
41:29 their works worthless;
44:12 smith with his tools works the iron
59:6 Their works consist of wrongdoing;
WORLD
10:14 I have gathered up the whole world
13:11 I have decreed calamity for the world,
14:17 turned the world into a wilderness,
14:21 and take possession of the world,
18:3 All you who live in the world,
23:17 out to all the kingdoms of the world
24:4 the world miserably perish;
26:9 the inhabitants of the world learn
26:18 that the inhabitants of the world
34:1 the world, and all who spring from it.
40:23 authorities of the world null and

WORLDS
45:17   worlds without end.
WORLD'S
14:9   of the world's leaders,
23:8   merchants the world's celebrities?
23:9   and the world's celebrities an utter
WORMS
14:11   you are covered with worms.
41:14   Be not afraid, you worms of Jacob;
66:24   against me, whose worms do not die
WORSHIP
19:21   worship by sacrifice and
36:7   Judea and Jerusalem to worship
46:6   they bow down to and worship.
66:23   all flesh shall come to worship
WORSHIPING
37:38   And as he was worshiping in the
WORTH
7:23   with a thousand vines worth
WORTHLESS
1:13   Bring no more worthless offerings;
41:29   their works worthless;
59:6   fabrications are worthless for cover
WOUND
30:26   and heals their open wound.
WOUNDEST
64:5   But thou woundest those of us
WOUNDS
1:6   only wounds and bruises and
53:5   and with his wounds we are healed.
WOVEN
38:12   My life is cut off like woven fabric;
WRAP
28:20   too narrow to wrap oneself in.
WRAPPED
59:17   wrapped himself in fury as in a robe.
WRATH
9:19   At the wrath of the Lord of Hosts
10:5   a staff—my wrath in their hand.
10:25   my wrath will become their undoing.
13:5   and the instruments of his wrath—
13:9   a cruel outburst of anger and wrath
13:13   in the day of his blazing wrath.
14:6   who subdued peoples in his wrath
26:20   until the wrath is past.
30:27   His wrath is kindled, heavy is his
48:9   name's sake I have bridled my wrath;
51:13   the wrath of the oppressor?
51:17   the cup of his wrath,
51:20   They have their fill of the wrath of
51:22   no more from the bowl of my wrath.
59:18   wrath upon his adversaries,
63:3   in my wrath I trampled them.
63:5   and my wrath, it assisted me.
WREAK
51:13   readies himself to wreak destruction?

WREATH
28:5   a crown of beauty and wreath of glory
WREATHS
28:1   has become as fading wreaths
28:4   And the fading wreaths, the crowns of
WRETCH
54:11   Poor wretch, tempest-tossed and
WRETCHED
24:4   of the earth shall be made wretched.
51:21   therefore hear this, O wretched one,
WRETCHEDLY
58:7   to bring home the wretchedly poor,
WRITE
8:1   Take a large scroll and write
30:8   Go now, write on tablets concerning
WRITTEN
38:9   illness, written upon his recovery:
65:6   See, it is written before me that I will
WRONGDOERS
1:4   the offspring of wrongdoers,
WRONGDOING
59:6   Their works consist of wrongdoing;
WRONGFUL
58:6   To release from wrongful bondage,
WROUGHT
26:18   We have not wrought salvation in the
42:8   nor my praise to wrought idols.
43:7   I have formed, molded and wrought
43:12   I who foretold and wrought salvation,
48:5   my graven and wrought images caused
YAH
26:4   the Lord Yah is an everlasting Rock.
YEAR
6:1   In the year of King Uzziah's death,
14:28   In the year King Ahaz died, came this
20:1   In the year the general who
21:16   to me, Within a year, as the term
29:1   Though you add year to year,
32:10   In little more than a year
34:8   the year of retribution on behalf of
36:1   In the fourteenth year of King
37:30   This year eat what grows wild,
37:30   and the following year what springs
37:30   But in the third year sow and harvest,
61:2   to herald the year of the Lord's favor
63:4   and the year of my redeemed had
YEARNINGS
63:15   The yearnings of thy bosom and thy
YEARNS
26:9   My soul yearns for thee in the night;
YEARS
7:8   within sixty-five years shall
16:14   Within three years, as the term
20:3   three years as a sign and portent
23:15   seventy years, the lifetime of a king.
23:15   And at the end of seventy years, Tyre
23:17   for after seventy years, the Lord

38:5 I will add fifteen years to your life.
38:10 deprived of the balance of my years?
65:20 aged who do not live out their years;
65:20 die young shall be a hundred years
YIELD
5:2 Then he expected it to yield grapes,
5:4 When I expected it to yield grapes,
5:10 vineyard shall yield but one bath,
YOKE
9:4 For thou hast smashed the yoke
10:27 their yoke removed from your neck:
10:27 the yoke that wore away your fatness
14:25 their yoke shall be taken from them,
47:6 weighed down heavily with your yoke.
58:6 to untie the harness of the yoke,
YOUNG
3:5 The young will be insolent to the
5:29 they are aroused like young lions:
7:14 give you a sign: the young woman
7:21 alive a young cow and a pair of sheep.
9:17 is not pleased with their young men,
11:6 the leopard lie down with young goats
11:6 calves and young lions will feed
11:7 their young will rest together;
13:18 bows shall tear apart the young.
18:5 are developing into young fruit,
20:4 and the exiles of Cush, both young
23:4 I no longer rear young men or raise
27:10 stripping bare the young branches of
30:6 on the backs of young asses,
31:4 As a lion or a young lion growls over
31:8 and their young men melt;
34:15 hatch them and brood over her young.
40:30 and young men slump down of
62:5 As a young man weds a virgin,
65:20 those who die young shall be a
YOUNGEST
60:22 the youngest a mighty nation.
YOUNGSTER
11:6 a youngster will lead them to pasture.
YOUTH
47:12 exerted yourself since your youth.
47:15 exerted yourself since your youth—
54:4 shall forget the shame of your youth
54:6 a wife married in youth only to be
YOUTHS
40:30 Youths grow faint and weary,
ZAPHON
14:13 in the utmost heights of Zaphon.
ZEAL
9:7 The zeal of the Lord of Hosts will
26:11 thy zeal for thy people
37:32 The zeal of the Lord of Hosts will
63:15 Where now are thy zeal and thy
ZEBULON
9:1 of Zebulon and Naphtali, but at

ZECHARIAH
8:2 Uriah the Priest and Zechariah
ZION
1:8 The Daughter of Zion is left
1:27 For Zion shall be ransomed by
2:3 For out of Zion shall go forth the law,
3:16 the women of Zion are haughty
3:17 of the women of Zion with baldness;
4:3 in Zion and they who remain
4:4 of the women of Zion and cleansed
4:5 Over the whole site of Mount Zion,
8:18 who dwells in Mount Zion.
10:12 Mount Zion and in Jerusalem,
10:24 O my people who inhabit Zion,
10:32 the mountain of the Daughter of Zion
12:6 sing for joy, O inhabitants of Zion,
14:32 The Lord has founded Zion;
16:1 the mountain of the Daughter of Zion
18:7 the place . . . Mount Zion.
24:23 in Mount Zion and in Jerusalem,
28:16 I lay in Zion a stone, a keystone,
29:8 amass to fight against Mount Zion.
30:19 O people of Zion, O inhabitants of
31:4 to wage war upon Mount Zion and
31:9 says the Lord, whose fire is in Zion,
33:5 righteousness he will replenish Zion.
33:14 The sinners in Zion are struck with
33:20 Behold Zion, the city of our solemn
34:8 year of retribution on behalf of Zion.
35:10 they shall come singing to Zion,
37:22 The Virgin Daughter of Zion holds
37:32 and from Mount Zion a band of
40:9 O Zion, herald of good tidings.
41:27 But to Zion, he shall be her
46:12 I will grant deliverance in Zion,
49:14 But Zion said, The Lord has forsaken
51:3 For the Lord is comforting Zion,
51:11 Let them come singing to Zion,
51:16 that I may say to Zion, You are my
52:1 clothe yourself with power, O Zion!
52:2 O captive Daughter of Zion.
52:7 saying to Zion, Your God reigns!
52:8 when the Lord returns to Zion.
59:20 But he will come as Redeemer to Zion
60:14 Zion of the Holy One of Israel.
61:3 to endow those who mourn in Zion,
62:11 Tell the Daughter of Zion,
64:10 Zion is a desert, Jerusalem a
66:8 Zion gave birth to her children.
ZION'S
62:1 For Zion's sake I will not keep silent;
ZOAN
19:11 The ministers of Zoan are utter fools;
19:13 The ministers of Zoan have been
30:4 For all their officials at Zoan,
ZOAR
15:5 its fugitives will reach Zoar

How to Use the Index

The Index consists of the main terms and expressions appearing in the literary analysis of Isaiah including its footnotes. However, general terms, such as *people*, *Israel*, and *Lord* do not appear in the Index.

Identify the main themes or message of Isaiah by observing the most commonly used words, such as *Zion*, *covenant*, *righteousness*, and *king*.

Identify the methodologies used to analyze Isaiah by observing such terms as *literary*, *pattern*, *composite*, and *type*.

Locate verbs under their noun form, viz., *oppress / oppressed* under *oppression*, *repents / repenting* under *repentance*, *heal / heals* under *healing*.

Look for compounds, such as *wandering* in the *wilderness*, *righteous warrior*, *rhetorical definition*, and *historical origins*, by locating a page on which both terms appear together.

Find the main areas of study on any subject by locating page groupings, such as the idea of a *remnant* of the Lord's people on pages 50–56, 61–66, 89–92; a latter-day *exodus* on pages 89–98, 134–42, 187–94; *progression* or *ascent* on a spiritual *ladder* on pages 77–84, 242–48, 261–66.

Do word studies on any variety of topics, such as *restoration*, *anointing*, *empowerment*, and *exaltation* by following their discussion throughout the text.

Index to the Literary Analysis of Isaiah

BIBLIOGRAPHY

Behr, J. W. *The Writings of Isaiah and the Neo-Babylonian Royal Inscriptions*. Pretoria, South Africa: Rubenstein & Co., 1937.

Blank, Sheldon H. "The Prophet as Paradigm." In *Essays on Old Testament Ethics*, edited by James L. Crenshaw and John T. Willis. New York: Ktav, 1974.

Bleeker, C. J. "Isis as Saviour Goddess." In *The Saviour God*, edited by S. G. F. Brandon. New York: Barnes and Noble, 1963.

Brandon, S. G. F. "The Ritual Technique of Salvation in the Ancient Near East." In *The Saviour God*, edited by S. G. F. Brandon. New York: Barnes and Noble, 1963.

Brownlee, William H. "The Manuscripts of Isaiah from Which DSIa Was Copied." *Bulletin of the American Schools of Oriental Research* 127 (October 1952): 16–21.

Brownlee, William H. *The Meaning of the Qumran Scrolls for the Bible*. New York: Oxford University Press, 1964.

Brueggemann, Walter. "From Dust to Kingship." *Zeitschrift für die alttestamentliche Wissenschaft* 84 (1972): 1–18.

Brueggemann, Walter. "Kingship and Chaos." *Catholic Biblical Quarterly* 33 (1971): 317–32.

Brueggemann, Walter. "Weariness, Exile and Chaos." *Catholic Biblical Quarterly* 34 (1972): 19–39.

Calderone, Philip J. *Dynastic Oracle and Suzerainty Treaty*. Manila: Ateneo University, 1966.

Carroll, R. P. "Second Isaiah and the Failure of Prophecy." *Studia Theologica* 32 (1978): 119–31.

Chamberlain, John V. "The Functions of God as Messianic Titles in the Complete Isaiah Scroll." *Vetus Testamentum* 5 (1955): 366–72.

Childs, Brevard. "The Enemy from the North and the Chaos Tradition." *Journal of Biblical Literature* 78 (1959): 187–98.

Coggins, Richard J. "The Problem of Isaiah 24–27." *Expository Times* 90 (1978–1979): 328–33.

Coleson, Joseph E. "Israel's Life Cycle from Birth to Resurrection." In *Israel's Apostasy and Restoration*, edited by Avraham Gileadi. Grand Rapids, Mich.: Baker Books House, 1988.

Cook, Margaret B. "A Suggested Occasion for Isaiah 9:2–7 and 11:1–9." *Journal of Biblical Literature* 68 (1949): 213–14.

Cooke, Gerald. "The Israelite King as Son of God." *Zietschrift für die alttestamentliche Wissenschaft* 73 (1961): 202–25.

Eaton, John H. "The King as God's Witness." *Annual of the Swedish Theological Institute* 7 (1968/69): 25–40.

Eissfeldt, Otto. *The Old Testament: An Introduction*. New York: Harper and Row, 1965.

Eissfeldt, Otto. "The Promises of Grace to David in Isaiah 55:1–5." In *Israel's Prophetic Heritage*, edited by B. W. Anderson and Walter Harrelson. New York: Harper and Row, 1962.

Engnell, Ivan. *Divine Kingship in the Ancient Near East*. Oxford: Basil Blackwell, 1967.

Erlandsson, Seth. *The Burden of Babylon*. Lund, Sweden: Gleerup, 1970.

Erman, Adolf. *The Ancient Egyptians*. New York: Harper and Row, 1966.

Faulkner, R. O. "The King and the Star Religion in the Pyramid Texts." *Journal of Near Eastern Studies* 25 (1966): 153–61.

Fensham, F. C. "Clauses of Protection in Hittite Vassal-Treaties and the Old Testament." *Vetus Testamentum* 13 (1963): 133–43.

Fensham, F. C. "Common Trends in Curses of the Near Eastern Treaties and *Kudurru*-Inscriptions Compared with Maledictions of Amos and Isaiah." *Zietschrift für die alttestamentliche Wissenschaft* 75 (1963): 155–75.

Fensham, F. C. "Malediction and Benediction in Ancient Near Eastern Vassal-Treaties and the Old Testament." *Zeitschrift für die alttestamentliche Wissenchaft* 74 (1962): 1–8.

Flemming, J., and H. Duensing, trans. "Ascension of Isaiah." In *New Testament Apocrypha, Vol. 2*, edited by Edgar Hennecke and Wilhelm Schneemelcher. Philadelphia: Westminster, 1965.

Fohrer, Georg. *Introduction to the Old Testament*. Nashville: Abingdon, 1968.

Fox, M. "Tôb as Covenant Terminology." *Bulletin of the American Schools of Oriental Research* 209 (1973): 41–42.

Frankfort, Henri. *Ancient Egyptian Religion*. New York: Columbia University Press, 1948.

Frankfort, Henri. *Kingship and the Gods*. Chicago: University of Chicago, 1948.

Frazer, James G.. *Adonis, Attis, Osiris*. New York: University Books, 1961.

Gardiner, Alan H. *Hieratic Papyri*, Third Series. London: British Museum, 1935.

Gaster, Theodore H. *Thespis: Ritual, Myth, and Drama in the Ancient Near East*. New York: Schuman, 1950.

Gordon, Cyrus H. "Leviathan: Symbol of Evil." In *Biblical Motifs*, edited by A. Altmann. Cambridge, Mass.: Harvard University Press, 1966.

Habel, Norman C. "He who stretches out the heavens." *Catholic Biblical Quarterly* 34 (1972): 417–30.

Hamlin, John E. "The Meaning of 'Mountains and Hills' in Isa. 41:14–16." *Journal of Near Eastern Studies* 13 (1954): 189.

Hayes, John H. "The Tradition of Zion's Inviolability." *Journal of Biblical Literature* 82 (1963): 419–26.

Hollenberg, D. E. "Nationalism and 'The Nations' in Isaiah XL–LV." *Vetus Testamentum* 19 (1969): 23–36.

Huffmon, H. B. "The Treaty Background of Hebrew *yādaʿ*." *Bulletin of the American Schools of Oriental Research* 181 (1966): 31–37.

Huffmon, H. B., and S. B. Parker. "A Further Note of the Treaty Background of Hebrew *yādaʿ*." *Bulletin of the American Schools of Oriental Research* 184 (1966): 36–38.

Jacobsen, Thorkild. *Toward the Image of Tammuz*. Cambridge, Mass.: Harvard University Press, 1970.

Jacobson, Thorkild. *The Treasures of Darkness*. New Haven, Conn.: Yale University Press, 1976.

Jones, G. H. "Abraham and Cyrus: Type and Antitype?" *Vetus Testamentum* 22 (1972): 311–16.

Kaiser, Otto. *Isaiah 1–12*. Phildadelphia: Westminster, 1972.

Kaiser, Otto. *Isaiah 13–39*. Philadelphia: Westminster, 1974.

Krause, Alfred E. "Historical Selectivity: Prophetic Prerogative or Typological Imperative." In *Israel's Apostasy and Restoration*, edited by Avraham Gileadi. Grand Rapids, Mich.: Baker Book House, 1988.

Lambert, W. G. *Babylonian Wisdom Literature*. Oxford: Clarendon Press, 1960.

Lowe, Benjamin F., Jr. "The King as Mediator of the Cosmic Order." Diss., Emory University, 1967.

McCarthy, D. J. "Notes on the Love of God in Deuteronomy and the Father–Son Relationship between Yahweh and Israel." *Catholic Biblical Quarterly* 27 (1965): 144–47.

McKenzie, John L. *Second Isaiah*. New York: Doubleday, 1967.

Mauchline, John. "Implicit Signs of a Persistent Belief in the Davidic Empire." *Vetus Testamentum* 20 (1970): 287–303.

May, Herbert G. "The Righteous Servant in Second Isaiah's Songs." *Zietschrift für die alttestamentliche Wissenschaft* 66 (1954): 237.

May, Herbert G. "Some Cosmic Connotations of *Mayîm Rabbîm*, 'Many Waters.' " *Journal of Biblical Literature* 74 (1955): 9–21.

Mendenhall, George E. "Covenant Forms of Israelite Tradition." *Biblical Archaeologist* 17.3 (1954): 50–76.

Merrill, Eugene H. "Pilgrimage and Procession: Motifs of Israel's Return." In *Israel's Apostasy and Restoration*, edited by Avraham Gileadi. Grand Rapids, Mich.: Baker Book House, 1988.

Millar, William R. *Isaiah 24-27 and the Origin of Apocalyptic*. Missoula, Mont.: Scholars Press, 1976.

Moran, W. L. "The Ancient Near Eastern Background of the Love of God in Deuteronomy." *Catholic Biblical Quarterly* 25 (1963): 77–87.

Moret, Alexander. *Kings and Gods of Egypt*. New York: Putnam's Sons, 1912.

Moret, Alexander. *Mystères Egyptiens*. Paris: Colin, 1913.

Muilenburg, James. *The Interpreter's Bible*. Vol. 5 (12 vols.). New York: Abingdon, 1956.

Nibley, Hugh. *The Message of the Joseph Smith Papyri*. Salt Lake City: Deseret Book, 1975.

Ogden, Graham S. "Moses and Cyrus." *Vetus Testamentum* 28 (1978): 201.

Otto, Eberhard. *Das ägyptische Mundoffnungritual*. Wiesbaden: Harrasowitz, 1960.

Patte Daniel. *Early Jewish Hermeneutic in Palestine*. Missoula, Mont.: Scholars Press, 1975.

Paul, Shalom M. "Deutero-Isaiah and Cuneiform Royal Inscriptions." *Journal of the American Oriental Society* 88 (1968): 180–86.

Pirenne, Jacques. "La politique d'expansion Hittite envisagée à travers les traités de vassalité et de protectorat." *Archiv orientàlui* 18:1 (1950): 373–82.

Pritchard, J. B., ed. *Ancient Near Eastern Texts*. Princeton, N.J.: Princeton University Press, 1969.

Pritchard, J. B. *The Ancient Near East in Pictures*. Princeton, N.J.: Princeton University Press, 1969.

Ringgren, Helmer. "Some Observations on Style and Structure in the Isaiah Apocalypse." *Annual of the Swedish Theological Institute* 9 (1973): 107–15.

Roberts, J. J. M. "The Davidic Origin of the Zion Tradition." *Journal of Biblical Literature* 92 (1973): 329–44.

Rosenberg, Roy A. "The God Sedeq." *Hebrew Union College Annual* 36 (1965): 161–78.

Scott, R. B. Y. *The Interpreter's Bible*. Vol 5 (12 vols.). New York: Abingdon, 1956.

Shalom, M. Paul. "Deutero-Isaiah and Cuneiform Royal Inscriptions." *Journal of the American Oriental Society* 88 (1968).

Smith, Gary V. "Alienation and Restoration: A Jacob-Esau Typology." In *Israel's Apostasy and Restoration*, edited by Avraham Gileadi. Grand Rapids, Mich.: Baker Book House, 1988.

Stuhlmueller, Carrol. *Creative Redemption in Deutero-Isaiah*. Rome: Pontifical Biblical Institute, 1970.

Stuhlmueller, Carrol. "The Theology of Creation in Second Isaiah." *Catholic Biblical Quarterly* 21 (1959): 429–67.

Vermes, G. "The Torah as a Light." *Vetus Testamentum* 8 (1958): 436–38.

Weinfeld, Moshe. "Berîth." In *Theological Dictionary of the Old Testament*. Vol. 2. Grand Rapids, Mich.: Eerdmans, 1975.

Weinfeld, Moshe. "The Covenant of Grant in the Old Testament and in the Ancient Near East." *Journal of the American Oriental Society* 90 (1970): 184–203.

Weizman, Z. "Anointing as a Motif in the Making of the Charismatic King." *Biblica* 57 (1976): 378–98.

Westermann, Claus. *Basic Forms of Prophetic Speech*. Trans. Hugh C. White. Philadelphia: Westminster, 1967.

Westermann, Claus. *Isaiah 40-66*. Philadelphia: Westminster, 1969.

Williamson, H. G. M. "The Sure Mercies of David." *Journal of Semetic Studies* 23 (1978): 330-49.

Wright, G. Ernest. "The Nations in Hebrew Prophecy." *Enc* 26 (1965): 225-37.

Wyngaards, J. "Death and Resurrection in Covenantal Context." *Vetus Testamentum* 17 (1967): 226-39.